Elgar Compan
Sustainable Cities
Strategies, Methods and Outlook

Edited by

Daniel A. Mazmanian

Professor of Public Policy, Sol Price School of Public Policy, University of Southern California, USA

Hilda Blanco

Research Professor, and Interim Director, Center for Sustainable Cities, Sol Price School of Public Policy, University of Southern California, USA

Edward Elgar
Cheltenham, UK • Northampton, MA, USA

Published by
Edward Elgar Publishing Limited
The Lypiatts
15 Lansdown Road
Cheltenham
Glos GL50 2JA
UK

Edward Elgar Publishing, Inc.
William Pratt House
9 Dewey Court
Northampton
Massachusetts 01060
USA

A catalogue record for this book
is available from the British Library

Library of Congress Control Number: 2014932511

This book is available electronically in the ElgarOnline.com
Social and Political Science Subject Collection, E-ISBN 978 0 85793 999 9

ISBN 978 0 85793 998 2 (cased)

Typeset by Servis Filmsetting Ltd, Stockport, Cheshire
Printed and bound in Great Britain by T.J. International Ltd, Padstow

Contents

List of contributors viii

1 The sustainable city: introduction and overview 1
Hilda Blanco and Daniel A. Mazmanian

PART I STRATEGIES

2 Rediscovering compact cities for sustainability 15
Peter Newman

3 Potable, stormwater and wastewater city strategies in the context of climate change 32
Blanca Jiménez Cisneros

4 Urban food systems strategies 57
Nevin Cohen

5 Sustainability strategies for consumer products in cities 86
Gregory A. Keoleian, Joshua P. Newell, Ming Xu and Erin Dreps

6 Strategies for growing green business and industry in a city 116
Karen Chapple

7 Strategies and considerations for investing in sustainable city infrastructure 133
Rae Zimmerman

8 Aligning fiscal and environmental sustainability 154
Richard F. Callahan and Mark Pisano

9 Gauging the health of a city: maximizing health and sustainability 166
Alek Miller and Richard J. Jackson

10 From information provision to participatory deliberation: engaging residents in the transition toward sustainable cities 188
Michaela Zint and Kimberly S. Wolske

11 Developing effective participatory processes for a sustainable city 210
Connie P. Ozawa

12 A measure of justice: environmental equity and the sustainable city 228
Manuel Pastor

PART II METHODS

13 Analyzing a city's metabolism 255
Christopher Kennedy, Larry Baker and Helge Brattebø

14 Developing sustainable cities indicators 283
Kent E. Portney

15 Climate action planning 302
Michael R. Boswell, Adrienne I. Greve and Tammy L. Seale

16 Climate change adaptation 320
Adrienne I. Greve and Michael R. Boswell

17 Economic resilience and the sustainability of cities in the face of climate change: an ecological economics framework 336
Adam Rose

18 A systems approach towards sustainable procurement 354
Laurie Kaye Nijaki

PART III THE FUTURE

19 Urban design and sustainability: looking backward to move forward 381
Tridib Banerjee

20 The future of sustainable economic development in cities 397
Edward J. Blakely

21 Sustainable cities and governance: what are the connections? 413
Daniel J. Fiorino

22 Technology and city sustainability 434
Bill Tomlinson

23 Conclusion 449
Daniel A. Mazmanian and Hilda Blanco

Index 469

Contributors

Larry Baker is a research professor in the Ecological Engineering Group in the Department of Bioproducts and Biosystems Engingeering, at the University of Minnesota, St. Paul, MN.

Tridib Banerjee is a professor and the James Irvine Chair in Urban and Regional Planning, in the Sol Price School of Public Policy, at the University of Southern California, Los Angeles, CA.

Edward J. Blakely is an honorary professor of Urban Policy at the United States Studies Centre at the University of Sydney, Sydney, NSW, Australia.

Hilda Blanco is a research professor and Interim Director of the Center for Sustainable Cities, in the Sol Price School of Public Policy, at the University of Southern California, Los Angeles, CA.

Michael R. Boswell is a professor in the City & Regional Planning Department in the College of Architecture and Environmental Design at Cal Poly, San Luis Obispo, CA.

Helge Brattebø is a professor in the Department of Energy and Process Engineering at the Norwegian University of Science and Technology, Trondheim, Norway.

Richard F. Callahan is the Department Chair and an associate professor in the School of Management – Public and Nonprofit Administration at the University of San Francisco, San Francisco, CA.

Karen Chapple is an associate professor of City & Regional Planning in the College of Environmental Design at the University of California Berkeley, Berkeley, CA.

Nevin Cohen is an assistant professor of Environmental Studies at The New School For Public Engagement, New York, NY.

Erin Dreps is a research associate in the Center for Sustainable Systems in the School of Natural Resources and Environment at the University of Michigan, Ann Arbor, MI.

Daniel J. Fiorino is the Distinguished Executive in Residence in the Department of Public Administration and Policy in the School of Public Affairs at American University, Washington, DC.

Adrienne I. Greve is an assistant professor in the City & Regional Planning Department in the College of Architecture and Environmental Design at Cal Poly, San Luis Obispo, CA.

Richard J. Jackson is a pediatrician who was Director of the National Center for Environmental Health with the Centers for Disease Control and Prevention for nine years. He currently teaches in the Department of Environmental Health Sciences at the University of California, Los Angeles, CA.

Blanca Jiménez Cisneros is the Director of the Division of Water Sciences and Secretary of the Interactional Hydrological Programme at UNESCO.

Christopher Kennedy is a professor in Civil Engineering at the University of Toronto, Toronto, Ontario, Canada.

Gregory A. Keoleian is a professor and the Director of the Center for Sustainable Systems in the School of Natural Resources & Environment at the University of Michigan, Ann Arbor, MI.

Daniel A. Mazmanian is a professor and the Director of New Initiatives at the USC Center for Sustainable Cities at the Sol Price School of Public Policy at the University of Southern California, Los Angeles, CA.

Alek Miller is an urban planner and public health practitioner in Los Angeles, CA.

Joshua P. Newell is an assistant professor in the School of Natural Resources & Environment at the University of Michigan, Ann Arbor, MI.

Peter Newman is a professor of Sustainability at Curtin University and Director of Curtin University Sustainability Policy Institute, Perth, Australia.

Laurie Kaye Nijaki is a postdoctoral research fellow at the Erb Institute for Global Sustainable Enterprise at the University of Michigan, Ann Arbor, MI.

Connie P. Ozawa is a professor and Director of the Nohad A. Toulan School of Urban Studies and Planning in the College of Urban & Public Affairs at Portland State University, Portland, OR.

Manuel Pastor is a professor of Sociology and American Studies and Ethnicity in the USC Dornsife College of Letters, Arts and Sciences at the University of Southern California, Los Angeles, CA.

Mark Pisano is a professor of the Practice of Public Administration at the Sol Price School of Public Policy at the University of Southern California, Los Angeles, CA.

Kent E. Portney is a professor of American Politics and Political Behaviour in the Department of Political Science at Tufts University, Medford, MA.

Adam Rose is a research professor for the Sol Price School of Public Policy and Coordinator for Economics at the Center for Risk and Economic Analysis of Terrorism Events at the University of Southern California, Los Angeles, CA.

Tammy L. Seale is a principal in Sustainability and Climate Change Services at PMC, San Luis Obispo, CA.

Bill Tomlinson is a professor of Informatics Department in the Donald Bren School of ICS at the University of California, Irvine, CA.

Kimberly S. Wolske is a postdoctoral research fellow at the Erb Institute for Global Sustainable Enterprise at the University of Michigan, Ann Arbor, MI.

Ming Xu is an assistant professor in the School of Natural Resources and Environment at the University of Michigan, Ann Arbor, MI.

Rae Zimmerman is a professor of Planning and Public Administration at New York University's Robert F. Wagner Graduate School of Public Service at New York University, New York, NY.

Michaela Zint is an associate professor in the School of Natural Resources and Environment at the University of Michigan, Ann Arbor, MI.

1. The sustainable city: introduction and overview

Hilda Blanco and Daniel A. Mazmanian

INTRODUCTION

The unprecedented urbanization of human populations around the world presents one of the most profound challenges of the twenty-first century. The causes and consequences are many, diverse and much debated. Yet the number of urban dwellers, along with the growth of, especially, medium, large and truly mega-cities continues unabated, with significant implications for the health and viability of their populations and their impact on nature's services.

We believe that in this context any meaningful path forward must weave together both intra- and intertemporal needs and challenges into a more comprehensive and thus sustainable cities approach. This approach must ultimately be spread globally, although not through the dictates of a central authority or even a binding global policy agreement, but through the cumulative action of path-breaking lead cities and their leaders around the world. Urban centers are the very places where societal challenges have throughout human history been confronted and overcome, through necessity, human ingenuity, experimentation and the diffusion of good ideas.

Cities today are already coming together in a shared concern with the challenges of today's urbanization, persuaded that the solutions can be found in charting a new course, that of becoming more sustainable: socially, economically and environmentally. The sustainable cities movement is beginning to emerge in a host of cities around the world, ranging from social and environmentally sensitive actions by groups of citizens, to implementing sustainable public policies, to embracing a comprehensive approach to sustainability that brings the major economic, social and environmental pieces together within a comprehensive 'systems' approach to the city, making it more resilient and livable.

We do not ignore the importance of global-level action when it comes to sustainability, but recognize that this is a long way off politically and will likely be based on what is learned through the efforts of cities in this transition period for human populations. In effect, cities' initiatives on sustainability are a critical step in the global transformation to sustainability, serving as exemplars, as pragmatic local ways of addressing both local and global issues, as means of empowering those who appreciate the significance of the challenges of moving toward a more sustainable future and choose to be a part of the process.

The present volume provides a framework for understanding the city as a critical building block of a more sustainable future. The city is approached in terms of becoming a 'sustainable system' in itself, nested within a broader subnational, national, continental context, and ultimately, a global systems context. It is a place where sustainable strategies are being devised, and methods and tools for achieving them applied. The volume is organized primarily to capture the two aspects of the transformation: Part I focuses on examples of social, economic, political and environmental policy strategies that are being developed. Part II brings to the fore methods and tools for applying the various strategies and analyzing the extent to which they are leading to greater sustainability, likewise, along social, economic, political and environmental lines. The authors bring to the discussion their diverse analytical and disciplinary trainings and backgrounds and, together, provide a wide array of strategic thinking and methods of analysis. Each strategy, each method, is a type of 'intervention' in what is inherently a complex system, with a myriad of interconnections and moving parts. However, cities, as any complex system, do not evolve or change automatically or holistically, but through interventions that leverage inflection points that move or steer them in new directions. In the contemporary parlance of change, interventions – imposed from outside a system or cultivated from within – are points of inflection and turning points (sometimes referred to as tipping points). In this case, strategies are interventions that turn cities in the direction of increasing sustainability.

The final part (Part III) provides several thought-provoking perspectives looking beyond current strategies and interventions, to more holistic futuristic visions of the sustainable city. Perspectives on urban form, the economic system, governance and technologies of the sustainable city are elaborated.

The volume is intended for use by scholars, practitioners and students interested in the role of, and prospects for, cities in the movement toward sustainability. It is designed to be a comprehensive source of contemporary research and knowledge about the array of methods and strategies in use, providing insights and actionable information organized around the environmental, social and economic dimensions of a sustainable city.

THE URBANIZATION CHALLENGE

An increasing population in a world of finite resources encapsulates the challenge of sustainability. Sustainability is further strained by the increasing and uneven rate of resource consumption. While the world's population tripled during the twentieth century, reaching seven billion in 2011, the use of water resources grew six-fold. One-sixth of the world's population lacks access to safe drinking water and one-third lacks adequate sanitation. Over the past two centuries, resource depletion and loss of biodiversity have accelerated. Increasing greenhouse gas (GHG) emissions threaten global climate patterns.

The world's population is not evenly distributed, but concentrated in human settlements. Further, in 2008 the world reached a momentous milestone: over half of the world's population now live in urban areas. This urbanizing trend will accelerate in the twenty-first century. As of 2010, over 82 percent of people in North America, over 73 percent in Europe, 83 percent in South America and 89 percent in Australia were already living in urban areas. Although Africa (39.3 percent urban population) and Asia (44.4 percent urban) are still mainly rural, by 2050, urban populations are projected to reach 57.7 percent in Africa and 64.4 percent in Asia (United Nations 2012).

Cities are the dominant human habitat. If we are concerned about the sustainability of the planet, then we need to focus on the sustainability of cities. Cities are the place where global challenges converge, ideas are tested, and solutions emerge. In order to discuss urban sustainability, we need first to clarify what we mean by sustainability and by urban settlements.

THE SUSTAINABILITY CHALLENGE

Sustainability has become a popular term, and there are likely hundreds of published definitions (Hempel 2009). The root of sustainability is the adjective 'sustainable', which the dictionary defines as the ability 'to be maintained at a certain rate or level: *sustainable fusion reactions*. *(Ecology)* (esp. of development, exploitation, or agriculture) conserving an ecological balance by avoiding depletion of natural resources . . .' (McKean 2005). According to the law of entropy, in the long run nothing is sustainable. Thus we should understand the term as a comparative, relative, not an absolute term, judging situations as more or less sustainable over a given time period, or cities as more or less sustainable compared to others.

Two major definitions of sustainability are important to understand: the Brundtland Commission's and 'balancing the three Es' definitions.

The canonical definition of sustainable development is that of the United Nations World Commission on Environment and Development Report published in 1987, commonly known as the Brundtland Report (after its Chairman, Harlen Brundtland):

> Sustainable development is development that meets the needs of the present generation without compromising the ability of future generations to meet their own needs. (UN WCED 1987)

This definition builds on the common meaning of the term, the ability to maintain an activity 'at a certain rate or level', and emphasizes retaining opportunities of development for present generations, especially the poor, and for future generations. It also refers to the more recent ecological meaning of sustainability, the natural environment's ability to meet human needs and functions. This idea implies that earth systems have a carrying capacity, a finite ability to sustain or carry life, and that at this point human activity is unsustainable.[1]

Development that balances the three Es, environment, equity and the economy, is a popular definition of sustainability (Daly and Cobb 1989; Elkington 1994; Campbell 1996; Godschalk 2004). On this definition, these three systems, the natural environment, along with the economy, and the social/political/ethical system that would guarantee a certain measure of equity, are assumed to be co-equal. Figure 1.1 is a popular way of depicting this idea. This balancing of the three spheres concept has been popularized for the business sector through the concept of the triple bottom line (TBL) or the three pillars: people, planet and profit. TBL has developed accounting systems that expand the traditional financial performance measures to incorporate social and environmental dimensions (Elkington 1998).

The definition of sustainability as a balance of the three spheres/dimensions, however, gives a misleading impression of the relationship among the three systems, environmental, social and economic. The relation is not of equals but of nested dependency. Figure 1.2 shows a more realistic schematic of the three systems, indicating the nested relations among the three. All human societies depend on the natural environment for land, goods, food, water, air and energy (Ross 2009). All manufactured goods are based on these natural goods. We have no substitutes for many of these natural goods, and thus the natural environment is the primary system on which all human societies depend. Economies, which are social constructs, dependent on human social organizations, vary across the world and across time. This relationship of dependency establishes an order of system adaptation in our pursuit of sustainable development: societies must strive to conserve natural resources and reduce resource degradation; and economies within these societies will require changes to facilitate the

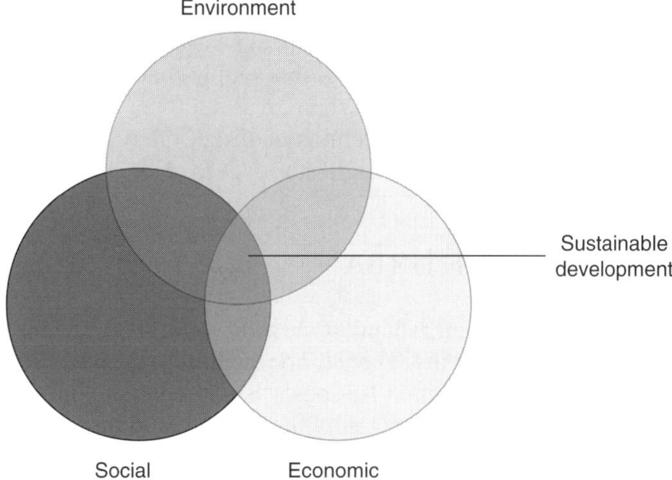

Figure 1.1 *Sustainable development as a balance or interface among three spheres*

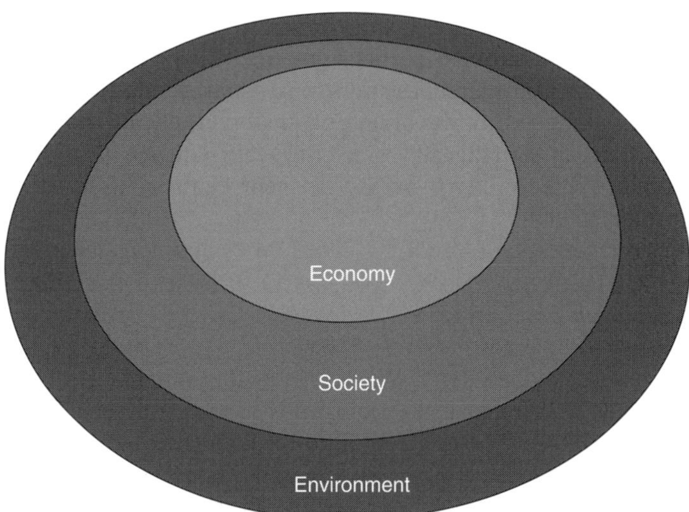

Figure 1.2 *The nested relationship among the three dimensions of sustainability*

conservation and quality of natural goods and services. How sustainability is to be achieved is all the more challenging in an age of growing economic globalization operating in a world of global supply chains where the traditional economic relations between urban areas and their rural regions are increasingly replaced by teleconnections or distal, often global, relations that are complex and only partly understood (Seto et al. 2012).

ON DEFINING THE URBAN

Defining the 'urban' in the urban milestone achieved in 2008 is almost as difficult as defining sustainability. There is no recognized, global definition of urban areas or cities. The United Nations, when it reports on urbanization or cities, uses countries' self-reports, with varying definitions. Urbanized land is typically defined as land in state-recognized cities (municipalities or local authorities), as land in agglomerations with threshold populations of from 1000 to 5000 persons, and in some countries in terms of density per unit area, ranging from 386 persons per square kilometers (USA), 1500 persons per square kilometer (People's Republic of China) to 4000 per square kilometer (Japan) (UN Population Division 2008).

Metropolitan areas are defined as integrated labor markets and commuting patterns rather than by density alone. They typically include at least one central city, other cities and towns, suburban areas, as well as the rural land in between. In this volume, we shall typically use the term cities and urban areas interchangeably to refer to areas with urban densities, and metropolitan areas to refer to areas that incorporate suburban areas and fringe rural lands.

SUSTAINABLE CITIES

What then is a sustainable city? We can respond in simple ways, such as to say that a sustainable city is an ecologically sustainable, socially just and economically viable city. But going beyond easy answers, this is a difficult question because sustainability is an integrative concept. It involves many dimensions, related in complex ways. As we discuss above, there are three major dimensions of sustainability widely recognized: environmental, social and economic. Two other aspects of sustainability central to the concept, but not as widely noted, are the 'interdisciplinary or integrative', and the 'systems-oriented' aspects of the concept. The interdisciplinarity, or better, the intent to integrate various dimensions in a situation, is the hallmark of a sustainability approach, which is implicit in the definition of sustainability as balancing the three Es. Thus, when applied to urban issues or urban sustainability, a sustainable approach requires 'substantive interdisciplinarity', beyond issues of environmental conservation, social justice or economic efficiency. That is, since urban issues are interdisciplinary, for example those of housing, land use, transportation and nature's services, whether development or urban life can be sustained over time requires knowing and taking into account the fundamental connections, for example, that housing has to transportation or to public health or other systems on which it is dependent or interdependent.

Figuring out how to make urban settlements more sustainable requires knowledge of how a local economy works, of how transportation systems are connected to land use and urban density, to economic activities, to the housing supply, to other public infrastructure and services, as well as to the distribution or accessibility of these services or goods for different groups within a city. The way urban systems work or fail to work together is a large part of the sustainability of an urban settlement. The complexity of varied, interrelated parts in these systems defies an explanation from a single discipline. Thus a sustainable approach fundamentally relies on interdisciplinary knowledge. Regarding the sustainability of cities, the three Es could be conceived as meta-criteria that rely on an integrative, systems-oriented, interdisciplinary knowledge base. That is, they are larger questions that can be posed of existing or proposed systems or projects once a rich understanding of a situation has been established: how can changes in such a situation conserve ecological systems; how can changes make systems more efficient; how can they improve social equity? Thus urban sustainability research could be conceived as essentially interdisciplinary research, with an overlay of environmental, social and economic criteria. Equally important, the sustainable city is where challenges and problems are addressed to meet the needs of the present without undermining or precluding the opportunities of future generations. A sustainable city, in this sense, is an active, evolving, organic community addressing problems of the present and foreseeable future while confronting ongoing challenges of economic development, equity and justice, and environmental protection.

CITIES AS COMPLEX SYSTEMS

The systems-oriented nature of the concept of sustainable cities, involving the complex interplay among urban systems of infrastructures, built environment, nature's services, organization and information systems that combine to facilitate urban life, is often also neglected.

Like all complex systems, cities involve hierarchies (ordered levels of subsystems). In particular, cities have been analyzed as open systems, that is, systems that have the ability to self-organize and sustain themselves by metabolizing inputs of energy, information and raw materials, and discharging into their environments wastes and disorder (entropy). The urban metabolism concept, a key method that is the subject of Chapter 13, is one example of how cities can be studied as complex systems. In a pioneering article on urban metabolism, Wolman (1965) analyzed a hypothetical city of one million as a complex open system, with energy, materials and water inputs and outputs. He estimated that, for one million inhabitants, 2000 tons of food, 4000 tons of fuel and 630 000 tons of water are needed daily as inputs. These are converted daily into 2000 tons of garbage, 500 000 tons of wastewater with 120 tons of solid particles, and 950 tons of atmospheric pollutants. This illustrates the tremendous flow of water moving through a city, as well as of materials and fuel.

Results from applying the method of urban metabolism analysis are in terms of flows, the main flows of water, energy and materials coursing through cities. The conduits for these flows are also complex urban systems, including transportation, water supply, wastewater treatment, solid waste disposal, energy and power systems, and information and communication systems.

Key to understanding urban complexity is the relation between urban systems and natural systems. For example, the built environment of cities composed of structures, combined with the sealed surfaces of streets, prevents precipitation from percolating into the ground and requires stormwater systems to prevent urban flooding. Another important impact of the sealed surfaces of cities is the heating of the local climate, also known as 'the heat island effect'. The removal of vegetation in cities and the concentration of asphalt and concrete, which absorb rather than reflect the sun's rays, increase the temperature of these surfaces as well as the ambient temperature surrounding them.

ORGANIZATION AND CONTENT

This volume does not attempt to focus on urban systems in themselves, but rather on strategies for improvement and methods and tools for achieving urban sustainability within a systems framework. Why this is imperative is underscored repeatedly throughout. Moreover, both strategies and methods aimed at urban sustainability need to be sensitive to the real-world subsystem addressed, as well as to the interconnections among systems to which a subsystem connects as part of the whole. We highlight all of the three Es, environment, equity and economy, but note that both strategies and methods overlap these dimensions; for example, there are environmental/spatial aspects to health and a sense of community.

Understanding cities as complex systems is essential in charting a path to sustainability. However, just as important is the need to understand more clearly the strategic points of entry into the city system in bringing about change, in guiding and steering the city – the system – toward sustainability. This entails human volition, vision, leadership, capacity, timing and 'luck'. This is why, in each of the sections of the volume, case studies and examples are provided. While there is no formulaic approach that can be universally applied, there are a number of promising emerging models and helpful examples.

STRATEGIES

The section on strategies highlights several critical dimensions of a sustainable city. It begins with a discussion of the major contemporary effort by planners to address sustainability through compact and smart growth strategies, by Peter Newman (Chapter 2). Strategies for making our cities more sustainable along several key dimensions follow in the subsequent chapters, beginning with the management of water, by Blanca Jiménez Cisneros (Chapter 3), food systems, by Nevin Cohen (Chapter 4), and consumer products, by Gregory A. Keoleian, Joshua P. Newell, Ming Xu and Erin Dreps (Chapter 5). Other strategies that focus on economic dimensions of sustainable cities include attracting green industry, by Karen Chapple (Chapter 6) investing in sustainable infrastructure, by Rae Zimmerman (Chapter 7) and confronting the inevitable reality that no city can be sustainable absent fiscal sustainability (Chapter 8), by Richard F. Callahan and Mark Pisano. Critically important social strategies for sustainability focus on human health, as in the chapter by Alek Miller and Richard J. Jackson (Chapter 9), education, by Michaela Zint and Kimberly S. Wolske (Chapter 10) and strategies for effective public participation, by Connie P. Ozawa (Chapter 11). The section concludes with a focus on justice as a central component of the sustainable city, by Manuel Pastor (Chapter 12).

METHODS

Moving from strategies to methods and tools, a first-order requirement is how to analyze a city's overall metabolism, dealt with by Christopher

Kennedy, Larry Baker and Helge Brattebø (Chapter 13), followed by developing a set of metrics that measure and track progress toward sustainability, by Kent E. Portney (Chapter 14). One of the most salient issues facing cities today is climate change, and as an important dimension of sustainability cities need an operational mitigation plan, which is addressed by Michael R. Boswell, Adrienne I. Greve and Tammy L. Seale (Chapter 15) and a climate adaptation plan, by Adrienne I. Greve and Michael R. Boswell (Chapter 16). In Chapter 17, Adam Rose provides a valuable approach to thinking about the economics of sustainability by framing the issue as one of economic resilience, which enables economists to think ecologically. Finally, it is important to be able to assess the economic value of ecosystem services to a city, and a very concrete transformative way for a city to accomplish this is through its own purchasing practices, as presented by Laurie Kaye Nijaki (Chapter 18).

LOOKING TO THE FUTURE

The above sections of the volume focus on current implementation strategies and methods and tools aimed at providing cities ways to become more sustainable. As such, they are bound by current knowledge and understanding. Yet we recognize, for a volume focused on a sustainable future-in-the-making, that the future is capable of surprising us. With this in mind, we invited scholars who are looking ahead not to what is, but to what ought to be, and what they surmise will be, to develop contributions that are more speculative about aspects of sustainability that are crucial to achieving a more sustainable future for our urban species. This includes a select number of assessments of what a more sustainable city will look and feel like. Tridib Banerjee places the sustainable city in the broad sweep of movements and orthodoxies in planning, looking back and looking ahead (Chapter 19). This is followed by, broadly speaking, a systems assessment of what meaningful sustainable development will need to entail, by Edward J. Blakely (Chapter 20). In Chapter 21, Daniel J. Fiorino unpacks the concept of sustainable governance, and discusses the future of governance for achieving sustainable cities. The role that technology will play in the future, enabling cities to quantify their activities, to become smarter in their resource use, to enable more localized city functions, and to share information widely, is next addressed by Bill Tomlinson (Chapter 22).

The volume closes with a summary and concluding chapter (Chapter 23) by the editors. It provides an overview of the chapters, reflects on the dimensions of sustainable cities addressed by the chapter authors, and raises issues for future research.

NOTE

1. For neo-classical economists, sustainability is interpreted as a 'problem of managing a nation's portfolio of capital (manufactured and natural) to maintain a constant level' (Ayres et al. 2001). Economists further distinguish between weak and strong notions of sustainability. Weak sustainability characterizes the view of neo-classical economists who believe that manufactured capital can be substituted for natural capital. Strong sustainability is the view that the existing stock of natural capital, such as the ozone layer, cannot be substituted by manufactured capital, and therefore must be maintained. This view holds that a minimum amount of different types of capital (economic, ecological and social) should be independently maintained to achieve sustainability (Brekke 1997).

REFERENCES

Ayres, R.U., J.C. van den Bergh and J.M. Gowdy (2001), 'Strong versus weak sustainability: economics, natural sciences, and "consilience"', *Environmental Ethics*, **23** (2), 155–68.

Brekke, Kjell A. (1997), *Economic Growth and the Environment: On the Measurement of Income and Welfare*, Cheltenham, UK and Lyme, USA: Edward Elgar Publishing.

Campbell, S. (1996), 'Green cities, growing cities, just cities? Urban planning and the contradictions of sustainable development', *Journal of the American Planning Association*, **62** (3), 296–312.

Daly, Herman E. and John B. Cobb, Jr (1989), *For the Common Good: Redirecting the Economy toward Community, the Environment, and a Sustainable Future*, Boston, MA: Beacon Press.

Elkington, J. (1994), 'Towards the sustainable corporation: win–win–win business strategies for sustainable development', *California Management Review*, **36** (2), 90–100, available at http://search.ebscohost.com/login.aspx?direct=true&db=buh&AN=9410213932&site=ehost-live (accessed 19 July 2009).

Elkington, John (1998), *Cannibals With Forks: The Triple Bottom Line of 21st Century Business*, Stony Creek, CT: New Society Publishers.

Godschalk, D.R. (2004), 'Land use planning challenges', *Journal of the American Planning Association*, **70** (1), 5–13.

Hempel, Lamont (2009), 'Conceptual and analytical challenges in building sustainable communities', in Daniel A. Mazmanian and Michael E. Kraft (eds), *Toward Sustainable Communities: Transition and Transformations in Environmental Policy*, Boston, MA: MIT Press, ch. 2.

McKean, E. (ed.) (2005), 'sustainable *adj.*', *The New Oxford American Dictionary, Second Edition*, Oxford: Oxford University Press, accessed 4 September 2010.

Ross, A. (2009), 'Modern interpretations of sustainable development', *Journal of Law and Society*, **36** (1), 32–54.

Seto, K.C., A. Reenberg, C.G. Boone, M. Fragkias, D. Haase, T. Langanke, P. Marcotullio, D.K. Munroe, B. Olah and D. Simon (2012), 'Urban land teleconnections and sustainability', *Proceedings of the National Academy of Sciences*, **109** (20), 7687–92.

United Nations (2012), *World Urbanization Prospects, the 2011 Revision*, Department of Economic and Social Affairs, Population Division, New York: United Nations, available at http://esa.un.org/unpd/wup/CD-ROM/Urban-Rural-Population.htm.

United Nations Population Division (2008), *World Urbanization Prospects: The 2007 Revision*, New York: United Nations, available at http://www.un.org/esa/population/publications/wup2007/2007WUP_Highlights_web.pdf (accessed 25 June 2009).

United Nations World Commission on Environment and Development (UN WCED) (1987), *Our Common Future*, Oxford: Oxford University Press, available at http://www.un-documents.net/wc.

Wolman, A. (1965), 'The metabolism of cities', *Scientific American*, **213** (3), 179–90.

PART I

STRATEGIES

2. Rediscovering compact cities for sustainability

Peter Newman

> Density is a key factor in the growth of cities, the happiness of cities, and the wealth of nations. And cities and regions where density is more concentrated near their urban cores – appear to gain the biggest economic advantage. (Florida 2012)

INTRODUCTION

Richard Florida's strong statement on the economic value of more compact cities has been understood for some time (e.g. Sassen 1994; Glaeser 2010). However, it is only in recent times that a more compact city form may be emerging in the world's automobile-dependent cities. To understand this historic trend it is necessary to understand how transport shapes cities and why cities are now rediscovering a more compact, sustainable form.

HISTORY OF URBAN FORM

Many historical and geographical features shape cities, but at any stage in a city's history the patterns of land use can be changed by altering its transportation priorities. Italian physicist Cesare Marchetti (1994) has argued that there is a universal travel time budget of around 1 hour on average per person per day. This 'Marchetti Constant' has been found to apply in every city in our Global Cities Database (Kenworthy et al. 1999; Kenworthy and Laube 2001; Kenworthy 2014) as well as in data on UK cities for the last 600 years (Standing Advisory Committee on Transport 1994). The biological or psychological basis of this Marchetti Constant seems to be a need for a more reflective or restorative period between home and work, but it cannot go on for too long before people become very frustrated due to the need to be more occupied rather than just 'wasting' time between activities.

The Marchetti Constant therefore helps us to see how cities are shaped (Newman and Kenworthy 1999). Cities grow to become 'one hour wide' based on the speed at which people can move in them. So far three city types have emerged.

Walking cities have existed for the past 8000 years, since walking was the only form of transport available to enable people to get across their cities, at speeds of around 5–8 km/h. Thus walking cities were and remain dense (usually over 100 people per ha), mixed-use areas with narrow streets, and are no more than 5–8 km across. They were the major urban form for 8000 years, but substantial parts of cities like Barcelona, Ho Chi Minh City, Mumbai and Hong Kong, for example, retain the character of a walking city. Kraców is mostly a walking city. In squatter settlements, the urban fabric is usually a walking city. In wealthy cities like New York, London, Vancouver and Sydney, the central areas are predominantly walking cities in character though they struggle to retain the walking city urban fabric due to the competing interests of car users. Many cities worldwide are trying to reclaim the fine-grained street patterns associated with walkability in their city centers and they find that they cannot do this without the urban fabric of ancient walking cities (Gehl 2010).

Transit cities from 1850 to 1950 were based on trams and trains that could travel at around 20–30 km/h. This meant they could spread out 20–30 km, with either linear tram-based development (trams being slower led to strips of walking urban fabric), or nodal dense centers along corridors following faster heavy rail lines with walking city urban fabric at stations, like pearls along a string. Densities could be lower (around 50 people per ha) as activities and housing could be spread out further. Most European and wealthy Asian cities retain this urban fabric, as do the old inner cores in US, Australian and Canadian cities. Many developing cities in Asia, Africa and Latin America have the dense corridor form of a transit city, but they do not always have the transit systems to support them, so they become car-saturated. Singapore, Hong Kong and Tokyo have strong densities in centers based on mass transit linkages. Cities like Shenzhen, Jakarta and Dhaka have grown very quickly, with dense, mixed-use urban fabric based only on buses and paratransit; the resulting congestion shows that their activity intensity demands mass transit. Most of these emerging cities are now building the transit systems that suit their urban form; for example, China is building 82 metro rail systems and India is building 16 (Newman et al. 2013). Cities without reasonable densities around train stations are finding that they need to build up the numbers of people and jobs near stations, otherwise not enough activity is there to support such sustainable transport.

Automobile cities from the 1950s onward could spread beyond the 20 km radius as far as 50–80 km, in all directions, and at low density because cars could average 50–80 km/h while traffic levels were low. These cities spread out in every direction due to the flexibility of cars and with zoning that separated activities. These cities provided limited transit, mostly bus services to support their sprawling suburbs. Canadian, Australian, US and New Zealand cities that were developed in this way are now reaching the limits of the Marchetti Constant of a half-hour car commute as they sprawl outwards. The freeways that service such areas are full at peak times and commuters are unable to keep within a reasonable travel-time budget (Newman 1995). This is now a serious political issue, as outer suburban residents are demanding fast rail links that can beat the traffic (McIntosh et al. 2013). At the same time, many people are leaving these areas and moving to better locations with walking city and transit city urban fabrics where they can live within their travel-time budget. The first evidence (see below) is now appearing that these automobile cities are densifying and reducing their car use – they are rediscovering a more compact city.

Cities of all kinds, whether growing megacities or rapidly sprawling ones, constantly face the need to adapt their land use or infrastructure to the travel-time budget. They may not realize that this is what they are doing, but if the Marchetti Constant is exceeded, then markets and politics over time bring about changes, enabling people to adapt by moving closer to their work or finding a better transportation option. The search for better options – in transport and land use – can form the basis of social movements that seek to provide more sustainable cities.

HOW DOES URBAN FORM RELATE TO SUSTAINABILITY?

Figure 2.1 from the Global Cities Database shows the huge range in per capita fuel use that characterizes cities across the world. They all have a combination of these three city types – walking, transit and automobile cities. The fuel use in a city is a surrogate indicator of automobile dependence and, in this case, it is easy to see how US and Australian cities are winning that race.

The city indicated – Barcelona – uses just 8 GJ per person per year compared to 103 GJ in Atlanta and yet they have similar per capita levels of wealth. The difference seems to be that Barcelona is substantially a walking city with some elements of a transit city and almost no trace of an automobile city, whereas Atlanta is almost completely an automobile city with just a little of the transit and walking city urban fabric.

The broader picture is expressed in Figure 2.2, where travel patterns (as reflected by either annual per capita car use or passenger transport energy use) are exponentially related to density of urban activity. Atlanta is 6 people per ha and Barcelona is 200 per ha.

The same patterns can be seen across cities where often the centers are walking cities, the middle suburbs are transit cities and the outer suburbs

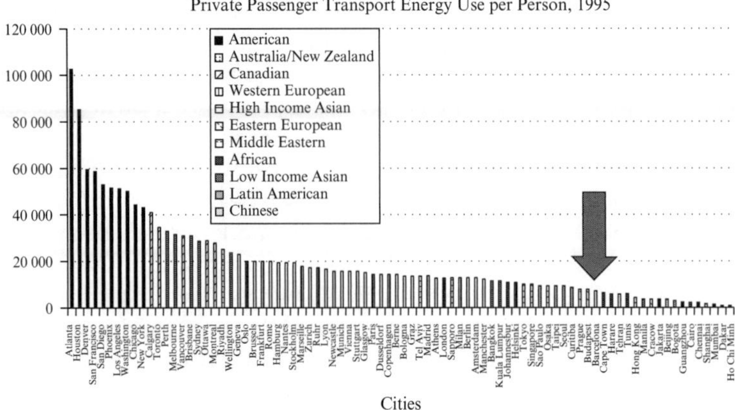

Sources: Kenworthy et al. (1999); Kenworthy and Laube (2001); Kenworthy (2014).

Figure 2.1 Fuel use per person in cities across the world

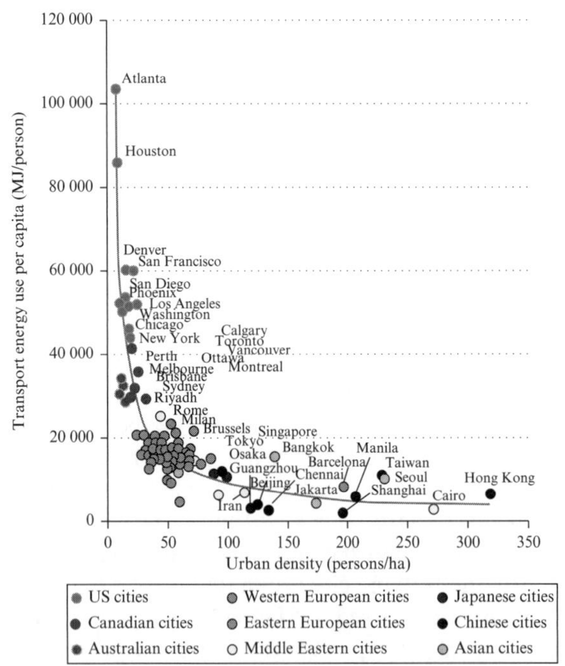

Sources: Kenworthy, J.R. (2010) *Cities Data Base for 2005*, CUSP; Newman and Kenworthy (2014).

Figure 2.2 Transport fuel per person and urban density (people per ha)

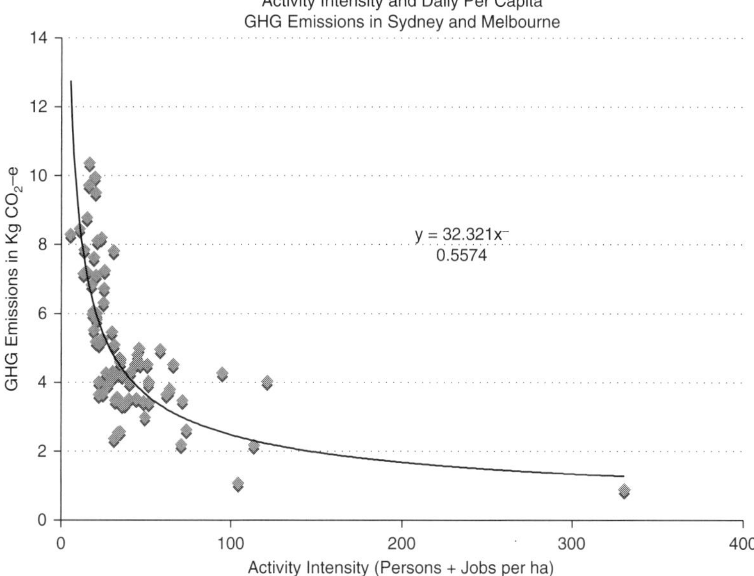

Source: Trubka et al. (2010).

Figure 2.3 Transport fuel use (expressed as CO_2e kgs per person) vs density (people and jobs per ha) in suburbs of Melbourne and Sydney

are automobile cities. This can be seen in Figure 2.3, where Melbourne and Sydney data are shown covering use of transport greenhouse gases per person by suburb versus the density of residents and jobs per ha.

Questions of wealth do not appear to be driving this phenomenon, as there is an inverse relationship between urban intensity and household income in Australian cities – outer suburbs are poorer and yet households in these areas can drive from three to ten times as much as households in the city center. As the data on Melbourne below (Table 2.1) indicate, the poorer households are driving more, using public transport less and walking less because of where they live.

There are obviously complex interactions that influence the intensity of activity and its effects on transport patterns. Ewing and Cervero (2010) have outlined how each of the urban fabric elements, such as density, the mixture or diversity of uses in a place, and design, influence travel. Other factors include the network of transit services provided, income, fuel prices, cultural factors and so on, but all of these can also be linked back to the intensity of activity in various ways. Thus, although many discussions

Table 2.1 Differences in wealth and travel patterns from the urban core to the fringe in Melbourne

	Core	Inner	Middle	Fringe
Percentage of households earning >$70 000 pa	12	11	10	6
Car use (trips/day/cap)	2.12	2.52	2.86	3.92
Public transport (trips/day/cap)	0.66	0.46	0.29	0.21
Walk/bike (trips/day/cap)	2.62	1.61	1.08	0.81

Source: Kenworthy and Newman (2014).

have tried to explain transport in non-land-use terms (e.g. Brindle 1994; Mindali et al. 2004), the data suggest that the physical layout of a city has a fundamental impact on movement patterns – the transport infrastructure priorities shape urban fabric and this in turn shapes transport. This chapter will now try to take the next step and explain how the relationship between transport and activity intensity works.

THE DEGREE OF COMPACTNESS TO FACILITATE WALKING AND TRANSIT

From the two density graphs above (Figures 2.2 and 2.3) and from data in areas where viable transit happens and where viable walking happens, there seems to be a density of around 35 people and jobs per ha for transit and around 100 people and jobs per ha for walking. How can these numbers be understood in terms of guidelines for development to ensure that transit and walking are viable options for more people? The results of work on these questions are in Newman and Kenworthy (2006) and are summarized below.

A pedestrian catchment area or 'ped shed', based on a 10-minute walk, creates an area of approximately 220 to 550 hectares for walking speeds of 5–8 km/h. Thus, for an area of around 300 hectares (a little over a square mile) developed at 35 people and jobs per hectare, there is a threshold requirement of approximately 10 000 residents and jobs within this 10-minute walking area. The range would be from about 8000 to 19 000, based on speeds of 5–8 km/h. Some centers will have many more jobs than others, but the important physical planning guideline is to have a combined minimum activity intensity of residents and jobs necessary for a reasonable local center and a public transport service to support it. Other authors endorse these kinds of numbers for viable local centers and public transport services (Pushkarev and Zupan 1997; Ewing 1996; Frank and Pivo

1994; Cervero 2004). The number of residents or jobs can be increased to the full 10000, or any combination of these, as residents and jobs are similar in terms of transport demand. Either way, the number suggests a threshold below which transit services become non-competitive without relying primarily on car access to extend the catchment area.

Many new car-dependent suburbs have densities more like 12 per hectare and hence have only one-third of the population and jobs required for a viable center. When a center is built for such suburbs, it tends to have just shops, with job densities little higher than the surrounding population densities. Hence the ped shed never reaches the kind of intensity that enables a walkable environment that can ensure viable transit. Many New Urbanist developments primarily emphasize changes to improve the legibility and permeability of street networks, with less attention to the density of activity (Falconer and Newman 2010). As important as such changes are to the physical layout of streets, we should not be surprised when the resulting centers are not able to attract viable commercial arrangements and have only weak public transport. However, centers can be built in stages with much lower numbers to begin with, provided the goal is to reach a density of at least 35 per ha by enabling infill at higher intensities.

If a walking city center is required, then a density of 100 per ha is needed. This gives an idea of the kind of activity that a town center would need: approximately 100000 residents and jobs within this 10-minute walking area. The range again is from around 70000 to 175000 people and jobs. This number could provide for a viable town center based on standard servicing levels for a range of activities. Lower numbers than this means that services in a town center are non-viable and it becomes necessary to increase the center's catchment through widespread dependence on driving from much farther afield. This also means that the human design qualities of the center are compromised because of the need for excessive amounts of parking. Of course, many driving trips within a walking ped shed still occur. However, if sufficient amenities and services are provided, then only short car trips are needed, which contributes to making the center less car-dependent. 'Footloose jobs', particularly those related to the global economy, can theoretically go anywhere in a city and can make the difference between a viable center or not. However, there is considerable evidence that such jobs are locating in dense centers of activity due to the need for networking and quick 'face-to-face' meetings between professionals. High-amenity, walking-scale environments are better able to attract such jobs because they offer the kind of environmental quality, livability and diversity that these professionals seek. As Florida (2012) says, 'Economic growth and development, according to several key measures, is higher in metros that are not just dense, but where density is more concentrated. This is true for productivity, measured as economic output per person, as well as both income and wages.'

Talent levels are also higher where density is more concentrated. This holds for both the share of college graduates and the share of knowledge, professional and creative workers (Glaeser 2010). Most citizens who experience car dependence, and have long commutes involving being stuck in traffic, can understand the need for more sustainable options, since they directly feel and bear the economic, social and environmental consequences of car dependence. They want other options provided for them. As cities continue to evolve, the politics of sustainable transport will demand both more livable and less car-dependent options for the future.

The key to this move towards sustainability is better provision of access to transit that is faster than cars along corridors, and better provision for walking and cycling in local areas, associated with a supportive land-use structure of intensive centers with minimum land-use activity intensity of 35 people and jobs per ha. This is due to a fundamental need to ensure that the more sustainable transport modes have a competitive speed advantage for long trips (transit) and for short trips (bike/walk) within centers.

WHAT IS NEXT – THE DEMISE OF THE AUTOMOBILE CITY?

In 2009 the Brookings Institution was the first to recognize a new phenomenon in the world's developed cities – declines in car use (Puentes and Tomer 2009). The data below confirm this trend. Peak car use suggests that we are witnessing the end of building cities around cars as the primary goal of planning – at least in the developed world – and probably the rediscovery of the compact city. Perhaps we are witnessing the demise of further automobile city building.

The Data on Car Use Trends

Puentes and Tomer (2009) first picked up the declining trend in per capita car use starting in 2004 in US cities. They were able to show that this trend was occurring in most US cities and by 2010 was evident in absolute declines in car use. The data are summarized in Figure 2.4.

Stanley and Barrett (2010) found a similar trend in Australian cities and that the peak had come at a similar time – 2004 – and car use per capita at least seemed to be trending down since then. We have since mapped this in all Australian cities, including small ones where congestion is no issue (Figure 2.5).

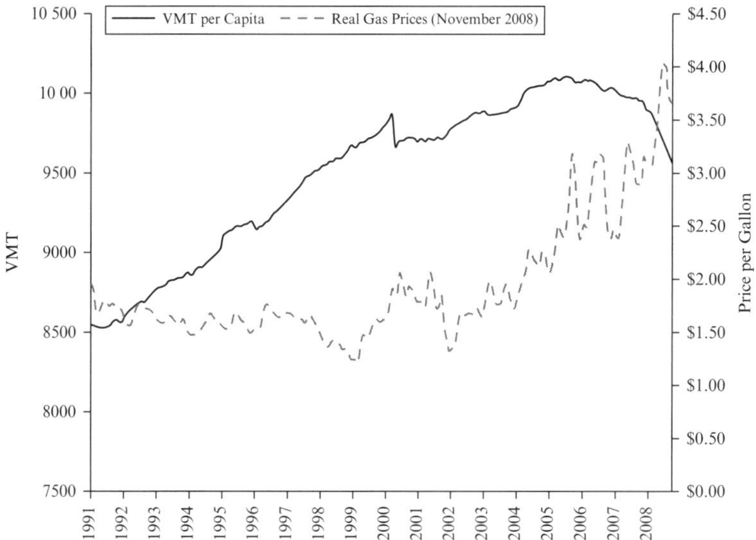

Source: Traffic Volume Trends and Energy Information Administration.

Figure 2.4 Peaking of US vehicle miles of travel (VMT)

Millard-Ball and Schipper (2010) examined the trends in eight industrialized countries that demonstrate what they call 'peak travel'. They conclude that

> Despite the substantial cross national differences, one striking commonality emerges: travel activity has reached a plateau in all eight countries in this analysis. The plateau is even more pronounced when considering only private vehicle use, which has declined in recent years in most of the eight countries . . . Most aggregate energy forecasts and many regional travel demand models are based on the core assumption that travel demand will continue to rise in line with income. As we have shown in the paper, this assumption is one that planners and policy makers should treat with extreme caution. (Ibid., p. 16)

The Global Cities Database (Kenworthy and Laube 2001; Kenworthy et al. 1999) has been expanding its global reach since the first data were collected in the 1970s. While the 2005–10 data are not yet complete, the first signs of a decline in car use can be gleaned from previous data. This was first recognized by us when we saw that cities in the developed world grew in car use per capita in the 1960s by 42 percent, in the 1970s by 26 percent, and the 1980s by 23 percent. The new data now show that the period 1995–2005 had a growth in car use per capita of just 5.1 percent, which is consistent with the above data on peak car use. The reductions started after this decade and appear to be continuing (Gargett 2012).

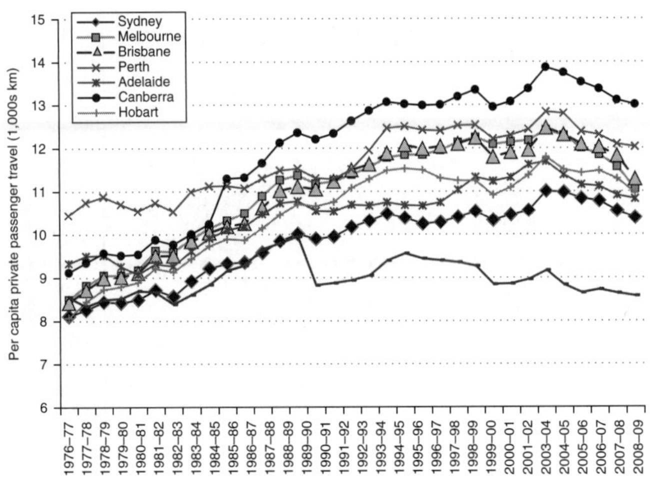

Source: Bureau of Transport and Resource Economics.

Figure 2.5 Peaking of car use in Australian cities

In the 26 cities that account for the 1995–2005 percentage increase in car VKT per capita, some cities actually declined in VKT per capita during this period. Some European cities show this pattern: London has declined 1.2 percent, Stockholm 3.7 percent, Vienna 7.6 percent and Zurich 4.7 percent. In the USA, Atlanta went down 10.1 percent, Houston 15.2 percent (both from extraordinarily high levels of car use in 1995), Los Angeles declined 2.0 percent and San Francisco 4.8 percent. The acceleration in decline has mostly been since that time.

Peak car use appears to be happening. It is a major historical discontinuity that was largely unpredicted by most urban professionals and academics. So what is causing this to occur?

The Possible Causes of 'Peak Car Use'

The following five factors are examined; they all suggest that a more compact city is emerging.

1. Hitting the Marchetti wall

As outlined above, the travel-time budget matters. Freeways designed to get people quickly around cities have become car parks at peak hours. Travel times have grown to the point where cities based around cars are becoming dysfunctional. As cities have filled with cars, the limit to the spread of the city has become more and more apparent, with the politics of road rage

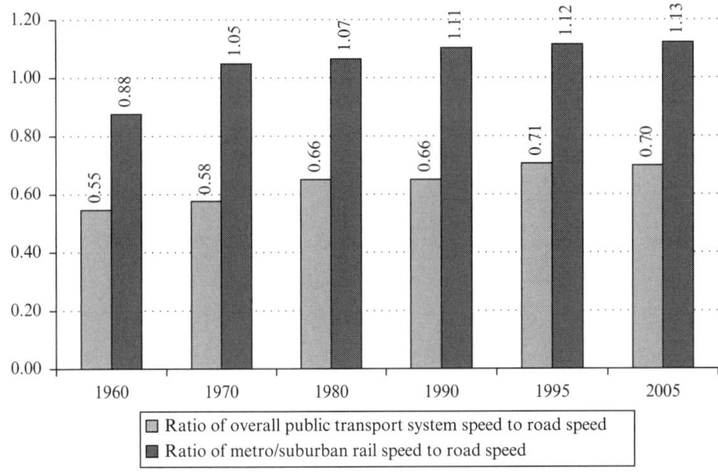

Source: Newman et al. (2013).

Figure 2.6 Relative speed of transit to car traffic and rail to car traffic in global cities, 1960–2005

becoming a bigger part of everyday life and many people just choosing to live closer in. The trends in relative speeds are shown in Figure 2.6.

The ratio of overall public transport system speed compared to general road traffic has increased from 0.55 to 0.70 between 1960 and 2005, the ratio of rail system speed to general road traffic has gone from rail being slower than cars in 1960 (0.88) to a situation in 2005 where rail was on average faster (1.13). Thus rail has become increasingly viable as an option in the world's cities. And with this trend, there will be a greater emphasis on rail-induced compact land-use patterns and a growing move away from freeway-induced land-use scatter. The data below support this. The automobile city seems to have hit the Marchetti wall.

2. The growth of public transport

The extraordinary revival of public transport globally and especially in car-dependent Australian and American cities is demonstrated in Figures 2.7 and 2.8.

Transport planners always saw the growth in transit as a small part of the transport task, and believed that car use growth would continue unabated. However, there is an exponential relationship between car use and public transport use that indicates how significant the impact of transit can be. By increasing transit per capita, the use of cars per capita is predicted to go down exponentially. This is the so-called 'transit leverage' effect (Neff 1996;

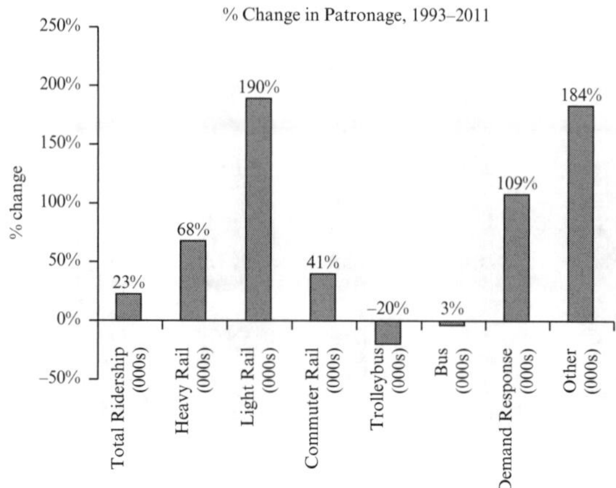

Source: American Public Transportation Association (2013).

Figure 2.7 Recent strong growth in US transit use, especially rail

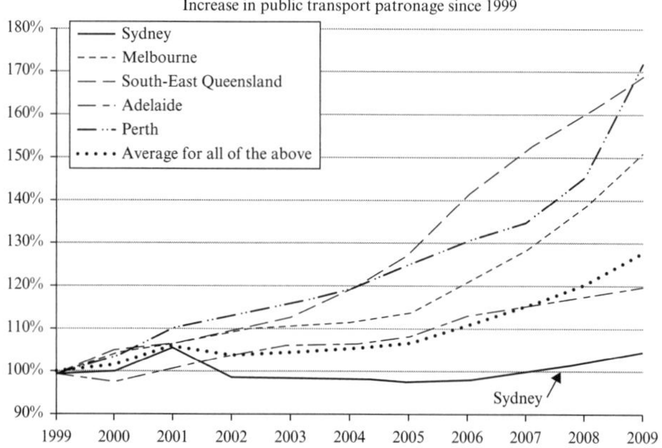

Source: Currie et al. (2008).

Figure 2.8 Growth in transit use in Australian cities since 1999

Newman et al. 2008). Thus, even small increases in transit can begin to put a large dent in car use growth and will eventually cause it to peak and decline.

3. The reversal of urban sprawl

The turning back in of cities leads to increases in density rather than the continuing declines that have characterized the growth phase of automobile cities in the past 50 years. The data on density suggest that the peak

Table 2.2 Trends in urban density in some US, Canadian, Australian and European cities, 1960–2005.

Cities	1960 Urban density persons/ ha	1970 Urban density persons/ ha	1980 Urban density persons/ ha	1990 Urban density persons/ ha	1995 Urban density persons/ ha	2005 Urban density persons/ ha
Brisbane	21.0	11.3	10.2	9.8	9.6	9.7
Melbourne	20.3	18.1	16.4	14.9	13.7	15.6
Perth	15.6	12.2	10.8	10.6	10.9	11.3
Sydney	21.3	19.2	17.6	16.8	18.9	19.5
Chicago	24.0	20.3	17.5	16.6	16.8	16.9
Denver	18.6	13.8	11.9	12.8	15.1	14.7
Houston	10.2	12.0	8.9	9.5	8.8	9.6
Los Angeles	22.3	25.0	24.4	23.9	24.1	27.6
New York	22.5	22.6	19.8	19.2	18.0	19.2
Phoenix	8.6	8.6	8.5	10.5	10.4	10.9
San Diego	11.7	12.1	10.8	13.1	14.5	14.6
San Francisco	16.5	16.9	15.5	16.0	20.5	19.8
Vancouver	24.9	21.6	18.4	20.8	21.6	25.2
Frankfurt	87.2	74.6	54.0	47.6	47.6	45.9
Hamburg	68.3	57.5	41.7	39.8	38.4	38.0
Munich	56.6	68.2	56.9	53.6	55.7	55.0
Zurich	60.0	58.3	53.7	47.1	44.3	43.0

Source: Newman and Kenworthy (2011).

in decline has occurred and cities are now densifying faster than they are spreading out. Table 2.2 contains data on a sample of cities in Australia, the USA, Canada and Europe showing urban densities from 1960 to 2005 that clearly demonstrate this turning point in the more highly automobile-dependent cities. In the small sample of European cities included in the table, densities are still declining due to shrinkage or absolute reductions in population, but the data clearly show the rate of decline in urban density slowing down and almost stabilizing as re-urbanization occurs.

The relationship between density and car use is also exponential, as shown above. If a city begins to slowly increase its density, then the impact on car use can be more extensive than expected. The compact city is being rediscovered.

4. The growth of a culture of urbanism

Commentators are increasingly picking up a renewed interest in living an urban and less suburban lifestyle (Leinberger 2007; Newman and Newman

2006). Puentes and Tomer (2009) suggest that this is not a fashion but a structural change based on the opportunities that are provided by greater urbanism. The cultural change associated with this urbanism is reflected in many aspects of popular culture, especially the use of mobile digital devices that enable freedom and connection without a car (Florida 2010).

5. The rise in fuel prices

The vulnerability of outer suburbs to increasing fuel prices was noted in the first fuel crisis in 1973–74 and in all subsequent fuel crisis periods when fuel-price volatility was clearly reflected in real-estate values (Fels and Munson 1974; Romanos 1978). The return to 'normal' after each crisis led many commentators to believe that the link between fuel and urban form may not be as dramatic as first presented by people like us (Newman and Kenworthy 1989; 1999). However, the impact of $140 a barrel oil on real estate in the USA led dramatically to the global financial crisis (sub-prime mortgagees were unable to pay their mortgages when fuel prices tripled).

Despite the global recession, the twenty-first century has been faced with a consolidation of fuel prices at the upper end of those experienced in the last 50 years of automobile city growth. Most oil commentators, including oil companies, now admit to the end of the era of cheap oil, even if not fully accepting the peak-oil phenomenon (Newman et al. 2009). The compact city is being driven by the transport factors outlined above, but fuel-price volatility will certainly add to the value of living closer to urban activity.

FACILITATING A MORE COMPACT CITY

Density increases are not easily achieved in any city, especially given an automobile city urban fabric. Rather than uniform increases everywhere, the urban planning profession has been developing ways to focus density in automobile cities. This model of the compact city is often called the polycentric city, as in Figure 2.9, with the rationale of reducing car dependence by creating small, walkable cities in the suburbs linked by fast, quality rail transit. This model has multiple sustainability advantages in terms of reductions in car use, oil use and building-energy use, better equity and health outcomes and stronger economies through agglomeration benefits (Schiller et al. 2010; Owen 2004; Newman and Kenworthy 1999; Newman et al. 2009).

Facilitating the more compact polycentric city needs a range of new and old planning tools. Old tools like strategic plans linked to infrastructure

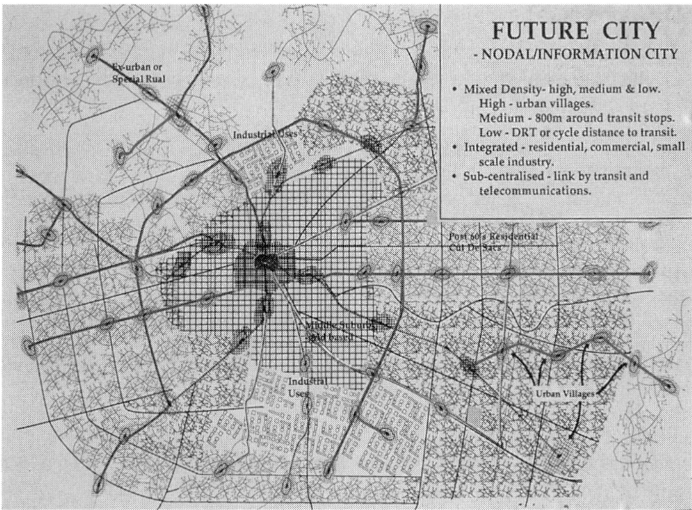

Source: Kenworthy et al. (1999).

Figure 2.9 The more compact polycentric city

plans are essential. Building fast rail out into the automobile city suburbs has been shown to work very successfully when the speed of transit is better than the car-based clogged freeways (McIntosh et al. 2013). New tools such as financing transit through value capture, new forms of governance that enable greater regional autonomy and more deliberative, participative processes, as well as new digital planning tools for assisting redevelopment, are all going to be needed (McIntosh et al. 2013; Briand and Hartz-Karp 2013; Glackin et al. 2013; Newton et al. 2012). In addition, the new techniques of biophilic urbanism that bring nature into urban buildings through green walls and green roofs, which are appearing in the many compact cities of Asia, are also needed (Newman and Matan 2013).

CONCLUSIONS

The compact city is being rediscovered. Only time will tell if this is a truly structural change or a small shift in a longer-term continuation of density declines over the past century or so. The evidence above suggests that it may be a structural change, and that a more sustainable city may finally be appearing to reduce the impact of automobile dependence. Tools to help accelerate this phenomenon are also emerging.

REFERENCES

American Public Transportation Association (2013), *Public Transportation Fact Book, Appendix A: Historical Tables*, Washington, DC: American Public Transportation Association.

Briand, M. and J. Hartz-Karp (2013), *From Surviving to Thriving: The Way of Participatory Sustainability*, Washington, DC: Island Press (in press).

Brindle, R.E. (1994), 'Lies, damned lies and "automobile dependence": some hyperbolic reflections', *Papers of the Australian Transport Research Forum*, **19**, 117–31.

Cervero, Robert (2004), *Transit Oriented Development in the United States: Experiences, Challenges and Prospects, Volume 102*, Washington, DC: Transportation Research Board, National Research Council.

Currie, G., J. Stanley and J. Stanley (2007), *No Way to Go: Transport and Social Disadvantage in Australian Communities*, Victoria: Monash University.

Ewing, Reid (1996), *Transit Oriented Development in the Sun Belt, Transportation Research Record, 1552, TRB*, Washington, DC, USA: National Research Council.

Ewing, R. and R. Cervero (2010), 'Travel and the built environment: a meta analysis', *Journal of the American Planning Association*, **76** (3), 265–94.

Falconer, Ryan and Peter Newman (2010), *Growing Up: Reforming Land Use and Transport in 'Conventional' Car Dependent Cities*, Saarbruecken, DE: VDM Verlag Dr. Müller.

Falconer, R., P. Newman and B. Giles-Corti (2010), 'Is practice aligned with the principles? Implementing New Urbanism in Perth, Western Australia', *Transport Policy*, **17** (5), 287–94.

Fels, M.F. and M.J. Munson (1974), 'Energy thrift in urban transportation: options for the future', Ford Foundation Energy Policy Project Report, New York: Ford Foundation.

Florida, R. (2010), *The Great Reset: How New Ways of Living and Working Drive Post-Crash Prosperity*, New York: HarperCollins.

Florida, R. (2012), 'Cities with denser cores do better', *The Atlantic* (28 November), http://www.theatlanticcities.com/jobs-and-economy/2012/11/cities-denser-cores-do-better/3911/ (accessed 10 February 2012).

Frank, L.D. and G. Pivo (1994), 'Impacts of mixed use and density on utilization of three modes of travel: single-occupant vehicle, transit, and walking', *Transportation Research Record: Journal of the Transportation Research Board*, **1466** (1980), 44–52.

Gargett, D. (2012), 'Traffic growth: modeling a global phenomenon', *World Transport Policy and Practice*, **18** (4), 27–45.

Gehl, Jan (2010), *Cities for People*, Washington, DC: Island Press.

Glackin, S., R. Trubka, P. Newman, P. Newton and M. Mouritz (2013), 'Greening the greyfields: trials, tools and tribulations of redevelopment in the middle suburbs', in *Planning Institute of Australia National Congress Program Handbook*, Canberra, ACT: Planning Institute of Australia.

Glaeser, Edward (2010), *The Triumph of the City: How Our Greatest Invention Makes us Richer, Smarter, Greener, Healthier and Happier*, London: Macmillan.

Kenworthy, J. (2014), 'Decoupling car use and metropolitan GDP growth', *World Transport Policy and Practice*, **19** (4), 8–21.

Kenworthy, Jeffery and Felix Laube (2001), *The Millennium Cities Database for Sustainable Transport*, Brussels: International Union of Public Transport (UITP).

Kenworthy, Jeffrey, Felix Laube, Peter Newman, Paul Barter, Tamim Raad, Chamlong Poboon and Benedicto Guia (1999), *An International Sourcebook of Automobile Dependence in Cities, 1960–1990*, Boulder, CO: University Press of Colorado.

Leinberger, Christopher B. (2007), *The Option of Urbanism: Investing in a New American Dream*, Washington, DC: Island Press.

Marchetti, C. (1994), 'Anthropological invariants in travel behaviour', *Technical Forecasting and Social Change*, **47** (1), 75–78.

McIntosh, J., P. Newman and G. Glazebrook (2013), 'Why fast trains work: an assessment of a fast regional rail system in Perth, Australia', *Journal of Transportation Technologies*, **3**, 37–47.

McIntosh, J., P. Newman, J. Scheurer and M. Mouritz (2014), 'Can value capture work in car-dependent cities?', *Transport Research Part A* (in press).

Millard-Ball, A. and L. Schipper (2010), 'Are we reaching peak travel? Trends in passenger transport in eight industrialized countries', *Transport Reviews*, **31** (3), 1–22.

Mindali, O., A. Raveh and I. Saloman (2004), 'Urban density and energy consumption: a new look at old statistics', *Transportation Research, Part A: Policy and Practice*, **38** (2), 143–62.

Neff, J.W. (1996), 'Substitution rates between transit and automobile travel', in *Association of American Geographers Annual Meeting*, Charlotte, NC.

Newman, C.E. and P.W.G. Newman (2006), 'Live-in culture: cars', in P. Beilharz and T. Hogan (eds), *Sociology: Place, Time and Division*, Melbourne: Oxford University Press, pp. 302–6.

Newman, P. (1995), 'The end of the urban freeway', *World Transport Policy and Practice*, **1** (1), 12–19.

Newman, Peter and Jeffrey Kenworthy (1989), *Cities and Automobile Dependence: An International Sourcebook*, Brookfield, VT: Gower Publishing.

Newman, Peter and Jeffrey Kenworthy (1999), *Sustainability and Cities: Overcoming Automobile Dependence*, Washington, DC: Island Press.

Newman, P. and J. Kenworthy (2006), 'Urban design to reduce automobile dependence', *Opolis*, **2** (1), 35–52.

Newman, P. and J. Kenworthy (2011), 'Peak car use: understanding the demise of automobile dependence', *World Transport Policy and Practice*, **17** (2), 32–42.

Newman, P. and J. Kenworthy (2014), 'Urban passenger transport energy consumption and carbon dioxide emissions', in R. Hickman, M. Givoni, D. Bonilla and D. Bannister (eds), *International Handbook on Transport and Development*, Cheltenham, UK and Northampton, MA, USA: Edward Elgar.

Newman, Peter and Anne Matan (2013), *Green Urbanism in Asia: The Emerging Green Tigers*, Toh Tuk Link, SG: World Scientific Publishing.

Newman, P., J. Kenworthy and G. Glazebrook (2008), 'How to create exponential decline in car use in Australian cities', *Australian Planner*, **45** (3), 17–19.

Newman, Peter, Timothy Beatley and Heather Boyer (2009), *Resilient Cities: Responding to Peak Oil and Climate Change*, Washington, DC: Island Press.

Newman, P., G. Glazebrook and J. Kenworthy (2013), 'Peak car and the rise and rise of global rail', *Transport Reviews* (forthcoming).

Newton P., P. Newman, S. Glackin and R. Trubka (2012), 'Greening the greyfields: unlocking the development potential of middle suburbs in Australian cities', *World Academy of Science, Engineering and Technology*, **71**, 138–57.

Owen, D. (2004), 'Green Manhattan: why New York is the greenest city in the US', *The New Yorker* (18 October).

Puentes, Robert and Adie Tomer (2009), 'The road . . . less travelled: an analysis of vehicle miles traveled trends in the US', *Metropolitan Infrastructure Initiatives Series*, Washington, DC: Brookings Institution.

Pushkarev, Boris and Jeffrey Zupan (1997), *Public Transportation and Land Use Policy*, Bloomington, IN and London: Indiana Press.

Romanos, M.C. (1978), 'Energy price effects on metropolitan spatial structure and form', *Environment and Planning A*, **10** (1), 93–104.

Sassen, Saskia (1994), *Cities in a World Economy*, Thousand Oaks, CA: Pine Forge Press.

Schiller, Preston L., Eric C. Bruun and Jeffrey R. Kenworthy (2010), *An Introduction to Sustainable Transportation: Policy, Planning and Implementation*, London: Earthscan.

Standing Advisory Committee for Trunk Road Assessment (1994), *Trunk Roads and the Generation of Traffic*, London: Department of Transport.

Stanley, John and Simon Barrett (2010), *Moving People – Solutions for a Growing Australia*, Kingston, ACT: Australasian Railway Association, Bus Industry Confederation and UITP.

Trubka R., P. Newman and D. Bilsborough (2010), 'Costs of urban sprawl: predicting transport greenhouse gases from urban form parameters', *Environment Design Guide*, **GEN 84**, 1–16.

3. Potable, stormwater and wastewater city strategies in the context of climate change

Blanca Jiménez Cisneros

SUMMARY

This chapter describes the challenges to supply water services for cities in the future, considering the impacts of climate change. Many of these challenges will be present even in the absence of climate variation as they are also caused by population growth, types of development and the inefficient management of urban water worldwide. Options to address the problems identified are presented, highlighting those specifically linked to climate change adaptation or mitigation measures. One important aspect is the need to review the concept of urban water services as it has been made urgent by the need to properly manage water in cities.

INTRODUCTION

In many countries, water accounts for a significant share of the costs of climate change impacts due to the many economic activities dependent upon it. Parry et al. (2009) estimated that the cost of adaptation of the water sector represents a similar investment to that needed to fulfill the MDG (Millennium Development Goals, costing US$9–11 billion per year, according UNFCCC 2007). To reduce these costs, strategies for adaptation are needed, notably for municipal water services. However, these are difficult to identify at a local level as impacts are the result of direct and indirect events and act through a long and complex chain of events that are not always obviously related (NACWA 2009). In this context, the literature recommends the development of 'a portfolio' of adaptation options, including 'low regret solutions' to reduce vulnerability and increase resilience to climate change. This chapter describes the impacts of climate change on urban water services and identifies measures that may be helpful in building such a portfolio.

MUNICIPAL WATER SERVICES

Municipal water services are those that the government has to provide for the population to allow access to safe water. Users include not only households, but also urban services, businesses and even industries that are connected to the municipal network. The water supply service is expected to provide water continuously, at reasonable price and of sufficient quantity and quality (in terms of drinking water). In addition, water utilities should also have a clear mandate to control the demand for water so they can proactively encourage its efficient and rational use.

Municipal water services also include the collection of wastewater, its treatment and disposal. Besides this, many other activities are necessary (Jiménez 2011), although these are not always considered in the legal and institutional frameworks of different countries. These include: (a) the collection and treatment of urban runoff; (b) the protection of people and their possessions from urban floods; (c) the reuse and safe reintegration of used water (wastewater) into the environment to protect the water sources; (d) the management of septic tanks and latrines (including the excreta contained in them and its periodic removal). In addition to the generally inadequate definition of sanitation services, they are provided throughout the world extremely unevenly, not only in terms of coverage but also in terms of quality. While in developed countries 99 percent of the wastewater is properly collected, treated and even reused, in developing ones this barely reaches 50 percent and almost always includes collection without treatment (WWAP 2009).

POTENTIAL IMPACTS OF CLIMATE CHANGE ON WATER SERVICES

Climate change has the potential to affect the way in which municipal water services are provided, not only in terms of how they are conceived but also in terms of infrastructure and methods of operation. It may affect not only the supply of drinking water but also its demand. Some effects of climate change are directly linked to climate, while others act indirectly as the result of a complex chain of events. Some of these may be anthropogenic, acting independently, in series or in parallel, to those originating from climate change (Figure 3.1). These effects are described below.

Direct Effects

Increased ambient temperature

Increased ambient temperature results in higher evaporation losses.

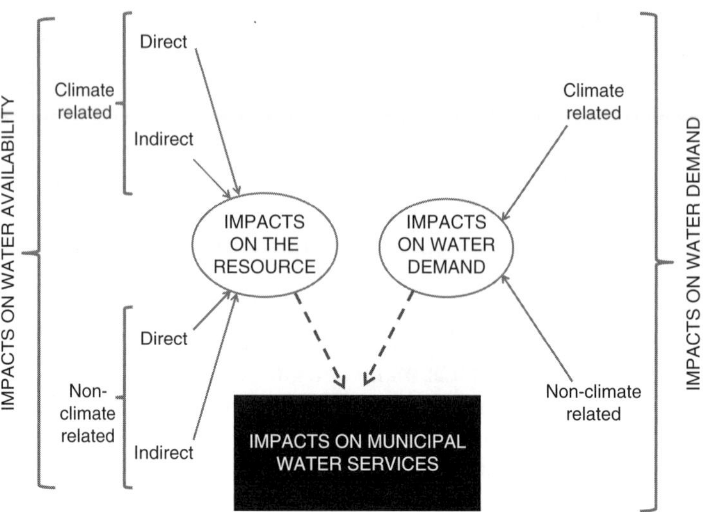

Figure 3.1 Impacts on municipal water services due to the impacts of climate change on water availability and water demand

Evaporation not only reduces the amount of water stored in lakes, dams and aquifers, but also affects resources transported by rivers and those contained in the soil as humidity. Dry soils need to absorb more water before runoff occurs. Thus, even when it rains, drier soil needs additional water before runoff supplying rivers and aquifers occurs (Zwolsman et al. 2010).

Snow and ice packs serve as reservoirs just like dams. Higher temperatures make them smaller, reducing the amount of stored water and hence its availability (Zwolsman et al. 2010). More than one-sixth of the world's population lives in basins fed from the melting of snow and ice, and thus this process is of considerable importance (Bates et al. 2008).

Higher ambient temperature is also the cause of higher water temperature. This may have different effects on the quality of water, depending on natural and anthropogenically moderated local conditions (Box 3.1). One example is the exacerbation of algal and blue-green bacterial blooms in natural and artificial reservoirs polluted with nutrients, resulting in taste and odour problems, and the presence of cyanotoxins in drinking water. Cyanotoxins have been linked to different diseases and even deaths in both developing and developed countries. The removal of these pollutants can only be accomplished using costly treatment processes, such as activated carbon (Van Vliet and Zwolsman 2008; Thorne 2008).

A higher ambient temperature, reducing the amount of available water, also reduces the dilution capacity for pollutants in water bodies. In addi-

BOX 3.1 EFFECT OF TEMPERATURE INCREASE ON WATER QUALITY

In Wuxi City, Jiangsu Province, China, water is supplied from Lake Taihu. The combination of an increased content of nutrients and higher atmospheric and water temperatures have led to the uncontrolled growth of cyanobacteria. The content of microcystins in water exceeded the WHO guideline of 1 μg/L. Due to this situation nearly two million people were forced to consume bottled water rather than tap water for over two months. (Qin et al. 2010)

BOX 3.2 TOXIC BY-PRODUCTS IN DISINFECTED WATER

At the Schoharie Creek Basin, New York, a higher and different composition of organic matter in the raw water is interfering with the disinfection process. The doses of chemicals required for treatment have increased. The total treatment costs have increased, not only because of this but also due to the need to control the disinfection by-products formed, and the need to treat and dispose of a greater amount of sludge. In addition, some water utilities in the northeast of the United States and Northern Europe have reported increases in the colour of raw water and the content of disinfection by-products linked to higher temperatures. (Zwolsman et al. 2010)

tion, a higher water temperature changes the composition of the aquatic flora and fauna and with it the content and nature of their metabolites in water. This frequently leads to the formation of by-products during disinfection of water at treatment plants (Box 3.2).

With regard to sanitation services, increased corrosion of sewers due to a higher release of sulphides with higher temperatures might be expected. However, on the other hand, wastewater treatment process, notably biological ones, may perform better as microorganisms depollute at a higher rate (Tchobanoglous et al. 2003).

Sea-level rise

In cities supplied by coastal aquifers or estuaries, saline intrusion due to sea-level rise might occur (Bonte and Zwolsman 2010). The extracted water will need treatment processes that are three to five times more expensive than those conventionally used to potabilize non-saline water. In sewers, the introduction of saline water to wastewater might occur, inhibiting its treatment. Additionally, discharge sites operated by gravity might no longer function (Boxall et al. 2009; Brooks et al. 2009; NACWA 2009; OFWAT 2009; Zwolsman et al. 2010). To control saline intrusion, there are several examples around the world in which water, and even reused water, is reinjected into the subsoil.

Changes in precipitation

Changes in rainfall affect water availability, not only due to its reduction or increase, but also its monthly, annual and even decadal variations.

Decreases Simply put, if it rains less, less water will be available. This affects not only the amount of available water but also its capacity to dilute pollutants (Van Vliet and Zwolsman 2008; Thorne 2008). In aquifers with already high contents of iron, manganese, arsenic or fluorine, these might be expected to increase further (Butscher and Huggenberger 2009; Dipankar et al. 2011).

Increases Wetter climates lead to increases in operating costs due to the more frequent need to clean water supply systems to remove sediments from rivers, bays, wetlands, water tanks and so on. Intense showers also sweep pollutants from the soil, for example in livestock areas, agricultural fields using manure, sewers, septic tanks, unsewered areas and even from the polluted urban air to surface and underground water sources (Brooks et al. 2009; Jiménez and Rose 2009). Several outbreaks of waterborne diseases during extreme rain events have been documented in the literature (Curreiro et al. 2001; Boxall et al. 2009; Jiménez and Rose 2009; Kundzewicz and Krysanova 2010; Dipankar et al. 2011; Butscher and Huggenberger 2009; Zwoslman et al. 2010).

Even if the annual amount of rainfall remains the same, more intense showers will lead to increased operating cost of sewers and even a need to increase their capacity (NACWA 2009; OFWAT 2009). Freas et al. (2008) calculated that, for climate change scenarios in which the number of storms demanding the use of the entire sewerage system increased by 35 percent, there would be a need to increase the storage volume by 57 percent. During wastewater treatment there will be a need to treat higher volumes of wastewater and urban storm runoff with a higher content of some types of pollutants. Besides increasing operating costs because of treatment, there will be a demand for additional costs to treat and dispose of increased levels of sludge. Eventually there will be a need to add extra

> **BOX 3.3 WATER AND HEALTH RISKS**
>
> In Philadelphia, a 9 percent increase in hospitalization of the population over 65 years of age due to diarrheic diseases was documented. This occurred nine days after the turbidity in the influent water of a local drinking water treatment plant increased, even though the plant fulfilled the standards set for treated water. Similar observations have been reported in the city of Belmont. (Schwartz et al. 2000)

treatment processes to address different types of pollutants or higher pollution loads.

Variable rainfall The main concern arising from variable rainfall is the lack of reliable water supply. This would also demand additional artificial storage capacity to match the variations in availability with the constant municipal water demand.

Extreme events (floods and droughts)

Droughts The water and wastewater networks have a greater risk of cracking in very dry soils that tend to shrink and put pressure on pipelines. For wastewater pipelines, in addition to their cost of replacement, the potential contamination of water sources from leaks should be considered.

Floods During flood events, failures of infrastructure may be experienced, even on a temporary basis, leaving the population with an unsafe supply and without protection from wastewater contamination. Chemicals, materials and equipment may also be damaged.

Indirect effects

Other factors linked to climate change which indirectly affect water resources may be identified. One example is deforestation. With higher atmospheric temperatures, forests become more sensitive to diseases, plagues and fires. Emelko et al. (2011) compared three sub-basins in the same region of Canada with different degrees of deforestation: one highly deforested as result of a recent fire: another under recovering conditions four years after a fire: and a third one undamaged and used as a reference. The comparison was based on the pollutant content in a river and the cost to treat its water for supply. For the damaged basins, the river water was not only highly polluted but the pollutant content was extremely variable throughout the year. These two situations affected not only the operating costs of the water treatment plant but also the reliability of the quality of the treated water. In addition, the pollutant composition was different in the different regions. In the damaged basins, odour, taste, potentially toxic organic compounds and even mercury were problematic. These issues were not observed in the undamaged basin. For mercury alone, its content was up to 60 percent higher than in the unaffected basin, with values surpassing the US EPA drinking water criteria by several times.

POTENTIAL IMPACTS OF CLIMATE CHANGE ON WATER DEMAND

Direct Effects

In relation to water demand, higher temperatures increase the consumption of water, not only by the inhabitants of cities but also by industry (for cooling, for instance) and agriculture. This situation puts additional stress on the competition for water among users. Extreme changes in climatic conditions or anthropogenic factors result in population migration, and with it changes in sites of water demand (Zwolsman et al. 2010).

Indirect Effects

Water demand may be affected by (Arnell and Delaney 2006; Butscher and Huggenberg 2009):

- population migration patterns that modify the distribution of water demand;
- tougher competition for water, as a result of the impacts of climate change on the agriculture and energy sectors; and
- the need to allocate specific amounts of water for ecosystems under warmer conditions.

CRITICAL GEOGRAPHIC CONDITIONS

Due to the challenges of providing municipal water services under climate change scenarios (Zwolsman et al. 2010), three geographical regions are considered to be the most vulnerable. These are:

- Lowlands and flat zones, such as those in river deltas or close to the ocean. These areas are flood-prone. This puts hydraulic infrastructure at risk and generally results in increased competition for water among users during dry conditions, for example for navigation, agricultural and power generation.
- Mountainous regions and elevated areas for which it is costly to raise water from lower basins to feed populated areas. Due to their geography, they need to rely on the water from their own basins.
- Arid and semi-arid regions that are already under critical situations of water stress. Any additional stressors put systems at high risk.

VULNERABILITY RELATED TO WATER SERVICES

It is important to assess the vulnerability of water services to climate change. This can be done for the service (including the infrastructure), but must also be applied to the population, considering different social classes and geographical conditions. In this context it also becomes evident that vulnerability is due not only to the impacts of climate change but many other factors acting in combination with it (Emelko et al. 2011; OFWAT 2009). However, the methodologies for these assessments are still under development, especially to deal with the uncertainty derived from the different climate change scenarios (NACWA 2009). These may be attributed partially or totally to the impacts of climate change.

COSTS OF ADAPTATION

To analyze the costs of adaptation measures it is necessary to consider the costs of impacts. These are difficult to define due to uncertainties of the different future scenarios, which include not only the effects of climate change but also population growth and changes in economic conditions, among others. Many of these scenarios fail to capture the future cost of water and the different ways in which it can be allocated, depending on social or political factors. Moreover, it is difficult to interpret costs when the same product (water) has prices with a 1000–10000 times difference within the same region, related to its different uses. As a result, there are no reliable estimations of the economic costs of climate change impacts (Parry et al. 2009) and those so far obtained are under- or overestimates (Ackerman and Stanton 2008; Kirshen 2007; Watkiss et al. 2007; Jiménez and Navarro 2010; Parry et al. 2009; Qin et al. 2010; Schwartz et al. 2000; Dipankar et al. 2011) because of different reasons.

UNDERestimates:

- Social and political costs
- Irreversible impacts
- Residual costs (cost of inaction)
- Private costs such as buying bottled water to address the lack of a reliable service

OVERestimates:

- Almost all of the adaptation measures considered are hard ones (use of infrastructure rather than the implementation of management tools)
- Municipal water is high-cost water and relatively well metered, compared to water used for other purposes (although it is the same water)

Most of the available estimations are for developed countries, although some examples are available for developing ones. At the global level, Kirshen (2007) reported that by 2030, to provide a sufficient water supply in more than 200 countries, the adaptation costs will amount to around US$531 billion in total. Of this, 85 percent is needed to address the requirements in developing countries, mainly in Asia and Africa. A second study, building upon the findings of the 2007 study, included the increased cost of reservoir construction (since the prime locations would already have been taken) and unmet irrigation demands (UNFCCC 2007). The costs obtained for 2030 were around US$898 billion. It was assumed that 25 percent of these costs would be specifically related to climate change, and hence the cost of adaptation to climate change in the water supply sector is estimated to be around US$225 billion by 2030. This is equivalent to US$11 billion/year (UNFCCC 2007). Ward et al. (2010) estimated the adaptation costs to provide enough raw water to meet future global industrial and municipal water demand, based on country-level demand projections up to 2050 through a combination of increased reservoir yield and alternative backstop measures, to be US$12 billion/year, with 83–90 percent of this cost to be incurred by developing countries. Preliminary estimations made by Ackerman and Stanton (2008) for the USA showed that the costs to supply municipal demand represented nearly half of the total costs for the water-related activities and impacts, even considering the cost for damages caused by floods or drought. NACWA (2009) considered the effects up to 2050 in the USA, and showed that investment and operating costs for water services could range from US$448 to US$944 billion, with drinking water representing around 70 percent and sanitation around

30 percent of the total. Data for developing countries on the costs of climate change adaptation are still scarce.

The limitations of the assessment costs may hinder their use for decision analyses. Nevertheless, these cost estimates can be used to identify projects and the funds needed to prepare for climate change impacts and mitigation measures.

ADAPTATION

Setting Goals

Above all, the main challenge for water utilities concerning climate change is to clearly distinguish its impacts, isolated as much as possible from other drivers of change – something that, in practice, is difficult. The next step would be to decide the main motivation for adaptation measures. Based on this, specific goals should be set for each component of water services. When it comes to assess the cost of adaptation, the challenge is to define goals, in order to

- maintain the same level of service;
- provide a higher level of service; and
- set up different types of service.

Table 3.1 shows some examples of goals for selected water services, highlighting those that may lead to a different selection of adaptation measures. These objectives should be openly discussed within society.

From the administration perspective, adaptation measures can be classified into five groups:

- Modification of actual processes, including users' water demands
- Adjustment of processes by introducing new operating, monitoring or regulation procedures
- Maintenance or rehabilitation of actual infrastructure or systems
- Introduction of new technologies that are more flexible and efficient
- Building new infrastructure

Adaptation Options

Table 3.1 shows adaptation options that can be used to address climate change impacts. Many of these options are currently in use or were developed to address problems stemming from causes other than climate

Table 3.1 Goals for adaptation

Overarching goals		
• To maintain the actual level of the service • To improve it • To provide additional or different type of the services		
Water supply	**Sewerage system**	**Wastewater treatment**
• Providing services with the same quality universally • Providing water to all, but not necessarily with the same quality of service • Rendering the service economically sustainable	• Conveying used water • Controlling urban floods	• Partially treating wastewater in order to allow the environment to complete the task • Providing treatment to allow water reuse • Treating used water to allow it to be safely reintroduced to a water source

change. Since the observed problems are the same, the solutions are also alike. The table highlights those measures that are more specific to address climate change impacts, as well as those that also contribute to mitigation. In the following sections some aspects regarding the adaptation options offered will be discussed in more detail.

Data

To adapt better, there is need to have relevant information. Climate change has made clear the need to obtain new information and organize it differently, but this will take some time. Such difficulties can be partially overcome by gathering relevant information that is dispersed in different public and private institutions, not all of which work specifically with water. This is a relatively quick solution with a small cost that can provide better tools to allow more informed decisions to be made. Research of existing data should not only be focused on technical aspects, but also on socio-economic ones. The production of new information is costly, and it is therefore important to use experts to optimize the process, in terms of both information needs and cost. This is a particular concern when compiling information on the impacts on water quality. Recommendations require 20–50 years of information, comparisons of pristine sites with anthropogenically impacted ones, or the identification of the contributions from different sources of pollution (Kundzewicz and Krysanova 2010; Emelko et al. 2011).

BOX 3.4 REDUCING WATER CONSUMPTION

In 2007 in Brisbane, Australia, the consumption of water was reduced from 300 L/person.d in 2005 to 130 L/person.d, by setting restrictions to water gardens, fill swimming pools, wash cars and even by limiting the time of showers to only 4 minutes. In many developing countries the water supply barely reaches 130 L/inhab.d, therefore further reductions in water demand are difficult to achieve even if water tariffs are increased, since this amount corresponds to the optimal amount of water use in cities. (McCafferty 2008)

Planning

Water utilities generally plan for periods of 20–40 years in advance; hence they have familiarity with medium-range scenarios, where climate change effects can be incorporated (NACWA 2009). What may have changed recently is the need to specifically identify the impacts of climate change and to select low-regret measures and those that also contribute to mitigation. In addition, future planning needs to consider a more global context in which food security, energy crises and the need to supply water to ecosystems have also become relevant. In this context, and due to the uncertainty of climate change scenarios, it is important to organize adaptation measures as a range of options that can be combined and used in a flexible way. This has been referred to as a portfolio of adaptation measures (NACWA 2009). Such a portfolio considers (Zwolsman et al. 2010):

- Solutions that address problems not only caused by climate change
- Solutions that can be quickly implemented at a low cost, such as modifying the operation of systems
- Expanding or building new infrastructure step by step
- Capacity building considering climate change

MITIGATION

In most locations, freshwater is already in use or has been allocated to users. As a result, because of population growth and to improve the quality of life, new water supply sources, which demand more energy, are being developed. For instance, the use of sea water or brackish water as a source consumes between two and six times more energy than the use

Table 3.2 Options to adapt water services to climate change impacts

Options	(1)*	(2)**	(3)***	Cost
General management of water				
Preparing adaptation plans to integrally manage water resources with the involvement of different governmental sectors and stakeholders	X		$	?
Identifying adaptation options with lower cost that can be implemented flexibly using a step-by-step approach	X		$	?
Designing decision-making methods under uncertain scenarios and considering multi-criteria objectives	X		???	$
Combining water and energy savings and sustainable management	X	X	?	$
Integrating a portfolio of options to flexibly and sustainably manage water	X		?	$
Securing the proper functioning of water services in the short and long term using public funds			?	$
Relocating activities with high water demand to areas/regions with high water availability		X	???	$$
Controlling erosion and deforestation in basins			??	$
Defining impacts and effects of climate change in order to set up proper and relevant adaptation and mitigation measures in different sectors, considering the impacts on water	X	X	?	$
Promoting fair and equitable interactions among institutions and stakeholders			$	?
Municipal water services				
Broadening the concept of water services to include the joint management of conventional and non-conventional water sources, water supply, urban flood control and management, sewer management, wastewater treatment and reuse, stormwater runoff management, reclamation of energy and materials from water, management of water and wastewater sludge and the reintegration of used water into the environment			??	$$$
Assessing the vulnerability of water utilities to extreme events and sea level rise	X		?	$
Using more sophisticated tools to optimize the management of water and address multi-criteria objectives	X		?	$
Combining soft and hard solutions	X		??	$
Supplying water services universally and in particular to the poor in order to reduce vulnerability and increase resilience to climate change impacts	X		??	$$
Combining centralized and decentralized systems			??	$$$
Building water utility networks to provide services at a regional level to increase resilience	X		?	$
Setting up plans and designing codes for hydraulic infrastructure that are flexible and can be adapted to seasonal and long-term climate change	X		?	$$

Recovering energy, materials (e.g. nutrients) and water from used water	X	X	?	$
Expanding the use of clean sources of energy (solar and wind, for instance) throughout water infrastructure		X	?	$
Urban water				
Designing cities considering water as an urban element, for instance by promoting areas for water infiltration and better urban designs that reduce soil erosion	X		?	$$
Combining inhabited areas with those used to produce food, reusing wastewater for irrigation		X	??	$
Certifying water-efficient buildings, industries, businesses and settlements	X	X	?	$
Distributing domestic appliances that consume less water at no cost	X	X	?	$$
Institutional				
Reinforcing water governance			?	$
Developing policies, laws and institutions to operate systems in a flexible and dynamic way to adapt to changing conditions	X		???	$
Building capacity within the water sector to address impacts of climate change	X			
Allocating budgets to put in place programs to address climate change impacts in a timely manner	X		?	$$
Considering, during the optimization of projects, not only economic criteria but also social and environmental factors along with the flexibility, redundancy and reliability of each solution	X		$???	
Legal				
Acknowledging the impacts of climate change on water as a resource in legal frameworks	X		?	$
Improving legal and financial frameworks to put in place selected adaptation measures in a step-by-step approach	X		?	$
Institutionally and legally granting ecosystems the entitlement to water			???	$
Socioeconomic				
Promoting economic growth considering water availability and protection in quantity and quality	X		???	$
Combining financial tools with social, environmental and political ones to assess the cost–benefit of a project, considering social justice and equality	X		??	$
Information				
Developing and gathering proper information and data to better understand climatic conditions in the future	X	X	?	$$
Defining the variation of water availability and water demand in the context of climate change	X		?	$
Assessing the vulnerability of water services, the population using them and ecosystems to address climate change	X		?	$
Sharing information among stakeholders, water utilities and governmental and academic institutions	X	X	?	$

Table 3.2 (continued)

Options	(1)*	(2)**	(3)***	Cost
Modifying monitoring programs to be able to obtain suitable information to assess impacts of climate change on water quality in the future	X		??	$$
Water sources management				
Identifying and monitoring the impacts of climate change on water sources	X		??	$
Implementing policies to protect water quality from point and diffuse sources of pollution by protecting the soil and air quality and by avoiding the exchange of pollutants between water, air and soil			??	$
Adopting cleaner production practices and promoting social responsibility in industries, in particular to avoid the presence in wastewater of pollutants that are recalcitrant to conventional treatment			?	$
Better protecting aquifers from overexploitation and pollution	X		??	$
Using treatment by wetlands and soil as key elements to naturally control non-point sources of pollution	X		?	$
Changing the concept of wastewater disposal to one of reintegration of water to the environment for its reuse	X		??	$$
Water demand management				
Controlling leaks in water networks by improving metering, using improved materials for pipelines, and providing better maintenance	X	X	?	$$$
Using water tariffs where there is flexibility to reduce water consumption, although not at sites where the amount of water required is barely provided			?	$
Re-leveling ground to improve irrigation efficiency in public gardens, parks etc.	X	X	?	$
Cascading water use and coupling the quality of available water to different uses	X	X	???	$$
Replacing activities demanding more water with those using less. This includes replacing golf courses with other types of sports areas	X	X	?	$
Water supply				
Relying on different sources of water, such as sea and saline water, pluvial water, waste, greywater and storm runoff of different qualities for different uses, rather than single water source	X		?	$$
Adapting the quality of the source to its use			??	$
Applying multi-criteria decision methods to jointly optimize the operation of dams and surface and groundwater reservoirs	X		???	$
Increasing and combining surface and groundwater storage capacity and use	X		?	$

Water treatment				
Constructing new drinking water treatment processes and ensuring existing ones can address the variations in the quality of influent water and as well new pollutants	X		?	$$
Promoting the use of potabilization methods at the household level and in some cases even providing them at no cost			?	$
Promoting the use of small rainwater storage devices at the household level			?	$
Reducing sludge production in drinking water plants by recovering the chemicals used or reducing the amount of chemicals added			?	$$
Sewerage systems				
Developing criteria to design sewers considering future climate conditions and not only historical data	X		?	$
Implementing additional pumping capacity and elevating stations to convey overflows into combined sewer systems	X		?	$$
Separating combined drainage to optimize the conveyance of sewage and pluvial water, where economically feasible			???	$$$
Using the capacity of aquifers to store storm runoff	X		?	$$
Combining green infrastructure with the management of sites to control urban runoff and improved drainage systems that store and treat sewer overflows	X		??	$
Reinforcing sewer facilities to reduce the infiltration of water	X		?	$
Wastewater treatment				
Providing sanitation and as a part of this considering the whole chain, including cleaning and the disposal/reuse of sludge			?	$
Reviewing the design and operation criteria of wastewater treatment plants to be efficient under changing conditions of water quality and quantity	X		?	$
Implementing fast wastewater processes to treat CSO (combined sewer overflows)			?	$
Combining green and grey infrastructure for sanitation			??	$
Increasing the level of treatment to compensate for the reduction in auto-depuration capacity of water sources	X		?	$$
Increasing the acceptance of the use of biosolids in agricultural soil and soil remediation		X	?	$
Recovering energy and materials from water and wastewater sludge	X	X	?	$
Practicing potable and non-potable reuse of water as a complementary tool for sanitation and ecosystem protection			??	$$

Table 3.2 (continued)

Options	(1)*	(2)**	(3)***	Cost
Floods				
Assessing the risk and vulnerability of the hydraulic infrastructure	X		?	$
Using robust, smart and flexible monitoring systems that combine sensors and communication tools for early warning systems to prevent floods, urban floods and pollution risk events	X		?	$$
Putting barriers in place to protect infrastructure from floods	X		?	$$
Including criteria to select sites, taking the risk of flooding of hydraulic infrastructure into account	X		?	$
Raising the level of hydraulic infrastructure	X		?	$$$
Storing equipment and chemicals at higher locations where they cannot be affected by floods	X		?	$
Combining green and grey infrastructure to prevent and control urban floods	X		?	$$
Promoting rainwater harvesting at the household level and green infrastructure as temporary storage systems to reduce the overloading of sewers	X		?	$
Adapting urban infrastructure to allow the natural drainage of basins and the minimizing of urban floods	X		???	$$
Properly running solid waste control systems to avoid the clogging of hydraulic infrastructure			?	$
Locating floating or hydroponic gardens in areas prone to flooding	X		?	$
Protecting and restoring coastal wetlands to reduce the negative impacts of floods	X		?	$
Reforesting upper basins to reduce storm runoff intensity and sediment transport	X		?	$
Learning to live with floods	X		?	$
Droughts				
Increasing the capacity of human resources to deal with drought; enforcing laws	X		???	$
Repairing and building new wells and pumping stations	X		?	$$
Temporarily using deep wells	X		?	$$
Sea level rise				
Use of dikes	X		?	$
Changing the use of land, considering the need to better design coastal cities, moving settlements inland and even relocating them	X		?	$$$
Artificially recharging aquifers to conserve the water resource and control saline intrusion in coastal areas	X		?	$$
Desalinating water	X		?	$$$

Combining water from different sources to reduce the salt content of those that are highly saline	X	?	$
Elevating discharge sites	X	?	$
Reinforcing infrastructure to avoid saline water entering sewers and reducing the efficiency of wastewater treatment plants	X	?	$
Education, social awareness, research and innovation			
Providing training on technology and climate change impacts and options to address them	X	?	$
Avoiding associating the perception of a better quality of life to the use of more water and energy	X	?	$
Changing the perception of wastewater as a waste product and the replacing the idea of disposing of wastewater with one of properly reintegrating it into the environment		?	$
Supporting research and innovation to address water problems at a local level	X	?	$

Notes:
1 This table lists water resources strategies and notes their relevance to climate change adaptation (column 1), climate change mitigation (column 2), difficulty of implementation (column 3), and cost.
* (1) If X, it is particularly relevant to climate change.
** (2) If X, it is also a mitigation option.
*** (3) Complexity or dificulty to implement X.

Sources: Andrews 2009; Bahri 2009; de Graaf and van der Brugge 2010; Dembo 2010; Dillon and Jiménez 2008; Elliot et al. 2011; Emelko et al. 2011; Foster et al. 1998; Godfrey et al. 2010; IAH 2011; Jiménez 2011; Jiménez and Asano 2008; Keller 2008; Marsalek et al. 2006; McCafferty 2008; Mayol 2008; Marshall and Randhir 2008; McGuckin 2008; Munasinghe 2010; NACWA 2009; OECD 2010; OFWAT 2009; Oxfam 2007; Mackay and Last 2010; Reiter 2009; Seah 2008; Sprenger et al. 2011; Thöle 2008; UNESCO 2011, UN HABITAT 2008 and 2010; Vörösmarty et al. 2000; Zwolsman et al. 2009; Zwolsman et al. 2011.

of a conventional source (Reiter 2009). This is one of the reasons why in the future it will be important to develop measures to reduce GHG emissions. So far, water utilities have been reducing their energy consumption motivated more by their energy bills than their GHG emissions. Globally, water and wastewater services are responsible for around 1.5 percent of the global CO_2 emissions and for 5–7 percent of the total emission of GHGs. With the growth of cities and population pressure this will likely rise to more than 7 percent of total GHG emissions (McGuckin 2008), although these figures may be different at a local level. For instance, in the State of California, however, the energy consumption of the water services sector in 2001 represented 15 percent of total energy consumption (Reiter 2009).

It is also important to identify the sources of GHG emissions. For the State of California, energy consumption per person for water services is around 1080 kWh/y/person, of which 20 percent goes towards supply, 5 percent to wastewater treatment and at least 36 percent to the residential use. In the UK, where the management of drinking water and wastewater contributes 1 percent of the total emissions of CO_2, nearly 66 percent is due to the provision of the services per se while the remaining 33 percent is due to the gases released during treatment and disposal practices (McGuckin 2008).

Mitigation Options

Among the activities to reduce GHG emissions in water utilities, the following have been recommended (OFWAT 2009; McCafferty 2008):

- Improving the sustainable management of basins to store carbon, to increase biodiversity and to stabilize flow in rivers
- Building water distribution networks demanding less energy
- Reducing water demand
- Increasing pumping efficiency
- Increasing the efficient use of water
- Improving energy use in buildings and using alternative sources of it (hydrogen generation, reuse of water heat, and energy production from sludge) to use less water for energy production
- Disposing off effluents in which the carbon contained in the biodegradable pollutant matter remains fixed into the soil
- More energy-efficient processes to treat water, wastewater and the sludge produced
- Recovering energy from wastewater and sludge
- Decarbonizing the electricity used by employing alternative sources of energy and even using the water infrastructure to generate energy

BOX 3.5 THE RUHRVERBAND WATER SYSTEM

The Ruhrverband Water System in Germany saved 44 GWh/year through a program applied to its wastewater treatment plants. Systematic energy audits were implemented through a financial rewards scheme in which personnel provided ideas to save energy. A total of 85 activities were identified, and 2.8 GWh/year, equivalent to 413 000€, were saved. The program was implemented because between 2000 and 2007, the price of electricity increased from 0.08 to 0.14 €/kWh and would reach a cost of 0.17 €/kWh in 2010. These energy savings along with the implementation of a co-fermentation process in anaerobic reactors, which were in fact the most important contributions to reducing GHG emissions, in total represented savings of only one percent of the total consumption. (Thöle 2008)

To finance adaptation and mitigation options, water utilities can use the principles of the carbon bonds market. Indeed, as water utilities use energy (approximately 4–5 percent of the total use in a country), by saving energy they can reduce their contribution to national GHG emissions and sell the corresponding amount saved as carbon credits to commercial or individual customers. The size of the carbon market bonds for water services has been estimated. For the EU and the USA alone, it is estimated to be US$92 billion with a projection to increase by 2020 to US$11 trillion as more stringent goals are set (McGuckin 2008).

Integrated assessment of mitigation options

In order to fully consider the entire water cycle, any option has to be analyzed in cost–benefit and social impact terms, not only from the perspective of the water utility but also from that of the users of water. To illustrate this, Cabrera et al. (2012) compared two situations in Spain. For Situation A, water utilities used 50 percent surface water and 50 percent groundwater for supply. For Situation B, water was supplied through desalination (WOB). The energy footprints for each case are of 0.296 kWh/m^3 and 3.65 kWh/m^3, respectively, from the source up to the site at which water enters the network. From this point onwards, energy consumption in both cases was the same, equivalent to 0.098 kWh/m^3. With regard to the energy source, two different scenarios were also considered. In the first scenario the proportions were: 29.8 percent of natural gas, 7.9 percent of oil, 22.5 percent of gas, 19.8 percent of nuclear, 9.7 percent of hydraulic and 10.4 percent of other. For

BOX 3.6 REDUCING WATER SAVING IN MELBOURNE

Because of water scarcity and intense droughts, the water utility in Melbourne, Australia, had to undertake an aggressive program to save water and energy involving the users from the Yarra Valley. The goal was to achieve a policy of neutral GHG emissions by reducing water demand by 30 percent by 2015. To achieve this, an energy density consumption map of water supply and sanitation services was developed, from the water sources to disposal sites. The energy consumption for different activities and the energy fluxes for the entire water cycle were described by empirical equations. The entire dataset was articulated using a GIS procedure that allowed re-engineering of the whole system, achieving net reductions in CO_2 of 25 000 tons between 2004 and 2008 (McCafferty 2008).

the second one, ES2, the proportions were 33.3 percent of natural gas, 33.3 percent of oil and 33.4 percent of carbon. The first, ES1, which is similar to the actual situation in Spain, was found to produce lower CO_2 emissions.

The carbon credit savings in a network with no water leaks compared to one with leaks depend not only on the amount of energy saved during the distribution phase, but also on the amount of energy used to extract water from the source. Therefore the combination of the previous scenarios leads to four possible situations: (a) WOA + ES1; (b) WOB + ES1; (c) WOA + ES2; and (d) WOB + ES2. The achievable savings depend on both the energy source and the water source, with the scenario involving the supply of water from desalination having the highest energy consumption. In addition, this study showed that savings are doubled considering the control of leaks alone. Furthermore, it was found that savings become of interest only above a certain population size (in this case, 25 000 people).

CONCLUSIONS AND RECOMMENDATIONS

There is still considerable confusion among water utilities with regard to what must be done to address climate change impacts. Uncertainty exists concerning impacts and their associated costs. There is therefore a need to increase knowledge in this field but also, at the same time, to develop adaptation portfolios to address possible impacts. Due to this situation, it is highly advisable to identify impacts that might be caused not only by climate change but also by other factors, in order to select the best possible low-regret solutions. To face the uncertainties of assessed cost it is important to use carbon market bonds wisely and as much as possible to set measures that jointly optimize the use of water and energy. For the specific case of developing countries, such carbon bond markets can also be used to deal with past deficiencies of the services.

From the above discussion, it can be seen that there are some key messages for water utilities and water policy makers. These include:

- Gathering existing relevant information and data to allow better assessment of the impact and vulnerability of water services to climate change. This can be achieved not only by producing new information, but also by sharing information among institutions and stakeholders. As this is a complex task, support from academia will be useful.
- Developing programs to address climate change impacts. For this, it is necessary to assess the vulnerability of different types of users and also that of water systems, including their infrastructure. This should be done with assistance of experts in order to reliably consider and assess uncertainties.
- Building capacity in the water sector to address climate change impacts proactively. In this respect, the active participation of professional networks such as associations is a practical means.
- Identifying activities to address climate change impacts in practice.
- Adopting more efficient design and operation procedures in the water sector, considering water and energy jointly.
- Reducing leaks in water networks, notably if they are over 30 percent. This is an important step in allowing water to and energy to be used efficiently, but also to reduce CO_2 emissions.
- Developing and sharing of case studies on adaptation and mitigation for different types of water utilities and situations.

REFERENCES

Ackerman, Frank and Elizabeth A. Stanton (2008), *The Cost of Climate Change: What We'll Pay if Global Warming Continues Unchecked*, New York: Natural Resources Defense Council.

Andrews, J. (2009), 'A new vision for Sydney: IN-FOCUS Asia Pacific', *Urban World*, **1** (5), 42–7.

Arnell, N.W. and E.K. Delaney (2006), 'Adapting to climate change: public water supply in England and Wales', *Climatic Change*, **78** (2–4), 227–55.

Association of Metropolitan Water Agencies (NACWA) (2009), 'Confronting climate change: an early analysis of water and wastewater adaptation costs', available at http://www.amwa net/galleries/climate-change/ConfrontingClimateChangeOct09.pdf.

Bahri, Akica (2009), 'Managing the Other Side of the Water Cycle: Making Wastewater an Asset', TEC Background Papers No. 13, Molnlycke: Global Water Partnership Technical Committee (TEC).

Bates, Bryson, Zbigniew W. Kundzewicz, Shaohong Wu and Jean Palutikof (2008), *Climate Change and Water: Technical Paper of the Intergovernmental Panel on Climate Change*, Geneva: Intergovernmental Panel on Climate Change (IPCC).

Bonte, M. and J. Zwolsman (2010), 'Climate change induced salinisation of artificial lakes in the Netherlands and consequences for drinking water production', *Water Research*, **4** (15), 4411–24.

Boxall, A., A. Hardy, S. Beulke, T. Boucard, T. Burgin, P.D. Falloon, P. Haygarth, T. Hutchinson, S. Kovats, G. Leonardi, L.S. Levy, G. Nichols, S.A. Parsons, L. Potts, D. Stone, E. Topp, D.B Turley, K. Walsh, E. Wellington and R. Williams (2009), 'Impacts of climate change on indirect human exposure to pathogens and chemicals from agriculture', *Environmental Health Perspectives*, **117** (4), 508–14.

Brooks J.P., A. Adeli, J. Read and M. McLaughlin (2009), 'Rainfall simulation in greenhouse microcosms to assess bacterial-associated runoff from land-applied poultry litter', *Journal of Environmental Quality*, **38** (1), 218–29.

Butscher, C. and P. Huggenberger (2009), 'Modelling the temporal variability of karst groundwater vulnerability, with implications for climate change', *Environmental Science and Technology*, **43** (6), 1665–9.

Cabrera, E., M.A. Pardo, R. Cobacho, F.J. Arregui and E. Cabrera, Jr (2012), 'Evaluation of carbon credits saved by water losses reduction in water networks', available at http://www.ita.upv.es/idi/descargaarticulo.php?id=226.

Curreiro, F.C., J.A. Patz, J.B. Rose and S. Lele (2001), 'The association between extreme precipitation and waterborne disease outbreaks in the United States, 1948–1994', *American Journal of Public Health*, **91** (8), 1194–9.

de Graaf, R. and R. van der Brugge (2010), 'Transforming water infrastructure by linking water management and urban renewal in Rotterdam', *Technological Forecasting and Social Change*, **77** (8), 1282–91.

Dembo, R. (2010), 'Why refitting buildings is key to reducing emissions', *Urban World*, **1** (5), 34–7.

Dillon, Peter J. and Blanca Jiménez (2008), 'Water reuse via aquifer recharge: intentional and unintentional practices', in Blanca Jiménez and Takashi Asano (eds), *Water Reuse: An International Survey of Current Practice Issues and Needs*, London: IWA Publishing, pp. 260–80.

Dipankar, C., D. Bhaskar and M.T. Murrill (2011), 'Examining India's groundwater quality management', *Environmental Science and Technology*, **45** (1), 27–33.

Elliot, Mark, Andrew Armstrong, Joseph Lobuglio and Jamie Bartram (2011), *Technologies for Climate Change Adaptation – The Water Sector*, Roskilde: UNEP Risoe Centre.

Emelko M., U. Silins, K.D. Bladon and M. Stone (2011), 'Implications of land disturbance on drinking water treatability in a changing climate: demonstrating the need for "source water supply and protection" strategies', *Water Research*, **45** (2), 461–72.

Foster, Stephen, Adrian Lawrence and Brian Morris (1998), 'Groundwater in Urban Development: Assessing Management Needs and Formulating Policy Strategies', *Technical Paper No. 390*, Washington, DC: The World Bank.

Freas, K., B. Bailey, A. Munevar and S. Butler (2008), 'Incorporating climate change in water planning', *Journal of the American Water Resources Association*, **100** (6), 92–9.

Godfrey S., P. Labhasetwar, S. Wate and B. Jiménez (2010), 'Safe greywater reuse to augment water supply and provide sanitation in semi-arid areas of rural India', *Water Science and Technology: A Journal of the International Association on Water Pollution Research*, **62** (6), 1296–303.

IAH Commission on Groundwater and Climate Change (2011), 'Groundwater and climate change', available at http://www.iah.org/gwclimate/gw_cc.html.

Jiménez, Blanca (2011), 'Safe sanitation in low economic development areas', in Peter Wilderer (ed.), *Treatise on Water Science, Volume 4*, New York: Oxford Academic Press, pp. 147–201.

Jiménez, Blanca and Takashi Asano (eds) (2008), *Water Reuse: An International Survey of Current Practice Issues and Needs*, London: IWA Publishing.

Jiménez, Blanca and Joan Rose (eds) (2009), *Urban Water Security: Managing Risks*, Paris: United Nations Educational, Scientific and Cultural Organization and Leiden: Taylor and Francis.

Jiménez, B. and I. Navarro (2010), 'Estimation of the cost of climate change impacts on the water sector in Central America', in *The Economics of Climate Change in Central America*, London: Department for International Development and Mexico City, MX: Economic Commission for Central America and the Caribbean.

Keller, J. (2008), 'From microbial fuel cells to bio electrochemical systems: how to convert organic pollutants to electric energy and more', Water and Energy Workshop Vienna, Austria, available at http://www.iwahq.org/templates/ld_templates/layout_633184.aspx?ObjectId=678195.

Kirshen, Paul (2007), 'Adaptation options and costs in water supply', available at http://unfccc.int/files/cooperation_and_support/financial_mechanism/application/pdf/kirshen.pdf.

Kundzewicz, Z.W. and V. Krysanova (2010), 'Climate change and stream water quality in the multi-factor context', *Climatic Change*, **103** (3–4), 353–62.

Mackay, R. and E. Last (2010), 'SWITCH city water balance: A scoping model for integrated urban water management', *Environmental Science Biotechnology*, **9** (4), 291–6.

Marsalek, Jiri, Blanca Jiménez, Per-Arne Malmquist, Mohammad Karamouz, Joel Goldenfum and Bernard Chocat (2006), *Urban Water Cycle Processes and Interactions: Urban Water Series, Volume 2*, Paris: United Nations Educational, Scientific and Cultural Organization and Leiden: Taylor and Francis.

Marshall, E. and T. Randhir (2008), 'Effect of climate change on watershed system: a regional analysis', *Climatic Change*, **89** (3–4), 263–80.

Mayol, I. (2008), 'Presentation at OECD conference', *Competitive Cities and Climate Change: OECD Conference Proceedings*, Milan: OECD.

McCafferty, P. (2008), 'Energy balances in water savings and reuse programs, energy use, saving and recovery at water and wastewater utilities', Water and Energy Workshop, Vienna, Austria, available at http://www.iwahq.org/templates/ld_templates/layout_633184.aspx?ObjectId=678195.

McGuckin, R. (2008), 'Carbon footprints and emerging mitigation/trading regimes', Water and Energy Workshop, Vienna, Austria, available at http://www.iwahq.org/templates/ld_templates/layout_633184.aspx?ObjectId=678195.

Munasinghe, Mohan (2010), 'Integrated solutions for water, sustainable development and climate change issues: applying the sustainomics framework', in Jan Lunqvist (ed.), *On the Water Front Volume 2: Selections from the 2010 World Water Week in Stockholm*, Stockholm: Stockholm International Water Institute (SIWI).

OECD (2010), *Cities and Climate Change*, Paris: OECD Publishing.

OFWAT (2009), 'Climate change – good practice from the 2009 price review: water today, water tomorrow', available at http://www.ofwat.gov.uk/publications/prs_inf_climate.pdf.

Oxfam (2007), 'Adapting to climate change: what's needed in poor countries, and who should pay', Oxfam Briefing paper 104, available at http://www.oxfam.org/sites/www.oxfam.org/files/adapting%20to%20climate%20change.pdf.

Parry, Martin, Nigel Arnell, Pam Berry, David Dodman, Samuel Fankhauser, Chris Hope, Sari Kovats, Robert Nicholls, David Satterthwaite, Richard Tiffin and Tim Wheeler (2009), *Assessing the Costs of Adaptation to Climate Change: A Review of the UNFCCC and Other Recent Estimates*, London: International Institute for Environment and Development and Grantham Institute for Climate Change.

Qin, B., G. Zhu, G. Gao, Y. Zhang, W. Li, H.W. Paerl and W. Carmichael (2010), 'A drinking

water crisis in Lake Taihu, China: linkage to climatic variability and lake management', *Environmental Management*, **45** (1), 105–12.
Reiter, P. (2009), 'Cities of the future and water: can we reshape urban water and urban design to achieve long term water security?' Presentation from the 2009 World Water Week in Stockholm, Stockholm: IWA.
Schwartz J., R. Levin and R. Goldstein (2000), 'Drinking water turbidity and gastrointestinal illness in the elderly of Philadelphia', *Journal of Epidemiological Community Health*, **54** (1), 45–51.
Seah, H. (2008), 'Water for all: conserve, value, enjoy', Water and Energy Workshop, Vienna, Austria, available at http://www.iwahq.org/ContentSuite/upload/iwa/Document/2008_Vienna_Day2_08.pdf.
Sprenger C., G. Lorenzen, I. Hülshoff, G. Grützmacher, M. Ronghang and A. Pekdeger (2011), 'Vulnerability of bank filtration systems to climate change', *Science of the Total Environment*, **409** (4), 655–63.
Tchobanoglous, George, Franklin L. Burton and H. David Stensel (2003), *Wastewater Engineering Treatment and Reuse*, 4th edn, New York: McGraw-Hill Metcalf and Eddy, Inc.
Thöle, D. (2008), 'Ways to identify possibilities of energy saving at wastewater treatment plants', Water and Energy Workshop, Vienna, Austria, available at http://www.iwahq.org/templates/ld_templates/layout_633184.aspx?ObjectId=678195.
Thorne, Olivia (2008), *A Practical Methodology for Assessing the Potential Impacts of Climate Change on Water Treatment Plant Operations*, Cambridge, UK: Submitted for the degree of Doctor of Philosophy.
UNESCO (2011), *The Impact of Global Change on Water Resources: The Response of UNESCO'S International Hydrology Programme*, Paris: United Nations Educational, Scientific and Cultural Organization, International Hydrological Programme.
United Nations Framework Convention on Climate Change (UNFCCC) (2007), *Investments and Financial Flows to Address Climate Change*, Bonn: United Nations Framework Convention on Climate Change (UNFCCC).
UN HABITAT (2010), *State of the World's Cities 2010/2011: Bridging The Urban Divide*, Nairobi: UN HABITAT.
Van Vliet, M. and J. Zwolsman (2008), 'Impact of summer droughts on the water quality of the Meuse River', *Journal of Hydrology*, **353** (1–2), 1–17.
Vörösmarty, C.J., P.J. Green, J. Salisbury and R.B. Lammers (2000), 'Global water resources: vulnerability from climate change and population growth', *Science*, **289** (5477), 284–8.
Ward, P.J., K.M. Strzepek, W.P. Pauw, L.M. Brander, G.A. Hughes and J.C.J.H. Aerts (2010), 'Partial costs of global climate change adaptation for the supply of raw industrial and municipal water: a methodology and application', *Environmental Research Letters*, **5** (4), 044011.
Watkiss, Paul, Francesco Bosello, Barbara Buchner, Michela Catenacci, Alessandra Goria, Onno Kuik and Etem Karakaya (2007), *Climate Change: The Cost of Inaction and the Cost of Adaptation, (Technical Report No 13/2007)*, Copenhagen, DK: European Environmental Agency (EEA).
World Water Assessment Programme (WWAP) (2009), *Water in a Changing World: The United Nations World Water Development Report* Paris, FR: UNESCO and London, UK: Earthscan.
Zwolsman, G., D. Vanham, P. Fleming, C. Davis, A. Lovell, D. Nolasco, O. Thorne, R. de Sutter, B. Fülöp, P. Satuffer and A. Johannessen (2010), 'Climate change and the water industry – practical responses and actions', *Perspective on Water and Climate Change Adaptation*, Amsterdam, NL: World Water Council, Cooperative Programme on Water and Climate, IUCN and International Water Association.

4. Urban food systems strategies

Nevin Cohen

INTRODUCTION

For much of the last century, food remained largely off the agenda of city planners and policy makers. Municipal officials viewed food production as a rural issue and food availability a private sector concern (Pothukuchi and Kaufman 1999). With the exception of conventional planning functions like the location of terminal markets or food production facilities, the planning literature ignored food and planners had neither the mandate nor the academic training to address urban food issues (Pothukuchi and Kaufman 2000). Within the past several years, this has changed rather dramatically as cities have engaged in food systems planning and policy making.

While the objectives, scope and design of food plans, policies and programs vary from place to place, officials no longer ignore the food system because it is increasingly understood as essential to public health, social equity, economic development and environmental sustainability. Cities are attempting to connect municipal domains that are related to food but which have traditionally been divided into discrete administrative agencies that have not considered food to be their responsibility (Wiskerke 2009). A number have reached beyond municipal boundaries with policies to procure food from regional producers and develop processing and distribution infrastructure to support regional farmers. Others have targeted particular policy issues, such as modifying zoning ordinances to accommodate urban agriculture (Hodgson et al. 2011; American Planning Association 2007; Pothukuchi 2009) or creating incentives for the sale of fruits and vegetables in low-income neighborhoods (Mukherji and Morales 2010; Hodgson 2012). The topic of food is incorporated in comprehensive plans, sustainability plans, regional plans and policy platforms. And because policy makers are networked globally, food policies are increasingly mobile, diffused widely through policy reports, conferences, and networks of elected officials and administrators, and adopted as so-called best practice policies from other communities (Peck 2011). Thus it is not unusual to see specific laws or regulations, such as those granting permission to raise chickens and bees, passed in city after city.

This chapter explains the drivers of food planning and policy making, how they have led to strategies to ensure that food systems contribute to broader urban sustainability goals, and the governance networks that have enabled the adoption of innovative policies. The chapter is based on data from interviews with 35 city officials and advocates in six cities in the USA and Canada, as well as a review of food planning and policy documents and the author's involvement in food policy development in New York City. It is not meant to identify exemplary food policies, nor is it a comprehensive guide to food policies, as food policy making is evolving rapidly. Reference documents with summaries of urban food policies are published by various planning and policy organizations.[1]

DRIVERS OF FOOD POLICY MAKING

As a result of global challenges, the food system is increasingly perceived to be unsustainable and in need of policy intervention (Morgan and Sonnino 2010). Worldwide, for example, some 870 million people suffer from hunger and malnutrition while an estimated 1.5 billion adults are overweight or obese (FAO, WFP and IFAD 2012; Institute of Medicine 2012). Food access has become increasingly difficult for low-income individuals as a result of food price increases. Since 2007, global commodity markets have been volatile, with food prices reaching their highest levels in 30 years during the summer of 2008, falling the following winter, and then rising again soon thereafter. Food price volatility and overall price increases are likely to increase as climate change results in more frequent extreme weather events, and water scarcity and soil depletion make growing food more challenging (FAO 2012). Population pressures will require expanding agriculture in more distant and less productive regions, resulting in greater yield variability and larger inputs of fertilizers, pesticides and transportation energy. And, since conventional food production depends heavily on petroleum inputs for transportation and fertilizers, petroleum price volatility will further contribute to food price spikes (FAO 2011).

Food safety remains another area of great anxiety, as globalization of the food supply and the increased scale of food production have amplified the impacts of outbreaks of food-borne illnesses. When contamination occurs, the numbers of consumers exposed can be very large, and it is more difficult to trace the source of contamination from processors using ingredients from a global marketplace. In the USA alone, roughly one in six Americans gets sick each year, 128 000 are hospitalized, and 3000 die of food-borne diseases (Centers for Disease Control and Prevention 2012). These food safety fears have combined with concerns about the impacts of new technologies (e.g. genetically modified organisms, pesticides, hormones) to increase uncertainty about the safety of the food supply and the impacts of agricultural technologies and production techniques on the ecosystem (Loeber et al. 2011).

The precariousness of the global food system has prompted advocacy at WTO meetings about international trade rules, and lobbying at the national level about federal agriculture policies. But activists and political leaders within cities have also focused on local manifestations of these global problems, along with urban-scale policy strategies. The issues that communities have focused on include the social justice and public health impacts of the food system, particularly in low-wealth communities, local and regional economic impacts of the food supply chain, and the effects of food systems on the urban and peri-urban environment.

Media coverage of the sustainability dimensions of the food system, as well as attention by businesses, advocacy organizations and political leaders, has also demonstrated to local policy makers the salience of sustainable food, encouraging them to allocate political capital to food-related policies. Increased interest in food has also prompted philanthropic organizations dedicated to urban sustainability to fund new urban food systems projects.[2] New projects and programs have increased the number of urban farmers, chefs, teachers and other 'everyday makers' working to create and scale up project-based food innovations that challenge rules, regulations and practices, prompting policy change in response (Bang and Sorensen 1999).

The focus on urban food systems strategies is also heavily influenced by the recession of 2008–09, which has forced municipal governments saddled with severe budget constraints to scale back government services and rely increasingly on individuals, NGOs and private businesses. Historically, economic downturns and fiscal crises have prompted cities to support urban agriculture as a form of self-provisioning and low-cost stewardship of vacant spaces (Lawson 2005). In this present economic crisis, cities have supported urban farms and gardens as sites of food production, land stewardship, youth and community development, education and ecosystem services. New York funded the creation of three urban farms as a lower-cost alternative to stormwater containment infrastructure (Cohen and Ackerman 2011). Cities have also linked food policies to local and regional economic development through support for food retail establishments and entrepreneurial food producers, by increasing enrollment in federal food benefits such as SNAP and the school lunch and breakfast programs, by facilitating the construction or renovation of food wholesale and retail distribution infrastructure, and by directing food procurement dollars to local and regional purveyors. The economic crisis has also encouraged individuals to engage in a broader range of economic activities, often for subsistence and also for new opportunities for social interaction based on ecological values (Conill et al. 2012). The rise in urban farming, craft food production and other food system ventures like community composting programs is a cultural as well as a pragmatic response to the severe recession.

The strategies employed by urban policy-making actors (e.g. nonprofit organizations, philanthropies, community groups, government agencies and elected officials, business leaders and entrepreneurs) are also influenced by efforts to link local-level policies and programs to larger-scale policy issues, from the ecological effects of industrialized food production to the mistreatment of laborers throughout the food supply chain. The attempt to employ local strategies, largely purchasing decisions by government agencies and consumers, but also community planning strategies, to address global issues is the result of political stalemate at the national level and the difficulty of influencing trade policy. It also reflects a greater awareness of the environmental and economic interconnections within a region's foodshed for municipal goals such as regional open space preservation, watershed protection, and regional economic development, and an appreciation of the potential impact of local actions on global policy, thanks to the work of organizations like ICLEI – Local Governments for Sustainability. Hence, Los Angeles adopted a local food procurement strategy that calls for products produced with fair labor and animal care practices, while city-funded neighborhood food planning in Vancouver aims to reduce greenhouse gas emissions to avert climate change.

DIMENSIONS OF URBAN FOOD SYSTEM SUSTAINABILITY

There has been a shift in the policy discussion from a nearly exclusive focus on the need to increase food production to the provision of sustainable diets, which the Food and Agriculture Organization defines as one with

> low environmental impacts, which contributes to food and nutrition security and to healthy life for present and future generations . . . [and which is] protective and respectful of biodiversity and ecosystems, culturally acceptable, accessible, economically fair and affordable; nutritionally adequate, safe and healthy; while optimizing natural and human resources. (Food and Agriculture Organization 2010; DeSchutter 2011)

Other dimensions of food system sustainability include the notion of community food security, which emphasizes the need for a food system that enables all people to obtain a safe, culturally acceptable, nutritionally adequate diet through a sustainable food system that is community based, environmentally sound and locally managed (Levkoe 2011). Proponents of food justice focus on undoing the structural oppression that creates inequity within the food system and argue access to justly produced, culturally appropriate food (food conventionally eaten by different ethnic, religious or culturally distinct groups) as a right (Sbicca 2012). Food sovereignty advocates emphasize the rights of communities to be able to produce their own culturally appropriate and healthy, just and ecological food (Fairbairn 2011).

Even among these different concepts of food system sustainability, problems can be bounded narrowly or broadly. For example, the loss of food sovereignty due to land appropriation and structural oppression has fueled the Via Campesina movement among landless peasants in the Global South (Anderson and Bellows 2012). But the notion of food sovereignty can also encompass the oppression faced by laborers throughout the food supply chain, ranging from farm workers to processing facility laborers to retail sales clerks in cities. Disempowerment and loss of sovereignty may also involve the culinary deskilling and loss of capacity to prepare healthy food from raw ingredients that results from food processing, refinement, breeding for longer shelf life, genetic modification, and packaging of industrially produced food (Kneen 1993; Jaffe and Gertler 2006).

Social Dimensions

Food insecurity, poor-quality diets, combined with the prevalence of high-calorie, low-nutrient density foods and the dearth of opportunities for physical activity have contributed to rising obesity levels that result in increased morbidity and mortality, and related health costs (though some dips in obesity among children have been observed recently in several cities and states) (Robert Wood Johnson Foundation 2012). In 2011, 14.9 percent of US households (17.9 million households) were food insecure, facing difficulty at some time during the year in providing enough food for all their family members due to a lack of resources, with cities faring slightly worse than nonmetropolitan areas (Coleman-Jensen et al. 2012, p. 11). In 2011, 5.7 percent of US households (6.8 million households) had very low food security, in which the food intake of some household members was reduced and normal eating patterns were disrupted at times during the year due to limited resources (ibid.). The economic downturn has exacerbated food insecurity. For example, between 2010 and 2011, 29 cities surveyed by the US Conference of Mayors reported an average increase of 15.5 percent in emergency food assistance requests (United States Conference of Mayors 2011).

Food insecurity results in diets high in carbohydrates and fats, contributing to excessive weight and obesity. In the USA alone, 73 million adults and 12 million children and adolescents are obese and require 21 percent of the nation's annual medical expenditures for treatment of obesity-related diseases (Institute of Medicine 2012, pp. 2, 17). Obesity is estimated to cause 112 000 deaths per year in the USA and contributes to the development of diabetes and other diseases (Finkelstein et al. 2009). Even national defense has been adversely affected: as of 2007–08, approximately 35 percent of military-age men and women were too overweight to meet the US military's height, weight and body mass requirements (Cawley and Maclean 2010). While rates vary from nation to nation, most developed countries and many emerging economies, particularly those with increasing rates of animal protein consumption, are experiencing rising rates of body mass and obesity.

Economic Dimensions

The poverty and low income that contribute to food insecurity, combined with business decisions and economic development strategies that have overlooked low-income, minority communities, has resulted in spatially disparate access to healthy food. A smaller proportion of supermarkets and a higher proportion of convenience stores selling processed packaged food, as well as high concentration of fast-food restaurants offering calorie-rich and nutrient-poor foods, are found in low-income and predominantly African-American neighborhoods compared to high-income and predominantly white neighborhoods (Gordon et al. 2011; Ver Ploeg et al. 2012). The Reinvestment Fund estimates that approximately 24.6 million people in the USA live in what they define as low supermarket access areas, which takes into account the relative accessibility between higher- and lower-income communities of the same density (The Reinvestment Fund 2011). The problem of food access is particularly serious for those 5.7 million households who live more than a half mile from a supermarket yet do not have access to a vehicle (Ver Ploeg et al. 2012).

The term 'food desert' has been used to describe these areas with limited access to retail stores selling healthy food.[3] Unfortunately, much of the food desert research has focused on the availability of conventional supermarkets, ignoring many other types of food retail options, from farmers' markets to family-owned greengrocers that provide access to fruits and vegetables in many low-income and minority communities (Short et al. 2007; Raja and Yadav 2008). Researchers have focused on supermarkets for various reasons, often pragmatic: databases of supermarket addresses are easily accessible; supermarkets often have a large assortment of food, including fresh food, making them a reasonable proxy for access to healthy food; and, because USDA defines food deserts as places bereft of food retailers that gross more than $2 million in revenue per year, studying supermarkets is more directly relevant to US food access policy (Ver

Ploeg et al. 2012). Apart from the limitations of focusing on supermarkets, studies often use simplified indicators of access that fail to reflect how people actually shop. More nuanced studies are emerging with various methods for measuring access, such as the relationship between the perceived quality of food retail establishments and purchasing decisions (Blitstein et al. 2012), measuring trips to markets from work and other locations (Kerr et al. 2012), and assessing perceptions of distance to food retailers in addition to physical proximity (Caspi et al. 2012).

Other dimensions of economic sustainability within the food system include the presence of a vibrant peri-urban and rural economy linked to the city; and job generation and economic development through food ventures. It also requires fair labor practices and living wages throughout the food supply chain. And it distinguishes those retail businesses that are designed primarily to serve local communities and that return a significant percentage of sales revenues to the local community.

Environmental Dimensions

Similar boundary issues exist with respect to the environmental impacts of the existing food system. Worldwide, agriculture contributes nearly one-third of global greenhouse gas emissions, including the clearing of forests for agriculture and ranching that requires burning (releasing CO_2) and removes a substantial carbon sink (Pelletier et al. 2011). With a relatively small number of large firms in control of the food industry, the supply chain is dominated by growing, processing and distribution systems that are highly energy and chemical intensive, increasingly reliant on monoculture and genetically modified organisms, and harmful to farm workers and residents of local communities exposed to pesticides, animal wastes and other impacts of industrial agricultural facilities (Lapping 2004). Pesticide use in the USA alone costs an estimated $10 billion per year in environmental and ecosystem services losses (Pimentel 2005). Rising incomes in emerging economies have led to increased consumption of animal protein, thus accelerating the adverse ecological impacts of deforestation and freshwater consumption to grow animal feed and support livestock, as well as the contribution of increasing amounts of greenhouse gases due to methane-emitting ruminants and their wastes (Satterthwaite et al. 2010). Since cities are the locations of higher-income consumers who demand products from the global food marketplace, and cities themselves purchase food for public institutions, urbanites and city governments contribute to the environmental impacts of agricultural production through their consumption patterns.

The food system also directly affects the urban environment. These impacts include motor vehicle traffic (some 2773 daily truck trips are made to NYC's Hunts Point food distribution center, located in one of the poorest neighborhoods in the nation that also suffers from high rates of asthma);[4] food and packaging waste disposal (40 percent of the available food in the USA is wasted, accounting for more than 25 percent of total freshwater consumption and 300 million barrels of oil per year (Hall et al. 2009)); and energy consumption for food processing and storage.

STRATEGIES FOR SUSTAINABLE URBAN FOOD POLICY

Cities have a number of ways to improve the sustainability of the food system through actions that are within the purview of municipal government.

Supporting Regional Producers

Industrialization and concentration in the food production process has led to the decline of mid-size farms, which find themselves too small to compete in global commodity markets yet too big to engage in direct sales through farmers' markets. The decline of 'agriculture of the middle' (Kirschenmann et al. 2008) has resulted in farmland conversion to non-agricultural uses at the edge of metropolitan areas, squandering high-quality soils, increasing automobile dependency as a result of low-density development, and threatening urban watersheds through the loss of pervious surfaces and increasing population in formerly rural areas. One strategy for cities to stem the loss of mid-size farms is to support farming in the peri-urban areas surrounding municipal borders. Definitions of local food vary significantly, from the 2008 Food, Conservation, and Energy Act (Farm Bill), which defines local as 'less than 400 miles from its origin, or within the State in which it is produced', to definitions based on market arrangements, such as sales through farmers' markets or direct from farm to institution (Martinez et al. 2010).

Local food is a small but growing market. The number of farmers' markets grew from 1755 in 1994 to approximately 7200 in 2011 (Oberholtzer et al. 2012). Community Supported Agriculture programs, in which consumers pay a farmer upfront for a season's worth of food, grew from two in 1996 to approximately 1400 in 2010 (ibid.). One municipal strategy is to support farmers' market infrastructure and permitting. City agencies can have complex and prohibitively costly rules and permitting requirements that prevent smaller farmers' markets from establishing and making a profit, particularly in lower-income neighborhoods (MBPO 2011). Cities can also support farmers' markets with zoning policies that make the markets legal in residential zones, allocate public space for markets, and provide support to NGOs that run the markets. Another strategy is to assist people in shopping at farmers' markets by providing financial incentives. Some cities offer incentives to low-income people to shop at farmers' markets, a policy that has been spread by organizations such as the NGO Wholesome Wave. These programs, which match dollars spent through federal programs like SNAP with additional incentive dollars provided by cities or philanthropic organizations, have grown in popularity and number, from only a few markets before 2008 to 150 markets in 2010 and over 350 markets in 2011 (Oberholtzer et al. 2012).

Cities can also spur the local and regional food economy by directing more of their purchases of food for schools, social programs and city functions, purchasing power that Morgan (2008) calls the 'public plate', to local farmers and food processors (Morgan and Sonnino 2008). By developing standards for government purchasing that take into account the sustainability dimensions of the food system, city governments can influence the market and ensure that the food served in public feeding programs is healthier, less environmentally disruptive and supports regional producers.

For example, New York City adopted Local Law 50 of 2011, legislation requiring the chief procurement officer to develop procedures to facilitate the purchasing of New York State food, defined as food grown, produced, harvested or processed in the state. New York City released guidelines that encourage municipal agencies to review their current 'menus' to identify where a currently procured product can be substituted by a product available from New York State. Additionally, city agencies may grant a 'price preference' for New York State food that is within 10 percent of the lowest responsive, responsible bidder's price, in situations where that low bidder does not offer New York State food products. In Los Angeles, Mayor Villaraigosa issued an executive directive that requires all City departments with food purchases of more than $10 000 annually to adopt a Good Food Purchasing Pledge which commits the agency to buy more nutritious food that is locally produced, sustainably grown by farms that 'treat their workers with respect and use humane animal treatment practices' (City of Los Angeles 2012). The directive requires agencies to increase annually the proportion of food that meets the good food criteria and to report annually on their progress. The good food criteria include sourcing food from: (1) small and mid-sized agricultural and food processing operations within the region; (2) production systems that conserve soil and water, emphasize good pest management practices, protect and enhance wildlife habitat and biodiversity, and offer healthy and humane care for livestock; (3) firms that offer safe and healthy working conditions and fair compensation for all food chain workers and producers from production to consumption; and

(4) foods that promote health and well-being by offering generous portions of vegetables, fruit and whole grains, and reducing salt, added sugars, fats and oils, and eliminating artificial additives (City of Los Angeles 2012).

Schools offer a significant opportunity to support regional food producers through local purchasing, public health through the nutritional quality of food served to students, and long-term sustainability by influencing the behavior of school children (Morgan 2008). In the USA, for example, some 30 million school children eat lunch five days a week, 180 days a year, creating market demand that can support sustainable agriculture while simultaneously improving children's health (Joshi and Ratcliffe 2012). US Public school districts for K-12 grades purchased more than $8.5 billion of food in school year 2009/10 (Young et al. 2012). The New York City Department of Education, which serves approximately 860 000 meals per day (the second-largest institutional food purveyor in the USA next to the US military) at an annual cost of $147.8 million, spent $23.9 million in 2011 for local produce, milk and yogurt ($20.8 million for milk and yogurt, and $3.1 million for produce).[5] The Los Angeles Unified School District (LAUSD), which serves 650 000 meals a day, shifted from a bid process for food to an RFP process that enabled the district to specify various dimensions of the food it wished to procure. In addition to enabling the school district to buy healthier and fresher food, the district also began to purchase items like milk exclusively from California dairies, began to eliminate canned fruits and vegetables in favor of fresh items, and increased the percentage of produce bought within a 200-mile radius from 9 percent in 2009 to 73 percent in 2012 (Center for Ecoliteracy 2012).

Farm-to-school programs, which attempt to preferentially support regional farmers through direct school food procurement, is a subset of a broader movement to use procurement as a tool for sustainable development (Nijaki and Worrel 2012). Farm-to-school also improves the freshness of the food served to children, thereby enhancing their diets and exposing them to healthier meals that may improve lifelong eating habits (Izumi et al. 2004). As of 2011, 33 US states had policies that directly supported farm-to-school programs, with ten states employing staff to manage these programs (Feenstra and Ohmart 2012).

While supporting regional food systems can be beneficial to the economy and preserve the working landscape of the peri-urban region, some have criticized efforts at food system localization as a 'local trap', pointing out that proximity and scale in and of themselves do not guarantee ethical or ecological production or economic viability (Born and Purcell 2006; Levkoe 2011). As is true for larger producers, small producers in the peri-urban area may use inefficient or ecologically damaging production methods, treat their workers poorly, abuse livestock, or otherwise engage in other unsustainable practices. And shorter supply chains can be created without regard to changed production methods.

Even the frequent emphasis on reducing food miles to reduce energy consumption and greenhouse gas emissions from the food system is not necessarily justified; shorter distribution routes relying on smaller delivery vehicles may translate into more trips, potentially requiring more fuel per ton of freight than long-distance rail or water transportation and larger, more efficient delivery vehicles. Moreover, according to one study, transportation accounts for only 11 percent of life-cycle greenhouse gas emissions in the food system, with the final delivery from producer to retail accounting for only 4 percent, suggesting the need to consider the energy requirements of the entire system, not merely transportation distance (Weber and Matthews 2008).

An effort to shift consumption to local sources also risks becoming a defensive strategy that, by reducing purchases from smallholder farmers and other producers in more distant regions and other countries, potentially hinders their economic development opportunities. Local foods can be more expensive than those produced in lower-cost regions, potentially creating wider gaps between high- and low-income consumers.

These factors suggest that policy makers should devise food procurement policies that account for production techniques and labor practices, as well as those that support smaller producers to attain these goals, rather than focusing merely on food produced within a specified geographic boundary. An equally important policy step is to design the food system of a city, including transportation, processing, storage and distribution infrastructure, in order to reduce the costs of production and procurement of food from local producers who meet sustainability criteria.

Expanding Urban Agriculture

In addition to responsibilities for public health and nutrition, land-use planning and regulation is typically a municipal responsibility. The popularity of urban agriculture has prompted advocates to urge cities to amend zoning ordinances that do not explicitly permit food production or farm stands. In some cases, fines against non-conforming urban farms (e.g. Oakland) and proposals for large-scale urban agriculture (e.g. Detroit), or illegal activities such as beekeeping (e.g. NYC), have prompted city officials to develop zoning changes to accommodate urban agriculture. Over the past few years a number of cities have revised their zoning ordinances to add urban farms and gardens as approved land uses, along with appropriate infrastructure such as compost bins and farm stands (Hodgson et al. 2011).

The details about where different types of agricultural activities can take place and the size and other standards for farms and gardens differ from city to city. Generally, cities have allowed community gardens in all parts of the city and larger farms in commercial and manufacturing zones. New York City, home to a number of large-scale rooftop farms, including commercial farms, non-profit educational farms and farms atop affordable housing developments, has adopted a zoning text amendment that excludes rooftop greenhouses atop commercial buildings from the lot's floor area ratio (FAR) and height limits, thus making more acres of rooftop space available for greenhouses (City of New York Department of Planning 2012).

In addition to zoning, the issue of land tenancy on public property is highly contested. In the case of New York City, the proposed development of community garden sites during the Giuliani administration, and more recently the creation of renewable leases for the gardens, has prompted policy debates about whether and to what extent gardeners should be granted long-term tenancy rights to public land. Many advocates viewed Detroit's recent sale of 140 acres of vacant city land to a single developer for $520 000 as an unfair giveaway that privileged large- over smaller-scale urban agriculture.

Indeed, growing space, whether on land or on rooftops, is one of the biggest constraints to the expansion of urban agriculture (Cohen et al. 2012). One strategy cities employ is to conduct land assessments to identify vacant parcels suitable for and worth allocating to urban agriculture. Portland, Vancouver, Oakland and San Francisco, among other cities, have conducted these surveys, often with the assistance of local universities (Mendes et al. 2008). In New York City, local law requires the city to conduct such an assessment of city-owned land suitable for urban agriculture and to publish the results. The NGO 596 Acres (www.596acres.org) is a grassroots effort to engage community residents in identifying ownership of vacant parcels and working with private owners or public officials to turn them into urban agriculture sites. Cities have also developed different types of land-tenure arrangements, from one-year renewable leases to the use of nonprofit land trusts to own land for farming and gardening in perpetuity.

A related issue is the potential risk of growing food in contaminated soil. In most cities, much of the soil on vacant land is contaminated with hydrocarbons, heavy metals such as lead, and other toxic chemicals, and such contaminated sites are particularly prevalent in low-income communities (McClintock 2012). Various government agencies, including some city health departments, have published guidelines on site assessment, soil testing and protocols to reduce the risk of exposure to the chemicals in the soil through direct contact with contaminated soil and through the ingestion of crops that have absorbed toxic chemicals (Toronto Public Health 2011; US EPA 2011). To minimize such risks, urban gardeners and farmers often choose to grow food in raised beds or containers filled with clean soil, and augmented with composted organic matter. Some urban farms located on highly contaminated sites, such as Greensgrow Farms in Philadelphia, use hydroponic systems elevated above the ground. In cities like New York, soil and compost are among the most significant resource needs for farms and gardens, and this suggests the importance of systems to recycle organic matter from households into compost for use by urban agriculture practitioners (Cohen et al. 2012).

Some cities have built food production into comprehensive plans, sustainability plans, or stand-alone plans focusing on urban agriculture. Seattle's 2005 comprehensive plan requires at least one community garden for every 2500 households in an urban village or neighborhood (City of Seattle 2005). Vancouver's Greenest City 2020 Action Plan establishes a specific target of increasing city and neighborhood food assets (including garden space) by at least 50 percent from 2010 levels (City of Vancouver 2011). New York's PlaNYC, its sustainability strategy, incorporates food as a crosscutting theme.

Minneapolis's stand-alone Urban Agriculture Policy Plan is perhaps the most comprehensive effort to expand food production. It calls on the city to 'prioritize local food production and distribution' when deciding on the use of city-owned and private property, including new development projects 'that could potentially affect existing local food resources'. It also requires the city to integrate farmers' markets into development plans, to identify policies to encourage green roofs for food production, and to incentivize developers to include space for food production, distribution and composting in new projects. The Minneapolis plan also calls for the creation of an 'overarching policy framework' to support urban agriculture, including an inventory of land for agriculture and food distribution, policies to support ownership or long-term tenure for growers and farmers' markets, policies to reduce liability and property taxes for urban farms and distribution facilities, and policies that make vacant and foreclosed properties more accessible for food growing and distribution (City of Minneapolis 2012).

Chicago's draft food systems plan (City of Chicago 2012), which recommends changes to the city's food environment to reduce obesity and strategies to improve education about food, nutrition and healthy eating habits, includes an innovative initiative to support urban food production at the neighborhood scale: the Green Healthy Neighborhoods project involves residents and NGOs in several South Side neighborhoods (Englewood, West Englewood, Washington Park, Woodlawn and parts of New City and Greater Grand Crossing) in developing a land-use strategy to create urban agriculture districts. The plan also calls for the creation of a 'system of farms and gardens', with the City joint-venturing with an NGO or land trust to develop city-owned vacant land into urban agriculture sites, including amalgamated scattered farm sites.

Cities are strategically integrating urban agriculture into the built landscape at multiple scales by creating incentives for developers to provide growing spaces in their projects. In New York City, a 202-apartment affordable housing project in the Bronx called Via Verde, created by the city's Housing Preservation and Development Department and developed by the Jonathan Rose Companies, includes a small apple orchard and rooftop community gardens. Via Verde was selected from a competitive Request for Proposals process that required respondents to consider incorporating access to nutritious food, physical fitness and places for social gathering, interpreted by the developer and architects as urban agriculture spaces (City of New York 2006). In December 2010, the New York City Housing Authority sold a parcel of land at a public housing project to a developer to build 124 units of affordable housing. The developer secured funds from the city to incorporate a 10 000-square-foot hydroponic rooftop greenhouse to grow produce on a commercial basis for the surrounding community (US HUD 2011).

Another strategy for creatively integrating food production into densely developed cities is to provide incentives for mobile or temporary farms and gardens on temporarily available land. In San Francisco, for example, city officials created a program called the Green Developer Agreement (GDA) to encourage temporary green uses of stalled development sites (San Francisco Planning Department 2010). This agreement allows developers to preserve their development approvals for a 5–8-year period as long as the site is used for a 'green' purpose, including urban agriculture. In 2010 Hayes Valley Farm (http://www.hayesvalleyfarm.com/) was able to open an interim-use urban farm project in San Francisco on a vacant parcel whose owner entered into a GDA with the city.

Cities are beginning to support urban agriculture as 'green' infrastructure that provides ecosystem services. For example, New York City's Department of Environmental Protection (DEP) funded three new urban agriculture projects to stem the flow of stormwater that, mixed with sewage, is discharged untreated as 'combined sewer overflow'. The US Clean Water Act requires cities to control this source of water pollution. To do so, DEP has committed to investing \$2.4 billion in green infrastructure, including 'blue roofs' that hold rainwater, extra-large street tree planters, 'green streets', parking lots paved with porous concrete, and vacant paved lots turned into gardens. This expenditure is much less than the \$6.8 billion in conventional infrastructure (e.g. larger sewers, holding tanks) required to accomplish the same pollution control.

Improving Distribution and Processing Infrastructure

A number of strategies can support sustainable and equitable distribution and processing of food, increasing access to fresh food in neighborhoods underserved by large grocers, making food distribution more efficient and thus more environmentally sound and economically viable, and encouraging entrepreneurship and job creation to support the local economy. These programs range from microenterprise development to conventional economic development support for larger businesses.

Mobile food vending is being deployed as a strategy for getting healthy food into some underserved communities (Tester et al. 2010). New York City's Department of Health and Mental Hygiene runs a 'green cart' program that offers 1000 additional mobile food-vending licenses to entrepreneurs (who are often very low-income individuals seeking an affordable business opportunity) who sell fresh fruits and vegetables from mobile carts in specific underserved communities (City of New York 2013). Other US cities like Chicago and Los Angeles are considering adopting this program and allowing other mobile vending opportunities such as food trucks vending healthy fare.

NGOs and city agencies throughout the USA have launched programs to help owners of *bodegas*, convenience stores, liquor stores and other small food establishments sell healthier food by offering loans for refrigeration and display equipment, business advice and connections to produce distributors. Evaluations have shown that these programs have been effective at increasing produce sales and health-related knowledge among consumers (Gittelsohn et al. 2012).

At the turn of the last century, cities began the process of rationalizing food distribution, building large terminal markets to accommodate the delivery by rail of food from distant markets, aggregating truck farms into larger markets, building public markets to remove pushcarts from city streets, and segregating noxious food production and processing facilities from residential and commercial zones (Donofrio 2007). Cities are now realizing that this effort at efficiency had the consequence of making it difficult for smaller farmers to distribute their produce and for smaller retailers to buy produce at wholesale. One potential solution that cities are trying is to create or renovate 'food hubs', locations to aggregate, store and process fresh produce into value-added products. Food hubs also serve as educational facilities (e.g. The Stop Community Food Centre in Toronto and Detroit's Eastern Market) and as wholesale farmers markets (e.g. Greenmarket Co. in NYC).

Cities have used a variety of strategies, from incentive zoning to financial support, to encourage large grocers to locate in low-income neighborhoods. Many of these initiatives are modeled after The Food Trust's Pennsylvania Fresh Food Financing Initiative, which helps finance food retailers through grants and loans (http://www.thefoodtrust.org). New York City's Food Retail Expansion to Support Health (FRESH) program, for example, combines zoning changes and financial incentives to induce developers to include supermarkets in their projects and to allow the construction of supermarkets in light manufacturing districts without a special permit. Under the Healthy Food Financing Initiative, the New Market Tax Credit Program, which provides credits against federal income taxes for qualified investments in low-income community development projects, is able to provide $32 million in tax credits for the creation of healthy food retail facilities (US Department of the Treasury 2012).

Finally, cities provide loans, incentives and incubator facilities to grow food-processing businesses. These can range from providing space for entrepreneurial food ventures to market their food, to community college training programs for jobs in the food industry, to space for farm stands, to licenses for food trucks to sell in designated parking spaces.

Increasing Access to and Use of Federal Food Benefits

The three major federal food assistance programs, Supplemental Nutrition Assistance Program (formerly Food Stamp Program), The National School Lunch Program, and the Special Supplemental Nutrition Program for Women, Infants, and Children (WIC), help low-income households obtain sufficient food. According to one study, receiving SNAP benefits reduces the likelihood of a household being food insecure by 30 percent and reduces the likelihood of being very food insecure by 20 percent (Ratcliffe et al. 2011). Ensuring that individuals use these federal benefits is important to a city's sustainability as it improves health, supplements household income, increases economic productivity, and contributes to the local economy. Every additional $5 billion of SNAP expenditures results in an increase in total economic activity of $9.2 billion and 82 100 additional jobs (Hanson and Golan 2002). SNAP benefits account for more than one-tenth of all spending for food eaten at home (Wilde 2012).

Cities attempt to expand the use of federal food benefits to purchase healthy food by funding wireless access at farmers' markets so that electronic benefits cards can be used to purchase produce (Bertmann et al. 2012). Various programs, some provided by the USDA (e.g. WIC and Senior Farmer Market Nutrition Program), and others sponsored by non-profit organizations with support from philanthropic organizations, increase the value of SNAP benefits redeemed at farmers' markets and thereby encourage SNAP recipients to use their benefits to purchase fresh vegetables (Young et al. 2011). The Fair Food Network in Michigan, for example, offers Detroit SNAP recipients double the value of their benefits when they shop at a farmers' market (Hesterman 2012).

In addition to the lack of access to fresh produce due to the absence of retail establishments, limited food preparation skills can be a significant barrier to the preparation of meals at home, leading households to eat a higher percentage of meals away from home. These meals tend to be higher in calories and fat than meals prepared and consumed at home (Soliah et al. 2011). Cooking classes and other efforts to re-skill individuals in food preparation encourage healthier eating (Brown and Hermann 2005). These are increasingly supported by cities and offered in public schools, community colleges, senior centers and other venues.

The school food environment is another major area of focus for food security advocates and policy makers. School food policy is critical for improving the health of a city's population given that students in schools consume one-third to more than half of their daily calories from school food during the school year (Ishdorj et al. 2012).[6] Pursuant to the Healthy Hunger-Free Kids Act of 2010, the USDA requires schools that participate in the USDA school meal programs to develop wellness policies that set standards for all food and beverages sold in school. In addition to the food served through USDA's school lunch and breakfast programs, most schools sell other food and beverages, known as competitive foods because they compete with the USDA meals. Some 40 percent of public school students eat or drink competitive foods (Guthrie et al. 2012). The Healthy, Hunger-Free Kids Act of 2010 required schools that offer the USDA school meal programs to limit competitive foods to those that meet nutrition standards based on the Federal Dietary Guidelines for Americans. USDA's Food and Nutrition Service has not (as of the publication date of this book) issued proposed nutrition standards, but is expected to do so soon. Among the many additional strategies to make school food more nutritious are proposals to ensure that all children eat a healthy breakfast by serving free school breakfasts to all students in their classrooms, easier registration for free school lunches to increase the number of eligible children who avail themselves of free or subsidized school food, and universal access to school lunches to remove the stigma associated with different groups of students eating lunch for free, for reduced price, or bringing food from home.

Cities are experimenting with a number of strategies to encourage people to consume fewer empty calories from products such as sugar-sweetened beverages and fast-food items. New York City has required menu labeling for chain restaurants since 2008 (this will soon be a national requirement under the Affordable Health Care for America Act), has run anti-obesity advertisements, and recently has approved a cap on the serving sizes of certain sugar-sweetened beverages (Young and Nestle 2012).[7] Other cities have adopted zoning ordinances that regulate the number and density of fast-food restaurants and their distances from schools and hospitals and specific neighborhoods (Eisenberg et al. 2011). Attempts by various municipalities to tax sodas, including through referenda, have not yet succeeded.

Managing Food Residuals

Strategies for reducing waste throughout the food supply chain include supporting food-marketing ventures, like community-supported agriculture (direct sales of weekly shares of produce), which can increase market opportunities for regional farmers and move more of their crops to market; relaxing standards for size and appearance of fruits and vegetables to enable more to be sold; providing better transportation, storage, processing and retail facilities to reduce spoilage and enable value-added processing of food that is at risk of spoilage; and providing consumer information and skills-building to encourage more efficient food use, food preservation (through canning, freezing or fermentation) and recycling of food waste through home composting. San Francisco's Department of Public Works operates a municipal fruit and nut tree-gleaning program, which provides residents with buckets and tools to harvest their trees, with the city providing harvesting assistance and donating the fruits and nuts to food banks, shelters, soup kitchens and hot-meal delivery programs (City of San Francisco 2013).

Post-disposal management of food waste is also important, as up to 25 percent of edible food is thrown away by households (Lee and Willis 2010). City waste management programs could support food waste composting and direct compost to urban gardens and urban and peri-urban farms. In addition to running a citywide composting program, Seattle's Public Utilities department created a backyard composting project and also supports food recovery from businesses as a waste reduction and food access strategy. Minneapolis requires that developers consider including space for food production, distribution and composting in new projects, allowing these spaces for urban agriculture to count towards green space 'set-aside' requirements and green building requirements.

Some organic waste, like oils and grease from commercial food establishments, must be collected and discarded by private waste haulers. Supporting specialty food waste recycling (e.g. biodiesel production from fats/oils/grease) requires processing infrastructure, assistance with facility siting, and policies to prime the pump, such as requirements that a certain percentage of homes in a jurisdiction operate their furnaces using biodiesel. For example, New York City's Local Law 43 of 2010 requires that, as of October 1, 2012, all heating oil used in the city must contain at least 2 percent biodiesel fuel.

FOOD SYSTEMS GOVERNANCE

Urban food policy making occurs through a combination of conventional policy making and networked governance. Conventional policy making involves decision making exercised by formal government institutions (e.g. a mayoral agency or the city council) backed by the authority of the state and spelled out in a city's charter and administrative code. Networked governance involves a mix of interdependent actors with different sources of institutional authority that work together to accomplish a public purpose, including public officials, corporations, interest groups, non-governmental organizations, researchers, philanthropic organizations, activists and ordinary citizens (Bulkeley 2005, p. 877; Dryzek 2010, p. 120).

Agency Integration

One of the challenges of food policy is that it is a boundary-spanning issue focused on in cities that were developed through 'mid-twentieth century institutional design' with divided, functional programs (in health, education, sanitation) that have their own policy communities divided into different sectors (Healey 2012, p. 21). Creating a sustainable urban food system requires breaking down silos between government agencies and supporting collaboration between government and non-governmental actors. How to bridge these functional divisions to address place-based issues such as food systems has been a challenge. For other place-based, cross-divisional issues, such as physical planning, coordinating departments, for example planning, were given the task of place-focused coordination (ibid.).

In many cities planning departments are involved in food policy, yet they have focused mainly on zoning and physical planning, not integrative policy planning. In some cities, agencies involved in sustainability planning or strategic planning have begun to weave together food policy issues, and in a small but growing number of cities food policy coordinators have been hired to encourage coordination across different silos of government. Governance fora such as food policy councils are also being invented in the spaces between government and civil society.

For example, Seattle developed a Food Action Plan (City of Seattle 2012), a blueprint to improve the city's food system. The recommendations in the plan include: expanding SNAP enrollment; creating a program to supplement SNAP benefits when redeemed at farmers' markets; expanding the city's P-Patch community gardening program and facilitating rooftop agriculture; investigating the viability of food hubs; helping corner stores sell healthy food; and promoting backyard composting.

The process for arriving at these recommendations follows what planners describe as a 'rational' planning model: (1) public participation to establish broad priorities; (2) translation of these priorities into goals; (3) establishment of criteria (feasibility, potential reach, inclusivity, community health impacts) to evaluate different recommended actions; and (4) evaluation of existing food-related activities and new policy ideas based on these criteria to arrive at final strategies, recommendations and specific actions. Yet, unlike other food planning processes, Seattle's efforts have a much greater emphasis on integration across agencies and the incorporation of food into existing planning processes. The city has a Food Interdepartmental Team (IDT), a working group of senior staff members from different agencies who collaborate on various food policy issues. The IDT has been successful at coordinating food policy work across different agencies, in part because it consists of energetic and dedicated individuals who see boundary spanning as part of their mission, and in large measure because the current mayor has directed them to do so.

Second, Seattle has focused on integrating policies into existing planning processes so that officials consider the needs of the food system as different types of infrastructure are developed, new land uses are planned, and projects are designed. This integrated planning approach is reflected in several strategies. For example, the Food Action Plan recommends integrating 'food access policies into the Comprehensive Plan, the Transportation Strategic Plan, Pedestrian and Bicycle Master Plans, the neighborhood planning process, and other relevant plans *so that planning processes include consideration of the availability of healthy food*' (emphasis added). In particular, the plan calls for new criteria that would be applied during the transportation planning process to ensure that food access is included as transportation infrastructure is developed. That means building 'pedestrian, bicycle, and transit connections between neighborhoods and community gardens, food banks, grocery stores and farmers' markets' as a matter of course as transportation engineers consider physical infrastructure and route planning.

The Food Action Plan also calls for integrating urban agriculture into the city's Comprehensive Plan, and recommends integrating supportive policies into additional plans and efforts, such as incentive programs to encourage green development. One such program, the 'Green Factor', requires developers of new projects to increase the use of landscaping. The

Green Factor provides a bonus for incorporating productive (vegetated) landscapes into new development. A second program, Priority Green, allows expedited permitting for projects that meet Seattle's sustainability goals, which includes the design of on-site food production into new projects. A third expands a program to require developers to purchase development rights from farmers in the region to meet the city's incentive zoning requirement in the downtown area and, it is hoped, to stem farmland conversion.

Food Policy Councils and Directors

Food policy councils can serve as a formal mechanism to meld the ideas and opinions of a wide range of stakeholders, both government officials and non-governmental actors. Food policy councils are groups of stakeholders who evaluate food systems issues for a municipality, county or state, identify problems that can be addressed through public policy, and recommend actions that governments should take. Most also educate the public about food policy issues. Councils may develop specific policy proposals, lobby for specific legislation, and participate in the regulatory process. Some food policy councils are involved in long-range food systems planning, while others focus on narrower issues related to food access. There are approximately 150 food policy councils in North America (Scherb et al. 2012).

A number of US and Canadian cities have food policy coordinators or directors to guide food systems policy and program development, often with input from food policy councils composed of various government and non-governmental stakeholders (Hatfield 2012). The location of food policy programs within the city bureaucracy, including proximity to elected officials, determines the direction or focus of the policy making and the likelihood that initiatives will be implemented. Eight of 13 food policy directors surveyed in 2012 were situated within sustainability-related departments or programs, with three of the eight also connected to a planning department. However, sustainability departments typically engage in strategic planning but lack regulatory authority or control over agencies. Food policy directors in these departments need to develop policy-making power by working closely with agencies that possess power through their control of land (e.g. parks, housing) or by virtue of their regulatory authority (e.g. health). Connection to and support of elected officials provides power to get local legislation and programmatic initiatives adopted. However, political pet projects designed without the support of the implementing agencies risk being neglected or subverted by the bureaucracy.

Locating food policy initiatives within a particular department may provide the food policy director with authority to launch programs or advance regulations. Yet being inside a department that has a specific mandate can be limiting because it focuses the efforts on issues that that agency is required and able to address. If a food policy director is in the city's health department, for example, it will be easier to implement policies addressing nutrition and diet-related diseases than transportation efficiency or the provenance of food purchased by the city.

Placing the food policy director position in a part of the city's administration that provides access to top agency officials across the administration (like the Mayor's Office) makes it easier for the director to link the efforts of disparate agencies. Creating an internal food advisory committee that consists of officials from those agencies is another strategy to get buy-in for policies across departmental silos. Of course, unless the food policy director is perceived to have power (perhaps by virtue of being supported by the mayor or a council member), senior officials from different departments may not attend and participate in a committee that is seen as merely advisory.

Given the importance of interdepartmental coordination for a cross-cutting issue like food policy, one of the key tasks of food policy coordinators is to ensure that agency programs and policies are in sync and working towards the same citywide goals. But the challenge is that, when city agencies do not see it as part of their mission to support sustainable food systems, any effort on the part of related agencies to contribute to the food system will be based solely on the interest and willingness of the agency head to do so. Creating structural change so that agency heads see improving the food system as part of their mission, and one they will be evaluated on, is key. One of the ways to do that is to ensure that existing systems for tracking agency performance, like citywide management reports, measure the extent to which an agency's actions contribute to the food system's sustainability. For example, the parks department might be required to track the conditions and productivity of the community gardens and farms under its purview, or the sanitation department might track the quantity of compost generated from organic waste that is returned to urban gardens and farms.

Food Plans

Increasing numbers of cities are developing plans to address the complex and interconnected dimensions of the food system. Chicago's draft food systems plan (City of Chicago 2012), *A Recipe for Healthy Places*, recommends changes to the city's food environment to reduce obesity and strategies to improve education about food, nutrition and healthy eating habits. The draft plan was developed through a process that included 26 public meetings held over 13 months, with more than 400 participants, and it suggests roles for both government and non-governmental entities. The plan was funded by a grant from the Centers for Disease Control and Prevention's (CDC) Communities Putting Prevention to Work (CPPW) Initiative, which is funded through the Affordable Care Act's Prevention and Public Health Fund. A number of other US cities, like Los Angeles and Seattle, are using CPPW funds to do food system planning.

Everyday Makers

The politically charged actions of what might otherwise be considered mundane, 'micropolitical' practices of everyday life are important mechanisms for policy development (Coleman 2007). The spaces in which the political activities of the micropolitical are grounded are less official and demarcated from everyday life than conventional policy making. These everyday experiences, and actions, are important in driving policy forward democratically (Marsh 2011, p. 76).

About a decade ago, a mix of city planners, academics, urban farmers, post-carbon activists, environmentalists, foodies, progressive farmers and others began to advocate for local-level policies to address the ills of the food system. Much of this advocacy took the form of practice-based activism, in which individuals design and prototype new products, services, business ventures, gardens and growing systems. These often require new laws and programs, and other technical, legal and social innovations. Sometimes individuals or groups will stretch or flout existing laws or regulations to produce, sell or consume the food they feel is healthier, more sustainable or more affordable, prompting policy innovation. These activities range from guerrilla gardening, to bee- and chicken-keeping, selling raw milk, harvesting wild edibles or animal slaughtering. Novella Carpenter's 'Ghost Town Farm', a West Oakland urban farm run by the author and blogger, mobilized the city's urban agriculture activists after a neighbor complained about Carpenter slaughtering animals on site and the city attempted to close the farm because of its non-compliance with zoning (McClintock et al. 2012).

CONCLUSIONS

The food system is as critical to urban sustainability as transportation, energy, water or any other essential infrastructure. Global ecological problems, opposition to industrial agriculture, economic crisis and attention to diet-related public health challenges are causing planners, policy makers, advocates and philanthropists to focus on strategies to make the urban food system more equitable and enable food to contribute to urban and regional sustainability. Strategies to improve the food system address all aspects of the food supply chain from production to waste disposal. Because the food system crosses institutional boundaries, cities are experimenting with governance systems to break down silos and develop integrated solutions. These include food policy councils to engage a wide range of actors in the planning process, food policy coordinators to direct the work of multiple agencies, and the efforts of everyday makers to push boundaries and incite policy making. No city has developed an exemplary food system, but cities such as Seattle, Toronto, New York, Minneapolis, Los Angeles and Chicago, and many others, have developed innovative planning processes that are operating at various scales, addressing different aspects of the food system, and engaging different mixes of stakeholders.

NOTES

1. See, for example, guides published by the American Planning Association, PolicyLink and ChangeLab Solutions.
2. See, for example, the Sustainable Agriculture Food Systems Funders (http://www.safsf.org/) and the community food funders (http://www.communityfoodfunders.org/).
3. Section 7527 of the 2008 Farm Bill defines a food desert as 'an area in the United States with limited access to affordable and nutritious food, particularly such an area composed of predominantly lower-income neighborhoods and communities' (see http://www.usda.gov/documents/Bill_6124.pdf).
4. http://nytelecom.vo.llnwd.net/o15/agencies/planyc2030/pdf/ll52_food_metrics_report_1012.pdf.
5. http://nytelecom.vo.llnwd.net/o15/agencies/planyc2030/pdf/ll52_food_metrics_report_1012.pdf.
6. See also http://www.letsmove.gov/healthy-schools.
7. The soda cap rule was struck down by the State Supreme Court on March 11, 2013 and is being appealed by the Bloomberg Administration. See http://www.nytimes.com/2013/03/12/nyregion/judge-invalidates-bloombergs-soda-ban.html?pagewanted=all&_r=0.

REFERENCES

American Planning Association (2007), 'Policy guide on community and regional food planning', available at http://www.planning.org/policy/guides/pdf/foodplanning.pdf on 12/15/12.

Anderson, M.D. and A.C. Bellows (2012), 'Introduction to symposium on food sovereignty: expanding the analysis and application', *Agriculture and Human Values*, **29** (2), 177–84.

Bang, H.P. and E. Sorensen (1999), 'The everyday maker: a new challenge to democratic governance', *Administrative Theory and Praxis*, **21** (3), 325–41.

Bertmann, F.M.W., P. Ohri-Vachaspati, M.P. Buman and C.M. Wharton (2012), 'Implementation of wireless terminals at farmers' markets: impact on SNAP redemption and overall sales', *American Journal of Public Health*, **102** (7), 53–5.

Blitstein, J.L., J. Snider and W.D. Evans (2012), 'Perceptions of the food shopping environment are associated with greater consumption of fruits and vegetables', *Public Health Nutrition*, **15** (6), 1124–29.

Born, B. and M. Purcell (2006), 'Avoiding the local trap: scale and food systems in planning research', *Journal of Planning Education and Research*, **26** (2), 195–207.

Brown, B.J. and J.R. Hermann (2005), 'Cooking classes increase fruit and vegetable intake and food safety behaviors in youth and adults', *Journal of Nutrition Education and Behavior*, **37** (2), 104–5.

Bulkeley, H. (2005), 'Reconfiguring environmental governance: towards a politics of scales and networks', *Political Geography*, **24** (8), 875–902.

Caspi, C.E., I. Kawachi, S.V. Subramanian, G. Adamkiewicz and G. Sorensen (2012), 'The relationship between diet and perceived and objective access to supermarkets among low-income housing residents', *Social Science and Medicine*, **75** (7), 1254–62.

Cawley, J. and J. Maclean (2010), *Unfit for Service: The Implications of Rising Obesity for US Military Recruitment*, Cambridge, MA: National Bureau of Economic Research, available at http://www.nber.org/papers/w16408.

Center for Ecoliteracy (2012), 'Rethinking school lunch: Los Angeles Unified School District: a new system for purchasing food for school meals', available at http://www.ecoliteracy.org/sites/default/files/uploads/shared_files/LAUSD_Procurement_Report_by_CEL.pdf (accessed 12 December 2012).

Centers for Disease Control and Prevention (2012), '2011 estimates of foodborne illness in the United States', available at http://www.cdc.gov/Features/dsFoodborneEstimates/ (accessed 12 December 2012).

City of Chicago (2012), 'Healthy places: food plan', available at http://www.healthyplaceschicago.org/food/food-plan-overview.lasso.

City of Los Angeles, Office of the Mayor (2012), *Executive Directive No. 24: Good Food Purchasing Policy*, Los Angeles, CA: City of Los Angeles, available at http://mayor.lacity.org/stellent/groups/ElectedOfficials/@MYR_Services_Contributor/documents/Contributor_Web_Content/LACITYP_023038.pdf.

City of Minneapolis (2012), 'Minneapolis city planning commission actions', available at http://www.minneapolismn.gov/meetings/planning/WCMS1P-085268.

City of New York (2006), 'Department of Housing Preservation and Development: New Housing New York legacy project request for proposals, issue date June 12, 2006'.

City of New York (2013), 'NYC green cart', available at http://www.nyc.gov/html/doh/html/diseases/green-carts.shtml.

City of New York Department of Planning (2012), 'Zone green', available at http://www.nyc.gov/html/dcp/html/greenbuildings/index.shtml.

City of San Francisco (2013), 'Urban harvesting program', available at http://sfdpw.org/index.aspx?page=1243.

City of Seattle (2005), *Seattle Comprehensive Plan, Urban Village Appendix B*, Seattle, WA: City of Seattle.

City of Seattle (2012), *Food Action Plan*, Seattle, WA: City of Seattle, available at http://www.seattle.gov/environment/documents/Seattle_Food_Action_Plan_10-24-12.pdf.

City of Vancouver (2011), *Administrative Report RR-1*, Vancouver, BC: City of Vancouver, available at http://vancouver.ca/ctyclerk/cclerk/20110712/documents/rr1.pdf.

Cohen, N. and K. Ackerman (2011), 'Breaking new ground', *The New York Times*, available at http://bittman.blogs.nytimes.com/2011/11/21/breaking-new-ground/ (published online 21 November 2011).

Cohen, Nevin, Kristin Reynolds and Rupal Sanghvi (2012), *Five Borough Farm: Seeding the Growth of Urban Agriculture in New York*, New York: The Design Trust for Public Space.

Coleman, S. (2007), 'Mediated politics and everyday life', *International Journal of Communication*, **1**, 49–60.

Coleman-Jensen, Alisha, Mark Nord, Margaret Andrews and Steven Carlson (2012), *Household Food Security in the United States in 2011: Economic Research Report Number 141*, Washington, DC: US Department of Agriculture, Economic Research Service.

Conill, Joana, Manuel Castells, Amalia Cardenas and Lisa Servon (2012), 'Beyond the crisis: the emergence of alternative economic practices', in Manuel Castells, Joao Caraca and Gustavo Cardoso (eds), *Aftermath: The Cultures of the Economic Crisis*, Oxford: Oxford University Press, pp. 210–31.

DeSchutter, Olivier (2011), *Report Submitted by the Special Rapporteur on the Right to Food*, Geneva: United Nations General Assembly Human Rights Council.

Donofrio, G.A. (2007), 'Feeding the city', *Gastronomica: The Journal of Food and Culture*, **7** (4), 30–41.

Dryzek, John S. (2010), *Foundations and Frontiers of Deliberative Governance*, Oxford: Oxford University Press.

Eisenberg, M.J., R. Atallah, S.M. Grandi, S.B. Windle and E.M. Berry (2011), 'Legislative approaches to tackling the obesity epidemic', *CMAJ: Canadian Medical Association Journal/Journal de l'Association Medicale Canadienne*, **183** (13), 1496–500.

Fairbairn, M. (2011), 'Framing transformation: the counter-hegemonic potential of food sovereignty in the US context', *Agriculture and Human Values*, **29** (2), 217–30.

Feenstra, G. and J. Ohmart (2012), 'The evolution of the school food and farm to school movement in the United States: connecting childhood health, farms, and communities', *Childhood Obesity*, **8** (4), 280–89.

Finkelstein, E.A., J.G. Trogdon, J.W. Cohen and W. Dietz (2009), 'Annual medical spending attributable to obesity: payer- and service-specific estimates', *Health Affairs (Project Hope)*, **28** (5), 822–31.

Food and Agriculture Organization of the United Nations (FAO) (2010), *International Scientific Symposium, Biodiversity and Sustainable Diets: United Against Hunger*, Rome: Food and Agriculture Organization of the United Nations, available at http://www.fao.org/ag/humannutrition/29186-021e012ff2db1b0eb6f6228e1d98c806a.pdf.

Food and Agriculture Organization of the United Nations (FAO) (2011), *The State of the World's Land and Water Resources for Food and Agriculture (SOLAW) – Managing Systems at Risk*, Rome: Food and Agriculture Organization of the United Nations and LondonK: Earthscan.

Food and Agriculture Organization of the United Nations, World Food Programme and International Fund for Agricultural Development (FAO, WFP and IFAD) (2012), *The State of Food Insecurity in the World 2012. Economic Growth is Necessary but not Sufficient to Accelerate Reduction of Hunger and Malnutrition*, Rome: FAO. See http://www.fao.org/docrep/016/i3027e/i3027e.pdf.

Gittelsohn, J., M. Rowan and P. Gadhoke (2012), 'Interventions in small food stores to change the food environment, improve diet, and reduce risk of chronic disease', *Preventing Chronic Disease*, **9**.

Gordon, C., M. Purciel-Hill, N.R. Ghai, L. Kaufman, R. Graham and G. Van Wye (2011), 'Measuring food deserts in New York City's low-income neighborhoods', *Health and Place*, **17** (2), 696–700.

Guthrie, J.F., C. Newman, K. Ralston, M. Prell and M. Ollinger (2012), 'Understanding school food service characteristics associated with higher competitive food revenues can help focus efforts to improve school food environments', *Childhood Obesity*, **8** (4), 298–304.

Hall, K., J. Guo, M. Dore and C. Chow (2009), 'The progressive increase of food waste in America and its environmental impact', *PLoS ONE*, **4** (11), e7940.

Hanson, K. and E. Golan (2002), *Effects of Changes in Food Stamp Expenditures across the US Economy: Food Assistance and Nutrition Research Report 26–6*, Washington, DC: US Department of Agriculture, Economic Research Service.

Hatfield, Molly M. (2012), *City Food Policy and Programs: Lessons Harvested from an Emerging Field*, Portland, OR: City of Portland, Oregon Bureau of Planning and Sustainability.

Healey, P. (2012), 'Re-enchanting democracy as a mode of governance', *Critical Policy Studies*, **6** (1), 19–39.

Hesterman, O.B. (2012), 'Double up food bucks: how advocates can help grow a healthy, sustainable food system', *Clearinghouse Review: Journal of Poverty Law and Policy*, **46**, 276–300.

Hodgson, Kimberley (2012), *Planning for Food Access and Community-Based Food Systems: A National Scan and Evaluation of Local Comprehensive and Sustainability Plans*, Chicago, IL: American Planning Association.

Hodgson, Kimberley, Marcia C. Campbell and Martin Bailkey (2011), *Urban Agriculture: Growing Healthy, Sustainable Places*, Chicago, IL: American Planning Association.

Institute of Medicine (IOM) (2012), *Accelerating Progress in Obesity Prevention: Solving the Weight of the Nation*, Washington, DC: The National Academies Press, p. 18.

Ishdorj, A., H. Jensen and M. Crepinsek (2012), 'Children's consumption of fruits and vegetables: do school environment and policies affect choice at school and away from school?', available at http://www.card.iastate.edu/publications/dbs/pdffiles/12wp531.pdf.

Izumi, B.T., K. Alaimo and M.W. Hamm (2004), 'Farm-to-school programs: perspectives of school food service professionals', *Journal of Nutrition Education and Behavior*, **42** (2), 83–91.

Jaffe, J.A. and M. Gertler (2006), 'Victual vicissitudes: consumer deskilling and the (gendered) transformation of food systems', *Agriculture and Human Values*, **23** (2), 143–62.

Joshi, A. and M.M. Ratcliffe (2012), 'Causal pathways linking farm to school to childhood obesity prevention', *Childhood Obesity*, **8** (4), 305–14.

Kerr, J., L. Frank, J.F. Sallis, B. Saelens, K. Glanz and J. Chapman (2012), 'Predictors of trips to food destinations', *The International Journal of Behavioral Nutrition and Physical Activity*, **9** (1), 58.

Kirschenmann, Fred, G.W. Stevenson, Fred Buttel, Thomas A. Lyson and Mike Duffy (2008), 'Why worry about the agriculture of the middle?', in Thomas A. Lyson, G.W.

Kneen, Brewster (1993), *From Land to Mouth: Understanding the Food System*, Toronto, ON: NC Press, pp. 37–53.

Lapping, M.B. (2004), 'Toward the recovery of the local in the globalizing food system: the role of alternative agricultural and food models in the US', *Ethics, Place and Environment*, **7** (3), 141–50.

Lawson, Laura J. (2005), *City Bountiful: A Century of Community Gardening in America*, Berkeley, CA: University of California Press.

Lee, Peter and Peter Willis (2010), *Waste Arisings in the Supply of Food and Drink to Households in the UK*, Banbury, UK: WRAP, available at http://www.wrap.org.uk/content/waste-arisings-supply-food-and-drink-uk-households.

Levkoe, C.Z. (2011), 'Towards a transformative food politics', *Local Environment*, **16** (7), 687–705.

Loeber, A., M. Hajer and L. Levidow (2011), 'Agro-food crises: institutional and discursive changes in the food scares era', *Science as Culture*, **20** (2), 147–55.

Manhattan Borough President's Office (MBPO) (2011), *Red Tape, Green Vegetables: A Plan to Improve New York City's Regulations for Community-Based Farmers Markets*, New York: Manhattan Borough President's Office.

Marsh, D. (2011), 'Late modernity and the changing nature of politics: two cheers for Henrik Bang', *Critical Policy Studies*, 5 (1), 73–89.

Martinez, Stephen, Michael S. Hand, Michelle Da Pra, Susan Pollack, Katherine Ralston, Travis Smith, Stephen Vogel, Shellye Clark, Loren Tauer, Luanne Lohr, Sarah A. Low and Constance Newman (2010), *Local Food Systems: Concepts, Impacts, and Issues, Economic Research Report Number 97*, Washington, DC: US Department of Agriculture, Economic Research Service.

McClintock, N. (2012), 'Assessing soil lead contamination at multiple scales in Oakland, California: Implications for urban agriculture and environmental justice', *Applied Geography*, **35** (1–2), 460–73.

McClintock, N., H. Wooten and A. Brown (2012), 'Toward a food policy "first step" in Oakland, California: a food policy council's efforts to promote urban agriculture zoning', *Journal of Agriculture, Food Systems, and Community Development*, **2** (4), 15–42.
Mendes, Wendy, Kevin Balmer, Terra Kaethler and Amanda Rhoads (2008), 'Using land inventories to plan for urban agriculture: experiences from Portland and Vancouver', *Journal of the American Planning Association*, **74** (4), 435–49.
Morgan, K. (2008), 'Greening the realm: sustainable food chains and the public plate', *Regional Studies*, **42** (9), 1237–50.
Morgan, Kevin and Roberto Sonnino (2008), *The School Food Revolution: Public Food and the Challenge of Sustainable Development*, London: Earthscan.
Morgan, K. and R. Sonnino (2010), 'The urban foodscape: world cities and the new food equation', *Cambridge Journal of Regions, Economy and Society*, **3** (2), 209–24.
Mukherji, N. and A. Morales (2010), 'Zoning for urban agriculture', *Zoning Practice*, **10** (3), 1–8.
New York City Council (2010), *FoodWorks: A Vision to Improve NYC's Food System*, New York: The New York City Council, p. 3.
Nijaki, L.K. and G. Worrel (2012), 'Procurement for sustainable local economic development', *International Journal of Public Sector Management*, **25** (2), 133–53.
Oberholtzer, L., C. Dimitri and G. Schumacher (2012), 'Linking farmers, healthy foods, and underserved consumers: exploring the impact of nutrition incentive programs on farmers and farmers' markets', *Journal of Agriculture, Food Systems, and Community Development*, **2** (4), 63–77.
Peck, J. (2011), 'Geographies of policy: from transfer-diffusion to mobility-mutation', *Progress in Human Geography*, **35** (6), 773–97.
Pelletier, N., E. Audsley, S. Brodt, T. Garnett, P. Henriksson, A. Kendall and K.J. Kramer (2011), 'Energy intensity of agriculture and food systems', *Annual Review of Environment and Resources*, **36** (1), 223–46.
Pimentel, D. (2005), 'Environmental and economic costs of the application of pesticides primarily in the United States', *Environment, Development and Sustainability*, **7**, 229–52.
Pothukuchi, K. (2009), 'Community and regional food planning: building institutional support in the United States', *International Planning Studies*, **14** (4), 349–67.
Pothukuchi, K. and J.L. Kaufman (1999), 'Placing the food system on the urban agenda: the role of municipal institutions in food systems planning', *Agriculture and Human Values*, **16** (2), 213–24.
Pothukuchi, K. and J.L. Kaufman (2000), 'The food system: a stranger to the planning field', *Journal of the American Planning Association*, **66** (2), 113–24.
Raja, S. and P. Yadav (2008), 'Beyond food deserts: measuring and mapping racial disparities in neighborhood food environments', *Journal of Planning Education and Research*, **27** (4), 469–82.
Ratcliffe, C., S. McKernan and S. Zhang (2011), 'How much does the Supplemental Nutrition Assistance Program reduce food insecurity?', *American Journal of Agricultural Economics*, **93** (4), 1082–98.
The Reinvestment Fund (2011), *Searching for Markets: The Geography of Inequitable Access to Healthy & Affordable Food in the United States*, Philadelphia, PA: The Reinvestment Fund, available at http://www.cdfifund.gov/what_we_do/resources/SearchingForMarkets_Report_web_Low_%20Res.pdf.
Robert Wood Johnson Foundation (2012), 'Declining childhood obesity rates – where are we seeing the most progress? Issue brief', available at http://www.rwjf.org/content/dam/farm/reports/issue_briefs/2012/rwjf401163.
San Francisco Planning Department (2010), *Executive Summary: Draft Green Development Agreement Legislation*, San Francisco, CA: San Francisco Planning Department.
Satterthwaite, D., G. McGranahan and C. Tacoli (2010), 'Urbanization and its implications for food and farming', *Philosophical Transactions of the Royal Society B: Biological Sciences*, **365** (1554), 2809–20.
Sbicca, J. (2012), 'Growing food justice by planting an anti-oppression foundation: oppor-

tunities and obstacles for a budding social movement', *Agriculture and Human Values*, **29** (4), 455–66.

Scherb, A., A. Palmer, S. Frattaroli and K. Pollack (2012), 'Exploring food system policy: a survey of food policy councils in the United States', *Journal of Agriculture, Food Systems, and Community Development*, **2** (4), 3–14.

Short, A., J. Guthman and S. Raskin (2007), 'Food deserts, oases, or mirages? Small markets and community food security in the San Francisco Bay area', *Journal of Planning Education and Research*, **26** (3), 352–64.

Soliah, L.A.L., J.M. Walter and S.A. Jones (2011), 'Benefits and barriers to healthful eating: what are the consequences of decreased food preparation ability?', *American Journal of Lifestyle Medicine*, **6** (2), 152–8.

Stevenson and Rick Welsh (eds), *Food and the Mid-Level Farm: Renewing an Agriculture of the Middle*, Boston, MA: The MIT Press, pp. 3–22.

Tester, J.M., S.A. Stevens, I.H. Yen and B.L. Laraia (2010), 'An analysis of public health policy and legal issues relevant to mobile food vending', *American Journal of Public Health*, **100** (11), 2038–46.

Toronto Public Health (2011), *Assessing Urban Impacted Soil for Urban Gardening: Decision Support Tool – Technical Report and Rationale*, Toronto, ON: City of Toronto, Department of Public Health.

United States Conference of Mayors (2011), *Hunger and Homelessness Survey, A Status Report on Hunger and Homelessness in America's Cities: A 29-City Survey*, Washington, DC: United States Conference of Mayors.

US Department of Housing and Urban Development, Office of Public and Indian Housing (HUD) (2011), *Final PHA Plan. Annual Plan for Fiscal Year 2012*, New York: New York City Housing Authority, p. 7.

US Department of the Treasury (2012), 'Community developments investments', available at http://www.occ.gov/publications/publications-by-type/other-publications-reports/cdi-newsletter/august-2012/healthy-foods-ezine-article-2-reinvestment-fund.html (accessed 12 December 2012).

US Environmental Protection Agency (US EPA) (2011), *Brownfields and Urban Agriculture: Interim Guidelines for Safe Gardening Practices*, Washington, DC: US Environmental Protection Agency, available at http://www.epa.gov/brownfields/urbanag/pdf/bf_urban_ag.pdf.

Ver Ploeg, Michele, Vince Breneman, Paula Dutko, Ryan Williams, Samantha Snyder, Chris Dicken and Phil Kaufman (2012), *Access to Affordable and Nutritious Food: Updated Estimates of Distance to Supermarkets Using 2010 Data, Economic Research Report*, Washington, DC: US Department of Agriculture, Economic Research Service.

Weber, C.L. and H.S. Matthews (2008), 'Food-miles and the relative climate impacts of food choices in the United States', *Environmental Science and Technology*, **42** (10), 3508–13.

Wilde, P.E. (2012), 'The new normal: the Supplemental Assistance Nutrition Program', *American Journal of Agricultural Economics*, advanced online publication, doi: 10.1093/ajae/aas043.

Wiskerke, J. (2009), 'On places lost and places regained: reflections on the alternative food geography and sustainable regional development', *International Planning Studies*, **14** (4), 369–87.

Young, C., A. Karpyn and N. Uy (2011), 'Farmers' markets in low income communities: impact of community environment, food programs and public policy', *Community Development*, **42** (2), 208–20.

Young, L.R. and M. Nestle (2012), 'Reducing portion sizes to prevent obesity: a call to action', *American Journal of Preventive Medicine*, **43** (5), 565–8.

Young, Nick, Salli Diakova, Thomas Earley, Justin Carnagey, Anne Krome and Cherie Root (2012), *School Food Purchase Study-III*, Alexandria, VA: US Department of Agriculture.

5. Sustainability strategies for consumer products in cities

Gregory A. Keoleian, Joshua P. Newell, Ming Xu and Erin Dreps

INTRODUCTION

The scholarly literature on urban sustainability, as well as policy and planning practice, has mostly dealt with cities as geographically bounded places. This research has emphasized how buildings, land-use patterns and transportation systems in cities contribute to energy consumption, GHG emissions, water use and other aspects of resource consumption, as well as how to integrate nature into the local urban fabric (Portney 2003; Wolch et al. 2004; Kellert et al. 2011; Brown et al. 2008; Wheeler and Beatley 2004; Beatley 2010; Cervero and Sullivan 2011).

As a result, strategies to promote sustainable communities are largely place-based, with the scale of such efforts ranging from single buildings, to urban districts, larger communities, cities or metropolitan regions. One example includes the widely used LEED certification programs for individual buildings and new communities, and efforts such as California's legislation (SB 375 or the Sustainable Communities and Climate Protection Act) that requires jurisdictions to craft land-use and transportation planning strategies to reduce GHG emissions.

Sustainably designed buildings, land-use patterns and transportation systems are clearly important, but so too is understanding the consumption impacts of urban dwellers. The larger material flows highlighted by ecological footprint analysis (Wackernagel et al. 2006) and urban metabolism studies (Kennedy et al. 2008) are frequently excluded from city-scale planning action. In particular, products and their consumption are often ignored, despite the enormous volume of materials and embodied energy used in their manufacture, distribution and disposal, and the geographically variable impacts of their supply chains.

Municipal solid waste (MSW) data – which exclude construction, demolition and nonhazardous industrial wastes – can be used to characterize urban consumption and product material flows. In 2010, 250 million tons of MSW were generated in the USA, 85 million tons of which were recovered through recycling or composting. Of the total waste generation, durable goods (products lasting three years or more) comprised 19.6 percent, non-durable goods (products lasting less than three years) comprised 21.3 percent, and containers and packaging comprised another 30.3 percent. These three categories together accounted for 71.2 percent of MSW (EPA 2011c), much of which can be categorized as consumer products together with their packaging. Food and yard waste accounted for the remaining waste fraction. Table 5.1 provides an estimate of the waste generation for each product category (durable, non-durable and containers/packaging) in the USA from 1960 to 2010 in pounds per capita. The contribution of each product category to the total generation in a given year is also presented as a percentage. This serves as a very rough picture of the average consumer product consumption (or metabolism) in cities. It assumes that consumer product purchasing is equal to the rate of product retirement.

In this chapter, we explore opportunities for improving urban sustainability through strategies focused on consumer products. Consumer products are defined as 'any article, or component part thereof, produced and distributed for sale to . . . or for the personal use, consumption or enjoyment of a consumer in or around a permanent or temporary household or residence, a school, in recreation, or otherwise' (Consumer Product Safety Commission 2011). Although food is outside the scope of this definition, it also serves as an illustrative example for select sustainability strategies.

We present several strategies for improving the sustainability of these products, using case examples to illustrate them. Along with highlighting the potential benefits inherent to each one, the chapter conveys the associated tradeoffs that can occur when assessing sustainability performance from a product life-cycle perspective. Some of the strategies presented here are in direct conflict with one another, and some are easy to implement but capable of lesser relative impact compared to those that are difficult to implement with much greater impact potential. The chapter does not serve as an endorsement of each strategy, much less all of them together, but rather as a presentation of the many opportunities available for making consumer products in cities sustainable, and the substantial benefits possible from doing so.

Impacts of products consumed in cities spread far beyond the city boundary, depending on the life cycle of the product. For example, a product's use, service, retirement and recovery phases may occur in the city, as well as impacts associated with these phases, while other phases of the product life cycle (i.e. raw material acquisition, processing, manufacturing, assembly and disposal) may happen in other parts of the country or even other parts of the world (Figure 5.1). Many examples occur where some manufacturing happens within city boundaries for larger industrialized cities, and landfills can also be cited as occurring within a city's boundary.

Table 5.1 MSW waste generation by product category

Products	Pounds per capita (Percentage)											
	1960	%	1970	%	1980	%	1990	%	2000	%	2010	%
Durable goods	**110.6**	**11.3**	**144.3**	**12.1**	**192.5**	**14.4**	**239.7**	**14.3**	**276.1**	**16.0**	**317.9**	**19.6**
Appliances	18.2	1.8	21.4	1.8	26.0	1.9	30.3	1.8	33.3	1.9	36.3	2.2
Furnishings and Carpet	24.0	2.4	27.9	2.3	42.0	3.1	68.0	4.1	75.0	4.4	92.5	5.7
Rubber Tires	12.5	1.3	18.6	1.6	24.0	1.8	29.0	1.7	35.0	2.0	33.6	2.1
Batteries, Lead-Acid	*	*	8.1	0.7	13.2	1.0	12.1	0h	16.2	0.9	20.7	1.3
Miscellaneous Durables	56.0	5.7	68.4	5.7	87.2	6.5	100.3	6.0	116.6	6.8	134.8	8.3
Nondurable goods	**193.3**	**19.7**	**246.6**	**20.7**	**303.9**	**22.7**	**419.5**	**25.0**	**454.9**	**26.4**	**344.2**	**21.3**
Printed Media (e.g. Newspaper, Magazines, Books)	100.7	10.2	117.9	9.9	127.5	9.5	143.5	8.6	134.6	7.8	80.7	5.0
Office-Type Papers	17.0	1.7	26.1	2.2	35.3	2.6	51.5	3.1	52.7	3.1	34.1	2.1
Bulk Mail and Other Commercial Printing	14.1	1.4	21.0	1.8	27.5	2.1	66.6	4.0	92.0	5.3	44.2	2.7
Tissue Paper and Towels	12.2	1.2	20.5	1.7	20.3	1.5	23.8	1.4	22.9	1.3	22.6	1.4
Paper Plates and Cups	3.0	0.3	4.1	0.3	5.6	0.4	5.2	0.3	6.8	0.4	8.7	0.5
Other Nonpackaging Paper	30.1	3.1	35.7	3.0	37.3	2.8	30.9	1.8	30.2	1.8	27.1	1.7
Disposable Diapers	*	*	3.4	0.3	17.0	1.3	21.7	1.3	23.0	1.3	24.2	1.5
Clothing and Footwear	15.2	1.5	15.9	1.3	19.2	1.4	32.2	1.9	46.0	2.7	58.0	3.6
Other Miscellaneous Nondurables	1.1	0.1	2.0	0.2	14.1	1.1	44.1	2.6	46.7	2.7	44.6	2.8
Containers and Packaging	**305.3**	**31.1**	**428.7**	**36.0**	**465.0**	**34.7**	**518.9**	**31.0**	**539.0**	**31.3**	**490.0**	**30.3**
Glass Packaging	69.0	7.0	117.3	9.8	12.3	0.9	95.1	5.7	78.5	4.6	60.6	3.7
Beer and Soft Drink Bottles	*15.6*	*1.6*	*54.9*	*4.6*	*59.5*	*4.4*	*45.4*	*2.7*	*40.6*	*2.4*	*36.7*	*2.3*
Wine and Liquor Bottles	*12.0*	*1.2*	*18.7*	*1.6*	*21.6*	*1.6*	*16.3*	*1.0*	*13.6*	*0.8*	*11.0*	*0.7*
Other Bottles & Jars	*41.4*	*4.2*	*43.7*	*3.7*	*42.2*	*3.2*	*33.5*	*2.0*	*24.3*	*1.4*	*12.9*	*0.8*

Steel Packaging	52.0	5.3	52.9	4.4	31.9	2.4	23.2	1.4	20.4	1.2	17.7	1.1
Beer and Soft Drink Cans	*7.1*	*0.7*	*15.5*	*1.3*	*4.6*	*0.3*	*1.2*	*0.1*	*	*	*	*
Cans	*41.9*	*4.3*	*34.8*	*2.9*	*25.2*	*1.9*	*20.4*	*1.2*	*18.7*	*1.1*	*14.9*	*0.9*
Other Steel Packaging	*2.9*	*0.3*	*2.7*	*0.2*	*2.1*	*0.2*	*1.6*	*0.1*	*1.7*	*0.1*	*2.9*	*0.2*
Aluminum Packaging	1.9	0.2	5.6	0.5	11.2	0.8	15.3	0.9	13.9	0.8	12.3	0.8
Beer and Soft Drink Cans	*	*	1.0	0.1	7.5	0.6	12.5	0.7	*10.8*	0.6	*8.9*	0.5
Other Cans	*	*	0.6	0.0	0.4	0.0	0.2	0.0	*0.4*	0.0	*0.5*	0.0
Foil and Closures	*1.9*	*0.2*	*4.0*	*0.3*	*3.4*	*0.3*	2.7	0.2	*2.7*	*0.2*	*3.0*	*0.2*
Paper & Paperboard Packaging	157.4	16.0	210.6	17.7	232.6	17.4	262.8	15.7	283.8	16.5	244.1	15.1
Corrugated Boxes	*81.8*	*8.3*	*125.6*	*10.5*	*150.8*	*11.3*	*193.1*	*11.5*	*214.7*	*12.5*	*188.2*	*11.6*
Other Paper & Paperboard Packaging	*75.6*	*7.7*	*85.0*	*7.1*	*81.8*	*6.1*	*69.7*	*4.2*	*441.4*	*25.6*	*55.9*	*3.5*
Plastics Packaging	1.3	0.1	20.6	1.7	30.0	2.2	55.5	3.3	79.5	4.6	88.6	5.5
Plastic Bottles, Jars, and Containers	*0.7*	*0.1*	*9.0*	*0.8*	*12.2*	*0.9*	*19.2*	*1.1*	*29.5*	*1.7*	*34.3*	*2.1*
Bags, Sacks and Wraps	*0.0*	*0.0*	*0.0*	*0.0*	*10.9*	*0.8*	*19.9*	*1.2*	*29.8*	*1.7*	*25.5*	*1.6*
Other Plastics Packaging	*0.7*	*0.1*	*11.6*	*1.0*	*7.0*	*0.5*	*16.4*	*1.0*	*20.2*	*1.2*	*28.8*	*1.8*
Wood Packaging	22.3	2.3	20.4	1.7	34.8	2.6	65.8	3.9	61.2	3.5	64.4	4.0
Other Misc. Packaging	1.3	0.1	1.3	0.1	1.1	0.1	1.2	0.1	1.7	0.1	2.2	0.1
Total Product Wastes	**609.2**	**62.0**	**819.6**	**68.8**	**961.3**	**71.8**	**1178.2**	**70.3**	**1270.0**	**73.7**	**1152.1**	**71.2**
Other Wastes	**373.6**	**38.0**	**371.8**	**31.2**	**377.4**	**28.2**	**496.6**	**29.7**	**453.7**	**26.3**	**466.4**	**28.8**
Food Scraps	136.1	13.8	126.0	10.6	114.8	8.6	191.9	11.5	211.9	12.3	225.2	13.9
Yard Trimmings	223.1	22.7	228.3	19.2	242.8	18.1	281.5	16.8	217.0	12.6	216.4	13.4
Miscellaneous Inorganic Wastes	14.5	1.5	17.5	1.5	19.9	1.5	23.3	1.4	24.9	1.4	24.9	1.5
Total MSW Generated	***982.8***	***100***	***1191.5***	***100***	***1338.7***	***100***	***1674.8***	***100***	***1723.7***	***100***	***1618.5***	***100***

Note: * Data not estimated or assumed to be negligible.

Source: US EPA (2011c).

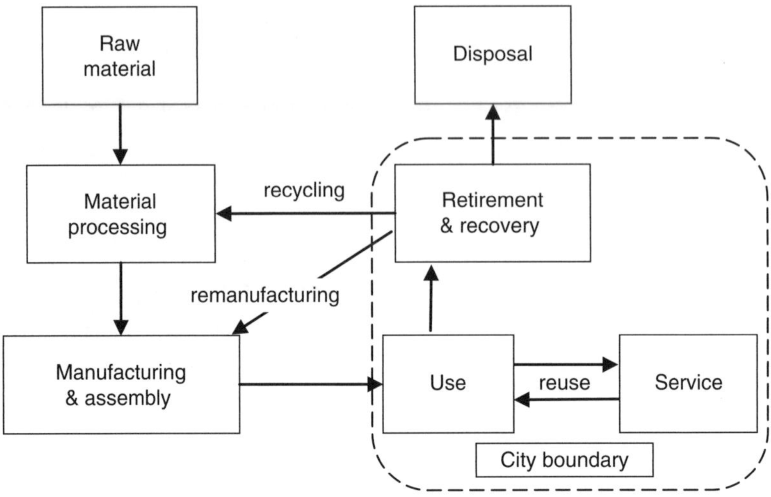

Source: Author.

Figure 5.1 Life cycle of a typical product consumed in cities

Therefore a holistic point of view is required to fully understand the impacts of consumer products and improvement strategies for cities.

Life-cycle assessment (LCA) is a comprehensive analytical tool to evaluate the full environmental impacts of a consumer product used in cities through various stages of its life cycle (ISO 2006). The major components of the LCA include: (1) goal and scope definition that establishes the objectives, audience and system boundaries of the study; (2) inventory analysis, which is a compilation of the inputs and outputs throughout the life cycle of the system; (3) impact assessment, which is a characterization of the magnitude and significance of the potential environmental impacts with respect to resource depletion and environmental and human health; and (4) interpretation, wherein the results of inventory analysis and impact assessment are combined to develop conclusions and recommendations.

The life-cycle inventory (LCI) is a fundamental phase of the LCA of consumer products and is compiled primarily using three methods: process-based; economic input–output; and the hybrid method. The process-based LCI quantifies energy/materials flows between unit processes from a 'bottom–up' perspective. Ideally, primary data for process-based LCI are collected from production facilities, or secondary data can be obtained from published studies and databases. Economic input–output LCI utilizes Leontief's (1986) economic input–output model to model the entire economy from a top–down perspective. Transactions between economic sectors are coupled with energy/materials flow data to compile LCI for a particular economic activity at industry level (Hendrickson et al. 1998). Government statistics are the primary source for economic input–output LCI. For the hybrid method, LCA practitioners often integrate the two methods to incorporate the best available data (Williams 2004). For consumer products, impacts occurring within the city (e.g. use, service) and close to the city (e.g. recycling, disposal) are relatively easy to measure using the process-based LCI, while economic input–output LCI may be more appropriate for examining impacts associated with upstream production processes if process-level data are not available.

Over the last three decades, LCA has developed rapidly and become a key tool for developing sustainability metrics and supporting sustainability-related research, policy making and practices in academia, government and industry (Keoleian and Spitzley 2006; Finnveden et al. 2009; Guinée et al. 2011). Recent development of spatially explicit LCA (Geyer et al. 2010a; 2010b; Newell and Vos 2012) and social LCA (Dreyer et al. 2006; Jorgensen et al. 2012) makes it possible, theoretically, to spatialize a consumer product's environmental and social impacts across its full life cycle. Finally, there is the life-cycle cost analysis of products – another measure of sustainability performance that accounts for the purchase, ownership and end-of-life management monetary costs and complements environmental and social indicators and metrics (Keoleian and Spitzley 2006).

CONSUMER PRODUCT SUSTAINABILITY STRATEGIES

A wide range of consumer-product-related strategies can be implemented for transforming the urban metabolism towards enhanced sustainability. These strategies foster environmental sustainability by reducing material and energy resource consumption throughout a product life-cycle system and also by limiting emissions and waste for production and consumption processes. These environmental and resource improvements can take place within or external to the city boundary in which the product is used. The strategies highlighted in this chapter were originally developed as part of a life-cycle design framework for integrating environmental objectives into product design (Keoleian and Menerey 1993; Keoleian and Menerey 1994; Keoleian et al. 1995). Similar strategies and principles for green design have also been formulated (Anastas and Zimmerman 2003; McDonough et al. 2003). Accordingly, we first present the role of product design in enhancing sustainability of cities. Subsequently, each sustainability strategy is presented along with specific case examples.

Fundamental Role of Product Design

Product design decisions affect the entire life-cycle environmental burden, and are thus a vital point of intervention in pursuing sustainability of consumer goods. Choosing and synthesizing sustainable design strategies to formulate successful products requires well-defined environmental goals and requirements, which must be balanced with other desired product features including functionality and aesthetics, cost and regulatory requirements.

Many of the strategies to improve the sustainability of products will be elaborated on in this chapter, and their efficacy hinges upon decisions made during product design and development. Product life extension can delay disposal and new consumption, and requires that designers target durability, adaptability, repairability, simplified maintenance or disassembly to enable remanufacture. Similarly, material life extension can reduce extraction of virgin materials, and requires that designers ensure the recyclability of products. Other design choices may include selecting sustainable materials, using fewer materials altogether, and improving the efficiency of processes and distribution. Decisions made during use and at the end of a product's life influence its life-cycle burden as well, but the range of options available at those stages is determined well in advance, at the point of product development (e.g. a consumer may wish to recycle a product at the point of retirement, but if it was not produced with recyclable materials, then this option is not available).

Examining the effect of product design on the full life cycle will ensure the fullest understanding of whether impacts are simply shifted from one phase to another (e.g. a less materially intensive product might reduce the extraction and distribution impacts, but it may also be less durable and therefore result in a greater waste burden), or are genuinely lessened. Nearly every design choice and sustainability strategy will entail some tradeoff, and only with an understanding of the product life cycle as well as consumer behavior and infrastructure for resource recovery can product developers identify opportunities to select the best approach for a given product.

Reducing Food Consumption and the Soda Ban in New York City

Industrialized production of food and rising incomes have combined to make food cheaper and, indirectly, promoted overconsumption. In 2000, per capita daily calorie availability reached an all-time high of 3900, while daily calorie consumption increased by an average of 300 over 1985 levels, with 23 percent of that increase coming from added sugars (Putnam et al. 2002). Predictably, over the past three decades, US obesity rates have risen alongside consumption (Smith et al. 2010). Added sugars are often consumed in the form of sugary drinks, namely sodas and juices, which numerous studies have linked to obesity (Drewnowski and Bellisle 2007; Smith et al. 2010; De Graaf 2011; Freudenberg et al. 2011). The soda ban is an example of city-scale planning action designed to reduce the impacts of consumption of a consumer product and therefore can be constructive in guiding similar efforts.

Through taxes and bans, municipal authorities have some leverage in influencing consumption within a city. A study by the Economic Research Service of the USDA found that soda taxes could reduce net calorie intake by 37 calories per day for adults and 43 for children, translating to 3.8 pounds and 4.5 pounds per year, respectively (Smith et al. 2010). Activists have disputed, however, whether such a tax would help the poor by making healthier choices more attractive, or whether it unfairly targets a consumer group already suffering from a lack of affordable food options. Seeking to support healthier consumption among its residents, the New York City Board of Health twice pursued a soda tax and was twice defeated due to lobbying from the soft-drinks industry (Freudenberg et al. 2011). Altering the approach, in September 2012 the New York City Board of Health approved a ban on the sale of sugary drinks over 16 ounces (Grynbaum 2012). The ban will be contested before it takes effect, and it has loopholes with respect to which establishments will be affected by it, but it represents a meaningful effort by a municipal government to reduce consumption.

Product Sharing

Joint ownership and product sharing is a potentially effective strategy for reducing consumption, although it is most applicable to expensive, durable goods that are used at irregular intervals (Mansvelt and Robbins 2011) and to which people do not become personally attached (Mont 2004a). The example of shared-use laundry facilities is provided here, which can be promoted in urban areas with high population density and a large proportion of multi-unit housing communities.

Communal laundry areas with shared use of machines can have a number of benefits, both to the environment and to the individuals involved. Among the benefits to individuals might be access to an item otherwise too expensive to afford (a high-quality washing machine, or a dryer) and relief from the burden of storing, maintaining and disposing of a bulky item. Benefits to the environment include a reduction in the overall number of items produced, and increased likelihood that more durable and efficient models will be employed (Mansvelt and Robbins 2011).

Higher intensity of use also means the washers and dryers will turn over more quickly and be replaced with still more efficient technologies as they are developed (Mont 2004b). As environmental performance increasingly contributes to competitiveness in the market, producers can also benefit from contracting with housing managers to maintain, upgrade and replace the machines, thereby regaining control over more life-cycle stages (Mont 2004b).

Also, sharing and renting equipment rather than buying less frequently used specialized equipment such as a power washer is an important strategy for better utilization of products.

Repair

Maintenance and repair of products can be an effective means of extending service lifetimes, thereby avoiding the environmental burdens associated with production and disposal (McCullough 2010). While the environmental tradeoffs of extending the useful lives of appliances that require substantial energy inputs during the use phase are described elsewhere in this chapter, for many products, repair remains an environmentally preferable alternative to replacement. Unfortunately, the service and repair sector for many goods has been declining in recent decades. Inexpensive overseas production has driven down the price of new products, while the price of repairs has increased due to a diminishing supply of labor in this field. This has skewed the value of repair and made replacement a more financially attractive option, despite the environmental burdens involved (McCullough 2009; 2010).

For certain categories of goods, extending the useful life through repairs can be both financially and environmentally preferable. Furniture, for example, does not stand to gain from efficiency improvements to new models because no use-phase energy is required. Its disposal does, however, comprise a portion of the 15.9 million tons of wood in US municipal solid waste (MSW) (in 2010), only 15 percent of which was recovered (Falk and McKeever 2012), and new furniture creates even larger upstream burdens from production processes. Because furniture is both expensive and durable, repairing it may be both financially and environmentally preferable to replacing it (Gregson et al. 2009). Small household appliances are another category of goods for which the repair sector is underdeveloped but which could represent substantial net environmental improvement from the avoidance of e-waste (McCullough 2009), with minimal compromise on use-phase energy efficiency.

Consumer choice and not product reparability play the biggest role in the repair/replace decision (Kinokuni 1999). Both the cost of repairs and consumer distrust or prior dissatisfaction with a repair experience leads consumers to favor replacement. Municipal or state governments can work to encourage repairs by eliminating sales tax on labor to make repairs more financially attractive, and by developing an easy-to-use system by which consumers can express grievances about repair technicians (McCullough 2009). Designing products to be repaired may be a step toward sustainability, but convincing consumers to take advantage of repair opportunities is likely to be a larger one.

Optimal Product Replacement

Extending the use phase of a product can avoid upstream environmental burdens associated with resource extraction and manufacturing as well as downstream energy inputs for recycling or contamination from landfill disposal. Despite decreased demand for production and disposal, the environmental benefits from extending a product's useful life depend on the environmental burdens associated with its use (Kim et al. 2003; Van Nes and Cramer 2006). For products without use-phase environmental burdens – for example shovels, which require no energy or water inputs and generate no emissions during their use – total life-cycle environmental impacts are indeed lessened by extending the product's lifetime, delaying disposal and additional production. For products with energy or water requirements for use, however, the optimal replacement time may come before the end of the product's useful life, in which case extending the use phase still further might cause net environmental harm (Kim et al. 2003; Van Nes and Cramer 2006).

A study of optimal replacement strategies for refrigerators determined that, because of ongoing technological advancements in energy efficiency, the optimal replacement time in terms of global warming potential from emissions and in terms of energy use was much shorter than the refrigerator's typical useful life (2–11 years, 2–7 years, and an average of 14 years, respectively). For refrigerators, the use phase dominates the total life-cycle energy requirement and related CO_2 emissions (Kim et al. 2006). In such cases, efficiency improvements in new models can result in sufficient use-phase environmental benefit to justify early replacement (ibid.; Van Nes and Cramer 2006). A study of optimal replacement time for air conditioning units revealed similar findings (De Kleine et al. 2011). Taken together, these studies suggest that, while extending the useful life of an appliance may be attractive from a cost perspective or in terms of production and disposal burdens, it comes with significant efficiency tradeoffs, and optimal replacement may be much sooner than the product's durability would otherwise permit.

Energy Efficiency/Grid Mix

Manufacturing efficient products can significantly contribute to reduced environmental burdens from their use, yet the true benefits gained from doing so depend on where they operate. Regional differences in the mix of primary energy sources used to provide electricity to the grid can significantly affect the emissions level and environmental impact associated with a product's manufacture and use (Marriott et al. 2010; MacPherson et al. 2012). Geography plays a large role in determining the source fuel used for power generation, and national averages fail to account for wide variations at regional scales: while the USA generates the majority of its energy using fossil fuels (nearly 70 percent from coal, natural gas and petroleum), coal specifically provides 96.18 percent of West Virginia's electricity, while Idaho gets 79.65 percent of its power from hydroelectric sources, and Vermont gets 73.61 percent from nuclear (EPA 2012). The carbon intensity of electricity use across the country is shown in Table 5.2. The life-cycle greenhouse gas emission factors to deliver one kilowatt hour (kWh) of electricity are provided for the 50 states in the USA. These data were derived from the US EPA EGrid Model and the Argonne National Lab GREET model. These results demonstrate that the use-phase greenhouse gas impacts from operating appliances and other products requiring electricity will vary widely ranging from 18 gCO_2-eq/kWh in Vermont (heavy nuclear) to 1109 gCO_2-eq/kWh in Wyoming (heavy coal). Smaller or larger grid boundaries could also be evaluated that would indicate different intensities for a city of interest.

The effect of grid mix on environmental performance of 'green' products can be so pronounced that in some places charging plug-in hybrid electric vehicles produces more emissions than the consumption of gasoline in traditional vehicles (MacPherson et al. 2012). In evaluating the life cycle of products the same product's carbon footprint may vary by as much as 50 percent depending on the grid mix where it is used (Weber 2012) – a level of detail often overlooked in life-cycle analyses, which lack standardized procedures to account for grid performance (Soimakallio et al. 2011).

Although grid boundaries are complex and unconfined by geographical borders, cities – where 75 percent of world energy consumption occurs and 90 percent of future population growth will be centered – have considerable leverage to promote renewable energy sources. Doing so will maximize the benefits of energy-efficient lighting and appliances as well as mitigate volatility in energy prices, support the local economy by creating jobs, and reduce GHG emissions both within the city and from upstream energy providers (Bhatt et al. 2010). Municipal governments can encourage the use of renewable energy by supporting renewable portfolio standards at the state level, or by initiating renewable energy targets of their own,

Table 5.2 State level greenhouse gas emissions from electricity usage

Total fuel cycle electricity greenhouse gas emission factor (gCO_2-eq/kWh) [cradle-to-wall outlet]

AK	655	MT	754
AL	566	NC	606
AR	600	ND	1049
AZ	612	NE	820
CA	368	NH	352
CO	943	NJ	331
CT	343	NM	983
DE	956	NV	643
FL	682	NY	343
GA	685	OH	921
HI	882	OK	819
IA	835	OR	228
ID	82	PA	608
IL	556	RI	579
IN	1046	SC	445
KS	864	SD	468
KY	1051	TN	557
LA	640	TX	713
MA	642	UT	994
MD	643	VA	541
ME	333	VT	18
MI	796	WA	167
MN	725	WI	791
MO	932	WV	1032
MS	626	WY	1109

Sources: Derived from the US EPA EGrid Model and the Argonne National Lab GREET model.

such as Ann Arbor, Michigan's target of 30 percent renewable energy by 2015 (Stanton 2011). In addition, individual households can contribute to renewable energy transformation through building integrated photovoltaics and small-scale wind turbines.

Recycling

Municipal solid waste (MSW) in the USA has increased significantly over the last half-century (from 88.1 to 250 million tons between 1960 and 2010), and recycling rates have climbed alongside (from 6.4 percent to 34.1 percent during the same period). Recycling rates took off noticeably in the mid-1980s, increasing from nearly 10 percent to 34.1 percent in the last 25 years alone (EPA 2011c), due in part to stricter EPA requirements for landfills and a growing sense that landfill space was becoming scarce, leading to the first introduction of curbside recycling programs (Jenkins et al. 2003). Despite its prevalence, recycling is generally less environmentally desirable than source reduction or reuse due to its energy input requirements and the sometimes lower-quality materials that it generates (King et al. 2006). On the other hand, when products are no longer suitable for reuse, recycling typically has the lowest total energy impact and global warming potential compared to final disposal alternatives like incineration or landfill (Björklund and Finnveden 2005). Energy recovery for discarded products, however, can be advantageous to recycling for some products. For example, the net non-wood (i.e. non-renewable energy) life-cycle energy in supplying one ton of kraft paper to consumers is 3.8 million Btu, with energy recovery compared to 14.3 and 14.7 million Btu for the landfill and recycling cases, respectively (Gaines 2012). For newsprint, on the other hand, recycling is the preferred strategy. Despite its shortcomings, recycling generally offers significant benefits and should be an important part of a city's sustainability strategy. Compared to landfill disposal, recycling improves air and water quality (Chester et al. 2008; EPA 2011a; Franchetti and Kilaru 2012), provides jobs, prevents disposal of valuable materials, and promotes resource conservation (EPA 2011a; 2011b). Recycling rates for a range of products and packaging are shown in Figure 5.2. Lead batteries from automobiles have the highest recycling rate, driven

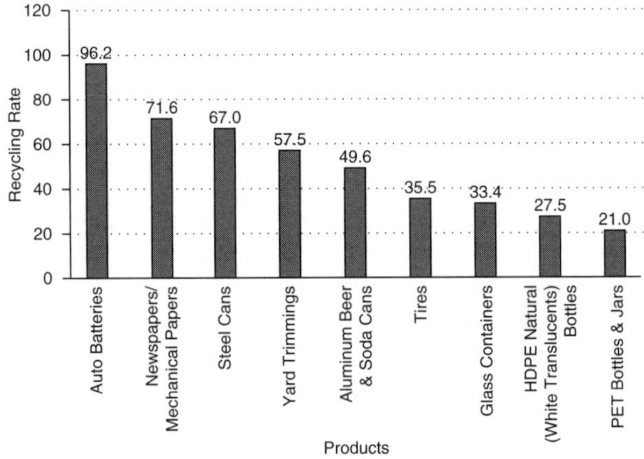

Source: US EPA (2011c).

Figure 5.2 Recycling rates of selected products, 2010

by regulations and disposal fees, while PET bottles and jars are at the lower end. In this latter case, only one-fifth of the states have bottle bills to drive collection. There is also tremendous opportunity for increasing recycling rates for many other consumer products such as clothing and footwear (14 percent), carpets and rugs (9 percent), small appliances (6.9 percent), and furniture and furnishings (0.1 percent).

Cities seeking to promote recycling within a sustainability plan have a variety of programs and strategies from which to choose. If establishing recycling for the first time within the city, even drop-off centers can encourage recycling, but curbside recycling increases participation significantly by making it more convenient (reducing burden of storing and transporting recyclables) and visible (Jenkins et al. 2003). Among curbside recycling programs, cities can choose to offer dual stream (where recyclables are sorted at point of collection, which requires more effort from residents) or single stream (where wastes are collected together, then sorted and processed later). While dual stream simplifies processing, single stream may be preferable as it leads to higher volumes collected (Chester et al. 2008). Cities can also make use of pay-as-you-throw programs for waste disposal, in which residents either pay a subscription fee for city-provided containers for trash collection or buy tags with which to label each bag at the curb (Jenkins et al. 2003). Doing so can divert waste from landfills and prevent improper disposal of recyclables, but the incentive to recycle is only indirect and its effectiveness may be limited. The cost may be low enough or its payment detached enough from the act of disposal that it provides only a very weak signal (Jenkins et al. 2003). Rather the reverse of pay-as-you-throw schemes, recycling rewards programs offer direct incentives. Usually these are monetary, as Recyclebank's rewards program through which participants earn Recyclebank dollars that can be redeemed for discounts at partner businesses, but can also be non-monetary rewards such as public recognition. In either case, incentives can be effective especially when awarded randomly – the chance of winning encourages participants to continue engaging in the behavior (North Carolina Department of Environment and Natural Resources, n.d.).

Perhaps the simplest strategy for a city looking to improve its sustainability through recycling is to reorganize its collection routes. Redesigning collection zones within a city can reduce the number of trucks needed, leading to energy and maintenance savings without investment in new equipment or infrastructure. Similarly, consolidating routes so that wastes and recyclables are collected on the same truck can reduce the miles traveled – in either case, providing meaningful improvements at minimal cost (Chester et al. 2008).

The city of Portland, Oregon has taken a multifaceted approach to reduce waste and increase recycling rates to 75 percent by 2015. The first phase of the new program included the addition of recycling and yard debris roll-carts, making curbside recycling even more convenient and increasing the volumes of recyclable and compostable materials collected. The types of materials collected for recycling were also expanded, and waste hauliers were required to use pre-printed forms to give feedback to residents whose recycling was contaminated with non-recyclables or whose trash contained recyclable or compostable material. The second phase expanded the list of compostable materials to include food scraps, including meat and bones, which are not recommended for backyard composting but which industrial composting facilities can handle. Compostable and recyclable wastes are collected weekly, and, given these expansions, residents can now opt for every-other-week garbage collection. Adjusting service fees based on size of garbage can or frequency of collection (weekly, every other week, or monthly) provides incentive for residents to reduce their waste and increase their recycling rates (City of Portland 2007).

Packaging: Plastic Bag Policies

Packaging is an important factor in the resource intensity of goods. Single-use plastic carry bags have become a common point of intervention for cities seeking to reduce materials requirements and plastic wastes. Worldwide, 4–5 trillion plastic bags are produced each year (Sharp et al. 2010), contributing to the 100 billion used annually in the USA (Murdoch 2010). Although plastic bags have been ubiquitous since the 1980s (Sharp et al. 2010), and offer the advantages of convenience, strength, durability and low cost, they pose a significant waste problem in that they do not biodegrade (Sanghi 2008; Murdoch 2010).

Policies have been implemented at a variety of scales – a national bag fee in Ireland, a state-wide ban in South Australia, and a city-wide ban in San Francisco – to reduce consumption of single-use plastic carry bags (Murdoch 2010; Sharp et al. 2010). The fee in place in Ireland reduced bag use by 90 percent and bag litter significantly. The ban in San Francisco was enacted after lobbying defeated a proposed $0.17 fee per bag, but in the end consumers predominantly switched to paper bags, which were still available and which impose their own set of environmental burdens (Murdoch 2010). The City of Los Angeles recently instituted a similar ban on plastic bags. In South Australia, the ban did not have the desired degree of impact, as many consumers treated the charge for single-use compostable bags (which were made available as an alternative to the traditional plastic bags) as a fee and made no effort to carry reusable bags or reduce the number. This suggests that consumers are not as attitudinally involved in reduced bag consumption as they might have been if allowed to come to the decision on their own, and implies that behavior change achieved through policy is unlikely to be durable in its absence. Despite these tradeoffs, a fee or ban on plastic bags (a policy easily implemented at a municipal scale) is an effective way to achieve behavior change quickly without relying on slower and less effective information campaigns (Sharp et al. 2010).

Dematerializing Packaging

When thinking through the sustainability of consumer products, one also needs to consider packaging. Packaging represents nearly one-third of municipal solid waste in the United States (EPA 2010), and although much of it is recycled, reducing the amount required is environmentally preferable. The concept of dematerialization refers broadly to the reduction of materials used by society over time and dematerialization studies have been done for products, businesses, regions, nations and even the globe (Vos and Newell 2010). The potential to dematerialize packaging has been demonstrated by European producers in response to EU regulations specifying that packaging must be of the minimum possible volume and weight necessary to meet safety, hygiene and other performance standards (Sinclair 2000; Huang and Ma 2004; Varzinskas et al. 2009). Pressure to dematerialize packaging can also come from retailers in order to save shelf space, reduce shipping costs, and minimize waste. One of the products targeted is laundry detergent, and indeed, since 2008, US liquid laundry detergent producers have shifted focus to concentrated detergents (Sauers and Mitra 2009). Other strategies can be implemented individually or in conjunction with dematerialization, including using safe, renewable or recycled materials; recovery and reuse or recycling of packaging wastes and so on (Sustainable Packaging Coalition 2011). None, however, is likely to provide greater benefits than an improvement in the amount of packaging relative to the product, or the 'product-to-package ratio' – in terms of materials required and waste generated, as well as efficiency of freight and associated emissions reductions (Parmer 2010).

The history of the aluminum beverage can is an instructive example of opportunities for dematerialization. When aluminum cans were first introduced 50 years ago, they weighed over 80 g, whereas today cans average closer to 13 g (International Aluminum Institute 2012). Modifications in the process of dematerializing the aluminum include reducing the thickness of can walls and altering the design to minimize the size of the heavier, more expensive end pieces (EPA 1999; Das and Yin 2007). Given that 200 billion aluminum cans are consumed annually (Das and Yin 2007), and half of these in North America alone (Fuller and Ottman 2004), significant benefits can result from modest improvements – a single gram of weight reduction can save over 200 000 tons of aluminum annually, in addition to the energy savings and CO_2 reductions during transport of the lower-weight cans (International Aluminum Institute 2012). Only 50 percent of aluminum cans used for beer and soda were recycled in the US in 2010 (EPA 2011c). Environmental benefits from dematerialization may have even greater benefits when applied to other products by reducing the throughput of materials that are less easily recycled.

Dematerialization can also be achieved by increasing volumes contained in a particular package. A life-cycle study of yogurt packaging found that 58 percent of life-cycle energy was attributable to production of primary packaging, and that solid waste generation was inversely related to container size (27.3 kg of solid waste associated with production of 32 oz. containers, compared with 42.8 kg for 6 oz. containers). Substantial improvements were achievable by changing manufacturing techniques such that the mass of the container was reduced (and its product-to-package ratio improved), shrinking energy consumption by 10 percent, solid waste by 8.8 percent, and life cycle GWP by 6.6 percent. Even with these improvements, the dematerialization benefits of purchasing higher-volume containers was still evident: yogurt consumed from 32 oz. rather than 6 oz. containers saves 14.5 percent of total life-cycle energy and reduces solid waste by 27.2 percent (Keoleian et al. 2004).

Dematerialization is also an important strategy for products. Table 5.3 shows the material production energy requirements and greenhouse gas emissions for commonly used materials from virgin and recycled sources. It can be used to estimate energy savings benefits from dematerialization of packaging and products. Less material translates into less energy consumed and greenhouse gas emissions as long as other life-cycle attributes are not compromised, such as durability.

Distribution: Digital versus Physical

In today's technologically advanced world, a considerable amount of media – including books, music and movies – is available electronically. Whether consuming via download is more sustainable than traditional methods of distribution is an important question as the prevalence of portable music players and e-book readers increases. Some amount of dematerialization of media may be possible through digital distribution and consumption, as well as avoided impacts from physical production and transport. These benefits, however, may be offset or overtaken entirely by the burdens from manufacture, transport, use and disposal of the

Table 5.3 Production energy and greenhouse gas (GHG) emissions for various materials from GREET 2.7, transportation life cycle model

Material		Total energy (MJ/kg)	GHG emissions [(kg CO_2e)/kg]
Steel			
	Primary	27	3.6
	Secondary	19	1.2
Cast iron		33	0.5
Aluminum			
	Primary (Ingot)	149	10
	Secondary (Ingot)	13	0.9
Lead			
	Primary	29	0.9
	Secondary	5	0.5
Nickel			
	Primary	148	12
	Secondary	37	2.9
Copper			
	Primary	111	8.5
Plastics			
	Polypropylene	49	3.7
	Polyester	87	6.9
	High-density polyethylene	53	4.1
Glass-fiber-reinforced plastic		85	4.8
Carbon-fiber-reinforced plastic		160	9.7
Glass		20	1.6
Fiberglass		21	1.5
Rubber		44	3.2
Nickel hydroxide			
	Primary	104	8.2
	Secondary	6	0.5
Potassium hydroxide		11	0.8
Cobalt oxide			
	Primary	148	12
	Secondary	37	3
Zinc		121	8.8
Magnesium		372	29
Platinum		199	16
Zirconium		226	16
Rare earth		336	27

Table 5.3 (continued)

Material	Total energy (MJ/kg)	GHG emissions [(kg CO_2e)/kg]
Manganese	121	8.8
Nafion 117 sheet	24	1.8
Nafion dry polymer	24	1.8
Polytetrafluoroethylene	113	8.4

Note: Updated values for new and existing materials have been developed by the Center for Sustainable System and are currently under review for inclusion in the GREET model.

Source: Keoleian and Sullivan (2012).

electronic equipment through which the digital media is accessed (Hogg and Jackson 2008). When considering only the delivery of music itself (and not the associated consumption of a digital music player), electronic downloads indeed reduce energy use and emissions compared with traditional retail or online shopping with home delivery (Weber et al. 2010). In studies that examine both the impact of data delivery and associated consumption of electronics, however, the results are less conclusive. Whether digital media results in true savings depends on the efficiency, frequency of use, and useful life of the device with which it is accessed, as well as the extent to which digital consumption displaces consumer travel to traditional retail (Sivaraman et al. 2007; Hogg and Jackson 2008; Moberg et al. 2011). Thus the potential for environmental benefits from digital distribution can be maximized when overconsumption is reined in through opportunities for upgrade and repair of digital devices and when there exists a robust system for the recycling of e-waste at the end of its useful life (Williams et al. 2008; Kahhat et al. 2008). Additional studies are available comparing e-books and electronic journals to traditional print (e.g. Gard and Keoleian 2002; Kozak and Keoleian 2003).

Distribution: Online Shopping with Home Delivery

The Internet enables not only digital consumption of media, but also online shopping with home delivery. While some environmental benefits may be derived from the ability to browse multiple retailers without physically traveling to each, the true impacts of online ordering are more complex. Whether online shopping provides any real improvement in environmental performance over traditional retail may depend heavily on context: in urban areas, where consumers could walk or use public transit with relative ease, online shopping with home delivery may actually perform worse environmentally. Conversely, in rural locations, where consumers may need to drive long distances to make in-person purchases, delivery may be environmentally preferable (Sivaraman et al. 2007). On the other hand, rural consumers may be more likely to bundle errands into a single trip, thus reducing the environmental burden of any single in-person purchase. Factors like this, as well as shipping distances, frequency of returns, amount of packaging and mode of transport (of freight, or of consumers to traditional retail centers) complicate the matter (Fichter 2003).

Physical: Distribution Efficiency

For the majority of products that lack a suitable digital substitute, physical distribution channels will be required. The mode in which products are moved through these channels can substantially influence their life-cycle energy and emissions impact (Cholette and Venkat 2009). Increasing global movement of goods often requires multiple modes of transport – including trucks, trains, ships and planes – contributing to air pollution at multiple scales. Freight is economically vital, both in terms of the goods delivered and the industry itself: the USA spent 6–7 percent of GDP on freight transport moving more than 4600 billion ton-kilometers of freight in 2002 alone, representing a value of over $8.3 trillion. The distribution phase can impact life-cycle environmental performance significantly; one study of yogurt packaging found that distribution was responsible for one-third of total life-cycle energy and that substantial improvements to GWP and energy use were available through improving freight efficiency and distances (Keoleian et al. 2004). Freight transport relies on fossil fuels, and the resulting emissions represent 25 percent of the total CO_2, 50 percent of total NO_x, and 40 percent of total particulate matter from all mobile sources (Corbett et al. 2007). These emissions, concentrated in high traffic points of distribution like ports and rail yards, can have substantial environmental and human health impacts (Hricko 2006). Thus, when the transport of goods cannot be avoided (i.e. local sourcing and production are not feasible), it is essential to utilize the mode of distribution that is most environmentally preferable. While none, using current technology, will avoid emissions altogether, rail and coastal shipping were found to offer the lowest carbon intensity, and any form of ground transportation was determined preferable to air freight, which should be avoided whenever possible (Cholette and Venkat 2009; Corbett et al. 2007). Rail freight emissions are 50–94 percent lower than those of truck transport, depending on the pollutant in question, while air freight emits 35 times more CO_2 than rail and 18 times more than road transport on a ton-mile basis (Facanha and Horvath 2006). Given the scale of freight transport, and the likelihood that it will increase in an ever more globalized economy, minimizing emissions through transport mode choice can make a significant impact.

Local Sourcing: Urbanwood

Urban areas do not have the resources or capacity to produce everything their populations require. As such, a majority of consumer goods are imported to the city from elsewhere, expanding its environmental footprint (Pincetl et al. 2012) – both in terms of the area required to support the city itself and in terms of the emissions and ecological burdens resulting from transporting goods. Great potential for improving the sustainability of cities lies, then, in exploiting opportunities for local production wherever feasible. Local production and consumption can support all dimensions of sustainability, stimulating local economies by keeping money circulating within the community, producing social development by providing jobs and connecting community members, and improving environmental quality by reducing burdens from shipping products long distances (Mayer and Knox 2006; Robinson 2010; Sustainable Connections 2012). In some cases, further environmental gains are achieved by diverting valuable local resources from the waste stream.

The recovery of lumber from urban trees is one opportunity for local sourcing of materials for the production of consumer goods. From the approximately 4 billion urban trees in the USA, 25 million dry tons of residues (chips, logs, tops, brush and stumps) are produced annually. Of these, only 25 percent is recycled or used for new production (Bratkovich et al. 2008). In southeastern Michigan, a push to better utilize urban tree wastes emerged in the wake of the emerald ash borer infestation. Urbanwood (2012a), a network of family-owned businesses, was born of this effort to recover good logs from dead urban trees to use for lumber and flooring. It is estimated that dead urban trees throughout southeast Michigan could provide enough lumber to build 362 average-sized homes (Think Local First 2009) or provide wood flooring to more than 2300. Although local wood sourcing and production face challenges, mainly in terms of the quantity and quality of available wood and the cost of sourcing it at small scales (Bratkovich et al. 2008), it also represents a significant opportunity to create value from waste, create local jobs, and reduce the environmental burden of importing goods produced elsewhere (Urbanwood 2012b; Robinson 2010; Bumgardner et al. 2011; Sustainable Connections 2012). Notably, however, these benefits are achieved in part because the material sourcing, as well as the production and consumption, occurs locally. In a study of the life-cycle impacts of food, transportation of the food from the point of production to the point of final consumption was found to make up only 11 percent of total GHG emissions (Weber and Matthews 2008). The benefits of local production and consumption, however, should also include the closer connection and enhanced stewardship that a community can develop with its local environment.

CONCLUSION

Consumer products, along with residential buildings and transportation vehicles, are the physical embodiment of our urban metabolism. Tremendous opportunities exist to enhance the sustainability of consumer product systems across all stages of the life cycle, which encompasses production, use and retirement. The greatest leverage begins with product design, which is controlled by the manufacturer. From the city perspective, retailers, consumers and municipal government have the ultimate responsibility for managing sustainability of consumer products. Table 5.4 provides a summary of the consumer product sustainability strategies for cities that were characterized in this chapter. This table indicates the point of intervention in the product life cycle for each strategy and the key stakeholders that have the most direct influence in the application of these strategies. The table also highlights the potential sustainability benefits and tradeoffs that may exist, depending on the specific context. Improvement is dependent on the current state of practice, usage patterns, infrastructure conditions, including the nature of recycling systems and grid systems, spatial configurations that can impact transportation and logistics and the upstream impacts from production activities that generally occur outside the city boundary. A comprehensive assessment of sustainability performance requires tools such as life-cycle assessment to measure system-wide impacts. However, these are not accessible for households to utilize on a routine basis. Therefore general observations drawing on case examples that demonstrate benefits serve as guidance for moving towards enhanced sustainability.

Consumers ultimately have the most direct and powerful role in shaping urban metabolism through their product purchasing decisions and their stewardship of these products. Retailers can influence consumer behavior through their merchandising and marketing of more sustainable product alternatives. Municipalities and local governments can enact regulations, invest in more sustainable infrastructure and provide economic incentives to promote more sustainable consumer products systems for addressing societal needs. Finally, sustainable transformation of urban metabolism will accelerate only when consumer product systems that are developed

Table 5.4 Summary of consumer product sustainability strategies: Points for intervention across the life cycle

Point of intervention/life-cycle stage	Strategy	Description	Sustainability benefits	Tradeoffs	Major actors
Production & distribution	Local sourcing/ production	Using local resources (materials and labor) to produce goods	Reduced emissions from distribution; creation of local jobs	More expensive if economies of scale are not possible; increased emissions if production occurs locally but materials are sourced elsewhere (then shipping in final product is better)	Producers/retailers/ local government
Production/end of life	Optimized replacement	Retiring energy-using products with newer models available at the best time to minimize environmental burden	Reduced use-phase energy requirement and emissions	More frequent replacement, meaning increased overall production with burdens from resource extraction, production and distribution; increased waste from retired products	Consumers/local government
Distribution	Digital delivery	Distribution of media in digital formats (e.g. MP3 files or online streaming of movies) rather than physical	Dematerialization resulting from less physical production of music or movie discs and their packaging; fewer emissions from distribution	Increased production and rapid replacement of digital devices plus energy requirement during their use	Consumers; producers
Distribution	Online shopping w/ home delivery	Internet browsing replaces physical travel to shopping centers, physical products delivered	Reduced emissions from travel for single-purpose shopping trips	Energy use of device used for browsing internet; more emissions from delivery if errands could have been bundled or if shopping were done on foot or using public transit	Consumers/ retailers

Distribution	Physical distribution efficiency	Using rail for distribution of products where possible, optimizing other modes as needed, avoiding air freight whenever possible	Reduced emissions (rail 50–94 percent lower than truck; air emissions 35 times higher than rail and 18 times higher than road transport)	Emissions never eliminated altogether	Producers; distributors
Distribution	Packaging bans	Banning, taxing, or requiring producer takeback of packaging or plastic carry bags	Dematerialization of packaging; reduced emissions from distribution (less excess packaging weight); less waste; faster adoption of pro-environmental behaviors than voluntary initiatives	Bag bans may lead to increased use of paper bags (with their own burdens) or increased production of 'green' bags; behavior change less durable than if self-motivated	Local governments; producers; consumers
Distribution	Dematerialized packaging	Lightweighting packaging through design and materials choice; concentrating liquid products; optimizing container volumes	Reduced burdens from resource extraction and distribution; less waste	May reduce opportunities for reuse if packaging is less durable (less problematic if it is easily recycled)	Producers
Use	Product sharing	Joint ownership of expensive, durable goods used at irregular intervals	Reduced production, resource conservation; faster replacement of energy-using goods with more efficient models, reducing overall energy use; improved access for individuals (social sustainability)	Unlikely to be adopted without effective management; may entail travel to use items, with resulting emissions	Consumers

Table 5.4 (continued)

Point of intervention/life-cycle stage	Strategy	Description	Sustainability benefits	Tradeoffs	Major actors
Use	Reducing consumption	Either voluntarily reduced consumption through 'slow living', or policy that encourages reduced consumption	Less overall production and waste, reducing burdens from all life-cycle stages	Difficult to implement: self-motivated reduced consumption are slow-acting and unreliable; consumer resistance to policy	Consumers; policy makers
Use	Repair	Extending products' useful life through maintenance and repair; producers facilitate repair by making products repairable	Reduced burdens from production and disposal since products are used longer; service job creation	Increased use-phase burdens from energy if the lifetimes of inefficient products is extended beyond optimal replacement time	Producers; consumers
Use/energy	Renewables in grid mix	Supporting state-wide Renewable Portfolio Standards or implementing municipal goals	Reduced emissions from cleaner energy; local jobs; reduced volatility in energy prices	Burdens from production of renewable generation equipment	Municipal governments; energy providers
Use/end of life	Reuse	Extending functional products' lifetimes through reuse by another consumer following initial retirement	Reduced production and resource use; less disposal of waste; improved access for individuals through secondhand markets	Increased use-phase burdens from energy if the lifetimes of inefficient products is extended beyond optimal replacement time; may supplement rather than replace new consumption	Consumers
End of life	Recycling	Materials recovery for new production	Reduced burdens from resource extraction; less waste; local job creation	Requires energy for recycling processes; resultant materials are sometimes lesser quality	Producers; consumers; municipal governments

Source: Author.

and managed for optimal life-cycle environmental performance also achieve optimal life-cycle cost performance; systems that achieve convergence of environmental, economic and social sustainability is the ultimate goal.

REFERENCES

Anastas, P.T. and J.B. Zimmerman (2003), 'Peer reviewed: design through the 12 principles of green engineering', *Environmental Science & Technology*, **37** (5), 94–101.

Beatley, T. (2010), *Biophilic Cities: Integrating Nature Into Urban Design and Planning*, Washington, DC: Island Press.

Bhatt, V., P. Friley and J. Lee (2010), 'Integrated energy and environmental systems analysis methodology for achieving low carbon cities', *Journal of Renewable and Sustainable Energy*, **2** (3), 031012, http://dx.doi.org/10.1063/1.3456367.

Björklund, A. and G. Finnveden (2005), 'Recycling revisited – life cycle comparisons of global warming impact and total energy use of waste management strategies', *Resources, Conservation, and Recycling*, **44**, 309–17.

Bratkovich, S., J. Bowyer, K. Fernholz and A. Lindburg (2008), *Urban Tree Utilization and Why It Matters*, Minneapolis, MN: Dovetail Partners, Inc.

Brown, M.A., F. Southworth and A. Sarzynski (2008), *Shrinking the Carbon Footprint of Metropolitan America*, Washington, DC: Brookings Institution.

Bumgardner, M., U. Buehlmann, A. Schuler and J. Crissey (2011), 'Competitive actions of small firms in a declining market', *Journal of Small Business Management*, **49** (4), 578–98.

Cervero, R. and C. Sullivan (2011), 'Green TODs: marrying transit-oriented development and green urbanism', *International Journal of Sustainable Development & World Ecology*, **18** (3), 210–18.

Chester, M., E. Martin and N. Sathaye (2008), 'Energy, greenhouse gas, and cost reductions for municipal recycling systems', *Environmental Science and Technology*, **42**, 2142–9.

Cholette, S. and K. Venkat (2009), 'The energy and carbon intensity of wine distribution: a study of logistical options for delivering wine to consumers', *Journal of Cleaner Production*, **17**, 1401–13.

City of Portland (2007), 'Portland Recycles! Plan, Office of Sustainable Development', available at http://www.portlandoregon.gov/bps/article/230043.

Consumer Product Safety Commission (2011), 'Consumer product safety act', available at http://www.cpsc.gov/businfo/cpsa.pdf.

Corbett, James J., James J. Winebrake, Erin H. Green, Prasad Kasibhatla, Veronika Eyring and Axel Lauer (2007), 'Mortality from ship emissions: a global assessment', *Environmental Science & Technology*, **41**(24), 8512–18.

Das, S. and W. Yin (2007), 'Trends in the global aluminum fabrication industry', *Journal of Metals*, **59** (2), 83–7.

De Graaf, C. (2011), 'Why liquid energy results in overconsumption', *Proceedings of the Nutrition Society*, **70** (2), 162–70.

De Kleine, R.D., G.A. Keoleian and J.C. Kelly (2011), 'Optimal replacement of residential air conditioning equipment to minimize energy, greenhouse gas emissions, and consumer cost in the US', *Energy Policy*, **39** (6), 3144–53.

Drewnowski, A. and F. Bellisle (2007), 'Liquid calories, sugar, and body weight', *American Journal of Clinical Nutrition*, **85** (3), 651–61.

Dreyer, L.C., M.Z. Hauschild and J. Schierbeck (2006), 'A framework of social life cycle impact assessment', *International Journal of Life Cycle Assessment*, **11** (2), 88–97.

Environmental Protection Agency (EPA) (1999), 'National source reduction characterization report for municipal solid waste in the United States', available at http://www.epa.gov/osw/conserve/rrr/pubs/r99034.pdf.

Environmental Protection Agency (EPA) (2011a), 'Recycling: a component of strong community development', available at http://www.epa.gov/region4/rcra/mgtoolkit/Community.html.
Environmental Protection Agency (EPA) (2011b), 'Source reduction and recycling: a role in preventing global climate change', available at http://www.epa.gov/region4/rcra/mgtoolkit/Climate_Change.html.
Environmental Protection Agency (EPA) (2011c), 'Municipal solid waste generation, recycling and disposal in the United States: tables and figures for 2010', available at http://www.epa.gov/wastes/nonhaz/municipal/pubs2010-Tables_and_Figures_508.pdf.
Environmental Protection Agency (EPA) (2012), 'eGRID2012 version 1.0 year 2009 summary tables', available at http://www.epa.gov/cleanenergy/documents/egridzips/eGRID2012V1_0_year09_SummaryTables.pdf.
Facanha, C. and A. Horvath (2006), 'Environmental assessment of freight transportation in the US', *International Journal of Life Cycle Analysis*, **11** (4), 229–39.
Falk, B. and D. McKeever (2012), 'Generation and recovery of solid wood waste in the US', *BioCycle*, 30–32.
Fichter, K. (2003), 'E-commerce: sorting out the environmental consequences', *Journal of Industrial Ecology*, **6** (2), 25–41.
Finnveden, G., M.Z. Hauschild, T. Ekvall, J. Guinee, R. Heijungs, S. Hellweg, A. Koehler, D. Pennington and S. Suh (2009), 'Recent development in life cycle assessment', *Journal of Environmental Management*, **91** (1), 1–21.
Franchetti, M. and P. Kilaru (2012), 'Modeling the impact of municipal solid waste recycling on greenhouse gas emissions in Ohio, USA', *Resources, Conservation and Recycling*, **58**, 107–13.
Freudenberg, N., J. McDonough and E. Tsui (2011), 'Can a food justice movement improve nutrition and health? A case study of the emerging food movement in New York City', *Journal of Urban Health: Bulletin of the New York Academy of Medicine*, **88** (4), 623–36.
Fuller, D.A. and J.A. Ottman (2004), 'Moderating unintended pollution: the role of sustainable product design', *Journal of Business Research*, **57** (11), 1231–8.
Gaines, L. (2012), 'To recycle, or not to recycle, that is the question: insights from life-cycle analysis', *MRS Bulletin*, **37** (04), 333–8.
Gard, D.L. and G.A. Keoleian (2002), 'Digital versus print: energy performance in the selection and use of scholarly journals', *Journal of Industrial Ecology*, **6** (2), 115–32.
Geyer, R., D.M. Stoms, J.P. Lindner, F.W. Davis and B. Wittstock (2010a), 'Coupling GIS and LCA for biodiversity assessments of land use part 1: inventory modeling', *International Journal of Life Cycle Assessment*, **15** (5), 454–67.
Geyer, R., D.M. Stoms, J.P. Lindner, F.W. Davis and B. Wittstock (2010b), 'Coupling GIS and LCA for biodiversity assessments of land use part 2: impact assessment', *International Journal of Life Cycle Assessment*, **15** (7), 692–703.
Gregson, N., A. Metcalfe and L. Crewe (2009), 'Practices of object maintenance and repair', *Journal of Consumer Culture*, **9** (2), 248–72.
Grynbaum, M. (2012), 'Health panel approves restriction on sale of large sugary drinks', *The New York Times*, 13 September, A24.
Guinée, J.B., R. Heijungs, G. Huppes, A. Zamagni, P. Masoni, R. Buonamici, T. Ekvall and T. Rydberg (2011), 'Life cycle assessment: past, present, and future', *Environmental Science & Technology*, **45** (1), 90–96.
Hendrickson, C.T., A. Horvath, S. Joshi and L. Lave (1998), 'Economic input–output models for environmental life-cycle assessment', *Environmental Science & Technology*, **32** (7), 184A–191A.
Hogg, N. and T. Jackson (2008), 'Digital media and dematerialization: an exploration of the potential for reduced material intensity in music delivery', *Journal of Industrial Ecology*, **13** (1), 127–46.
Hricko, A. (2006), 'Ships, trucks, and trains: effects of goods movement on environmental health', *Environmental Health Perspectives*, **114** (4), A204.
Huang, C. and H. Ma (2004), 'A multidimensional environmental evaluation of packaging materials', *Science of the Total Environment*, **324** (1), 161–72.

International Aluminum Institute (2012), 'Lightweight', available at http://packaging.world-aluminum.org/benefits/lightweight.html.
International Organization for Standardization (ISO) (2006), *Life Cycle Assessment: Principles and Framework, ISO 14040*, Geneva: International Organization for Standardization.
Jenkins, R.R., S.A. Martinez, K. Palmer and M.J. Podolsky (2003), 'The determinants of household recycling: a material-specific analysis of recycling program features and unit pricing', *Journal of Environmental Economics and Management*, **45** (2), 294–318.
Jorgensen, A., L.C. Dreyer and A. Wangel (2012), 'Addressing the effect of social life cycle assessments', *International Journal of Life Cycle Assessment*, **17** (6), 829–39.
Kahhat, R., J. Kim, M. Xu, B. Allenby, E. Williams and P. Zhang (2008), 'Exploring e-waste management systems in the United States', *Resources, Conservation & Recycling*, **52** (7), 955–64.
Kellert, S.R., J. Heerwagen and M. Mador (2011), *Biophilic Design: The Theory, Science and Practice of Bringing Buildings to Life*, Hoboken, NJ: Wiley.
Kennedy, C., J. Cuddihy and J. Engel-Yan (2008), 'The changing metabolism of cities', *Journal of Industrial Ecology*, **11** (2), 43–59.
Keoleian, G.A. and D.A. Menerey (1993), *Life Cycle Design Guidance Manual: Environmental Requirements and the Product System*, Cincinnati, OH: Environmental Protection Agency.
Keoleian, Gregory A. and Dan Menerey (1994), 'Sustainable development by design: review of life cycle design and related approaches', *Air & Waste* **44** (5), 645–68.
Keoleian, G.A. and D.V. Spitzley (2006), 'Life cycle based sustainability metrics', *Sustainability Science and Engineering*, **1**, 127–59.
Keoleian, G.A. and J.L. Sullivan (2012), 'Materials challenges and opportunities for enhancing the sustainability of automobiles', *Material Research Society Bulletin*, **37** (4), 365–73.
Keoleian, G.A., J.E. Kock and D. Menerey (1995), *Life Cycle Design Framework and Demonstration Projects: Profiles of AT&T and Allied Signal*, Washington, DC: Environmental Protection Agency.
Keoleian, G.A., A.W. Phipps, T. Dritz and D. Brachfeld (2004), 'Life cycle environmental performance and improvement of a yogurt product delivery system', *Packaging Technology and Science*, **17** (2), 85–103.
Kim, H.C., G.A. Keoleian, E. Darby and J.C. Bean (2003), 'Life cycle optimization of automobile replacement: model and application', *Environmental Science and Technology*, **37** (23), 5407–413.
Kim, H.C., G.A. Keoleian and Y.A. Horie (2006), 'Optimal household refrigerator replacement policy for life cycle energy, greenhouse gas emissions, and cost', *Energy Policy*, **34** (15), 2310–23.
King, A.M., S.C. Burgess, W. Ijomah and C.A. McMahon (2006), 'Reducing waste: repair, recondition, remanufacture or recycle?', *Sustainable Development*, **14** (4), 257–67.
Kinokuni, H. (1999), 'Repair, market structure, product durability, and monopoly', *Australian Economic Papers*, **38** (4), 343–53.
Kozak, G.L. and G.A. Keoleian (2003), 'Printed scholarly books and e-book reading devices: a comparative life cycle assessment of two book options', *Conference Record: 2003 IEEE International Symposium on Electronics and Environment*, Boston, MA: IEEE Computer Society.
Leontief, Wassily (1986), *Input–Output Economics*, 2nd edn, New York: Oxford University Press.
MacPherson, N.D., G.A. Keoleian and J.C. Kelly (2012), 'Fuel economy and greenhouse gas emissions labeling for plug-in hybrid vehicles from a life cycle perspective', *Journal of Industrial Ecology*, **16** (5), 761–73.
Mansvelt, J. and P. Robbins (eds) (2011), 'Product sharing', *Green Consumerism: An A-to-Z Guide*, Thousand Oaks, CA: Sage Publications, pp. 363–5.
Marriott, J., H.S. Matthews and C.T. Hendrickson (2010), 'Impact of power generation mix on life cycle assessment and carbon footprint greenhouse gas results', *Journal of Industrial Ecology*, **14** (6), 919–28.

Mayer, H. and P.L. Knox (2006), 'Slow cities: sustainable places in a fast world', *Journal of Urban Affairs*, **28** (4), 321–34.
McCullough, J. (2009), 'Factors impacting the demand for repair services of household products: the disappearing repair trades and the throwaway society', *International Journal of Consumer Studies*, **33** (6), 619–26.
McCullough, J. (2010), 'Consumer discount rates and the decision to repair or replace a durable product: a sustainable consumption issue', *Journal of Economic Issues*, **44** (1), 183–204.
McDonough, W., M. Braungart, P.T. Anastas and J.B. Zimmerman (2003), 'Peer reviewed: applying the principles of green engineering to cradle-to-cradle design', *Environmental Science & Technology*, **37** (23), 434A–441A.
Moberg, A., C. Borggren and G. Finnveden (2011), 'Books from an environmental perspective – part 2: e-books as an alternative to paper books', *International Journal of Life Cycle Assessment*, **16** (3), 238–46.
Mont, O. (2004a), 'Institutionalisation of sustainable consumption patterns based on shared use', *Ecological Economics*, **50** (1), 135–53.
Mont, O. (2004b), 'Reducing life-cycle environmental impacts through systems of joint use', *Greener Management International*, **45**, 63–77.
Murdoch, M. (2010), 'The road to zero waste: a study of the Seattle green fee on disposable bags', *Environmental Practice*, **12** (1), 66–75.
Newell, J.P. and R.O. Vos (2012), 'Accounting for forest carbon pool dynamics in product carbon footprints: challenges and opportunities', *Environmental Impact Assessment Review*, **37**, 23–36.
North Carolina Department of Environment and Natural Resources (n.d.), 'Division of Pollution Prevention and Environmental Assistance: incentives', available at http://p2pays.org/socialmarketing/incentives.asp.
Parmer, N. (2010), 'Green packaging: improve your product-to-package ratio', available at http://multichannelmerchant.com/opsandfulfillment/0199-green-packaging-improve-your-product-to-package-ratio.
Pincetl, S., P. Bunje and T. Holmes (2012), 'An expanded urban metabolism method: toward a systems approach for assessing urban energy processes and causes', *Landscape and Urban Planning*, **107**, 193–202.
Portney, Kent E. (2003), *Taking Sustainable Cities Seriously: Economic Development, the Environment, and Quality of Life in American Cities*, Cambridge, MA: MIT Press.
Putnam, J., J. Allshouse and L.S. Kantor (2002), 'US per capita food supply trends: more calories, refined carbohydrates, and fats', *Food Review*, **25** (3), 2–12.
Robinson, Nandi (2010), *Why Buy Local? An Assessment of the Economic Advantages of Shopping at Locally Owned Businesses*, Lansing, MI: Michigan State University Center for Community and Economic Development.
Sanghi, S. (2008), 'Use of plastic bags: factors affecting ecologically oriented behavior in consumers', *Abhigyan*, **26** (3), 34–45.
Sauers, L. and S. Mitra (2009), 'Sustainability innovation in the consumer products industry', *Chemical Engineering Progress*, **105** (1), 36–40.
Sharp, A., S. Hoj and M. Wheeler (2010), 'Proscription and its impact on anti-consumption behaviour and attitudes: the case of plastic bags', *Journal of Consumer Behavior*, **9** (6), 470–84.
Sinclair, A.J. (2000), 'Assuming responsibility for packaging and packaging waste', *Electronic Green Journal*, **1** (12), 2–26.
Sivaraman, D., S. Pacca, K. Mueller and J. Lin (2007), 'Comparative energy, environmental, and economic analysis of traditional and e-commerce DVD rental networks', *Journal of Industrial Ecology*, **11** (3), 77–91.
Smith, Travis, Bing-Hwan Lin and Jong-Ying Lee (2010), *Taxing Caloric Sweetened Beverages: Potential Effects on Beverage Consumption, Calorie Intake, and Obesity*, Washington, DC: Economic Research Service, US Department of Agriculture.
Soimakallio, S., J. Kiviluoma and L. Saikku (2011), 'The complexity and challenges of deter-

mining GHG (greenhouse gas) emissions from grid electricity consumption and conservation in LCA (life cycle assessment) – a methodological review', *Energy*, **36** (12), 6705–13.
Stanton, R. (2011), 'Ann Arbor officials will consider wind options to meet city's new renewable energy goals', AnnArbor.com, available at http://www.annarbor.com/news/new-city-of-ann-arbor-renewable-energy-goals-will-look-at-wind-options-in-michigan/.
Sustainable Connections (2012), 'Think Local First: why buy locally owned?', available at http://sustainableconnections.org/thinklocal/why.
Sustainable Packaging Coalition (2011), 'Definition of sustainable packaging', available at http://www.sustainablepackaging.org/content/?type=5&id=definition-of-sustainable-packaging.
Think Local First (2009), 'The Urbanwood Project', available at http://www.thinklocalfirst.net/aboutus/The%20Urbanwood%20Project.
Urbanwood (2012a), 'About the Urbanwood Project', available at http://urbanwood.org/about.
Urbanwood (2012b), 'Frequently asked questions', available at http://urbanwood.org/faq.
Van Nes, N. and J. Cramer (2006), 'Product lifetime optimization: a challenging strategy towards more sustainable consumption patterns', *Journal of Cleaner Production*, **14** (15), 1307–18.
Varzinskas, V., J. Staniskis, A. Lebedys, E. Kibirkstis and V. Miliunas (2009), 'Life cycle assessment of common plastic packaging for reducing environmental impact and material consumption', *Environmental Research, Engineering and Management*, **4** (50), 57–65.
Vos, Robert O. and Joshua P. Newell (2010), 'Dematerialization', in Paul Robbins, Nevin Cohen and Geoffrey J. Golson (eds), *Green Business: An A-to-Z Guide*, Thousand Oaks, CA: SAGE Publications.
Wackernagel, M., J. Kitzes, D. Moran, S. Goldfinger and M. Thomas (2006), 'The ecological footprint of cities and regions: comparing resource availability with resource demand', *Environment and Urbanization*, **18** (1), 103–12.
Weber, C.L. (2012), 'Uncertainty and variability in product carbon footprinting: case study of a server', *Journal of Industrial Ecology*, 16 (2), 203–11.
Weber, C.L. and H.S. Matthews (2008), 'Food-miles and the relative climate impacts of food choices in the United States', *Environmental Science & Technology*, **42** (10), 3508–13.
Weber, C.L., J.G. Koomey and H.S. Matthews (2010), 'The energy and climate change implications of different music delivery methods', *Journal of Industrial Ecology*, **14** (5), 754–69.
Wheeler, Stephen M. and Timothy Beatley (2004), *The Sustainable Urban Development Reader*, London: Routledge.
Williams, E. (2004), 'Energy intensity of computer manufacturing: hybrid analysis combining process and economic input–output methods', *Environmental Science & Technology*, **38** (22), 6166–74.
Williams, E., R. Kahhat, B. Allenby, E. Kavazanjian, J. Kim and M. Xu (2008), 'Environmental, social, and economic implications of global reuse and recycling of personal computers', *Environmental Science & Technology*, **42** (17), 6446–54.
Wolch, Jennifer, Manuel Pastor and Peter Dreier (eds) (2004), *Up Against the Sprawl: Public Policy and the Making of Southern California*, Minneapolis, MN: University of Minnesota Press.

6. Strategies for growing green business and industry in a city

Karen Chapple

INTRODUCTION

Cities around the globe are trying to figure out how to 'grow green' – that is, how to generate economic activity that preserves and enhances environmental quality while using natural resources more efficiently. Although the path to reducing human impact on the environment is relatively clear, we are less sure about how to grow our economies and benefit society's least advantaged members at the same time – in other words, how to link the three Es (environment, economy and equity) of development.

Sustainable economic development joins sustainability goals to economic development:

> Sustainable economic development enhances equitable local income and employment growth without endangering local fiscal stability, degrading the natural environment, or contributing to global climate change. It challenges the model of growth based on pure consumption rather than human happiness, takes into account long-term goals as well as short-term needs and is sensitive to local context and history. (Gage and LoPresti 2012, p. 1)

How is growing a green economy related to sustainable economic development? Green growth meets many sustainability goals: for instance, it leads to more fiscal stability by reducing energy usage and reliance on fossil fuels; it reduces consumption by promoting recycling and reuse; and it focuses on local context by improving quality of life and supporting local business. Yet the transition to a low-carbon economy does not necessarily promote equitable local income and employment growth. Such outcomes, then, must result from intentional economic development strategies. The goal of this chapter is to outline the strategies that can ensure that green urban growth is sustainable as well.

As is typical of emergent phenomena, there is considerable confusion about what constitutes a green economy, as well as what strategies are effective in growing it. This chapter begins by defining green economic activity and providing a framework for evaluating economic development approaches. It then outlines policies and programs that facilitate green, sustainable growth. Evidence from a recent survey of green businesses shows their preferences in terms of location and policy approaches. Finally, two brief case studies, one of a strong-market city (Portland) and the other of a weak-market region (Riverside–San Bernardino) in a strong regulatory state (California), show what localities are doing to grow the green economy. A conclusion discusses how current approaches are falling short and how to integrate green and sustainable economic development more effectively.

FRAMING THE GREEN ECONOMY AND ECONOMIC DEVELOPMENT

Defined as economic activity that reduces energy consumption and/or improves environmental quality, the green economy encompasses both new and traditional sectors. Innovation in the green economy might thus occur through the creation of new products, the transformation of production processes, or the development of new markets. Energy provides a simple example. New industries, such as biofuels, may introduce new products that reduce dependence on traditional or dirty sources of energy. Traditional industries, such as utilities, may be changing the way they source power, relying more on renewable energy and alternative fuels (i.e. innovating in how they produce energy). Individual households might install solar photo voltaic panels, thus joining an emerging market of energy consumers.

Most studies use existing industrial classification systems to define the green economy. Major studies count the number of jobs in states and metropolitan areas, finding that about 2 percent of all jobs are in the green economy, mostly in manufacturing, utilities, transportation, construction and professional services sectors (Pew Charitable Trust 2009; Muro et al. 2011). The shortcoming of the counting method is that it is not possible to measure the 'greening' of existing businesses or the activity of emerging industries not yet classified in the industry codes.

Based on a review of 25 reports on the green economy, Figure 6.1 presents a framework for thinking about the green economy. Each of 18 industry sectors listed contains multiple industries, and not all firms in all industries are necessarily green. The figure also highlights how frequently each industry sector is mentioned in the literature, with the darkest shades representing the sectors cited most frequently.

The figure presents the range of green business categories along two axes. The vertical axis shows the range, from traditional businesses, such as utilities and professional services that are greening their operations, to businesses in emerging industries (some 'cleantech'), such as biofuels research, solar panel manufacturing and ecotourism. Since they are late in

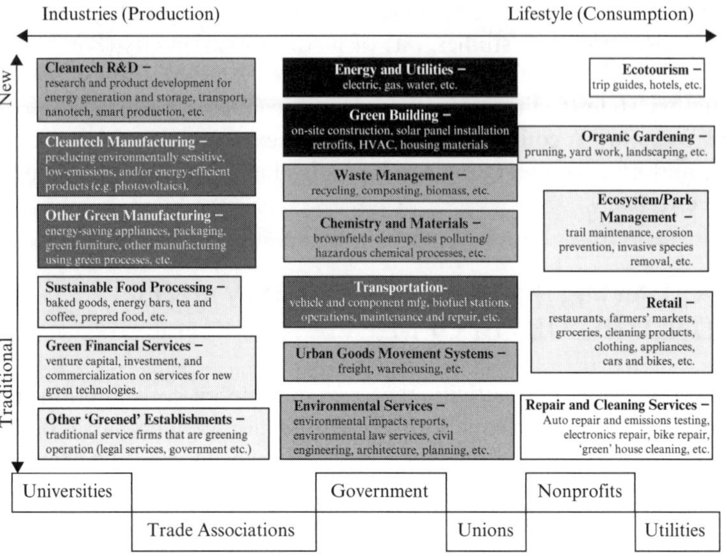

Source: Adapted from Chapple (2008).

Figure 6.1 Defining the green economy

the product cycle, the traditional businesses are more likely to be greening their production processes, while the emerging industries are innovating new green products.

On the horizontal axis, businesses move from those that produce green products, such as manufacturers and food processors, to those that sell green products or participate in the green lifestyle economy, such as farmers' markets and local park maintenance operators. Many of these types of businesses pursue designations as green-certified businesses in city or county registry programs. Business categories located in the middle of the horizontal axis contain both production and consumption aspects. Within the green economy, businesses interact with and are influenced by the government agencies, universities, non-profit organizations, unions, utilities and trade associations (shown at the bottom of the figure).

Green Economic Development in the Context of Traditional Economic Development

Policies to grow a green economy tend to fall into two major categories: stimulating production or stimulating consumption. Both can lead to sustainable economic development. Growing production can attract capital into a local economy, creating jobs and raising incomes. Growing consumption – or shifting consumption from traditional to green products – can help keep spending local, creating equitable income growth and improving local quality of life. Ultimately, both can enhance the capacity of local areas and their residents to compete in the global economy.

Production

Early in the twentieth century, economists identified the importance of exports in generating local income to support urban economies. Ever since, the idea of an 'economic base' of export or 'driving' sectors has dominated economic development approaches. To stimulate production, cities rely heavily on both carrots and sticks: economic incentives to attract and retain business; and green standards and regulations. As a long-term stimulus, many are also trying to build local capacity to compete in the green economy. Local incentives typically include fee exemptions, low-cost loans and in-kind contributions (e.g. of land or infrastructure). Green standards and regulations that stimulate production are typically goals to green the way goods and services are produced by spurring renewable energy use or greater energy efficiency. Another set of programs, from cluster initiatives to green campuses to workforce development, build local capacity to compete in the green economy over the long term.

Consumption

Despite the focus on production, in recent times, local-serving jobs account for at least two-thirds of all jobs and higher rates of job growth than export sectors (Porter 2003; Markusen et al. 2004). There are four reasons to support local-serving jobs as a sustainable economic development strategy. First, investing in local quality of life is key to attracting and retaining businesses and their workers, meaning more stability (Florida 2002). Second, local services play a critical support role in industry clusters, tying jobs to place (Porter 2003; Warner and Liu 2006). Third, local services from education to health care and child care are public goods because of their critical role in local human development (Committee for Economic Development 2004; Sen 1999). And fourth, providing these services locally means that they are not imported and thus a drag on the local economy (Williams 1997).

Cities are increasingly recognizing the importance of consumption-driven economic development by adopting four types of green policies: green standards and regulations for energy use (described above); green building incentives; environmentally preferable purchasing; and 'buy local' initiatives. These policies may or may not help develop local businesses, depending on how mandates are framed (e.g. whether local purchasing standards accompany them). However, they still play an important role by raising awareness of the environment and thus indirectly helping to build the market for green goods and services. Most common are energy efficiency programs, for example ratepayer surcharges to create public benefits funds for renewable facilities, R&D and education. Although these are not direct economic development programs, they at least help to support green innovation and develop a new market for green products. Another common consumption incentive is the solar panel installation tax credit or permit fee waiver.

Conclusion
Either a production or consumption focus can help meet sustainable economic development goals. Over the long term, cities and regions need to produce goods in order to avoid dependency and grow local jobs and incomes. Incentives to attract businesses are popular with politicians and practitioners, but they are very risky; businesses may fail or move on as they mature. Thus a focus on local-serving sectors may be the most effective way to change local consumption patterns – and could lead to exports in the long run. The toolkits for both include incentives, regulations and standards, but the extent to which they enhance sustainability depends on whether they emphasize economic growth or development, as explained in the next section.

Policies to Support Growth versus Development

In this era of global competition and local fiscal constraint, cities increasingly seek to develop and maintain a vibrant economy. Yet few cities have adopted comprehensive economic development strategies, and even if they have articulated explicit economic development goals, they rarely adopt the right types of policies to support them. In the push to stimulate the green economy, cities are often confused about whether to pursue economic growth or development, as well as whether to seek high-quality jobs or simply job creation of any kind. Despite the rallying cry for green jobs as pathways out of poverty, a green economy does not necessary mean well-paying, green-collar jobs and sustainable economic development unless local job standards and training programs, as well as long-term strategies, are in place. Even though we might expect a net gain in jobs, many cities have underestimated the potential for job loss, since many businesses will shed jobs in the process of producing green products or becoming more green.

Simply put, economic growth is an increase in output through the efficient use of resources, while economic development is a change in functional capacity that generates new resources for growth – in other words, that can make growth sustainable. Growth is quantitative change (in numbers of new businesses, jobs, per capita income, buildings etc.), while development is qualitative, structural change that can help foster innovation and improve productivity (Malizia and Feser 1999). Development will probably increase growth – but only over the long term. Growth can lead to development, if the new resources it generates are reinvested in businesses, people or places; if not, it is probably unsustainable.

On the growth side, the most common goals are creating new jobs, growing new or expanding existing businesses, and thus expanding the tax base. Both green business incentives and green standards and regulations are likely to produce these outcomes.

Business incentives to spur the green economy may include tax credits, fee exemptions, low-cost loans, permit streamlining and in-kind contributions (e.g. of land or infrastructure). For example, the City of San Francisco Clean Energy Business Exclusion is a payroll tax exemption for businesses with over ten employees. For large-scale incentives, such as tax credits and abatements, cities usually turn to state programs, such as the Texas Emerging Technology Fund. Via enterprise zones, many states also offer tax credits and loans for the purchase of capital equipment, which can in turn help further innovation. Some California regions have implemented Recycling Market Development Zones, a state program that combines recycling with economic development not only to reduce the amount of waste produced but also to encourage new businesses, expand existing ones and create more jobs within California. In these designated zones, the state provides low-interest loans for land and equipment purchases as well as leasehold improvements and working capital.

Green regulations and standards provide goals to green the way goods and services are produced by spurring renewable energy use, greater energy efficiency or improved environmental quality. Federal and state environmental policies and regulations, such as California's regulation of carbon emissions via Assembly Bill 32 (AB 32), are without a doubt a significant driving force in motivating local jurisdictions, businesses and individuals to try to reduce greenhouse gas emissions. Many cities and states have adopted renewable energy portfolio targets, specifying that utilities generate a certain amount of electricity from renewable sources, often local. Washington State's Renewable Energy Standards mandate local ethanol and biofuels purchasing, but only when local businesses demonstrate sufficient capacity for production. A growing number of cities are adopting green building regulations, from mandating LEED standards in government buildings to setting these standards for all large development. Recycling standards to reduce waste from construction and demolition can help spur the local recycling industry. In order to use such regulations to grow local business, however, cities need to pair them with preferential purchasing clauses or marketing programs (such as green certification programs) for local businesses.

But some caveats apply. Many green standards simply require the substitution of energy-efficient for traditional inputs, and as such are unlikely to result in net increases of jobs or materials. They could even result in job loss, as firms figure out how to produce goods or services more efficiently or hire fewer workers. New regulations will undoubtedly result in job loss in carbon-intensive industries. In order to result in growth or even retention, the regulations will have to grow the overall market. For instance, green building retrofits may create a new market, as households undertake rehabilitation projects they would otherwise not pursue, but green cleaning products may not, as consumers substitute eco-sensitive for traditional cleansers. Likewise, incentives will be ineffective unless they include clawback provisions to keep businesses from leaving; moreover, since business expansions are far more common than relocations, the most sustainable subsidies target existing and startup businesses (Leroy 2005; Neumark et al. 2005).

Further, none of these approaches alone is likely to lead to the equitable income growth sought. Certain industry sectors are much more likely to provide high-paying jobs for low-skilled workers, especially heavily unionized sectors such as utilities and construction. If cities target industry sectors that hire a large share of low-wage workers (such as retail, waste management, trucking or business services), yet are interested in job quality, they will need to implement provisions for job standards. These might include living wage and benefit ordinances, certification programs, sector-based strategies, local hiring clauses and project-specific community benefits agreements (Foshay et al. 2008).

Development goals range from improving business functions and knowledge, to city quality of life, to worker human capital. Over time, these will make cities more competitive in the green economy. Attaining these goals requires considerable investment, often long-term, in cluster initiatives, R&D, business incubators, marketing, transportation and land use, workforce development and other programs. Although they create only a few jobs, at least in the short run, they may generate more high-quality jobs.

Cluster initiatives facilitate the networking that connects core businesses with suppliers and new technologies. The East Bay Green Corridor Partnership brings together a variety of public, university and private sector partners to coordinate and market green economic development activities for nine cities in San Francisco's East Bay. Penn Future is an environmental organization that advocates for regulatory changes in support of renewable energy and educates the public about buying green. Green business incubators, as in Austin and Sacramento, provide logistical support and financing for startups, while eco-industrial campuses, such as that proposed in the South Bronx, convert brownfields into green campuses. Finally, a number of cities across the country provide workforce development programs, typically focused on green building construction programs: for instance. Richmond Build trains local youth in solar panel installation and experiences 90 percent placement rates due to close relationships with both unions and industry.

But again, results will depend on which industry sectors cities invest in. Cluster initiatives facilitating technology transfer from university to businesses tend to create jobs mostly for high-skilled workers (with graduate-level education) (Marcelli et al. 2000). Cleantech R&D will generate innovations, but few new jobs. Later phases of the product cycle will produce far more jobs and output, but mass assembly and manufacturing are likely to occur far from the original city. The experience of business incubators has been that sectors vary in how much they will benefit from shared infrastructure, management and supplies. Improving quality of life will enhance environmental quality and attract a more competitive workforce, but may displace existing residents if protections are not in place. Workforce development programs are most successful in just a few sectors; it is easiest to create quality jobs and career ladders in unionized sectors like construction and health care (Conway et al. 2007).

One approach that can combine both growth and development is building the market for green products and services. Cities and states support local business and transform consumers' spending habits) – through standards, incentives, purchasing policies and marketing. For instance, by offering free or low-cost assistance with green building codes, cities encourage energy-efficient construction and design. By providing incentives for solar energy, federal and state tax credit programs leverage significant private spending. By enacting bike-friendly programs, Sunday Streets or marketing campaigns for buying local, cities educate their residents about alternatives. New interest in green products and services not only grows the pie, but also develops new local knowledge and capacity.

Finally, across the country, city governments are implementing climate action plans. Although these are non-binding, they guide policy from municipal energy use to transportation planning to building codes, and as such may spur innovation and/or job creation. Perhaps most importantly, they create new awareness, which in turn can lead to different consumption patterns (Wheeler 2008).

Choosing a Strategy

Many different levels of government are involved in enacting regulations and policies. The federal, state and local government can all provide business incentives. Permitting processes exist at the state level (for environmental concerns) and municipal level (for buildings and solar installation). Local infrastructure spending decisions are made at the state, regional, county and municipal levels. While higher levels of government can help incentivize local household spending primarily through tax policy, local government can promote markets through regulation and technical assistance, in addition to property taxes and impact fees. Federal and state governments shape the availability of funding for higher education and workforce development, while local areas have some say over workforce development programming. R&D investment comes mostly from the federal government, but increasingly from the state as well.

Intervention will be most effective if it builds upon local strengths and chooses appropriate policies to meet local sustainability goals. Is the economic development goal local income growth? Cities should consider enacting policies such as green building standards with provisions for local purchasing and hiring. Is the goal local quality of life? Cities might stimulate consumption through green building policies, support for open space amenities, and technical assistance for retailers. Is the aim equitable job growth? Cities might look to sectors that have traditionally provided well-paying, career-track jobs, with established job training programs and relationships with unions, such as utilities and transportation. Or is the goal innovation, in order to spur growth over the long term? Incentivizing the cleantech sector with funding for R&D and technical assistance for startups may be the best approach.

New green standards, regulations, incentives, technical assistance and marketing programs can help spur the green economy, but they will not actually create local economic development in the absence of supporting policies. Local purchasing and hiring requirements, labor standards and clawback provisions will need to be part of the green economic development package if green policies are to have an impact on the economy and equity as well as on the environment – and if they are to support local sustainability.

As with any new economic development initiative, green economic policies will be most successful to the extent that they build on existing strengths in the city or region. Existing stakeholders, from government agencies to universities, nonprofits, trade associations, utilities and unions, need to be involved. Green economic development programs should take advantage of existing, often surplus, capacity in job training programs, business incubators, small business assistance centers and other organizations. New green programs should build on successful existing programs and organizations (e.g. the Berkeley First Source hiring program, the MIT Entrepreneurship Center and the New York Industrial Retention

Network). In order to incorporate this cross-sectoral landscape of existing stakeholders and programs, initiatives will need individuals with effective leadership skills, not just organizational leadership but also political, visionary and team leadership (Crosby and Bryson 2005). Drawing on existing strengths will not only generate more endogenous development, but also will help to create a more sustainable green economy over time.

EVIDENCE ON GREEN BUSINESS AND INDUSTRY

At about 2 percent of the overall economy, the green economy is very small; green industry is not likely to drive the economy in the same way that sectors such as manufacturing or information technology have done. On the other hand, in omitting the consumption aspects of the green economy, studies may be underestimating its impact. Whatever the numbers, the green economy is growing faster than the overall economy, with concentrations (both absolute and in share of employment) in the Washington, New York, San Francisco, Philadelphia and Atlanta regions (Muro et al. 2011). But how do these concentrations emerge? To answer this question, we draw on a unique business survey, which sampled 8000 green and traditional businesses in California (Chapple and Hutson 2010). Overall, the ability to develop a concentration of green business depends on (1) overall locational issues, (2) the relationship of the business to local markets and networks, and (3) local policy. The following looks at each in turn, and then briefly presents two case studies.

Overall Location Trends and Business Preferences

Location theory increasingly emphasizes how less tangible factors – such as personal preferences of executives, quality of life or local networks – strongly influence location and relocation decisions (O'Sullivan 1996). For green businesses, two of these factors dominate – the role of the executive's residence and local quality of life – as well as a third, the existence of a strong local market. Other factors are more minor; these include the availability and quality of the labor pool in the region, the availability of space, the existence of other firms in the area, proximity to a university or research institution, the availability of financial capital and the existence of suppliers. The emphasis among green businesses on the local quality of life and market reflects their focus on consumption.

Many economic development programs, particularly the incentives meant to attract new businesses, assume that businesses are footloose, despite research that finds low mobility rates (Neumark et al. 2005). But, compared to other businesses, green companies are more tied to location and less concerned with strict regulations and high taxes. Other distinct characteristics include a focus on local markets, strong local network connections and a willingness to embrace government intervention.

Local markets provide both feedback about new products and demand for goods and services. Private households constitute the largest market for green businesses, followed by private firms, with relatively less reliance on the public sector. Moreover, green companies are more likely than other types of businesses to serve markets within their cities or regions, as opposed to national and international destinations.

Research has long shown that firm innovation and growth depends on business networks with competitors, partners, suppliers and support organizations such as trade association within and outside the home region (Porter 2001). Green firms tend to be more embedded in local/regional networks and markets than traditional firms; their competitors, suppliers and partners are more likely to be located within the home city or region of the firms than nationally or globally. When partnering with other firms or organizations, green firms are more likely to choose partners within the local region, and they tend to interact more often with both local firms and government. The cross-sectoral complexity of these networks probably leads to a need for strong leadership.

Asked what types of policies they value, most businesses will mention a business-friendly climate, with reduced regulation and taxes. But green companies have a particular notion of the factors that make their region more competitive, and a much more positive view of the role of public policy and government regulation in the economy than their traditional counterparts. Instead of demanding government assistance to lower the costs of doing business, green businesses tend to ask for more government incentives, not only for businesses (financial incentives), but also to increase the demand for green products among consumers (market incentives/market education). Other types of incentives requested include tax credits for buying 'green', utility rebates, subsidies for energy-efficient equipment installation, and low-cost loans for home improvement. Green businesses also place importance on issues such as quality of life and public transportation/infrastructure, and thus tend to support restrictive land-use and green building regulations.

Yet green businesses also emphasize the necessity of removing barriers and streamlining permit processes in order to develop standards and best practices. Many businesses simply wish to see general improvements in how government and the overall economy are functioning. But also, standardized processes in different cities and regions would allow companies to scale up their business and have easier access to a larger market. The building and solar manufacturing industries are especially insistent that this will improve regional competitiveness. For the case of solar, in addition to state and national-level organizations such the Solar Energy Industry Association, region-specific industry organizations like SolarTech in Silicon Valley have emerged recently to accelerate the process of permit streamlining and gains associated with economies of scale.

Green businesses tend not to see improving the labor pool as a major issue, perhaps because they are still too small to make use of external training providers. Small firms tend to have diverse labor needs, from managerial to technical to administrative skills, so job training programs may accommodate only a few of their workers. Thus most green businesses rely primarily on in-house training.

In sum, the green economy is increasingly integrated with the overall economy. However, green businesses have unique needs, with implications for policy. They are particularly oriented to local markets and rely heavily on local networks of nonprofits, government and similar businesses. Driving their location are three factors: the local market for the firm's product or service; the executive's place of residence (of particular importance for small firms); and the quality of life. In contrast to other businesses, green businesses perceive public intervention very positively.

The distinction between small and large green firms is significant and should be considered in planning any local economic development or support strategy. Smaller firms are characterized by a focus on the local market, and many choose a location close to the executive's residence, while larger firms are more focused on the labor market and on access to financial capital in making a location choice. Large green firms show more interest in using outside training, particularly certificate programs, than do other types of firms – another opportunity for economic development strategies.

The growth of the green economy depends on embeddedness in the local market and strength of the local regulatory system. This suggests that the country's most distressed metropolitan regions may be able to boost their own green economies through carefully crafted regulations that incentivize the growth of local green markets. This, in turn, can build the capacity of local firms to compete in global markets. But if the green economy is to be the panacea promised by many, it will require the focused and coordinated action of governments, firms and communities. The next section shows how two places – a strong-market city (Portland) and a weak-market region in a strong regulatory state climate (Riverside–San Bernardino counties in California) – have focused their efforts.

Growing Green Business Sustainably: Two Cases

Portland

As is suggested in other chapters of this volume, any list of model green cities would include Portland, Oregon. Due to supportive land-use and transportation policies at the regional and state levels, Portland has been able to create model sustainability programs and transform itself into one of the country's most livable cities. Yet its job growth tends to lag the region's, and household income is declining.

As a result, regional business groups such as the Portland Business Alliance have long urged economic development policies that focus on its strengths: the ability to attract young talent; a culture of research and entrepreneurship; and relatively high productivity. Whether or not due to local government intervention, Portland has experienced rapid growth in green sectors, specifically in solar power manufacturing, biofuels, wind energy, green building and environmental services. Although the 2012 Portland Plan emphasizes its strengths in traded sectors, it also suggests developing import substitution strategies. Local production can expand consumer choices in food, energy, building materials and other areas, reducing dependence on other regions (City of Portland 2012).

But it is the city's ability to implement energy efficiency retrofits that has brought it national attention. Working with a variety of government, non-profit and utility partners, and using a combination of federal and local finance, the city ran a pilot project, Clean Energy Works, that helped 500 homeowners finance and install energy efficiency upgrades. The project included a landmark community workforce agreement requiring that 80 percent of the jobs go to local residents and wages be equal to at least 180 percent of the state median. Local policy success led to replication at the state level, where Clean Energy Works Oregon is now supported by the US Department of Energy and other funding sources. The state program continues to link equity to environmental goals, with set-asides for disadvantaged workers (Clean Energy Works Oregon 2012). This example of policy learning is arguably made possible by Portland's overall support for sustainability goals.

Riverside–San Bernardino

Although the Inland Empire (Riverside and San Bernardino counties) initially developed due to the citrus industry, most recently it has expanded due to spillover growth from the strong-market regions of Los Angeles and San Diego directly to the west and south. The Inland Empire now boasts a population of nearly 4 million. Following the recession of the 1970s, the 1980s brought an unprecedented boom. Riverside and San Bernardino counties experienced some of the highest growth rates in Southern California due to the influx of manufacturing from Los Angeles, a growing immigrant and commuter population, and a booming construction industry. Today, the strong industries in the area are industrial: manufacturing, logistics and energy production related to the region's significant wind, solar and geothermal resources. But the recent recession has impacted the Inland Empire more than many California regions, due in large part to its dependence on the homebuilding industry, as well as its large first-time homeowner population, hit hard by the foreclosure crisis.

The Inland Empire has seen extraordinary growth across the green economy, with rates of increase exceeding California's in employment, establishments and sales. Within the region, the City of Riverside has driven growth, with a 9 percent annual growth rate (compared to 3 percent in the region as a whole). One reason for this growth is the leadership of Riverside's mayor, Ron Loveridge, who draws from his experience sitting on the California Air Resources Board, as well as the fortuitous city ownership of the local public utility. The mayor has convened a Clean & Green Taskforce and rebranded suburban Riverside as the 'Clean & Green City', making early progress on green goals, such as a 50 percent renewable energy standard for the utility, a tree-planting program, and a city fleet powered solely by alternative fuels (it is currently at 60 percent). The city has built infrastructure for obtaining natural gas or even hydrogen fuel, and required LEED certification standards for new buildings. Ownership of the public utility has given the city funding for R&D, so it has funded research at UC-Riverside on combining organic and inorganic materials to create growth in photovoltaic cells and flexible batteries. The city's green initiatives are boosted by Riverside's February 2009 designation as an Emerald City, part of the California Department of Conservation's Emerald City Pilot Project. Emerald City status will give Riverside access to state funding and expertise in the realization of the city's Green Action Plan. Thus the mayor's leadership is not just about political savvy and vision, but the ability to leverage informal contacts and facilitate cooperation of players in a complex organizational landscape (Sweeting 2002).

Another possible reason for this growth is the institutional density. Active in the region's green network are the Inland Empire Economic Partnership (a regional business group similar to Joint Venture: Silicon Valley), the Riverside County EDA, Cal State San Bernardino, and UC Riverside's College of Engineering–Center for Environmental Research and Technology (CE–CERT), which acts as a readily accessible public interface for environmental problem-solving. Also, the Green Valley Initiative (GVI) is an ambitious cluster strategy that aims to establish the

Riverside–San Bernardino region as a center for green technology, with more than 500 stakeholders and 30 regional cities involved, helping the region to leverage federal funding.

Finally, state regulation has played a pivotal role. Attorney General Jerry Brown sued San Bernardino County for not taking AB 32 into account in its general plan. The settlement required the county to invest in hybrid vehicles, replace diesel with natural gas vehicles, follow LEED Silver standards for all new buildings and major renovations, and improve its solid waste and recycling programs. All that is lacking is market demand. Although residents of the City of Riverside support its initiatives and often invest in their own solar energy systems, residents of the eastern part of the region are less interested.

The Inland Empire case provides an interesting example of a strong state regulatory framework driving green economic growth in a weak-market region. Yet it is where that top–down regulation is met by local initiative, as in the City of Riverside, that growth is particularly rapid. But is it sustainable? Although local institutions are involved, there is no clear focus on developing long-term capacity to compete.

Lessons from the evidence

Evidence from a survey of green businesses, as well as two cases, suggests the challenges of linking green business growth to broader sustainable economic development goals. Most green businesses help to reduce carbon emissions in some way and many reduce or transform consumption. Green businesses tend to reflect (and flourish in) local contexts with a strong culture of environmental consciousness, and in many cases regions are building a support structure for green businesses that promotes stable, long-term growth. However, if sustainable economic development is to 'enhance equitable local income and employment growth', cities, regions and states are falling short. Although there are examples across the country of green policies that give preference to local businesses and ensure livable wages, and the Portland case provides a great example of a city innovation that is then scaled up to the state level, these are the exceptions, not the rule.

GROWING THE FUTURE GREEN ECONOMY

Governments have many tools to help grow and develop the green economy, including regulations and standards, incentives, market-building approaches and cluster strategies. But the appropriate toolkit will vary from region to region, city to city. Thus the more proactive local governments, with capacity for facilitative leadership, will probably emerge as the winners, at least initially, in the green economy.

The state remains a critically important actor in promulgating local green economy growth; its regulation helps to level the playing field across strong- and weak-market cities and regions. Still, the heavy hand of the state will not be uniformly popular, and regions dependent on manufacturing are not likely to embrace green and sustainable economic development.

Although cities are learning how to promote green growth and development, the jury is out on whether these green strategies can be integrated with sustainable economic development goals. Policy makers have yet to acknowledge many of the contradictory goals in environmental and economic programs. For instance, incentives for cleantech R&D may ultimately increase local carbon emissions or result in little job creation as firms mature and offshore their jobs, with products imported across long distances. Likewise, Buy Local programs benefit high-cost developed regions with high emissions per capita at the expense of less carbon-intensive places.

However, the amount of innovation – and rate of adoption – in both green and sustainable development is promising, in terms of both technological advances and new policies. Although the state and federal regulatory framework provides the structure for change, cities and regions offer the greatest opportunities for sustainable and green economic development; it is at the local level where individuals feel empowered to act, learning takes place, and behaviors change.

REFERENCES

Chapple, Karen (2008), *Defining the Green Economy: A Primer on Green Economic Development*, Berkeley, CA: Center for Community Innovation.

Chapple, Karen and Malo Hutson (2010), *Innovating the Green Economy in California Regions*, Berkeley, CA: Center for Community Innovation.

City of Portland (2012), 'The Portland Plan', available at http://www.portlandonline.com/portlandplan/index.cfm?c=45722 (accessed 6 October 2012).

Clean Energy Works Oregon (2012), 'Clean energy works high road outcomes: new faces, career pathways and increasing influence', available at http://www.cleanenergyworksoregon.org/wp-content/uploads/2012/09/HighRoad_Short_090612.pdf (accessed 6 October 2012).

Committee for Economic Development (2004), *A New Framework for Assessing the Benefits of Early Childhood Education*, Washington, DC: Committee for Economic Development.

Conway, Maureen, Amy Blair, Steven L. Dawson and Linda Dworak-Muñoz (2007), *Sector Strategies for Low-Income Workers: Lessons from the Field*, Washington, DC: Aspen Institute.

Crosby, B.C. and J.M. Bryson (2005), 'A leadership framework for cross-sector collaboration', *Public Management Review*, **7** (2), 177–201.

Florida, Richard (2002), *The Rise of the Creative Class: And How It's Transforming Work, Leisure, Community and Everyday Life*, New York: Basic Books.

Foshay, Elena, Deric Licko, Ana Mileva and Josh Mukhopadhyay (2008), *Ensuring that Green Jobs are Quality Jobs*, Berkeley, CA: Center for Labor Research and Education and Center for Community Innovation.

Gage, Alea and Anthony LoPresti (2012), *Sustainable Economic Development Policy Overview (Policy Overview 01–2012)*, Berkeley, CA: Institute of Urban and Regional Development.

Leroy, Greg (2005), *The Great American Jobs Scam*, San Francisco, CA: Berrett-Koehler Publishers.

Malizia, Emil and Edward Feser (1999), *Understanding Local Economic Development*, New Brunswick, NJ: The State University of New Jersey Press.

Marcelli, Enrico, Sundari Baru and Donald Cohen (2000), *Planning for Shared Prosperity or Growing Inequality? An In-Depth Look at San Diego's Leading Industry Clusters*, San Diego, CA: Center on Policy Initiatives.

Markusen, Ann, Greg Schrock and Elisa Barbour (2004), *Making the City Distinctive: A Guide for Planners and Policymakers*, Minneapolis, MN: Project on Regional and Industrial Economics.

Muro, Mark, Jonathan Rothwell and Devashree Saha (2011), *Sizing the Clean Economy: A National and Regional Green Jobs Assessment*, Washington, DC: Brookings Institution.

Neumark, David, Junfu Zhang and Brandon Wall (2005), 'Employment dynamics and business relocation: new evidence from the national establishment time series', NBER Working Paper 11647, Cambridge, MA: National Bureau of Economic Research.

O'Sullivan, Arthur (1996), *Urban Economics*, Chicago, IL: Irwin.

Pew Charitable Trust (2009), *The Clean Energy Economy: Repowering Jobs, Businesses and Investments Across America*, Washington, DC: Pew Charitable Trust.

Porter, Michael (2001), 'Regions and the new economics of competition', in Allen Scott (ed.), *Global City-Regions: Trends, Theory, Policy*, New York: Oxford University Press, pp. 139–57.

Porter, M. (2003), 'The economic performance of regions', *Regional Studies*, **37** (6–7), 549–78.

Sen, Amartya (1999), *Development as Freedom*, New York: Knopf.

Sweeting, D. (2002), 'Leadership in urban governance: the mayor of London', *Local Government Studies*, **28** (1), 3–20.

Warner, M. and Z. Liu (2006), 'The importance of child care in economic development: a comparative analysis of regional economic linkage', *Economic Development Quarterly*, **20** (1), 97–103.

Wheeler, S. (2008), 'State and municipal climate change plans: the first generation', *Journal of the American Planning Association*, **74** (4), 481–96.

Williams, Colin (1997), *Consumer Services and Economic Development*, London and New York: Routledge.

7. Strategies and considerations for investing in sustainable city infrastructure

Rae Zimmerman

INTRODUCTION

Infrastructure comprises a very large and diverse set of physical systems and social services, and financial strategies inevitably reflect the breadth of the concept. Infrastructure systems are essential to urban sustainability, and can resonate with urban and natural environments depending on their design. Over more than a century, for example, the water supplies of urban areas have been supplemented and supported by water sources often located many hundreds of miles away from where they are used (Zimmerman 2009, p. 229), and this practice is often not without conflicts. Energy resources including fuels have been similarly drawn from long distances to serve cities and their regions. New technologies and behavioral changes have been emerging to promote sustainability, supplementing and, in some cases, replacing traditional infrastructures that rely on distant resources, and these new approaches will present challenges to infrastructure finance.

The extent to which infrastructure finance reflects urban sustainability goals will require public buy-in. Public opinion polls have shown that infrastructure categories tend to rank low as a priority; however, the areas that infrastructure impacts either directly or indirectly tend to rank higher. For example, the Pew Research Center for the People and the Press (Dimock et al. 2013, p. 1) surveys of public priorities over the first decade of the twenty-first century show that, of the public priorities included in their polls (ranked as "top priority for president and Congress"), "improving infrastructure" when ranked against numerous non-infrastructure priorities typically ranked second to the bottom (30 percent indicating it as a top priority); and energy ranked higher in the 2013 poll (45 percent), but according to the Pew polls the percentage for energy has been declining. However, economic outcomes of investment in general, such as the economy and jobs, to which infrastructure indirectly contributes, tended to obtain the highest ranks with 86 percent and 79 percent of the respondents ranking those areas as top priorities respectively. Other areas related to indirect impacts of infrastructure in the 2013 poll included 'protecting environment' with 52 percent indicating it as a top priority, and that percentage represents a steady increase over previous polls. Global warming, another area linked to infrastructure, however, obtained the lowest rank, at 28 percent. The 2013 poll also reported bi-partisan differences in priorities, with Republicans giving lower ranks than Democrats for environmental protection, climate change and transportation infrastructure (Dimock et al., p. 2). The 2014 Pew Center survey results show that the percentage indicating transportation as a priority increased (39 percent versus 30 percent in 2013), energy and global warming remained about the same, and environment declined (49 percent from 52 percent in 2013) (Doherty et al. 2014, p. 1).

Many reasons have been given for the general lack of direct interest in infrastructure by the public (see, e.g. Seley 1983; Perry 1995). One is the lack of an overall constituency for the general category of infrastructure. Rather, constituencies tend to form around more specific infrastructure subcategories or sectors such as transportation, energy, water and even more detailed components. Another reason is that for a long time infrastructure was taken for granted. It was expected to support development and not necessarily be an aim in itself, and the basic needs of people for water, sanitation, transportation and electric power were assumed to be public goods that were automatic. Infrastructure, especially in urban areas, is often beneath the surface, underground, and thus not noticed until something goes wrong. For these reasons and others the word 'infrastructure', according to Altshuler (1989, p. 506) does not even appear in vocabularies until the 1980s (also discussed in Zimmerman 2012a, p. 438).

The emergence of extreme events has brought renewed attention to infrastructure, and these events have often produced enormous, unexpected and highly uncertain demands on infrastructure financing. The importance of protecting infrastructure has been emphasized at the federal level, especially in the context of these extremes, and for a number of years the Obama administration designated December as critical infrastructure protection month (described by Zimmerman 2012b, p. 235) and more recently as 'critical infrastructure security and resiliency month' (US White House 2013b), which seems to provide a closer connection to the objective of sustainability.

Even if financing for infrastructure is supported, the level and nature of investments for sustainability are often unclear. The level of investment often emphasizes direct investment and not indirect needs such as supporting or lowering infrastructure resource use 'footprints' and reducing adverse environmental and social impacts to promote sustainability.

Multiplier Effects from Infrastructure Investments

Infrastructure systems are not only indispensable for urban living, but investment in infrastructure has multiplier effects for the economy. The multiplier effects from infrastructure investment have been a constant source of study and debate for many years (Hulten and Schwab 1995). Yet it is often difficult to assess with certainty in which sectors these benefits will be located and how large they will be. Zimmerman (2012a, p. 438) summarizes some estimates of infrastructure's multiplier effects, for example, citing an estimate by the World Bank (2011, p. 7) that as infrastructure capital investment doubles, a 15 percent increase in gross domestic product (GDP) occurs. The US Department of the Treasury and Council on Economic Advisors (2012) concluded that infrastructure investments improve the economy, jobs (primarily in construction) and businesses, as well as lowering transportation costs. Not all of the estimated impacts pertain to capital investments. The US Department of the Treasury and Council on Economic Advisors (ibid., p. 8), citing the work of Gramlich (1993), points to the benefits of increasing investment in highway maintenance. At a smaller geographic scale, numerous property value studies have pointed to the positive effects of infrastructure investments of all kinds (ibid., p. 9); however, environmental and visual impacts can also have negative effects on properties in close proximity to infrastructure. Shatz et al. (2011) evaluated the impacts of highway infrastructure and productivity, economic output and employment changes using a review and meta-analysis of the literature. They underscored the variable nature of the findings due to differences in the way studies were conducted, and found some significant positive linkages between highway infrastructure and certain aspects of the economy (ibid., p. xvii).

Not all investment strategies are directly monetary in nature, although non-monetized effects have implications for investment needs. First, the shortening of timeframes for permits and environmental review processes is a type of investment that is expected to have multiplier effects by expediting infrastructure projects, and hence lowering their cost, and a number of projects have been targeted by the federal government in a presidential memorandum of August 31, 2011 for such expedited reviews (US Department of the Treasury and Council on Economic Advisors 2012, p. 2; see Zimmerman 2012b, pp. 161–2 for a review of similar actions). Second, for transportation infrastructure, certain transportation plans and programs are exempt from environmental impact assessment requirements under the National Environmental Policy Act (NEPA). Third, in emergencies, the government has mechanisms in place to grant exemptions to regulations in order to ease the cost and difficulty of restoration. These encompass requirements for debris removal, fuel requirements under the

Clean Air Act, and various water discharge permits under the Clean Water Act (Zimmerman 2012b, pp. 205–6), as well as expedited environmental reviews in connection with rebuilding after emergencies (Disaster Relief Appropriations Act 2013).

Another perspective focuses on the value of infrastructure assets as a basis for prioritizing investments (Zimmerman 2012a, pp. 437–8). Valuing infrastructure, however, has been challenging and very much depends on how one defines assets and their value. Some estimates of assets reach into the many trillions of dollars, and for transportation and utilities the US Census has estimated a 2009 value of several trillions of dollars (US Census Bureau 2012, cited by Zimmerman 2012a, p. 438). Heintz et al. (2009, p. 1), citing the Bureau of Economic Analysis, give a figure of $8.2 trillion for the 2007 value of US non-defense public assets including infrastructure, of which $2.6 trillion is for roads (Ibid., p. 14).

Scope of Urban Infrastructure Facilities: Definitions and Types

Infrastructure is usually defined or categorized in terms of the types of physical facilities and the services it provides. The scope of infrastructure and the types of facilities and services included within it vary widely. The American Society of Civil Engineers (ASCE 2009) uses 15 categories. These can be grouped into the following broad areas: energy (1 category); transportation, including aviation, bridges, roads, rail and transit (5 categories); water, including supply, dams, levees and waterways (4 categories); waste management, including solid waste and wastewater, among others (3 categories); schools (1 category); and parks and recreation (1 category), acknowledging that the sectors within each category can overlap. The US government has defined 'critical infrastructure and key resources (CIKR)' for the purpose of security from an 'all-hazards' perspective. Those categories encompass 18 sectors (US Department of Homeland Security 2009, p. 3) of which seven and possibly parts of others are infrastructures covered by the ASCE. This chapter focuses on a core set of infrastructures for energy, transportation, communication, water and waste management.

INFRASTRUCTURE INVESTMENT PATTERNS AND TRENDS

Historic and Current Investment Estimates

In two major infrastructure sectors, transportation and water, the US Congressional Budget Office (CBO) (2007, pp. 10, 14) has identified a number of distinct patterns and trends in public spending. The following patterns and trends are apparent in the CBO analysis, as summarized by Zimmerman (2009, p. 227): highways dominate the allocation of infrastructure funding by the federal, state and local governments; federal spending on infrastructure has increased but its share of total federal spending has declined at least for the two decades prior to 2004; infrastructure expenditures as a share of US Gross Domestic Product (GDP) has been declining or at least not changing; state and local infrastructure spending has been increasing as federal spending has declined in the early part of the twenty-first century; spending on operations has been exceeding capital expenditures.

The ASCE (2011a, p. 5) estimates for the electric power sector began with the spending trends: 'From 2001 through 2010, annual capital investment averaged $62.9 billion, including $35.4 billion in generation, $7.7 billion in transmission, and $19.8 billion in local distribution systems (in 2010 dollars).' They noted a wide variation from year to year in these investments. The Edison Electric Institute (2012) reported a $30 billion investment in 2011 in electricity transmission and distribution, which represented an 8.4 percent increase for transmission and a 13 percent increase for distribution over 2010 investment levels.

Needs Estimates and Investment Gaps

The ASCE (2013) infrastructure report card of 2013 estimated a need of $3.6 trillion (in 2010 dollars) by 2020, up from $2.122 trillion in the 2009 report card (ASCE 2009) and $1.6 trillion in the 2005 report card (ASCE 2005) across the infrastructure categories they measure. In 2009, when they subtracted spending of $903 billion and the allocations under the American Recovery and Reinvestment Act (ARRA) of $71.76 billion, the shortfall across the infrastructure sectors they cover was just over one trillion dollars; roads and bridges accounted for almost half of the needs and the shortfall, and rail and transit combined account for about 15 percent (ASCE 2009, p. 7). In the 2013 estimates, the overall shortfall had increased to $1.6 trillion (ASCE 2013).

ASCE's 2011 detailed updated estimates for transportation alone showed an average annual investment needed between 2010 and 2040 of about $220 billion, with highways accounting for the majority of the need (about 90 percent), and ASCE's estimates indicated that the gap is growing (ASCE 2011b, pp. 9–10). The American Public Transportation Association (APTA) (2012, p. 11) reported generally steady upward trends in both capital and operating funding for public transportation between 1995 and 2010 with a slight downturn beginning in state and local funding sources around 2008 or 2009 for capital funding. This trend in capital funding continued in 2011 regardless of the funding source (APTA 2013a, p. 11; APTA 2013b, p. 29).

The ASCE (2011a, p. 5) has estimated need and spending gaps in the electric power sector: 'funding gaps in electric generation, transmission, and distribution . . . are projected to grow over time to a level of $107 billion by 2020, about $11 billion per year, and almost $732 billion by 2040.' They estimate an additional amount needed for households and businesses due to the impact of failing to close the investment gap in electric power (ASCE 2011a, p. 9).

In the water sector, the American Water Works Association (2012, pp. 6–7) has estimated that $2.1 trillion (in 2010 dollars) is the 'current replacement value' for water pipes in the USA. The US EPA (2008) report on 2004 needs already indicated large estimates for stormwater and combined sewer overflow abatement needs, which together were about equal to the needs for wastewater treatment (p. x).

Sources of Investment Funds and Mechanisms for Infrastructure Financing

Infrastructure investments comprise an extensive mix of sources of funding, which tend to vary depending on the type of infrastructure.

Copeland and Tiemann (2010, p. x) provide an extensive history of the provision of grants and loans for wastewater treatment and water supply, and to some extent the allocations were supported by needs assessments.

For public transportation, APTA (2013a, p. 9) reported that in 2011, passenger fares and other funds directly generated by public transportation agencies accounted for about 44 percent of operating funds for public transportation and government sources accounted for the rest, with local funds accounting for about a fifth, state funds accounting for a quarter, and federal funds accounting for about percent. In contrast, about 44 percent of capital funds have come from federal sources and only about a quarter of capital funds are from transit agency generated funds (APTA 2013a, p. 9).

Private spending tends to be more unevenly spread across infrastructure sectors, not as easy to categorize, and often includes more unusual examples. Some have argued that private spending has been increasing (Uchitelle 2008). In the transportation area, for example, where public spending tends to dominate, examples of privately run infrastructures exist, as well as with private support ranging from the purchase of whole airports and roadways (Zimmerman 2009, p. 228) to contributing to the support of road segments in return for naming. A total of 95 percent of worldwide provision of water supply and water sanitation services is considered to be from public sources, though the private role has been expanding (Palaniappan et al. 2006, p. 131). In the energy sector, however, private ownership and operation are typically more pervasive. The US Government Accountability Office (GAO) (2006, p. 1) has indicated that about 85% of US critical infrastructure is privately owned.

TRADITIONAL, CONDITION-DRIVEN PERFORMANCE ISSUES AND EXTREME EVENTS AS A BASIS FOR COST ESTIMATES AND INVESTMENT

Condition Measures and Drivers of Funding for Selected Infrastructure Categories

As indicated above, based on condition ratings, the ASCE has produced estimates for future infrastructure investment needs by type of infrastructure.

ASCE's overall rating for all infrastructure in 2013 was D+, up from D in 2005 and 2009, and in 2013 the ratings varied for individual categories with navigable waterways and levees being the lowest with a D– and the highest B– for solid waste, with rail and bridges being second highest with a C+ (ASCE 2005; 2009; 2013). The ratings focused primarily on condition of the physical infrastructure and congestion but did not generally incorporate the extra needs due to environmental factors, such as exposure to extreme events or security risks or take into account new sustainable technologies for infrastructure to meet those needs and others.

Supply and Environmental Factors and Characteristics Affecting Performance, Condition and Cost

Age of infrastructure

Age is often used to signal deterioration of infrastructure structures and function. Data from the National Bridge Inventory, for example, show a generally positive relationship between age and increasing structural deterioration and functional obsolescence (US Department of Transportation 2012, pp. 3–20 and 3–21). When it comes to catastrophic collapses, however, age is not necessarily related to collapse. Zimmerman (2012b, pp. 198–9) analyzed over two dozen bridge collapses for which the National Transportation Safety Board had issued reports, and found that two-thirds of the bridges had opened in the 1950s and one-fifth of the collapsed bridges were built in the 1920s–30s or earlier. The correlation coefficient for the age of the collapsed bridges versus those in the National Bridge Inventory was only 0.2 (with 1.0 indicating a perfect correlation) (Zimmerman 2012b, p. 199).

Thus factors other than age, such as design, operation and maintenance, and inspection can contribute to investment needs to avoid catastrophic failures.

Environmental factors: extreme events

Many infrastructure sectors confront increasingly stringent environmental, health and safety standards that translate into ongoing investment needs. Extreme events are likely to be among the largest potential contributors to the cost of infrastructure if current trends continue.

Extreme events often produce disruption over many weeks after the event, not to mention the immediate loss of life and property. According to the Federal Emergency Management Agency (FEMA), major declared disasters of all kinds have been increasing over time, and the first decade of the twenty-first century has reached existing records, with 2011 ranking first and the first decade of the century accounting for one-third of the declared disasters since 1956 (Zimmerman 2012a, p. 184, citing FEMA 2012a). Zimmerman (2012b, p. 187, citing Blake et al. 2011, pp. 9, 11) summarized some trends for hurricanes alone: 'nine out of the ten most costliest hurricanes exceeding $7 billion in damages occurred since 2000 (without adjusting for inflation) and six out of the top ten exceeding $11 billion occurred since 2000 when adjusting for inflation using a 2010 deflator'. By 2011, the top two weather events were Hurricane Katrina at $108 billion and Hurricane Ike at $30 billion (unadjusted for inflation) (ibid., p. 11). They estimated that, during the period 1851 through 2010, 'About two major hurricanes every three years made landfall somewhere along the Gulf or Atlantic coast' (ibid. p.15). Estimates for the Atlantic coast for the 2013 hurricane season by Colorado State University indicated greater numbers and intensity than for the 1981–2010 average (Klotzbach and Gray 2013), though those conditions were not realized. Zimmerman (2009, p. 231) summarized the infrastructure impacts of Hurricane Katrina, with major outages in electric power and communications initially occurring over a period of a week to two weeks, with lingering effects thereafter. The US Department of Energy (2009) comparisons of the 2005 Hurricanes Katrina and Rita and the 2008 Hurricanes Gustav and Ike indicated distinct profiles over time ranging across the energy cycle from refinery shutdowns through customer outages, with the recovery time periods for the 2005 hurricanes far exceeding those for hurricanes in 2008.

When Hurricane Sandy made landfall on the US portions of the east coast on October 29, 2012, it produced extensive damage to the area's infrastructure, with an overall estimated damage cost ranking second to Hurricane Katrina (Blake et al. 2013, p. 1). The scale of Sandy, given that it targeted the largest metropolitan area in the USA, presents very new challenges to building a resilient and sustainable urban environment. In the month following the hurricane, New York, New Jersey and Connecticut requested close to $82 billion for damages and increasing resilience (Hernandez and Baker 2012), and on December 7, 2012 President Obama asked Congress for $60 billion, of which over 10 percent covered various infrastructure categories, primarily transportation (Executive Office of the President 2012). On January 15, 2013 the US House of Representatives approved emergency legislation for $50.7 billion (Hernandez 2013) including coverage of infrastructure. Electric power was also funded in other ways. One of the major utilities affected by the hurricane, Consolidated Edison, indicated before the hurricane that it could cost $250 million for adaptation to secure its infrastructure against the impacts of sea level rise (Navarro 2012). The US Department of Transportation's Federal Highway Administration provides emergency funding following disasters for 'federal-aid highway facilities' under its Emergency Relief Program of $100 million per year or more, and eligibility is subject to a number of requirements (Kirk 2014, pp. 2–4). Special-purpose legislation for funding following emergencies and disasters often contains provisions for the funding of infrastructure repair and reconstruction, such as the Disaster Relief Appropriations Act of 2013 that provided funds for public transportation systems following Hurricane Sandy and complemented support from a number of other federal legislative sources since 1998 (Disaster Relief Appropriations Act 2013; Kirk 2014, pp. 7–9). The Disaster Relief Appropriations Act of 2013 (P.L. 113–2) also provides funding for water and wastewater facilities through state revolving funds. US Department of Housing and Urban Development (HUD) (2014, p. 4) summarized allocations for recovery under the Disaster Relief Appropriations Act of 2013 for infrastructure systems by the end of 2013 identifying allocations of $18 billion for 12 programs, encompassing the utility and transportation sectors (which "includes projects specifically designed to promote infrastructure resiliency"). Similar infrastructure cost estimates have been developed for other catastrophes, such as earthquakes. It is often difficult to separate out infrastructure costs from other costs for many of these catastrophes.

The real challenge is whether funds will fully cover hardening infrastructure against future extreme events for example, the many recommendations of the NYS 2100 Commission (2013) that are transferable to other areas and at what level. The allocations under the Disaster Relief Appropriations Act (2013) for Hurricane Sandy have specifically included some of those prevention costs (US Department of Housing and Urban Development (HUD) 2014, p. 4). Healy and Mehotra (2009) pointed out the greater amount of disaster funding spent for response rather than for more long-term efforts to prevent damages. Among their findings for a set of disasters was that 'a $1 increase in preparedness spending resulted in approximately a $7.37 decrease in disaster damage' (ibid., p. 396), which, among their other findings, suggests that if this is applied to infrastructure, investment in prevention can reduce the costs of damage following an extreme event. At the federal level, several shifts toward preparedness were evident between 2009 and 2013 in the appearance of the US Department of Homeland Security's National Preparedness Goal and Presidential Policy Directive PPD-21, 'Critical Infrastructure Security and Resilience' of 2013 (US White House 2013a).

Terrorist attacks against infrastructure, both physical and cyber, are also extreme events that have had major implications for infrastructure (Zimmerman 2012a, p. 441) and its financial needs. US and worldwide trends vary (ibid., p. 443), and a number of foiled planned attacks demonstrate that the threats continue. Financial support to harden infrastructure against such attacks as well as to recover from them is covered under a number of federal programs. Given the 'all-hazards' approach in federal homeland security policy (US Department of Homeland Security 2009, p. 11), these funds could also be applicable to unintentional acts of destruction such as natural hazards (Zimmerman 2012b). The US Department of Homeland Security (DHS) finances infrastructure hardening as well as response to and recovery from disasters resulting in losses to infrastructure and its users. Zimmerman (ibid., p. 236) summarizes the grant programs as follows: there are five programs within the homeland security grant programs (HSGP), two of which are probably more related to infrastructure – the Urban Area Security Initiative (UASI) and the State Homeland Security Program (SHSP). A grant program specifically for infrastructure is the US DHS Infrastructure Protection Program (IPP), which includes a transit program – the Transit Security Grant Program (TSGP) (ibid., pp. 236–9; FEMA 2012b). FEMA has other 'Non-Disaster' grant programs for preparedness that cover other infrastructure areas such as intercity rail and ports (FEMA 2012b). There are other sector-specific sources of federal funding primarily for the response and recovery phases of disasters and the infrastructure repair needed as a result of both intentional and unintentional acts of destruction (Zimmerman 2012b). For transportation infrastructure, for example, after disasters occur FEMA provides disaster assistance, which can include some infrastructure such as vehicles. The US Department of Transportation (DOT) has funding for 'Quick Release Emergency Relief Funds' for transportation recovery (described in ibid., pp. 239–40). Some estimates of financial need for other specific infrastructure sectors exist. For example, in the water sector, Copeland and Tiemann (2010, p. 2) cite the AWWA figure of $1.6 billion to secure US water systems.

Pervasiveness of information technologies in infrastructure operation and maintenance practices

New developments in technology are likely to influence infrastructure costs and hence investment strategies. One key factor is the use of information technologies for operations and maintenance in many infrastructure sectors, which provides support and may increase vulnerabilities (Zimmerman 2012a, p. 452). Examples of information technology usage for the transportation sector have been covered by Zimmerman (2012b, ch. 7, citing US DOT 2008, pp. 2–18); they include the use of Supervisory Control and Data Acquisition (SCADA) systems for road traffic, train controls and computerized automobile controls at the individual vehicle level. This does not come without its downsides – for example the costs associated with cyber security. The US Department of Homeland Security (2013, p. 4), using US Computer Emergency Readiness Team (US-CERT) data, reported that cyber incidents against three entities – critical infrastructure, federal agencies and industrial partners of US DHS as a group – had increased 68 percent over 2011 levels. In the electric power sector, the US Government Accountability Office (2012, p. 9) summarized some of the cyber threats as follows:

> an increased number of entry points and paths that can be exploited by potential adversaries and other unauthorized users; use of new system and network technologies; wider access to systems and networks due to increased connectivity; and an increased amount of customer information being collected and transmitted, providing incentives for adversaries to attack these systems and potentially putting private information at risk of unauthorized disclosure and use.

The Industrial Control Systems Cyber Emergency Response Team (ICS–CERT, 2012, p. 5), using a database of 198 cyber intrusions, identified the energy sector as a leading target for attacks, accounting for 41 percent of the attacks, with the water sector following with 15 percent. A US CERT evaluation of 256 cyber incidents in 2013 found that energy again led as a target, accounting for 59%, water and transportation each accounted for 5%, and others under 5% (ICS–CERT 2014, p. 1). There has been a widespread effort to address cyber security for critical infrastructures, for example, the passage of Executive Order 13636, 'Improving Critical Infrastructure Cybersecurity in 2013'. These new threats will involve different investments than those previously emphasized to promote security.

Demand Characteristics and Selected Relationships with Infrastructure Investment

Population-related drivers of infrastructure demand

The move to outlying portions of urban areas accompanied by increasing per capita use of land has traditionally increased the cost of providing infrastructure for those areas. The form these population movements take varies but the direction of the effects on infrastructure costs is similar. The US EPA (2000, p. 6) noted that metropolitan area population and land development trends showed that the ratio of the percentage of growth in land development and the percentage in population growth always exceeds one for some major metropolitan areas. Later on, census trends indicated that smaller areas, typically more spread out, are growing the fastest (Romero-Lankao and Dodman 2011, p. 114), and Zimmerman (2012b, pp. 12–13) evaluated US Census Bureau (2011) data, noting that faster-growing areas are not the most populous, are also often growing faster than the states they are in, and are in states that are auto-dependent. The Brookings Institution studies have shown an increasing suburbanization of the poor (cited in Zimmerman 2012b, p. 15). Whatever the pattern, suburbanization creates increasing infrastructure costs, since more transmission and capacity are required per capita to service these outlying areas than it costs to service core areas with higher densities (Burchell et al. 2005).

Moreover, population and population density in many coastal counties have been growing faster than in non-coastal areas, and coastal areas tend to be more susceptible to extreme weather events in the form of hurricanes (Wilson and Fischhetti 2010). In those areas, the concentration of infrastructure in coastal areas in many cities such as New York City (Zimmerman and Faris 2010; Zimmerman 2012b) will require investments for greater protection against sea level rise associated with climate change and storm surge from increasing storm activity.

Equity and infrastructure investment needs

Equity issues arise in the form of infrastructure access, affordability, quality, impacts near infrastructure facilities, and processes for obtaining and distributing infrastructure resources in the context of both the routine deployment of infrastructure and infrastructure considerations in extreme events. Below are just a few illustrations.

Palaniappan et al. (2006, p. 117) identify a number of global justice issues in water resources connected with access, pointing out that, worldwide, the number of people without access is about 2.5 billion for sanitation and over 1 billion for safe water supply. With respect to the quality of water supply in developing countries, these authors cite UN and WHO estimates for deaths from water-related diseases of over 2 million per year.

Considerable attention has been given to equity issues in the transportation infrastructure sector especially in the context of extreme events. Wright and Bullard (2007) clearly underscore some of the problems with transportation equity in New Orleans. They note that African Americans tend to have a much smaller share of car ownership than the US population as a whole; before Hurricane Katrina, these populations relied on public transportation (about a quarter); and there were disabled and elderly populations in the city that would have difficulty escaping (ibid., p. 190, citing other studies).

Zimmerman et al. (2007) reported that about 7.3 million elderly or one-fifth of the elderly population nationwide reside in counties in which at least one hurricane or tropical storm occurred during the 1995–2005 decade. Florida, in particular, has relatively high concentrations of both elderly and storms. The elderly have generally less access to transportation, own relatively fewer cars, and usually need assistance when using transportation of any kind (Litman 2006).

Thus, prioritizing equity issues creates special infrastructure investment needs.

NEW INFRASTRUCTURE TO PROMOTE SUSTAINABILITY

Sustainability Objectives for Infrastructure

Infrastructure plays a key part in sustainability. This occurs particularly with respect to infrastructure's contribution to greenhouse gases (GHGs), which are a key measure of climate change and overall resource use. Thus any investment strategy for sustainable infrastructure needs to strive to reduce the GHG emissions and adverse effects of climate change to which infrastructure contributes.

Infrastructure contributions to greenhouse gases and climate change

Addressing climate change concerns and greenhouse gas reduction from infrastructure will require additional infrastructure investments. Transportation and energy sectors alone account for a substantial share of GHG emissions. Carbon dioxide, used as an indicator of all GHGs expressed as carbon dioxide equivalents, accounts for most GHG emissions. The US EPA (2014, pp. ES-7) found that in 2012 carbon dioxide accounted for 'approximately 82.5 percent of total greenhouse gas emissions'. Fossil fuels accounted for 94.2 percent of carbon dioxide GHG emissions in 2012 (ibid., pp. ES-8), and energy generation and transportation accounted for 40 percent and 34.4 percent of the GHG emissions within the fossil fuels category respectively (ibid., pp. ES-11). Waste and wastewater treatment processes also produce greenhouse gases (US Environmental Protection Agency 2014).

Resource use

Traditional infrastructure accounts for substantial use of natural resources such as energy, water and land. Reducing resource demand by infrastructure, a key input for urban sustainability, is likely to require new or reoriented infrastructure investments. In the transportation sector, energy intensity of alternative ways of providing infrastructure services is an important first step in understanding the benefits of alternative modes of travel, which have energy savings, as well as benefits from reducing transportation emissions. In addition to energy intensity, the use of different forms of energy by different infrastructure sectors provides a critical perspective on infrastructure resource use, and hence potential investment needs to manage consumption of those resources. For fossil fuels alone, according to the US Department of Energy (September 2012, p. 37), in 2011, 92 percent of coal, 100 percent of nuclear power and about a third of natural gas was used by the electric power sector and 71 percent of petroleum was used in the transportation sector (accounting for 93 percent of the energy in that sector) (updated from Zimmerman and Faris 2011, p. 184). On the other hand, renewable energy (discussed in more detail in the next section) was used by a number of infrastructure sectors, which potentially reduces resource use: about half of the renewable energy was used for electric power and about 13 percent was used for transportation (US Department of Energy September 2012, p. 37). Water use by other infrastructure sectors also illustrates resource use patterns that can have investment implications. The electric power industry consumption of water is exemplified by the fact that according to Averyt et al. (2011, p. 12) the average daily freshwater withdrawal of US water-cooled thermoelectric power plants in 2008 was 60 billion to 170 billion gallons and 5–10 percent of that was consumed.

Alternatives to Traditional Infrastructure and Cost Implications for Investment

Alternatives to traditional infrastructures tend to lower resource use and GHG emissions depending on how they are designed, and can, thereby, promote sustainability. Costs are difficult to assess overall, given the variety and relative newness of these options, but some initial estimates are provided.

Renewable energy

The renewable energy sector still accounts for under 10 percent of total energy use in the USA, according to the US Department of Energy, Energy Information Administration (US Department of Energy, September 2012) and recent statistics provided by the Intergovernmental Panel on Climate Change (IPCC) (Edenhofer et al. 2011, p. 9) indicate that renewable energy accounted for 12.9 percent of the supply of energy globally and 19 percent of the supply of electricity globally in 2008. Internationally, the United Nations Environmental Program (UNEP) (2011, p. 13) reports that financial investment in renewables has been increasing and between 2004 and 2010 the compound annual growth rate of investment in the entire renewables sector increased overall by 36 percent. They further report that solar energy has shown by far the largest investment increase of 91 percent; wind energy follows with a 43 percent rate (ibid., p. 13).

Streets as infrastructure finance engines

Streets are now extensively used to promote environmentally sustainable objectives not only for transportation but for energy and water use as well (Zimmerman 2012b). For example, stormwater control is now a well-known use for streets by taking advantage of using adjoining vegetation and porous pavement for water absorption. Although this is a widespread practice, Chicago is often cited as a notable example (US EPA 2010, p. 19). Streets are a means for waste recycling when recyclable materials are used for their surfaces, and New York City's attempt at using recycled glass for street surfacing material is one such initiative, although it met with obstacles (Zimmerman 2012b, p. 150). Other innovations in using streets for waste recycling include using plastic bags (ibid., citing Khullar 2009). Streets have been designed for multiple transportation modes through careful design and usage. They traditionally have been utility corridors or conduits for utility distribution lines. Finally, the use of street surfaces, parking lots and pavement to generate energy has been suggested that can then be used by vehicles using the streets (see references and description in Zimmerman 2012b, pp. 150–51). All these initiatives provide examples of promoting sustainability principles at the street scale.

The indirect economic benefits of street design can be substantial, generating private investment. For example, the NYC Department of Transportation (DOT) (2012, p. 4) found over a ten-fold increase in sales retail businesses following the installation of bike lanes in a study area in Manhattan.

In identifying key urban places, Davidson (2012, p. 15) describes the street as a financial engine, housing key bastions of economic development, singling out Grant Street in Pittsburgh as having played a key part in twentieth-century industry, with train stations, government buildings and office towers. Streets, he notes, became the focal point of local economies and their investment.

New innovative forms of infrastructure investment will be needed to achieve the sustainability goals for infrastructure described above. Although these innovative measures are now incorporated throughout many programs in the USA and beyond, the means to provide the infrastructure investment are often not apparent and are generally provided only on an ad hoc basis.

Alternative modes of transportation

Alternative modes of transportation create benefits not only in terms of reducing environmental emissions but also in terms of energy intensity savings. The US DOT, FHWA National Bicycling and Walking Study shows an increase not only in the use of bicycling but also a steady rise at the end of the first decade of the twenty-first century in its funding (US Department of Transportation 2010, pp. 5, 6). Whether this is sufficient to support biking innovations is yet to be seen. There has been a considerable infusion of private funds into biking, especially to support bike share programs by private vendors. This, and changes in the street networks needed to support biking in general, is usually funded by government agencies. Some data support the lower energy intensity of biking and walking. For example, the Sightline Institute (2008) gave a range of pounds of carbon dioxide as carbon dioxide equivalents per passenger-mile of practically zero for biking and walking, and identified the highest categories as single drivers in SUVs (1.6) and cars (1.2).

Financing Strategies to Promote Infrastructure Investment for Sustainability

Although traditional financing strategies abound in the infrastructure sector to promote both conventional and innovative infrastructure approaches, and extend from research and development (R&D) through usage, the mechanisms have not in the past been sufficient to cover the monetary shortfalls that ASCE and others have estimated, nor the costs of newer technologies to support environmental and security aims. The mechanisms include grants for R&D for new technologies, grants for planning and construction that have been typical of wastewater treatment plant and highway construction, loans and loan guarantees to producers (such as manufacturers) and users (such as residents and businesses), and various tax incentives. Other incentive systems, some bordering on regulatory requirements, exist to encourage alternative routing, timing and extent of use of infrastructure resources and services. There are also more broadly based financial structures such as infrastructure banking and revolving funds backed by government funds. For example, the

Clean Water State Revolving Fund has provided almost $10 billion in loans (US EPA 2014). The US CBO (2012) has described the structure, advantages and disadvantages of a federal infrastructure bank for surface transportation. The difficulty lies in designing financial mechanisms that can address distributional issues, that is, the relationship between those who bear the costs and those who obtain the benefits (both directly and indirectly). Regressive impacts are critical to avoid also for equity reasons. For the support of renewable resource-based infrastructure, paralleling the decentralization and dispersal of infrastructure that renewables have fostered is a decentralization of infrastructure financing. These technologies and their financing reach remote dispersed populations. Mohiuddin (2005–06), for example, underscores the role of microfinance for renewable resource use.

CONCLUSIONS

In conclusion, estimates for infrastructure investment needs are enormous and growing, as is the demand, especially given the newer demands that sustainability and resilience pose. A number of themes emerge as informing infrastructure investment strategies in light of sustainability. First, the growing backlog of the need for repair, replacement and renewal is pervasive across many types of infrastructure, and these undermine the ability to achieve sustainability, at least in the short term. Second, in order to be more effective in addressing the backlog, investment strategies need to be aware of dramatic changes that have been under way in how infrastructure is delivered to promote sustainability. Renewable resources and new modes of delivering energy, transportation and water are an important part of this. Technologies in these areas tend to move and change rapidly. These new technologies incur costs that are not always predictable and are initially high during the development stages. This suggests new approaches to investing in infrastructure that incorporate R&D. Third, different types of extreme events are increasing, whether in number, in severity of the consequences, or in the form they take. In spite of the trends in extreme events, changes in population distribution tend to increase the severity of the consequences. The events and their impacts tend to be magnified by infrastructure crises and society's dependence on infrastructure. Fourth, equity issues are a dimension of infrastructure financing that is pervasive and continuous. Thus, infrastructure finance is facing numerous challenges and sustainability and resiliency principles provide a unifying theme to guide new directions for financial resource strategies.

REFERENCES

Altshuler, A. (1989), 'Institutional investment', *Journal of Policy Analysis and Management*, **8** (3), 505–8.

American Public Transportation Association (APTA) (2013a), 'Public transportation investment background data updated, 8th edition', December 12, Washington, DC: APTA, available at http://www.apta.com/resources/reportsandpublications/Documents/Public-Transportation-Investment-Background-Data.pdf.

American Public Transportation Association (APTA) (2013b) *2013 Public Transportation Fact Book*, October, Washington, DC: APTA, available at http://www.apta.com/resources/statistics/Documents/FactBook/2013-APTA-Fact-Book.pdf.

American Society of Civil Engineers (ASCE) (2005), '2005 report card for America's infrastructure', available at http://www.asce.org/reportcard/2005/index.cfm (accessed 7 November 2005).

American Society of Civil Engineers (ASCE) (2009), '2009 Report card for America's infrastructure', available at http://www.infrastructurereportcard.org/2009/sites/default/files/RC2009_full_report.pdf.

American Society of Civil Engineers (ASCE) (2013), '2013 report card for America's infrastructure', available at http://www.infrastructurereportcard.org/a/#p/grade-sheet/previous-grade.

American Society of Civil Engineers (ASCE) (2011a), *Failure to Act: The Economic Impact of Current Investment Trends in Electricity Infrastructure*, Reston, VA: American Society of Civil Engineers.

American Society of Civil Engineers (ASCE) (2011b), *Failure to Act: The Economic Impact of Current Investment Trends in Surface Transportation Infrastructure*, Reston, VA: American Society of Civil Engineers.

American Water Works Association (AWWA) (2012), *Buried No Longer: Confronting America's Water Infrastructure Challenge*, Washington, DC: American Water Works Association.

Averyt, K., J. Fisher, A. Huber-Lee, A. Lewis, J. Macknick, N. Madden, J. Rogers and S. Tellinghuisen (2011) *Freshwater Use by U.S. Power Plants: Electricity's Thirst for a Precious Resource* Cambridge, MA: Union of Concerned Scientists, November.

Blake, E.S., C.W. Landsea and E.J. Gibney (2011), 'The deadliest, costliest, and most intense United States tropical cyclones from 1851 to 2010 (and other frequently requested hurricane facts): NOAA technical memorandum NWS NHC-6', available at http://www.nhc.noaa.gov/pdf/nws-nhc-6.pdf.

Burchell, R.W., A. Downs, B. McCann and S. Mukherji (2005), *Sprawl Costs. Economic Impacts of Unchecked Development*, Washington, DC: Island Press.

Copeland, C. and M. Tiemann (2010), *Water Infrastructure Needs and Investment: Review and Analysis of Key Issues*, Washington, DC: Congressional Budget Office.

Davidson, M. (2012), 'The thirty great places in America: neighborhoods, streets and public spaces', *Planning*, 12–17.

Dimock, M., C. Doherty and A. Kohut (2013), *Public's Policy Priorities: 1994–2013 Deficit Reduction Rises on Public's Agenda for Obama's Second Term*, Washington, DC: Pew Research Center for the People and the Press, available at http://www.people-press.org/files/legacy-pdf/01-24-13%20Prioritie%20Release.pdf (published online 24 January 2013).

Disaster Relief Appropriations Act, 2013, P.L. 113–2 (2013), Washington, DC: US Government Printing Office, available at http://www.gpo.gov/fdsys/pkg/PLAW-113publ2/pdf/PLAW-113publ2.pdf.

Doherty, C., A. Tyson and M. Dimock (2014), 'Deficit reduction declines as public priority', Washington, DC: Pew Center for People and the Press, January, available at http://www.people-press.org/files/legacy-pdf/01-27-14%20Policy%20Priorities%20Release%202.pdf.

Edenhofer, O., R.P. Madruga, Y. Sokona, K. Seyboth, P. Matschoss, S. Kadner, T. Zwickel, P. Eickemeier, G. Hansen, S. Schlömer and C. von Stechow (eds) (2011), 'Summary for policymakers', in *IPCC Special Report on Renewable Energy Sources and Climate Change Mitigation*, Cambridge, UK and New York: Cambridge University Press.

Edison Electric Institute (2012), *EEI Survey Shows Transmission and Distribution Investment*, Washington, DC: EEI, December 20.

Executive Office of the President, Office of Management and Budget (2012), 'Letter; appendix: detailed estimates of necessary federal resources', available at http://www.whitehouse.gov/sites/default/files/supplemental__december_7_2012_hurricane_sandy_funding_needs.pdf (published online 7 December 2012).

Federal Emergency Management Agency (FEMA) (2012a), 'Declared disasters by year or state', available at http://www.fema.gov/news/disaster_totals_annual.fema.

Federal Emergency Management Agency (FEMA) (2012b), 'Preparedness (non-disaster) grants', available at http://www.fema.gov/preparedness-non-disaster-grants.

Gramlich, E. (1993), 'Infrastructure investment: a review essay', *Journal of Economic Literature*, **32** (3), 1176–96.

Healy, A. and N. Malhotra (2009), 'Myopic voters and natural disaster policy', *American Political Science Review*, **103** (3), 387–406.

Heintz, J., R. Pollin and H. Garrett-Peltier (2009), *How Infrastructure Investments Support the U.S. Economy: Employment, Productivity and Growth*, Amherst, MA: Political Economy Research Institute (PERI), available at http://www.americanmanufacturing.org/files/peri_aam_finaljan16_new.pdf.

Hernandez, R. and P. Baker (2012), 'Obama proposes $60.4 billion storm-recovery bill', *The New York Times*, available at http://www.nytimes.com/2012/12/08/nyregion/obama-proposes-hurricane-recovery-bill.html (published online 8 December 2012).

Hulten, C.R. and R.M. Schwab (1995), 'Infrastructure and the economy', in J. Michael Pogodzinski (ed.), *Readings in Public Policy*, Cambridge, MA: Blackwell, pp. 213–34.

ICS-CERT (2014) ICS-CERT Monitor Oct-Dec 2013, available at https://ics-cert.us-cert.gov/sites/default/files/Monitors/ICS-CERT_Monitor_Oct-Dec2013.pdf.

Industrial Control Systems Cyber Emergency Response Team (2012), 'ICS-CERT monitor', available at http://ics-cert.us-cert.gov/sites/default/files/ICS-CERT_Monthly_Monitor_Oct-Dec2012_2.pdf.

Khullar, M. (2009), 'Plastic roads offer greener way to travel in India', *The New York Times*, available at http://www.nytimes.com/2009/11/14/ business/global/14plastic.html?_r=1&scp=1&sq=India%20roads%20from%20plastic&st=cse (14 November 2009).

Kirk, R.S. (2014), *Emergency Relief for Disaster Damaged Roads and Transit Systems: In Brief*, Washington, DC: Congressional Research Service, 28 January.

Klotzbach, P.J. and W.M. Gray (2013), *Extended Range Forecast of Atlantic Seasonal Hurricane Activity and Landfall Strike Probability for 2013*, Fort Collins, CO: Colorado State University, Department of Atmospheric Science.

Litman, T. (2006), *Lessons from Katrina and Rita: What Major Disasters Can Teach Transportation Planners*, Victoria, BC, Canada: Victoria Transport Policy Institute.

Mohiuddin, S. (2005–06), 'Expanding the role of microfinance in promoting renewable energy access in developing countries', *Georgetown Public Policy Review*, **11** (1), 119.

Navarro, M. (2012), 'New York is lagging as seas and risks rise, critics warn', *The New York Times*, available at http://www.nytimes.com/2012/09/11/nyregion/new-york-faces-rising-seas-and-slow-city-action.html (11 September).

New York City Department of Transportation (NYC DOT) (2012), 'Measuring the street: new metrics for 21st century streets', available at http://www.nyc.gov/html/dot/downloads/pdf/2012-10-measuring-the-street.pdf.

New York State 2100 Commission (2013), *Recommendations to Improve the Strength and Resilience of the Empire State's Infrastructure*, Albany, NY: New York State 2100 Commission.

Palaniappan, M., E. Lee and A. Samulon (2006), 'Environmental justice and water', in Peter H. Gleick (ed.), *The World's Water 2006–2007*, Washington, DC: Island Press, pp. 117–35.

Perry, D.C. (1995), 'Building the public city: an introduction', in D.C. Perry (ed.), *Building the Public City*, Thousand Oaks, CA: Sage, pp. 1–20.

Romero-Lankao, P. and D. Dodman (2011), 'Cities in transition: transforming urban centers from hotbeds of GHG emissions and vulnerability to seedbeds of sustainability and resilience', *Current Opinion in Environmental Sustainability*, **3** (3), 113–20.

Seley, J.E. (1983), *The Politics of Public-Facility Planning*, Lexington, MA: Lexington Books.

Shatz, Howard J., Karin E. Kitchens, Sandra Rosenbloom and Martin Wachs (2011), *Highway Infrastructure and the Economy Implications for Federal Policy*, Santa Monica, CA: The Rand Corporation.

Sightline Institute (2008), 'How low-carbon can you go: the green travel ranking', available at http://www.sightline.org/maps/charts/climate-CO2byMode.

Uchitelle, L. (2008), 'As public works languish, private cash sets the agenda', *The New York Times*, p. 1 and 'A shift in money', p. 18 (6 January).

United Nations Environmental Program (UNEP) (2011), 'Global trends in renewable energy investment', available at http://www.unep.org/pdf/BNEF_global_trends_in_renewable_energy_investment_2011_report.pdf.

US Census Bureau (2011), 'Population distribution and change: 2000 to 2010', available at http://www.census.gov/prod/cen2010/briefs/c2010br-01.pdf (accessed 21 November 2011).

US Census Bureau (2012), 'Table 781: Net stock of private fixed assets by industry: 2000 to 2009', available at http://www.census.gov/compendia/statab/2012/tables/12s0781.pdf.

US Congressional Budget Office (2007), 'Trends in public spending on transportation and water infrastructure, 1956–2004', available at http://www.cbo.gov/ftpdocs/85xx/doc8517/08-08-Infrastructure.pdf.

US Congressional Budget Office (2012), 'Infrastructure banks and surface transportation', available at http://www.cbo.gov/sites/default/files/cbofiles/attachments/07-12-2-InfrastructureBanks.pdf.

US Department of Energy (2009), 'Comparing the impacts of the 2005 and 2008 hurricanes on U.S. energy infrastructure', available at http://www.oe.netl.doe.gov/docs/HurricaneComp0508r2.pdf.

US Department of Energy, Energy Information Administration (September 2012), *Annual Energy Review 2011*, Washington, DC: US EIA.

US Department of Homeland Security (2009), *National Infrastructure Protection Plan*, Washington, DC: US Department of Homeland Security.

US Department of Homeland Security (2013), Written testimony of NPPD Office of Cybersecurity & Communications Acting Assistant Secretary Roberta Stempfley, and National Cybersecurity and Communications Integration Center Director Larry Zelvin for a House Committee on Homeland Security, Subcommittee on Cybersecurity, Infrastructure Protection and Security Technologies hearing titled 'Facilitating Cyber Threat Information Sharing and Partnering with the Private Sector to Protect Critical Infrastructure: An Assessment of DHS Capabilities', 16 May, Washington, DC: US DHS.

US Department of Transportation (DOT), Federal Highway Administration (FHWA) (2010), 'The national bicycling and walking study: 15-year status report', available at http://drusilla.hsrc.unc.edu/cms/downloads/15-year_report.pdf.

US Department of Transportation (DOT) (2008), *Status of the Nation's Bridges, Highways, and Transit Conditions & Performance*, Washington, DC: US DOT.

US DOT FHWA and Federal Transit Administration (FTA) (2012), *2010 Status of the Nation's Highways Bridges and Transit: Condition & Performance. Report to Congress*, Washington, DC: US DOT http://www.fhwa.dot.gov/policy/2010cpr/pdfs/cp2010.pdf.

US Department of the Treasury and The Council on Economic Advisors (2012), 'A new economic analysis of infrastructure investment', available at http://www.treasury.gov/resource-center/economic-policy/Documents/20120323InfrastructureReport.pdf.

US Environmental Protection Agency (EPA) (2000), *Development, Community and Environment. Our Built and Natural Environments*, Washington, DC: US Environmental Protection Agency.

US Environmental Protection Agency (EPA) (2008), *Clean Watersheds Needs Survey 2004 Report to Congress*, Washington, DC: US EPA.

US Environmental Protection Agency (EPA) (2010), *Green Infrastructure Case Studies:*

Municipal Policies for Managing Stormwater with Green Infrastructure, Washington, DC: US EPA, available at http://www.epa.gov/owow/NPS/lid/gi_case_studies_2010.pdf.
US Environmental Protection Agency (EPA) (2012), 'Clean water state revolving fund', http://water.epa.gov/grants_funding/cwsrf/cwsrf_index.cfm.
US Environmental Protection Agency (EPA) (2013), *Inventory of US Greenhouse Gas Emissions and Sinks: 1990 –2011*, Washington, DC: US EPA.
US Government Accountability Office (GAO) (2012), 'Cybersecurity: challenges in securing the electricity grid', Washington, DC: US Government Accountability Office.
US Government Accountability Office (2006) *Critical Infrastructure Protection: Progress Coordinating Government and Private Sector Efforts Varies by Sectors' Characteristics* GAO-07–39, Oct 16, Washington, DC: US Government Accountability Office. available at
US Department of Housing and Urban Development (HUD), Sandy Program Management Office (PMO) (2014), 'Monthly Public Financial Update', Washington, DC: US HUD, 23 January, available at http://portal.hud.gov/hudportal/documents/huddoc?id=HSTFSupp_Rpt123113.pdf
US White House (2013a), Presidential Policy Directive – Critical Infrastructure Security and Resilience, Presidential Policy Directive/PPD-21, February 12, Washington, DC: The White House, available at http://www.whitehouse.gov/the-press-office/2013/02/12/presidential-policy-directive-critical-infrastructure-security-and-resil
US White House (2013b), Presidential Proclamation 'Critical Infrastructure Security and Resilience Month, 2013', 31 October, available at http://www.whitehouse.gov/the-press-office/2013/10/31/presidential-proclamation-critical-infrastructure-security-and-resilienc.
Wilson, S.G. and T.R. Fischetti (2010), *Coastal Population Trends in the US: 1960–2008*, Washington, DC: US Census Bureau, available at http://www.census.gov/prod/2010pubs/p25-1139.pdf. The World Bank (2011), 'How much does infrastructure contribute to GDP growth?', *World Bank Research Digest*, **5** (4), 7, available at http://siteresources.worldbank.org/DEC/Resources/ 84797-1154354760266/2807421-1288872844438/7530108-1313070714827/GDP_Growth.pdf.
Wright, B. and R.D. Bullard (2007), 'Washed away by Hurricane Katrina: rebuilding a "new" New Orleans', in Robert D. Bullard (ed.), *Growing Smarter: Achieving Livable Communities Environmental Justice, and Regional Equity*, Boston, MA: MIT Press, pp. 189–214.
Zimmerman, R. (2009), 'Making infrastructure competitive in an urban world', *The ANNALS of the American Academy of Political and Social Science*, **626** (1), 226–41, doi: 10.1177/0002716209344842.
Zimmerman, R. (2012a), 'Critical infrastructure and interdependency revisited', in David G. Kamien (ed.), *The McGraw-Hill Homeland Security Handbook*, 2nd edn, New York: The McGraw-Hill Companies, pp. 437–60.
Zimmerman, R. (2012b), *Transport, the Environment and Security: Making the Connection*, Cheltenham, UK and Northampton, MA, USA: Edward Elgar Publishing.
Zimmerman, R. and C. Faris (2010), 'Infrastructure impacts and adaptation challenges', *Annals of the New York Academy of Sciences*, **1196** (1), 63–85, available at http://onlinelibrary.wiley.com/doi/10.1111/j.1749-6632.2009.05318.x/pdf.
Zimmerman, R. and C. Faris (2011), 'Climate change mitigation and adaptation in North American cities', *Current Opinion in Environmental Sustainability*, **3** (3), 181–7, doi:10.1016/j.cosust.2010.12.004.
Zimmerman, R., C.E. Restrepo, B. Nagorsky and A.M. Culpen (2007), 'Vulnerability of the elderly during natural hazard events', *Proceedings of the Hazards and Disasters Research Meeting*, Boulder, CO: Natural Hazards Center, pp. 38–40, available at http://www.colorado.edu/hazards/workshop/hdrm_proceedings.pdf.

8. Aligning fiscal and environmental sustainability

Richard F. Callahan and Mark Pisano

INTRODUCTION

The future of environmental sustainability will be driven by the capacity of local, state and federal levels of government to develop fiscal sustainability. For example, in the case of the Alameda Corridor in Los Angeles County environmental sustainability advanced only because of the fiscal sustainability of the project. The environmental improvements of reducing particulate car and truck pollutants, as well as remediation of underground water pollution, were financed by the innovative public–private partnership that generated revenues to pay for long-neglected environmental degradations (Callahan 2007).

The Alameda Corridor rail construction case illustrates a small but emerging set of cases showing local government leaders linking fiscal decisions to environmental issues (Wang et al. 2013), as well as the connection of public administration and environmental sustainability (Fiorino 2010). In research on leadership adaptation to fiscal stress, a recent set of case studies offered practical lessons for connecting fiscal and environmental sustainability (Pisano and Callahan 2012; 2013). These practices include: framing fiscal stress as a catalyst for addressing long-term natural resource needs, done recently in San Bernardino County; developing fiscal expertise before a crisis, in Los Angeles County; and more inclusive budget processes to develop trust, as found in the Whittier School District (Rubio-Cortes 2012). The findings from these and other cases offer actionable lessons for leaders in the public sector and communities to link environmental and fiscal sustainability. This chapter describes examples of fiscal sustainability that can fund environmental sustainability.

In part, this chapter draws on the recent findings from a three-year research project on local government fiscal sustainability funded by the Haynes Foundation. In this research, local government is not synonymous with small units of government. The eight case studies include a fiscal giant of local government, Los Angeles County, with over a $23 billion annual budget; San Bernardino, the largest geographic county in the USA; and the large cities of Long Beach (McGrath 2012b) and Santa Ana with populations of over 200 000 each, as well as smaller cities and school districts. The research findings from these cases develop from the following questions: do the findings on fiscal sustainability have implications for the understanding of environmental sustainability? Do the findings on fiscal decision-making processes and strategy offer insights for institutional design and strategy that shift from short-term outlooks to accounting for long-term fiscal and environmental impacts?

This chapter's findings illustrate an interconnectedness of local government fiscal sustainability and environmental fiscal sustainability. One of the cases, San Bernardino County (Pisano and Callahan 2013), offers a vivid example strategy in the context of budget shortfalls that nonetheless moved forward by bringing together city governments and other stakeholders to address long-term environmental needs, in particular water allocation and growth, through a general plan coordinated across various cities and county government.

This chapter outlines the nested relationship between fiscal sustainability and environmental sustainability in local and regional governments. Of practical application are the ways that the varied findings explain how leaders can change organizational behaviors through institutional redesign to advance both environmental and fiscal sustainability. If 'all politics are local', in the aphorism attributed to former Speaker of the House, Tip O'Neil, then all environmental impacts are likewise political with local impacts. The first section of this chapter addresses emerging practices of fiscal sustainability; the second section reviews the challenges of aligning fiscal and environmental decision making; the third section considers how to connect land use, housing, transportation and air quality; the fourth section offers a case study that links long-range planning and budgeting, including practices on water sustainability and an international fiscal study; the final section suggests three central features for effective political strategy to advance sustainability.

EMERGING PRACTICES FOR FISCAL SUSTAINABILITY

The evolution of budget deliberations has shifted fundamentally to a context of scarcity. No longer are there discussions of how to increase funding for expanded and new programs; rather, there is recognition of limited financial resources (Pisano and Callahan 2012) leading to a question of what can be funded. An expert panel review of the fiscal sustainability case studies outlined a conflict in world views as to whether the economic downturn is temporary, calling for fiscal strategies that bridge the gap in revenues until an upturn, in contrast to a view that the downturn is permanent with continued fiscal deficits.

Research forecasts a new normal of increasing fiscal constraints for decades, driven by revenue stagnation and demographics of aging taxpayers (US GAO 2012; Pisano 2013). Additionally, there are pressures that are cyclical, structural and intergovernmental (Chapman 2008), coupled with expectations from residents wanting increased services with decreased taxation (Korey 2011). These constraints suggest the need to rethink policies developed in times of relative abundance. The duration of fiscal stress at all levels of government – but experienced most harshly at the local and state levels, where operating deficits are not constitutionally permissible – will drive transformation and change. The cases researched on fiscal sustainability suggest practices that shift from short-term focuses to decision-making processes that account for long-term impact. The lessons from research on eight case studies of fiscal sustainability (Callahan 2012; Pisano and Callahan 2012; McGrath 2012a; 2012b; Rubio-Cortes 2012; Pisano and Callahan 2013) collectively suggest the following effective practices:

1. Leadership needs a robust understanding of fiscal sustainability. For some, sustainability simply refers to the ability to balance the budget from year to year. There are conceptual and practical limits in considering sustainability as simply balancing the budget through expenditure reductions. The complexity of intergovernmental financial flows, the need to understand enterprise financing and variable economic conditions, requires an increasing fiscal literacy.
2. Long-term thinking needs to account for the full cost of projects both for construction and lifetime maintenance for capital projects of collective bargaining, and of externalities. The difference between budgeting and fiscal sustainability was addressed by Los Angeles County leadership using the following definition: 'include only known resources in the annual budget and make decisions based on long term and full costing; manage strategically to maximize resources; and develop partnerships and innovation in financing to accomplish the needs of the county'. This approach has led to fiscal integrity that keeps options open for future generations, potentially a transformative redefinition of budgets.
3. Trust is a journey. Earning and retaining trust as a 'reserve', allows public organizations to be sustained in a variable financial world. The leadership of the Whittier Union High School District exemplified the practices of building trust in the community in both educational quality and the effective management of financial resources.

Leadership practices of transparency, meaningful engagement and effective communication increased trust that enabled difficult public elections on property tax increases to succeed in difficult economic times.

4. Leaders change the organizational culture to advance fiscal integrity. Organizational culture developed from committing to fiscal integrity, working across departments and programs, engaging key stakeholders as problem solvers, developing administrative expertise, and shifting toward risk-adverse fiscal models. Finally, clear and transparent executive accountability is needed to for difficult decision making, efficient execution and adherence to budget targets.
5. There is a need to see fiscal sustainability as part of a system. The systems view provided an analytical framework to identify leverage points that can affect outcomes in the long term. Leadership both reduced the cost of services and developed innovative ways to maintain services. A systems approach integrated initiatives, found economies of scale, developed incentives, and identified impacts across silos, departments and units of a jurisdiction.

THE CHALLENGES OF ALIGNING FISCAL AND ENVIRONMENTAL DECISION MAKING

The first practical, but surprisingly difficult, step for connecting fiscal and environmental sustainability is to confront the actual reality. The lack of alignment between fiscal and environmental sustainability results from societal discussions trapped in outdated ways of thinking and acting. Conventional practice in the public sector at the local, regional, state and federal levels does not connect fiscal and environmental sustainability. Current governmental practices create an adversarial context between fiscal and environmental sustainability. Elected officials conduct budget deliberations and environmental impact reports in separate contexts and in different public hearings. The processes for fiscal issues and environmental issues differ in the authorizing legislation, with divergent practices evolving over the past several decades.

Similarly, local government processes typically do not connect comprehensive general plans with the budgeting activity of local and state government. Comprehensive land-use and transportation plans have long-term horizons; budgets seldom extend beyond one year. Good comprehensive plans are linked to a business plan with return on investment calculations needed for fiscal sustainability. The budgets of state and local/regional governments are year to year, with the Legislative Analyst of the State of California looking ahead five years. Comprehensive plans, as well as environmental plans, look at the effects of demographic cycles on their decisions. All budget practices at the local and state levels fail to look at the changing demographic cycles and fail to rethink fundamental assumptions.

The challenge in fiscal and environmental sustainability is linking these unconnected elements. This linkage would leverage assets for long-term outcomes, measurable in time and amount. Framing the public sector decision-making processes as a strategy puzzle that considers the range of assets provides a context for considering the budget and the environment as a set of assets rather than two distinct sets of constraints. A range of examples in transportation and air quality at the regional and federal levels offers evidence of the disconnection between financing and environmental approvals. Spending on transportation planning and environmental documents on environmental externalities can have a statement of overriding consideration, ultimately making it hard to realize the desired goals. In California, as well as in the federal system, institutional design penalizes itself by not linking environmental sustainability with fiscal sustainability.

In project decision making, sustainability calls for developing a business plan for the project that is based on the utility of the investments, the amount consumers are willing to pay, and building the project on this agreed financial structure. The Alameda Corridor and the toll roads in Orange County were planned and developed using a business plan model. These projects were required to achieve transportation, environmental and equity goals before being included in the Regional Plan of SCAG that conformed to the region's air quality plan. Finally, these projects align those who benefit with those who pay. This approach to project development requires users and consumers to be supportive and willing to pay for project development.

CONNECTING LAND USE, HOUSING, TRANSPORTATION AND AIR QUALITY

There are examples that link land use, housing, transportation and air quality with encouraging results. The blueprint of strategies of the Southern California Association of Governments and the Sacramento Area Council of Governments that linked transportation, energy and air quality showed gains in all aspects at a reduced cost, leading to the passage of state law SB 375 that required development of the Sustainability Community Program. Each region has developed a long-range land-use plan that links new development patterns with transportation investments. A practical step has been the focus of these plans on outcome-based processes. The combined sustainability strategy was required to demonstrate vehicle miles traveled, CO_2 emissions and energy consumption reductions. Connecting more efficient land use with transportation improvements benefits each and can be accomplished at less cost.

In the case of SCAG, the regional land-use plan was based on a regional return on investment strategy that linked land-use policies and transportation investments to return on investments calculations that would provide economic and financial sustainability. The distinctive feature of the *2012 SCAG Transportation Plan* was the effort to work with local government through workshops at the local, sub-regional and regional levels, as opposed to imposing mandates on local government. The sustainability of the environmental goals became linked to developing shared commitments across local governments. Building the regional plan from the bottom up was made possible by the regional systems modeling and information processes. CO_2 reductions of the regional plans are submitted to the Air Resources District for approval as part of the state's climate change initiative.

Financing remains the ultimate test of whether a sustainability strategy that is less costly can be implemented, which means that annual fiscal and budgeting decisions remain in place. If sustainability strategies can be shown as less costly, and have a positive return on investment (ROI) calculation, then revenues can be generated by the participating entities. Revenues can be derived by jurisdictions providing they have the right institutional design to captures these efficiencies and ROI. The lessons learned from the budgets in the case studies suggest practices for the 186 jurisdictions in the SCAG and the 27 jurisdictions in the SACOG region to help formulate approaches that capture revenues, creating budgets that are more sustainable.

Infill development with mixed use that is distributed throughout the region is the dominant urban form in these strategies. While the state has eliminated redevelopment as a tool for financing, there are a number of other California statutes that have been enacted in the past and can be used now, such as the Infrastructure Financing Investment Act and the Infrastructure Financing Act or Assessment Districts. Another possible source for financing the investments for these sustainability plans is the Cap and Trade Program that the State of California has developed to assist in implementing the state's Climate Change Program. The Air Resources Board (ARB) charges emitters of CO_2 and pays reducers. If the resulting emission reductions of the regional sustainability program are achieved, and are cost-effective as envisioned, the cities and counties could obtain resources under the Cap and Trade Program for these investments. To be successful, these financing provisions require new institutional designs.

The lessons gained from the case studies become a way to develop institutional designs that realize fiscal gains.

LINKING LONG-RANGE PLANNING AND BUDGETING: A SURVIVAL GUIDE

The leadership of the County of San Bernardino had struggled with the economic downturn and public corruption issues in the past decade. This county, perhaps more than any other area of the country, has been shocked by the economic transformation of the country: housing bubble burst, industrial closings and military base closures, and other dysfunctional internal stresses. The major city in the county, the City of San Bernardino, has filed for bankruptcy. The county turnaround began with new leadership (Pisano and Callahan 2013) that outlined a ten-year budget plan framework to project the future costs of previously adopted policies. Starting in 2010, the county leadership initiated reform and transformation that directly link long-range planning with long-range budget reform. The practical steps that leadership in San Bernardino County applied were similar to other cases, particularly the County of Los Angeles:

- included only actual – not projected – revenues;
- considered the long-term costs and revenue projects;
- calculated life-cycle costs in developing the general fund budget;
- developed partnerships beyond the current budget year.

The linkage between budgetary and environmental sustainability in this case study offers evidence for the possibility of success in times of profound fiscal stress. The most important practical step for the County of San Bernardino County's chief executive officer was to engage all the public jurisdictions and districts in a long-run growth and development discussion. The county used the staff, skills, and tools of planning and communications within the county government and across the cities in the county. The Council of Governments for the county convened a process that developed an economic growth strategy as well as a partnering strategy with cities and the county in this vast geographical area to share in the delivery of services and the management of parks. Key in the long-run vision were the issues of housing foreclosures and water supply. The plan operationalized annual targets and milestones that had budgetary consequences tied back to the county-elected and -appointed officials' deliberations on the long-run budget.

The partnership strategy that is essential in resolving fiscal and environmental sustainability is found in the County of San Bernardino. Its leadership demonstrated that fiscal sustainability and environmental sustainability do not have to be separate decision-making processes. Along similar lines, the budgetary process is linking a county-wide coordinated city and county general plan to assist in the resolution of the housing and economic base rebuilding. An important innovation tested in the county-wide plan was the inclusion of a pioneering initiative in the City of Ontario. This initiative included in the general plan an economic strategy as its foundational starting point for zoning. The city started with an economic strategy that would support the needs of its citizens as well as the fiscal long-term needs of the city. A key element of the plan was the development of the airport infrastructure of Ontario Airport and the related logistics sector that springs from it. The city- and county-coordinated plan extended Ontario's approach to the joint county-wide effort to rebuild the economic base of the county and the adjacent County of Riverside. A strategy for revitalizing the housing stock, devastated by the housing market collapse, also included use of the Sustainable Cities Strategy of the SCAG Regional Transportation Plan.

The County of San Bernardino leadership concluded that the issue that most threatened both future fiscal and environmental sustainability was water supply – not surprising for a desert region. As part of the visioning effort, the water agencies were charged to develop a strategy that would address this issue through coordination and cooperation of all entities within the vast region. The approach deliberately did not just rely on past practices of water management, acquiring water from beyond the region. Strategies of conservation, new urban development forms, changes in the economic base that are less demanding, reuse of the scarce resource, capture of runoff and green development were all considered. Lastly, costs and financing that would need to be part of the annual budgeting process of jurisdictions and faced by consumers and businesses were a major consideration, so as not to jeopardize the county's competitiveness. Actions needed to develop a more sustainable, diverse and decentralized water supply will require new ways of doing business in the future.

The approach taken in San Bernardino is now being extended to other parts of Southern California. The Metropolitan Water District's Blue Ribbon Committee MWD 2060 developed a similar strategy for the entire region. The key design feature of this regional strategy is decentralized activity that relies on more efficient and lower-cost strategies emerging through new institutional design, similar to the practices being followed in the examples of air quality and transportation.

Shifting to an international example, fiscal sustainability research partners in Germany have identified decentralized sustainability programs where municipalities are a key building block for these initiatives. The research team that conducted the local government fiscal sustainability case studies has undertaken a joint research program with the University of Kehl, to explore how fiscal and environmental sustainability are being implemented. Germany requires that all budgets have a three-year time horizon. The City of Freiburg, which is in the research area, has voluntarily extended this to a ten-year time frame for many of the reasons cited in the above examples. The development of policy for solid waste disposal is an example of linking environmental sustainability and cost reductions in that city's long-term budget.

POLITICAL STRATEGY TO ADVANCE SUSTAINABILITY

Fundamentally, the question for fiscal and environmental sustainability is: how does cooperation emerge in a political environment that presently is highly charged? This challenge is shared across contemporary American experience with constitutional democracy as characterized by turbulence and a search for reasonableness (Newland 2012). In effect, the challenge of accounting for fiscal and environmental sustainability in a turbulent public decision-making processes is the challenge of politics.

As part of a political strategy, innovations in technology have proven effective in advancing sustainability. Technological advances, in part, mitigated the dire forecasts of the Club of Rome report in the 1970s. Changes in technology involve risk, further emphasizing the need for a political strategy that focuses on risk identification, risk mitigation and risk management, and away from risk avoidance. To accomplish this change, procurement processes will need to become outcome based and not specification based and employ the same systems, life-cycle and institution design principles. The system evaluation capacities that have been developed in space and military successes by the Aerospace Corporation for NASA and the US Air Force can be adapted for domestic needs and environmental needs. The National Academy of Public Administration, undertaking institutional and policy design, and the Aerospace Corporation, undertaking systems and technical evaluations, have developed a partnership to advance this connection.

In effect, challenges of a transforming context and turbulent public decision-making processes are challenges of politics. What is missing is political strategy on how to develop a constituency for fiscal and environmental sustainability and the tools to link these constituencies. Developing a constituency for environmental and fiscal sustainability is difficult to attain for our collective goods goals because we have not linked these objectives to implement either. This has been done in the national cultural changing constituency for clean air, water and parks over the past several decades. The constituencies across a range of stakeholders, individual and associations, for environmental protection emerged only in the 1960s. At the core of various ideologically driven questions is the uncertainty of a future capacity to pursue fiscal and environmental sustainability.

Developing constituencies for fiscal sustainability calls for a transition from partisan politics to a strategy that includes a range of associations, from environmental, fiscal watch dogs, business, government and labor, and individuals who are not transitory but can regularly engage, over a period of a decade or more, in policy-making discussion and electoral politics. San Bernardino County's approach is an example. A strategic approach will engage citizens beyond special-purpose interest to use all resources, both environmental and financial, in more effective ways. Moreover, the need to look long term will bind these interests into a set of mutual interdependencies that will require trust building, which was the case in Los Angeles County, where the pension negotiations that followed these characteristics have generated a sustainable large-scale pension program (Pisano and Callahan 2012).

Strategy also needs to communicate the similarity of the rules of the game – in effect the institutional features common to both fiscal and environmental sustainability, as well as the need to redesign institutional features to move from ineffective path dependency. More effective communication is needed to deal with the fiscal and financial debt threat at all levels of government. As part of a communication strategy, iterative dialogue through learning forums (Moynihan 2008) offers tangible practices that can improve performance over time. The practices of effective communication include discussion of the long-term impacts, the use of the tools of system planning, information systems, pricing and consumer information. This iterative dialogue can develop an organizational culture that engages each of the sectors, creates a political strategy that binds us together and reverses the divisions that are pulling us apart.

The strategy that is emerging from all the cases and examples described above is to complement the use of existing revenues derived from our tax base with partnerships and the nexus of beneficial use payments of consumers. The dynamics needed are to align the beneficiaries who are consumers and taxpayers. When this is done, individuals become the decision makers and, in the process, over time, both change their behavior and become part of the problem solving of both issues. More revenue is brought to the table and more problem solvers are involved and new coalitions emerge. Ignoring this strategic approach and failing to add capacity to address the common goods results in those who are affected most, the disadvantaged, suffering the greatest harm. The inability to build a political solution to the fiscal and environmental sustainability challenges will result in larger numbers of those least able to afford or absorb the impact being adversely affected. A political strategy is needed to include more of the benefits of a sustainable society, to advance the three Es: economics, environment and equity.

CONCLUSION

Environmental sustainability has been disconnected from financial decisions, with budgets and financing operating with a short-term focus, not connected to principles of sustainability, and with both goals thought to be unattainable and incompatible. Our research on fiscal sustainability suggests the potential for practical steps that link environmental and fiscal sustainability in local government decision making. These are steps that in the aggregate can address the most fundamental challenges facing local, state and national levels of government.

The starting point is to change the decision-making process for both budgets and environment to outcomes and results that can be explained in ways that the public can relate to and understand without referencing specific programs, projects and initiatives. The tools of planning need to be used in both processes so that assumptions can be made explicit and understood, using a language that enables decision makers to anticipate both the immediate as well as the long-term costs. Given the advanced information and analytical tools that we have today, the long-term cost can include the externalities that decisions have on society where the impacts of one decision form part of the costs of another. Actual environmental and fiscal returns on investments can occur, for example in the City of Brea's purchase of a solar system built by Chevron on top of their city hall to reduce their electricity bill as part of their budget decision making (McGrath 2012a).

Getting life-cycle costs correct – including externalities – creates opportunities for more sustainability in project development. Aligning those who benefit with those who pay for new projects can also create fiscal and environmental returns on investments. This principle is based on a recent change, with world consumers of private and public goods becoming the primary decision makers. Coupling planning and information systems with a redesign of institutions will enable public sector leaders to replicate in the public space what is happening in the market space. These changes will enable individuals to be consumers, taxpayers and providers by changing their behavior.

Shifting from a perspective of environmental sustainability as an abstraction to the connection of fiscal sustainability practices in local government advances both concepts. The practical steps outlined in the chapter advance a connection of environmental and fiscal sustainability, facilitating future iterations of the budget processes to use environmental and fiscal resources more wisely.

REFERENCES

Callahan, R.F. (2007), 'Governance: the collision of politics and cooperation', *Public Administration Review*, **67** (2), 290–301.

Callahan, R.F. (2012), 'Moving beyond magical thinking: finding leadership, strategy, and fiscal sustainability in local government', *National Civic Review*, **101** (1), 8–10.

Chapman, J.I. (2008), 'State and fiscal sustainability: the challenges', *Public Administration Review*, **68** (S1), S115–S131.

Fiorino, D.J. (2010), 'Sustainability as a conceptual focus for public administration', *Public Administration Review*, **70** (S1), S78–S88.

Korey, J.L. (2011), 'California: a failed state or too big to fail?', *The California Journal of Politics & Policy*, **3** (2), 1–21.

McGrath, M. (2012a), 'Case study IV: fiscal sustainability and bottom-up change in Brea, California', *National Civic Review*, **101** (1), 30–34.

McGrath, M. (2012b), 'Case study II: fiscal sustainability and political culture in Long Beach, California', *National Civic Review*, **101** (1), 18–23.

Moynihan, Donald P. (2008), *The Dynamics of Performance Management: Constructing Information and Reform*, Washington, DC: Georgetown University Press.

Newland, C. (2012), 'Values and dignity in public administration: post NPM global fracture and search for human dignity and reasonableness', *Public Administration Review*, **72** (2), 293–301.

Pisano, M. (2013), 'Demography is Economic Destiny', America 2050, Regional Plan Association, pp. 3–4.

Pisano, M. and R.F. Callahan (2012), 'Case study I: fiscal sustainability in Los Angeles County', *National Civic Review*, **101** (1), 11–17.

Pisano, M. and R.F. Callahan (2013), 'County of San Bernardino', *National Civic Review*, **102** (1), 3–6.

Rubio-Cortes, G. (2012), 'Case study III: Whittier Union High School District fiscal solutions', *National Civic Review*, **101** (1), 24–9.

Southern California Association of Governments (1994), *Regional Comprehensive Plan*, Los Angeles, CA: SCAG.

Southern California Association of Governments (2004), *Compass: Charting the Course for a Sustainable Southland*, Los Angeles, CA: SCAG.

Southern California Association of Governments (2008), *Comprehensive Regional Plan*, Los Angeles, CA: SCAG.

United States General Accountability Office (US GAO) (2012), 'State and local fiscal outlook: April 12th update', available at http://www.gao.gov/assets/590/589908.pdf.

Wang, X., C.V. Hawkins, N. Lebredo and E.M. Berman (2013), 'Capacity to sustain sustainability: a study of US cities', *Public Administration Review*, **72** (6), 841–52.

9. Gauging the health of a city: maximizing health and sustainability

Alek Miller and Richard J. Jackson

INTRODUCTION

'Sustainable development is development that meets the needs of the present generation without compromising the ability of future generations to meet their own needs' (UN WCED 1987). As the United Nations World Commission on Environment and Development defines sustainable development, it is clear that the primary reason to work for sustainability is to bolster the well-being of people across time. Sustainability and health go hand in hand in pursuit of this goal. However, organizations employ a wide variety of strategies that fall under the umbrella of environmental sustainability and that sometimes fail to consider their implications for human health. Not every measure that is sustainable is necessarily healthy and the reverse is also true: not everything that is healthy is also sustainable. The goals of this chapter are three-fold: to explain how health is affected by physical and social conditions of urban life; to discuss the intersection of sustainability and health; and to identify and critically examine tools for measuring health and sustainability at each level of the built environment. This chapter will first introduce a few basic concepts of public health that will be useful for the academic, practitioner, student, policy maker, or layperson concerned about sustainability – for present and future generations. In discussing tools for evaluating these strategies, the chapter will also address the gray area where sustainability and health do not align in order to promote thoughtful critique of the tools we use for the lofty goals of promoting the well-being of future generations and the planet.

DEFINING HEALTH

Since 1948, the World Health Organization has defined health as 'a state of complete physical, mental, and social well-being, and not merely the absence of disease or infirmity' (WHO 1948).[1] This emphasis on the interconnectedness of individual health and the social environment is critically important for public health. The Institute of Medicine defines public health as 'what we, as a society, do collectively to assure the conditions in which people can be healthy' (IOM 2002). Assuring the conditions in which people can be healthy includes understanding and advocating for a built environment that facilitates, rather than impedes, health. This is a broad definition that includes ensuring the well-being of current and future generations and has a parallel in the goals of sustainability.

As authors in earlier chapters have noted, the city is the primary habitat for people today. As the world's population becomes more urbanized, the consequences of urban planning and public policy become magnified. High density is often touted as a key strategy for making cities more sustainable, in part by reducing the need for travel and concentrating infrastructure and resources (Eidlin 2010). However, high density in cities causes more people to be exposed to environmental risks. For example, when neighborhoods located near pollution sources – such as a highway or a polluting factory – are densely populated, the large number of people exposed magnifies the ill effects of the pollutants from those sources. As a recent analysis by Schweitzer and Zhou (2010) demonstrates, the evidence about the health effects of infill and compact development when it comes to their effect on air quality is mixed. These types of urban form may reduce emissions from mobile sources, but they can also concentrate people where air quality is poor, exposing greater numbers to risks. The number of people exposed to ozone and fine particulate matter remains high in compact neighborhoods (Schweitzer and Zhou 2010). On the other hand, the health benefits from measures to improve sustainability in cities are multiplied as well. By promoting active modes of travel, thereby reducing the amount of auto traffic and cold starts that take place in and around densely populated neighborhoods, high numbers of people can benefit. For this reason, increased density as a goal of sustainability and a fact of an urbanizing world must be approached with an understanding of public health goals and strategies.

Urban planning emerged as a discipline with complementary goals to those of public health in a quickly urbanizing USA. In 1664, zoning was first used to separate land uses in order to protect the health of the people living near 'noxious sites', and to protect land values. Zoning has been a widely used tool for separating uses in the USA since New York City adopted the first comprehensive zoning ordinance in 1916. Although it fulfills many goals, including mitigating the risks of investing in real estate, zoning has also long been used as a tactic for containing disease and the hazards of industry (Maantay 2001).

CONCEPTS FOR UNDERSTANDING DISEASE AND INJURY

In the field of public health, there are concepts that are important to understand when thinking about the effects of planning decisions on public health. First, public health examines outcomes at the level of populations, which can be at the level of a city, neighborhood, group of employees, racial or ethnic group and so on (Gordis 2009). This means that public health is well equipped to examine long-term trends that accompany measures to promote sustainability and climate change.

DESCRIBING OCCURRENCE OF DISEASE AND INJURY

At the level of a population, disease and injury are measured in terms of incidence and prevalence. Incidence measures the number of new cases of a disease occurring over a given period of time. Prevalence gives a snapshot of the proportion of people in a population affected by a disease at a given time at any point in their treatment, so prevalence includes new cases and people who have been affected for some time (Gordis 2009). These two concepts are important for understanding how public health studies and professionals describe the occurrence of disease and injury – while prevalence tells us how widespread a disease or phenomenon is, incidence tells us the rate at which new people are becoming affected.

PREVENTION

As the old adage goes, an ounce of prevention is worth a pound of cure. This is true, but there is an important distinction to be made between the types of prevention: primary, secondary and tertiary. Primary prevention is prevention in its truest sense: that is, reducing or eliminating exposure to a risk factor. Secondary prevention is early detection of a disease, while tertiary prevention is reducing the harm of the disease. To many public health professionals, primary prevention has great promise, especially when it comes to human health and the built environment. By preventing exposure to risks, urban planning for sustainability offers some promise for improving human health at the city level.

HOW DOES URBAN PLANNING INTERACT WITH PUBLIC HEALTH?

The built environment interacts with social cues, behavioral choices and genetics to create both negative and positive health outcomes – in physical activity, occurrence of injury and death (as a result of motor vehicle accidents), in nutrition (including access to healthy food), in social capital, in mental health, and a wide range of others.

Physical Activity

First, in terms of physical activity, the built environment is a major factor in determining who has the opportunity to commute, socialize and play outdoors. Cities that are planned to prioritize automobile travel may make pedestrian and bicycle commuting unappealing and dangerous, thereby eliminating one very important type of incidental physical activity that has been a part of daily life for centuries. Consider the policy of many cities that mandates that businesses provide a minimum number of parking spots for automobiles, but no minimum amount of space for bicycle racks or requirements for pedestrian-friendly entrances: these policies perpetuate the idea *and the reality* that driving is truly more convenient than active modes and, importantly, that each car trip has a low marginal cost (Manville and Shoup 2004). These policies limit the amount of incidental physical activity that people can get in daily life and contribute to a sedentary lifestyle. A sedentary lifestyle is a contributing factor for several chronic diseases that have increased in prevalence over the past several decades, such as type 2 diabetes and some cancers (Manson et al. 2004). Additionally, cities that offer little open space reduce the options that residents have for passive and active physical activity. Open space for recreational activity is also efficient at meeting other necessary environmental goals, such as absorbing water runoff and maintaining biodiversity.

Injuries and Death

The risks of injury and death are also influenced by the planning decisions made in cities. One unfortunately common example of this is the leading cause of death for people between the ages of five and 34: motor vehicle crashes (Centers for Disease Control 2011). In the USA, over 30 000 people were killed in motor vehicle crashes and many more people were injured in 2010, some of which could be prevented or made less severe with more careful planning (National Highway Traffic Safety Administration 2011). To the extent that dispersed development increases vehicle miles traveled, which is correlated with an increased risk of injury and death in motor vehicle crashes, efforts to reduce vehicle miles driven could also have an effect.

Resiliency to Disasters

Policies related to planning and sustainability that influence injuries in cities include those standards that affect resiliency to disasters. Resilient buildings maintain their integrity in extreme weather and are more sustainable in the sense that they do not need replacement after major weather events. Resilient buildings can also prevent injuries and deaths in disasters. For example, puncture wounds are highly common injuries following hurricanes and tornadoes, typically from nails in buildings that do not withstand the extreme weather. Neighborhoods and cities that have resilient characteristics – both in physical durability and in culture and character – predict how humans fare in disasters. This will become increasingly important as extreme weather events become more common. Sustainability links long-term consequences of climate change to human health and wellness.

Nutrition and Access to Healthy Food

One of the major health problems facing the USA today is that of nutrition – Americans are becoming overweight or obese at unprecedented rates. In the USA, food insecurity is 'experienced when there is (1) uncertainty about future food availability and access, (2) insufficiency in the amount and kind of food required for a healthy lifestyle, or (3) the need to use socially unacceptable ways to acquire food'. At the household level, this condition contributes to overweight and obesity, and to anxiety and stress due to this uncertainty (National Research Council 2006).

Undoubtedly, this experience is linked to poverty and low income, but there is a spatial component to it that must be addressed as well. As part of a national effort to relieve food insecurity, the Healthy Food Financing Initiative was created in 2009. It is an interagency working partnership between the US Treasury Department, Agriculture Department, and Department of Health and Human Services. The working group defines a food desert as 'communities, particularly low-income areas, in which residents do not live in close proximity to affordable and healthy food retailers. Healthy food options in these communities are hard to find or are unaffordable' (US Department of Health and Human Services 2012). This reflects the spatial and community-level experience of food insecurity. Communities that experience high rates of food insecurity caused by a lack of access to healthy, affordable food choices often also experience an abundance of calorie-dense, unhealthy food choices. Intake of fruits and vegetables has been linked to proximity to supermarkets (Cannuscio and Glanz 2011, pp. 50–62). Rates of urban disinvestment escalated through the 1970s and 1980s, creating a trend toward fewer, larger supermarkets located outside city centers while 'price wars' drove many smaller grocers out of business. This trend toward focusing investment outside of cities because of negative assumptions about urban customers came to be known as 'supermarket redlining'. Urban areas saw a decline of major chain stores through the 1990s and, as one report notes, 'in 1995, the poorest 20 percent of urban neighborhoods had 44 percent less retail supermarket space than the richest 20 percent' (Eisenhauer 2011, pp. 126–8). This trend is compounded by the fact that supermarkets now often occupy many thousands of square feet and companies must buy enormous amounts of space to accommodate them and the accompanying parking lots required by cities.

Social Capital

Putnam defines social capital as 'the features of social organization, such as trust, norms, and networks that can improve the efficiency of society by facilitating coordinated actions' (cited in Eicher and Kawachi 2011, p. 118). The trustworthiness that people feel is present in their community correlates with rates of depression, but there is not an overwhelming amount of evidence of the causal relationship between social capital and health (ibid., pp. 117–28).

Bonding and bridging capital foster this feeling of trustworthiness and connection to community. Bonding describes the connection between socially homogeneous groups, such as people who share the same religious or political beliefs. Bridging describes connection between people from different groups. Bridging is also known as the 'strength of weak ties', as Granovetter described it, and plays a role in how safe people feel in public – bridging capital is best built through informal interactions (Eicher and Kawachi 2011, pp. 117–28). Eicher and Kawachi point out that, of course, the interaction of planning and social capital is most present where there are places where informal interactions between neighbors and community members can occur. These places – parks, restaurants, bars, grocery stores – may be intentionally included or zoned out of neighborhoods and communities, but must be considered as a contributor to the social capital and overall well-being that people feel in their community. Social capital plays a major part in the community-driven side of recovery from disasters, as social cohesion is important to the psychosocial and physical elements of recovery, and to the popular narrative of recovery.

Mental Health

Density has a range of effects on mental health. For example, consistent ambient noise detracts from the ability to concentrate and has been shown to contribute to stress, anxiety and behavioral problems in children. Crowding can contribute to aggression and violence by causing excessive, unwanted interactions between people. This aggression and violence, then, takes a profound toll on residents touched by it, particularly on children (Sullivan and Chang 2011).

On the other hand, density can also have positive effects on mental health. Mental health and social capital are highly interconnected in this way. Planning that enhances social capital by encouraging connection between neighbors also enhances mental health by reducing isolation. Walkability is associated with lower levels of depression (Sullivan and Chang 2011, p. 112). Additionally, access to open space and places to connect with nature has mental health benefits for people in dense, stressful environments and should be maintained in cities.

Extreme Weather Events and Health

Extreme heat and cold events, such as heat waves and blizzards, also interact with planning and public health in profound ways. Each year, more people die because of extreme heat events than because of any other type of extreme weather (Stone et al. 2010). This interacts with urban planning because communities that have sufficient social cohesion may be able to respond to these events by allowing vulnerable people to access a cooling center, such as the ones set up in many cities by community centers or senior centers.

For all these reasons, planners and policy makers should consider the nuanced effects that urban planning has on public health in seeking remedies for sprawl and promoting sustainability. Conducting planning and design projects with these consequences in mind could have significant upstream benefits.

SUSTAINABILITY AND HEALTH

As illustrated by the preceding section, the effects of urban planning on public health are complex and far-reaching. For this reason, measures that seek to promote sustainability should take public health into consideration. It is particularly useful to approach both problems at a range of scales. For example, reducing greenhouse gases at the regional level, which is a necessary step toward slowing climate change, will not combat social isolation. Nor can a quarter-acre community garden make the grand-scale impact that policy change can, but both and all scales of tools are necessary for creating a sustainable and healthy society. The following section will address problems in the built environment that affect human health. Each section will include possible solutions that support sustainability and public health at the scale of the building, neighborhood, city and region. The solutions include practices that are already in place, some that are more theoretical in nature, and are not meant to be a comprehensive guide to fixing these problems. Rather, we present a few solutions of a world of possibilities intended to be an inspiration for creating a healthier, more sustainable world.

Building Scale

Efforts to promote sustainability at the scale of the individual building are important for sustainability because the buildings where we work and live consume vast amounts of energy while affecting the health of people inside and outside of them.

The problem

Buildings can be responsible for making their occupants sick. When we say 'air quality', people typically think of smog and emissions that occur outdoors. But indoor air quality is important because people spend so much time indoors, in schools, offices, homes, restaurants and shops. The term 'sick building syndrome' describes a set of adverse symptoms that affect occupants during the time they are in a building where they live or work (Environmental Protection Agency 2012b). Sick building syndrome generally describes 'irritation of the nose, eyes, and mucous membranes; fatigue; dry skin; and headaches' (Frumkin and Fox 2011, p. 222). Sick building syndrome can be the result of several sources: poor outdoor air quality brought indoors; the acoustics and air flow of the building; emissions from products used inside; odors; and inadequate air flow.

Indoor air quality can also affect the health of occupants by inadequately protecting them from poor outdoor air quality, especially when buildings are located near major pollution sources, like highways and industrial areas. Even the most tightly sealed windows and doors allow particulate matter and other pollutants into buildings and, subsequently, lungs. Rates of childhood asthma are higher for children who live near highways and are exposed to a high volume of traffic-related pollution (Gauderman et al. 2005). Building intakes that are located near pollution sources are hazardous for human health and worsen indoor air quality.

One solution

The movement to 'green' workplaces and other buildings has made great strides, particularly in schools and hospitals. School and hospital designs that increase energy efficiency in an effort to be more sustainable have also found success in improving outcomes for students and patients. These are just two examples of the successful building-scale applications of principles of sustainability and public health. Air quality is a major component of making buildings more sustainable and healthy, although it is just one of many areas where programs have made improvements.

Schools Evidence tells us that academic performance improves when indoor air quality is well managed through proper ventilation and cleaning, operable windows, and monitoring temperature (Environmental Protection Agency 2012a). By managing air quality to reduce ozone, schools have seen reductions in student and teacher absenteeism, as well as improved teacher health and greater student achievement (National Research Council 2006).

Hospitals and health care settings Health care settings have great potential for affecting the environment because they consume about 4 percent of all energy produced in the USA (Zimring and DuBose 2011, pp. 203–15). In recent years, hospitals have embraced sustainability as a part of their mission to heal. 'Evidence-based design', or basing decisions about facility design on credible research, was part of creating the momentum to consider the design of health care facilities as a critical part of patients' experiences (ibid.). Alongside evidence-based design, the momentum has grown to reduce the environmental footprint of hospitals. Aside from air quality, hospitals have embraced other elements of sustainability, such as making access to views of nature and daylight a priority, which have been demonstrated to improve patient outcomes.

Neighborhood Scale

Neighborhoods accommodate a wide variety of uses. They are a major determinant of the air we breathe, how we obtain our food, and how we interact with neighbors. They are the beginning and end of most trips outside the home. Neighborhoods are the locus of human life in cities and any effort to promote sustainability must consider its effect on neighborhoods where people live.

Problem

Because neighborhoods are expected to fulfill so many responsibilities in our lives, it has become clear that auto-centric street design makes neighborhood streets inhospitable to other uses. Planners and designers have, in many cases, chosen to accommodate high speeds for automobile traffic and reserved space for parking at the expense of other valuable uses of public space. For example, auto-centric streets can be uncomfortable places to walk and bike; they can cause runoff of pollutants into nearby water bodies, and are unsafe and uncomfortable places to spend time. Auto-centrism is unhealthy for many of these same reasons, in addition to promoting a transportation mode that contributes to air pollution, causes injury and death, and discourages physical activity.

One solution

One strategy for changing the orientation of streets from cars to people is by pursuing 'Complete Streets' policies, which explicitly seek to fulfill the complementary goals of sustainability and health. Complete Streets ensure that streets are designed to serve people of all ages and abilities, and typically include space so that people can walk and bicycle, as well as drive, on public streets. Complete Streets policies should apply to both new projects and retrofit projects (National Complete Streets Coalition 2010). Because there is no prescriptive street design for Complete Streets, these policies can be especially useful for decision makers because they take local conditions and needs into account, such as the climate and other attributes of the local population. Complete Streets are sustainable because they promote non-motorized transportation modes, like walking and biking. They also often add vegetation and pervious surfaces to the streetscape to reduce the width of the street and capture runoff. Some cities, like Portland and Boston, use swales for this, which contribute to a stormwater management strategy.

Complete Streets benefit public health in several ways: they encourage physical activity by making streets safer for active transportation; they contribute to preventing or reducing the severity of injuries from auto accidents by reducing speeds; and they promote mental health and social capital by providing space for people to congregate and play.

City Scale

At the scale of the city, problems of health and sustainability are a concern because high numbers of people are exposed to health risks in densely populated areas. The governing bodies of cities also have great potential to promote innovative solutions to far-reaching problems and to regulate dangerous and unhealthy patterns of development.

Problem

At the city scale, two examples offer insights into the intersection of health and the built environment. First, public health professionals and environmental organizations have identified the 'urban heat island effect' as a major problem in cities. This effect is the phenomenon whereby temperatures of urban areas are consistently higher than those of surrounding, less-dense areas. This is attributed to the high volume of heat-absorbing asphalt and lack of vegetation. On average, cities can be 1–5.4 degrees Fahrenheit (°F) warmer than surrounding areas. This is a concern for public health because hundreds of deaths each year are attributed to excessive heat exposure (Centers for Disease Control and Prevention 2006). Additionally, higher temperatures, particularly in Los Angeles, lead to more smog, which also exacerbates health problems such as asthma (Horowitz 2011). The urban heat island effect also has serious implications for energy consumption because it increases demand for electricity for air conditioning. In fact, the effect is considered to be responsible for 5–10 percent of demand for electricity (Environmental Protection Agency 2008). The production of electricity, too, can degrade the air quality where it is produced, depending on its source. The self-perpetuating problems of the urban heat island effect and climate change present serious public health and environmental risks that demand action.

Second, the lack of local food production in cities in the USA presents a different type of challenge. The current system of agriculture, which necessitates the transport of food for hundreds of miles, contributes to food insecurity and climate change. Because of zoning policies and the high costs of building supermarkets in cities, some major grocery stores and distributors of fresh produce either cannot fit into older neighborhoods or choose not to because of perceived risks of investing in poor neighborhoods.

Solutions

Because of the vast amount of energy that buildings consume, and their tendency to absorb heat, cool roofs show some promise for addressing the urban heat island effect. By reducing the amount of energy buildings use in cities, and the amount of heat they emit, there is a great deal of potential for cool roofs and, especially, inexpensive cool roof coatings to have an impact on the urban heat island effect. Cool roof materials reflect heat away from buildings and have demonstrated energy savings of 10 to 70 percent. They are effective at reducing energy use in both warm and cool climates because net benefits from reduced cooling in the summer outweigh the small added need for heating in the winter (Environmental Protection Agency 2008).

Policies that encourage creation of urban gardens serve several complementary goals of sustainability and health. Urban gardens can promote productive, sustainable use of otherwise vacant land; they can reduce vehicle miles traveled (VMT) used for food production, and provide community members with low-cost fresh produce. The people who volunteer or work in urban gardens benefit from physical activity, contact with nature, and with each other. Urban gardens may also function as a gathering space and a reason to connect with neighbors, which builds social capital. Many community groups are working to combat the issue of food deserts and the abundance of calorie-dense fast-food restaurants from both sides of the problem. Many cities are capping the number of fast-food restaurants within their city limits, while others promote 'cornerstore conversions', which refers to assisting convenience store owners to stock healthy, fresh foods while remaining profitable (Public Health Law and Policy 2009).

Region Scale

As cities grow and spread, combining into hyphenated mega-metropolitan areas, their effects are felt throughout entire regions.

Problem

Air quality has an important impact on the lives of large numbers of people across regions. Motor vehicle travel is responsible for many of the pollutants that cause air pollution, in addition to stationary sources of pollution, like factories and refineries. Air pollution can cause adverse health effects and may exacerbate asthma symptoms in children and reduce lung function (Samet 2011, p. 72).

Solutions

Efforts to cut down on air pollution and greenhouse gas emissions at the regional scale can have positive consequences for the lives of people in cities. This is especially true for those who live and work near ports and highways, depending on strategies used for reducing greenhouse gases. For those strategies that are focused on mobile sources and the air pollution caused by travel, strategies may focus on reducing vehicle miles traveled (VMT) or on improving fuel economy of automobiles. Because the broadest gains for human health in cities will likely be found in strategies that reduce VMT, we focus on those strategies here.

There are several strategies to reduce air pollution at the regional level. Many planners suggest pricing road use through tolls or a VMT fee so that consumers can fully understand the costs of their travel. However, road pricing is often maligned as regressive and is not politically feasible on a broad scale. An alternative and complementary strategy is to improve public transit and ensure that alternative travel modes are safe and attractive. Some transit agencies work to entice more riders onto transit by making improvements to transit systems, which, of course, must be safe, clean, convenient and affordable to be effective. The federal Clean Air Act requirements have been bolstered by some statewide measures, such as California's Fleet Rule, which requires transit agencies and other government agencies with large vehicle fleets to retire or retrofit their vehicles by a certain point in time. Many transit agencies have also switched to compressed natural gas fuel to improve air quality and reduce diesel consumption. Meanwhile, other transit agencies have added filters to diesel buses for the remaining years of use. Reducing VMT accomplishes the complementary environmental goals of improving air quality and reducing greenhouse gas emissions. This strategy reduces harm from poor air quality and reduces risk of injury and death from traffic crashes.

TOOLS FOR MEASURING HEALTH IN CITIES

Long-term sustainability is a lofty goal for any individual, community or region; the best way for us to know if we are moving in the right direction is to develop tools that can measure our progress. Tools have been developed to measure the success of projects in becoming more sustainable at every scale. The following are a few stand-out examples.

Building Scale

At the scale of the individual building, the US Green Building Council's (USGBC) Leadership in Energy and Environmental Design (LEED) certification program has gained prominence over the past decade. LEED is a third-party system that certifies buildings as having been constructed using green building practices. The system encompasses a variety of these practices, such as water use and stewardship of resources, and emissions reductions. It has also evolved to take into account the different needs of buildings for different uses, rather than one catch-all certification. The USGBC now offers special categories of certification for homes, schools, health facilities, retail and even entire neighborhoods (USGBC 2012).

Some have cited the program's reliance on predicted results, rather than real performance, as a weakness (Cater 2010). However, in recent years LEED has begun requiring building owners to report energy use to maintain their status. The USGBC has also begun to include points in its certification system for qualities that affect the health of buildings' occupants, such as indoor air quality and acoustics (Cater 2010).

One alternative to the LEED system is the Living Building Challenge. This is another certification tool for developments at a wide variety of scales. Projects are certified after a year of operation, rather than prior to their use. The Living Building Challenge standards also include 'imperatives' standards that specifically aim to ensure development that is healthy for people, as well as sustainable. For example, development should be created to accommodate a walkable human scale, rather than one better suited to automobiles. Other imperatives also recognize the human need for democracy, social justice and contact with nature (International Living Future Institute 2010).

Building certification tools, while useful in some ways, also have their limitations. Buildings that are LEED certified tell a buyer or lessee that the building meets certain standards for energy efficiency and offer some basic certainty about how the building will consume energy and retain value over time. However, designing for efficiency alone may not be effective even in that aspect. For example, a building that uses very little energy for heating and cooling may inadvertently encourage inefficient habits in its occupants if they are uncomfortable – such as personal air conditioning units or heaters. Careful commissioning of buildings is also necessary to ensure that their systems are installed and operate as designed. Some improvements in efficiency, especially in ventilation, may improve the health of occupants, but can also overlook opportunities for biophilic design. The reverse may also be true – designing for health and comfort alone may overlook opportunities to make buildings more efficient.

Neighborhood Scale

At the neighborhood scale, two similar indices have been developed to describe walkability. WalkScore (2012) is a widely known, user-friendly index that rates neighborhoods on a scale of 1 to 100, with the highest scores being the most walkable. WalkScore primarily uses proximity of businesses to the address entered to determine its walkability. It has gained traction in the real-estate world and has been integrated into several real-estate websites in order to give prospective buyers and renters a sense of the neighborhood. This is a welcome development because it gives viewers a somewhat neutral basis on which to compare neighborhoods and to anticipate whether they will be able to include incidental physical activity in daily life. The developers also recently released BikeScore, the tool's bikeability counterpart.

WalkScore has been widely embraced in part because of its transparency.

The developers have been clear about how it works, and the places where flaws remain. For example, as a part of its algorithm, WalkScore uses the number of businesses in a neighborhood as a way to determine whether it is a 'walker's paradise', and whether most errands can be completed on foot. This can lead to overestimating the walkability of neighborhoods because it does not make a distinction between types of businesses. For example, a tattoo shop may provide a valuable service for some, but it does not necessarily make a neighborhood more walkable. However, like LEED and other similar tools, WalkScore has made great progress in making the tool more responsive to its users' needs, including by offering an apartment search application that specifically searches for places with groceries, schools and restaurants nearby.

A second example of neighborhood-scale tools for measuring sustainability and health, the Pedestrian Environmental Quality Index (PEQI), was developed by the San Francisco Department of Public Health (2012). The PEQI is used to measure a wide variety of characteristics that affect the pedestrian experience, including street design, intersection safety and land use. Importantly, the PEQI is implemented by trained observers and has the distinct advantage of capturing the subjective feelings of being on the street in a quantitative way. It is intended to help decision makers compare street segments and intersections in order to prioritize pedestrian improvements (San Francisco Department of Public Health 2012). Of course, this also means that it is not as easy to use for the broad audience that WalkScore can reach, but it serves a different purpose entirely.

Both of these tools are welcome additions to the conversation about sustainability and health. They allow us to compare neighborhoods and remind us that subjective experiences, such as how safe a street or a corner feels, make a difference to how we experience neighborhoods.

Neighborhood Scale and Larger

Health Impact Assessment (HIA) is a tool used to shine light on the health consequences of policies, programs and projects from the neighborhood up to the state and regional level (Board on Environmental Studies and Toxicology 2011). HIAs examine the ways that projects or policies might affect human health through a variety of pathways, including exposure to pollutants as well as social and economic relationships (UCLA 2008). HIAs include an emphasis on equity and eliminating health disparities, as well, by giving special attention to how health consequences will be distributed across the population. As a tool, HIAs are very flexible, and have been used by policy makers, community groups and private companies to anticipate the health effects of decisions prior to implementation

(Board on Environmental Studies and Toxicology 2011). The basic steps of an HIA involve identifying appropriate projects, the health effects that should be considered, and the people who will be affected. Next, recommendations are developed to mitigate negative health consequences and report to decision makers. Finally, the group conducting the HIA monitors the impacts of the HIA on the decision-making process (Dannenberg and Wendel 2011, pp. 309–12). HIAs are recommended by the US Department of Health and Human Services as part of implementing the interagency Healthy People 2020 program, in part because of the potential for reducing health disparities (US DHHS 2011).

HIA success story

Residents of Baltimore suffer from negative health outcomes at higher rates than other Marylanders, which results in comparatively shortened life spans and diminished quality of life. Within the city, too, there are vast health disparities between income and racial groups, with low-income and African American people faring much worse than their wealthier and white counterparts (Thornton et al. 2010). So, in 2010, when the City of Baltimore released a draft of its new zoning code for public comment, it presented an opportunity to influence decisions about the built environment where the city's residents' health is shaped. This was the first comprehensive revision of the zoning code in nearly 40 years. A group of researchers from several nearby universities collaborated with the Baltimore City Health Department to conduct an HIA to determine how a revision of the zoning code could influence health outcomes (Thornton et al. 2010; Salkin and Ko 2011).

In keeping with the spirit of HIAs' purpose, their report had two stated objectives: to inform stakeholders of the zoning code's potential for improving health outcomes; and to make recommendations for how the city could magnify the positive effects and minimize unanticipated negative consequences of changes to the code (Thornton et al. 2010).

The report that the research group produced is derived primarily from the first three phases of HIA. First, in the screening step of the process, they established that there was a need for a HIA in the first place. A literature review established that there is a strong relationship between zoning and health (Thornton et al. 2010). Next, the scoping step of HIA determines which health impacts should be evaluated in relation to the project or policy. An examination of public health data and interviews with experts revealed which negative health outcomes most affect Baltimore's residents and where disparities are most dramatic. Through the scoping process, the researchers determined that the most important health outcomes relative to zoning were violent crime, obesity and its related illnesses, physical activity and pedestrian safety, and diet and nutrition (Thornton et al. 2010).

The research from the first two phases of the HIA then informed the authors' recommendations. These were based on the proposed changes to the zoning code, an analysis of the percentage and distribution of the population that would be exposed to their effects, and a review of the literature to understand how those changes might affect the four health outcomes of interest (Thornton et al. 2010).

To their credit, the city planners who wrote the first draft of the revised zoning code considered many of the ways that the first changes to zoning code could affect Baltimoreans' health (Thornton et al. 2010). For that reason, each of the recommendations in the HIA includes a section highlighting 'supported changes' where the draft improves conditions from the existing code, as well as 'recommended revisions' where the code could go further to improve health. For example, in terms of crime, the HIA found that many of the changes to improve the pedestrian environment, such as promoting mixed-use and other design improvements, will likely reduce crime. However, without distinguishing between retail outlets that do and do not allow off-site alcohol sales in the definition of mixed-use retail, the authors raised a concern about the potential to increase the incidence of crime. They recommend reducing the number of retail outlets that sell alcohol for off-site consumption because of the proven correlation of this type of sale with increased violence. Their analysis also found that the draft code's changes would disproportionately negatively affect low-income Baltimoreans by concentrating liquor stores in their neighborhoods (Thornton et al. 2010).

This HIA is among the first that analyzes a comprehensive zoning code rewrite. Now that the final zoning code has been approved by City Council and published, the authors will be able to conduct the final step of the HIA – monitoring and evaluation, where they evaluate how their recommendations influenced the decision-making process and whether their recommendations are implemented as intended.

KEY ORGANIZATIONS AND PROGRAMS

There are several governmental and professional organizations that work to remedy the many problems at the intersection of health and the built environment, through creating sustainable and healthy solutions.

The federal government offers a few shining examples. First, the Centers for Disease Control and Prevention began the Healthy Community Design Initiative, which is part of the National Center for Environmental Health's

Division of Emergency and Environmental Services. The Healthy Community Design Initiative seeks to link urban design with health by educating decision makers and combining public health surveillance with community design. The Initiative also offers technical assistance on creating HIAs to communities (Centers for Disease Control and Prevention 2012). Next, the US Department of Agriculture has developed a toolkit that nonprofits and community planners can use to identify problems of food insecurity. The toolkit offers guidance on data collection and analysis and how to conduct a food assessment at the community level, as well as understanding how to analyze food insecurity at the household level (Cohen et al. 2002).

Professional organizations, such as the American Planning Association, have also embraced the mission to improve public health while making communities more sustainable. The American Planning Association's Planning and Community Health Research Center is a strong example of this commitment. This national research center brings together planners who want to build healthier communities by advocating for healthy policies, educating decision makers, and conducting research and outreach in service of that goal. The Research Center has also developed principles for creating healthy, sustainable food systems through collaborating with professionals from the Academy of Nutrition and Dietetics, the American Nurses Association and the American Public Health Association (American Planning Association 2012). By facilitating these cross-disciplinary collaborations, professional organizations like these are making great strides to put a wide variety of skills to work to solve the complex problems of sustainability and health.

On a global scale, the World Health Organization has developed its Healthy Cities Initiative to offer technical assistance and policy guidance to countries and local governments around the world when dealing with the complex problems of urban health. The Healthy Cities Initiative is a part of its broader Healthy Settings program, which is a place-based approach to health promotion and sustainable development. Healthy Settings include workplaces, rural areas, cities and hospitals, among others. The Healthy Cities Initiative has been implemented in all the WHO's regions since its inception in the 1980s, and represents a commitment on the part of community members and decision makers to achieve a high quality of life for all the city's residents. The Healthy Cities Initiative also specifically includes measures to address inequality and the environmental determinants of health (World Health Organization 2012).

At the national, state and local levels in the USA, Safe Routes to School programs promote walking and biking for students. This fulfills the goals of promoting walking and biking as alternatives to arriving at school by automobile, as well as increasing physical activity for students while teaching them safe habits when using active transportation. Federal grants are distributed through the Federal Highway Administration, while some states have their own programs to supplement the federal one. Importantly, some state Safe Routes to School programs fund different components of these projects – some focus on infrastructure around schools, such as bike lanes and sidewalks, while others emphasize encouraging healthy behaviors and promoting safe habits. Of course, for school administrators and parents who want to get students walking and biking, infrastructure and healthy behavior are never mutually exclusive and the overarching goal is to provide students with safe, healthy choices for getting to school (National Center for Safe Routes to School n.d.).

CONCLUSION

Our pursuit of sustainability as a goal, with its inherent consideration of preserving resources for future generations, must also be accompanied by an understanding of the complex ways that pursuit interacts with human health. Generally, the goals of public health and sustainability are complementary and mutually reinforcing. Establishing tools and frameworks to measure how projects and policies affect the environment and human health, as many organizations have, is an appropriate step in the right direction. Our hope is that, as we move forward in making a healthier and more sustainable world, we will continue to seek out and maintain a nuanced and comprehensive understanding of how the two goals interact and reinforce one another.

NOTE

1. 'Preamble to the Constitution of the World Health Organization as adopted by the International Health Conference', New York, 19–22 June 1946; signed on 22 July 1946 by the representatives of 61 States (Official Records of the World Health Organization, no. 2, p. 100) and entered into force on 7 April 1948.

REFERENCES

American Planning Association (2012), 'Planning and community health research center', available at http://www.planning.org/nationalcenters/health.

Board on Environmental Studies and Toxicology (2011), *Improving Health in the United States: The Role of Health Impact Assessment*, Washington, DC: National Academies Press, available at http://dels.nas.edu/Report/Improving-Health-United-States/13229.

Cannuscio, Carolyn and Karen Glanz (2011), 'Food environments', in Andrew L. Dannenberg,

Howard Frumkin and Richard J. Jackson (eds), *Making Healthy Places: Designing and Building for Health, Well-being, and Sustainability*, Washington, DC: Island Press, pp. 50–62.

Cater, Franklyn (2010), 'Critics say LEED program doesn't fulfill promises', *National Public Radio*, available at http://www.npr.org/templates/story/story.php?storyId=129727547 (8 September).

Centers for Disease Control and Prevention (2006), 'Heat-related deaths – United States, 1999–2003', available at http://www.cdc.gov/mmwr/preview/mmwrhtml/mm5529a2.htm.

Centers for Disease Control and Prevention (2011), 'Motor vehicle safety', available at http://www.cdc.gov/motorvehiclesafety/index.html.

Centers for Disease Control and Prevention (2012), 'Designing and building healthy places', available at http://www.cdc.gov/healthyplaces.

Cohen, Barbara, Margaret Andrews and Linda Scott Kantor (2002), *Community Food Security Assessment Toolkit*, Washington, DC: United States Department of Agriculture, Economic Research Service, available at http://www.ers.usda.gov/publications/efan-electronic-publications-from-the-food-assistance-nutrition-research-program/efan02013.aspx.

Dannenberg, Andrew L. and Arthur M. Wendel (2011), 'Measuring, assessing, and certifying healthy places', in Andrew L. Dannenberg, Howard Frumkin and Richard J. Jackson (eds), *Making Healthy Places: Designing and Building for Health, Well-being, and Sustainability*, Washington, DC: Island Press, pp. 308–18.

Eicher, Caitlin and Ichiro Kawachi (2011), 'Social capital and community design', in Andrew L. Dannenberg, Howard Frumkin and Richard J. Jackson (eds), *Making Healthy Places: Designing and Building for Health, Well-being, and Sustainability*, Washington, DC: Island Press, pp. 117–28.

Eidlin, E. (2010), 'What density doesn't tell us about sprawl', *Access*, **37**, 2–9, available at http://www.uctc.net/access/37/access37_sprawl.shtml.

Eisenhauer, E. (2001), 'In poor health: supermarket redlining and urban nutrition', *GeoJournal*, **53** (2), 125–33.

Environmental Protection Agency (2008), 'Reducing urban heat islands: Compendium of strategies, cool roofs', available at http://www.epa.gov/heatisld/resources/pdf/CoolRoofsCompendium.pdf.

Environmental Protection Agency (2012a), 'Improved academic performance: IAQ tools for schools', available at http://www.epa.gov/iaq/schools/student_performance/index.html.

Environmental Protection Agency (2012b), 'Indoor air quality glossary of terms', available at http://www.epa.gov/iaq/glossary.html.

Frumkin, Howard and Jared Fox (2011), 'Healthy schools', in Andrew L. Dannenberg, Howard Frumkin and Richard J. Jackson (eds), *Making Healthy Places: Designing and Building for Health, Well-being, and Sustainability*, Washington, DC: Island Press, pp. 216–28.

Gauderman, W.J., E. Avol, F. Lurmann, N. Kuenzli, F. Gilliland, J. Peters and R. McConnell (2005), 'Childhood asthma and exposure to traffic and nitrogen dioxide', *Epidemiology*, **16** (6), 737–43.

Gordis, Leon (2009), *Epidemiology*, 4th edn, Philadelphia, PA: Elsevier/Saunders.

Horowitz, Cara (2011), *Anthony Pritzker Environmental Law and Policy Briefs, Issue Brief No. 2*, Los Angeles, CA: Emmett Center on Climate Change and the Environment, available at http://cdn.law.ucla.edu/SiteCollectionDocuments/Centers and Programs/EmmettCenteronClimateChangeandtheEnvironment/Pritzker_02_Bright_Roofs_Big_City.pdf.

Institute of Medicine (IOM) (2002), *The Future of the Public's Health in the 21st Century*, Washington, DC: National Academies Press, available at http://www.nap.edu/catalog.php?record_id=10548.

International Living Future Institute (2010), *Living Building Challenge Standard*, Seattle, WA: International Living Future Institute, available at http://living-future.org/lbc/about.

Maantay, J. (2001), 'Zoning, equity, and public health', *American Journal of Public Health*, **91** (7), 1033–41.

Manson, J.E., P.J. Skerrett, P. Greenland and T.B. VanItallie (2004), 'The escalating pandemics of obesity and sedentary lifestyle: a call to action for clinicians', *Archives of Internal Medicine*, **164** (3), 249–58.

Manville, M. and D. Shoup (2004), 'Parking, people, and cities', *Access*, **25**, 2–8.

National Center for Safe Routes to School (n.d.), 'Safe routes', available at http://saferoutesinfo.org.

National Complete Streets Coalition (2010), 'Fundamentals', available at http://www.completestreets.org/complete-streets-fundamentals.

National Highway Traffic Safety Administration (NHTSA) (2011), *Traffic Safety Facts 2009: A Compilation of Motor Vehicle Crash Data from the Fatality Analysis Reporting System and the General Estimates System, DOT HS 811 402*, Washington, DC: USDOT, NHTSA, available at http://www-nrd.nhtsa.dot.gov/Pubs/811402.pdf.

National Research Council (2006), 'Concepts and definitions', in Gooloo S. Wunderlich and Janet L. Norwood (eds), *Food Insecurity and Hunger in the United States: An Assessment of the Measure*, Washington, DC: The National Academies Press, available at http://www.nap.edu/openbook.php?record_id=11578&page=41.

Public Health Law and Policy (2009), *Healthy Corner Stores – The State of the Movement*, Oakland, CA: ChangeLab Solutions.

Salkin, P.E. and P. Ko (2011), 'The effective use of health impact assessment (HIA) in land-use decision making', *Zoning Practice*, available at http://www.healthimpactproject.org/resources/document/Salkin-201_Effective-Use-of-HIA-in-Land-Use.pdf.

Samet, Jonathan M. (2011), 'Community design and air quality', in Andrew L. Dannenberg, Howard Frumkin and Richard J. Jackson (eds), *Making Healthy Places: Designing and Building for Health, Well-being, and Sustainability*, Washington, DC: Island Press, pp. 63–76.

San Francisco Department of Public Health (2012), 'Program on health, equity and sustainability: Pedestrian Environmental Quality Index', available at http://www.sfphes.org/elements/24-elements/tools/106-pedestrian-environmental-quality-index.

Schweitzer, L. and J. Zhou (2010), 'Neighborhood air quality, respiratory health, and vulnerable populations in compact and sprawled regions', *Journal of the American Planning Association*, **76** (3), 363–71.

Stone, B., J.J. Hess and H. Frumkin (2010), 'Urban form and extreme heat events: are sprawling cities more vulnerable to climate change than compact cities?', *Environmental Health Perspectives*, **118** (10), 1425–28.

Sullivan, William C. and Chun-Yen Chang (2011), 'Mental health and the built environment', in Andrew L. Dannenberg, Howard Frumkin and Richard J. Jackson (eds), *Making Healthy Places: Designing and Building for Health, Well-being, and Sustainability*, Washington, DC: Island Press, pp. 106–16.

Thornton, Rebecca L.J., Caroline M. Fichtenberg, Amelia Greiner, Beth Feingold, Jonathan M. Ellen, Jacky M. Jennings, Madeleine A. Shea, Joseph Schilling, Ralph B. Taylor, David Bishai and Maureen Black (2010), *Zoning for a Healthy Baltimore: A Health Impact Assessment of the TransForm Baltimore Zoning Code Rewrite*, Baltimore, MD: Johns Hopkins University Center for Child and Community Research, available at http://www.hopkinsbayview.org/pediatrics/zoning/files/FullReportColor.pdf.

United Nations World Commission on Environment and Development (UN WCED) (1987), *Our Common Future*, Oxford: Oxford University Press.

University of California, Los Angeles Health Impact Assessment Clearinghouse (UCLA) (2008), 'HIA guide', available at http://www.hiaguide.org/.

US Department of Agriculture, Economic Research Service (USDA ERS) (2013), 'Food desert locator', available at http://www.ers.usda.gov/data-products/food-desert-locator.aspx.

US Department of Health and Human Services (US DHHS) (2011), 'Objective development and selection process', available at http://www.healthypeople.gov/2020/about/objectiveDevelopment.aspx.

US Department of Health and Human Services, Administration for Children & Families

(2012), 'CED Data Healthy Food Financing Initiative', http://www.acf.hhs.gov/programs/ocs/resource/healthy-food-financing-initiative-0.
US Green Building Council (USGBC) (2012), 'Rating Systems', available at http://www.usgbc.org/DisplayPage.aspx?CMSPageID=222.
WalkScore (2012), 'Walk score: drive less, live more', available at http://www.walkscore.com.
World Health Organization (WHO) (2012), 'Introduction to healthy settings', available at http://www.who.int/healthy_settings/about/en.
Zimring, Craig and Jennifer DuBose (2011), 'Healthy health care settings', in Andrew L. Dannenberg, Howard Frumkin and Richard J. Jackson (eds), *Making Healthy Places: Designing and Building for Health, Well-being, and Sustainability*, Washington, DC: Island Press, pp. 203–15.

10. From information provision to participatory deliberation: engaging residents in the transition toward sustainable cities

Michaela Zint and Kimberly S. Wolske

BACKGROUND

Among the many challenges cities face in transitioning toward sustainability is the question of how to involve local residents. Achieving urban sustainability goals will require not only broad political support (Carvalho and Peterson 2012), but also changes in residents' consumption and lifestyle choices (Dietz et al. 2009). This chapter explores how cities can actively engage their residents in meeting these goals. Borrowing from others, we define engagement to mean a 'personal state of connection' in which individuals are not only aware of sustainability issues, but are concerned, motivated and able to take appropriate actions (Lorenzoni et al. 2007; Whitmarsh et al. 2011).

Cities are experimenting with a variety of strategies to foster citizen engagement. These can include communication and education efforts aimed at raising awareness and knowledge of sustainability challenges; behavior change interventions that encourage residents to make more sustainable choices in their personal lives; and participatory approaches that involve residents in the visioning, planning and implementation of sustainability initiatives. Because cities are employing all these strategies for the purpose of engaging target audiences, we will refer to them collectively as 'engagement strategies' in the remainder of this chapter.

There are a growing number of resources and opportunities to inform cities' sustainability engagement practices. For example, ICLEI – Local Governments for Sustainability has created several guides on how to engage community members and communicate about climate change (ICLEI – Local Governments for Sustainability 2009; Knapp 2011). The Urban Sustainability Directors Network encourages members to share relevant strategies and best practices through one of its user groups focused on fostering sustainable behavior among residents and employees.

Professional meetings are also beginning to focus on the challenge of engaging residents in city sustainability. In 2011, the Garrison Institute began hosting an annual symposium for mayors, city planners and transportation directors to discuss emerging behavior change strategies and climate change communication techniques. At a global level, the United Nations recently held a symposium on sustainable cities and climate change education (Inter-Agency Committee of the UN Decade of Education for Sustainable Development 2009), and the 2013 World Environmental Education Congress has sustainable cities as one of its main themes (World Environmental Education Congress 2013).

Despite growing interest in engagement strategies as a means to help achieve cities' sustainability goals, little is known about existing engagement programs and their effectiveness. Documentation, including results from program evaluations, is scarce, and academic literature on engagement strategies to promote sustainable cities is extremely limited. Of the peer-reviewed articles that address this topic, most identify only the need for greater public involvement (e.g. Wheeler 2008); few publications address the role of engagement in depth (e.g. Moser 2006) or offer insights based on empirical research. Consequently, for cities interested in engaging local residents in sustainability, finding examples of proven approaches or programs is difficult.

This chapter, therefore, aims to shed light on the roles that engagement strategies can play in transitioning cities toward sustainability and to highlight case studies that demonstrate their potential for success. We begin by introducing a range of engagement strategies and examining how they might contribute to the creation of an engaged and sustainability-minded citizenry. These strategies include information provision and persuasion, psychology-based behavior change tools, and participatory, deliberative approaches. We then look at a selection of eight case studies from cities in North America and Australia to explore how these strategies can be successfully implemented. Challenges to strengthening the role of engagement strategies in cities' sustainability initiatives are discussed next, followed by recommendations for researchers and practitioners.

AN INTRODUCTION TO SUSTAINABILITY ENGAGEMENT STRATEGIES

Information Provision and Persuasion

Many programs intended to engage individuals in sustainability rely primarily on information-based strategies. In the context of promoting action on climate change, the focus of many cities' sustainability engagement efforts, these often take the form of public service announcements, mass media campaigns, educational websites and brochures, or other forms of online communications. The underlying assumption of these programs is that, once individuals are aware of and understand the problems associated with unsustainable patterns of behavior, they will develop favorable attitudes toward sustainability and be motivated to act accordingly. Research has repeatedly shown, however, that even if campaigns are successful in raising awareness and changing attitudes, they rarely lead to changes in behavior (e.g. Environment Canada 2006; Staats et al. 1996; see also Abrahamse et al. 2005; Hines et al. 1987).

There are a number of explanations for this 'attitude–behavior gap'. While people may be aware of and concerned about environmental problems, they may not know what actions to take nor have the skills needed to carry them out. People are often confused, for example, about the types of actions they can take to help reduce climate change, with many people assuming that recycling is a sufficient strategy (Whitmarsh 2009). Even among people who understand the importance of reducing fossil fuel use, there are misconceptions about which energy-saving behaviors have the greatest impact (Attari et al. 2010; Kempton et al. 1985). Providing procedural information about appropriate action strategies and their relative effectiveness may help overcome some of these challenges, but other barriers are likely to persist. Individuals may have difficulty adopting behaviors if they lack necessary resources such as access to public transportation or the money to buy energy-efficient products. Even when individuals have the knowledge, skills and resources needed to take action, many are deterred by the perception that it will take too much effort or require sacrificing their quality of life (Lorenzoni et al. 2007; Norgaard 2006).

For others, the magnitude of problems such as climate change can be overwhelming. Communications that emphasize the negative impacts of environmental problems without providing details of how to effectively reduce those impacts may lead people to engage in defensive coping strategies. These might include avoiding additional information about the problem, justifying their current unsustainable behaviors, or deflecting blame to others (Norgaard 2006; Stoll-Kleemann et al. 2001). Such outcomes have been observed, for example, with carbon footprint calculators – a tool commonly used by city governments as part of their outreach efforts. This intervention assumes that people will be inspired to adopt a less resource-intensive lifestyle once they understand the direct impact of their choices on the environment (Sutcliffe et al. 2008). Research has shown, however, that these calculators tend to have the opposite effect. Learning the immense size of one's carbon footprint can lead to feelings that sustainability is impossible to achieve, which in turn lessens the likelihood of engaging in sustainability behaviors (Brook 2011; Warburton 2008). This outcome has been observed even when footprint calculators are accompanied with a list of energy-saving actions and information to enhance self-efficacy (Truelove 2009).

In summary, information and persuasion-based communications can have an important role in fostering sustainability, but cities must recognize their limitations. These strategies are best used when the objective is to increase awareness and knowledge of sustainability issues or to promote favorable attitudes toward sustainability. Program designers must be attentive, though, to the needs of target audiences and recognize that some types of information may be more effective than others. Furthermore, even the best-designed communications are unlikely to lead to behavior change on their own.

Psychology-based Tools

Research in environmental and conservation psychology has revealed a number of tools that, when combined with well-designed communications, can increase the likelihood of effecting behavior change (Stern 2011). These tools work by specifically addressing some of the psychological barriers that information-based strategies are ill-equipped to handle. For example, commitments, which consist of verbal or written pledges to undertake a specific behavior or goal (e.g. reduce household energy consumption by 5 percent), can be effective. They are thought to promote behavior change by increasing the salience of one's pro-environmental attitudes, thus encouraging individuals to act in ways that are congruent with what they believe (Lokhorst et al. 2013). Providing individuals with feedback about their progress toward meeting a goal (e.g. kilowatt hours of energy used) can also be an effective strategy, as it helps people learn the impact of their actions and rewards their efforts. Feedback is generally more effective the more frequently it is given (Abrahamse et al. 2005). Because many sustainable behaviors require changing ingrained habits, short, simple reminders – or prompts – to perform a behavior can be effective as well (Hopper and Nielsen 1991; Kurz et al. 2005). Behavior can also be influenced by tapping underlying social motives. Programs that use peers to model desired behaviors tend to be more effective than those that use impersonal communications or strangers (Aronson and O'Leary 1982–83; Burn 1991). Likewise, people are sensitive to prevailing social norms. Interventions that highlight the prevalence with which others have adopted desired behaviors have shown to be successful in a number of contexts (Cialdini 2003; Nolan et al. 2008). For the reader interested in learning more about these techniques, McKenzie-Mohr and colleagues (McKenzie-Mohr 2011; McKenzie-Mohr et al. 2012) provide additional guidance about how and when to use each of these tools.

Engagement strategies such as those described above are typically used when program managers have specific behavioral objectives in mind, such as seeking compliance to meet predetermined energy conservation goals. Using engagement strategies in such instrumental ways may be appropriate when there is widescale agreement about the desirability of particular behaviors or goals. A limitation of this approach, however, is that it assumes that experts 'know' that particular behaviors are the 'right' ones and privileges those that implement these strategies as reformers (De Young 2011; Jickling 2005).

Participatory Deliberation Processes

One disadvantage of the engagement strategies just described is that they are unlikely to lead residents to feel that they have ownership over their cities' sustainability visions and solutions. Moreover, they tend not to enable and empower residents to effect change in themselves and others. These concerns have led to calls for emancipatory engagement approaches (Wals 2011; Wals and Corcoran 2012), often referred to as participatory processes. The idea underlying these approaches is that citizens, not just technical experts or politicians, have important local knowledge and should have the opportunity to determine their own future as well as how to realize their visions. Calls for participatory processes are relatively common, as they are believed to be key to facilitating the more difficult, fundamental societal changes needed for sustainability (Brulle 2010). Despite their promise, however, the use of participatory strategies at a city-wide level is rare within sustainability contexts. Thus, relatively little is known about their effectiveness in fostering change compared to other sustainability engagement strategies.

CASE STUDIES

This section describes a variety of engagement strategies to meet cities' climate mitigation and, in some instances, adaptation goals. The selected cases are not meant to provide a comprehensive review of the types of programs that exist, but rather to showcase strategies that can be effective depending on a program's goals and available resources. Cases were also selected to illustrate the spectrum of potential audiences. The initial cases target individuals and households, subsequent cases describe programs that take advantage of existing social groups, and the final cases look at programs that focus on entire communities or cities. Though coincidental, our arrangement of cases also illustrates how programs can range from top–down approaches to ones that are participant driven.

'Ann Arbor Energy Challenge'

Engagement strategy

Cities often have limited budgets and staff for engagement programs. This constraint leads many to rely on websites, brochures and other printed communications as a means of informing or persuading residents to change their behavior. As discussed previously, information about environmental problems or behaviors rarely leads to behavior change when used alone (Gardner and Stern 2002). The following program illustrates how carefully designed print media can be combined with proven behavior change techniques to effectively engage residents – without requiring significant resources.

Program summary and results

This program was developed as part of a dissertation research study and implemented in collaboration with the City of Ann Arbor, Michigan (Wolske 2011). The program challenged households to reduce their carbon footprint by 2 percent during the one-month program period. Program materials explained that, if global emissions were reduced by 2 percent each and every year, we would achieve an 80 percent reduction in emissions by 2050 and avoid catastrophic climate change. The Energy Challenge was presented as an opportunity for households to do their part. A random sample of 2825 households received a letter from the City's Energy Office inviting them to participate, and about 200 signed up for the challenge.

All participants received an informational booklet identifying 34 climate-friendly behaviors related to dietary choices, household energy use and personal transportation. This booklet was unique in that it included (1) rationales for these behaviors based on specific carbon savings and health benefits, (2) suggestions for how to engage in these behaviors in Ann Arbor, and (3) explanations of common misperceptions associated with these behaviors.

All participants were asked to track their efforts through an online log each week of the challenge and were randomly assigned to one of three treatment groups. These groups received one of the following: (1) feedback at the end of the month about their total carbon savings; (2) weekly feedback about their cumulative carbon savings; or (3) weekly feedback about their cumulative carbon savings as well as 'stories' consisting of anecdotes from other participants about their successes. Participants also received weekly emails from the City to remind them to complete the online logs.

The majority of participants (78 percent), regardless of treatment, achieved the desired 2 percent goal, with median carbon savings of 6 percent. In addition, the study showed that participants with less conservation experience and those who received weekly feedback were more likely to engage in a broader set of behaviors. A survey conducted one month after the intervention indicated that participants maintained their behaviors. A year and a half later, the program was repeated, with the contents of the informational booklet posted on a website. Similar participation rates and CO_2 savings were achieved.

'Turn It Off', 'Clean Air at Schools: Engines Off!' and 'Clean Run Behavior Change Initiative'

Engagement strategy

Programs targeting specific, concrete behaviors tend to be more effective than programs that focus solely on changing individuals' knowledge and attitudes, or groups of behaviors (Stern 2011). This is in part because the barriers and benefits to engaging in different behaviors vary.

Community-based social marketing (CBSM) draws on these insights as well as social marketing principles to offer practitioners a framework for designing behavior change programs (McKenzie-Mohr et al. 2012). CBSM involves five steps: (1) selecting a specific behavior to target; (2) researching the barriers and benefits associated with the behavior in the targeted community; (3) developing strategies to reduce the barriers to the behavior while increasing the behavior's perceived benefits; (4) piloting the strategies to test their effectiveness; and (5) implementing and evaluating the program at the community level. As suggested by the final two steps, CBSM stresses the need for an evaluative approach. This helps to ensure that programs are improved before they are adopted on a large scale, and thus prevents resources from being wasted.

The CBSM approach appears to be gaining popularity among cities as a means to promote sustainable behavior (Tools of Change 2012) and is particularly suitable when the goal is to change specific behaviors (e.g. encouraging individuals to ride a new transit system). The examples below describe how CBSM has been used to reduce automobile emissions in cities.

Program summary and results: Turn It Off

Turn It Off is an anti-idling program that was first tested in Toronto (McKenzie-Mohr et al. 2012). The initial program sought to reduce idling in school parking lots and commuter 'Kiss and Ride' sites, locations where idling is particularly common. Research on the barriers and benefits that motorists associated with idling informed the development of strategies to change their behavior. In addition to placing signs at the above locations, motorists were approached by trained university students on behalf of the city and asked to place a 'no idling' sticker in the front window of their car. The purposes of this sticker were to remind motorists to turn their engines off, illustrate their public commitment to the behavior, and contribute to the development of social norms by making the behavior visible. They also received a card with information about associated benefits including cost savings, decreased air pollution, and reduced CO_2 emissions. Of the 1296 individuals approached, over half (51 percent) made a commitment to turn off their car engines when parked and one in five (20 percent) affixed the sticker to their windshields. Pilot testing examined the effectiveness of signs used alone compared to the combined strategies above and to a control group. For ten days over 8000 observations were obtained to assess changes in the frequency and duration of idling at 12 locations. Signs alone did not reduce idling, whereas the intervention of combined strategies reduced idling by 32 percent and its duration by 73 percent. Based in part on these findings, Natural Resources Canada created a 'turnkey' toolkit that has been used by over 100 municipalities to implement their own anti-idling campaigns (Natural Resources Canada 2010).

Program summary and results: Clean Air at Schools: Engines Off!

Turn It Off has inspired similar programs such as Clean Air at Schools: Engines Off! (CASEO) in Denver (Engines Off Colorado 2012). Based on preliminary research of the barriers and benefits that parents associated with idling, the program's messages focus on the health benefits to children from reducing vehicle exhaust. The program also involves students throughout the process. Students collect baseline data on idling rates, which are subsequently shared with parents through a letter from the schools' principals. 'Children breathing – no idle zone' signs are posted, and information about idling and associated health concerns is disseminated through brochures and events. Parents are asked to pledge to their children that they will not idle at school.[1] These pledges are posted publicly in the schools, and the classes with the most pledges win a pizza party. Students give key chains to drivers to help them remember not to idle. At the end of the program, students collect another round of observations to measure results and to ask parents for feedback about the program. Between 2008 and 2012, the percentage of idling vehicles decreased by 25–71 percent and total daily idle duration declined 25–93 percent at the 17 schools where CASEO was implemented (Engines Off Colorado 2012). Parent surveys from the pilot year suggest that idling in other locations was reduced, too.

Program summary and results: Clean Run Behavior Change Initiative

One way to strengthen the CBSM approach is to make it collaborative by working with target audiences to decide on a behavioral goal as well as to select and implement strategies to achieve it. For example, the Clean Run Behavior Change Initiative in Australia modified the traditional CBSM methodology by involving members of its target audience of professional truck drivers. Based on drivers' input, 'keeping idling to a minimum' was selected as the target behavior because drivers felt this was completely within their control. Four sets of intervention strategies were tested, again based on drivers' input. Across all four groups, idling was reduced on average by 72 percent, and drivers reported that they also reduced idling of their personal vehicles. The intervention with the greatest combination of behavior change strategies resulted in an 87 percent reduction in idling. This intervention's strategies consisted of signs, stickers, posters, a notice board, 'leakage' (i.e. word of mouth, peer pressure), commitment, MDT[2] messaging and feedback meetings. The program's overall success was attributed largely to the sense of ownership that resulted from the program being developed 'by drivers for drivers' (MacRae and Stockport 2008).

'Baltimore Energy Challenge' (BEC)

Engagement strategy

One of the challenges of engaging residents in energy reduction and other environmental behaviors is motivating audiences with limited interest in environmental problems. Competitions of the type below, developed and implemented in close collaboration with or by community organizations, appear to be able to overcome this challenge. In these programs, communications occur through established community networks headed by 'block' or other 'influential' leaders who model desired behaviors. The effectiveness of this type of approach has been attributed to the credibility of these messengers (Burn 1991; Meneses and Palacio 2007), expectations of trust and reciprocity among community members (Berry 2010), and social norms (Cialdini et al. 2004). Because community-based programs tend to rely heavily on partnerships and volunteers, they can help to significantly leverage limited resources (Berry 2010). In light of their reliance on volunteers, however, they also require thoughtful management of volunteer recruitment and retention.

Program summary and results

The goal of the Baltimore Energy Challenge (BEC) is to reduce energy use by creating a competition between neighborhoods. To achieve this goal, the City works with neighborhood associations, schools and communities of faith to recruit volunteer 'energy captains', as well as with partners such as the city's Weatherization Assistance Program. About 10 to 20 captains and junior captains per neighborhood or school are trained by AmeriCorps staff to inform residents about reducing energy and utility costs. The program expects initial energy-efficiency behaviors to lead to reduced utility bills and these, in turn, to influence households to take additional steps such as weatherizing their home and replacing old, inefficient appliances.

The captains create outreach plans that typically include sharing information through door-to-door canvassing, house meetings, community events and articles in neighborhood newsletters. As part of their outreach plans, captains ask community members for a written commitment to adopt energy-saving behaviors outlined in a toolkit. Residents also receive free or subsidized energy efficiency resources (e.g. compact fluorescent lamps – CFLs) and, in some instances, assistance with installation by AmeriCorps staff. Neighborhoods and schools may receive a $1000 stipend and are recognized as leaders for taking action on energy use.

In its 2009 pilot year, over 100 volunteers from eight Baltimore neighborhoods recruited 750 participants and distributed over 1000 pledge kits to participant homes. The mean reductions in winter electricity use (compared to baseline measures) were 6.6 percent (range: 1.8 percent to 12.8 percent). Participants in the lowest-income neighborhood had the greatest reduction in energy use, which appeared attributable to particularly motivated senior citizen captains. A post-intervention survey also suggested that participants engaged in a variety of energy-efficiency behaviors. For example, 77 percent reported that they installed CFLs, 46 percent turned down the water heater temperature, 44 percent added caulking and weather stripping, and 41 percent wrapped their water heaters (Baltimore Neighborhood Energy Challenge n.d.).

Based on the success of this pilot, BEC shifted its focus from these neighborhoods to a new set of 12 neighborhoods and also adopted the same model to foster changes in energy efficiency behaviors in schools, businesses and religious institutions.

'EcoTeams'

Engagement strategy

One of the distinguishing characteristics of the next case example, EcoTeams (http://www.empowermentinstitute.net/, www.globalactionplan.com/), is that the program seeks to foster changes in behavior through social diffusion (Rogers 1995). Social diffusion refers to how technologies, ideas, behaviors or other innovations spread through communication among members in a particular network of influence. The theory suggests that, once a critical mass of adoption occurs, broad-scale adoption will ensue, resulting in more generalized societal change.

Several factors influence the rate of diffusion. In particular, the theory recognizes early adopters – those attracted to innovation and experimentation – as change agents that are key to influencing others. This suggests that focusing on 'recruiting the choir' is appropriate, as it will be the choir who will mobilize the rest of society. The theory thus offers yet another explanation for why peer-to-peer communication tends to be more effective than top–down, expert-driven communication.

Other contextual factors can increase the likelihood that innovations will be adopted. These include when individuals: (1) can experiment with the innovation without making a huge commitment; (2) have an opportunity to observe others' adoption; and (3) have social support (Rogers 1995). EcoTeams have several of these characteristics.

Program summary and results

Over 150 000 individuals in cities around the world have participated in the EcoTeam program (Davidson 2011; Rabkin and Gershon 2007). Each EcoTeam is initiated by a leader who recruits four to eight individuals from other households, businesses, city departments, schools, communities and so on to form a group. Groups meet regularly over a period of several weeks or months to help each other try to adopt new behaviors. The teams' efforts are guided by a workbook, organized around themes. The original workbook (*Green Living Handbook*) addresses actions related to waste, recycling, electricity, gas and water usage, whereas a subsequent workbook focuses exclusively on ways to reduce carbon emissions (*Low Carbon Diet*). There are other workbooks as well, including *All Together Now*, which was designed to help New York City residents prepare for emergencies in order to create more disaster-resilient communities. Team participants monitor their individual behaviors and impacts, in part to build self-efficacy (i.e. feelings that individuals' actions make a difference). The program concludes with culminating activities such as a meeting to celebrate impacts and a review of the group's aggregate achievements.

In contrast to many other programs implemented in cities, considerable evidence exists to support EcoTeams' effectiveness. Research reveals that the program leads to changes in a variety of behaviors and that these are maintained for up to three years after the program has ended (Burgess and Nye 2008; Staats et al. 2004). Early changes typically consist of easier behaviors, but toward the end of the program and later, participants tend to adopt more difficult behaviors (Baxter 2009, cited in Whitmarsh et al. 2011). Moreover, there is some evidence to suggest that team leaders become politically engaged (Davidson 2011). In terms of environmental impact, self-reports from about 20 000 EcoTeam participants suggest that they produced 40 percent less solid waste, used 32 percent less water and 14 percent less energy, traveled 8 percent fewer vehicle miles and generated 15 percent less CO_2 emissions in one year (Empowerment Institute 2013).

'Chicago's City–Community Partnerships' and 'Geraldton 2029 and Beyond'

Engagement strategy

The engagement strategies reviewed so far in this chapter have the potential to foster and support changes in residents' behaviors and thus can contribute to cities' transition toward sustainability. The types of profound and essential societal changes needed to achieve sustainability, however, are likely to require participatory processes. By participatory processes, we do not mean token involvement or even consultation. Instead, we are referring to collaborative governance that is inclusive, deliberative and influential (Carson and Hartz-Karp 2005) and requires authorities to relinquish some of their power. A genuinely participatory, deliberative democracy approach has the potential to (1) motivate participation, (2) develop ownership over visions for desired, sustainable futures, and (3) generate support for implementing the changes needed to achieve these visions (Carson and Hartz-Karp 2005). Participatory approaches do not impose visions or solutions but involve residents in developing their own visions as well as the strategies for achieving these visions.

Many agree on the need for participatory approaches to support transitions toward sustainability (Brulle 2010; Johnson 2012). Yet few cities appear to be using these engagement strategies. Two exceptions are described next. The first case, Chicago's City–Community Partnerships, is unique in that it draws on anthropological methods and involves a large variety of partners to engage diverse communities in leading the design and implementation of community action projects. The second case, Geraldton 2029 and Beyond, also rare in its approach, employs an assortment of deliberative processes to engage residents and has led to mitigation efforts for which policy makers thought they lacked support.

Program summary and results: Chicago's City–Community Partnerships

The City of Chicago contracted with The Field Museum in 2008 to help engage local communities in implementing the city's climate action plan (Hirsch et al. 2011). To accomplish this goal, The Field Museum focused on several Chicago communities, which were selected based on their geographic, ethnic, racial and socioeconomic diversity. Rapid ethnographic inventories including interviews, focus groups and participant observation were conducted in each community. The purpose of these inventories was to identify (1) community assets, both tangible (e.g. organizations, infrastructure, individuals with relevant skills) and intangible (e.g. cultural values and traditions), (2) community concerns, and (3) barriers to engagement.

Another notable aspect of this program is that front-end research efforts were conducted in close collaboration with community partners. These partners helped connect researchers to community leaders and also participated in all phases of the research, including the completion of final reports. In addition, the researchers used creative data collection methods such as drawing, visual prompting and object-based storytelling. Researchers felt that these techniques gave them insights into cultural and historical contexts that they would not have been able to obtain through traditional data collection means (Hirsch et al. 2011).

As a result of the above process and with support from The Field Museum, new community partnerships were formed between for-profit and not-for-profit organizations, representing a range of social service and environmental missions. These partnerships ultimately led to several community action projects. All of these projects link climate action to respective communities' concerns and assets. For example, in one community with many immigrants from the Mexican state of Michoacán, a vacant lot was converted into a Monarch butterfly[3] garden, linking the community's concerns over immigration rights with climate messages about habitat and open space (see Chicago Community Climate Action Toolkit at http://climatechicago.fieldmuseum.org/ for descriptions of this and other community projects).

Community action projects were also designed to create a sense of ownership among participating organizations. The hope was that organizations would become climate action leaders in their communities and, thus, would continue to pursue community-based actions on climate change. There are some early signs that this goal has been achieved as several Chicago communities have expanded their projects and obtained grants to advance their climate mitigation efforts.

Program summary and results: Geraldton 2029 and Beyond

Since 2010, the Greater Geraldton City Region of Western Australia, in collaboration with Curtin University, has worked to improve its sustainability and resilience through meaningful engagement of its citizens in collaborative problem solving and decision making (Hartz-Karp 2012). The initiative provides the entire community with opportunities for discourse on issues that matter to the future sustainability of the city region.

Consistent with adaptive management, a range of participatory, deliberative processes has been instituted to foster ownership of sustainability challenges and opportunities. Public deliberations have been led by government, community and industry groups. They have ranged from small to large scale, included both face-to-face and online formats, and have employed a variety of traditional and innovative social media.

Efforts have included a deliberative poll, with 3000 randomly sampled residents receiving questionnaires to determine their understanding of and views on various sustainability issues. Around 200 respondents then deliberated for a day, with the aim of exchanging perspectives and learning more about the issues from different viewpoints. At the end of the day, they completed the questionnaire again. Responses showed that views shifted even further in the direction of the city taking more proactive steps to become sustainable including through striving for carbon neutrality.

Around 40 Community Champions volunteered to encourage deliberation among community members. After being trained in facilitation, each Champion held one or more small group meetings, with residents deliberating and developing ideas to create a more sustainable city. Other groups worked online to develop proposals using an innovative online platform, CivicEvolution (www.civicevolution.org). The Champions and other community members prioritized these proposals, which were then fast-tracked through the City's Council. Priorities currently being implemented include planting one million trees, becoming the 'bicycle capital of the west', creating an Aboriginal cultural center, and forming a youth council.

A randomly sampled Citizens' Jury worked with an international IBM team on a 'Smarter Cities Challenge' to develop the City's digital future. This has resulted in a far-reaching plan based on local knowledge and values as well as expert input, with immediate outcomes such as rapid uptake of smart meters.

Using 21st Century Town meeting deliberative technology, a charette was held over four days with about 300 residents to create a sustainable future plan for the city region. The resulting visionary plan is in the process of becoming a statutory document. Planning in accordance with this document is being rolled out, precinct by precinct, beginning with the most socioeconomically deprived areas. Related deliberations involving over 50 local residents and expert planners also focused on participatory budgeting for the present, with a budget of around \$50 000 being allocated to prioritized initiatives.

Public deliberations not only addressed emerging issues, but also led to the development of a 'Citizens' Charter' based on the pillars of sustainability. This charter forms the basis of the Community Strategic Plan driving the City's operations. In addition, public deliberations have helped spawn a growing community of social entrepreneurs (see www.wildpollinators.org). Moreover, public deliberations have led to new partnerships, including with local media, to champion the 2013–14 participatory budgeting initiatives (Hartz-Karp 2012). For the first time, industry and government are also collaborating to determine if Geraldton could be the first region powered by alternative energy.

Overall, the deliberations revealed that community members were far more supportive of actions to support sustainability and less conservative in their views than government decision makers anticipated. This has allowed government decision makers to implement more comprehensive and ambitious actions on climate change and sustainability than they previously thought possible.

MOVING FORWARD

The previous section shared examples of different types of engagement strategies that cities are employing to transition toward sustainability. These engagement strategies range from top–down, one-way information transmission, persuasion and social marketing to bottom–up, social diffusion and participatory, deliberative democracy approaches. Each of these strategies has its strengths and limitations (Corner and Randall 2011; Johnson 2012) and serves different purposes, depending on desired goals.

The purpose of this section is to explore how to strengthen the contributions of engagement strategies in transitioning cities toward sustainability. We begin with a description of challenges that appear to limit their potential contributions, followed by recommendations for overcoming these challenges.

One significant concern is how little information is available about the sustainability engagement strategies cities are using. Internet searches suggest that cities all over the world are employing a range of these strategies, but documentation describing their respective programs' goals, underlying theories of change, specific strategies and, particularly, evaluation results are difficult to obtain. Research on this topic is scarce as well. This means that cities cannot benefit from each other's experiences or insights. As such, cities may be 'reinventing the wheel', implementing ineffective approaches, and not making the most of limited resources.

It is also important to note that, of the information that is accessible, most focuses on top–down information provision, persuasion or social marketing programs that target individuals or households in cities of Western countries. Information about engagement strategies implemented in developing countries, which target influential stakeholders (e.g. building owners or managers, architects), or are about programs that employ bottom–up approaches, is particularly hard to find.

A related challenge is that we do not know how representative this chapter's examples are of the types of sustainability engagement strategies employed in cities. The chapter's case examples were selected, in part, because (1) we could obtain documentation about the respective programs, (2) they tended to explicitly apply research-based best practices, and (3) there were some evaluation or research results to show that the program contributed to the city's sustainability efforts. Based on the types of programs we found during our search for case studies, it appears that most cities use top–down approaches in their sustainability efforts. Chicago and Geraldton were notably the only cities we could identify through extensive searches that have adopted a participatory approach. Similarly, it appears that many sustainability engagement efforts are not as closely integrated with cities' policy, market and infrastructure interventions as they could be (Stern 2011). One exception, to illustrate what we mean by an integrated program, is 'Solarize Portland'. To achieve the goal of increasing residential solar PV installations, Portland residents have access to significant tax rebates (which by themselves are insufficient to incentivize large-scale adoption), and the city collaborates with neighborhood associations and other stakeholders to facilitate volume purchases to reduce the price of solar installation. Community-based social marketing and diffusion strategies address misperceptions related to the sufficiency of available sunlight, focus on residents' concerns such as the suitability of their properties, and serve to create supportive social norms. The city credits this integrative approach with tripling solar installations in three years. Again, if our difficulty in identifying these types of cases is indicative of how rarely they are used, then the full potential of sustainability engagement strategies is not being realized in many cities.

In light of the above challenges, we offer the following recommendations for strengthening the role of engagement strategies in transitioning cities toward sustainability:

- *Support efforts to document and disseminate information about cities' sustainability engagement programs*

It is important that those involved in developing, implementing and evaluating cities' sustainability engagement programs be encouraged to improve their documentation of these programs. Helpful documentation would include information about programs' goals, underlying theories of change, the specific tools and strategies used, as well as results from implementation and outcome evaluations. Such documentation should be broadly disseminated, along with 'lessons learned'. ICLEI, the Urban Sustainability Directors Network, and the Garrison Institute are among the groups facilitating this type of dissemination, but additional efforts are needed to serve the needs of a larger and more diverse group of potential program providers and partners. Special attention should also be given to support networking between Western and developing countries, as both are likely to benefit from each other's insights. Such interactions would be particularly useful for improving knowledge of effective engagement strategies around climate change adaptation in light of the risks climate change poses to poor urban populations.

- *Draw on research and resources from related disciplines to inform cities' sustainability engagement efforts*

Several disciplines have much to offer in informing and supporting cities' sustainability engagement efforts. These disciplines include sustainability and climate communication; sustainability, environmental and health education; as well as conservation psychology and others. These fields offer research on theories and interventions that support changes in individual and collective behaviors (Dietz and Stern 2002; Heimlich and Ardoin 2008; Zint 2012) and thus can inform the design of engagement strategies' theories of change. There are also numerous books and guides to inform the development, implementation and evaluation of engagement strategies. Examples of relevant guides include Futerra's *Engage: Campaign Guidebook for Cities* (www.citiesengage.eu), Climate Access's *Climate Communication and Behavior Change* (www.climateaccess.org), the National Audubon's Society's *Tools of Engagement* (web4.audubon.org/educate/toolkit), the North American Association for Environmental Education *Guidelines of Excellence* series (www.naaee.net/publications), the environmental education program evaluation website of one of the authors (www.meera.snre.umich.edu), and many others. Moreover, all these disciplines have professional conferences and meetings through which applicable insights can be gained and partnerships developed. The Behavior, Energy, and Climate Conference (http://beccconference.org), for example, would be relevant for those interested in enhancing cities' climate change communication efforts.

- *Encourage researchers to investigate questions surrounding sustainability engagement strategies in cities*

There are many unanswered questions about cities' sustainability engagement strategies that researchers could explore. These questions include: what sustainability engagement strategies are used in cities (e.g. how representative is the use of strategies like those highlighted in this chapter) and to what extent do factors like a city's green urban identity (Solecki and Leichenko 2006) explain differences in their adoption and implementation? What are the barriers to using different strategies and how can these barriers be overcome? For example, is the prevalence of information-based strategies due to the assumption that the public just needs to be 'educated' or because of a lack of expertise and resources? Likewise, are approaches such as participatory deliberative democracy avoided because expert-based solutions are assumed to be superior or because of a lack of awareness of this strategy's potential? Finally, what are the relative short- and long-term contributions of different engagement strategies in transitioning cities toward sustainability, and what are the underlying processes to which their outcomes and impacts can be attributed? Such research can also apply and advance theory of how to engage individuals in personal, collective and societal change.

- *Strengthen collaborations and partnerships with a range of stakeholders*

Many of the engagement programs described in this chapter attribute their successes in great part to their collaborations with partnering organizations. Partners in these programs include various city departments, community and non-profit organizations, businesses, universities, schools and museums, among others. Partners provide different types of expertise and resources, facilitate access to networks, and help leverage limited resources. Partners are also critical to minimizing duplication and supporting greater coordination. As part of the National Science Foundation funded Climate and Urban Partnership, for example, partners across four cities will support collaborations across physical, virtual and temporal communities as well as communities of practice. The program aims to reduce the likelihood of audiences receiving potentially conflicting and confusing messages as well as to enhance participating cities' capacities for climate change mitigation and adaptation communication.

CONCLUDING THOUGHTS

These are exciting times for those in cities with an interest in, and commitment to, sustainability engagement strategies. The roles these approaches can play and their value is increasingly being recognized, and they appear to be employed in cities with ever more sophistication and creativity. As long as engagement strategies are grounded in research-based practices and informed by lessons learned through evaluation, we have no doubt that they have the potential to make significant contributions toward fostering the individual, collective and societal changes needed for sustainability.

At the same time, it will be important to keep in mind the advice of one of our colleagues. De Young (2011) reminds us that bringing about change is a difficult and slow process. We should not look at sustainability engagement strategies as quick fixes, nor attempt to force or rush large-scale transformations. Instead, if we are to bring about durable change, sustainability engagement strategies must be implemented over the long run. To fulfill these strategies' promise we must, as he suggests, balance both urgency and patience.

ACKNOWLEDGMENTS

The authors are grateful to University of Michigan graduate students Lindsay Bienick, Sara Cole, Tim Hessen, Meghan Jacokes, Meghan Kelly, Samuel Little, Carrie Robble and Emily Wedes for their assistance with identifying and reviewing literature and programs described in this chapter. We also thank the leaders who reviewed our descriptions of their programs to ensure that these depictions were accurate and who provided additional suggestions for improving the chapter. Feedback by Drs Janette Hartz-Karp and Jennifer Hirsch was particularly helpful.

NOTES

1. Research on intergenerational learning supports that appropriately designed programs can foster behavior change in both youth and adults (Duvall and Zint 2007).
2. This is an external device, such as a Garmin, that allows for two-way communication between drivers and others.
3. Monarch butterflies migrate between Mexico (several colonies overwinter in Michoacán reserves) and the USA and Canada. Monarch butterfly numbers are declining due to climate change.

REFERENCES

Abrahamse, W., L. Steg, C. Vlek and T. Rothengatter (2005), 'A review of intervention studies aimed at household energy conservation', *Journal of Environmental Psychology*, **25**, 273–91.

Aronson, E. and M. O'Leary (1982–83), 'The relative effectiveness of models and prompts on energy conservation: a field experiment in a shower room', *Journal of Environmental Systems*, **12** (3), 219–24.

Attari, S.Z., M.L. DeKay, C.I. Davidson and W. Bruine de Bruin (2010), 'Public perceptions of energy consumption and savings', *Proceedings of the National Academy of Sciences*, **107** (37), 16054–9.

Baltimore Neighborhood Energy Challenge (n.d.), 'Baltimore Neighborhood Energy Challenge phase 1 report', available at http://cleanergreenerbaltimore.org/uploads/files/BNEC%20Pilot%20Results%20Report.pdf.

Berry, D. (2010), 'Delivering energy savings through community-based organizations', *The Electricity Journal*, **23** (9), 65–74.

Brook, A. (2011), 'Ecological footprint feedback: motivating or discouraging?', *Social Influence*, **6** (2), 113–28.

Brulle, R.J. (2010), 'From environmental campaigns to advancing the public dialog: environmental communication for civic engagement', *Environmental Communication*, **4** (1), 82–98.

Burgess, J. and M. Nye (2008), *An Evaluation of EcoTeams as a Mechanism for Promoting Pro-environmental Behaviour Change at Household and Community Scales*, London: Global Action Plan.

Burn, S.M. (1991), 'Social psychology and the stimulation of recycling behaviors: the block leader approach', *Journal of Applied Social Psychology*, **21** (8), 611–29.

Carson, Lyn and Janette Hartz-Karp (2005), 'Adapting and combining deliberative designs: juries, polls, and forums', in John Gastil and Peter Levine (eds), *The Deliberative Democracy Handbook: Strategies for Effective Civic Engagement in the Twenty-first Century*, San Francisco, CA: Jossey-Bass, pp. 120–38.

Carvalho, Anabela and Tarla Rai Peterson (eds) (2012), *Climate Change Politics: Communication and Public Engagement*, Amherst, NY: Cambria Press.

Cialdini, R.B. (2003), 'Crafting normative messages to protect the environment', *Current Directions in Psychological Science*, **12** (4), 105–9.

Cialdini, Robert B., Raymond R. Reno and Carl A. Kallgren (2004), 'A focus theory of normative conduct: recycling the concept of norms to reduce littering in public places', in Elliot Aronson (ed.), *Readings About the Social Animal*, 9th edn, New York: Worth, pp. 56–79.

Corner, A. and A. Randall (2011), 'Selling climate change? The limitations of social marketing as a strategy for climate change public engagement', *Global Environmental Change*, **21**, 1005–14.

Davidson, Scott (2011), 'Up-scaling social behaviour change programmes: the case of EcoTeams', in Lorraine Whitmarsh, Saffron O'Neill and Irene Lorenzoni (eds), *Engaging the Public With Climate Change: Behavior Change and Communication*, Washington, DC: Earthscan, pp. 180–99.

De Young, R. (2011), 'Slow wins: patience, perseverance and behavior change', *Carbon Management*, **2** (6), 607–11.

Dietz, T., G.T. Gardner, J. Gilligan, P.C. Stern and M.P. Vandenbergh (2009), 'Household actions can provide a behavioral wedge to rapidly reduce US carbon emissions', *Proceedings of the National Academy of Sciences*, **106** (44), 18452–6.

Dietz, Thomas and Paul C. Stern (eds) (2002), *New Tools for Environmental Protection: Education, Information, and Voluntary Measures*, Washington, DC: National Academies Press.

Duvall, J. and M. Zint (2007), 'A review of research on the effectiveness of environmental education in promoting intergenerational learning', *Journal of Environmental Education*, **38** (4), 14–24.

Empowerment Institute (2013), 'Sustainable lifestyle campaign: benefits of the program', available at http://www.empowermentinstitute.net/index.php/community/green-living/sustainable-lifestyle-campaign.

Engines Off Colorado (2012), 'Schools', available at http://www.enginesoff.com/2_4_schools.htm.

Environment Canada, Audit and Evaluation Branch (2006), 'Evaluation of the one-tonne challenge program', available at http://www.ec.gc.ca/ae-ve/default.asp?lang=en&n=E0530F2A-1.

Gardner, Gerald T. and Paul C. Stern (2002), *Environmental Problems and Human Behavior*, 2nd edn, Boston, MA: Pearson Custom.

Hartz-Karp, J. (2012), 'Laying the groundwork for participatory budgeting – developing

a deliberative community and collaborative governance: Greater Geraldton, Western Australia', *Journal of Public Deliberation*, **8** (2), Article 6.
Heimlich, J. and N. Ardoin (2008), 'Understanding behavior to understand behavior change: a literature review', *Environmental Education Research*, **14** (3), 215–37.
Hines, J.M., H.R. Hungerford and A.N. Tomera (1987), 'Analysis and synthesis of research on responsible environmental behavior: a meta-analysis', *The Journal of Environmental Education*, **18** (2), 1–8.
Hirsch, J., S. Van Deusen Phillips, E. Labenski, C. Dunford and T. Peters (2011), 'Linking climate action to local knowledge and practice: a case study of diverse Chicago neighborhoods', in Helen Kopnina and Eleanor Shoreman-Ouimet (eds), *Environmental Anthropology Today*, New York: Routledge, pp. 267–96.
Hopper, J.R. and J.M. Nielsen (1991), 'Recycling as altruistic behavior: normative and behavioral strategies to expand participation in a community recycling program', *Environment and Behavior*, **23** (2), 195–220.
ICLEI – Local Governments for Sustainability (2009), 'ICLEI resource guide: outreach and communications', available at http://www.icleiusa.org/action-center/engaging-your-community/outreach-and-communications-guide/Outreach%20and%20Communications%20Guide.pdf.
Inter-Agency Committee of the UN Decade of Education for Sustainable Development (2009), *Symposium on Climate Change Education and Sustainable Cities*, Nairobi, Kenya: United Nations.
Jickling, B. (2005), 'Sustainable development in a globalizing world: a few cautions', *Policy Futures in Education*, **3** (3), 251–9.
Johnson, B.B. (2012), 'Climate change communication: a provocative inquiry into motives, meanings, and means', *Risk Analysis*, **32** (6), 973–91.
Kempton, Willet, Craig K. Harris, Joanne G. Keith and Jeffrey S. Weihl (1985), 'Do consumers know "what works" in energy conservation?', in John Byrne, David A. Schulz and Marvin B. Sussman (eds), *Families and the Energy Transition*, New York: Haworth Press, pp. 115–33.
Knapp, Don (2011), *Climate Communication for Local Governments*, Oakland, CA: ICLEI – Local Governments for Sustainability.
Kurz, T., N. Donaghue and I. Walker (2005), 'Utilizing a sociological–ecological framework to promote water and energy conservation: a field experiment', *Journal of Applied Social Psychology*, **35** (6), 1281–300.
Lokhorst, A.M., C. Werner, H. Staats, E. van Dijk and J.L. Gale (2013), 'Commitment and behavior change: a meta-analysis and critical review of commitment-making strategies in environmental research', *Environment and Behavior*, **45** (1), 3–34.
Lorenzoni, I., S. Nicholson-Cole and L. Whitmarsh (2007), 'Barriers perceived to engaging with climate change among the UK public and their policy implications', *Global Environmental Change*, **17** (3–4), 445–59.
MacRae, G. and T. Stockport (2008), 'Turn your key – reducing truck idling', *Australian Journal of Environmental Education*, **24**, 55–66.
McKenzie-Mohr, Doug (2011), *Fostering Sustainable Behavior: An Introduction to Community-based Social Marketing*, 3rd edn, Gabriola City, BC: New Society Publishers.
McKenzie-Mohr, Doug, Nancy R. Lee, P. Wesley Schultz and Philip A. Kotler (2012), *Social Marketing to Protect the Environment: What Works*, Washington, DC: Sage.
Meneses, G.D. and A.B. Palacio (2007), 'The response to the commitment with block-leader recycling promotion technique: a longitudinal approach', *Journal of Nonprofit & Public Sector Marketing*, **17** (1–2), 83–102.
Moser, S.C. (2006), 'Talk of the city: engaging urbanites on climate change', *Environmental Research Letters*, **1**, 1–10.
Natural Resources Canada (2010), 'Welcome to the idle-free zone', available at http://oee.nrcan.gc.ca/idling/idling.cfm.
Nolan, J.M., P.W. Schultz, R.B. Cialdini, N.J. Goldstein and V. Griskevicius (2008), 'Normative social influence is underdetected', *Personality and Social Psychology Bulletin*, **34** (7), 913–23.

Norgaard, K.M. (2006), '"People want to protect themselves a little bit": Emotions, denial, and social movement nonparticipation', *Sociological Inquiry*, **76** (3), 372–96.
Rabkin, Sarah and David Gershon (2007), 'Changing the world one household at a time: Portland's 30-day program to lose 5,000 pounds', in Susanne C. Moser and Lisa Dilling (eds), *Creating a Climate for Change, Communicating Climate Change and Facilitating Social Change*, New York: Cambridge University Press, pp. 292–302.
Rogers, Everett M. (1995), *Diffusion of Innovations*, 4th edn, New York: Simon & Schuster.
Solecki, W.D. and R.M. Leichenko (2006), 'Urbanization and the metropolitan environment: lessons from New York and Shanghai', *Environment: Science and Policy for Sustainable Development*, **48** (4), 8–23.
Staats, H., P. Harland and H.A.M. Wilke (2004), 'Effecting durable change: a team approach to improve environmental behavior in the household', *Environment and Behavior*, **36** (3), 341–67.
Staats, H.J., A.P. Wit and C.Y.H. Midden (1996), 'Communicating the greenhouse effect to the public: evaluation of a mass media campaign from a social dilemma perspective', *Journal of Environmental Management*, **46** (2), 189–203.
Stern, P.C. (2011), 'Contributions of psychology to limiting climate change', *American Psychologist*, **66** (4), 303–14.
Stoll-Kleemann, S., T. O'Riordan and C.C. Jaeger (2001), 'The psychology of denial concerning climate mitigation measures: evidence from Swiss focus groups', *Global Environmental Change*, **11**, 107–17.
Sutcliffe, M., P. Hooper and R. Howell (2008), 'Can eco-footprinting analysis be used successfully to encourage more sustainable behaviour at the household level?', *Sustainable Development*, **16** (1), 1–16.
Tools of Change (2012), 'Tools of change: proven methods for promoting health, safety and environmental citizenship', available at http://www.toolsofchange.com.
Truelove, Heather Barnes (2009), 'An investigation of the psychology of global warming: perceptions, predictors of behavior, and the persuasiveness of ecological footprint calculators', unpublished doctoral dissertation: Washington State University, Pullman.
Wals, A.E.J. (2011), 'Learning our way to sustainability', *Journal of Education for Sustainable Development*, **5** (2), 177–86.
Wals, Arjen E.J. and Peter B. Corcoran (eds) (2012), *Learning for Sustainability in Times of Accelerating Change*, Wageningen, Netherlands: Wageningen Academic Publishers.
Warburton, Diane (2008), *Evaluation of WWF-UK's Community Learning and Action for Sustainable Living (CLASL)*, Surrey, UK: WWF-UK.
Wheeler, S.M. (2008), 'State and municipal climate change plans: the first generation', *Journal of the American Planning Association*, **74** (4), 481–96.
Whitmarsh, L. (2009), 'Behavioural responses to climate change: asymmetry of intentions and impacts', *Journal of Environmental Psychology*, **29** (1), 13–23.
Whitmarsh, Lorraine, Saffron O'Neill and Irene Lorenzoni (2011), *Engaging the Public with Climate Change: Behaviour Change and Communication*, Washington, DC: Earthscan.
Wolske, Kimberly S. (2011), 'Encouraging climate-friendly behaviors through a community energy challenge: the effects of information, feedback, and shared stories', unpublished doctoral dissertation: University of Michigan, Ann Arbor, MI.
World Environmental Education Congress (2013), 'Environmental education in cities and rural areas: seeking greater harmony', available at http://www.weec2013.org/en/congress-overview/congress-theme.html.
Zint, Michaela (2012), 'Advancing environmental education program evaluation: insights from a review of behavioral outcome evaluations', in Robert B. Stephenson, Michael Brody, Justin Dillon and Arjen E.J. Wals (eds), *International Handbook of Research in Environmental Education*, New York: Routledge, pp. 298–309.

11. Developing effective participatory processes for a sustainable city

Connie P. Ozawa

Transitioning from a city based on consumption levels untethered to resource renewal and reproduction will require a massive collective effort. Participation is important for educating and preparing city residents to deal with tomorrow's challenges. Moreover, sustainability, as contested as the term is, shares qualities with other difficult-to-define but widely utilized terms such as resilience, eco-city and low-carbon urbanization. These future-oriented concepts are inherently imbued with uncertainty. City leaders need to help cultivate cultural norms to collectively accept this uncertainty and plan with it rather than deny it. In the absence of a clear and agreed destination and due to the inherent uncertainties involved, a critical component of an effective strategy is putting in place a strong social base and a process for negotiating and renegotiating agreement as the future unfolds.

Public involvement in public affairs is a popular concept but one that varies widely in meaning, expectations and practice, and raises a plethora of questions. First, who is the public? How are they represented? And, how and when in a public process is the public involved and what is the nature of their involvement? Decision making for a sustainable city adds another layer of complexity. Not only is the question of what exactly constitutes a 'sustainable city' ambiguous, but the desire to anticipate conditions generations into the future brings forward challenges of dealing with uncertainty and unknowable change. Finally, the realities of a globalizing world complicate participatory processes due not only to differences in languages among the public, but also to differences in cultural practices, lifestyle choices and value systems that may impose distinct demands on the physical form of our cities and impede efforts to create comfortable and safe urban environments for all the city's residents.

While policy makers, public managers and their professional staff have recognized and respected the important need for public participation in a democratic society, public involvement methods and techniques are often added into the larger decision framework as a routine and formulaic appendage rather than as a thoughtfully crafted, integrated strategy. Moreover, participation is often viewed as a legal, procedural obligation or as a minor step within a larger process aimed to achieve a narrowly defined instrumental end.

Participatory methods at a very basic level are necessary to inform the public or to solicit perceptions or opinions from persons or groups not otherwise involved in the inner circle of decision making. In one-way communication flows, however, terminology and meanings are not negotiated and the potential for misunderstanding is not avoided, nor are errors detected or corrected. In fact, whether such methods are participatory or not is questionable. More intensive participation methods include public workshops, charrettes, open houses and citizen advisory committees. These interactive events intended to attract residents or businesses or other stakeholders may be convened at multiple points in the decision-making process to help set the agenda, formulate the problem or envision a desired future, collect technical data and information on preferences and values, and even select a preferred alternative solution. Multidirectional communication flows are possible and probable, enabling the deciphering of specialized terminology or clarifying taken-for-granted assumptions, but the extent to which shared meanings and understanding are generated is highly variable and contingent on factors specific to the issues at hand as well as the micropolitics of the institutional context, history, interests and even the specific personalities involved. Unless shared meanings or learning from one another are specifically identified as important objectives of the process, the quality and effectiveness of the participatory process may fall short.

For all methods, in addition to questions about the participants mentioned earlier, key questions also include: (1) are the decision makers listening to the public's input? (2) how are they balancing what they hear with other relevant imperatives? and (3) how is the decision makers' reasoning communicated back to the public? Ultimately, answers to these questions are reflected in the implementation of the decision reached. The degree to which the public feels heard, in turn, will have implications for the attitudes of the public in future processes over the long term. Thus participatory processes aiming to create sustainable cities must consider the full cycle of public decisions, from agenda-setting through implementation.

How is public involvement for sustainability different from our past conceptions? Many of the same issues persist, but fundamentally sustainability forces us to consider processes as part of long-term systems evolution. Individual events should not be viewed as discrete and separate from what occurs following and further into the future, but as the basic building blocks or foundation for future possibilities. Public involvement for sustainability requires greater attention to strategies that exploit the benefits of information sharing, strengthen the adaptive capacity of relationships among the actors, as well as deepen the sense of collective responsibility.

The aim of this chapter is to stimulate thinking about the special aspects of participatory processes pertinent to moving toward more sustainable cities. This chapter begins with a brief listing of participation methods in wide use today and considers their functions and the social goals they aim to achieve. We turn next to a discussion of the special demands of decision making for sustainable cities. Then, I present three participatory strategies to stimulate thinking about how critical elements can come together to establish a positive social foundation for a sustainable city. Participatory processes are always embedded within particular circumstances at a particular time and place, and reflect the institutional contexts, histories and personalities involved. Although direct comparisons and transferability may be limited, these examples nonetheless provide strong leads for further innovation and research.

ELEMENTS OF PARTICIPATORY PROCESSES: A MENU OF METHODS

Figure 11.1 shows commonplace methods that have been developed to facilitate participation, the functions served by these methods, and the social goals stated in the literature as part of the rationale for a participatory process (Beierle and Cayford 2002).

As can be seen in Figure 11.1, public notices play a limited role in achieving the social goals of public involvement, fulfilling a basic level of the social contract by informing the public of upcoming events or decisions, and optimally by this act generating public acceptance and trust in institutions. Surveys similarly inform the public of potential topics for the public agenda while also gathering limited data from those surveyed. The information is limited to the extent that the issues are framed by the survey author and questions are closed-ended rather than open-ended. The remaining methods can also be seen largely as information-gathering tools. The extent to which any of these tools meets specific social goals depends, of course, on the specific parameters, context and microdynamics of the processes.

Notably only workshops/charrettes and committees with citizen members offer consistent (though not always successfully realized) opportunities for deliberation and negotiations that can lead to not just technically sounder decisions, but also to refinement of knowledge, an increase in community intelligence and community capacity, and developing a sense of citizenship, which is essential for nurturing social responsibility. These

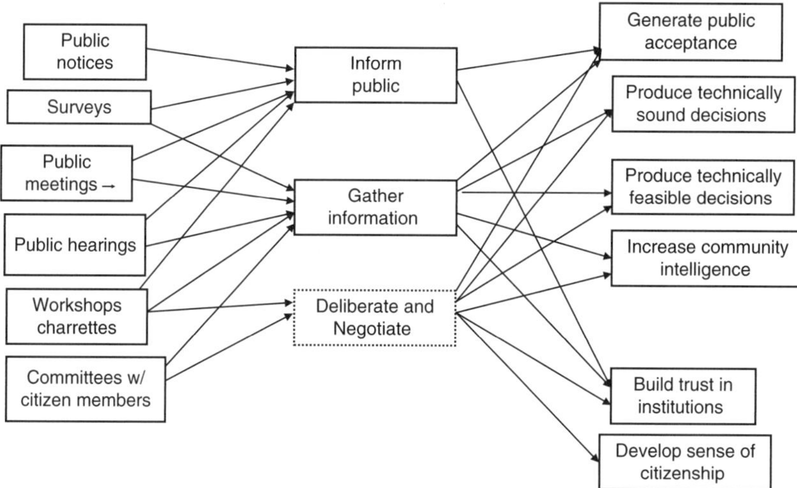

Figure 11.1 Methods of public involvement, functions and social goals

latter participatory methods are highly interactive. They are also more exclusive strategies as they tend to attract a narrower range of persons, are relatively costly in terms of human and material resources, and are logistically constrained in terms of the overall number of persons who can effectively participate.

In fact, any given public decision-making process in the USA today would probably include a suite of methods and techniques applied concurrently, sequentially and iteratively during various phases. An effective strategy for moving our cities toward sustainability will make use of several of these techniques. Stopping short of asserting a technical definition of sustainability, which is contested and continually evolving, certain logics suggest that social goals of decision making for sustainability should include: (1) increase community intelligence: sharing data and information to create as sound an understanding about natural and human-made systems as possible given the state of knowledge and the range of stakeholder perspectives; (2) increase community capacity: cultivating a sense of mutual respect arising from acknowledgment of a common fate and recognition of multiple perspectives; and (3) increase a sense of citizenship: accepting the shared responsibility of shared decision making. Achieving these social goals requires open and multidirectional communication flows and other process dynamics that are elaborated in the following section, which considers the key drivers of public decision-making processes, the participants.

ELEMENTS OF PARTICIPATORY PROCESSES: THE PEOPLE, STRUCTURE AND DYNAMICS OF THE PROCESS

Initiating a participatory process begins with the question of who should be expected to participate. Twenty-five years ago, Susskind and Cruikshank (1987) offered a useful framework for public managers to identify whom they ought to invite to participate in mediated negotiations to effectively resolve public disputes. Their recommendations are informative also for participatory processes more generally. Moving beyond referencing what might be viewed as an amorphous 'public', Susskind and Cruikshank asserted that public decision making should include four categories of stakeholders: those persons or organizations with (1) legal authority, such as a landowner or an agency with a public mandate, (2) economic resources, such as a firm with capital for construction or restoration work, (3) legal standing, as recognized by existing laws, or (4) moral standing, such as organized rights groups or religious organizations or those likely to be directly adversely affected by the proposed activity. In fact, it is difficult to imagine a project of any scope that would not involve a public agency and a private landowner or developer, and it is noteworthy that including public agencies directly in the process provides a link to our representative democratic infrastructure and thereby avoids the potential privatization of public decisions. Those who initiate a major action presumably command resources for implementation, and their commitment to a project would require consideration of their interests and they must be part of any conversation. The prescription to involve those with legal standing is intended to avoid lengthy implementation delays that might arise from litigation by those opposing a decision. Finally, Susskind and Cruikshank's advice to include those with moral standing might be seen as a preemptive, cautionary approach to anticipate those who may not have legal standing under current law but who may soon obtain it or those who currently enjoy substantial public support for their viewpoints despite their lack of legal standing. Given the dynamic nature of the meaning of 'sustainability', this last category is particularly relevant here.

More recently, Innes and Booher (2010, p. 35) have suggested 'Diversity, Interdependency, Authentic Dialogue', or DIAD, as both descriptive and normative guidelines for successful collaboration. Their prescription for diversity of participants is intended as a means to ensure that a broad and deep array of political and technical information is brought into the process. This diversity element also has special significance in our rapidly internationalizing world, and one that may suggest additional barriers at first. As cities become increasingly cosmopolitan, working together to build a sustainable urban future demands attention to groups whose first language may be different from ours, whose housing preferences may be multigenerational rather than nuclear-family occupancy, whose experiences with authority may be one of oppression, not service (Fincher and Iverson 2008; Sandercock 2003). For example, some immigrants come from countries in which government was regarded with caution and distrust. Such persons are often highly suspicious of questioning by government representatives and attending a public meeting to voice their concerns about government practices simply would be inconsistent with their own survival strategies. The needs and preferences of these groups may stretch our preconceived notions of participatory processes and burden our previously practiced methods, but we would be negligent if we failed to acknowledge them and modify our approaches accordingly. The varied life experiences and cultural preferences of such groups may expand the array of options we ultimately consider. In other words, attending to inclusion and expanding the diversity of participation is essential in a globalizing world and may deliver new ideas for urban innovations.

A second dimension to consider is how the public is represented. Are all stakeholders directly involved in deliberative meetings or are groups represented by designated spokespersons?

Involving all individuals falling into the categories suggested by Susskind and Cruikshank is often theoretically and pragmatically challenging, especially in more intensive participatory processes such as advisory committees or workshops. Developers may be formally involved in public decision-making processes through hired consultants with an explicit contractual obligation. If an affected party includes a large number of individuals, for example, residents in a neighborhood or parents of schoolchildren, a spokesperson for that group may be chosen (by the group itself, ideally) to participate. Are neighborhood residents, even if members of a neighborhood association or a parent–teachers' organization, held to a similar level of accountability as the hired consultant? How formal is the relationship between spokespersons and the groups they represent? More importantly, what is the flow of information exchanged and the level of learning among the entire stakeholder group that occurs when representatives are involved? Does such an approach constitute 'public participation' at all?

In fact, more commonly, participants in public workshops and advisory committees are targeted or selected for their 'representativeness', or the presumed ability of that person to understand and express the needs of the group for whom they are assigned representation. The appropriateness of one approach or the other will vary, depending on circumstances (Beatley and Brower 1994).

Clearly, public involvement is a concept that is fraught with dilemmas.

A third critical element is the quality of relationships among all the groups involved. Innes and Booher's guideline of 'interdependency' among interests speaks to ensuring cooperation among participants whose attainment of goals is dependent on the consent and actions of others. This interdependency also delivers *de facto* recognition of the legal and moral legitimacy of participants. In *The Deliberative Practitioner*, John Forester has provided numerous quotes from planners regarding the importance of recognition and its effect on relationships. One Israeli transportation planner makes a simple statement about the value of listening to others. He says, 'If you give legitimacy to the needs of your opponent, even if you can't answer them, even if you can't come up with a solution, then they act differently toward you' (Forester 1999, p. 109). Sustainable cities require the actions and cooperation of multiple actors. Therefore acknowledgment of others' legitimacy and our interconnectedness is critical.

Investing in developing solid social relationships is not easy. However, the City of Seattle, WA, provides a promising illustrative example of how a focus on relationship-building and social capital might be operationalized. For more than a decade, the city has committed to enabling neighborhoods to create planning agendas for their local community. The city's strategy includes placing professionals throughout the city to serve as community liaisons to spur outreach and engagement activities. This infrastructure lays a consistent and continuing social foundation for the range of activities that arise sporadically from any of the various city departments. In 2009, this effort was expanded to address the increasing diversity of the city with the creation of 'Public Outreach and Engagement Liaisons' (POELs), persons culturally and linguistically fluent in one of the ethnic groups prevalent in the host neighborhood to serve as bridge builders.

'Authentic dialogue' is the third element of Innes and Booher's model, and it may appear idealistic and overly demanding, if even achievable. However, Innes and Booher suggest that, if participants recognize their dependency on others, they will see the need to communicate accurately to others to ensure that technically sound and politically stable problem-solving is achieved. In other words, 'authentic dialogue' may be understood as simply a commitment to communicate accurately.

Another vital component of a participatory process to consider is the level of trust and social capital among participants. On a practical level, sustained interactions among participants provide greater opportunity for the development of cognition-based trust than one-shot or multiple, but intermittent, interactions. Cognition-based trust is rational, developed over time with the collection of experiences that match words with behaviors, demonstrate competencies, and build and reinforce understanding of others' interests and interdependence (Kasperson et al. 1992; Ozawa 2010).

A simple example of cognition-based trust is the trust that pedestrians hold when stepping into a crosswalk on a busy street. Pedestrians 'trust' drivers to stop. While it is true that it is illegal for a driver *not* to stop for a pedestrian in a crosswalk in the USA, the legality is second to the expectation. Pedestrians learn quickly that the level at which they should 'trust' drivers varies from city to city, based on their observations and experiences, or cognition. Similarly, residents in a city with a history of open and transparent decision making coupled with congruent actions will tend to 'trust' government representatives when compared to residents in a city where public actions appear routinely to contradict public statements. Processes deliberately intending to cultivate trust must allow sufficient opportunities for interactions and adequate time for reflection and appreciation of those interactions in order for trust to grow.

Social capital refers to the quality of individuals sharing cultural norms, purposes and pursuits. Robert Putnam has identified two distinct types of social capital, bonding and bridging. In general terms, bonding social capital is that which exists among members of a homogeneous group; bridging social capital is that which exists between members of heterogeneous groups. Social capital allows for candid exchanges of political interests and other potentially risky information sharing. Social capital may result when such information sharing yields positive outcomes (Putnam 2000). Thus an effective participatory process is one that both utilizes and produces social capital, especially the type that bridges unlike groups.

Finally, in contrast to a community subject to 'top–down' or 'command-and-control' approaches, a community that understands the reasoning behind actions and their objectives is better prepared to adapt if conditions do not unfold as expected. When participants understand the limits of knowledge, lack of certainty is forgiven. In a sense, this is decentralized decision making: shared control also implies shared blame, which quickly translates into no blame when the future does not unfold as planned. Given the current lack of surety or consensus about what constitutes a truly sustainable system, decision making today for a sustainable city will undoubtedly require corrections along the way. The ability of groups to adapt to changing knowledge bases and conditions is a goal and consequence of effective participatory processes for sustainability.

In summary, participatory processes for a sustainable city should be inclusive, diverse, generate a shared understanding of interdependency, invite multiple sources and types of information in order to build together as strong a knowledge base as possible, and build social capital among all participants, including government representatives. An effective participatory process would be designed to allow for sharing of participants' hopes, dreams and fears, what they care about, or, stated more drily, their political interests. A 'good' process would engender trust among the participants to prepare them to confront changes in expected future conditions, to adapt together. In fact, while not yet pervasive, promising examples of participatory processes exist. In the following pages, three examples of participatory processes, each successful in its own way, are presented.

COMMUNITY PARTNERSHIPS: THE OREGON SOLUTIONS APPROACH

Community partnerships are voluntary associations of residents, businesses and government to pool resources to resolve commonly viewed problems. Watershed stewardship groups are an example that can be found across the USA. Watershed groups are voluntary organizations that undertake non-regulatory approaches to restore damaged watersheds and prevent future harm. Their work ranges from outreach and education about the assets of urban streams to the organization of volunteer work groups to remove invasive plant species or restore eroded stream banks. The level of public funding awarded, the degree of formal institutional linkages and support, and other logistical details vary from one stewardship group to another. What is emblematic of watershed organizations is the shared commitment of members to an articulated goal, watershed health.

For the past decade, a small but influential program called 'Oregon Solutions' has offered technical support and guidance to community residents, businesses and elected leaders to undertake projects to solve local problems. The program started with the passage of the state Sustainability Act of 2001, and moved from the governor's office to the National Policy Consensus Center at Portland State University in 2002. Similar in many ways to the public support given to watershed councils, the program has assisted communities across the state to develop partnerships to design and implement more than 60 projects as of 2012 (orsolutions.org 2013). Projects have ranged in scale from the site-specific to regional, and have varied in focus from creation of interpretive centers to highlight a local asset, such as fossil beds, to planning for a biomass facility in a timber town with a declining economic base, to completion of a recreational trail system. The basic principle underlying the Oregon Solutions approach is that collaboration among diverse stakeholders can optimize a community's resources to focus efforts to design and implement a project to achieve a significant community goal.

Oregon Solutions invites local community leaders – who may be an elected official, a businessperson, or a leader of a local community organization – to seek assistance in bringing together a diverse array of residents, businesses, local government and others to address a mutually recognized challenge. Through a consensus-seeking framework, the program provides technical information and support, but meetings are facilitated by a member of the local community and the process moves forward only on the energy and will of participants. In other words, Oregon Solutions is clear that it expects ownership of the project to rest not with the program but with community members. Project participants are as varied as the projects themselves, but they typically involve public entities such as local, state or federal government agencies, public schools, private businesses, industry groups and local non-profit organizations.

Although the focus of the work may be fairly bounded in time and space, such as the construction of a trail, the social relationships that develop are often as lasting as the gravel laid down for the pathway. The consensus framework for decision-making nurtures an understanding of personalities, values, preferences and political interests among the participants that goes beyond the specific issues at hand (Henderson 2010). In fact, in most cases, the initiating problem behind the Oregon Solutions project does not end with simple resolution. Ongoing relationships must be continually renegotiated as project conditions change both in the local environment as well as in the external economic and political context and as the individuals themselves move through their lives and play different roles in the community. The creation of the interpretive center, for example, requires ongoing cooperation for the development, operation and maintenance of the facility. The Oregon Solutions approach captures local energy for immediate projects and builds capacity for the future. In ways similar to watershed councils across the national landscape, the capacity of the individuals involved increases as they interact with others toward a shared goal.

PARTICIPATORY PLANNING: THE EAST PORTLAND ACTION PLAN

Community-based, participatory planning processes represent an approach to public involvement that requires a substantial commitment of resources by a sponsoring organization to sustain a mechanism over an indefinite period of time. The process can begin as early as the agenda-setting stage and continue through implementation of not just one, but many, projects. One exemplary case of participatory planning is occurring in Portland, Oregon, ongoing since 2007.

East Portland represents the largest land area annexed by the city since the mid-1980s and, in 2010, was home to about one-quarter of the City of Portland's population (593 820, according to 2012 US census estimates). It is an area that has experienced a variety of earth-shaking events. Just prior to annexation in the 1970s, East Portland neighborhoods were bifurcated by the construction of an interstate freeway (I-205); a major consequence of annexation to residents in the 1990s was a forced transition from septic tanks to city sewer lines, which imposed severe stress on household budgets. Today, as closer-in neighborhoods gentrify, East Portland is drawing large numbers of residents in search of affordable housing. While the area hosts a strong school system, compared to other Portland neighborhoods, the physical infrastructure remains unimpressive, lacking in public parks, transit access, bike lanes and even sidewalks. East Portland is also showing a notable demographic shift, from nearly 90 percent white in 1990 to just over 70 percent white in 2013, and 40 percent of the population of non-white or Hispanic heritage.

State and local elected officials and community leaders assembled in late 2007, and sought to address the area's deficiencies, particularly the under-investment of public funds, and the impending challenges of an increasingly culturally diverse community. The purpose of creating the East Portland Action Plan was to provide 'leadership and guidance to public agencies and other entities on how to strategically address community-identified issues and allocate resources to improve livability for neighborhoods in the East Portland Neighborhood Office (EPNO) coalition area' (City of Portland 2009, p. 2).

The agenda was huge. Relationships had been strained. The process could easily have been overwhelming. City, county and state elected officials, more than two dozen city and county staff, special service districts, business and community organizations, and hundreds of residents met at community workshops, in small work groups and at advisory committee meetings. Together, over the course of eight months, they identified 268 problems needing attention. The Portland City Council approved the plan in February 2009, and partnership projects were quickly initiated. As of January 2013, the city has committed more than $1.3 million to improvement projects. But the 'plan' did not end with the publication of the document or even the funding of action items, several of which have been fully implemented as of 2013. The planning staff continues to convene monthly meetings at the local high school, providing language assistance upon request and dinner for those who attend the early evening meetings, and maintaining the dialogue over how best to suit the needs of its residents as East Portland moves into the future. A website keeps a record of past aspirations and achievements, and updates on projects and future agendas. The monthly meetings continue to be heavily attended by neighborhood residents, and membership on committees, which requires relatively minor but definite indicators of commitment, continues to grow.

These ongoing and interactive meetings reflect the recognition by the city of the need to maintain close connections with the neighborhood in order to improve conditions and ensure livability that suits current residents. In fact, one of the Plan's action items implemented was the hiring of a community planner specifically to steward the East Portland Action Plan. The healthy attendance of these meetings reflects a sense of effectiveness and satisfaction among the residents. Consequently, four years after its approval, the Plan lives on as a participatory process, engaging the residents of the community and local public agencies, and as broadcast from its active website, http://eastportlandactionplan.org/.

COMMUNITY BENEFITS AGREEMENTS: THE STAPLES CENTER

A third strategy for involving the public constructively in development decisions entails creating written agreements between a developer or business and the local community. Non-profit organizations such as the LA Alliance for a New Economy and Strategic Actions for a Just Economy in Los Angeles and Good Jobs New York in New York City, representing community, labor and environmental interests, have found that they can leverage their moral authority around expected, adverse impacts to their neighborhoods to obtain legally enforceable concessions from developers and operators of large-scale projects.

Community benefits agreements (CBAs) are reminiscent of 'good neighbor agreements', which date back to the late 1970s. Good neighbor agreements emerged from residents' concerns about workers' safety, jobs and local environmental effects from the operations of industrial facilities, particularly with respect to their use of toxic chemicals and contaminants. Good neighbor agreements with industrial facilities rely on the strength of local organizations to establish their legitimacy in a public decision-making process, such as permit renewal for plant operations or proposed facility expansion. In the mid-1980s, non-governmental organizations were bolstered by the 1986 amendments to the Superfund Amendments and Reauthorization Act (SARA), which made public the emission reports on hundreds of common industrial chemicals, many highly toxic. The local facility's dependence on a local workforce and good community relations provided the incentive for plant managers to participate in negotiations that were largely separate from the formal regulatory process and did not involve public officials in any official capacity. Consequently, enforcement of a non-binding agreement can be problematic if the facility is owned by a corporate entity with weak ties to the local community, but in smaller communities where plant operators and management are also members of the local community good neighbor agreements have been effective.

In contrast, CBAs are legal documents appended to formal public decisions granting approval for a proposed project. These agreements are developed after the initiating agency (whether it be a private business or a permitting authority) has a fairly complete idea of the proposed project and associated activities.

The CBA is negotiated and signed by the developer and a community representative, and signifies community support for project permit applications and other types of local government endorsements. They are intended not only to mitigate downstream physical harms in the local community and compensate for expected economic losses, but also to enable the sharing of expected benefits from proposed urban development. Items included in CBAs include provisions for traffic congestion management, the construction of new amenities for the community, or the assignment of first rights to jobs.

A pathbreaking and widely cited model is an agreement over the second phase of downtown Los Angeles' Staples Center district. The community, which was represented by a coalition of 29 community groups, including 300 immigrant residents from the area, was sufficiently organized to pose a credible threat to the developers, who needed not only permit approvals from local government, but also substantial public subsidies. From the industry or developer's perspective, an agreement with the community can not only better ensure favorable decisions by government bodies, but also more positive media coverage of their enterprises (Romney 2001) and, potentially, a healthier, safer and more attractive local environment for their investment.

CBAs, in theory, could address any number of issues ranging from environmental quality and economic opportunities, to local governance. The Staples Center agreement included provisions for parks and park improvements, living-wage jobs, local hiring preferences and job training for displaced residents, subsidized residential parking, and construction of affordable housing units. Although representatives of the community hammered out the details of the negotiation, periodic updates were given to the community at large and, over time, residents' mood reportedly changed. What started as an adversarial and angry posture toward the developer and later become more respectful (Romney 2001).

DISCUSSION

These processes illustrate to varying degrees successful attainment of social goals central to addressing the long-term welfare and well-being, the sustainability, of a city. Oregon Solutions projects are a prime example of successful community-based initiatives, supported by a public entity that lends technical expertise in process design, but does not lead the process, and can serve as one suggestive participatory model for moving toward sustainability. When public entities stay in the background, space is created for community members to assume ownership and agency, helping to create not just a physical but also a social environment for their future. The process is soup-to-nuts, involving not only the formulation of the problem but also project planning through to implementation and ongoing maintenance. The repeated opportunities for interaction among participants sets the stage for information sharing and social learning, building community capacity and increasing collective intelligence about the issues facing the community. The 'scrappiness' that often characterizes Oregon Solutions projects means that all types of resources are valued and respected: hard dollars to purchase construction materials or to hire additional expertise, residents' sweat equity, as well as the wisdom gained through experience of older community members. The experience of producing a tangible product for the community is a visible and long-lasting reminder of an effort, and of the positive relationships that were built.

Similar to watershed councils, however, as a voluntary association, Oregon Solutions projects are not by design open to a broad array of participants. In fact, one might argue that the opposite is true: the premise of collaboration that ignites the process may discourage the inclusion of dissident voices. In other words, community members working to achieve a specific objective might be inclined to invite like-minded individuals rather than potential naysayers into the group. This may be true to the extent that others in the community are not holding key economic or political resources and, if true, these sorts of community-based participatory processes arguably generate 'bonding social capital' but deliver less on 'bridging social capital'. In fact, Oregon Solutions projects tend to involve a wide range of community groups often with divergent concerns. Not only are difficult public issues rarely handled without the input of traditional allies and enemies, but often it is the anticipation of conflict that motivates communities to seek assistance from Oregon Solutions in the first place.

In contrast, the East Portland Action Plan is an example of the dynamism of good planning and a participatory process that is self-consciously designed to broaden its outreach to groups historically underrepresented in public decision making. The city responded to the deficits of a neighborhood that had arisen over time. Whether the spatial inequity in the city was a product of intentional discrimination or simple neglect, the city leaders committed to investing in listening to the residents of the area to determine how best to improve the living conditions of their neighborhoods. Early evidence of the city's responsiveness spurred the residents to move forward from past hurts and motivated them to engage in discussions with the city. The city's hiring of a full-time planner to shepherd this process, and the planner's attention to basic needs to enable residents to attend meetings, such as providing food, childcare and language interpreters, were minor but meaningful gestures that reinforced a sense of mutual respect. Trust between residents and the city leadership was further rebuilt as concerns brought forward in the public meetings were answered by action, signaling the city's intent. Four years down the road, the monthly community meetings continue to draw new residents and the now more familiar faces from the neighborhood are stepping into leadership roles. New projects continue to be identified as past issues are addressed and resolved. The city seems to have proven to the increasingly cultural diverse residents of East Portland that it cares about the neighborhood, acknowledges their mutual interdependence and that working together to build a better future is a shared goal. Good working relationships for collaborative planning are essential ingredients for our efforts to not just 'manage our co-existence in shared space', paraphrasing Patsy Healey from her book on collaborative planning (Healey, 2006), but to aggressively confront the challenges of sustainability.

The third technology in participatory processes presented here is the community benefits agreement. CBAs are an effective strategy for turning adversarial relationships between a developer and local neighborhood into a constructive partnership. The Staples Center experience also illustrates the ability to use CBAs to address physical, social and economic dimensions of a neighborhood's future. Although the engagement of the community with decision making may be viewed as relatively constrained since negotiations typically occur after many details of financing and project design are completed, important improvements may be added to enhance the product for existing residents, future residents, the developers and public and private investors. In the Staples case, park space and affordable housing units amid the upscale development were added during the negotiations. If constructed properly, the park can provide non-threatening, informal spaces for residents of different socioeconomic status to encounter one another. Possibly, with the aid of children or dogs, today's social unifiers, residents can grow familiar with 'strangers' and enjoy a less alienating urban environment. To the extent that social harmony is considered essential for sustainable cities, the impact of thoughtfully and deliberately crafted CBAs around major urban developments can help to weave a more sustainable social fabric (Fincher and Iverson 2008).

Distinct from the other two examples of participatory processes, CBAs do not directly engage community residents. The highly technical language of the document requires oversight if not a leading role by professional advocates rather than direct participation by residents. CBAs are legal documents and their monitoring and enforcement are conducted in the shadow of the court. Consequently, social goals such as increasing community intelligence or capacity are not predictable by-products of this strategy. It is also worth noting that CBAs require a relatively high level of interest-group organization prior to initiation. Nonetheless, they are significant and effective tools to utilize in the context of what is often a hostile and adversarial situation, and can be an important component of a larger strategy of participatory processes to move toward a sustainable city.

CONCLUSION

In their intriguing study published in 2010, Portney and Berry compared the cities with local sustainability policies against survey data and found that residents in cities that that have made a commitment to sustainability are more likely to sign petitions, demonstrate in the streets, join local reform groups and participate in neighborhood associations. While their examination was rather broad, they concluded that 'sustainable cities are participatory cities' (Portney and Berry 2010, p. 133).

Portney and Berry also acknowledge that their work is silent on causality. Does participation yield a concern for sustainability, or does a commitment to sustainability create a demand for participation or an investment in participatory processes? In many regards, the directions of causality matter less than the nature of that participation, especially given the fact that most cities are currently undertaking participatory processes on a fairly regular if not ongoing basis.

Participatory processes that can move us forward toward sustainability come in many forms. There is no magic bullet or one-size-fits-all model. The three examples reviewed here offer three different strategies for building community capacity, increasing community intelligence and strengthening relationships and a sense of citizenship. The Oregon Solutions approach highlights the latent capacity of communities to actively collaborate. The East Portland Action Plan process is an excellent strategy for generating bridging capital within a community undergoing demographic change, not only because of the projects or objectives of its work, but also by providing space for people from diverse backgrounds to come together and to get to know one another. Community benefits agreements rely on a formal legal structure and are relatively weak tools for generating social capital. Nonetheless, the objective of CBAs, the material benefits to the community, may be structured to generate a more positive social environment for nurturing informal means of increasing community capacity. In all cases, the participation was meaningful because it yielded tangible results.

The future unfolds with each day. Each opportunity for public decisions presents a chance to improve the sustainability of our cities by strengthening the social foundation for confronting the hard decisions that are needed to transition our cities from centers of consumption to agglomerations of people informed about the biophysical and social consequences of their actions. Careful and critical examinations of participatory processes such as the three reviewed here should encourage further innovations. Key points to bear in mind are the need to increase community intelligence so that we can work with a solid understanding of the biophysical and social components of our world; to increase our capacity to work together because the complexity of transforming from a consumption-based economy to a sustainable one is monumental and will not be achieved without a broad, collaborative effort; and to increase our sense of collective vulnerability and success because we are ultimately, in fact, all in this together.

REFERENCES

Beatley, T. and D.J. Brower (1994), 'Representation in comprehensive planning: an analysis of the Austin plan process', *Journal of the American Planning Association*, **60** (2), 185–97.

Beierle, Thomas C. and Jerry Cayford (2002), *Democracy in Practice: Public Participation in Environmental Decisions*, Washington, DC: Resources for the Future.

City of Portland Bureau of Planning and Sustainability (2009), *East Portland Action Plan, Adopted February 18, 2009*, Portland, OR: City of Portland.

Fincher, Ruth and Kurt Iveson (2008), *Planning for Diversity: Redistribution, Recognition and Encounter*, New York: Palgrave Macmillan.

Forester, John (1999), *The Deliberative Practitioner: Encouraging Participatory Planning Processes*, Boston, MA: MIT Press.

Healey, Patsy (2006), *Collaborative Planning: Shaping Places in Fragmented Societies*, 2nd edn, New York: Palgrave Macmillan.

Henderson, Tia S. (2010), 'The foundation to collaborate: understanding the role of participant interests', Portland, OR: Portland State University (unpublished dissertation).

Innes, Judith and David Booher (2010), *Planning with Complexity: An Introduction to Collaborative Rationality for Public Policy*, New York: Routledge.

Kasperson, R., D. Golding and S. Tuler (1992), 'Social distrust as a factor in siting hazardous facilities and communicating risks', *Journal of Social Issues*, **48** (4), 161–87.

Oregon Solutions (n.d.), 'Oregon Solutions', available at orsolutions.org (accessed 4 March 2013).

Ozawa, Connie P. (2005), 'Putting science in its place', in Bruce Stiftel and John Scholz (eds), *Adaptive Governance: Florida's Water Conflicts*, Washington, DC: Resources for the Future, pp. 185–95.

Ozawa, Connie P. (2011), 'Planning resilient communities: insights from experiences with risky technologies', in Bruce Goldstein (ed.), *Collaborative Resilience: Moving Through Crisis to Opportunity*, Boston, MA: MIT Press, pp. 19–38.

Portney, K.E. and J.M. Berry (2010), 'Participation and the pursuit of sustainability in US cities', *Urban Affairs Review*, **46** (1), 119–39.
Putnam, Robert (2000), *Bowling Alone: The Collapse and Revival of American Community*, New York: Simon & Schuster.
Romney, L. (2001), 'Community, developers agree on Staples plan', *Los Angeles Times*, Home Edition, A-1.
Sandercock, Leonie (2003), *Cosmopolis II: Mongrel Cities of the 21st Century*, London and New York: Continuum.
Susskind, Lawrence and Jeffrey Cruikshank (1987), *Breaking the Impasse: Consensual Approaches to Resolving Public Disputes*, New York: Basic Books.

12. A measure of justice: environmental equity and the sustainable city

Manuel Pastor

INTRODUCTION

The concept of environmental justice has its origins in both community organizing and academic research. Many date the organizing part of the equation to a set of protests in 1982 by a predominantly low-income and African-American community in Warren County, North Carolina. Seeking to stop plans to build a toxic dump in their region, concerned residents joined forces with the National Association for Advancement of Colored People (NAACP) and the United Church of Christ (UCC) in a protest in which 500 people were arrested – and together, they were able to both block the development of the dump and effectively launch a new social movement (Bullard 1994; Cole and Foster 2000).

Research and measurement was an early and important part of this effort. The Warren County protest led the US General Accounting Office to conduct an initial analysis that suggested that there were indeed racial disparities in the location of toxic sites in three southeastern states (US General Accounting Office (GAO) 1983). This prompted the UCC Commission for Racial Justice to conduct the first nationwide study that demonstrated a correlation between hazardous waste facilities and neighborhoods of color called *Toxic Wastes and Race in the United States* (United Church of Christ 1987). A wave of other studies followed and, by 1994, the idea that disparities in environmental amenities and disamenities might have racial and income dimensions was so accepted that then-President Clinton signed Executive Order #12898 on Environmental Justice.

The executive order mandated that each federal agency had to 'make achieving environmental justice part of its mission by identifying and addressing, as appropriate, disproportionately high and adverse human health or environmental effects of its programs, policies, and activities on minority populations and low-income populations' (Clinton 1994). Specifically, this meant that projects and decisions should: (1) avoid, minimize, or mitigate disproportionately high burdens; (2) ensure the full participation by all potentially affected communities; and (3) prevent denial of, reduction in, or significant delay in receipt of benefits. And the adoption of the executive order eventually led to a cascade downward to states that then launched their own efforts to investigate and ameliorate environmental inequities (Bonorris 2010).

Since the era of the Warren County protests, the early empirical research and the 1994 executive order, researchers, policy makers and community leaders have grappled with a series of important questions, including: (1) does the relationship between race, income and the environment really hold up across more complicated studies that take into account other locational factors?; (2) if such a relationship is found, what are the proactive tools to both measure environmental disparity and adopt policies to prevent over-exposure and excess concentration?; and (3) what, if any, is the relationship between efforts to address environmental injustice and broader efforts to address the environment?

This chapter looks at the second and third of these questions, particularly in the context of how cities and regions seeking to be more sustainable might measure, incorporate and address environmental inequity in the course of their work.[1] While we know that some think the first of these questions remains a controversy for some analysts, we will spend little time on it precisely because we think it is not: while there are exceptions in any particular location and for any particular media, a landmark comprehensive meta-study concluded that disparities do exist, even when one uses multivariate analysis, and that race is actually a more consistent and significant predictor of environmental 'bads' than income (Ringquist 2005). In explaining that pattern, we have suggested that it is less about race *per se* than it is about voice in the political process, something that suggests why it is important to develop proactive tools that help those with less influence to be shielded before disparities occur – exactly the topic of this chapter (Pastor et al. 2001; Pastor et al. 2005; Morello-Frosch 2002).

Thus, here we look at the second and third issues: why environmental justice might matter for sustainability and how regional planners and others might measure environmental disparities in meaningful ways. We argue in this chapter that, while environmental justice seems like a local affair and has often been addressed at a federal or national level, it really ought to be considered region by region. We also suggest that any such approach needs to be cumulative: to truly reflect the realities of disadvantaged communities, it should consider the multitude of sources that impact people at a neighborhood level and account for social vulnerability. Finally, we argue that this is an area in which community engagement is as important as community outcomes and talk about why such participation should be a key element in the sustainability toolkit.

We begin the chapter with a brief discussion of environmental justice and why and how it matters for sustainability. We then take up the issues mentioned above – the need to take a regional approach, the importance of considering cumulative impacts, and the benefits of community engagement – and offer a few practical tools along the way. We then take up the current state of the metrics of measurement: it turns out that our state, California, is doing pretty well and several methods are emerging, including one we have helped develop, that will likely be in more widespread use in the future. Finally, we conclude with some recommendations for planners, including a warning about why getting to the commons might actually involve a bit of conflict.

WHAT HAS ENVIRONMENTAL JUSTICE GOT TO DO WITH SUSTAINABILITY?

Sustainability is widely understood to be composed of three interdependent components: equity, environment and economy, also known as the three Es (World Commission on Environment and Development 1992; Campbell 1996; Portney 2003; Vos 2007). In some sense, then, equity in environmental conditions is baked into the notion of sustainability – but the reality is that the three Es are often conceptualized as being somewhat in competition or tension, with the planner's objective being to strike a balance between different interests (Campbell 1996).

This tradeoff framework is most familiar for the case of equity and the economy, with the standard story being that too much equality could smother incentives and reduce economic growth. Interestingly, a new body of evidence is beginning to challenge this supposed tension through comparisons between countries, considerations of the USA over time, and analyses of the experiences of various metropolitan regions in the USA (Eberts et al. 2006; Pastor and Benner 2008; Berg and Ostry 2011; Stiglitz 2012). Each of these studies finds that equity and inclusions can prompt faster or more long-lasting growth; the underlying notion is that at some point too much inequality (and we seem to have gotten there in recent years) can be harmful, partly because it can trigger underinvestments in human capital, create damaging social tensions, and impede consensus on growth strategies moving forward (Benner and Pastor 2012).[2]

What about the relationship of equity to the environment? Parallel to the equity–economy consideration, there has long been a framework that we have a sort of environmental Kuznets curve in which the initial process of development is associated with environmental degradation; attention to environmental protection is consider to be the province of wealthier societies (Stern 2004). The domestic analogy to the Kuznets curve is essentially a cross-sectional variant on that longitudinal story: it is thought that less economically advantaged individuals might tend to be less protective of the environment and more willing to sacrifice protecting the planet if it means protecting their jobs.

Interestingly, that attitudinal frame is not found in California, a state where environmental restrictions are generally cutting-edge and where the demographic change over the last 30 years foreshadows what the USA is expected to go through over the next 70. Recent state polling, for example, has indicated that communities of color are actually more concerned than the state's white residents about air quality and climate change, and are also even more willing than whites to make economic tradeoffs, should there be any, to improve the environment.[3]

This suggests a political-economy reason why more equity might produce a better environment: by paying attention to communities that may face the worst environmental conditions, we can strengthen the base of public support for sustainability. After all, lower-income individuals may experience problems with localized pollution most directly and hence the implicit domestic Kuznets curve on policy preferences about environmental protection would not hold, particularly in more democratic settings (Farzin and Bond 2006).[4] Conversely, saddling the brunt of the challenge on marginalized groups with the least voice in the policy-making process ensures that the problem receives less policy attention. Interestingly, this may have large overall impacts on environmental quality: by making the commons less common and thereby deteriorating the collective will to tackle challenges, environmental conditions might worsen for everyone.

Is there evidence for this perspective? In an intriguing recent effort – with one of the best article titles we have ever seen, 'Is environmental justice good for white folks?' – economists Michael Ash, James Boyce, Grace Chang and Helen Scharber compare American metropolitan regions and find that where the gap between the industrial pollution burden experienced between people of color and white people is wider, the toxic exposure to whites as well as to people of color is also higher. In other words, wherever toxic exposure is worse for some, it is worse for all. As a result, the authors suggest that '[e]fforts to reduce disparities in pollution burdens could foster improvements in environmental quality that benefit all Americans' (Ash et al. 2013, p. 663).

This is a novel, but not singular, finding. Other researchers have shown that addressing inequality, particularly in terms of income, helps improve national environmental sustainability metrics (such as biodiversity), while others find that nations with a greater commitment to societal equality have stricter environmental regulations, resulting in lower emissions of some pollutants (Torras and Boyce 1998; Mikkelson et al. 2007). A similar exercise looking at just the USA found that greater levels of inequality in power within states led to weaker environmental regulations, resulting in greater environmental degradation and adverse health conditions (Boyce et al. 1999).[5]

Meanwhile, another set of studies, using various years of data from the National Air Toxics Assessment, established that counties in California that were more segregated by income and race had worse measures of predicted health risk and that metropolitan areas throughout the USA with higher levels of racial residential segregation have both higher racial/ethnic disparities in health risks from air toxics exposures (which makes sense, given the geographic separation of living space) but also higher levels of air pollution exposures overall (Morello-Frosch 1997; Morello-Frosch and Jesdale 2005).

All of this suggests that equity is not just one of the three legs of the sustainability triangle but also that it may play a positive role in promoting sustainability overall. There is therefore reason to be concerned about the fairness aspect of sustainability for its own sake and also for its contribution to a more inclusive polity and a wider set of environmental coalitions. And that leads us immediately to consider: how then do you measure environmental justice in a way that is meaningful, easy to implement, and useful to policy makers?

MEASURING, MONITORING AND MAKING ENVIRONMENTAL JUSTICE

From its humble beginnings in protest and its research antecedents in demonstrating disparity, one might think that environmental justice is merely about equalizing the probability that any particular community will be overburdened with hazards or health risks. While this sort of defensive definition – one with a focus on just the relative incidence of pollution – may have been appropriate in an earlier era, the field has certainly shifted in the last 30 or so years.

Environmental justice (EJ) is now generally defined more positively as the belief that all people, regardless of race, ethnicity, gender or income, have the right to a clean and healthy environment in which to live, work, go to school, play and pray.[6] Accompanying this definition is a sense that it is as much about equal access to decision-making processes as it is about the actual distribution of benefits and burdens of new projects and plans. And EJ is increasingly not simply about leveling the playing field but cleaning up the field altogether, including the provision of access to open space, fresh food and public transit.

It is also the case that such a broad definition of EJ can lead one all over the issue as well as all over the geographic map. EJ advocates are increasingly concerned not simply about the siting of hazards or the routing of high-polluting traffic, but also the mismatch of jobs and housing, the existence of 'food deserts' (low-income communities with few sources of fresh produce), clear gaps in disaster preparedness – the list goes on and on (Bullard et al. 2004; Bullard 2007; Gottlieb 2009; Bullard and Wright 2012). Indeed, EJ authors have taken on very broad issues of global sustainability, climate change and a range of other topic areas (Agyeman 2005; Hoerner and Robinson 2008).

We appreciate the breadth – and think that there is much to be gained from bringing the equity lens to every aspect of our natural and built environment. We also think that many of the more positive attributes, such as access to open space, can be measured and tracked over time. However, in this chapter, we confine our attention to looking mostly at the hazards (or negative side) of the equation, partly given the constraints of space and partly because of our desire to be focused. At the end, we discuss how the sort of EJ measures we suggest could be broadened to include other areas.

Thus we focus here on the three issues for measuring environmental disparity in terms of exposure: the scale at which to measure; the cumulative nature of what to measure; and the democratic method that should be used to measure. We specifically suggest that measurement should take place on a regional scale, be of multiple pollutants, explicitly consider the intersection of environmental burden and social vulnerability, and that community engagement is the best method for developing metrics and ensuring the democratic participation that is central to the vision of EJ.

We acknowledge that this arena of EJ measurement is just emerging and there is actually no agreed-upon framework for measuring environmental disparities in cities, regions and states (Payne-Sturges et al. 2012). The literature also evidences some confusion between demonstrating disparity (the stuff of regression analysis) and documenting areas for policy action (the stuff of online and other policy-friendly tools). Maguire and Sheriff (2011) provide a broad overview of all those issues but leave the reader unsettled as to what is next; we are taking the easier path of focusing in on the three dimensions above, a task that makes our focus more limited but also easier.

It Takes a Region

When considering EJ patterns, there are multiple scales that analysts need to keep in mind. The hyper-local matters – it is where residents near power plants or highly trafficked roadways experience decreased lung capacity and higher rates of asthma (Perez et al. 2012). The national experience also matters, as this is the level where policies such as Executive Order #12898 set a context for all lower levels of government. But we would suggest – particularly for a volume about sustainable cities – that the metropolitan region is a critical level at which to measure and address EJ.

This is partly because environmental inequity is often a regional affair. The reason is that the distribution of pollution across the USA by region is largely a result of the sorts of industrial and economic clusters that are rooted in, and so vary by, metropolitan areas: software programming and other high-tech activities dominate Silicon Valley, Seattle and Austin; auto production has a base in the industrial Midwest and parts of the South; and chemical production has a very high location quotient in the metro areas of New Jersey (Storper 1997). Comparing pollution exposures between these places may not be as revealing – or as susceptible to actions by city planners – as comparing the burden of different neighborhoods within specific metros.[7]

Some researchers have found that patterns of environmental disparity are indeed sensitive to the choice of geographic scale, although there were relatively consistent findings with regard to race (Lester et al. 2001). One especially intriguing study looked more directly at the distribution of toxic releases by race and region and suggested that national-level analysis might 'wash out' racial effects within regions (Ash and Fetter 2004). For example, using a multivariate regression analysis (with what are called 'fixed effects' to control for the regional location of populations), they found disparities for African Americans both across the nation and within specific metropolitan regions; they also found that Latinos tend to live in less polluted metropolitan regions but in more polluted areas within those regions.

A purely national approach misses this type of racial disparity within regions and could understate the problem. This is partly why an EJ screening method we have developed for the California Air Resources Board (discussed in more detail below) ranks neighborhood exposures relative to the region (or air basin) in which they occur (Sadd et al. 2011).[8] Note the word 'rank': we have argued that a more typical regulatory approach, setting a sort to threshold (such as whether pollution impacts high-minority and/or high-poverty neighborhoods) does not allow for the specific targeting that a relative risk approach can produce.[9]

One measure of environmental inequality at the regional level that meets the standard is a modified Gini coefficient.[10] The Gini coefficient is frequently used in economics as a measure of inequality, particularly income inequality, and summarizes differences between the distribution of assets (such as income) or deficits (such as pollution) by simply arraying those with the least to the most of any attribute (income or pollution) and asking which share they bear. Derived from a resulting 'Lorenz curve' analysis, there are two 'ideals', one where pollution burdens are totally equal and one in which the entire burden is borne by a tiny sliver of the population. The closer the Gini is to zero, the more equal is the distribution of pollution; the closer it is to one, the more unequal is the distribution of the pollution burden.

Several researchers have used the Gini approach, including Millimet and Slottje (2002), who used the Gini coefficient to compare distribution of air and water pollution at the county and state levels, partly on the way to investigating the relationship between environmental regulation and the distribution of emissions.[11] In keeping with our emphasis on the need to scale down measurement, the authors find that emissions are distributed much more unevenly at the county than at the state level (Millimet and Slottje 2002). Marshall and colleagues (2006) also utilize a Gini coefficient, in this case to look at air emissions in Southern California, and these authors suggest that the distribution is much more unequal than is the distribution of income.

There is one key limit to a straightforward Gini coefficient: it is generally based on the ranking of a population along the same attribute one is trying to measure – so we may know that pollution burdens are unequally experienced, but a simple Gini calculation does not necessarily suggest if there are differential burdens by other characteristics, such as race and income. These socioeconomic dimensions are key when measuring EJ, given both its social movement origins and its particular legal basis in civil rights law and an executive order.

Tackling this issue, Su and colleagues (2009) calculated a Cumulative Environmental Hazard Inequality Index for Los Angeles County, utilizing census tract-level information to array the degree of pollution burden against the share of the population that is either non-white or living in a household with an income that is below twice the poverty line. In a follow-up effort, Su and colleagues (2012) replicated the work across three urban counties, this time including heat stress as well as key air pollution measures – and they found important variations. All this suggests that scale matters and that distributional disparities can be measured – and so a follow-up question is: what is the nature of the burden we need to measure?

It Takes a Cumulative Approach

We have argued that environmental justice (EJ) ranges across a wide array of issues and that, because of this, it may be useful to focus in on a few key dimensions of the EJ measurement questions: the scale of measurement, the nature of what to measure, and the role of community members in the measurement process. In this second arena of what to measure, we apologize in advance for going pretty wide: we think that even if some parsimony is involved in terms of focusing on environmental bads rather than environmental goods, one should try to measure as much as possible and all at once.

This thinking reflects the newest 'wave' in EJ research, activism and policy making: the insistence that policy makers pay attention to cumulative impacts (CI). In essence, the old regulatory approach was to look at pollution burdens emission by emission, source by source, and media by media – and then to set and enforce standards accordingly. The problem with this approach is that the real aim of environmental policy should be to protect people who may be affected by multiple sources. Partly as a result, new measurement approaches are trying to score areas based upon multiple exposures in a geographic area from combined emissions and discharges, from all sources, whether single- or multi-media.

This is consistent with a key aspect of sustainability strategies: the hope to move past a siloed approach to the world and instead consider how all the parts of our economy and society intersect to create better planetary health over the long haul. Yet another aspect of a cumulative approach is the attempt to consider the complementary role of social and biological factors. After all, assessing pollution level without taking into account the nature of the affected population – are there many old or young people? Do residents have access to healthcare? Are they socially isolated? – is likely to miss the actual impact any level of pollution might actually have. As Hynes and Lopez (2007, p. 30) note, '[s]ocial inequalities compound occupational, physical, and built environment risks, resulting in greater health disparities among minorities and the poor'.

For example, in the face of heightened exposure and lessened preparedness and/or ability to cope, vulnerable populations (often concentrated among urban poor and racial/ethnic minorities) suffer from increased and compounded health problems (Fox et al. 2002; Krieg and Faber 2004). In one community-level assessment of risk exposure for low- and middle-income white children in upstate New York, Evans and Marcynyszyn (2004) identified residential crowding, interior noise level and housing quality as variables that increased youths' overnight endocrine levels, which are indicative of chronic stress and associated with the development of cardiovascular disease and low immune functioning. Single risk factors were not associated with increased physical stress for either low- or middle-income children, indicating that the combination of risk factors increased negative health outcomes.

This, of course, significantly complicates the task at hand: we cannot just measure one thing; instead we are forced to combine what seems to be the environmental burden apples with the social vulnerability oranges. But this is exactly the approach taken by a number of emerging 'screening' methods, including one we have developed as part of work with the California Air Resources Board (Sadd et al. 2011). Known as the Environmental Justice Screening Method (EJSM), this approach uses a GIS based map and a set of scores based on ranking along three different dimensions: hazard proximity, air-related health risk and social vulnerability.

Box 12.1 lists the three dimensions and the basic data sources we used. Of the three dimensions, the one that is perhaps the most complicated is the hazard proximity measure. Without going too far into detail, we essentially start from a very small geographic level (city blocks and land parcels), count up various hazards nearby, weight the closest ones more highly, attribute an extra point if the actual land use is 'sensitive' (say, a school), then population-weight the resulting scores up to the level of the census tract (because that is the level for which the other variables are readily available). The results are then ranked from one to five, and a similar but simpler ranking is done for both modeled exposure to poor or toxic air, and social vulnerability.[12]

The total cumulative impacts score is simply the sum of the categorical scores (which ranges from 3 to 15, given the quintile ranking for each of the three dimensions). Figure 12.1 shows these scores across the LA metro region, and readers who know Los Angeles will see that the picture squares with both intuition (a higher score around the ports and in the industrial corridor of southeast Los Angeles) as well as the sort of 'surprise' that in retrospect makes great sense (challenges in the San Gabriel Valley, a location in which lower-income immigrants have settled and wind patterns drive pollution from the western side of the region).

While this is but one example of a cumulative approach, there are three aspects of the EJSM that are worth stressing. First, we have developed an application of the approach for the San Francisco Bay Area, the San Diego area, and a significant swath of the San Joaquin Valley; in each case, it does its ranking within regions, partly because of the regional nature of exposures noted earlier. Second, the EJSM uses a complex and multifaceted notion of social vulnerability. We think using more rather than fewer SES indicators is superior; for example, using only poverty can lead one to identify neighborhoods with university dorms as vulnerable, where the student income there is really just temporarily low (or at least we professors offering high-priced university education hope that is so).[13]

A third aspect of the EJSM deserves fuller discussion (and the general topic gets it in the next section): while the EJSM was subject to the usual peer review, it was also developed in a way that involved community reviewers making suggestions at the earliest design phase, community leaders providing input throughout (often side by side with agency personnel), and community-based organizations testing the potential validity of the findings through a procedure called 'ground truthing' (Los

BOX 12.1 CUMULATIVE IMPACT INDICATORS BY CATEGORY

1: PROXIMITY TO HAZARDS AND SENSITIVE USES SCORE

Sensitive Uses
Childcare facilities
Healthcare facilities
Schools
Senior housing facilities
Urban playgrounds
Hazardous Facilities
AB 2588 "Hot Spots" stationary source facilities
Chrome-platers
Hazardous waste sites
Hazardous Land Uses
Railroad facilities
Ports
Airports
Traffic volume
Refineries
Intermodal distribution

Cumulative Impact Score =

Hazard Proximity and Sensitive Land Use Score (1-5) + Health Risk and Exposure Score (1-5) + Social and Health Vulnerability Score (1-5)

2: HEALTH RISK AND EXPOSURE SCORE

Risk Screening Environmental Indicators (RSEI) toxic concentration
National Air Toxics Assessment (NATA) cumulative respiratory hazard
NATA estimated cumulative cancer risk PM2.5 estimated concentration Ozone estimated concentration

3: SOCIAL AND HEALTH VULNERABILITY SCORE

Race/ethnicity – % people of color (total pop non-Hispanic white)
Poverty – % below twice the Federal Poverty Level
Homeownership – % living in rented households
Housing value – median house value
Educational attainment – % > age 24 with < high school
Age of residents – % < age 5
Age of residents – % > age 65
Linguistic isolation – % residents < age 4 in households where no one > age 13 speaks English well
Voter turnout – % votes cast in general election
Birth outcomes – % preterm and small for gestational age

Note: Analysis updated to reflect the most recent data for all indicators.

Source: Sadd et al. (2011).

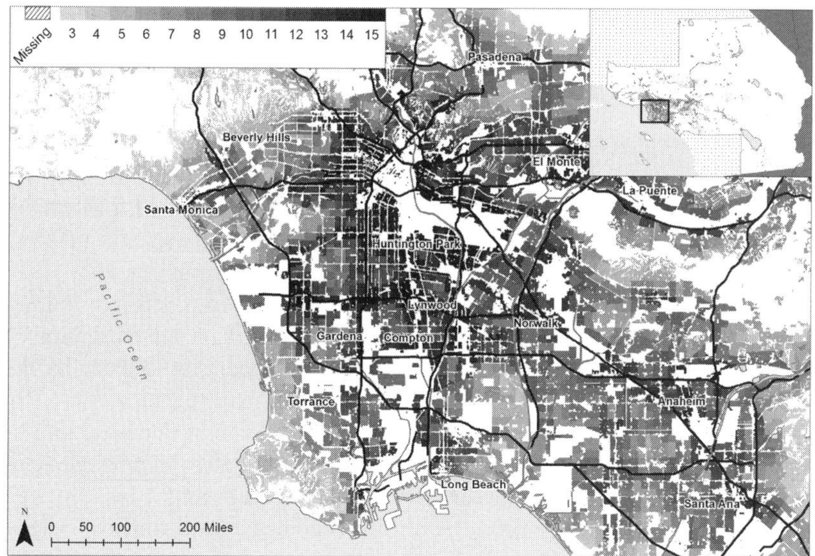

Note: Analysis updated to reflect the most recent data for all indicators.

Source: Sadd et al. (2011).

Figure 12.1 Tract-level cumulative impact score, Los Angeles metro

Angeles Collaborative for Environmental Health and Justice 2010). Such community engagement is important for ensuring accuracy as well as 'buy-in' – and it is an often overlooked part of sustainability efforts (see also Ozawa's chapter on this topic in this volume – Chapter 11).

It Takes a Community

Part of taking a more holistic approach to measuring EJ involves taking a more holistic approach to who should be involved. As noted by Corburn (2005; 2009), at nearly every stage in an assessment and measurement process, the expert status bestowed on those with specialized, scientific skills privileges the 'objective' voice above those of community members. The risk is that this can result in a failure to operationalize variables and key factors that are seemingly more difficult to quantify but actually speak to the full scope of issues of concern for affected communities. And if sustainability is about the long-term ability to maintain measurement over time, surely getting that community engagement is critical.

This is partly because the research demonstrates that it is, in part, a lack of community engagement that leads to the placement of environmental negatives (Pastor et al. 2001). In a less EJ-focused, more public health-centric and forward-looking volume, Jason Corburn argues that 'the frames for moving towards healthy city planning include consideration of population health, a relational view of place, processes of governance, and relations of power' (2009, p. 12). From both perspectives, one important part of protecting health and restoring power to these communities (not to mention making democracy more real in America) is taking community input seriously.

As a result, new approaches should not just identify impacted communities but also develop partnership models that can incorporate community-level expertise that has heretofore often been excluded from science-based assessments (Dietz and Stern 2008). To do this will require a new approach to community engagement, one that is more authentic, relational and mutually respectful (Freudenberg et al. 2011). It will also require that engagement be translated into suggestions for effective remediation and a bias toward action (Hynes and Lopez 2007). And we would argue that this is all especially important in the context of a sort of brand-new frontier of environmental planning – and one that can seem extremely abstract: sustainability.

In a recent paper originally written for the US EPA, Freudenberg, Pastor and Israel consolidate academic literature as well as their own collective experience into a set of recommendations to government agencies to promote community engagement (Freudenberg et al. 2010; Freudenberg et al. 2011). The authors argue that government agencies often worry that participation will increase conflict and costs, but suggest that the benefits of new knowledge and new voices will actually improve outcomes. They recommend three basic strategies: get people involved early; provide them with resources so they can fully participate; and ensure that outcomes reflect participation and local needs.

Early involvement signals to communities that their input will be taken seriously and can address distrust that may exist between communities and government agencies from previous bad experiences (Hale 2008; Minkler 2004). Such involvement can also involve providing communities with resources to fully participate, particularly through capacity-building efforts such as community-based participatory research and the creation of innovative and interactive workshops that draw on ideas and desires of local residents (Minkler et al. 2008). Finally, results matter: nothing convinces a community that it was heard than when its issues are actually addressed.

A prime example of mucking up this mix is the experience with what must be one of the most significant frontiers for sustainability in the USA, California's 2006 Global Warming Solutions Act. Partly because some key EJ actors were involved in mustering support for passage of the legislation, the Act mandated the creation of an Environmental Justice Advisory Committee (EJAC) and specific attention to ensuring that gains from the law would accrue to some of the most disadvantaged communities in California (Sze et al. 2009). However, early recommendations by the EJAC were not given much attention, EJAC members felt that their committee was understaffed, and these members were also concerned about the State's seeming unwillingness to reconsider a 'cap-and-trade' system that they felt could create uneven reductions in co-pollutants.

This tension eventually led to a 2009 lawsuit by EJ advocates alleging that the California Air Resources Board (CARB) had not adequately considered alternatives to cap-and-trade; a 2011 ruling led to a redo of the environmental review and CARB was given permission to go ahead with cap-and-trade in 2012. But the damage was done: there are uneasy relations about the proper approach to addressing global warming between agencies, mainstream environmentalists and EJ advocates. In a state where the EJ advocates can be critical and the people of color population now tops 60 percent, this is not a recipe for political sustainability.

Contrast this with a procedure in which we were engaged: the development of the Environmental Justice Screening Method (EJSM) for the California Air Resources Board. Early in the process, we realized that such a technical tool might be perceived as yet another outside scientific effort and thus lose credibility in the community's eyes. While we tried to address this by soliciting input and using a scoring strategy that was transparent, simple and easy to explain, we also developed a parallel 'ground truthing' project that allowed residents to compare our results from secondary data with maps they created by walking the communities being studied, as well as to conduct actual air monitoring (Los Angeles Collaborative for Environmental Health and Justice 2010).

The result: significant confidence in the EJSM, so much so that the state's EJ groups have lobbied for it to be a main tool for resource allocation in proposed (but ultimately unsuccessful) legislation about distributed solar power. The point: if you want to have confidence, you need to do confidence building. And if you want to have sustainability, you need sustainable relationships between experts, policy makers and community residents.

STATE OF THE METRICS

While some of the above discussion has been in broad strokes, the good news is that the metrics to gauge EJ have been in steady development in recent years. A recent EPA review reports that 23 states have developed 36 different types of EJ assessment methods, ranging from analysis of demographic indicators to complex quantitative analysis, which inform a variety of programs and policies (Payne-Sturges et al. 2012).

The EPA itself has gotten into the game, starting first with the Environmental Justice Strategic Enforcement Assessment Tool (EJSEAT), an approach that included a number of the indicators in the EJSM review above but also contained information on compliance. EJSEAT has been the subject of some criticism, partly because of the enforcement metric – is finding a large number of violations a sign of a bad actor or good policing? – but also because it did not drive some of the health metrics down to a sufficiently local level. Partly as a result of the controversy (as well as subsequent evolution in the field), it is soon to be replaced by a new nationally consistent EJ screening tool, as part of US EPA's Plan EJ 2014.[14]

Perhaps unsurprisingly, California has been a first mover in this arena of measuring EJ. The state is generally ahead of the curve on environmental issues but it has also been at the forefront of legislation and administrative action with regard to EJ (Bonorris 2010) – and so too with measurement of cumulative impacts and environmental justice. Aside from the EJSM described above, researchers at the University of California, Davis, have developed an approach that is similar but somewhat better tailored to rural areas in that it includes measures of pesticide use (Huang and London 2012). Meanwhile, the State's Office of Environmental Health Hazard Assessment is developing a new cumulative impacts screening methodology for the state that is going by the working title 'California Communities Environmental Health Screening Tool' (Cal-EnviroScreen).

Cal-EnviroScreen (or whatever turns out to be the ultimate name of the method) is likely to be the one of these tools that becomes the standard, partly because it is being sponsored and developed internally and so responds more directly to regulatory concerns. EnviroScreen takes into consideration environmental hazards as well as social and health vulnerability factors, and includes a very broad range of indicators. However, it eschews the more complicated land-use calculations that are in the EJSM and its ranking procedure currently goes across the whole state rather than taking the regional approach of the EJSM (Alexeeff et al. 2012). The latter suggests one of the inevitable tensions with tools that are developed by state agencies: because they need to respond to political pressures (like a mandate to take a statewide approach or to not explicitly consider race), they can wind up making choices that are not as reflective of the state of the science.

In any case, this is a field very much in development. Table 12.1, taken partly from a report we prepared for the Sustainable Communities Initiative being spearheaded by the US Department of Housing and Urban Development (Pastor et al. 2012), shows a range of online EJ-related tools that map multiple neighborhood-level environmental, health

Table 12.1 Other environmental justice, climate change and health-related tools

Environmental health tools	
EJView	EJView is a mapping tool hosted by the US EPA that allows users to create maps and generate reports examining multiple variables that may affect human and environmental health within a community or region. Users can search by address, area, or EPA facility. Key data: Institutions, EPA reporting sites, health service areas, health risk/demographic, natural boundaries/water features
NEPAssist	NEPAssist is a mapping tool that facilitates the environmental impact review (EIR) process and project planning in relation to environmental considerations. Users can search by address, area, geographic coordinates, watershed, or congressional district. Key data: Institutions, EPA reporting sites, health service areas, health risk/demographic, natural boundaries/water features, transportation, soil maps, FEMA flood warning areas, topography maps
National-Scale Air Toxics Assessment (NATA) dataset and mapping tool	NATA is a dataset compiled by the US EPA that provides broad estimates of health risks over geographies nationwide. NATA estimates risks from breathing air toxics that are emitted from a variety of sources, and the latest version, 2005, includes 178 air toxics. The EPA also provides interactive GoogleEarth maps so users can view the distribution of risks in specific geographic areas. Key data: Stationary, mobile, background, secondary formation air toxics
National Environmental Public Health Tracking Network	The National Environmental Public Health Tracking Network is a tool of the Center for Disease Control and Prevention, which provides information on environmental hazards, exposures, and chronic health conditions. This tool allows users to select environmental risks/health conditions, demographics and geography, and displays data through mapping, charts and tables. It also allows users to examine trends over time. Key data: Health, air quality, climate change, demographic

Table 12.1 (continued)

Environmental health tools	
EnviroMapper for Envirofacts	EnviroMapper is a mapping tool drawing on several US EPA data sources to display the location of activities that may affect water, air, and land anywhere in the US, from the neighborhood to national levels. Key data: Facilities with potentially toxic emissions, chemical, industries
Community-Focused Exposure and Risk Screening Tool (C-FERST)	Although this tool is not yet available, it will soon operate as a one-stop-shop community mapping and assessment tool for better understanding cumulative impacts.
Public health tools	
Health Landscape	Health Landscape is an interactive, web-based mapping tool that allows users to analyze and display demographic and health-related information at a variety of geographic levels nationwide. The tool draws from a variety of health, socio-economic, and health data sources, and can also be used to create maps from publically available data sources. Key data: Health care facilities, health status/risks, demographic
Health Professional Shortage Areas (HPSA)	The US Department of Health and Human Services developed this tool to allow users to identify areas that have a shortage of health professionals or are considered medically underserved. Key data: Health professional shortage areas, medically underserved areas and populations
Climate change and disaster planning tools	
On The Map for Emergency Management	This tool is operated by the US Census Bureau and maps current natural hazard and emergency related events ranging from the city to the national level. Key data: Natural disaster (including date and time information)
Sea Level Rise Maps	This tool is run by the Pacific Institute, and allows users to map potential flood warning zones and coastal erosion zones and layer the locations of at-risk infrastructure. Key data: Hazard zones, infrastructure at risk

Source: Pastor et al. (2012).

and demographic indicators, allowing users to visualize community environmental stressors. Most sites are fairly easy to navigate and provide ready-to-use data and maps, which governmental agencies, such as metropolitan planning organizations (MPOs), can use to define, delineate and profile communities with EJ concerns.

It is safe to say that these are but a beginning to what is likely to be a continually growing area of research. With the debate about environmental justice largely over (there is indeed injustice!), with new research suggesting that engaging equity can actually promote sustainability, and with the rapid development of new databases, GIS techniques and measurement strategies, we suspect that the field will continue to expand and mature. The trick will be not to develop better and fancier metrics, but to remember the purposes to which they should be put: a set of new policies that can ensure that inclusion of all and fairness in the allocation of burdens and gains is part of our sustainable future.

WHAT LIES AHEAD

In a recent volume considering another intersection of the three Es of sustainability – economy and equity – Pastor and Benner suggest that one key step to wedding the concerns of prosperity and inclusion is the creation of epistemic communities where 'facts are accepted, values are shared, and destinies are intertwined amongst a broad and diverse set of constituencies' – especially business, labor and community groups, but also universities, governments, philanthropy and others (Benner and Pastor 2012, p. 186). In their view, economic sustainability and the search for win–win solutions require a shared base of facts, goals and metrics.

Measuring EJ effectively is one part of ensuring that another couplet in the three Es – equity and the environment – are linked in a new and broader commitment to the sustainable city. We have argued that environmental justice is indeed key to sustainability, not simply because equity is one of the pillars of sustainability but also because fairness in the sharing of benefits and burdens makes the commons a real concept and one that is more broadly supported at a political or policy level. We have further argued that measurement is possible, that the metropolitan region is the best level at which to measure, that measurements should be as comprehensive as possible and include social vulnerability as well as exposure, and, finally, that the process of measuring should engage as many community actors in the co-creation as possible.

All of these measurement approaches should be proactive, focusing on prevention rather than clean-up after the fact (Raffensperger and Tickner

1999). Such a 'precautionary approach' may be particularly important for one of the newest sustainability challenges, climate change, which evidence suggests is likely to disproportionately affect people of color and low-income communities in the USA (Shonkoff et al. 2009). Fortunately, there are now a number of efforts aimed at measuring climate vulnerability for less advantaged populations and these are likely to bear interesting results and policy implications in years to come (English et al. 2009).

Another imperative for future research: documenting access (and lack thereof) to environmental positives. While we have mostly focused on how to gauge negative impacts and social risks, there has been extensive mapping of access to open space and parks, with the results demonstrating disparities that can be ameliorated by better policy and enhanced resources (Garcia and Strongin 2011; Wolch et al. 2005). There are also significant opportunities for future research throughout the metropolitan areas of America with regard to better access to fresh food as well as public transit, and mapping and data will be useful in this as well (Bullard 2007).

Finally, a warning for planners: talk of a sustainable future often conjures up images of living in harmony with nature and each other. That surely is the goal – but along the path can lie a series of obstacles in the form of those who profit from environmental degradation, those who deny climate change, and those who fund the politics that has stymied sustainability efforts in the nation. Likewise, the path to achieving environmental justice has its resistant elements, including polluters who would prefer to place burdens on those with less political leverage and those who, despite the strong evidence, suggest that the pattern of disparity must be related just to income, industrial structure or some other benign cause.

Sustainability, in short, is not for the faint of heart. It will likely require the messiness of conflict, something planners and government actors often seek to avoid (Pastor and Benner 2011). It will necessitate raising issues of racial and income disparity, never the most comfortable of topics. But no one said protecting the planet would be easy – just that it was necessary. A better world is possible, and better measurements of environmental protection and environmental justice will be part of the process of getting there.

ACKNOWLEDGEMENTS

This research and analysis was partially supported by W.K. Kellogg Foundation Grant #: P3023394.

NOTES

1. A related question is what environmental justice policies and practices are the most effective at addressing disparities, a topic that has received very little attention until recently. A new report addressing this research gap has just come out (Callahan et al. 2012) and we refer readers to that; for this chapter, we focus on the documentation of disparities as a first step.
2. There is also an argument about how sharp inequalities in wealth can lead to excessive financialization of the economy and hence risks of bubbles, but because this has less of a parallel with the equity–environment relationship we attempt to sketch, we leave it to one side here.
3. In a 2010 *Los Angeles Times*/University of Southern California poll of Californians, Latino and Asian Americans were significantly more concerned about global warming, air pollution and water and soil contamination than non-Hispanic white respondents; the black sample in that poll (which oversampled on Latinos and Asians) was too small to draw definitive conclusions. This is not a unique finding. The 2011 Statewide Survey by the Public Policy Institute of California (Baldassare et al. 2011) found that blacks (42 percent) and Latinos (41 percent) were more likely than Asian Americans (28 percent) and whites (19 percent) to consider regional air pollution a serious health threat and that blacks and Latinos (69 percent each) were more likely than Asian Americans (53 percent) and whites (51 percent) to think the State should act now to curb greenhouse gas emissions even if it hurts the economy.
4. In a series of case studies we have completed on Los Angeles, we found that actors primarily concerned with social, economic and environmental justice have helped to drive a series of broad environmental efforts in Los Angeles, including a remarkable reduction in regional air pollution driven partly by the organizing of low-income communities directly abutting the region's ports (Pastor and McMorrow 2010).
5. See also Vornovytskyy and Boyce (2010) for a look at interregional differences in Russia.
6. 'Environmental justice', US Environmental Protection Agency, http://www.epa.gov/environmentaljustice/, (accessed 18 July 2012).
7. Geographer Laura Pulido also asserts that race, space and the environment intersect at the regional level, arguing that '[p]ollution concentrations are inevitably the product of relationships between distinct places, including industrial zones, affluent suburbs, working-class suburbs, and downtown areas, all of which are racialized' (2000, p. 13).
8. Regions are also important environmentally because this is where part of the work to address climate change must be done. For example, in California, a complement to 2006 legislation mandating significant reductions in greenhouse gas emissions was Senate Bill 375, a measure that required metropolitan planning organization to prepare a 'sustainable communities strategy'. That strategy involves meeting greenhouse gas emission reduction goals through reductions in vehicle miles traveled, something that can only be achieved through a better jobs–housing balance at the metropolitan level.
9. This is why we do not sketch out any threshold strategies below. We show in one report that a threshold approach taken by, for example, the California Energy Commission, leads to screening 'in' or 'out' too many areas, leaving very little ability to differentiate by relative risk (Pastor et al. 2010).
10. Such a measure is in keeping with Harper and Lynch's 2010 comprehensive study of methods to measure cancer-related health disparities in which the authors present a menu of 'measures of average disproportionality' (Harper and Lynch 2010).
11. Their findings are consistent even when they use other standard measures of inequality (Millimet and Slottje 2002, p. 96).
12. The EJSM profiled in this section is based on the method outlined in Sadd et al. (2011), 1441–59. However, the map presented in this chapter was updated to use more data from CARB's Community Health Air Pollution Information System (CHAPIS), Southern California Air Quality Management District's AB2588 Air Toxics 'Hot Spots' Program, Cal-EPA's Toxic Air Contaminant Hexavalent Chromium Activity database (chrome

plating facilities), the CA Department of Toxic Substances Control's Treatment, Storage and Disposal Facilities database, the National Air Toxics Assessment for mobile and stationary sources, the US EPA's Risk Screening Environmental Impacts project (which is built up from the Toxics Release Inventory and air modeling), CARB's estimates of ozone and particulate matter, the Southern California Association of Governments land-use spatial layers and the US Census, among others.

13. We would also stress the importance of including such variables as linguistic isolation, particularly since research is emerging that recent immigrants may be especially vulnerable to disproportionate siting, partly because of their lack of knowledge and partly because of their lack of civic participation (Pastor et al. 2007).
14. For more, see: 'EJSEAT', US Environmental Protection Agency, http://www.epa.gov/compliance/ej/resources/policy/ej-seat.html (accessed 25 August 2012), and 'Plan EJ 2014', US Environmental Protection Agency, http://www.epa.gov/compliance/ej/resources/policy/plan-ej-2014/plan-ej-information-2011–09.pdf (accessed 25 August 2012).

REFERENCES

Agyeman, Julian (2005), *Sustainable Communities and the Challenge of Environmental Justice*, New York: NYU Press.

Alexeeff, G.V., J.B. Faust, L.M. August, C. Milanes, K. Randles, L. Zeise and J. Denton (2012), 'A screening method for assessing cumulative impacts', *International Journal of Environmental Research and Public Health*, **9** (2), 648–59.

Ash, M. and T.T. Fetter (2004), 'Who lives on the wrong side of the environmental tracks? Evidence from the EPA's risk-screening environmental indicators model', *Social Science Quarterly*, **85** (2), 441–62.

Ash, M., J.K. Boyce, G. Chang and H. Scharber (2013), 'Is environmental justice good for white folks? Industrial air toxics exposure in urban America', *Social Science Quarterly*, **94** (3), 616–36.

Baldassare, Mark, Dean Bonner, Sonja Petek and Jui Shrestha (2011), *Californians and the Environment*, San Francisco, CA: Public Policy Institute of California.

Benner, Chris and Manuel Pastor (2012), *Just Growth: Inclusion and Prosperity in America's Metropolitan Regions*, New York: Routledge.

Berg, Andrew G. and Jonathan D. Ostry (2011), *Inequality and Unsustainable Growth: Two Sides of the Same Coin?*, Washington, DC: International Monetary Fund, available at http://www.imf.org/external/pubs/cat/longres.aspx?sk=24686.

Bonorris, Steven (2010), *Environmental Justice for All: A Fifty State Survey of Legislation, Policies and Cases*, 4th edn, Berkeley, CA: University of California, Berkeley, Hastings Law School, available at http://www.uchastings.edu/public-law/docs/ejreport-fourthedition.pdf.

Boyce, J.K., A.R. Klemer, P.H. Templet and C.E. Willis (1999) 'Power distribution, the environment, and public health: a state-level analysis', *Ecological Economics*, **29** (1), 127–40.

Bullard, Robert D. (2007), *Growing Smarter: Achieving Livable Communities, Environmental Justice, and Regional Equity*, Boston, MA: MIT Press.

Bullard, Robert D. (1994), *Unequal Protection: Environmental Justice and Communities of Color*, San Francisco, CA: Sierra Club Books.

Bullard, Robert D. and Beverly Wright (2012), *The Wrong Complexion for Protection: How the Government Response to Natural and Unnatural Disasters Endangers African American Communities*, New York: New York University Press.

Bullard, Robert D., Glenn Johnson and Angel Torres (eds) (2004), *Highway Robbery: Transportation Racism and New Routes to Equity*, Boston, MA: South End Press.

Callahan, Colleen, J.R. DeShazo and Cristin Kenyon (2012), *Pathways to Environmental Justice: Advance a Framework for Evaluation*, Los Angeles, CA: Luskin Center for

Innovation, UCLA Luskin Center for Public Affairs, available at http://luskin.ucla.edu/sites/default/files/Pathways%20to%20Environmental%20Justice.pdf.

Campbell, S. (1996), 'Green cities, growing cities, just cities?: Urban planning and the contradictions of sustainable development', *Journal of the American Planning Association*, **62** (3), 296–312.

Clinton, William J. (1994), 'Executive Order: Federal Actions to Address Environmental Justice in Minority Populations and Low-Income Populations', retrieved 17 August 2012 from http://www.epa.gov/region2/ej/exec_order_12898.pdf.

Cole, Luke and Sheila Foster (2000), *From the Ground Up: Environmental Racism and the Rise of the Environmental Justice Movement*, New York: New York University Press.

Corburn, Jason (2005), *Street Science: Community Knowledge and Environmental Health Justice*, Boston, MA: MIT Press.

Corburn, Jason (2009), *Toward the Healthy City: People, Places, and the Politics of Urban Planning*, Boston, MA: MIT Press.

Dietz, Thomas and Paul Stern (eds) (2008), *Public Participation in Environmental Assessment and Decision Making*, Washington, DC: National Academies Press.

Eberts, Randall, George Erickcek and Jack Kleinhenz (2006), 'Dashboard indicators for the Northeast Ohio economy: prepared for the Fund for Our Economic Future', Working Paper 06–05, Cleveland, OH: The Federal Reserve Bank of Cleveland, available at http://www.clevelandfed.org/Research/Workpaper/2006/wp06-05.pdf.

English, P.B., A.H. Sinclair, Z. Ross, H. Anderson, V. Boothe, C. Davis, K. Ebi, B. Kagey, K. Malecki, R. Schultz and E. Simms (2009), 'Environmental health indicators of climate change for the United States: findings from the state environmental health indicator collaborative', *Environmental Health Perspectives*, **117** (11), 1673–81.

Evans, G.W. and L.A. Marcynyszyn (2004), 'Environmental justice, cumulative environmental risk, and health among low- and middle-income children in upstate New York', *American Journal of Public Health*, **94** (11), 1942–4.

Farzin, Y.H. and C.A. Bond (2006), 'Democracy and environmental quality', *Journal of Development Economics*, **81** (1), 213–35.

Fox, M.A., J.D. Groopman and T. Burke (2002), 'Evaluating cumulative risk assessment for environmental justice: a community case study', *Environmental Health Perspectives*, **110** (S2), 203–9.

Freudenberg, Nicholas, Barbara Israel and Manuel Pastor (2010), *Community Participation in Environmental Decision-Making Processes: Can it Reduce Disproportionate Impact?*, Washington, DC: US Environmental Protection Agency, available at http://www.epa.gov/ncer/events/calendar/2010/mar17/abstracts/communitycapacity.pdf (accessed 28 September 2012).

Freudenberg, N., M. Pastor and B. Israel (2011), 'Strengthening community capacity to participate in making decisions to reduce disproportionate environmental exposures', *American Journal of Public Health*, **101** (S1), S123–S130.

Garcia, Robert and Seth Strongin (2011), *Healthy Parks, Schools and Communities: Mapping Green Access and Equity for Southern California*, Los Angeles, CA: The City Project.

Gottlieb, R. (2009), 'Where we live, work, play . . . and eat: expanding the environmental justice agenda', *Environmental Justice*, **2** (1), 7–8.

Hale, Charles R. (2008), *Engaging Contradictions: Theory, Politics, and Methods of Activist Scholarship*, Berkeley, CA: University of California Press.

Harper, Sam and John Lynch (2010), *Methods for Measuring Cancer Disparities: Using Data Relevant to Healthy People 2010 Cancer-Related Objectives*, Ann Arbor, MI: University of Michigan, Center for Social Epidemiology and Population Health.

Hoerner, J. Andrew and Nia Robinson (2008), *Climate of Change: African-Americans, Global Warming and Just Climate Policy*, Oakland, CA: Environmental Justice and Climate Change Initiative, available at http://issuu.com/theejcc/docs/climateofchange (accessed 2 October 2012).

Huang, G. and J.K. London (2012), 'Cumulative environmental vulnerability and

environmental justice in California's San Joaquin Valley', *International Journal of Environmental Research and Public Health*, **9** (5), 1593–608.
Hynes, H. and R. Lopez (2007), 'Cumulative risk and a call for action in environmental justice communities', *Journal of Health Disparities Research and Practice*, **1** (2), 29–57.
Krieg, E.J. and D.R. Faber (2004), 'Not so black and white: environmental justice and cumulative impact assessments', *Environmental Impact Assessment Review*, **24** (7–8), 667–94.
Lester, James P., David W. Allen and Kelly Marie Hill (2001), *Environmental Injustice in the United States: Myths and Realities*, Boulder, CO: Westview Press.
Los Angeles Collaborative for Environmental Health and Justice (2010), *Hidden Hazards: A Call to Action for Healthy, Livable Communities*, Los Angeles, CA: Liberty Hill Foundation, available at http://www.libertyhill.org/document.doc?id=202.
Maguire, K. and G. Sheriff (2011), 'Comparing distributions of environmental outcomes for regulatory environmental justice analysis', *International Journal of Environmental Research and Public Health*, **8**, 1707–26.
Marshall, J.D., P.W. Granvold, A.S. Hoats, T.E. McKone, E. Deakin and W.W. Nazaroff (2006), 'Inhalation intake of ambient air pollution in California's south coast air basin', *Atmospheric Environment*, **40** (23), 4381–92.
Mikkelson, G.M., A. Gonzalez and G.D. Peterson (2007), 'Economic inequality predicts biodiversity loss', *PLoS ONE*, **2** (5), E444.
Millimet, D.L. and D. Slottje (2002), 'Environmental compliance costs and the distribution of emissions in the US', *Journal of Regional Science*, **42** (1), 87–105.
Minkler, M. (2004), 'Ethical challenges for the "outside" researcher in community-based participatory research', *Health Education and Behavior*, **31** (6), 684–97.
Minkler, M., V.B. Vásquez, M. Tajik and D. Petersen (2008), 'Promoting environmental justice through community-based participatory research: the role of community and partnership capacity', *Health Education and Behavior*, **35** (1), 119–37.
Morello-Frosch, Rachel (1997), *Environmental Justice and California's "Riskscape": The Distribution of Air Toxics and Associated Cancer and Non-cancer Health Risks Among Diverse Communities*, Berkeley, CA: University of California, Berkeley, Department of Health Sciences.
Morello-Frosch, R. (2002), 'Discrimination and the political economy of environmental inequality', *Environment and Planning C: Government and Policy*, **20** (4), 477–96.
Morello-Frosch, R. and B.M. Jesdale (2005), 'Separate and unequal: residential segregation and estimated cancer risks associated with ambient air toxics in US metropolitan areas', *Environmental Health Perspectives*, **114** (3), 386–93.
Pastor, Manuel and Chris Benner (2008), 'Been down so long: weak market cities and regional equity', in Richard M. McGahey and Jennifer S. Vey (eds), *Retooling for Growth: Building a 21st Century Economy in America's Older Industrial Areas*, Washington, DC: Brookings Institution Press, pp. 89–118.
Pastor, Manuel and Chris Benner (2011), 'Planning for equity, fighting for justice: planners, organizers, and the fight for metropolitan inclusion', in Ethan Seltzer and Armando Carbonell (eds), *Regional Planning in America: Practice and Prospect*, Boston, MA: Lincoln Institute of Land Planning, p. 296.
Pastor, Manuel and Erin McMorrow (2010), 'Looking forward: sustainability and the future of Los Angeles', in Ali Modarres (ed.), *State of Los Angeles, 2010*, Los Angeles, CA: Pat Brown Institute, California State University, Los Angeles.
Pastor, Manuel, Mirabai Auer and Madeline Wander (2012), *Advancing Environmental Justice through Sustainability Planning*, Los Angeles, CA: University of Southern California, Program for Environmental and Regional Equity.
Pastor, Manuel, Rachel Morello-Frosch and James Sadd (2010), *Air Pollution and Environmental Justice: Integrating Indicators of Cumulative Impact and Socio-Economic Vulnerability into Regulatory Decision-Making*, Sacramento, CA: California Air Resources Board, available at http://www.arb.ca.gov/research/apr/past/04-308.pdf.
Pastor, M., R. Morello-Frosch and J. Sadd (2005), 'The air is always cleaner on the other side:

race, space, and ambient air toxics exposures in California', *Journal of Urban Affairs*, **27** (2), 127–48.

Pastor, M., J. Sadd and J. Hipp (2001), 'Which came first? Toxic facilities, minority move-in, and environmental justice', *Journal of Urban Affairs*, **23** (1), 1–21.

Pastor, Manuel, James Sadd and Rachel Morello-Frosch (2007), *Still Toxic After All These Years: Air Quality and Environmental Justice in the San Francisco Bay Area*, Santa Cruz, CA: Center for Justice, Tolerance and Community, University of California, Santa Cruz.

Payne-Sturges, D., A. Turner, J. Wignall, A. Rosenbaum, E. Dederick and H. Dantzker (2012), 'A review of state-level analytical approaches for evaluating disproportionate environmental health impacts', *Environmental Justice*, **5** (4), 173–87.

Perez, L., F. Lurmann, J. Wilson, M. Pastor, S.J. Brandt, N. Kunzli and R. McConnell (2012), 'Near-roadway pollution and childhood asthma: Implications for developing "win–win" compact urban development and clean vehicle strategies', *Environmental Health Perspectives*, **120** (11), 1619–26.

Portney, Kent E. (2003), *Taking Sustainable Cities Seriously: Economic Development, the Environment, and Quality of Life in American Cities*, Boston, MA: MIT Press.

Pulido, L. (2000), 'Rethinking environmental racism: white privilege and urban development in Southern California', *Annals of the Association of American Geographers*, **90** (1), 12–40.

Raffensperger, Carolyn and Joel Tickner (1999), *Protecting Public Health and the Environment: Implementing The Precautionary Principle*, Washington, DC: Island Press.

Ringquist, E.J. (2005), 'Assessing evidence of environmental inequities: a meta-analysis', *Journal of Policy Analysis and Management*, **24** (2), 223–47.

Sadd, J., M. Pastor, R. Morello-Frosch, J. Scoggins and B.M. Jesdale (2011), 'Playing it safe: assessing cumulative impact and social vulnerability through an environmental justice screening method in the south coast air basin, California', *International Journal of Environmental Research and Public Health*, **8** (5), 1441–59.

Shonkoff, S.B., R. Morello-Frosch, M. Pastor and J. Sadd (2009), 'Minding the climate gap: environmental health and equity implications of climate change mitigation policies in California', *Environmental Justice*, **2** (4), 173–7.

Stern, D.I. (2004), 'The rise and fall of the environmental Kuznets curve', *World Development*, **32** (8), 1419–39.

Stiglitz, Joseph E. (2012), *The Price of Inequality: How Today's Divided Society Endangers Our Future*, New York: W.W. Norton & Company.

Storper, Michael (1997), *The Regional World: Territorial Development in a Global Economy*, New York: Guilford Press.

Su, J.G., R. Morello-Frosch, B.M. Jesdale, A.D. Kyle, B. Shamasunder and M. Jerrett (2009), 'An index for assessing demographic inequalities in cumulative environmental hazards with application to Los Angeles, California', *Environmental Science & Technology*, **43** (20), 7626–34.

Su, J.G., M. Jerrett, R. Morello-Frosch, B.M. Jesdale and A.D. Kyle (2012), 'Inequalities in cumulative environmental burdens among three urbanized counties in California', *Environment International*, **40**, 79–87.

Sze, J., G. Gambirazzio, A. Karner, D. Rowan, J. London and D. Niemeier (2009), 'Best in show? Climate and environmental justice policy in California', *Environmental Justice*, **2** (4), 179–84.

Torras, M. and J.K. Boyce (1998), 'Income, inequality, and pollution: a reassessment of the environmental Kuznets curve', *Ecological Economics*, **25** (2), 147–60.

United Church of Christ (1987), *A National Report on the Racial and Socio-economic Characteristics of Communities with Hazardous Waste Sites*, New York: United Church of Christ, Commission for Racial Justice.

US General Accounting Office (GAO) (1983), *Siting of Hazardous Waste Landfills and Their Correlation With Racial and Economic Status of Surrounding Communities*, Washington, DC: US Government Printing Office.

Vornovytskyy, Marina S. and James K. Boyce (2010), *Economic Inequality and Environmental*

Quality: Evidence of Pollution Shifting in Russia, Amherst, MA: University of Massachusetts, Amherst, Political Economy Research Institute (PERI), available at http://www.peri.umass.edu/fileadmin/pdf/working_papers/working_papers_201-250/WP217.pdf.

Vos, R.O. (2007), 'Defining sustainability: a conceptual orientation', *Journal of Chemical Technology and Biotechnology*, **82** (4), 334–9.

Wolch, J., J. Wilson and J. Fehrenbach (2005), 'Parks and park funding in Los Angeles: an equity-mapping analysis', *Urban Geography*, **26** (1), 4–35.

World Commission on Environment and Development (WCED) (1992), *Report of the World Commission on Environment and Development (WCED): Our Common Future*, Rio de Janeiro: United Nations Conference on Environment and Development (UNCED), available at http://www.un-documents.net/wced-ocf.htm.

PART II

METHODS

13. Analyzing a city's metabolism

Christopher Kennedy, Larry Baker and Helge Brattebø

1. INTRODUCTION

Collection of urban metabolism (UM) data is required for assessing the sustainability of cities. A UM study involves quantification of the inflows, outflows, storage and production of energy and materials within an urban boundary. Such data can serve a variety of purposes, whether as input to city greenhouse gas (GHG) inventorying, for determination of urban ecological footprints, or sustainability assessment in specific areas such as water use, air pollution, waste, materials management and so on. About 20 relatively comprehensive UM studies have been published in academic literature (Kennedy et al. 2011). The World Bank has also conducted several studies of cities (Hoornweg et al. 2012), and many more cities are collecting data on some aspects of UM as part of GHG inventorying.

The objective of this chapter is to provide practical guidance for undertaking a UM study. In particular this will involve description of data collection techniques and estimation methods, and potential pitfalls to avoid in determining various components of UM. For example, it will describe how transportation fuel consumption can be determined from vehicle counts, sales data and/or transportation models; and how material stocks can be scaled up from studies of individual buildings/infrastructure segments. It is very much a 'how to do it' guide for both city managers and academics.

Figure 13.1 provides a generic framework for assessing the UM, broadly including inflows, outflows, internal flows, storage and production of biomass, energy, minerals and water. This is a comprehensive framework that integrates methods of water, energy and substance flow analysis with the Eurostat system of material flow analysis (Kennedy and Hoornweg 2012). The framework captures all biophysical stocks and flows within the system boundary, including natural components (e.g. solar radiation, groundwater flows), peri-urban activities (e.g. food production, forestry), as well as a broad range of anthropogenic stocks and flows.

For any of the materials or substances shown in Figure 13.1, there is a mass balance:

$$\text{Inflow} + \text{Net production} = \text{Increase in storage} + \text{Outflow} \quad (13.1)$$

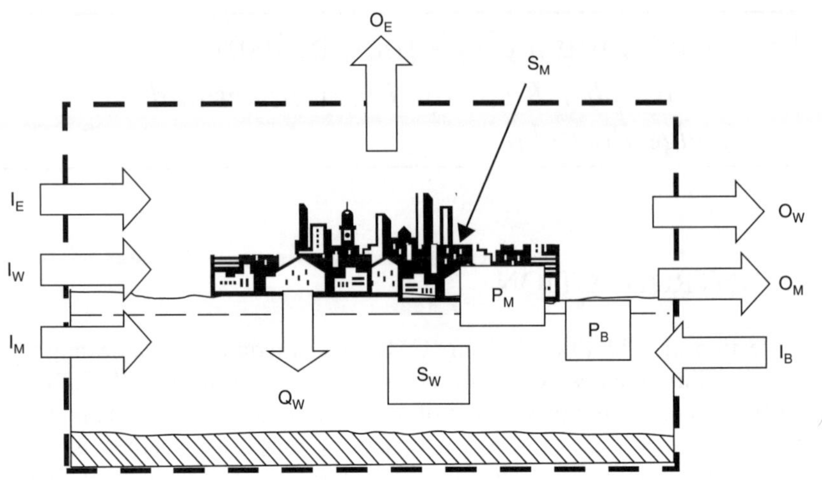

Notes:

Inflows
Biomass [t & J]
  food
  wood
Fossil Fuel [t & J]
  transport
  heating/industrial
Minerals [t]
  metals
  construction materials
Electricity [kWh]
Natural energy [J]
Water [t]
  Drinking (surface & groundwater)
  Precipitation
Substances [t]
  e.g. nutrients
Produced goods [t]

Production
Biomass [t & J]
Minerals [t]

Outflows
Waste Emissions [t]
  gases
  solid
  wastewater
  other liquids
Heat [J]
Substances [t]
Produced goods [t]

Stocks
Infrastructure / Buildings [t]
  construction materials
  metals
  wood
  other materials
Other (machinery, durable) [t]
  metals
  other materials
Substances [t]

Source: Adapted from: Kennedy and Hoornweg (2012).

Figure 13.1 Urban metabolism classification system showing inflows (I), outflows (O), internal flows (Q), storage (S) and production (P) of biomass (B), minerals (M), water (W) and energy (E)

Equation (13.1) is the basis of the method of material flow analysis (MFA), described further in Sections 3 and 5, which is used for analyzing material parameters in the UM. A similar equation, expressing the conservation of energy, applies to the analysis of energy flows in the UM.

There are potentially many parameters that could be measured within the UM, so some reduction to key basic quantities is necessary. To take an inventory of all individual goods or all chemical elements would be overwhelming. Hence Table 13.1 provides a practical list of quantities that would ideally be included in a basic UM study. Depending on the context, data availability and key environmental challenges of a specific city, the suggested list in Table 13.1 may be longer or shorter. The table shows the UM parameters required for greenhouse gas accounting for cities, including direct and indirect emissions. It also shows other parameters, including flows of water, nutrients, materials and pollutants that are of importance for urban sustainability.

A completed UM study would aim to determine the parameters of Table 13.1 within an urban region for a calendar year. In many instances, the urban region will be determined by the political boundaries of a city, or the amalgamation of city boundaries to form a metropolitan region. Clear definition of the urban region should be given in reporting on a UM, along with background information such as population, gross area and year of study. UM parameters should ideally be reported in SI units, mainly in tonnes and Joules, as per Figure 13.1.

Research in recent years has extended the analysis of UM by including upstream and/or downstream environmental life-cycle impacts associated with flows into or out of urban regions. Much of this analysis has developed from GHG inventorying approaches for cities, which includes emissions occurring outside cities as a result of driving activities inside them (i.e. scope 2 and 3 emissions). An early example is the work done by the French Agency for the Environment and Energy Management on the inventory tool Bilan Carbon (ADEME 2007). Various approaches to adding life-cycle extensions to urban metabolism have been published (e.g. Ramaswami et al. 2008; Schulz 2010; Chavez and Ramaswami 2011; Chester et al. 2012). In a study of ten cities by Kennedy et al. (2009), upstream emissions for heating, industrial and transportation fuels were found to be between 7 percent and 24 percent of the direct emissions for these sectors. Extending UM to include life-cycle impacts of GHG emissions is demonstrated further in Section 4 of this chapter.

The rest of this chapter describes how the UM parameters of Table 13.1 are collected in practice. Sections 2 to 5 discuss methodology and data collection techniques grouped under each of the four main elements of metabolism: energy, materials, water, nutrients. This is then followed by a concluding section discussing diagrammatic representation of UM.

Table 13.1 Data requirements for basic urban metabolism studies

Quantity	Required for GHG calculation	Notes
Inflows		
Food	✓*	
Water (imports)	✓*	
Water (precipitation)		Standard climate data
Groundwater abstraction	✓*	
Construction materials	✓*	Primarily cement, aggregates, steel
Fossil fuels (by type)	✓	
Electricity	✓	
Total incoming solar radiation	✓	Standard climate data
Nitrogen & phosphorus		Example nutrients
Produced		
Food	✓*	
Construction materials	✓	Cement and steel
Stocks		
Construction materials		In the building stock
Nitrogen & phosphorus		
Landfill waste	✓	Accumulated
Construction/demolition waste		
Outflows		
Exported landfill waste	✓	
Incinerated waste	✓	Air emission plus accumulated mass
Exported recyclables		
Wastewater	✓	
Nitrogen & phosphorus		
SO_2		
NOx		
CO		
Volatile organics		
Particulates		
Methane	✓	
Ozone	✓+	
Black carbon	✓+	

Notes:
* has upstream (embodied) GHG emissions.
+ typically omitted from GHG calculations due to difficulty of estimation.

Source: Adapted from Kennedy and Hoornweg (2012).

2. ENERGY

Energy consumption in cities can be broadly divided into stationary uses and mobile uses. In both cases energy use should be reported first by the type of fuel or source, and second, where possible, by the type of user, for example residential, commercial, industrial.

Stationary Energy Use

Energy consumption data for each type of fuel typically have to be obtained from local utilities or fuel providers. In some cases these may be publicly owned utilities, which may make data publicly available; in other cases access to data from private companies may be required.

The number and complexity of sources of stationary energy use in a city can differ significantly between cities. For example, in many North American cities natural gas supplied by a single utility can account for over 95 percent of the fuels used for heating and industrial purposes. In other cities, particularly older ones, there can be significant use of fuel oils or coal. Obtaining data on the use of these truck-delivered fuels can be more difficult if there are multiple companies in the market. A more extreme case of complexity is the example of Bangkok, which has a wide variety of fuel sources (at least 13), including substantial use of wood, rice-husk and bagasse (Table 13.2).

Table 13.2 Heating and industrial fuel use for Bangkok in 2006

Fuel type	Use (TJ)
Wood	8725
Fuel oil	32217
Natural gas	15407
LPG	12041
Kerosene	322
Gasoline	595
Diesel	6033
Coal and coke	20331
Lignite	22035
Anthracite	632
Rice husk	8449
Bagasse	33427
Charcoal	314

Sources: Kennedy et al. (2010); Phdungsilp (2006).

Electricity is still typically provided a by a single utility in most cities, but attention should be given to a growing amount of generation from dispersed sources. Where electricity is supplied by more than one source, the amounts supplied and means of generation should be reported separately. This is particularly the case when electricity is generated from renewable sources within the urban boundary. Care should also be taken to note whether electricity is reported based on final consumption, which excludes transmission and distribution losses, or from the power generators' or utilities' perspective, which may or may not include such line losses.

The special case of combined heat and power (CHP) generation is perhaps best treated as a separately reported item from both heating fuels and electricity use. Sometimes when CHP plants are located within a city it may not be possible to distinguish the data on source fuels from total source fuels for the city; if this is the case then CHP becomes incorporated under heating fuels by default. Another case to watch out for is district heating, when the heating source is located outside city boundaries, with typically hot water or steam pumped to the city along a heat pipe.

Mobile Energy Use

Most of the energy required for transportation in cities is in the form of gasoline or diesel, mainly combusted in automobiles or trucks. Other fuels include liquified petroleum gas (LPG), natural gas and biofuels, as well as electricity used to power subways, rail and street cars.

Three methods may be used to quantify transportation fuel use within the study area. Typically the preferred method involves multiplication of the within-boundary vehicle kilometres travelled (VKT) by the fuel economy (L/km) for each vehicle grouping, for example automobile, motorcycle, SUV and various categories of truck. The VKT must be determined from vehicle counts or surveys, often supported by computer models. The design of surveys and computer models is often unique to each city, but there are guidelines for determining VKT in some countries (see, e.g., the US Department of Transport Federal Highway Administration, or Leduc 2008, for the European Union).

Data on fuel sales, for example from gasoline stations within the study area, can also be used, but generally should be avoided unless the boundaries of the area correspond to a commutershed; that is, the amount of travel into or out of the area is small (less than 5 percent) relative to travel within the area. This may be the case if the UM study is being conducted for a metropolitan region. One potential pitfall with using fuel sales data, however, is that some commercial traffic may obtain fuel on bulk contracts, and hence be missed from data based on retail sales. In other words, fuel sales data may be suitable for estimating energy use by automobiles in a commutershed, but not by trucks.

When neither VKT data or fuel sales data are available or appropriate, a third approach is to estimate fuel consumption from data for a higher-level state, province or region. Typically this would involve scaling based on population or vehicle registrations. In a study of ten global cities, Kennedy et al. (2010) found that differences in the fuel consumption estimates using scaling, fuel sales and VKT methods were up to about 5 percent. Having established fuel use for mobile and stationary purposes, this can be converted into greenhouse gas emissions by multiplying by an emissions factor (Kennedy et al. 2010).

In addition to ground transportation within a city, there can also be substantial quantities of fuel loaded onto planes, ships and trains within cities. Combustion of these fuels might mainly occur outside city boundaries, but since these vehicles serve cities, their energy use is sometimes included in scope 3 greenhouse gas emissions. Often the amount of fuel loaded onto planes and ships can be provided by airports or marine ports. Where this is not available, estimates may be scaled from higher-level data based on the number of passenger boardings, or freight tonnage.

3. MATERIAL STOCKS AND FLOWS

The stocks and flows of materials for cities can be quantified with differing degrees of refinement, from bulk materials, through to individual goods and individual substances.

At the broadest level, material stocks and flows for cities can be classified using the Eurostat system of groupings: (i) biomass; (ii) fossil fuels; (iii) metallic minerals; (iv) non-metallic minerals; and (v) non-specified (Table 13.3). Examples of studies that have reported material flows using this system include those for Hamburg, Leipzig, Limerick, Lisbon, London and Vienna (Bongardt 2002; Browne et al. 2009; Hammer and Giljum 2006; Niza et al. 2009). Other studies have used different frameworks (see review by Weisz and Steinberger 2010), some of which may include so-called 'hidden flows' such as removal of overburden during mining or waste trimmings from forestry. Inclusion of such hidden flows will generally increase the amount of materials ascribed to cities (see, e.g., the study of York, UK by Barrett et al. 2002).

Construction materials constitute the largest stocks and flows of materials for cities. (This is aside from water, which is treated separately; see Section 4.) Quantifying the bulk stocks and flows of aggregates, cement, glass, steel, wood and so on for cities is challenging. Essentially bottom–up

Table 13.3 Material groups under the EUROSTAT system

Material group	Material examples
Biomass	Agriculture, forestry, fishery, livestock and others
Fossil fuels	Coal, petroleum and natural gas
Metallic minerals	Iron ores and non-ferrous metal ores
Non-metallic minerals	Stone and industrial use (chalk and dolomite, slate, chemical and fertilizer minerals, salt, other mining and quarrying products)
	Bulk minerals for construction (limestone and gypsum, gravel and sand, clays and kaolin, and excavated soil)
Non-specified	Items that do not fall into the above four groups

Source: Gou (2012).

and top–down approaches may be employed. The bottom–up approach typically involves classifying the buildings and other infrastructure in a city into representative groups with typical material characteristics, for example detached homes, roads and highway bridges, and collecting data on the annual additions, demolitions and stocks of each group. Statistically representative quantities for the material components of each group then need to be established; this may be done with the help of local architects and engineers who have bills of quantities from projects completed in the city. The top–down approach may involve engaging local industry groups concerned with sales of materials in the city to obtain estimates of bulk material flows for a given year. Alternatively, material quantities might be estimated from state-, province- or regional-level data weighted by building starts or infrastructure investment data.

Unless special surveys are conducted, or market research is accessed, information on flows of consumer goods into cities is most likely to be obtained by scaling from national or other higher-level data. At the national level, flows of many different types of goods are quantified, at least in economic terms, in national import, export, production and consumption statistics.

Quantification of substance flows, for example of a specific nutrient, metal or other element, will usually involve first undertaking studies of relevant goods or bulk materials, including their waste streams, and then drawing upon knowledge of the fractional component of the substance in the goods, bulk materials and wastes. The methodologies used in substance flow analysis are described further in the case of nutrients in Section 5.

Having established suitable data on material stocks and flows for cities, formal methods of material flow accounting (MFA, including substance flow accounting) may be applied. Several books describe MFA methodology (e.g. Brunner and Rechberger 2004; Baccini and Brunner 2012). These provide formal procedures for forming systems boundaries, representing processes, stocks and flows, with associated definitions and terminology. The methods have also been incorporated into software packages, such as SIMBOX (Baccini and Bader 1996) and STAN (Cencic and Rechberger 2008). As conservation of mass lies at the heart of MFA, applying the formal methodology may help to either verify or fill gaps in material flows data.

4. WATER

Despite the importance of maintaining a sustainable urban water metabolism, many cities have not developed comprehensive water balances and are hence vulnerable to changes in water use or climatic regime. Several components of urban water balances can be derived simply, but others require extensive analysis. Withdrawals are generally well documented; in the USA, the US Geological Survey documents water withdrawals (surface and groundwater) by type of use, at the county level, and finer-scale analysis can often be done via state agencies, which may maintain public data files for each withdrawal. Within the municipal system, water used for external irrigation can be estimated by comparing water use during the growing season with water use during winter. In some suburban communities with well-maintained lawns, outside irrigation can use several times more water than interior water uses. Residential end uses of water in several cities throughout the USA have been documented by Mayer et al. (1999). This study showed that nearly all the variation in household water use occurs in outside water use (mostly irrigation); interior use is remarkably similar (around 70 gallons/capita/year). Similarly, sewage flows are generally well documented and readily available in developed countries. Gains or losses of sewage flows are often measured by municipal sewage agencies, which need this information to guide maintenance operations.

Water balances for urban landscapes are more troublesome. Flows of urban runoff are often measured in US cities, as is precipitation, allowing ready calculation of yields (cm/yr). What is more difficult is the apportionment of the remaining water into evaporation and recharge, except in desert regions where most of the evaporation is the result of landscape irrigation.

Groundwater balancing is generally accomplished through modeling. Groundwater models can account for regional groundwater inflows and outflows, inflows and outflows from rivers and lakes, withdrawals and recharge, with the latter often as the 'unknown'. Once calibrated, groundwater models can then predict the effect of changes in withdrawal or recharge. The latter is greatly influenced by urbanization: as impervious surface area increases, groundwater recharge is reduced.

From a UM point of view, the role of water and the water balance of a city is of course important, due to the large quantities of water flowing through a city. Even when all natural water of rivers not collected, processed or transported by man-made systems within a city is excluded, the flows of urban water services in water supply and wastewater (stormwater and sewage) management will totally dominate the flow quantity (kg/year) and the flux quantity (kg/cap/year) of the material balance within a city.

Despite the fact that distribution, pumping and processing of water – upstream and downstream to the consumers – consume energy carriers, various construction (stock) materials and operation chemicals and transport services, and create a variety of by-products and emissions to water, air and soil, these are often poorly understood, quantitatively. So are also the associated potential environmental impacts, both the direct impacts from activities within the city and the indirect impacts from processing activities (chemicals, energy carriers, transport work) elsewhere in the global system.

Along with a growing attention to the role of UM and the search for solutions for sustainable cities, it is indeed necessary to better understand and document the quantitative relationships between the flows of water, materials, chemicals, energy carriers, emissions and wastes in cities, as well as how these factors influence the social, environmental and economic dimensions of sustainability. Such an understanding can be facilitated by a metabolism model approach to the urban water cycle services. The starting point of this approach is a generic metabolism model system definition, within which any city in principle could be studied; see Figure 13.2.

The system definition illustrates that inside a system boundary (the city total hydraulic catchment area) water is flowing from the source via the water supply subsystem to the water demand subsystem, and further via the wastewater subsystem to the recipient. This is normally a linear flow; however, future systems will probably increasingly include water reuse and recycling concepts, and therefore the system definition also includes a cyclic water recovery subsystem. Finally, there is a resources recovery subsystem, which is relevant for energy, nutrients and sludge recovery from the water and wastewater subsystems.

The first important message is that each of these subsystems must be connected in a mass-balance consistent way with respect to water. Hence the starting point is to define all relevant water flows ($Q_{i,j}$) from an origin i to a destination j. Then a quantitative mathematical model of these flows must be developed, assuring mass balance. The drivers within the system are water demand ($Q_{1,3}$), wastewater generation ($Q_{2,3}$) and stormwater runoff ($Q_{0,3}$).

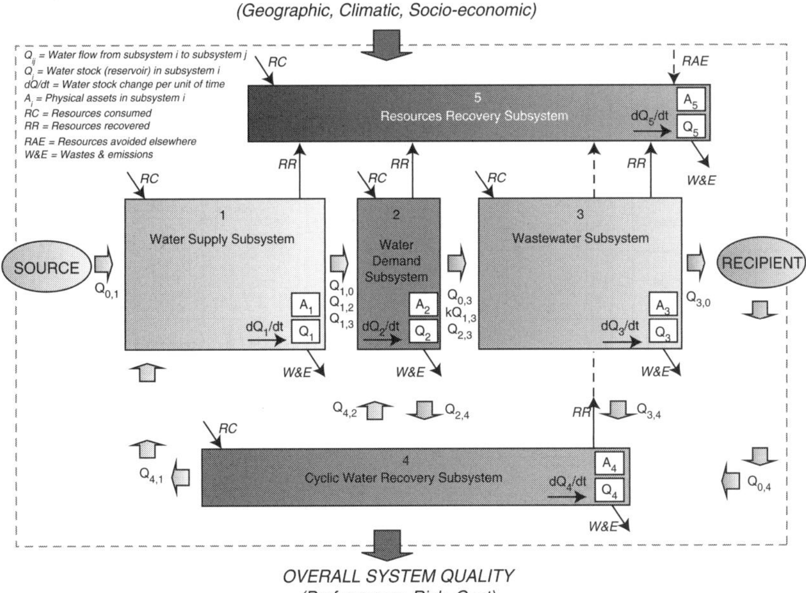

Source: Venkatesh (2011).

Figure 13.2 Metabolism model system definition of urban water services

A second important message is that each subsystem can be broken down into a set of processes or sub-subsystems. Each sub-subsystem will have to be mathematically described in terms of water flows. And each of these processes has a given function, such as particle separation in water treatment plants, pumping in distribution networks, pipe transport in wastewater collection networks, and sludge stabilization in wastewater treatment plants – and this function is provided by use of a given technology (equipment types, artifact designs). For a given technology, and a given water throughflow specification (quantity and quality), any process activity will mobilize a given flow of resources consumed (RC, such as chemicals, materials, energy carriers) and wastes and emissions (W&E, such as direct and indirect emissions of CO_2 to the atmosphere, nitrogen and phosphorus substances to water, and solid wastes to soil). The metabolism modeling challenge for this kind of system is indeed simple, yet challenging! One has to develop an overall model that is mass-balance consistent at different levels of detail, so that all activities in the system are correctly related, and when this is done, the remaining task is to add the required set of specific coefficients for input resources, output wastes and emissions (such as the

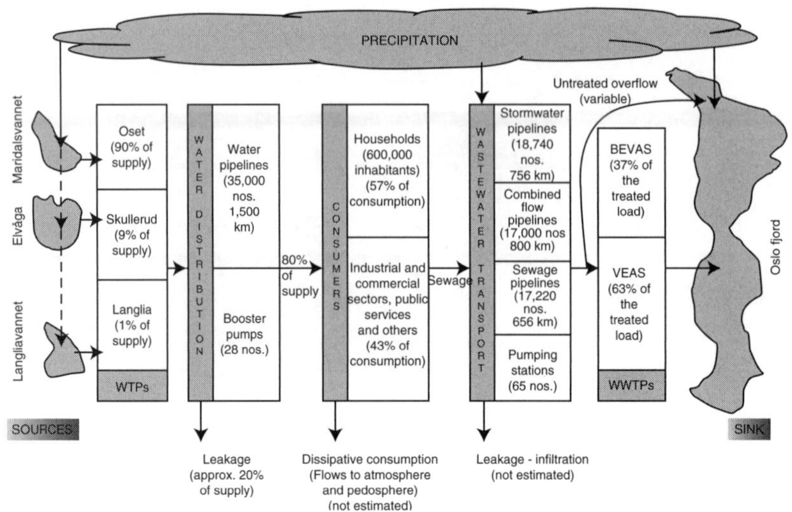

Source: Venkatesh (2011).

Figure 13.3 The urban water services of the city of Oslo

relative consumption of specific energy carriers and chemicals per m^3 of water, in kWh/m^3 and kg/m^3). Once this is done, and the model is calibrated for a given city, it will provide quantitative estimates for all metabolic flows and fluxes within the system, for a given year. Such physical information (for water, energy, chemicals, materials, wastes and emissions) can easily be further used for environmental assessment, such as by use of life-cycle assessment (LCA) methods, or for economic assessment. A model like this can also be used for examining changes over time in the past, from accounting and operations data within the water utility of a given city. It can also be used for evaluating scenarios for the future metabolism and its associated environmental impact, on the basis of prognosis for population growth, industrial water demand, changes in technologies and so on. This is more complex, and points towards a dynamic model approach.

What we can obtain from such methods, or related types of models and calculations, is a variety of information. As an example, the urban water system of Oslo (Norway) is briefly outlined in Figure 13.3, serving a population of about 600 000 inhabitants in households (57 percent of water consumption) and various industrial, commercial and public services (43 percent of water consumption), adding up to about 150 m^3/cap/year total demand.

The urban water services in the city of Oslo have been examined by the metabolism model approach since 2007, partly in close collaboration with

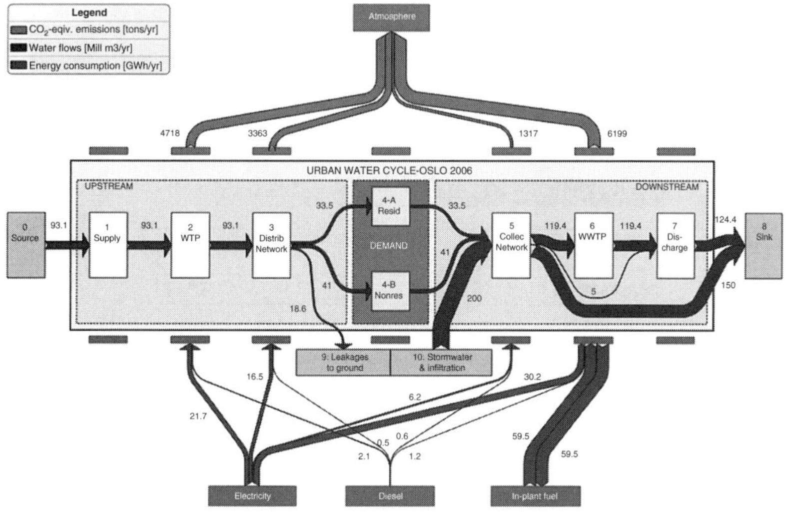

Source: Authors.

Figure 13.4 *The water/energy/CO_2 nexus of urban water services in Oslo*

the city's water utility, Oslo VAV. Results from this research have been published in a series of papers by Venkatesh and Brattebø (2011a; 2011b; 2012a; 2012b) and by Venkatesh et al. (2011). These studies cover issues such as material flows, energy flows, emissions, environmental life-cycle impacts and economic impacts associated with selected subsystems as well as the system as a whole. Other studies, similar to that done in Oslo, are being carried out for selected other cities: Nantes (France), Toronto (Canada) and Turin (Italy). The metabolism model approach is also being developed further within a EU project called TRUST (http://www.trust-i.net/), with the aim to develop dynamic metabolism models for the evaluation of 'TRransitions to the Urban water Services of Tomorrow' and testing such models for a number of cities in Europe.

In regard to the city of Oslo, Figure 13.4 shows a Sankey diagram of the so-called 'water/energy/carbon nexus' profile of urban water services in 2006. The central section of the figure presents the water flows (in million m^3 per year) from the source to the sink. Shown also is the split between residential and non-residential demand, the high share of water losses due to leakage in the water distribution network, and the dominant role of stormwater flows downstream to the use phase as well as the share of wastewater discharged via combined sewers and the wastewater treatment plant. In the bottom section of the figure are shown flows of direct energy

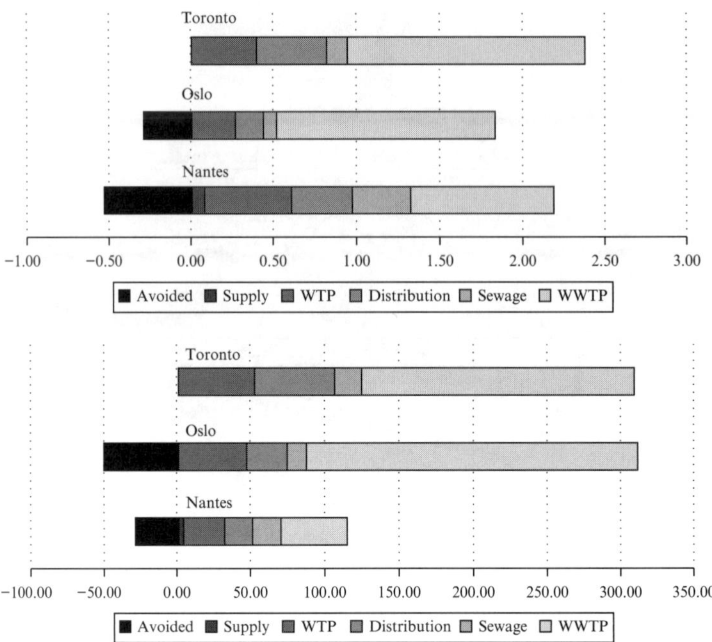

Source: Author.

Figure 13.5 Total energy consumption in the urban water services of Nantes, Oslo and Toronto, by subsystem (upper chart in kWh/m³ and lower chart in kWh/cap)

demand to each of the subsystems (in GWh/year), including heat generation and reuse from sludge fermentation in the wastewater plant, and the split between energy carriers. In the top section are shown the estimated direct emission to air flows of greenhouse gases (in tons/year of CO_2 equivalents). Metabolic quantifications like this, derived from the turnover of water in the urban water cycle, offer good insight into opportunities for environmental improvements, in this case how direct energy consumption and direct greenhouse gas emissions can be understood and, it is hoped, reduced.

By use of environmental LCA methods and models it is possible to develop further the system-wide profile (direct and indirect) of emissions and environmental impact. While direct emissions can fairly easily be measured or estimated from water/energy balance measurements, as explained above, the quantification of indirect and system-wide emissions is more difficult. Selected results from such analysis are presented in Figures 13.5, 13.6 and 13.7 with more complete and detailed data for

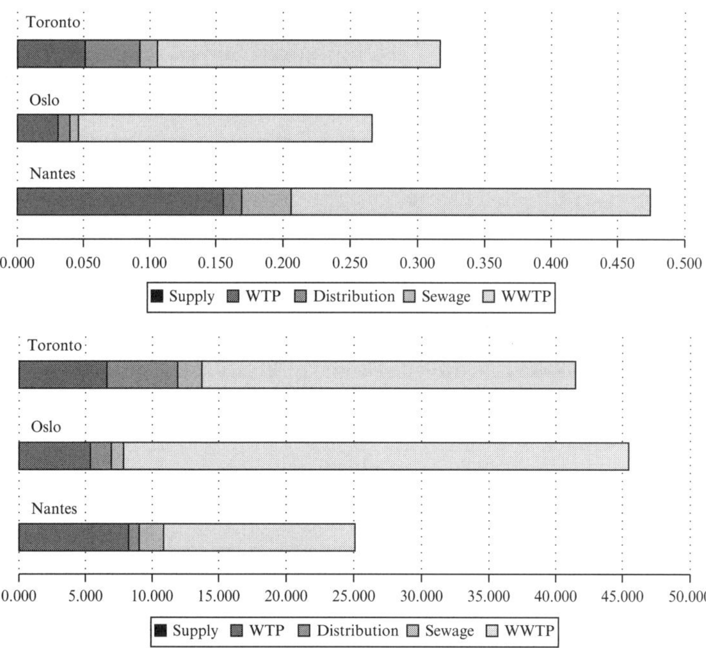

Source: Author.

Figure 13.6 Total GHG emissions in the urban water services of Nantes, Oslo and Toronto, by subsystem (upper chart in $kgCO_2$*-eq/m*^{3} *and lower chart in* $kgCO_2$*-eq/cap)*

urban water-related direct and indirect energy and greenhouse gas emissions, for Nantes, Oslo and Toronto.

As can be seen from Figures 13.5 and 13.6, there are significant differences between cities, in both energy consumption and greenhouse gas emissions. For energy, this is due to several local conditions, such as topography and distances (water pumping), treatment processes used for water and wastewater, and how energy recovery opportunities are implemented from sludge or outflow wastewaters. When the figures are presented on a per capita basis it is also important to appreciate the importance of per capita water demand and the share of water leakages.

For greenhouse gas emissions, one should also take into consideration the share of different energy carriers. As seen in the upper chart of Figure 13.7, this distribution is indeed different between cities, and one should bear in mind that the technologies for electricity generation (i.e. the mix of primary energy sources in power generation) are very different

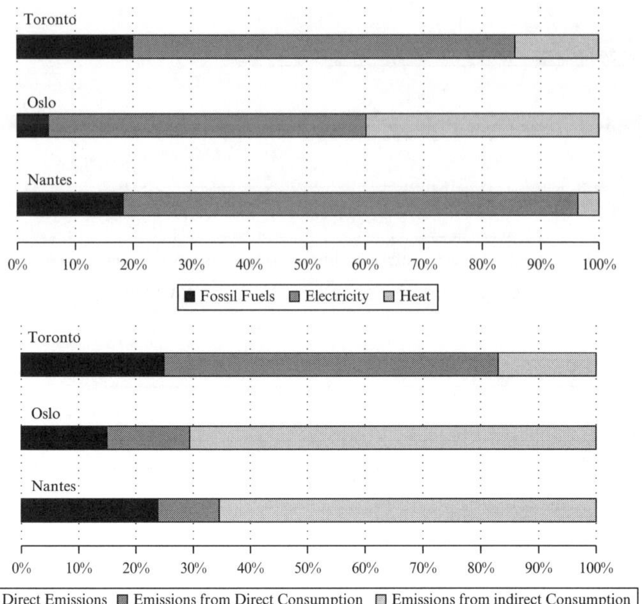

Source: Author.

Figure 13.7 Distribution of energy carriers consumed (upper chart) and direct and indirect GHG emissions (lower chart) from urban water services of Nantes, Oslo and Toronto

from country to country. Norway, for instance, has close to 100 percent of its electricity generated from hydropower, with very low CO_2 emissions per kWh.

An important finding is shown in the lower chart in Figure 13.7, which presents the sources of greenhouse gas emissions for the urban water services. Despite some differences between the cities, the share of direct emissions (direct process emissions and combustion of fuels within the system) is only a minor part of the total, while emissions from direct consumption and indirect consumption (of products such as electricity, process chemicals and infrastructure materials) account for the majority of total emissions. This means that sectors such as urban water services should not focus mainly on their direct emissions if they want to be sustainable in their activities regarding energy and greenhouse gas emissions. They must think about and analyse their activities in a system-wide perspective, and take advantage of methods such as MFA and LCA. This proves that urban metabolism modeling approaches also have a role to play in the urban water sector.

5. NITROGEN, PHOSPHORUS AND SALTS

Problems Caused by Poor Metabolism of Water, Nutrients and Salts

Understanding water balances (discussed in Section 4) is first necessary to deal with the essential role of nutrients (nitrogen and phosphorus) and salts in maintaining sustainable cities. Severe mismanagement of the flows of these materials often causes deterioration of urban ecosystems. Most obviously, either too much or too little water can cause serious loss of human well-being, especially during periods of climate extremes – too much or too little precipitation. Urban water problems are often associated with groundwater stored in aquifers below the city. Groundwater is often the preferred source of municipal water supply, because it often lies directly underground, is often plentiful (at least during early development), and is generally naturally 'clean', requiring little or no treatment prior to consumption. Over time, however, groundwater supplies are often depleted and/or become polluted (see examples in Kennedy et al. 2007). Groundwater depletion is often accompanied by land subsidence (sometimes by a meter or more), with damage to infrastructure. Over time, aquifers become depleted or polluted, withdrawals are often halted, and groundwater levels rise, which may flood underground structures (Foster et al. 1998; Shananan 2009). Many cities also utilize surface water, initially from rivers flowing nearby, but often imported from great distances as cities expand. Cities also discharge sewage, in various levels of treatment, urban runoff and, in the case of older cities, often 'combined' sewage (sanitary + urban runoff), often causing eutrophication of downstream rivers and estuaries.

One of the most prevalent pollutants of urban groundwater is nitrate (Wakida and Lerner 2005; Xu and Usher 2006; Xu et al. 2007). Nitrate is extremely mobile in soil; hence additions of nitrogen at the surface often result in downward migration of nitrate through the vadose zone to underlying aquifers. These inputs include fertilizers, leakage of fecal material to latrines, leaky sewer pipes and animal wastes. As a result, aquifers underlying many cities are contaminated to the point they do not meet WHO water quality standards (Wakida and Lerner 2005).

Nitrogen and phosphorus from agricultural runoff, urban sewage and urban runoff also contaminate lakes, rivers and estuaries, causing eutrophication, with severe impacts on human utilization (Carpenter et al. 1998). In addition, phosphate rock (the penultimate source of P entering cities) is a finite, non-renewable resource. In the USA, for example, the phosphate rock resource would be depleted in just 40 years if it continued to be used at current rates, compelling the USA to import P fertilizer from other parts of the world, or to move toward a 'circulate economy', recycling P that moves into cities back to farms. Finally, salt contamination is a major concern for many cities in the world: in north-temperate regions, road salt has become a major contaminant of groundwater and urban streams (Kaushal et al. 2005); coastal cities throughout the world suffer from seawater intrusion as the result of drawdown of freshwater aquifers; and inland desert cities face the problem of concentration of salts by evaporation (Baker et al. 2002).

Material Flow Analysis (MFA) of Nutrients and Salts

Much about the metabolism of nutrients and salts can be learned from material flow analysis (MFA), which traces the flows of these materials through systems. (Note that MFA is a generic methodology; when applied to individual elements it can also be called substance flow analysis, SFA.) In the context of urban ecosystems, MFA is a hybrid approach that borrows from several fields: hydrology, industrial ecology and biogeochemistry. MFA is essentially a mass balance accounting of the flows of any material, in terms of mass/time through a system. These systems can be of any size; for cities, some scales of interest are urban regions, watersheds within urban regions, and households. For an urban region, a material flows through various pathways (e.g. a human food system), may be stored within a subsystem (e.g. phosphorus in residential lawns), be transformed (e.g. by fixation of atmospheric N_2 gas to NOx by combustion), and exit the system (e.g. nutrients in sewage may exit as biosolids, treated effluent and gases).

An MFA for phosphorus in the Minneapolis–St Paul region illustrates the idea (Figure 13.8). This analysis revealed that only 4 percent of P entering the MSP region was recycled, whereas 31 percent leaked (sewage effluent + runoff) to the Mississippi River, and 64 percent was stored, mostly in landfills. The latter included incinerated sewage biosolids, garbage and landscape waste, along with storage in vegetated landscapes. Reconfiguring the system (using MFA) in a 'conservation scenario' reduced P inputs and greatly reduced storage and leakage of P, while conserving enough P to supply about half of that needed to provide food to the urban region.

System boundaries

Because many data sources are from governmental databases, most MFA studies for nutrients and salts have been developed on the basis of governmental units. For urban regions, these sources might include municipalities, metropolitan regional governments (often focused on water, sewage, solid waste, transportation or planning), county or state governments,

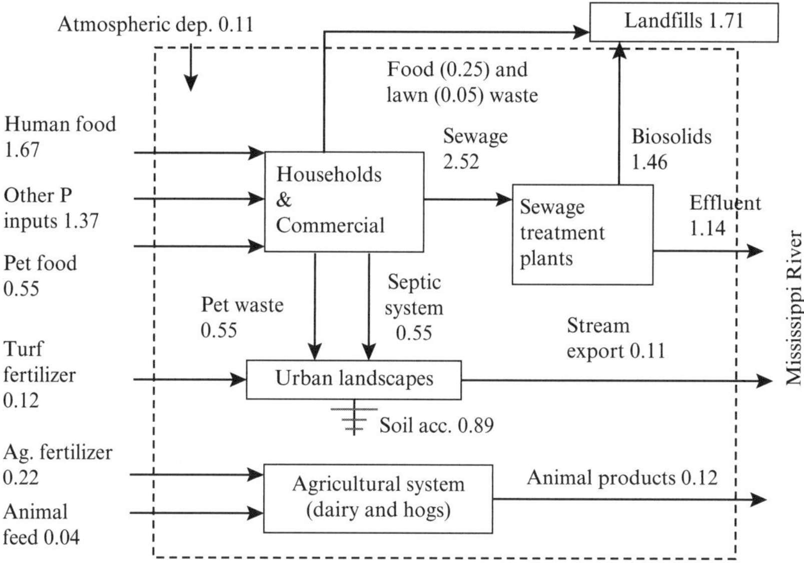

Source: Baker (2011).

Figure 13.8 Phosphorus balance for the Minneapolis–St Paul urban region

and federal agencies (Table 13.4). For some fluxes, disaggregated data can sometimes be obtained. An example is the US Department of Energy's household energy databases, which can be disaggregated to the household unit, though only at coarse scales (climate regions). To some extent, data from larger surveys can be 'mapped' into smaller geographic units using other types of data that are acquired at smaller scales (e.g. US Census 'block-level' data) based on factors such as population distribution, race and ethnicity, age and income.

Data sources

Much of the data needed to develop urban nutrient balances can be acquired from readily accessible public databases (Table 13.4). With increasing resolution of satellite imagery, the growing using of LIDAR for fine-scale topographic mapping, the nearly universal adoption of GIS mapping by all but the smallest cities, and increasing accessibility and transparency of data made possible through the Internet, the technique of MFA is becoming a practical tool for urban management of nutrients, salts and other substances.

Table 13.4 Examples of data sources that have been used in urban MFA studies

	Original source of data	Typical unit of government	Common spatial resolution for reporting
Impervious surface	Land Sat images; LIDAR imagery	State	Variable, 0.6–10 m < 0.2 m (vertical)
Land cover/land use	Satellite or air photo	State	Variable, 0.6–10 m
Crop production	Surveys of farmers	National Agricultural Statistical Survey (NASS)	County
Agricultural fertilizer use	Surveys of farmers	NASS	State
Population characteristics	Nationwide census	US Census	Census blocks
Housing characteristics	Surveys	US Census, American Housing Survey	Metropolitan areas
Watershed boundaries	Digital topographic maps	Some states	Variable
Sewershed	Ground-based mapping	Municipality or regional sewage authority	Delineated by individual hookups
Water withdrawals	Measured withdrawal + chemical characteristics	Varying, often state agencies or water management districts; county-level summaries by USGS	Individual withdrawals
Sewage and treated effluent; biosolids	Direct measurement at sewage treatment plants	Municipality or regional sewage authority	Individual sewage treatment plants
Land parcel information	Ground-based mapping and reporting	Local governments	Individual properties

Solid waste disposal	'Tipping' studies at landfills	Cities or regional authorities; national summaries	Cities
Animal feedlots (type and size)	Ground-based reporting	State government (Minnesota)	Varying – about 30 animal units in Minnesota
Animal production	Ground-based reporting	State government; aggregated by NASS	County
Animal feed consumption	Analysis of animal operations (various studies)	None	None
Human nutrient consumption	National surveys based on 24-hour dietary recall	Federal government – Continuing Survey of Foods Study	Federal
Pet food	NAS (2006)	Pet incidence studies	
Lawn fertilizer use	Local lawn fertilizer studies. Also see Fissore et al. (2011)	Various (not systematic)	Various

Source: Adapted from Baker (2009).

Development of new methods

As the fields of industrial ecology, urban ecology and planning converge on the topic of urban sustainability, new types of studies will yield new types of information to explain the flows of materials through cities. MFAs for nitrogen and phosphorus at the scale of urban regions are becoming common enough that 'typologies' of cities with respect to nutrient fluxes may soon be possible. At the scale of small watersheds, studies of nutrient flows through urban landscapes (Kaushal et al. 2011; Groffman et al. 2004) are providing better understanding of the dynamics of materials moving from rooftops and lawns to streets, storm sewers and streams. Baker et al. (2014) have quantified C, N, P and solids fluxes removed by street sweeping in relation to tree canopy cover, which translates to reduction of these materials entering storm sewers. The Central Arizona–Phoenix Long-Term Ecological Research Project (CAP-LTER) project has developed a spatial survey approach by which randomly sampled points throughout the urban area are sampled for soil and biota at 200 points at five-year intervals, providing a survey conducted every five years, an approach that could provide direct measurement of materials accumulating in soil (Hope et al. 2005). This will prove a great improvement on the traditional approach of estimating accumulation 'by difference' that is now used in most urban MFA studies. The Twin Cities Household Ecosystem Project (TCHEP) developed a hybrid approach using surveys, energy bills, parcel data and onsite vegetation surveys to quantify flows of C, N and P through households in relation to their demographic, social and behavioral attributes (Fissore et al. 2011; Nelson et al. 2008); also see methodologies at tchep.umn.edu. Finally an MFA study of salt in five municipal water systems in the Southwest USA used a hybrid approach that involved measurements of salts in source waters and sewers, computation of salts added by water treatment based on chemical additions; estimation of salt by human excretion from mineral intakes estimated in a national food survey, and modeled inputs of salts from water softeners, informed by a household survey of water softeners and their use (Thompson et al. 2006).

6. UM DIAGRAMS

Given the substantial amount of information contained in a UM study, some form of diagram may be useful for presenting results. A few options for UM diagrams are briefly reviewed here, although these are by no means exhaustive. Also, a UM diagram would typically be supplemented with one or more data tables.

One of the most creative UM diagrams was that presented by ecologists Duvigneaud and Denayeyer-De Smet for Brussels in the early 1970s

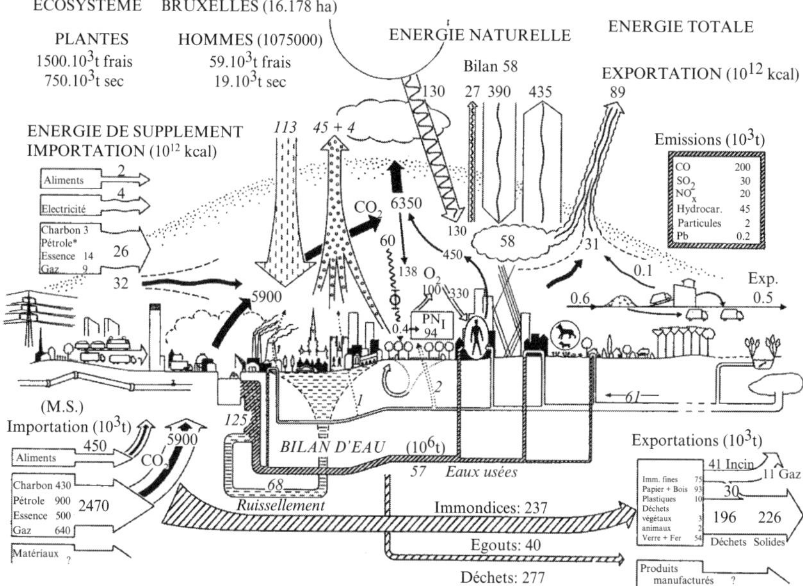

Source: Duvigneaud and Denayeyer-De Smet (1977).

Figure 13.9 The urban metabolism of Brussels, Belgium in the early 1970s

(Figure 13.9). The Brussels diagram presents the stocks and flows in an attractive way, with some attention to artistic detail. That said, while Figure 13.9 is visually appealing, it is a bit too busy for details to be picked out during a PowerPoint presentation, although it might still be used as a quick guide to the complexity of the UM.

A much simpler, but less aesthetically pleasing, approach is shown in Figure 13.10, where the UM of Greater Toronto is compared to that of Hong Kong. Much less information is displayed for each city, so that it is possible to see the results easily. The approach of constructing a UM diagram out of simple boxes and arrows can be taken further, using for instance the methods used to construct MFA diagrams (e.g. Brunner and Rechberger 2004).

A further approach to presenting the UM is by use of a Sankey diagram (Figures 13.4 and 13.11). This is particularly useful for displaying upstream energy transformations and losses, as well as showing energy flows by fuel type and end use. The UM of Amman in Figure 13.11 is a customized diagram, but there are also commercially available software packages for constructing Sankey diagrams.

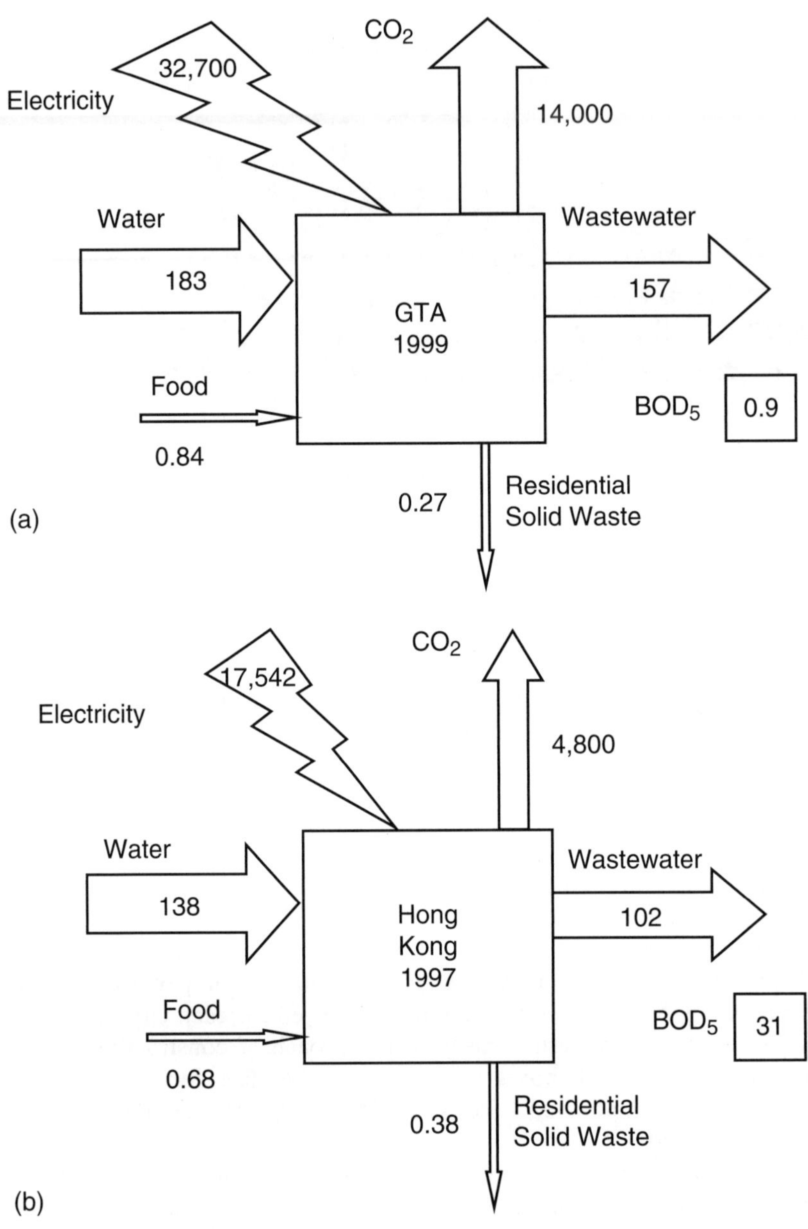

Source: Sahely et al. (2003).

Figure 13.10 Comparison of urban metabolism of (a) the GTA 1999 and (b) Hong Kong 1997

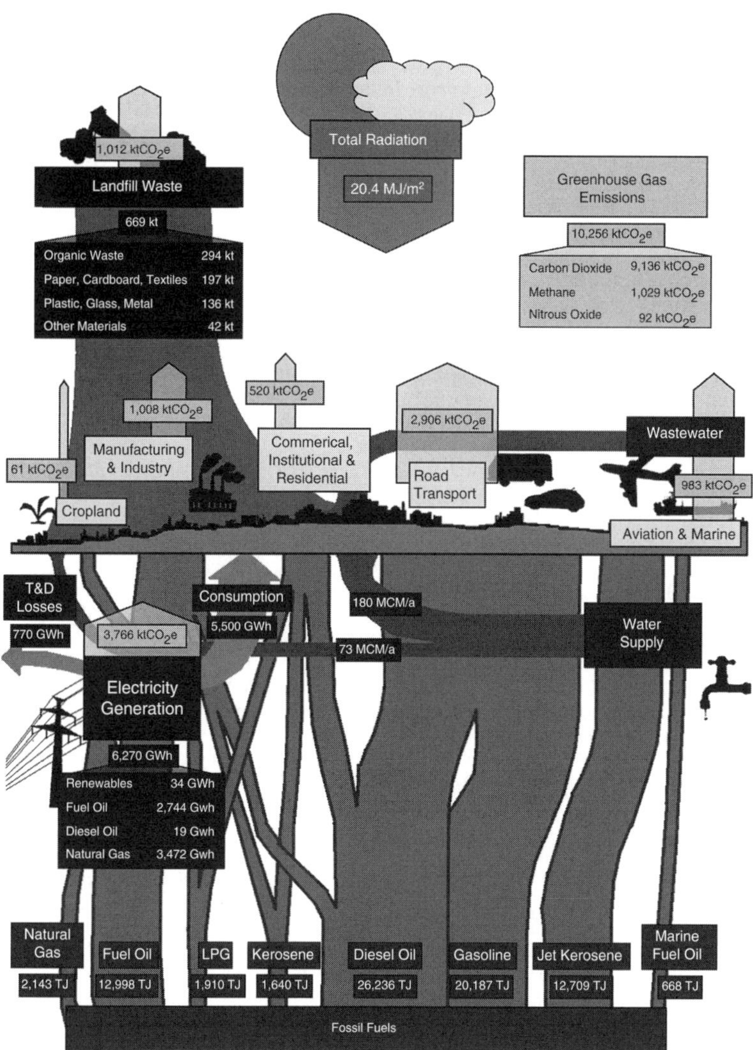

Source: Sugar et al. (2013).

Figure 13.11 *Urban metabolism of Amman*

REFERENCES

ADEME (French Environment and Energy Management Agency) (2007), *Bilan Carbone™ Companies and Local Authorities Version Methodological Guide (Version 5.0): Objectives and Principles for the Counting of Greenhouse Gas Emissions*, Paris: ADEME.

Baccini, Peter and Paul H. Brunner (2012), *Metabolism of the Anthroposphere: Analysis, Evaluation Design*, 2nd edn, Boston, MA: MIT Press.

Baccini, Peter and Hans-Peter Bader (1996), *Regionaler Stoffhaushalt*, Berlin: Spektrum Akademicher Verlag.

Baker, L. (2009), 'Introduction: New directions in management of urban pollution', in L. Baker (ed.), *The Water Environment of Cities*, Lowell, MA: Springer Science, pp. 1–16.

Baker, L. (2011), 'Can urban P conservation help to prevent the brown devolution?', *Chemosphere*, **84** (6), 779–84.

Baker, L.A., A.J. Brazel, N. Selover, C. Martin, N. McIntyre, F.R. Steiner, A. Nelson and L. Musacchio (2002), 'Urbanization and warming of Phoenix (Arizona, USA): impacts, feedbacks, and mitigation', *Urban Ecosystems*, **6** (3), 183–203.

Baker, L., P. Kalinosky, S. Hobbie, R. Bintner and C. Buyarski (2014), 'Quantifying nutrient removal by enhanced street sweeping', *Stormwater Magazine*, February/March.

Barrett, John, Harry Vallack, Andrew Jones and Gary Haq (2002), *A Material Flow Analysis and Ecological Footprint of York: Technical Report*, Stockholm: Stockholm Environment Institute.

Bongardt, Bertold (2002), 'Material flow accounting for London in 2000', Social Ecology Working Paper 67, Vienna: Institute for Interdisciplinary Studies at Austrian Universities.

Browne, D., B. O'Regan and R. Moles (2009), 'Assessment of total urban metabolism and metabolic inefficiency in an Irish city-region', *Waste Management*, **29** (10), 2765–71.

Brunner, Paul H. and Helmut Rechberger (2004), *Practical Handbook of Material Flow Analysis*, Boca Raton, FL: Lewis Publishers.

Carpenter, S.R., N.F. Caraco, D.L. Correll, R.W. Howarth, A.N. Sharpley and V.H. Smith (1998), 'Nonpoint source pollution of surface waters with phosphorus and nitrogen', *Ecological Applications*, **8** (3), 559–68.

Cencic, O. and H. Rechberger (2008), 'Material flow analysis with software STAN', *Journal of Environmental Engineering and Management*, **18** (1), 3–7.

Chavez, A. and A. Ramaswami (2011), 'Progress toward low carbon cities: approaches for transboundary GHG emissions footprinting', *Carbon Management*, **2** (4), 471–82.

Chester, M., S. Pincetl and B. Allenby (2012), 'Avoiding unintended tradeoffs by integrating life-cycle impact assessment with urban metabolism', *Current Opinion in Environmental Sustainability*, **4** (4), 451–7.

Duvigneaud, P. and S. Denayeyer-De Smet (1977), 'L'ecosystème urbain bruxellois', in P. Duvigneaud and P. Kestemont (eds), *Productivité en Belgique*, Bruxelles: Travaux de la Section Belge du Programme Biologique International, pp. 581–97.

Eurostat (2009), *Economy-Wide Material Flow Accounts: Compilation Guidelines for Reporting to the 2009 Eurostat Questionnaire (Version 01: June 2009)*, Luxembourg: Eurostat.

Fissore, C., S.E. Hobbie, J.Y. King, J.P. McFadden, K.C. Nelson and L.A. Baker (2011), 'The residential landscape: fluxes of elements and the role of household decisions', *Urban Ecosystems*, DOI 10.1007/s11252-011-0189-0.

Foster, Stephen S.D., Adrian Lawrence and Brian Morris (1998), *Groundwater in Urban Development: Assessing Management Needs and Formulating Policy Strategies, Number 390*, New York: The World Bank.

Gou, T. (2012), *Review of Material Flows in Cities (Masters of Engineering Thesis)*, Toronto, ON: University of Toronto, Civil Engineering Department.

Groffman, P.M., N.L. Law, K.T. Belt, L.E. Band and G.T. Fisher (2004), 'Nitrogen fluxes and retention in urban watershed ecosystems', *Ecosystems*, **7** (4), 393–403.

Hammer, Mark and Stefan Giljum (2006), 'Materialflussanalysen der Regionen Hamburg, Wien und Leipzig (Material flow analysis of the regions of Hamburg, Vienna and Leipzig)', Working Paper 6, Hamburg: NEDS.

Hoornweg, Daniel A., Gisela Campillo, Dennis Linders, Artessa N. Saldivar-Sali and Lorraine Sugar (2012), *Mainstreaming Urban Metabolism: Advances and Challenges in City Participation*, Barcelona: Sixth Urban Research and Knowledge Symposium.

Hope, D., W. Zhu, C. Gries, J. Oleson, J. Kaye, N. Grimm and L.A. Baker (2005), 'Spatial variation in soil inorganic nitrogen across an arid urban ecosystem', *Urban Ecosystems*, **8** (3–4), 251–73.

Kaushal, S.S., P.M. Groffman, L.E. Band, E.M. Elliott, C.A. Shields and C. Kendal (2011), 'Tracking nonpoint source nitrogen pollution in human-impacted watersheds', *Environmental Science & Technology*, **45**, 8225–32.

Kaushal, S.S., P.M. Groffman, G.E. Likens, K.T. Belt, W.P. Stack, V.R. Kelly, L.E. Band and G.T. Fisher (2005), 'Increased salinization of fresh water in the northeastern United States', *Proceedings of the National Academy of Sciences*, **102** (38), 13517–20.

Kennedy, C.A. and D. Hoornweg (2012), 'Mainstreaming urban metabolism', *Journal of Industrial Ecology*, **16** (6), 780–82.

Kennedy, C., J. Cuddihy and J.Y. Engel (2007), 'The changing metabolism of cities', *Journal of Industrial Ecology*, **11** (2), 43–59.

Kennedy, C., J. Steinberger, B. Gasson, T. Hillman, M. Havránek, Y. Hansen, D. Pataki, A. Phdungsilp, A. Ramaswami and G.V. Mendez (2010), 'Methodology for inventorying greenhouse gas emissions from global cities', *Energy Policy*, **37** (9), 4828–37.

Kennedy, C., J. Steinberger, B. Gasson, T. Hillman, M. Havránek, Y. Hansen, D. Pataki, A. Phdungsilp, A. Ramaswami and G.V. Mendez (2009), 'Greenhouse gas emissions from global cities', *Environmental Science and Technology*, **43** (19), 7297–302.

Kennedy, C.A., S. Pincetl and P. Bunje (2011), 'The study of urban metabolism and its applications to urban planning and design', *Journal of Environmental Pollution*, **159** (8–9), 1965–73.

Leduc, G. (2008), *Road Traffic Data: Collection Methods and Applications*, European Commission, JRC 47967.

Mayer, Peter W., William B. DeOreo, Eva M. Optiz, Jack C. Kiefer, William Y. Davis, Benedykt Dziegielewski and John O. Nelson (1999), *Residential End Uses of Water*, Denver, CO: American Water Works Association.

National Research Council (2006), *Nutrient Requirements of Dogs and Cats*, Washington, DC: The National Academies Press.

Nelson, Kristen, S. Graczyk, J. King, S. Hobbie, L. Baker and J. McFadden (2008), *Our Household Choices in Urban Living Survey*, St Paul, MN: University of Minnesota.

Niza, S., L. Rosado and P. Ferrão (2009), 'Urban metabolism: methodological advances in urban material flow accounting based on the Lisbon case', *Journal of Industrial Ecology*, **13** (3), 384–405.

Phdungsilp, Aumnad (2006), *Energy Analysis for Sustainable Megacities (Licentiate of Engineering Thesis)*, Stockholm: Royal Institute of Technology, Department of Energy Technology.

Ramaswami, A., T. Hillman, B. Janson, M. Reiner and G. Thomas (2008), 'A demand-centered, hybrid life-cycle methodology for city scale greenhouse gas inventories', *Environmental Science and Technology*, **42** (17), 6455–61.

Sahely, H.R., S. Dudding and C.A. Kennedy (2003), 'Estimating the urban metabolism of Canadian cities: GTA case study', *Canadian Journal for Civil Engineering*, **30** (2), 468–83.

Schulz, N.B. (2010), 'Delving into the carbon footprints of Singapore: comparing direct and indirect greenhouse gas emissions of a small and open economic system', *Energy Policy*, **38** (9), 4848–55.

Shananan, Peter (2009), 'Groundwater in the urban environment', in Lawrence A. Baker (ed.), *The Water Environment of Cities*, New York: Springer, pp. 29–48.

Sugar, L., C.A. Kennedy and D. Hoornweg (2013), 'Synergies between climate adaptation and mitigation in development: case studies of Amman, Jakarta, and Dar es Salaam', *International Journal of Climate Change Strategies and Management*, **5** (1), 95–111.

Thompson, Ken, Wendy Christofferson, Dan Robinette, Jason Curl, Lawrence A. Baker,

John Brereton and Kenneth Reich (2006), *Characterizing and Managing Salinity Loadings in Reclaimed Water Systems*, Denver, CO: American Water Works Research Foundation.

Venkatesh, G. (2011), 'Systems performance analysis of Oslo's water and wastewater system', doctoral thesis, Norwegian University of Science and Technology.

Venkatesh, G., J. Hammervold and H. Brattebø (2011), 'Methodology for determining life-cycle environmental impacts due to material and energy flows in wastewater pipeline networks: a case study of Oslo (Norway)', *Urban Water Journal*, **8** (2), 119–34.

Venkatesh, G. and H. Brattebø (2011a), 'Energy consumption, costs and environmental impacts for urban water cycle services: case study of Oslo (Norway)', *Energy*, **36** (2), 792–800.

Venkatesh, G. and H. Brattebø (2011b), 'Environmental impact analysis of chemicals and energy consumption in wastewater treatment plants: case study of Oslo, Norway', *Water Science and Technology*, **63** (5), 1019–32.

Venkatesh, G. and H. Brattebø (2012a), 'Assessment of environmental impacts of an ageing and saturated water supply pipeline network – City of Oslo, 1991–2006', *Journal of Industrial Ecology*, **16** (5), 722–34.

Venkatesh, G. and H. Brattebø (2012b), 'Environmental impact analysis of chemicals and energy consumption in water treatment plants: case study of Oslo, Norway', *Water Science and Technology: Water Supply*, **12** (2), 200–211.

Wakida, F.T. and D.N. Lerner (2005), 'Non-agricultural sources of groundwater nitrate: a review and case study', *Water Research*, **39** (1), 33–16.

Weisz, H. and J. Steinberger (2010), 'Reducing energy and material flows in cities', *Current Opinion in Environmental Sustainability*, **2** (3), 185–92.

Xu, Y., L. Baker and P. Johnson (2007), 'Trends in ground water nitrate contamination in the Phoenix, Arizona region', *Ground Water Monitoring & Remediation*, **27** (2), 49–56.

Xu, Yongxin and Brent Usher (eds) (2006), *Groundwater Pollution in Africa*, London: Taylor and Francis.

14. Developing sustainable cities indicators

Kent E. Portney

One of the earliest manifestations of the push for sustainability in American cities is contained in a number of cities' efforts to develop indicators of sustainability, and to develop these indicators within the context of an indicators project. This chapter examines four major aspects of sustainable cities indicators. First, it briefly describes the indicators projects or efforts in six cities selected here for comparison – Austin, Texas; Boston, Massachusetts; Jacksonville, Florida; Minneapolis, Minnesota; Santa Monica, California; and Seattle, Washington. The focus here is on what specific cities have actually done in their indicators projects, not on trying to prescribe in any comprehensive way what cities could or should do in their indicators initiatives. Second, it looks at a sampling of the indicators used to measure the environmental, social and economic dimensions of sustainability, and indicators that stand at the intersection of these three dimensions. This includes a discussion of the promises and pitfalls of relying on a relatively small number of indicators as a method of trying to understand the sweeping idea of sustainability. Third, it looks at the processes used by sustainability indicators projects in cities – the processes used to develop indicators. And fourth, it examines recent trends in some cities to incorporate indicators projects into their performance management systems in order to maximize the chances that improvements in sustainability results will be achieved as a matter of public policy. This chapter does not seek to challenge the inclusion of any particular indicators in specific cities. It merely seeks to explain what some specific cities have included.

THE ADVENT OF SUSTAINABILITY INDICATORS PROJECTS

Perhaps starting in earnest with the indicators projects that got under way in the late 1980s and early 1990s in Jacksonville, Florida and Seattle, Washington, cities, counties and metropolitan areas all around the USA have embarked on efforts to define and measure how sustainable they are. Often building on analogous livability and healthy cities indicators projects, sustainability indicators projects sought to give tangible meaning to the broad and, at that time, rather amorphous concept of sustainability. This turns out to be no small task given the challenges of defining, in objective terms, what sustainability means, and using the definitions to guide local planning and policy (Brugmann 1997a; Pinfield 1997; Brugmann 1997b; Maclaren 1996).

Jacksonville's efforts, spearheaded by the Jacksonville Community Council, Inc., a local philanthropic nonprofit organization, are reflected in its 'Indicators of Progress' project. Seattle's sustainability indicators project was spearheaded by what evolved into a nonprofit citizens' group called Sustainable Seattle, Inc. Informal, open, public meetings in 1990 eventually developed into a broad-based local effort to measure and track sustainability through measuring dozens of different characteristics, as discussed later. Since that time, many other cities have developed their own indicators projects, including those profiled here – Santa Monica, California; Boston, Massachusetts; Minneapolis, Minnesota; and Austin, Texas (the Central Texas Sustainability Indicators Project). Other cities with notable sustainable indicators projects include Cambridge, MA (Kline 1995a; Kline 1995b); Portland, OR (City of Portland 2012); Scottsdale, AZ (City of Scottsdale 2000; 2006); and Santa Barbara, CA (Santa Barbara 1999; Zachary 1995) – to name a few.[1]

Sustainable cities indicators projects often serve multiple purposes. Sometimes spearheaded by local government agencies, and sometimes by local nonprofit organizations, sustainability indictors are typically designed to hold a mirror in front of a community so that it can see where it stands and where problems may exist for future policies, programs and actions. Sustainability indicators' progress reports (sometimes referred to as 'report cards') provide measurements over time, producing information about whether the community is moving in the right, the sustainable, direction or not. More broadly, such projects are sometimes used to raise awareness about problems or issues that have not made their way onto the local public agenda, perhaps nudging local officials to take action, to adopt policies and programs, when they would not otherwise be inclined to do so. And the process of developing sustainability indicators is often seen as a way to engage the general public and to crystallize a vision of a city's sustainable future while building a base of political support for the programs that local officials may decide to pursue. In any case, there is ongoing debate, as will be discussed later, as to which of these goals is most important, and what kinds of processes ought to be used to develop sustainability indicators.

A BRIEF OVERVIEW OF SELECTED CITIES' INDICATORS PROJECTS

This chapter provides details of the indicators projects in six cities. These six cities are selected here because they demonstrate the wide range of approaches and forms of local indicators projects. They are not, in any systematic sense, meant to be representative of all cities' sustainability indicators projects. Indeed, the vast majority of US cities do not have any sort of indicator project at all. According to a 2010 survey of US cities and towns sponsored by the International City Management Association, only 42 percent of cities of 100 000 population or larger, and only 14 percent of municipalities larger than 2500 population, reported having any sort of sustainability or quality of life indicators project (ICMA 2010). These six cities do, however, show how varied cities projects are, at least with respect to what kinds of indicators are included, and what kind of organization or agency has taken primary responsibility for the development and maintenance of the indicators project.

Before discussing the indicators themselves, a brief description of the projects sets the stage for understanding how these projects and their reports are defined and operate. Table 14.1 provides a glimpse into the origins and operations of the indicators projects in six cities. This table reveals that some cities prefer to operate their indicators project within the formal confines of city government, as in Santa Monica and Minneapolis. Other cities rely on local nonprofit organizations, as in Jacksonville, Austin and Boston. And in at least one case, Seattle, the initial indicators project of a dedicated nonprofit became incorporated into the performance management efforts of the city government. Table 14.2 (below) provides the general outline of each city's indicators project, showing the main categories or groups of indicators found in the most recent report. As noted below, many of these indicators projects have undergone changes over time, so the categories or groupings of indicators reflected in Table 14.2 (below) may be somewhat different from what was reported earlier. Later in this chapter, additional information will be provided about the specific indicators included in different cities' projects.

All six of the indicators projects discussed in this chapter make substantial efforts to provide regular reports and updates based on their respective efforts to monitor trends toward becoming more or less sustainable. In some cases, updates are provided annually, and in others less frequently. Typically, the frequency of updated trends depends on availability of data, and the indicators projects are usually at the mercy of other agencies, such as a local or regional planning agency, a state or county environmental office, the US Bureau of the Census, or others, to measure and report such data. With the possible exception of some of the city government-based indicators in Seattle, none of the six cities' indicators projects discussed here has its own independent capacity to monitor and measure its selected indicators.

One of the toughest challenges facing any sustainability indicators project is what to do when the selected indicators show that the city is becoming less sustainable. If, after reporting for, say, five years, a city discovers that its air quality is getting consistently worse (thus, is becoming less sustainable), how does the indicators project respond? In most cases, the project includes the specification of 'interventions' or 'actions' that can and should be taken to try to alter the unsustainable trend. Yet, as discussed below, one of the limitations of indicators projects conducted outside of city government is that the organization sponsoring the project may not have any capacity or explicit authority to intervene. On the other hand, when the indicators project is operated within city government, efforts can be made to adopt and implement specific programs to try to move toward greater sustainability. Perhaps in the best case, as in Seattle, the city's performance management system (as reflected in its strategic plan) outlines explicit interventions and assigns city agency responsibility for making the changes necessary.

Seattle

As noted earlier, a number of these projects have their origins in nonprofit organizations. Seattle's project arose from the Sustainable Seattle Forum, formed in 1990, and the indicators project, spearheaded by the nonprofit organization Sustainable Seattle, Inc., grew out of this forum (AtKisson 1996; Corson 1993). Table 14.1 implies that there is a separate indicators project in Seattle, that associated with the city government's strategic plan, subtitled 'Toward a Sustainable Seattle' (City of Seattle 2005). In short, the long-term strategic plan incorporates a number of different indicators, many of which are used as benchmarks in the city's performance management system.

Jacksonville

The indicators project in Jacksonville, Florida, one of the oldest and longest-running city indicators projects in the USA, was developed by the Jacksonville Community Council, Inc., a nonprofit community foundation working in collaboration with other community-based and nonprofit groups, including the local Chamber of Commerce. The Community Council published its first indicators report in 1985, and has issued updates and progress reports nearly every year since then. The specific indicators

Table 14.1 The origins and operations of sustainable indicators projects in selected cities

Seattle, Washington	Santa Monica, California	Jacksonville, Florida	Boston, Massachusetts	Central Texas (Austin)	Minneapolis, Minnesota
Sustainable Seattle, Inc. (nonprofit organization) and the City of Seattle	City of Santa Monica	Jacksonville Community Council, Inc. (nonprofit organization)	The Boston Foundation, Inc. (nonprofit organization)	Central Texas Sustainable Indicators Project, Inc. (nonprofit organization)	City of Minneapolis

and their broader categories have undergone several changes, and the order in which the indicators are presented has also changed. Contemporary reports distinguish a small number of 'key indicators', such as the unemployment rate, the quality of the air and water, from 'supporting indicators', such as the amount of open space and the percentage of the population with a college education. The project provides no rationale or explanation for why some indicators are considered 'key' and others 'supporting'.

Boston

In Boston, the indicators project has its origins around the year 2000, when the Boston Foundation, Inc., a nonprofit community foundation, produced its first comprehensive indicators report (Boston Foundation 2000). The Foundation issued subsequent indicators progress reports under various titles in 2002, 2004 and 2008, with the latest in 2012 (Boston Foundation 2012). Each report appears to emphasize a different aspect of the indicators, with the most recent reports seemingly interested in promoting and emphasizing economic growth and development. The indicators report from 2000 was entitled *The Wisdom of Our Choices: Boston's Indicators of Progress, Change, and Sustainability*. Subsequent reports were issued under different titles, and the idea of sustainability was either downplayed, or disappeared almost altogether.

Austin

The Central Texas Indicators Project, the product of another nonprofit organization, focused on a number of counties with Austin, Texas, as its core. The number of counties expanded from three in its first inception, now covering Bastrop, Burnet, Caldwell, Hays, Travis and Williamson counties. Austin is in Travis County. This ambitious project issues regular progress reports where the reports make a systematic effort to compare each county with the state as a whole and sometimes with other cities around the USA. When notable changes in indicators are reported (an indicator suggests that the city or county is moving in a more sustainable or less sustainable direction), a brief explanation is provided. Figure 14.1 shows a sample page graphically presenting the time series measures of an indicator of hazardous waste.

Santa Monica and Minneapolis

Two of the cities profiled in Table 14.1 have developed their sustainability indicators fully within the context of their city governments. The indicators project in Santa Monica is the product of the city's Office of Sustainability and the Environment. And the project in Minneapolis, Minnesota, was developed by the Minneapolis Sustainability Office.

Santa Monica's indicators project is rooted firmly in the city's overall sustainability plan, and is grounded in a set of ten 'guiding principles'. These principles include: the concept of sustainability guides city policy; protection, preservation and restoration of the natural environment is a high priority of the city; environmental quality, economic health and social equity are mutually dependent; all decisions have implications for the long-term sustainability of Santa Monica; community awareness, responsibility, participation and education are key elements of a sustainable community; Santa Monica recognizes its linkage with the regional, national and global community; those sustainability issues most important to the community will be addressed first, and the most cost-effective programs and policies will be selected; the city is committed to procurement decisions that minimize negative environmental and social impacts; cross-sector partnerships are necessary to achieve sustainable goals; and the precautionary principle provides a complementary framework to help guide city decision-makers in the pursuit of sustainability. The Santa Monica indicators project has its origins in 1994, when work began in earnest on the city's sustainability plan. At that time, indicators of sustainability were developed in four key areas: resource conservation, transportation, pollution prevention and public health protection, and community and economic development. Subsequently, in 2001 and 2002, the indicators and goals were changed, based on extensive stakeholder and public input, and the currently used indicators are those developed as of 2006.

Minneapolis' indicators project evolved over time, starting perhaps in 1993 with the city's first efforts to engage in climate protection and the measurement of carbon emissions. The project is sanctioned by the city

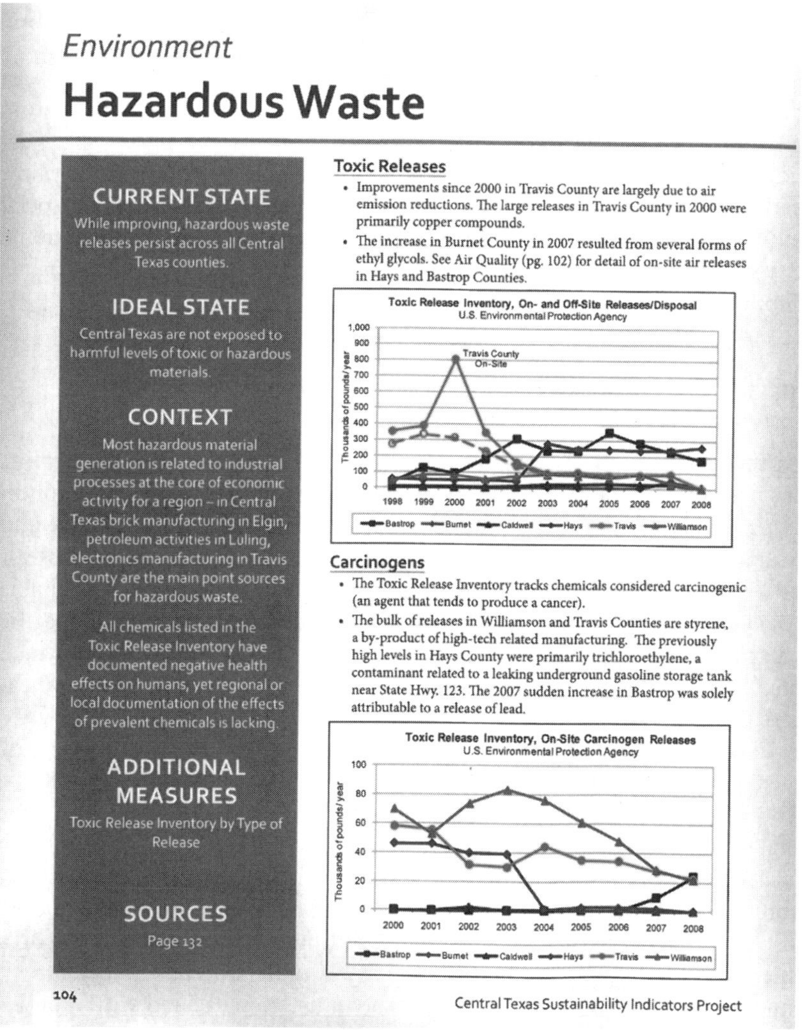

Environment

Hazardous Waste

CURRENT STATE

While improving, hazardous waste releases persist across all Central Texas counties.

IDEAL STATE

Central Texas are not exposed to harmful levels of toxic or hazardous materials.

CONTEXT

Most hazardous material generation is related to industrial processes at the core of economic activity for a region – in Central Texas brick manufacturing in Elgin, petroleum activities in Luling, electronics manufacturing in Travis County are the main point sources for hazardous waste.

All chemicals listed in the Toxic Release Inventory have documented negative health effects on humans, yet regional or local documentation of the effects of prevalent chemicals is lacking.

ADDITIONAL MEASURES

Toxic Release Inventory by Type of Release

SOURCES

Page 132

Toxic Releases

- Improvements since 2000 in Travis County are largely due to air emission reductions. The large releases in Travis County in 2000 were primarily copper compounds.
- The increase in Burnet County in 2007 resulted from several forms of ethyl glycols. See Air Quality (pg. 102) for detail of on-site air releases in Hays and Bastrop Counties.

Carcinogens

- The Toxic Release Inventory tracks chemicals considered carcinogenic (an agent that tends to produce a cancer).
- The bulk of releases in Williamson and Travis Counties are styrene, a by-product of high-tech related manufacturing. The previously high levels in Hays County were primarily trichloroethylene, a contaminant related to a leaking underground gasoline storage tank near State Hwy. 123. The 2007 sudden increase in Bastrop was solely attributable to a release of lead.

104

Central Texas Sustainability Indicators Project

Source: Central Texas Indicators (2009).

Figure 14.1 Hazardous waste indicators from the Central Texas Indicators Project (2009)

council, which periodically reviews and approves the indicators and targets for achieving future improvements. In January 2012, the Minneapolis city council approved a set of 26 indicators along with associated targets and timetables for improvement. The indicators project itself now reports progress only on its website (City of Minneapolis 2012a), and divides the initiative into three distinct pieces. The first is entitled *Living Well – Sustainability Report*, which focuses largely on health indicators such as infant mortality, disease incidence, teen pregnancy and other indicators discussed below. The second is entitled *Minneapolis Greenprint*, a collection of largely environmental and energy-related indicators. And the third, entitled *Minneapolis – A Vital Community*, includes an array of social indicators. Virtually all the indicators in this project are also reflected in the city's long-term comprehensive plan, *The Minneapolis Plan for Sustainable Growth* (City of Minneapolis 2012b).

THE SUSTAINABILITY INDICATORS

At the heart of any sustainable cities indicators project are the indicators themselves. Sustainability indicators are measures of factors and conditions in the city that are thought to be relevant to the sustainability and livability of the city. How does one know whether a city is sustainable or not? How does one know whether a city is becoming more sustainable over time? The argument underlying indicators is that a number of specific characteristics must be measured and tracked. Decisions about which measures ought to be used make up the core of any sustainability indicators project.

Each indicators project ends up focusing on some finite number of measures, although the number of measures may well change over time. The real challenge for most sustainability projects is to select measures that represent key elements of sustainability, and that can actually be measured. Not everything that might be considered important to sustainability has available data, and much of the data that are available may not capture the essence of sustainability. Embedded in this is a bit of a dilemma: on the one hand, sustainability is understood as a very broad, multidimensional concept that inevitably must be measured with a larger number of indicators; on the other hand, there is a limit to how many indicators can be managed, and when there are very large numbers of indicators, it is often difficult to know what story they are telling. The Sustainable Seattle project devised an initial list of some 99 indicators, but later decided that this was too many to be useful, so this list was subjected to review by a 'civic panel', which winnowed the list down to some 40 indicators (AtKisson 1996). Some indicators projects deal with the dilemma by distinguishing 'primary' or 'key' indicators from 'secondary' or 'supporting' measures. The challenge gets even more complicated when the issue turns to interventions – what a city can do to work toward becoming more sustainable. Traditionally, cities have thought of themselves as rather impotent influences on all but the most fundamental aspects of livability and sustainability. What can a city do about air pollution, for example? When a city concludes that it cannot influence a particular outcome, such as reducing air pollution, it may see no need to measure that outcome, as important as it might be in terms of environmental quality, among its indicators of sustainability. As discussed later, these kinds of issues inevitably arise in the process of developing indicators. In any case, for the purposes of the discussion in this chapter, indicators will be divided into groups that correspond to the three legs of the sustainability stool: those that relate to the environment; those that relate broadly to society (including equity); and those that relate to the local economy and economic performance. In addition, there is a category of indicators at the intersection of these three dimensions – indicators that capture other aspects of sustainability – including indicators related to public health.

Although sustainability indicators projects have been in operation in cities for many years, and there is considerable information available concerning what any one city might be doing in terms of developing and reporting on indicators, there is surprisingly little detailed commonality among the selected indicators from one city to another. All indicators projects contain measures of environmental quality, for example, but it often seems as if no two cities use exactly the same indicator. For many indicators areas, cities seem to feel they should tailor the selected indicators to their own needs. Thus, when it gets down to details, essentially each city defines sustainability in its own way. The range that cities have used is discussed below.

One commonality among cities' sustainability efforts is that they tend to divide the indicators into groups, categories or indicators areas. As noted above, all cities' sustainability indicators include those that relate to the environment. But cities differ in what they call such indicators, or which group they belong to. As shown in Table 14.2, for example, Jacksonville's Community Indicators project includes an area called 'Natural Environment' and the indicators project in central Texas (which covers Austin) includes a section on the 'Environment'. Santa Monica includes a section combining 'Environment and Public Health', and Minneapolis's indicators effort includes a section entitled 'Greenprint Report', a large section that includes 'Energy and Emissions', 'Urban Design and Mobility', 'Clean Water' and 'Green Economy'.

The bottom line is that the organizations that engage in creating and reporting on sustainability indicators are free to define and organize them as they wish. One can only speculate as to why some cities decide to organize their indicators differently from others. Moreover, while this may be

Table 14.2 Areas or groups of indicators contained in sustainable indicators projects in selected cities

Seattle		Santa Monica, California	Jacksonville, Florida	Boston, Massachusetts	Central Texas (Austin)	Minneapolis, Minnesota
Sustainable Seattle, Inc.	Seattle City government					
Environment	Urban villages	Resource conservation	Educational excellence	Civic vitality	Public safety	Living Well – Sustainability Report:
Population and resources	Land use	Environmental and public health	Vibrant economy	Cultural life and the arts	Education and Children	Healthy Life
Economy	Transportation	Transportation	Natural environment	Economy	Social equity	Vital Community:
Youth and education	Housing	Economic development	Social well-being and harmony	Environment and energy	Public and Civic engagement	Affordable Housing
Health and community	Capital facilities	Open space and Land use	Arts, culture and recreation	Housing	Economy	Homelessness
	Utilities	Housing	Health	Public Health	Environment	Brownfield Sites
	Economic development	Community education and civic participation	Responsive government	Public Safety	Health	Violent Crime
	Neighborhood planning	Human dignity	Moving around efficiently	Technology	Land use and mobility	Community Engagement
	Cultural resources		Community safety	Transportation		Arts and Economy
	Environment					Graduation Rate

Sources: Sustainable Seattle, Inc. 1992–93; City of Seattle 2005; City of Santa Monica 2011; Jacksonville Community Council, Inc. 2011; Boston Foundation 2012; Central Texas Indicators 2009; City of Minneapolis 2012a; 2012b.

somewhat difficult to document, a city's sustainability project goes through a process in which the specific indicators and their categories are modified over time. Often, indicators are added or deleted without explanation. Such changes may reflect changes in emphasis, priorities or strategies, or may simply reflect the lack of recurring data available to track specific indicators.

Indicators of the Environment

Measuring the quality of the biophysical environment is at the core of any sustainability indicators project. Typically, such indicators of the environment focus on air, water, and soil and land use, but there are many other aspects of the environment that are important because of implications for the environment. For example, measuring amounts and types of energy used in a city is important because of its implications for air quality and climate change. Measuring amounts of solid or hazardous waste recycled is important because it represents mitigation of contamination of the soil and perhaps the water. While a perusal of the indicators used across cities reveals hundreds of variations on the environmental theme, the quality of the biophysical environment is central to any sustainable indicators project. All the six cities' projects profiled here include aspects of the environment as major categories of sustainability. An overview of the environmental indicators used by a number of cities, and some examples from specific sustainable indicators projects, will illustrate projects' experiences.

Indicators of air quality

Every sustainable indicators project incorporates measures of air quality or air emissions. Traditionally, the only measures of air quality available to cities focused on ambient air quality – the amount and type of air pollution in the air at given points in time, and the number of days in a given year when the air quality could be said to be poor, given a threshold measure of air pollution. Typically, such ambient air quality data would be gleaned from US EPA and state air monitoring information, and take the form of the Pollutant Standards Index, a measure adopted in the Sustainable Seattle indicators. The Central Texas Indicators Project also measures the amount of ground-level ozone, and the amount of air pollutants released as reported to the Toxic Release Inventory. In Minneapolis, the primary measures of air quality focus on the number of days with high particulate matter, and high ground-level ozone. Partly as a means for addressing high levels of some pollutants, Minneapolis includes measures of the size of the tree canopy in the city. Jacksonville's key air quality measures focus on the number of days that the air quality index was 'good' during the previous year.

In recent years, some specific indicators related to air emissions have become incorporated into cities' climate action plans. The advent of the climate action plan ushered in an era in which the focus changed from ambient air quality (the amount of pollutants in the air) to air emissions (the amount of specific pollutants, particularly greenhouse gas (GHG) emissions that result from human activity within the city itself). Climate action plans call for cities to measure their carbon (and carbon equivalents) emissions produced within the city, to track trends in these emissions by comparing them with emissions from some earlier benchmark time (usually 1990), and to take actions to reduce carbon emissions if they exceed desired target levels. The indicators measuring carbon emissions are discussed more fully in Chapters 15 and 16.

Indicators of water quality

Many indicators projects include measures of some aspects of water. This is often defined fairly broadly to include the quality of drinking water, but also includes issues related to nutrient content and overload found in various bodies of water, such as local lakes, rivers, streams or other resources. Particularly in areas where access to water resources is limited or threatened, indicators try to capture some aspect of how well protected the water resources are. Water indicators might also include, as in the Sustainable Seattle indicators, measures of fluctuations in water levels in various bodies of water, at least partly an indicator of how well managed water usage is. The Central Texas Indicators Project measures the amount of water used, the average depth of the wells used as a water source, official notices of water quality violations, and the number of officially impaired bodies of water. Minneapolis uses indicators that measure the amount of rainwater or stormwater runoff, the number of installed rain gardens, and the number of lake beach closings due to high levels of pollutants. Jacksonville focuses on measures of average daily water usage, as well as the number of streams that meet dissolved O_2 and bacteria standards. Santa Monica has developed indicators of the amount of water consumed from local (as opposed to imported) sources, and the amount of wastewater generated and treated.

Solid waste management and recycling

Sustainability is often thought to require significant attention to solid waste streams, with the goal of reducing the amount of material that is landfilled or incinerated. Since recycling is a core strategy for reducing the amount of waste that is disposed of, indicators often focus on how extensive the local solid waste recycling effort is, usually focusing on the percentage of the total amount of solid waste generated that is recycled. All the cities' sustainability projects profiled here include such solid waste and recycling indicators. The Central Texas Indicators Project also includes measures of the amount of illegally disposed materials, and the amount of electronics waste that is recycled, and also includes measures of hazardous wastes. Figure 14.1, for example, shows a page from this indicators project where the measure is the amount (in thousands of pounds per year) of toxic releases in each county over time. Minneapolis' indicators include a measure of the source-separated organic material that is diverted from landfills or incinerators.

Energy

Because energy use is so closely connected to the quality of the environment, particularly air quality, and the issue of climate change, sustainability indicators often include measures of energy usage. This usually focuses on the amount of various fossil fuels consumed, or the amount of renewable energy (electricity from solar, wind or biogas, for example) generated and consumed. Nearly all cities that have an indicators project try to measure the amount of energy consumed from renewable sources. The Sustainable Seattle project measured the number of vehicle miles traveled by Seattle residents, and the amount of fuel consumed, as energy indicators. In the Central Texas Indicators Project, a measure documents the number of Green Choice option participants in the city's renewable energy program. Also related to energy and the environment are indicators of public transit. Although many cities develop a separate category of indicators related to transportation, the purpose of such indicators is to measure the extent to which a city's energy is used efficiently, and public transit plays a major role in this (Zegras 2006). The Boston indicators project, for example, has indicators of the percentage of houses and jobs that are within a quarter mile of a public transit node – a subway station or bus stop. It also measures the level of public transit ridership.

Many other measures of environmental quality are possible, as developed in some cities' projects. For example, the Central Texas Indicators Project measures aspects of land use, focusing on the amount of open space and the population density in newly developed areas of the city, where greater density is understood to be much more energy efficient and environmentally friendly. Boston's indicators project includes measures of parks and greenspace, as well as its ecological footprint.

Social Indicators

Many indicators projects recognize that sustainability has important social aspects. Such projects recognize that sustainability is about more than the quality of the biophysical environment. Yet there is probably no category of indicators that is more varied across cities than social aspects. In other words, cities that have sustainable indicators projects vary widely in terms of the specific social aspects that they think should be measured and tracked. Social indicators often include such issues as the quality and character of the cultural and arts communities, the level of crime as a matter of public safety, levels of ethnic and racial diversity (and other measures of equity), educational attainment (such as the high-school graduation rate and the rate of adult literacy). In the Sustainable Seattle initiative, social indicators, under the category of Youth and Education, included the ethnic diversity of public school teachers, and under the category of Health and Community, included library and community center usage. The Central Texas Indicators Project includes a wide array of social indicators, including those related to public safety, such as the number of victims of child or elder abuse, the number of victims of family violence and other violent crime, equity in law enforcement, child care access and availability, public school quality and performance, and civic engagement and volunteerism, among many others. Boston's indicators project includes measures of racial and ethnic diversity, voter participation, opportunities for civic discourse, and the city's ranking on the United Way's 'Caring Index'. A number of cities try to track (and reduce) the number of homeless people, as in Minneapolis and Santa Monica. The Santa Monica indicators project includes measures of community engagement, including participation in neighborhood associations, and even involvement in the development of the sustainable indicators plan itself.

One of the more challenging aspects of sustainability relates to achieving greater equity of various sorts. Either as part of social indicators or indicators of the local economy, cities often include measures of some aspects of equity. These include, for example, the levels of poverty and unequal distribution of incomes, availability of affordable housing for those on low incomes, and levels of diversity in employment. The indicators project in Jacksonville includes measures of the perception of racism as a problem.

Indicators of the Economy and Economic Performance

Economic performance is without doubt a significant element in measuring local sustainability. As the Brundtland Commission stated, sustainability is 'economic development activity that meets the needs of the present without compromising the ability of future generations to meet their own needs' (WCED 1987, p. 8) Where there was once an understanding that economic growth would have to be sacrificed in order to protect and improve the quality of the environment, sustainability often seeks to engage in vigorous economic development while protecting the environment. Thus understanding local economic performance represents an important aspect of sustainability. Indicators of the local economy can be quite varied, but almost always include basic measures of change in personal or family income levels. They may also include measures of the unemployment rate, and the character of the local employment base. For example, the Sustainable Seattle Project used the percentage of the jobs in Seattle accounted for by the top ten largest employers, where a higher percentage was considered less sustainable than a lower percentage. This project also used the distribution of personal income, housing affordability and the amount of 'community capital' (the total deposits of consumers in local banks) as indicators of the health and sustainability of the local economy.

The Central Texas Indicators Project includes a number of indicators of economic performance, such as the availability of labor and jobs, exports to other countries, the total amount of venture capital invested, the number of green jobs, and entrepreneurship and innovation, measured by the three-year new business survival rate. In Boston, indicators of economic performance include the number of patents issued per capita, the amount of private and public R&D funding, and the amount of venture capital invested, very similar to the business investment indicator in Jacksonville. Minneapolis is particularly interested in measuring the number of green jobs created, and the number of green companies. Santa Monica's project is not just interested in the number of jobs in the employment base; it is also interested in measuring the number of new jobs in the city that carry above-average pay levels.

Indicators at the Intersection

Some classes of indicators are not easily categorized because they cut across different areas. Two such areas are public health and arts and culture. Cities' efforts to create indicators of sustainability frequently recognize that there is a connection between the environment, economic performance and society on the one hand, and public health on the other. In such cities, an explicit effort is made to develop and measure indicators of public health.

Numerous cities have discovered that sustainability requires explicit attention to the character of local arts and culture. Although sometimes treated as social indicators, these issues are often included in indicators projects in their own right, and sometimes they are considered as an element of civic and community engagement. In either case, a healthy and thriving arts and culture community is often thought to be integral to sustainability. For example, the Sustainable Seattle project included measures of how much arts instruction there is in the city. The Central

Texas Indicators Project focuses on the frequency of attendance at cultural events, the public perception of arts opportunities, and participation in various forms of artistic expression. Boston's indicators project includes measures of the strength of the nonprofit sector, and the amount of public funding and support for the arts.

One might argue that the health and well-being of the residents of a city is the ultimate goal of sustainability. Clearly, indicators of community health are frequently developed by cities' indicators projects. These usually include measures of infant health, such as the frequency of low birth weights, or the frequency of specific diseases such as asthma. Sometimes cities include measures of perceived quality of life or well-being. The Sustainable Seattle project included a measure of the frequency of child hospitalization for asthma, among others. The Central Texas Indicators Project includes measures of the number of people without health insurance, the level of enrollment in Medicaid and Medicare, the number of doctors, the rate of cigarette smoking and several measures of mental health. The Boston indicators project also looks at leading causes of hospitalizations, and tracks these causes with an eye toward reducing them. The Minneapolis project also includes measures of teen pregnancy, and the incidence of lead poisoning, asthma and obesity. In Jacksonville, health indicators also include incidence of cancer, HIV and STDs.

THE CHALLENGES, PROMISES AND PITFALLS OF SUSTAINABILITY INDICATORS

Decisions to develop and use sustainability indicators are based on the assumption that it is possible to measure and track progress toward becoming more sustainable (Bell and Morse 2008). Yet this assumption is often questioned if for no other reason than the concept of sustainability is so broad, and the elements of sustainability are so interrelated (Portney 2013, pp. 37–83). Pragmatically, the challenge for any city's sustainable indicators project is to select indicators that are understood to be closely linked to sustainability, and that, when taken together as a whole, reflect the totality of sustainability in that place. No city's indicators project has found a way to develop a fully integrated set of indicators that can, in any true sense, be considered comprehensive and holistic. So the ever-present question persists: if a city is able to adopt policies and programs that cause all its indicators to move in the sustainable direction, can anyone say that the city is truly becoming more sustainable? This is a question that has no definite answer; it is a question that is answered largely by assuming that it is.

A second challenge has to do with the pragmatic availability of data to measure progress. Cities frequently find that they cannot get data for many of their indicators, and even when data are available, they may not be reported frequently enough to be of much programmatic use. A city may rely on data from the US Bureau of the Census decennial census, but these data are available only every ten years. So unless the Census Bureau makes an effort to measure and report more frequently, the city may not be able to measure the indicators they think are important.

A third challenge is that the indicators and progress reports, by themselves, are understood to be inadequate to achieving greater sustainability. Unless the indicators represent areas where city government has the capacity and authority to take actions, and unless city government links the indicators to specific policies, programs and actions, there is no reason to believe that developing an indicators project will make any difference (Brugmann 1997a). While the Central Texas Indicators Project probably does as good a job as any indicators project in tracking changes to a wide variety of sustainability-related indicators, it is not at all clear whether the Austin city government takes any actions when indicators are moving in the unsustainable direction. In the best indicators projects, measurement of progress is explicitly linked to policy and program goals and timetables of city government. The indicators effort in Minneapolis represents a good case in point. There, the indicators, along with targets, goals and timetables, are ratified by the city council, with links to specific programs designed to achieve those targets and goals. The need for explicit attention to the link between indicators and city programs has been long recognized (AtKission 1996; Brugmann 1997a).

The need for such linkage has been addressed in some cities through the incorporation of sustainability indicators and goals into comprehensive plans. Of the six cities discussed above, at least two – Seattle and Minneapolis – have done just that. Each city's comprehensive strategic plan includes measures of program goals related to sustainability, tracks progress toward achieving those goals, and often prescribes actions if the goals are not met. In this way, indicators can be systematically used as part of a performance management system or plan.

CONCLUSION

This chapter set out to review what a number of cities have done to develop indicators of sustainability and quality of life. It focused on the indicators projects or efforts in six cities – Seattle, Santa Monica, Jacksonville, Austin (Central Texas), Boston and Minneapolis. It provided some historical background, and showed the wide array of different indicators used to measure important aspects of environment, energy, health, economic performance and development, arts, culture and society. Indicators projects in four cities – Seattle, Jacksonville, Boston and Austin – were spearheaded by major nonprofit organizations. Two other cities – Santa Monica and Minneapolis – developed their indicators projects within city government. And Seattle's city government incorporated many aspects of the nonprofit-based indicators into the city's comprehensive plan. Although many cities end up adopting very similar or identical indicators, they vary considerably in how they organize these indicators. Indeed, the categories used to report the indicators vary considerably from city to city. To the extent that the categories of indicators, as well as the order in which they are reported, might reflect local values and preferences, cities may well differ considerably.

NOTE

1. For a fairly comprehensive listing of sustainability and community indicators projects, see the Community Indicators Consortium (2012) and the Global Compact Cities Programme (2012) websites.

REFERENCES

AtKisson, A. (1996), 'Developing indicators of sustainable community: lessons from sustainable Seattle', *Environmental Impact Assessment Review*, **16** (4), 337–50.

Bell, Simon and Stephen Morse (2008), *Sustainability Indicators: Measuring the Immeasurable?* 2nd edn, London: Earthscan.

Boston Foundation (2000), 'The wisdom of our choices: Boston's indicators of progress, change, and sustainability', available at http://www.tbf.org/Indicators2006/News/detail.asp?id=2999.

Boston Foundation (2011), 'A great reckoning: healing a growing divide. A summary of the Boston indicators report 2009', available at http://www.bostonindicators.org/Indicators2008/.

Boston Foundation (2012), 'City of ideas: reinventing Boston's innovation economy', available at http://www.bostonfoundation.org/content.aspx?ID=19382.

Brugmann, J. (1997a), 'Is there a method in our measurement? The use of indicators in local sustainable development planning', *Local Environment*, **2** (1), 59–72.

Brugmann, J. (1997b), 'Sustainability indicators revisited: getting from political objectives to performance outcomes – a response to Graham Pinfield', *Local Environment*, **2** (3), 299–302.

Central Texas Indicators (2000), *Sustainability Indicators Project of Hays, Travis, and Williamson Counties: A Report on the Economic, Environmental, and Social Health of the Central Texas Region*, Austin, TX: Central Texas Indicators Project.

Central Texas Indicators (2009), 'Central Texas sustainability indicators project: 2009 data report', available at http://www.centex-indicators.org/annual_rept/ar2009.pdf.

City of Minneapolis (2012a), 'Sustainability indicators', available at http://www.minneapolismn.gov/sustainability/indicators/index.htm and http://www.minneapolismn.gov/www/groups/public/@citycoordinator/documents/images/wcms1p-093724.pdf.

City of Minneapolis (2012b), 'The Minneapolis plan for sustainable growth', available at http://www.minneapolismn.gov/cped/planning/plans/cped_comp_plan_2030.
City of Portland (2012), 'Comprehensive plan goals and policies', available at http://www.portlandonline.com/bps/index.cfm?c=34249.
City of Santa Monica (2011), 'Sustainable city progress report', available at http://www.smgov.net/Departments/OSE/progressReport/default.aspx.
City of Scottsdale (2000), *Scottsdale Seeks Sustainability: 2000 Indicators Report*, Scottsdale, AZ: City of Scottsdale Environmental Planning and Design.
City of Scottsdale (2006), 'Sustainability indicators report 2006–2007', available at http://www.scottsdaleaz.gov/Assets/Public+Website/ecogecko/SustainabilityBook.pdf.
City of Seattle (2005), 'Comprehensive plan: toward a sustainable Seattle', available at http://www.seattle.gov/dpd/cms/groups/pan/@pan/@plan/@proj/documents/web_informational/dpdp020401.pdf.
Community Indicators Consortium (2012), 'Community indicator projects', available at: http://www.communityindicators.net/efforts.
Corson, Walter (1993), *Measuring Urban Sustainability*, Washington, DC: Global Tomorrow Coalition.
Global Compact Cities Programme (2012), 'Measuring urban sustainability', available at http://citiesprogramme.com/archives/research/measuring-urban-sustainability-a-review-of-indicator-systems.
ICMA (2010), 'Local government sustainability polices and programs, 2010', available at http://icma.org/en/icma/knowledge_network/documents/kn/Document/301646/ICMA_2010_Sustainability_Survey_Results.
Jacksonville Community Council, Inc. (2002), 'Quality of life in Jacksonville: 2002 indicators for progress', available at http://issuu.com/jcci/docs/qualityoflife2002/1.
Jacksonville Community Council, Inc. (2011), 'Quality of life indicators in Jacksonville: indicators for progress', available at http://www.jcci.org/quality-of-life-report.
Kline, Elizabeth (1995a), *Sustainable Community Indicators*, Medford, MA: Consortium for Regional Sustainability, Tufts University.
Kline, Elizabeth (1995b), *Sustainable Community Indicators: Examples from Cambridge, MA*, Medford, MA: Consortium for Regional Sustainability, Tufts University.
Maclaren, V.W. (1996), 'Urban sustainability reporting', *Journal of the American Planning Association*, **62** (2), 184–202.
Pinfield, G. (1997), 'The use of indicators in local sustainable development planning: a response to Jeb Brugmann', *Local Environment*, **2** (2), 185–7.
Portney, Kent E. (2013), *Taking Sustainable Cities Seriously: Economic Development, the Environment, and Quality of Life in American Cities*, 2nd edn, Cambridge, MA: MIT Press.
Santa Barbara (1999), *Community Indicators*, Santa Barbara, CA: South Coast Community Indicators Project.
Sustainable Seattle, Inc. (1992–93), *Proposed Key Indicators of Sustainable Community (Version 5, December 1992; and Version 6, January 1993)*, Seattle, WA: Sustainable Seattle Indicators Project.
World Commission on Environment and Development (WCED) (Brundtland Commission) (1987), *Our Common Future*, New York: Oxford University Press.
Zachary, Jill (1995), *Sustainable Community Indicators: Guideposts for Local Planning*, Santa Barbara, CA: Community Environmental Council, Inc.
Zegras, C. (2006), 'Sustainable transport indicators and assessment methodologies', available at http://web.mit.edu/czegras/www/Zegras_LAC-CAI_Bkgd.pdf.

15. Climate action planning

Michael R. Boswell, Adrienne I. Greve and Tammy L. Seale

> We will respond to the threat of climate change, knowing that the failure to do so would betray our children and future generations.
> President Barack Obama, Inaugural Address, 21 January 2013

Climate action plans (CAPs) are strategic policy instruments that cities and counties across the USA are using to establish how they will address the challenge of climate change. Although these plans principally address how a community will reduce greenhouse gas (GHG) emissions, primarily caused by the burning of fossil fuels, CAPs increasingly focus on how to prepare for the impacts of climate change, referred to as climate adaptation. As of 2012, over 200 US communities have adopted a stand-alone CAP based on a GHG inventory, and about the same number have a climate action plan currently in progress. A total of 1054 communities around the country have signed the Mayors Climate Protection Agreement (http://www.usmayors.org/climateprotection/agreement.htm), which commits them to adopting a plan to reduce GHG emissions.

The methods and tools for preparing CAPs have matured and robust best practices have emerged. In the book, *Local Climate Action Planning*, Boswell, Greve and Seale document the state of practice and provide communities with a framework for preparing CAPs (Boswell et al. 2012). Although many communities are undertaking a wide array of activities to address climate change, a CAP represents a strong approach for developing and implementing policy. In addition, many communities have discovered that preparing CAPs creates a potential to discuss other 'good planning' principles in their communities, often referred to as co-benefits (see Figure 15.1). For example, a community may choose to facilitate residential energy efficiency upgrades to reduce energy consumption and ultimately GHG emissions. These actions will also produce benefits to homeowners, through lower utility bills and increased comfort in the home. Another example is the promotion of bicycling for transportation, which has co-benefits of reduced traffic congestion, better air quality and improved personal health. Climate action planning is planning that can provide an array of benefits to a community when done well.

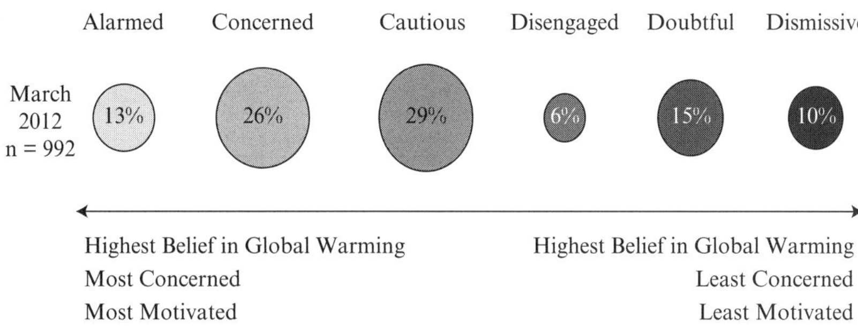

Source: Leiserowitz et al. (2012).

Figure 15.1 Proportion of the US adult population in the Six Americas, March 2012

PLANNING FOR REDUCING GHG EMISSIONS

GHG emissions are related to everyday choices that affect the combustion of fossil fuels, such as how energy is used and how people move throughout communities, decisions that are often directly or indirectly affected by land-use patterns and resource availability. The typical contents of a CAP are an inventory of the GHG emissions a community is releasing into the atmosphere, a forecast of emissions based on growth expectations, a set of targets delineating the community's desired GHG emissions reductions, and a set of actions the community will take to achieve the targets (see Figure 15.2 for an example of GHG emissions by sector). This method embodies a practical approach to planning for two reasons. First, the quantification of current emissions and the establishment of a future emissions reduction target create a clear, measurable goal for planning. Second, the quantification of emissions reduction strategies allows a community to determine precisely what must be done in order to reach the target.

PLANNING FOR ADAPTING TO CLIMATE CHANGE IMPACTS

In addition to reducing GHG emissions, some communities also consider how they will address the changes in the climate that may directly impact the community. Addressing climate impacts should be viewed as complementary to GHG emissions reduction. Climate change is already occurring and some impacts cannot be avoided solely through emissions reduction. Adaptation prepares for these unavoidable consequences. Communities that

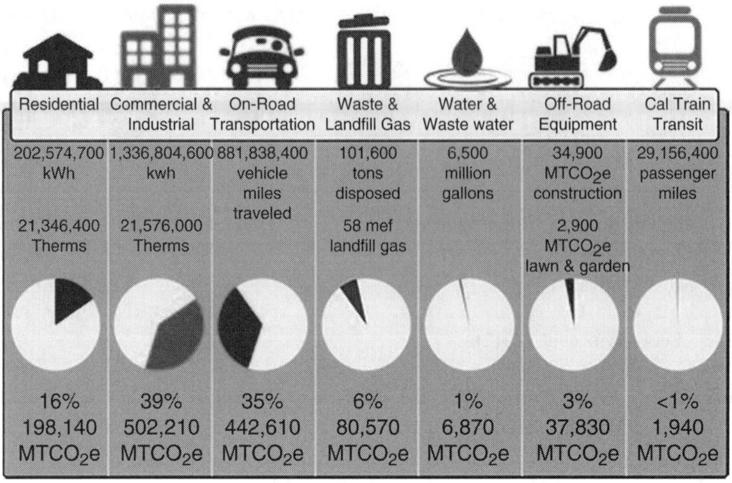

Residential	Commercial & Industrial	On-Road Transportation	Waste & Landfill Gas	Water & Waste water	Off-Road Equipment	Cal Train Transit
202,574,700 kWh	1,336,804,600 kwh	881,838,400 vehicle miles traveled	101,600 tons disposed	6,500 million gallons	34,900 $MTCO_2e$ construction	29,156,400 passenger miles
21,346,400 Therms	21,576,000 Therms		58 mef landfill gas		2,900 $MTCO_2e$ lawn & garden	
16%	39%	35%	6%	1%	3%	<1%
198,140 $MTCO_2e$	502,210 $MTCO_2e$	442,610 $MTCO_2e$	80,570 $MTCO_2e$	6,870 $MTCO_2e$	37,830 $MTCO_2e$	1,940 $MTCO_2e$

Source: PMC.

Figure 15.2 Example of GHG emissions by sector

want to include climate adaption in their CAPs must conduct a vulnerability assessment, which includes identifying the forecasted regional changes to the climate and determining the community assets that will be affected by these changes. For example, a community affected by sea-level rise may need to consider infrastructure located in low-lying coastal areas. The vulnerability assessment would then be used to develop appropriate adaptive policy.

CLIMATE ACTION PLANNING PROCESS

The most commonly referenced climate action planning process is ICLEI – Local Governments for Sustainability's 5 Milestone Process (ICLEI 2013):

1. Conduct a baseline emissions inventory and forecast.
2. Adopt an emissions reduction target.
3. Develop a Local Climate Action Plan.
4. Implement policies and measures.
5. Monitor and verify results.

While ICLEI's milestone approach identifies core steps in CAP development, there are several steps missing or embedded within the milestones that are critical to the CAP process.

We propose a three-phase climate action planning process based on our experience and that of others in preparing climate action plans: (1) preliminary activities; (2) climate action plan development; and (3) implementation and monitoring.[1] Although the steps are presented in numerical order, many of them overlap or are iterative, and thus they should be applied as a general organizing principle rather than a stepwise 'cookbook' for planning. When moving through these steps it is important to adhere to the principles for a good planning process such as transparency and documentation, participation, justification and consistency.
Phase I: Preliminary activities:

1. Establish community commitment.
2. Build community partnerships.
3. Establish the role of the plan.
4. Assemble a climate action team (CAT).
5. Consider the logistics of plan development.
6. Establish a public education and outreach program.
7. Audit existing community policies and programs.

Phase II: Climate action plan development:

8. Conduct a baseline GHG emissions inventory and interim forecast.
9. Conduct a climate vulnerability assessment.
10. Formulate plan vision and goals (including a GHG emissions reduction target).
11. Develop, evaluate and specify strategies.
12. Quantify GHG emissions reduction strategies.

Phase III: Implementation and monitoring:

13. Develop and administer an implementation program.
14. Monitor and evaluate implementation and goal attainment.
15. Modify and update the plan.

These three phases of CAP development reinforce each other. Given this is a new area of planning, communities need to be willing to experiment, innovate, change course, admit failures and promote successes. The freedom to develop and implement aggressive, innovative emissions reduction and climate adaptation strategies in Phase II relies on the strength of the organizational steps taken in Phase I and the monitoring and evaluation feedback loop provided by Phase III. Experimentation and innovation is possible only with careful monitoring and a firm commitment to revise and adapt strategies based on observed effectiveness.

Phase I: Preliminary Activities

In Phase I, the community establishes a commitment to taking action on climate change; builds community partnerships; specifies the role of the CAP; makes logistical choices such as identifying a funding source, a timeline for plan development, and CAP author (e.g. city, consultant, stakeholder, task force); establishes a climate action team (CAT); develops a public outreach and education program; and conducts an audit of exiting community policies and programs. The order of these preliminary tasks is not critical and will vary based on community needs.

(1) Establish community commitment

In order to move forward with climate action planning, a community should make a formal commitment. Common forms of this commitment include passing a resolution, joining ICLEI – Local Governments for Sustainability, and signing the US Conference of Mayors Climate Protection Agreement. Since the preparation of a community CAP requires cooperation among government agencies, utility providers and local stakeholders, this commitment signals to all parties and the community at large the importance of the effort. Moreover, some communities choose to celebrate the commitment with fairs, workshops, visioning meetings and other community events to celebrate, educate and inspire.

Communities vary in why they choose to engage in climate action planning. A 2012 survey of US communities with CAPs identified the following top five reasons for adopting a CAP (in order of importance):[2]

1. Commitment to increase energy efficiency and save money
2. Recognition of the threat posed to the community by climate change
3. Acknowledgment of an ethical commitment to help solve the climate change crisis
4. Opportunity to raise public awareness of the climate change issue and build support for more ambitious future efforts
5. Desire to create a sustainability or green image for the community, possibly to promote tourism or economic development

(2) Build community partnerships

The endorsement of a formal agreement should be quickly followed with the building and solidifying of partnerships among government agencies, utility providers and local stakeholders to share information, resources or expertise in the planning process. Stakeholders may include local colleges and universities, environmental groups, business associations and neighboring communities.

When engaging in partnerships, several questions should be addressed. First, who will prepare the plan? Typically climate action plans are prepared by government agencies, but there are notable examples, such as Evanston, Illinois and Aspen, Colorado, which were led by citizen groups. Second, what is the role of each partner? Potential roles include leadership and logistics, technical assistance, funding, and education and outreach. Third, how will communication, coordination and dispute resolution be handled? Some communities have chosen to establish community advisory committees or task forces to facilitate these issues.

(3) Establish the role of the plan

Clearly defining the purpose or role of the plan, especially as it relates to other community plans, will help refine the planning process. As mentioned above, communities choose to engage in climate action planning for a variety of reasons. These reasons will be reflected in the role of the plan. Communities may already have a variety of existing plans and programs that directly or indirectly address climate change. Communities also vary considerably in size, economic base, demographics, wealth, culture, politics and a host of other factors that will affect the role of a CAP. In the state of California, some communities are adopting CAPs for the sole purpose of facilitating environmental review of proposed development, given the state's legal mandate to address GHG emissions.

A review of CAPs in the USA shows that a few common roles have emerged. Some communities choose to create a CAP that is a broad, visionary document intended to inspire or guide future action. Other communities create CAPs with detailed implementation mechanisms that coordinate with capital improvement plans, zoning codes, comprehensive plans and/or economic development strategies. Some communities adopt CAPs as a chapter or section of a broader sustainability plan or comprehensive/general plan. Finally, some communities adopt plans that serve largely as an umbrella for a variety of existing polices, programs and actions already being undertaken, whereas others will use the CAP as a progressive instrument for driving change.

(4) Assemble a climate action team (CAT)

Since CAPs require significant data and analysis for conducting GHG inventories and climate vulnerability assessments, it is generally wise to establish a climate action team (CAT), sometimes also called a 'green team'. The CAT comprises individuals who have access to data and information regarding identified areas of GHG emissions (e.g.

transportation, land use, energy) and climate vulnerabilities (e.g. public health, natural hazards, sea-level rise). Since CAPs are usually prepared by local governments, the CAT will usually consist of representatives from such departments as planning and building, public works, transportation, engineering, public safety, natural resources, public health and administration.

(5) Consider the logistics of plan development

There are several key questions regarding the logistics of preparing a CAP. First, what is the desired or required planning time frame? A CAP will usually take one to one and a half years from initiation to adoption. If the CAP is being prepared to meet an outside deadline (e.g. a grant application or a legal obligation), then workload, cost and level of sophistication of the plan will have to be adjusted accordingly.

Second, how much will it cost to prepare the CAP? A CAP will require roughly 1000 to 2500 staff hours. If a consultant were to prepare the plan, the cost would be in the range of $50 000 to $300000. The cost is primarily driven by five factors (more of each representing higher initial costs): (1) level of public education and outreach; (2) amount of work needed to prepare or update a GHG emissions inventory and forecast and a climate vulnerability assessment; (3) specificity of the strategies developed in the plan; (4) level of review by outside or governing bodies; and (5) level of consultant support. It is quite possible that higher levels of sophistication in the planning process could pay off during the implementation of the plan, if this investment resulted in a higher-quality plan.

Third, what expertise is needed, will external help be necessary, and who will lead the planning effort? These questions can be addressed as part of establishing partnerships and creating a CAT. Experts will be needed for GHG inventory and forecast, climate vulnerability assessment, policy development in a variety of areas, public education and outreach, and plan writing and management. Many communities have looked to consultants and local colleges and universities to provide this expertise. For example, students and faculty at California Polytechnic State University, San Luis Obispo, prepared CAPs for the cities of Benicia and San Luis Obispo. Also communities are increasingly creating municipal staff positions tasked with creating and implementing sustainability, climate and energy polices. This is an emergent profession that is filling the niche for specialized expertise in climate action planning.

(6) Establish a public education and outreach program

Public participation is a well-established area of planning and public policy. The brief discussion here focuses on three aspects of participation unique to climate action planning: the recognition of the 'Six Americas', the co-benefits framing, and the knowledge-deficit theory of climate change denial.

Survey research from Yale University and George Mason University shows that the American public can be segmented 'into six audiences that range along a spectrum of concern and issue engagement from the Alarmed, who are convinced of the reality and danger of climate change and highly supportive of personal and political actions to mitigate the threat, to the Dismissive, who are equally convinced that climate change is not occurring and that no response should be made' (Leiserowitz et al. 2012, p. 4). The Six Americas segmentation can be used by planners to first recognize that the public is diverse in its perspectives on climate change, and then to design participation programs that are appropriate to each audience.

The co-benefits framing suggests that the public is likely to be more supportive of action on climate change when there are multiple benefits of such action, such as monetary or personal health benefits, or when climate change is framed around other moral obligations. Research shows that frames for climate change action more likely to produce positive action include:

- Need to be caring and friendly towards others (Bain et al. 2012, pp. 600–603)
- Social/economic/technological development (ibid.)
- Public health benefits (Myers et al. 2012, pp. 1105–12)
- Ensuring that future generations (aka 'our children and grandchildren') do not suffer from our actions and enjoy a better future (Markowitz and Shariff, 2012, pp. 243–7)

Finally, the knowledge-deficit theory of climate change denial suggests that the more people know about the science and impacts of climate change, the more likely they will be concerned and motivated to take action. Some studies have called this into question, however (Kahan et al. 2012; Kellstedt et al. 2008, pp. 113–26). For practice, this indicates that a focus on benefits and co-benefits during a public education and outreach process, rather than science and trying to convince skeptics, is the best approach.

(7) Audit existing community policies and programs

Many communities already have polices, programs and activities that are reducing GHG emissions, and are adaptive to climate change, and these should be documented through an audit. The audit allows a community to identify opportunities for action and to take credit for actions already under way. The focus of the policy audit will typically be existing policy documents such as comprehensive or general plans, and existing operational procedures.

The audit may also reveal existing polices, programs and activities that are exacerbating GHG emissions or increasing a community's climate vulnerability. For example, the community may have land-use policies that exacerbate sprawl and dependence on single-occupant vehicles or place infrastructure close to the coast and susceptible to sea-level rise. There may also be polices, programs and activities that reduce GHG emissions but increase climate vulnerability or vice versa. For example, a cooling center that provides relief during heatwaves may consume significant electricity, resulting in GHG emissions. This could be optimized, however, by shifting the cooling center's electricity to a renewable source or even building cooling centers that make the most of energy-efficient building techniques and technologies. These conflicting policies deserve special attention to see if they can be optimized to maximize benefits and minimize costs.

Phase II: Climate Action Plan Development

In Phase II, the community conducts a baseline GHG emissions inventory and develops an interim forecast of future GHG emissions; conducts a climate vulnerability assessment; formulates a vision and goals (including a GHG emissions reduction target); develops GHG emissions reduction strategies; develops climate adaptation strategies; and quantifies the amount of GHG emissions reduction from adopted strategies. This phase is usually iterative; often the forecast is adjusted based on the policy audit and the reduction target may be adjusted as the community evaluates potential reduction strategies.

(8) Conduct a baseline GHG emissions inventory and interim forecast

A GHG emissions inventory accounts for activities within a defined jurisdiction for a defined year. Typical activities that generate emissions include vehicle travel, electricity and natural-gas usage, landfill material decomposition and agricultural practices. Some of these activities generate emissions directly in the jurisdiction (referred to as Scope 1 emissions) and some generate emissions outside the jurisdiction but are caused by activities within the jurisdiction (referred to as Scope 2 emissions). At this time, life-cycle emissions (referred to as Scope 3 emissions) are not typically included in a community GHG emissions inventory. Inventories are usually conducted for the most recent year for which complete activity data are available.

A GHG emissions forecast is based on local population and economic growth assumptions, and assumes that the community will undertake no new actions to reduce emissions; it is a 'no-action' or 'worst-case' scenario.

The forecast will show the baseline year emissions from the inventory and the emissions forecast out to specific years consistent with targets. In addition, it may account for external factors such as technology change or state and federal policy, the assumption being that, even if a local community did nothing, emissions growth would be less due to these external activities (Boswell et al. 2010, pp. 451–62). In future steps, the forecast can show the emissions reduction targets (step 10) and the potential reduction from baseline and forecast based on the implementation of quantified strategies (step 12).

The methods and tools for conducting a GHG emissions inventory and forecast require specialized training and knowledge, but are accessible to most professionals. The most widely accepted protocols for best practice are (see resources section below for additional detail):

- For quantifying emissions from local government operations: Local Government Operations Protocol: For the Quantification and Reporting of Greenhouse Gas Emissions Inventories, Version 1.1.
- For quantifying emissions from community-wide activities: US Community Protocol for Accounting and Reporting of Greenhouse Gas Emissions, Version 1.0.

Many communities will hire a consultant or work with university experts to complete this portion of the climate action planning process due to its technical nature.

(9) Conduct a climate vulnerability assessment

A climate vulnerability assessment evaluates the extent to which projected climate impacts have the potential to affect a community. Climate change directly impacts a community through changes such as sea-level rise or increased temperature. A comprehensive vulnerability assessment also includes how these direct impacts interact with local biophysical and socioeconomic factors to result in a wide range of secondary impacts such as altered economic continuity, reduced water supply, or reduced public health and safety. This climate vulnerability assessment process has four steps that allow a community to identify and carefully assess potential impacts: exposure, sensitivity, potential impact and adaptive capacity.

Climate change varies spatially. The exposure step identifies the changes projected for a particular community, including the difference from current conditions and speed with which the change is anticipated to occur. The next step, sensitivity, determines whether or not these projected changes have the potential to affect a community. Three broad categories are used to identify areas of potential impact: structures (buildings and infrastructure), populations and functions. The points of sensitivity are evaluated to determine the level of disruption to community function that the impact would cause and the permanence of this effect. For example, a sea-level rise in a large marine port could dramatically impact the movement of goods and services in a community. This disruption of transportation would impact the local economy and employment base. The final step is an evaluation of the existing ability to address the projected impacts. The current level of preparation is called adaptive capacity.

Completion of all of these steps depends on the CAT identifying potential impacts, and local capacity requires input from those most familiar with the affected area of city operation or function. The completed vulnerability assessment serves as a basis for adaptation strategy development.

(10) Formulate plan vision and goals (including a GHG emissions reduction target)

A key step in any planning process is to develop plan vision and goals. In climate action planning the focus is usually on achieving a GHG emissions reduction target. This target is based on a desired reduction from the GHG inventory baseline by a certain year. For example, California has a target of reaching 1990 GHG emissions levels by 2020 and 80 percent below 1990 levels by 2050. Most communities should look to their state for guidance on appropriate reduction targets. Alternatively, communities may choose the provisional US target of 17 percent below 2005 by 2020 or may choose their own target based on local emissions levels and community values. Climate adaptation has no similar specific issue or target; the adaptation needs that emerge from the vulnerability assessment must be prioritized based on speed of onset and the potential level of disruption. This prioritization can be used to establish goals for reducing community vulnerability.

(11) Develop, evaluate and specify strategies

Once goals are set, the community can decide what should be done to reach them. Strategies can aim at establishing new regulations, fees or taxes, programs, policies, capital projects and so on. In climate action planning, strategies should be robust and crafted, as much as possible, to include co-benefits. Robust climate policy has seven characteristics:

1. Quantified (for GHG emissions reduction strategies only): GHG emissions reductions that would result from successful implementation of the strategy have been quantitatively estimated (in CO_2 or CO_2e).
2. Specified: sufficient detail for action is provided.
3. Costed: cost of implementation is estimated.
4. Funded: funding sources for implementation are identified.

5. Scheduled/prioritized: a timeline, schedule or priority for implementation is identified.
6. Assigned: a specific individual or entity with primary responsibility for implementation is identified.
7. Monitored: monitoring of implementation is specified.

Co-benefits are the benefits of implementing a particular strategy in addition to the climate change benefits (see Figure 15.2). For example, implementing a program to get more people on bicycles, thus reducing automobile GHG emissions, may also enhance public health. A program to move coastal infrastructure landward in advance of sea-level rise could be coordinated with enhanced coastal recreational opportunities.

GHG emissions reduction strategies Strategies for reducing GHG emissions will vary depending on the sources of emissions identified in the inventory. Typical areas include the following:

- Renewable energy focuses on centralized and decentralized generation of energy through renewable sources such as solar, wind and hydro; it may include nuclear if the standard is 'low-carbon' energy.
- Energy conservation consists of practices intended to reduce the consumption of fossil-fuel-based energy and includes actions such as insulation upgrades, energy-efficient equipment (e.g. EPA Energy Star), green buildings, LED lighting and so on.
- Land use and transportation aims to shift people away from single-occupant vehicles and into lower-carbon modes such as transit, walking and bicycling. This is addressed through coordinated improvements in alternative transportation service and facilities and programs to increase mixed-use, infill, and smart-growth type development.
- Water, wastewater and solid waste focuses on reducing consumption since it is linked to energy demand and increasing the efficiency of transportation and disposal. Also, methane capture in wastewater treatment and landfill practices is a priority since it is a potent GHG.
- Agricultural operations focuses on improving energy efficiency in agricultural operations and methane capture and reduction in livestock operations.
- Sequestration aims to capture atmospheric carbon, most often through agricultural and silvicultural practices, including urban tree programs.

Climate adaptation strategies Climate adaptation strategies vary based on the identified risks in the vulnerability assessment. The adaption needs identified in a vulnerability assessment typically fall into several categories or sectors:

- Public health and equity focuses on impacts that disproportionately impact particular groups of people either due to intrinsic (e.g. age, gender, ethnicity, health) or extrinsic (e.g. occupation, financial resources) factors.
- Ocean and coastal resources are impacted by sea-level rise, intensification of coastal storms and ocean acidification, which can have a range of consequences for coastal communities, from damage to structures to disruption of marine ecosystems.
- Water resources are influenced by the alteration of the timing of precipitation events and the annual temperature regime, which alter water supply, flood frequency and aquatic ecosystem health.
- Biodiversity, habitat and terrestrial ecosystem strategies focus on the climate impact of altered seasonal patterns. Seasonal pattern alters fire frequency, habitats and the species that rely on them, and the industries directly reliant on ecosystem health such as agriculture or forestry.
- Natural hazards such as flooding, fire,or landslides can increase in frequency and/or severity due to the influence of climate change. Strategies associated with natural hazards can build on those already part of local hazard mitigation plans or safety elements in a comprehensive plan.

(12) Quantify GHG emissions reduction strategies

A particular and somewhat unusal step in climate action planning is the quantification of GHG emissions reduction strategies. Since communities are aiming to achieve an overall, specific, quantified reduction of emissions, they should identify whether the suite of identified strategies will allow them to reach this goal. This is accomplished by calculating the GHG reduction potential of each strategy. This information is also useful for identifying whether enough strategies have been adopted and deciding over what time frame implementation will have to occur to achieve the desired reduction target. There are two commonly used approaches for quantifying GHG emissions reduction: ICLEI CAPPA software and CAPCOA GHG quantification resource report.

> The Climate and Air Pollution Planning Assistant (CAPPA) is an Excel-based decision-support tool designed to help U.S. local governments explore and identify potential opportunities to reduce greenhouse gas emissions and other air pollution emissions. CAPPA provides a starting point for two major tasks: determining an achievable emissions reduction target and selecting strategies to include in a local government–operations or community-scale emissions-reduction plan, commonly called a climate action plan. CAPPA users can compare the relative benefits of a wide variety of emissions reduction and clean air measures, and identify those most likely to be successful for their community based on its priorities and constraints. (ICLEI 2013, FAQs)

The California Air Pollution Control Officers' Association (CAPCOA) *Quantifying Greenhouse Gas Mitigation Measures: A Resource for Local Government to Assess Emission Reductions from Greenhouse Gas Mitigation Measures* report focuses primarily on quantifying project-level GHG emissions. It can be used, however, as a resource for quantifying community-wide GHG emissions reduction strategies. Although the information was developed for California communities, much of it is generic enough or can be adapted for use in other states.

Phase III: Implementation and Monitoring

In Phase III the community develops and administers an implementation program, implements the adopted policies and strategies, monitors and evaluates implementation, assesses whether the GHG emissions reduction target is being attained or if vulnerability needs are being met, and then modifies and updates the plan based on the evaluation and the changing policy environment. The last two steps are critical but often overlooked. Since a CAP establishes a clear, specific numeric target for GHG emissions reduction, accounting for plan success is a relatively straightforward endeavor. Adaptation can be more complicated because climate science is evolving and the projection of impact has high levels of uncertainty. This complexity increases the importance of monitoring and subsequent adjustment. CAPs should explicitly establish how this will be done and plan stakeholders should commit to making needed changes and updates.

(13) Develop and administer an implementation program

Although implementation is often treated as a late step in the climate action planning process, the keys to successful implementation are often established early on. As noted above, strategies for GHG emissions reduction and climate adaptation should be robust and incorporate key elements for implementation. A 2012 study of city CAP implementation revealed numerous keys to success:[3]

- Create agency-wide staff buy-in and institutionalize/routinize implementation and accountability, especially through a municipal 'green team'.
- Get the technical assistance and financial support of utility providers.
- Develop and facilitate an active and engaged citizenry, possibly creating a citizen advisory group.
- Cultivate climate champions (who can be elected officials, staff members or citizens).
- Identify and communicate co-benefits, especially cost savings.

- Cultivate community partnerships for implementation.
- Lead by example by implementing and showcasing municipal actions.
- Allocate some general fund revenue for implementation programs.

If these lessons are heeded during the climate action planning process, then the community should be able to develop a robust program for implementation that designates who will implement the strategy, in what time frame, and how.

The biggest 'how' of implementation tends to be funding. Since community funding is often limited, communities should go about securing external funding, developing creative approaches, and leveraging community partnerships. State and federal governments have created programs for funding development and implementation of climate action plans. At the federal level, the US EPA regularly announces funding opportunities. States vary considerably, but in California, for example, the State's Strategic Growth Council awarded $45 million in Sustainable Community Planning Grants. Communities have also identified creative approaches to funding implementation, such as the Phoenix Energy Conservation Savings Reinvestment Fund to take the money saved from energy efficiency projects and reinvest in additional energy-efficiency projects.

Finally, community partners can provide funding or act as direct implementers themselves. For example, in Bellingham, Washington local business leaders formed Sustainable Connections with a mission 'to be the local forum where businesses come together to transform and model an economy built on sustainable practices' (Sustainable Connections 2013) Sustainable Connections has been a key partner with the city in implementing portions of the climate action plan, especially related to green building programs. In Benicia, California the Benicia Tree Foundation has been a key partner in implementing tree programs for carbon sequestration.

(14) Monitor and evaluate implementation and goal attainment

Strategies that have been adopted should be monitored to determine whether they are being implemented and whether they are working. Implementation can be compromised by lack of funding, lack of administrative clarity and follow-through, or resistance. Strategies that are implemented may not work for a host of reasons. The results of monitoring should be regularly reported to the public and decision-makers. One approach to monitoring is to develop a set of indicators that can be consistently tracked over time that relate to GHG emissions activities – for example tracking bicycle trips, solar panel installations, or residential electricity use.

(15) Modify and update the plan

Although this is the final step in the process, it signals that climate action planning is a continuous, iterative process that reacts to implementation successes and failures, changes in social, economic and environmental conditions, and changes in scientific and technological knowledge. As a general rule, CAPs should be updated every 3–5 years, based on the degree to which the identified conditions have changed.

RESOURCES

This chapter provides a basic outline and key considerations for preparing a community climate action plan. These resources provide additional detail and constitute a sufficient set of resources for practice. Since climate action planning is an emergent field, the state of practice continues to evolve rapidly. Those working in this area should keep track of the latest developments in the field. Organizations such as the US Environmental Protection Agency (EPA) and ICLEI – Local Governments for Sustainability have a variety of resources available for keeping track of the latest developments.

Planning Guides

Boswell, Michael R., Adrienne I. Greve and Tammy L. Seale (2012), *Local Climate Action Planning*, Washington, DC: Island Press. http://www.islandpress.org/ip/books/book/islandpress/L/bo8070543.html.

California Emergency Management Agency and California Natural Resources Agency (2012), *California Adaptation Planning Guide*, Sacramento, CA: author. http://resources.ca.gov/climate_adaptation/local_government/adaptation_policy_guide.html.

Center for Research on Environmental Decisions (2009), *The Psychology of Climate Change Communication: A Guide for Scientists, Journalists, Educators, Political Aides, and the Interested Public*, New York: Center for Research on Environmental Decisions. http://guide.cred.columbia.edu/index.html.

ICLEI – Local Governments for Sustainability (2006), *U.S. Mayors' Climate Protection Agreement: Climate Action Handbook*, Oakland, CA: ICLEI. http://www.iclei.org/documents/USA/documents/CCP/Climate_Action_Handbook-0906.pdf.

GHG Emissions Accounting Guides and Tools

Guidance

California Air Resources Board, California Climate Action Registry, ICLEI – Local Governments for Sustainability, and The Climate Registry (2010), *Local Government Operations Protocol: For the Quantification and Reporting of Greenhouse Gas Emissions Inventories, Version 1.1*, Sacramento, CA: California Air Resources Board. http://www.theclimateregistry.org/resources/protocols/local- government-operations-protocol/.

ICLEI – Local Governments for Sustainability (2012), *U.S. Community Protocol for Accounting and Reporting of Greenhouse Gas Emissions, Version 1.0*. Oakland, CA: Author (October). http://www.icleiusa.org/tools/ghg-protocol/community-protocol/us-community-protocol-for-accounting-and-reporting-of-greenhouse-gas-emissions.

California Air Pollution Control Officers' Association (2010), *Quantifying Greenhouse Gas Mitigation Measures: A Resource for Local Government to Assess Emission Reductions from Greenhouse Gas Mitigation Measures* (August). http://www.capcoa.org/wp-content/uploads/2010/11/CAPCOA-Quantification-Report-9–14-Final.pdf.

Software

ICLEI – Local Governments for Sustainability. Climate and Air Pollution Planning Assistant (CAPPA) Version 1.5.
http://www.icleiusa.org/tools/cappa.
This is an Excel-based decision support tool designed to help US local governments explore, identify and analyze potential climate and air pollution emissions reduction opportunities.

Blogs and Email Lists

ScienceDaily: Global Warming News,
http://www.sciencedaily.com/news/earth_climate/global_warming/.

Climate Central Blogs,
http://www.climatecentral.org/blogs.

Climate Compass Blog,
http://www.c2es.org/climatecompass.

ICLEI Local Action Blog,
http://www.icleiusa.org/blog.

ICLEI Connection,
http://www.icleiusa.org/news/e-newsletter.

EPA Smart Growth Listserv,
http://www.epa.gov/smartgrowth/.

NOTES

1. This is slightly different than, though consistent with, the three-phase, 15-step process proposed in our book, *Local Climate Action Planning*. The modifications here show a clearer integration of climate adaptation.
2. Unpublished research by the chapter authors.
3. Unpublished research by the chapter authors.

REFERENCES

Bain, P.G., Hornsey, M.J., Bongiorno, R. and Jeffries, C. (2012), 'Promoting pro-environmental action in climate change deniers', *Nature Climate Change*, **2**(8), 600–603. doi:10.1038/nclimate1532.

Boswell, M.R., Greve, A.I. and Seale, T.L. (2010), 'An assessment of the link between greenhouse gas emissions inventories and climate action plans'. *Journal of the American Planning Association*, **76**(4), 451–62. doi:10.1080/01944363.2010.503313.

Boswell, M.R., Greve, A.I. and Seale, T.L. (2012), *Local Climate Action Planning*, Washington, DC: Island Press.

ICLEI (2013), 'ICLEI's five milestones for climate mitigation', available at http://www.icleiusa.org/action-center/getting-started/iclei2019s-five-milestones-for-climate-protection.

ICLEI (2013, FAQs), 'Frequently asked questions', available at http://www.icleiusa.org/tools/cappa/faqs.

Kahan, D.M., Peters, E., Wittlin, M., Slovic, P., Ouellette, L.L., Braman, D. and Mandel, G. (2012), 'The polarizing impact of science literacy and numeracy on perceived climate change risks', *Nature Climate Change*. doi:10.1038/nclimate1547.

Kellstedt, P.M., Zahran, S. and Vedlitz, A. (2008), 'Personal efficacy, the information environment, and attitudes toward global warming and climate change in the United States', *Risk Analysis: an official publication of the Society for Risk Analysis*, **28**(1), 113–26. doi:10.1111/j.1539–6924.2008.01010.x.

Leiserowitz, A., Maibach, E., Roser-Renouf, C. and Hmielowski, J. (2012), *Global Warming's Six Americas, March 2012 & Nov. 2011*, Yale University and George Mason University, New Haven, CT: Yale Project on Climate Change Communication. P.4.

Markowitz, E.M. and Shariff, A.F. (2012), 'Climate change and moral judgement', *Nature Climate Change*, **2**(4), 243–47. doi:10.1038/nclimate1378.

Myers, T., Nisbet, M., Maibach, E.and Leiserowitz, A. (2012), 'A public health frame arouses hopeful emotions about climate change', *Climatic Change*, **113**(3), 1105–12. doi:10.1007/s10584–012–0513–6.

Sustainable Connections (2013), 'Sustainable Connections', available at http://sustainable connections.org/.

16. Climate change adaptation

Adrienne I. Greve and Michael R. Boswell

Climate change adaptation is the assessment of community vulnerability to climate change impacts and the development of strategies to reduce them. It is complementary to the development of strategies to reduce a community's greenhouse gas (GHG) emissions. Both types of strategies are needed and often fall under the broader umbrella of climate action planning.

Reducing GHG emissions (often referred to as 'mitigation') addresses the root cause of climate change by aiming to limit atmospheric concentrations of heat-trapping gases. But due to the persistence of these gases in the atmosphere, observable slowing of the progression of climate change would be many decades away even if aggressive GHG emissions reductions were to occur today. Changes to the climate are already occurring and are projected to continue well into the future regardless of the level of GHG emissions reduction achieved (Field et al. 2012; Solomon et al. 2007). Climate change adaptation refers to actions taken to address these unavoidable climate impacts.

While action must be taken at all scales, cities are critical to the development and implementation of effective climate adaptation measures. Despite being a global problem, the impacts of climate change will be felt most severely at the local level. The challenge of climate adaptation is that direct climate impacts such as sea-level rise, temperature changes, including extreme heat events, and change in precipitation patterns have a variety of secondary impacts on community conditions. These secondary impacts can include adverse impacts on human health and safety, economic continuity, ecosystem integrity, and hazard severity and frequency. Because secondary impacts vary spatially and are a product of local characteristics such as biophysical setting, community culture, economic base and available resources, policy is often most effective when implemented at smaller regional and local scales.

The challenge for regional and local scales is that effective adaptation strategy development is based on evolving climate science that describes a global phenomenon. The uncertainty associated with projecting global climate change impacts is amplified at regional and local scales (Solomon et al. 2007). Further complicating the issue is that projecting potential climate impacts is inexact because local impacts often result from the interaction of community characteristics that vary from the physical built form to local cultural and behavioral norms. Handling the inherent uncertainty and complexity of climate adaptation in a planning context requires communities to carefully evaluate potential impacts and embrace a willingness to iteratively adjust as knowledge and adaptation needs evolve.

While it may appear that adaptation lags behind GHG emissions reduction in terms of publicity and policy action, this can be misleading as adaptation can include the programs and local strategies that are part of typical city operation. For example, communities often have a local hazard mitigation plan, public health strategies, a plan for water management, and more. Climate impacts can be addressed in a single, stand-alone plan or these strategies can be integrated throughout the plans, programs and policies that already govern city function. In this case, a community may be implementing adaptation strategies such as cooling centers for extreme heat days without explicitly identifying the action as climate adaptation. The most common difference between the two means of addressing adaptation needs is the extent to which the measures are backed by a vulnerability assessment. Stand-alone plans represent a concentrated effort to comprehensively address climate impacts and are more likely to be based on a vulnerability assessment. Impact-specific measures are likely to be based on perceived need or vulnerability, but are less likely to benefit from an assessment that takes a broader view of projected impacts and potential outcomes.

CLIMATE IMPACTS

There is a limited number of direct climate impacts: altered temperature patterns including extreme heat; changed seasonal precipitation patterns, including drought, reduced snowpack and intense rainfall; sea-level rise; and ocean acidification. The direct impacts of climate change cannot be treated in isolation. In any one location, the experienced climate impacts result from the combination of interacting direct climate impacts and a host of socioeconomic factors and existing built forms. For example, reduced rainfall and increased temperature can lead to higher wildfire risk. The extent to which this threatens communities depends on factors such as the local emergency response capacity, surrounding vegetative habitat, the distribution of structures, community evacuation procedures, and the location and integrity of infrastructure such as transportation and water.

Because of the number of factors that contribute to local vulnerability, it can be more effective to view climate change through the lens of impact sectors rather than individual climate impacts such as sea-level rise or increased temperature. Many climate adaptation resources are organized using sectors. While the specific definition of these sectors varies, the overall intention does not. The sectors most likely to be of particular interest for cities are listed below.

Public Health and Equity

Many climate impacts have the potential to impact public health, from the human consequences of temperature extremes, to altered disease vectors, to air quality, to access to basic needs such as water and food. These impacts do not affect all groups or locations equally. In many cases, specific groups may be disproportionately sensitive to these impacts due to either intrinsic (e.g. age, gender, ethnicity, health) or extrinsic (e.g. occupation, financial resources) factors (Parry et al. 2007; Portier et al. 2010; Cal EMA and CNRA 2012).

Ocean and Coastal Resources

Sea-level rise, intensification of coastal storms and ocean acidification all have the potential to dramatically impact coastal communities, from flooding and erosion that damages both built structures and coastal ecosystems, to intrusion of saltwater into groundwater aquifers, to the disruption of marine ecosystems and associated industries such as shellfish (Snover et al. 2007; Parry et al. 2007; Cal EMA and CNRA 2012).

Water Resources

Climate change may result in the alteration of the timing of precipitation events and the annual temperature regime. These changes, such as reduced snowpack and drought, have the potential to influence both the availability of and demand for water. In addition to impacts on water supply, two other impacts to freshwater systems may be experienced: intense storms and rapid snowmelt may result in flooding; and aquatic ecosystems will be impacted by both changed water levels and temperature regimes (e.g. Parry et al. 2007; Backlund et al. 2008; Schwarz et al. 2011).

Biodiversity, Habitat and Terrestrial Ecosystems

Climate change alters the seasonal patterns of temperature, precipitation and, as a result, disturbance regimes such as wildfire. These impacts together can result in habitat alteration, species loss, increased invasive species range, including pests, and altered growing ranges for vegetation. These impacts together influence ecosystem health, but also agricultural productivity, including livestock health and forestry operations (Parry et al. 2007; Backlund et al. 2008; Cal EMA and CNRA 2012).

Natural Hazards

The influence of climate change on natural hazard frequency and severity is closely related to the above impact categories, but given the specific nature of these impacts and the close relationship to the practice of hazards planning, it has been separated. Climate change may increase the frequency and severity of hazards such as flooding, wildfire and landslides. In addition, this is an area that allows for specific evaluation of the vulnerability of linear infrastructure such as roads, rail, water (pipes, canals and dams), electricity, gas and communication. Hazards not only have the potential to impact public safety, but overall community function too (IPCC 2012; Backlund et al. 2008; Cal EMA and CNRA 2012).

TAKING ACTION

Although climate change is happening now, many of the most damaging potential impacts are projected to occur many decades into the future. While this distance can lead decision makers to hesitate to take action (Binder et al. 2010), it should be viewed as an opportunity. The longer time frame means that there is a greater number of viable options for adapting to climate change. In addition, it allows time for development of proactive policies that may take a long time to implement, such as land-use shift or diversification of economic base. The relative cost of taking action now is likely to be much less than that of reactively addressing impacts in the future.

Taking action on climate adaptation need not come at the cost of addressing more immediate community needs. The most effective adaptation policy is integrated within normal city operation and governance. Economic stability, public safety, public health, environmental quality and reduced GHG emissions are all potential short-term co-benefits to long-term adaptation action. Integration of adaptation as an additional consideration in the typical plan-making and plan-update process is identified as a primary contributor to successful adaptation strategy implementation (Urwin and Jordan 2008; Binder et al. 2010)

GETTING STARTED

Before beginning the adaptation strategy development process, a community can take several steps to better position itself for long-term effectiveness. While the impacts of climate change will vary from community to community, those communities with demonstrated success in implementing climate adaptation measures share a few common characteristics, including committed political leadership, establishment of an adaptation team, and stakeholder engagement throughout the process from initiation to implementation (Binder et al. 2010).

Commitment to the process of climate adaptation should be formalized through actions such as passing resolutions by the city council or inclusion in the capital improvement plan. Actions by city leadership send a clear message to both city staff and residents that adaptation strategies are a priority (Smit et al. 2000; Smith et al. 2009). Another effective way to demonstrate commitment is to dedicate staff, funding and other resources to the effort. A formal city commitment also can serve as the basis for formation of a climate adaptation team.

The diversity of potential impacts associated with climate change means that nearly every department within city government may be affected and will have a role in developing and implementing strategies to address the impacts. Accounting for these multiple viewpoints necessitates assembling a climate adaptation team. Adaptation measures rely on specific information about the manner in which climate change is likely to impact a city. This information is best developed by those staff and community members most familiar with the affected population, function or structure. In addition, this information is also critical to identifying current capacity to adapt and strategies most likely to be locally effective (Smit and Wandel 2006). The adaptation team facilitates integration across departmental boundaries and spatial scales. Members of the adaptation team should include representatives of the following departments: planning, community development, building, engineering, public works, emergency management, police, fire, finance, public health and environment. The climate adaptation team may also include community groups, chamber of commerce and other local stakeholders.

Ongoing public engagement is vital to successful policy development and implementation. Stakeholders, defined as those who may be impacted, should be included in the policy-making process in order to ensure their needs are met, to foster support for the resulting policy, and to reduce potential conflict. It is difficult for community leaders to take action without some level of consensus around approaches to address climate change impacts. Building an informed and engaged community not only provides political support, but also lays a foundation for ongoing efforts. It may be this fostered community support that can maintain momentum, even in the face of change in elected officials or staff turnover. Community engagement also ensures that measures identified and adopted address community needs, are equitable and can be efficiently implemented (Boswell et al. 2012; Cal EMA and CNRA 2012).

CLIMATE CHANGE ADAPTATION PLANNING PROCESS

Climate adaptation strategies address unavoidable climate impacts with the aim of reducing community vulnerability and increasing local capacity to adapt. The process of developing strategies can be broken into two phases: (1) vulnerability assessment and (2) strategy development (see Figure 16.1). This process can vary, depending on the level of detail a community desires; however, even comprehensive, highly detailed efforts still face the challenge of policy development in the context of uncertainty. The lack of precision can mean that decision makers feel reluctant to take action. One increasingly common strategy for making policy choices in the face of uncertainty is decision analysis tools (Smith et al. 2009).

Vulnerability Assessment

The first phase of the climate change adaptation planning process is the vulnerability assessment. The goal of vulnerability assessment is the identification of adaptation needs that demand strategy development. The definition of adaptation need is based on an evaluation of a community's exposure to projected climate impacts, their sensitivity to those impacts, the potential consequences of the impacts, and the existing local capacity to address the impacts (FEMA 2001; Snover et al. 2007; Glick et al. 2011; Cal EMA and CNRA 2012).

Exposure

The first step in vulnerability assessment is an evaluation of the projected climate impacts for a particular location. A major challenge is applying global-scaled climate change scenarios to regions and localities. In most cases, these scenarios will not have a spatial resolution that easily accommodates a local planning process. For example, even downscaled climate models at best usually have between 5 and 12 km resolution (e.g. Solomon et al. 2007; Cayan et al. 2011). While the precision of these models is likely to improve with time, it is not critical to taking action. The information

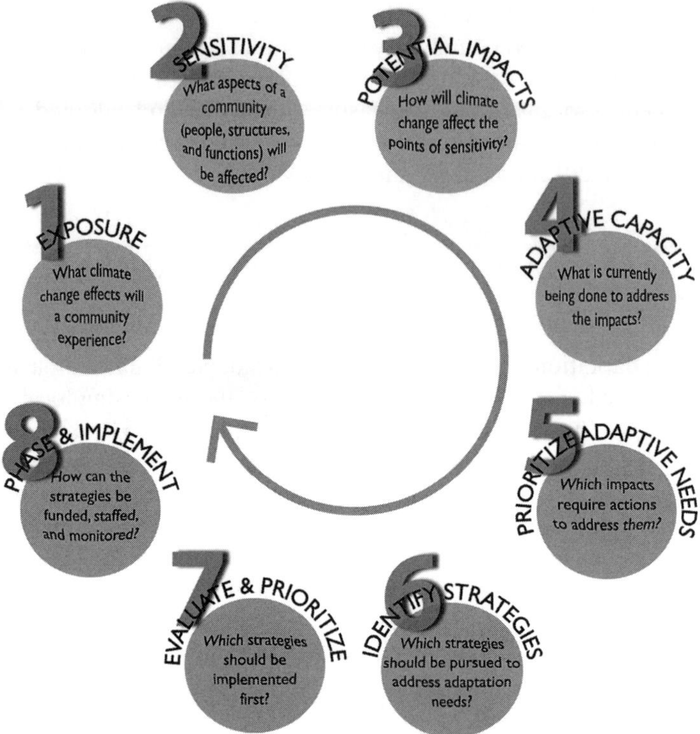

Note: The process has two phases: vulnerability assessment and strategy development.

Sources: Adapted from Cal EMA and CNRA (2012).

Figure 16.1 Steps in adaptation strategy development process

needed to taking the first step in devising adaptation policy is to develop a local climate change profile that includes how much local conditions are projected to change, the speed with which the change will occur, and its spatial extent.

The information gathered as part of the assessment of exposure to climate change impacts plays a critical role in prioritizing adaptation needs and associated strategies. Large or fast-moving changes from current conditions are likely to be those for which a community is least prepared. Because this step relies on climate science, which is most often developed on larger national or international spatial scales, this step can be bolstered through direct inclusion of regional or state scientific collaborators. Inclusion of the scientific community in the team assembled to develop policy can speed the diffusion of up-to-date climate science and further ensure consistency in the policy approach at multiple scales (Binder et al. 2010).

The outcomes from assessing exposure should be scenarios of potential local climate changes at different future time periods. Depending on location, this could include expected sea-level rise and coastal inundation, changes in precipitation patterns and amounts, changes in frequency of heat waves and droughts, and changes in acidity of coastal waters. These can be mapped and carry explanations regarding the time frame of changes, likelihood of changes and their magnitude/frequency. Strides have been made in making scientific projections easily accessible to local jurisdictions. Tools such as NOAA's sea-level rise viewer (http://www.csc.noaa.gov/digitalcoast/tools/slrviewer) or the Public Interest Energy Research (PIER) Cal-Adapt tool (cal-adapt.org) provide an easy way to for communities to conduct an initial assessment of exposure to climate impacts.

Sensitivity and potential impact

The completion of a climate change profile (exposure) is the first step in understanding the potential consequences of climate change for a community. The next step is to identify the range of potential secondary impacts, which can include public safety, human health, and social, economic and cultural stability. For each potential impact such as increased temperature, flooding or reduced water supply, a systematic evaluation of impacted community resources must be conducted. This evaluation begins with a basic identification of those aspects of a community potentially impacted. This initial step is similar to the checklists commonly used to assess natural hazards (FEMA 2001). The assessment of potential impacted community resources can be categorized into three sectors: structures, populations, and functions (Cal EMA and CNRA 2012). These three categories are closely related. For example, disruption of transportation networks (structure) would also impact economic continuity (function).

Structures This broad category encompasses not only the existing and planned buildings that make up a city, but also the infrastructure that connects them (e.g. transportation, water, energy or communication). Climate change results in physical damage to structures due to impacts such as flooding, landslide or fire, as well as impacts on the efficiency and structural integrity of systems such as energy transmission. Of particular importance in this sector is identification of critical nodes where damage or loss would have far-reaching impacts, such as to endanger residents, disrupt the local delivery of goods and services, or isolate particular populations.

Communities should specifically identify and evaluate the extent to which critical infrastructure might be disrupted, such as evacuation routes or water distribution. Certain parts of these networks, such as those located near coastal areas threatened by sea-level rise, should be identified. Similarly, buildings of particular community importance should be carefully evaluated, such as hospitals, emergency services, economic centers and cultural hubs.

Populations Climate change poses disproportionate risk to some populations due to factors such as health, age, language, employment or housing quality. Those populations that are most vulnerable must be identified. Vulnerability can be amplified due to extrinsic factors such as where someone lives or works. For example, extreme heat can result in reduced energy, heat stroke or worse. Those individuals who lack access to air conditioning, have poor insulation in their home, or work outside (i.e. construction workers) are at greater risk for heat-related impacts. Intrinsic factors such as age or health can also indicate greater risk. The elderly or those with already compromised health will also be at great risk during extreme heat events. Identifying those populations at risk for each of the climate impacts projected to occur in a community allows for specific strategies to be devised that are tailored to local needs.

Functions Closely related to structures and populations are the various services and functions that define day-to-day operations in a city. Climate change can disrupt city functions such as economic continuity, emergency response, social services, recreation and others. For example, climate change can alter the viability of some industries, such as tourism in a mountain community reliant on the ski industry. The losses experienced by this industry have the potential to impact the overall employment base and community financial security. Similarly, impacts to ecological functions can have a cascade effect that alters disaster resistance, disease vectors, agricultural productivity and more. Individual communities may have specific traditions or functions that have particular local relevance or importance. The climate adaptation team should seek to identify the manner in which impacts can interact and propagate.

Identifying the community resources (structures, populations and functions) that may be affected by climate change, points of sensitivity, leads to an assessment of potential impact. Identification of the potential impacts of climate change on a city relies heavily on the climate action team. Each point of sensitivity will affect the community; the task of the climate action team is to carefully determine to what extent. This step can be completed through qualitative assessment by developing descriptive scenarios. The potential impact should be based on input from the adaptation team members most familiar with the affected community resource. This description should be as specific as possible and detail the expected duration of the impact, whether or not it will result in permanent changes, if it endangers local populations, or will disrupt normal community function, including provision of services, ecosystem health, or economic, continuity (Cal EMA and CNRA 2012). These descriptions are locally specific. The same impact may have very different consequences or importance in different biophysical or socioeconomic settings.

Each point of impact should evaluate the potential extent of the impact. This description should include the following (Cal EMA and CNRA 2012):

- The temporal extent of the impact.
- The spatial extent of the impact.
- The permanence of the impact.
- The level of disruption to normal community function.

Adaptive capacity

The complement to the assessment of potential impacts is a review of existing local policy to evaluate the extent to which a community is prepared for the projected impacts. It identifies pre-existing adaptive capacity and highlights areas most in need of policy revision or new policy development. An audit of existing policy aims to identify policies and programs that reduce climate change vulnerability, as well as local policies or behaviors that increase it (Klein et al. 2001; Cal EMA and CNRA 2012). The review of the local level of preparation in tandem with the assessment of potential impacts is used to identify the adaptation needs. It is this identification of need that serves as the basis for policy development.

Because many of the impacts of climate change are already being experienced, such as reduced water supply, heat waves, or increased coastal erosion, many communities already have policies in place. The evaluation of adaptive capacity will indicate the extent to which those policies are adequate to address future change. In some cases, a simple bolstering of existing policy may be enough to address projected changes; in others, projected impacts may be too much for existing policy and demand a new approach. The evaluation of adaptive capacity measures the extent to which a community is prepared.

Plans, programs, resources and existing collaborations should all be included in an assessment of local adaptive capacity. For each potential impact, the following steps should be taken (Cal EMA and CNRA 2012):

- Identify actions in progress, planned, or readily implemented to address the issue.

- If the policy or program is not yet implemented, evaluate the time and resources needed for implementation.
- Assess the extent to which the existing policy or program addresses potential impacts ('is it enough?').
- Note the degree to which the existing policy or program could be strengthened.

Adaptation Strategy Development

The second phase of the climate change adaptation planning process is strategy development. The information developed in the vulnerability assessment serves as the basis for climate adaptation strategy development. To develop strategies, projected climate change, potential impacts and adaptive capacity must be combined with policy considerations such as cost, political feasibility and time. Much of the information available to inform strategy development is either qualitative in nature or associated with high levels of uncertainty. As discussed above, one way in which to manage a complex decision with competing interests and high uncertainty is through the use of decision analysis tools such as decision matrices (Smith et al. 2009, ACCAP 2009; Cal EMA and CNRA 2012).

A decision matrix can be used to identify the highest adaptation needs by considering various factors such as the magnitude/frequency/onset/duration/uncertainty of an impact and the adaptive capacity of the community, among others. It is infeasible for a city to address every adaptation need. The decision matrices assist in narrowing the list of impacts that require strategy development. Figure 16.2 is a decision matrix that considers the community's adaptive capacity to a climate change impact, and the magnitude of such an impact. The use of a matrix requires only that potential impacts and adaptive capacity are rated high, medium or low, usually by the climate adaptation team.

A next step can prioritize adaptation needs based on how quickly an impact is projected to occur and the level of certainty associated with the projected impact. Decision matrices can be populated with a variety of local priorities and impact characteristics. What can be powerful about this strategy is that it can provide clear policy direction based only on simply qualitative categorizations. These categories can be based on the level of disruption to community function for each impact, its speed of onset, and the level of certainty.

Adaptation strategies characteristics

The highest-priority adaptation needs require strategy development. This iterative process relies heavily on insights from the adaptation team. These strategies should draw on local experience with types of strategies that

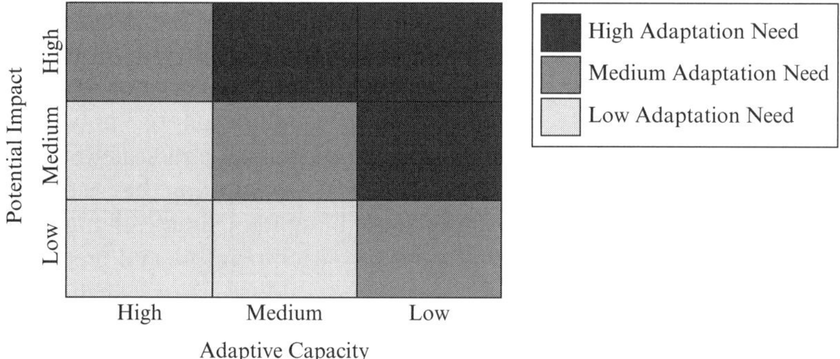

Sources: Cal EMA and CNRA (2012).

Figure 16.2 A matrix to identify high adaptation needs by accounting for potential impacts and adaptive capacity

have proved locally effective. The following list covers some key characteristics of effective adaptation measures (Boswell et al. 2012; Cal EMA and CNRA 2012).

- *Flexible*: Smith (1997) defines flexible climate adaptation strategies as robust and resilient. It is policy that is applicable under a wide range of conditions. This is critical due to the evolving nature of climate science and our understanding of potential impacts. Flexibility is one response to policy development in a context of uncertainty. Taking the idea of flexibility even further, de Loe et al. (2001) advocate for reversibility as a policy goal.
- *Cost-effective*: Co-benefits are a commonly cited priority for climate-related strategy development. It may be more accurate to view the idea of co-benefits as economically efficient. Policies that can address adaptation needs simultaneously with other community priorities can have both long-term and short-term benefits. This can be critical for building support for these strategies because the benefits of adaptive measures may not be realized for many years, if not decades.
- *Targets irreversible impacts*: Smith (1997) suggests that three situations are most appropriate for adaptation policy development: (1) irreversible impacts such as extinction, loss of an ecosystem (e.g. the Everglades), or extreme weather (e.g. hurricanes); (2) unfavorable trends where enacting adaptation measures now is more feasible than it is likely to be in the future (e.g. limiting population density in coastal areas); and (3) decisions, such as those regarding infrastructure, that have long life spans.

- *Specific*: Anticipatory adaptation should target a specific climate impact and impact type. Uncertainty is best evaluated in the context of a specific issue or potential impact in need of resolution (Smit and Wandel 2006). Most climate impacts that require adaptive policy will have an expected speed of onset, rate of change and scale (Smit et al. 2000). Policy will be more effective if tailored using the best available information about the anticipated impact. Climate change acts directly on climate characteristics such as temperature and precipitation, but adaptive policy may focus on secondary impacts such as the impact of change in temperature on human health. Depending on the specific impact, the resulting policy may vary.
- *Feedback loops and adaptive policy*: Climate adaptation policy must have indicators that allow for evaluation of policy success. These data, in combination with advances in climate science and development of new technology, must inform revision of adaptation policy.

Prioritize strategies

Following identification of adaptation strategies, they can be evaluated by the adaptation team for a range of feasibility considerations such as co-benefits, political support, cost, and time required for implementation. Based on these data, strategies can be phased into near, mid and long term using another decision matrix. The use of the matrices and clear communication of the criteria used for categorization make the process transparent and more easily communicated. Information helpful for systematic assessment includes the following (Smit et al. 2000; Smith et al. 2009; Boswell et al. 2012; Cal EMA and CNRA 2012):

- *Costs*: This includes the financial costs of implementation and operation. In addition, other resource requirements should be included, such as costs to other aspects of community function, for example ecosystems and social continuity.
- *Community co-benefits*: Co-benefits refers to the extent to which a strategy not only meets adaptation needs, but also addresses other local priorities. It is particularly helpful if the co-benefits are projected to be experienced in the near term. This can offset the long-term benefits associated with many adaptation strategies.
- *Duration of implementation*: There are two parts to assessment of implementation time: the time to initiate a strategy and the time needed to complete implementation. This can vary widely, based on the strategy being assessed. Time can be added based on the availability of technology, the level of political resistance to a strategy, or the pace with which a strategy can be implemented (e.g. land-use change).

- *Social acceptance*: In many cases, adaptation strategies, like other planning measures, require feedback from the community and approval by advisory bodies and elected officials. Strategies that have low levels of support may experience delays and increased costs due to the need to build the support necessary for adoption. Popular strategies that enjoy broad public support are likely to have more successful implementation due to political support, funding and social acceptance.

Implementation

The final stage is devising a plan for ensuring that the adaptation strategies are effective. Success at climate adaptation does not occur when strategies are adopted. It is experienced many decades into the future when a community demonstrates resilience in the face of unavoidable climate impacts. Long-term success requires that cities establish a system where implementation can be sustained for the long term. Several steps can be taken preemptively, at the time of strategy development, to increase the likelihood of long-term, effective implementation.

The identification of an agency, department or staff member responsible for implementation should accompany each strategy. The responsible party should be funded specifically for the task or have the task added explicitly to their job description. In addition to defining a responsible party, strategies should have an identifiable funding source or potential funding source. By having a responsible party and funding mechanism, the identified phasing plan is most likely to be implemented.

The other critical component of long-term effectiveness is the establishment of monitoring systems and feedback loops. Climate adaptation is a fairly new area of policy development, and climate science is evolving quickly. Adaptation strategies should be monitored and the monitoring data evaluated regularly to ensure that intended changes are taking place and that they continue to be adequate for addressing projected climate impacts. In the event that strategies are not as effective as anticipated or new climate data indicate that impacts may be more severe than anticipated, a system for adjustment or revision of strategies should also be established.

REFERENCES

Backlund, Peter, Anthony Janetos, David Schimel, Jerry Hatfield, Mike Ryan, Steven Archer, Dennis Lettenmaier, Kenneth Boote, Philip Fay, Leroy Hahn, Cesar Izaurralde, Bruce A. Kimball, Terry Mader, Jack Morgan, Donald Ort, Wayne Polley, Allison Thomson,

David Wolfe, Richard Birdsey, Cliff Dahm, Linda Heath, Jeff Hicke, David Hollinger, Travis Huxman, Gregory Okin, Ram Oren, James Randerson, William Schlesinger, David Major, Leroy Poff, Steve Running, Lara Hansen, David Inouye, Brendan P. Kelly, Laura Meyerson, Bill Peterson and Rebecca Shaw (2008), *The Effects of Climate Change on Agriculture, Land Resources, Water Resources, and Biodiversity in the United States: A Report by the US Climate Change Science Program and the Subcommittee on Global Change Research*, Washington, DC: United States Department of Agriculture.

Binder, L.C.W., J.K. Barcelos, D.B. Booth, M. Darzen, M.M. Elsner, R. Fenske, T.F. Graham, A.F. Hamlet, J. Hodges-Howell, D.D. Huppert, J.E. Jackson, C. Karr, P.W. Keys, J.S. Littell, N. Mantua, J. Marlow, D. McKenzie, M. Robinson-Dorn, E.A. Rosenberg, C.O. Stockle and J.A. Vano (2010), 'Preparing for climate change in Washington State', *Climatic Change*, **102** (1–2), 351–76, doi:10.1007/s10584–010–9850–5.

Boswell, Michael R., Adrienne I. Greve and Tammy L. Seale (2012), *Local Climate Action Planning*, Washington, DC: Island Press.

California Emergency Management Agency (Cal EMA) and California Natural Resources Agency (CNRA) (2012), 'California adaptation planning guide', available at http://resources.ca.gov/climate_adaptation/local_government/adaptation_policy_guide.html.

Cayan, Dan, Mary Tyree, Mike Dettinger, Hugo Hidalgo, Tapash Das, Ed Maurer, Peter Bormirski, Nicholas Graham and Reinhard Flick (2011), *Climate Change Scenarios and Sea Level Rise Estimate for the California 2009 Climate Change Scenarios Assessment (CEC-500–2009–014-F)*, Sacramento, CA: California Climate Change Center, available at http://www.energy.ca.gov/2009publications/CEC-500-2009-014/CEC-500-2009-014-F.PDF.

de Loe, R., R. Kreutzwiser and L. Moraru (2001), 'Adaptation option for the near term: climate change and the Canadian water sector', *Global Environmental Change*, **11** (3), 231–45.

Federal Emergency Management Agency (FEMA) (2001), 'Understanding your risks: identifying hazards and estimating losses (FEMA 386–2)', available at http://www.fema.gov/library/viewRecord.do?id=1880.

Field, Christopher B., Vicente Barros, Thomas F. Stocker, Qin Dahe, David J. Dokken, Kristie L. Ebi, Michael D. Mastrandrea, Katharine J. Mach, Gian-Kasper Plattner, Simon K. Allen, Melinda Tignor and Pauline M. Midgley (2012), *Managing the Risks of Extreme Events and Disasters to Advance Climate Change Adaptation: Special Report of the Intergovernmental Panel on Climate Change*, Cambridge, UK and New York: Cambridge University Press.

Glick, Patty, Bruce A. Stein and Naomi A. Edelson (eds) (2011), *Scanning the Conservation Horizon: A Guide to Climate Change Vulnerability Assessment*, Washington, DC: National Wildlife Federation.

IPCC (Intergovernmental Panel on Climate Change (2012), *Managing the Risks of Extreme Events and Disasters to Advance Climate Change Adaptation. A Special Report of Working Groups I and II*, Cambridge, UK and New York: IPCC.

Klein, R.J.T., R.J. Nicholls, S. Ragoonaden, M. Capobianco, J. Aston and E.N. Buckley (2001), 'Technological options for adaptation to climate change in coastal zones', *Journal of Coastal Research*, **17** (3), 531–43.

Parry, Martin L., Osvaldo Canziani, Jean Palutikof, Paul van der Linden and Clair Hanson (2007), *Climate Change 2007: Impacts, Adaptation and Vulnerability. Contribution of Working Group II to the Fourth Assessment Report of the Intergovernmental Panel on Climate Change*, Cambridge, UK and New York: Cambridge University Press.

Portier, C.J., K. Thigpen Tart, S.R. Carter, C.H. Dilworth, A.E. Grambsch, J. Gohlke, J. Hess, S.N. Howard, G. Luber, J.T. Lutz, T. Maslak, N. Prudent, M. Radtke, J.P Rosenthal, T. Rowles, P.A. Sandifer, J. Scheraga, P.J. Schramm, D. Strickman, J.M. Trtanj and P. Whung (2010), *A Human Health Perspective On Climate Change: A Report Outlining the Research Needs on the Human Health Effects of Climate Change*, Research Triangle Park, NC: Environmental Health Perspectives/National Institute of Environmental Health Sciences, doi:10.1289/ehp.1002272, available at www.niehs.nih.gov/climatereport.

Schwarz, A., S. Marr, K. Schwinn, E.S. Townsley, A. O'Callaghan, J. Andrew, T. Quasebarth, E. Lopez-Calva, P. Kullis, G. Pelletier, T. Cox, D. Rodrigo, B. Brown, J. Hinchcliff and J. Tijero (2011), 'Climate change handbook for regional water planning', available at http://www.water.ca.gov/climatechange/docs/Climate_Change_Handbook_Regional_Water_Planning.pdf.

Smit, B. and J. Wandel (2006), 'Adaptation, adaptive capacity and vulnerability', *Global Environmental Change*, **16** (3), 282–92.

Smit, B., I. Burton, R.J.T. Klein and J. Wandel (2000), 'An anatomy of adaptation to climate change and variability', *Climatic Change*, **45** (1), 223–51.

Smith, J.B. (1997), 'Setting priorities for adapting to climate change', *Global Environmental Change*, **7** (1), 251–64.

Smith, J.B., J.M. Vogel and J.E.Cromwell III (2009), 'An architecture for government action on adaptation to climate change: An editorial comment', *Climatic Change*, **95** (1–2), 53–61.

Snover, A.K., L.W. Binder, J. Lopez, W.J. Kay, D. Howell and J. Simmonds (2007), *Preparing for Climate Change: A Guidebook for Local, Regional, and State Governments*, Oakland, CA: ICLEI – Local Governments for Sustainability.

Solomon, Susan, Dahe Qin, Martin Manning, Melinda Marquis, Kristen Averyt, Melinda M.B. Tignor, Henry L. Miller and Zhenlin Chen (2007), *Climate Change 2007: The Physical Science Basis: Contribution of Working Group I to the Fourth Assessment Report of the Intergovernmental Panel on Climate Change, Summary for Policymakers*, Cambridge, UK and New York: Cambridge University Press.

Urwin, K. and A. Jordan (2008), 'Does public policy support or undermine climate change adaptation? Exploring policy interplay across different scales of governance', *Global Environmental Change*, **18** (1), 180–91, doi:10.1016/j.gloenvcha.2007.08.002.

17. Economic resilience and the sustainability of cities in the face of climate change: an ecological economics framework

Adam Rose

I. INTRODUCTION

Cities are major agglomerations of population and economic activity. Their very existence and size are an indication of their economic vitality. However, any given city will not thrive forever. A city may deplete critical resources within its own boundaries or its hinterlands, lose its comparative advantage in cross-border trade or suffer severe social ills. It may also be subjected to external shocks from natural and man-made disasters. Recent examples include Detroit's downturn due to structural changes in the auto industry in the USA and abroad, and New Orleans being the bull's eye of Hurricane Katrina. Thus, in addition to long-term concerns about a lasting resource base, adequate community infrastructure and rising sea levels, cities must be resilient, or able to rebound from short-run disasters to be sustainable as well.

This chapter examines the role of economic resilience in the sustainability of cities. The next section identifies features of cities that make them both vulnerable and resilient, followed by a section on the relationship between resilience and sustainability. In Section IV, I then define economic resilience and offer an operational metric. I discuss individual tactics to implement it in Section V and summarize studies on the relative effectiveness of resilience tactics and their costs in Section VI. Section VII examines the relationship between resilience and adaptation in relation to climate change. In Section VIII, I outline an ecological economics framework for the evaluation of resilience strategies to address climate change in cities. In Section IX, I conclude with a discussion of broader strategies to make cities more resilient to disasters in the short run and emphasize the importance of translating them into adaptations for long-run sustainability.

II. VULNERABILITY AND RESILIENCE

Cities are vulnerable to disasters for a number of reasons: first, they represent large concentrations of population in the built environment, including complex infrastructure. This concentration makes them more susceptible to contagion effects associated with the spread of disease, fire and building collapse. Concentration also makes evacuation in anticipation of disasters more difficult. The complexity of cities stems primarily from their overall interdependence and the more sophisticated nature of economic and social activity than in other areas. This, together with the faster pace of life, makes cities relatively rigid, meaning less flexibility and hence leading to less resilience.

The basic economic rationale for cities often places them in more highly vulnerable locations, such as along coasts or major rivers. They represent larger targets for terrorists as well. In the case of major disasters, the very size of cities makes them more likely to be overwhelmed in providing emergency response services, such as fire and health care.

With respect to climate change in particular, cities contribute relatively more to the problem per capita than other areas through industrial production and traffic congestion. They are also more likely to exacerbate the effects of climate change through heat-island effects and overloaded water and storm systems.

Despite their overall and per capita wealth, cities typically also house large percentages of low-income and other disadvantaged population groups. These groups have higher vulnerability to temperature extremes and susceptibility/mortality to vector-borne diseases, whose spread has been linked to higher temperatures and moisture levels. These groups also have lower resilience capacities than others in terms of education, social connectivity, material resources and political clout.

At the same time, cities also have some distinct advantages with respect to resilience. They are more diversified economically, and thus more likely to be able to withstand a severe shock to any given sector. While overall they may not have a higher proportion of excess capacity at a given point in time than population centers of other sizes, unless the disaster is especially widespread, cities have a greater absolute amount of excess capacity to absorb displaced businesses and residents. They also contain a greater amount of resources for recovery and reconstruction, as well as more specialized skills and expertise. Cities typically are centers of innovation, a key ingredient of resilience, as will be discussed below. Cities are also likely to have greater prominence and political power, and thus are able to command greater transfers of resources from outside their boundaries.

At the same time, all the examples provided in the previous paragraph are effective up to some threshold, at which point resilience can be overwhelmed. In these cases the sheer size of the city becomes a liability.

Several striking examples exist of the grand resilience of cities, including the rapid rebuilding following the Chicago fire of 1876 and the San

Francisco earthquake of 1906. This also includes the enormous resilience of the New York City area following the 11 September 2001 terrorist attacks, where 95 percent of the businesses located in the World Trade Center area were able to relocate relatively rapidly nearby because of the large supply of excess office space (Rose, Oladosu et al. 2009). New Orleans is an excellent example of a city whose resilience was overwhelmed by a major hurricane and subsequent technological failure that resulted in massive flooding. Subsequently, however, New Orleans, which lost a large percentage of its population, perhaps permanently, has had its downtown and tourist business cores rebound because of the strong demand for goods and services produced there (Robertson 2009).

III. RESILIENCE AND SUSTAINABILITY

Several ecologists and ecological economists have linked resilience to the concept of sustainability, which refers to long-term survival at a non-decreasing quality of life. A major feature of sustainability is that it is highly dependent on natural resources, including the environment. Destroying, damaging or depleting resources undercuts our longer-term economic viability, a lesson also applicable to hazard impacts, where most analysts have omitted ecological considerations. Klein et al. (2003) note that, from an economic perspective, sustainability is a function of the degree to which key hazard impacts are anticipated. However, I agree with the position that it is also a function of a society's ability to react effectively to a crisis, and with minimal reliance on outside resources (Mileti 1999).

In the context of longer-term disasters, such as climate change, Timmerman (1981) defined resilience as the measure of a system's capacity to absorb and recover from the occurrence of a hazardous event. In the climate change context, however, most researchers now refer to this as 'adaptation' (Metz et al. 2007). Dovers and Handmer (1992) note an important feature that distinguishes man from the rest of nature in this context – human capacity for anticipating and learning. They then bifurcate resilience into reactive and proactive, where the latter is uniquely human. I maintain that proactive efforts can enhance resilience by increasing their capacity prior to a disaster, but that resilience is operative only in the response/recovery/reconstruction (often referred to as 'post-disaster') stages. Adaptability is not just applicable to long-term events, but is a major attribute of resilience to disasters. Moreover, this adaptability requires that we consider a revised equilibrium state in measuring stability and resilience. Most ecological economists view flexibility and adaptability as the essence of resilience. This makes intuitive sense for natural disasters as well, given their 'surprise' nature in terms of infrequency and large consequences.

Godschalk (2003) makes the point that 'resilient cities are constructed to be strong and flexible, rather than brittle and fragile'. It is this flexibility (adaptability) that is the key to resilience as interpreted by others (Comfort 1999; Zolli 2012). Foster (1997) interprets this in terms of coping with contingencies. He put forth 31 principles for achieving resilience, among them, in the general systems realm, such characteristics as being diverse, renewable, functionally redundant, with reserve capacity achieved through duplication, interchangeability and interconnections.

What is the relationship between resilience and sustainability? Resilience is usually used in the context of responding to specific shocks, and thus relates to short-run survival and recovery. This contributes to long-run survival, a key aspect of sustainability, along with improving the quality of life and the environment. However, the distinction is blurred in several key ways:

- Resilience in the short run can be carried over to adaptation in the long run.
- Disasters open up opportunities to rebuild and improve outcomes, including mitigating future disasters.
- Disasters provide a valuable learning experience of how to cope with extreme stress.
- Disasters provide outside economic stimulus to the affected economy through insurance and through private and public sector assistance.

IV. DEFINING ECONOMIC RESILIENCE

Previously, I defined economic resilience in a manner that builds on considerations from other disciplines but focuses on the essence of the economic problem (Rose 2004, 2009):

- *Static economic resilience*: The ability of a system to maintain function when shocked. This is the heart of the economic problem, where ordinary scarcity is made even more severe than usual, and it is imperative to use the remaining resources as efficiently as possible at any given point in time during the course of recovery.
- *Dynamic economic resilience*: Increasing the speed of recovery from a shock. This refers to the efficient utilization of resources for repair and reconstruction. Static resilience pertains to making the best of the existing capital stock (productive capacity), while this aspect is all

> about enhancing capacity. As such, it is about dynamics, in that it is time-related. Investment decisions involve diverting resources from consumption today in order to reap future gains from enhanced production.

Note that the definition is couched in terms of function, typically measured in economics as the 'flow' of goods and services, such as gross domestic product (GDP), as opposed to property damage. It is not the property (capital stock) that directly contributes to economic well-being, but rather the flows that emanate from these stocks. Two things should be kept in mind. First, while property damage takes place at a point in time, the reduced flow, often referred to as business interruption (BI), begins at the time of the disaster but continues until the system has recovered or attained a 'new normal'. Second, the recovery process, and hence the application of resilience, depends on the behavior of economic decision-makers and public policy.

Ability implies that a level of attainment will be achieved. Hence the definition is contextual: the level of function has to be compared with the level that would have existed had the ability been absent. This means that a reference point or type of worst-case outcome must be established first. Further discussion of this oft-neglected point is provided below.

Another important distinction is between 'inherent' and 'adaptive' resilience. The former refers to aspects of resilience already built into the system, such as the availability of inventories, excess capacity, input substitution, contractual arrangements accessing suppliers of goods from outside the affected area (imports), and the workings of the market system in allocating resources to their highest-value use on the basis of price signals. Adaptive resilience arises out of ingenuity under stress, such as draconian conservation otherwise not thought possible (e.g. working many weeks without heat or air conditioning), changes in the way goods and services are produced, and new contracting arrangements that match customers who have lost their suppliers with suppliers who have lost their customers.

V. QUANTIFICATION OF ECONOMIC RESILIENCE

In this section, I provide admittedly crude mathematical definitions of resilience in both static and dynamic contexts. Direct static economic resilience (DSER) refers to the level of the individual firm or industry (micro and meso levels) and corresponds to what economists refer to as 'partial equilibrium' analysis, or the operation of a business or household entity itself. Total static economic resilience (TSER) refers to the economy as a whole (macro level) and would ideally correspond to what is referred to as 'general equilibrium' analysis, which includes all the price and quantity interactions in the economy throughout its integrated supply chains (Rose 2004).

An operational measure of DSER is the extent to which the estimated direct output reduction deviates from the likely maximum potential reduction given an external shock, such as the curtailment of some or all of a critical input. In essence, DSER is the percentage avoidance of the maximum economic disruption that a particular shock could bring about. A major measurement issue is what should be used as the maximum potential disruption. For ordinary disasters, a good starting point is a linear, or proportional, relationship between an input supply shortage and the direct disruption to the firm or industry. Note that, while a linear reference point may appear to be arbitrary or a default choice, it does have an underlying rationale. A linear relationship connotes rigidity, the opposite of the 'flexibility' connotation of static resilience defined in this chapter.

Analogously, the measure of total economic resilience to input supply disruptions is the difference between a linear set of indirect effects, which implicitly omits resilience, and a non-linear outcome, which incorporates the possibility of resilience.

Also, while the entire time-path of resilience is key to the concept for many analysts, it is important to remember that this time-path is composed of a sequence of individual steps. Even if 'dynamics' are the focal point, it is important to understand the underlying process at each stage, that is, why an activity level is achieved and why that level differs from one time period to another. As presented here, static resilience helps explain the first aspect, and changes in static resilience, along with repair and reconstruction of the capital stock, help explain the second.

I illustrate the application of the definition with the following case study. Rose, Oladosu et al. (2009) found that potential business interruption losses were reduced by 72 percent from a worst-case scenario by the rapid relocation of firms in the World Trade Center area in the aftermath of the 11 September 2001 terrorist attacks. Moreover, this resilient strategy, dependent of course on excess office capacity, saved an expensive rebuilding campaign. This more intensive use of resources is also the theme of the recovery in the current great recession in the USA and other countries, as employment recovery significantly lags the recovery of output. The experience of New Orleans and New York thus signals a significant change in approaches to disaster recovery and long-run sustainability in the USA; recovery had typically emphasized prompt rebuilding. Equipped with stronger requirements for mitigation and, it is hoped, some general accumulated wisdom, the cities are recovering less by reflex action and more by intelligent planning (Vale and Campanella 2005).

Of course, what is ultimately important in the 9/11 case is that New York City, and the USA as a whole, clearly survived (Chernick 2005). Any single disaster taking place in a large, vital city is unlikely to threaten its sustainability because of its various capacities to rebound. Severe repeated disastrous events in a concentrated area have not yet been experienced, and this would open up other possibilities. This is one of the reasons that climate change is so important, in that it lays open the possibility of a greatly increasing number of short-run disasters, such as hurricanes and floods, or the likelihood of long-run disaster, such as would be caused by sea-level rise.

VI. ECONOMIC RESILIENCE OPTIONS

There are many ways to achieve and enhance economic resilience relative to the use of inputs and the production of outputs at the microeconomic level of individual firms, households or organizations. Economic resilience operates at two other levels of the economy as well: the mesoeconomic refers to economic sector, individual market or cooperative group, and the macroeconomic refers to all individual units and markets combined, including interactive effects.

At the microeconomic level, Rose (2009) has used a production function approach to identify and calibrate an extensive list of resilience 'tactics'. These include input substitution, conservation, stockpiling, excess capacity, technological change, management effectiveness and relocation. Individual businesses in relation to their supply chains are also highly resilient (Sheffi 2005). Recent disasters have caused firms to rethink strategies such as just-in-time inventories, and to focus on a broader picture, including improved emergency planning; however, they have not radically changed their way of doing business. Economies are composed of many atomistic decision-makers, and their adaptive behavior can lead to a smooth transition in the aftermath of disasters. Below we will discuss their effectiveness and cost.

Resilience at the mesoeconomic (sector or market) level includes pricing mechanisms, industry pooling of resources and information, and sector-specific types of infrastructure such as railroad tracks. What is often less appreciated by disaster researchers outside economics and closely related disciplines is the inherent resilience of market prices that act as the 'invisible hand' to guide resources to their best allocation in the aftermath of a disaster. Some pricing mechanisms have been established expressly to deal with such a situation, as in the case of non-interruptible service premia that enable customers to estimate the value of a continuous supply of electricity and to pay in advance for receiving priority service during an outage. The price mechanism is a relatively costless way of redirecting goods and services. Those price increases, to the extent that they do not reflect 'gouging', serve the useful purpose of reflecting highest-value use, even in the broader social setting. Moreover, if the allocation does violate principles of equity (fairness), the market allocations can be adjusted by income or material transfers to the needy.

At the macroeconomic level, there is a large number of interdependencies through both price and quantity interactions that influence resilience. This means that resilience in one sector can be greatly affected by activities related to or unrelated to resilience in another. This makes resilience all the more difficult to measure and to influence in the desired manner. In this context, macroeconomic resilience is not only a function of individual business or household actions, but also that of all the entities that depend on them or that they depend on directly or indirectly. There are also several other types of macro resilience. Macroeconomic structure refers to features such as economic diversity, which reduces vulnerability to overall impacts when some individual sectors are greatly affected. Geographic proximity to other economies makes it easier to import goods and receive aid from neighboring communities. Agglomeration economies refer to advantages of large city size in reducing costs of production that can remain intact and keep the city competitive after a disaster (Chernick 2005). All these forms of static resilience have dynamic counterparts as the macroeconomy changes during the reconstruction process.

The role of markets in disaster recovery is not often appreciated. Horwich (1995) and Boettke et al. (2007) have emphasized their important role in recovery following the Kobe Earthquake and Hurricane Katrina, respectively. The market has actually served as a stabilizing influence in these cases and has usually set resource allocation on the right course. This implies that there are in fact features in economies that will keep them from being entirely transformed by a disaster. A related feature is the growing use of insurance, as well as broader reinsurance markets, to spread the losses from disasters. This is yet another stabilizing influence that helps ensure survival.

Of course, many local and even regional markets are especially challenged in the aftermath of a major disaster. Some short-term centralized planning may be required. Otherwise, the major long-term role of planning applies during the course of repair and reconstruction, when a comprehensive approach may be preferred to the patchwork quilt outcome of economic decisions (Blanco et al. 2009). The planning approach in this instance has the advantage of being able to incorporate the various aspects of externalities and public goods so that the built environment is structured in society's overall best interest.

The effectiveness of various resilience tactics has been measured in several recent studies (e.g. Rose and Lim 2002; Chang and Shinozuka 2004; Rose et al. 2007; Kajitani and Tatano 2007; Rose, Oladosu et al. 2009). Many resilience tactics are low cost and some are even cost saving. Conservation often more than pays for itself, the exception being the few instances where, for example, energy-saving equipment must be purchased and where these costs cannot entirely be recouped from savings. However, the case of adaptive conservation in a crisis is likely to be a more straightforward example of doing more with less. Other tactics are relatively inexpensive. Input substitution imposes a slight cost penalty, as in most cases the substitute was not the cheapest alternative in the first place. For import substitution, the penalty may simply be additional transportation costs. Production recapture (rescheduling) requires only overtime pay for workers. Relocation costs may involve only moving costs or additional travel cost for workers; also some of the costs may be offset by lower rents in the new location, as in the case of the relocation after the 9/11 attacks. Inventories need to be built up ahead of time, but they are not actually used until after the event; hence the cost is only the opportunity cost (interest payment on the set-aside for the stockpile), rather than the value of the inventory itself.

Many of these options are much cheaper than mitigation measures, which generally require widespread interdiction or 'hardening' of many and massive targets (e.g. electric power plants, steel mills, major bridges). Moreover, a major cost advantage that resilience offers over mitigation stems from the fact that resilience is implemented after the event is known to occur, thereby allowing for fine-tuning to the type of threat and character of a particular event, rather than being a 'one-size-fits-all' approach. The major cost advantage of resilience, however, comes from the fact that it need not be implemented until the event has actually occurred. Thus the risk factor need not involve the multiplication of the benefit term by the probability of occurrence, which reduces the potential benefits in the case of mitigation for major events in the range of 10^{-2} to 10^{-3}.

One way to lower the cost of resilience, apart from mitigation, is to make it multi-purpose, so that it applies to a broad range of hazard threats. Emergency planning drills are amenable to this, as are inventory buildup and backup information technology systems.

VII. CLIMATE CHANGE: RESILIENCE AND ADAPTATION

While mitigation of the causes of climate change is the preferred approach, the reality is that some amount of climate change is inevitable given that greenhouse gases (GHGs) are 'fund' pollutants (i.e. they have long residence times in the atmosphere, and hence any emissions in a given year add to the existing concentrations). Even large cutbacks in emissions will still result in an increased atmospheric concentration of GHGs (Metz et al. 2007).

The second-best response to climate change is adaptation – actions to minimize losses for the climate change that does occur (Pacific Council on International Policy 2010). Typically, adaptation is associated with long-term, or chronic, climate change, as opposed to short-term climate variability.

There are as many adaptation strategies as there are resilience strategies, and many overlap. Examples of adaptation include the creation of drought-resistant crops, construction of seawalls, safeguards against wildfires and population migration.

We begin with the hypothesis that resilience can be thought of as a short-run version of adaptation, geared toward dealing with disasters related to climate change. However, some subtle differences arise. Building a levee or a seawall mitigates riverine floods or ocean storm surge, but is an adaptation strategy with respect to climate change. Also, if resilience refers to bouncing back, population migration is the antithesis, though there is an increasing realization that the optimal recovery from the disaster is not necessarily to return to prior population and economic levels if they are not sustainable (e.g. New Orleans following Hurricane Katrina). Still, many ways of translating resilience into sustainable practices can also extend resilience to adaptation practices (see below).

One key institution relating to both resilience and adaptation is the market. Ideally, price signals would help allocate resources efficiently. In both cases, there are likely to be severe market failures, owing to various types of damages, myopia and uncertainty. In the case of disasters, a short-term destruction of productive capacity leads to market disarray and the propensity for gouging that obscures market signals. In the case of adaptation, these signals are more likely to be obscured by lack of information and awareness of the risk.

Economists emphasize the power of the profit motive and market signals in guiding decisions toward efficient allocations of resources even in the dynamic settings applicable to sustainability. At the same time, economists are aware of market failure, especially in relation to environmental resources (see expanded discussion below). We have also long emphasized market failure in dealing with disasters, including myopia, principal–agent problems, moral hazard and so on, regarding why sufficient resources are not devoted to mitigation and why people do not purchase sufficient flood insurance (e.g. Kunreuther et al. 2013).

Equity is more complicated in the case of long-run climate change, since one needs to consider not only the fair sharing of costs and benefits within a given time period, but across generations. This dynamic, or intergenerational equity issue, is an especially thorny problem. The interest rate is a type of price that reflects the intertemporal tradeoffs in resource allocation. However, over long periods, any positive interest rate 'discounts' future generations, and if the rate is low enough or the time period long enough (e.g. in excess of 5 percent or more than 50 years), the present value discounting essentially results in stipulating that 'future generations don't count' (e.g. Brennan 1999). One solution is to preserve present value discounting but to establish a set-aside fund to enhance the capacity of future generations to adapt to climate change.

VIII. AN ECOLOGICAL ECONOMICS FRAMEWORK FOR RESILIENCE AND SUSTAINABILITY

The application of resilience to dealing with short-run aspects of climate change is at an advanced stage in some ways and in its infancy in others. Yes, we have improved our resilience capacity with respect to individual hurricanes, floods, wildfires and droughts. However, we have not necessarily witnessed the frequency and magnitude of such events that climate change portends. Nor are we adequately prepared for the simultaneous or compound events that are likely to occur in the future. And nor are we prepared for unprecedented or unknown short- and long-term events that could emanate from climate change, such as flooding in locations that have never witnessed such events before or the 'deep-freeze' prospect for Europe in case of a 'flipping' of the North Atlantic conveyer-belt.

A new framework is needed to address economic resilience in the context of this new and broad issue. In this section, we compare two approaches: environmental economics and ecological economics, and the potential for both to contribute to analyzing key issues of resilience and sustainability in the face of climate change.

Environmental economics is a traditional applied field of economics dating back to the 1960s (Tietenberg 2006). Nearly all of it has evolved out of the neoclassical economics paradigm and its standard tools. The essence is the assumption of maximizing behavior on the part of individual producers and consumers, and the substitutability among production inputs and consumer products. The profit maximization assumption also provides the basic rationale for pollution – in the absence of regulation and enforceable individual ownership rights in the environment, it is profitable to pollute (it is less costly than mitigation). The major insight from environmental economics is that the solution to the problem is to penalize pollution (e.g. a carbon tax) or to make it profitable not to pollute by giving a stake in the environment (e.g. cap-and-trade). Extensive work has been done on the design of these and other policy instruments and their macroeconomic and distributional impacts (e.g. Sterner and Coria 2012; Rose, Wei et al. 2009; Rose et al. 2012).

Environmental economists have also pioneered research on assessing environmental damage through non-market valuation (Freeman 1993). This is critical to valuing the benefits of mitigation and resilience. However, work on evaluation of ecological services lags behind, in part because of the limitations of environmental economics and also due to the complexities of the issue. Overall, environmental economics is limited because it is focused so heavily on the economy and still considers pollution a side-effect (albeit a pervasive one), and sees pollution mitigation and resilience as a diversion of resources from otherwise productive uses. Moreover, the environment itself is not typically modeled to any sophisticated degree and is simply viewed in terms of its ability to provide resources for human beings.

In contrast, ecological economics views the situation holistically. The economy and the environment are at least on par, and one apt characterization is that the economy is nestled in the womb of the biosphere. Moreover, ecological economics places great emphasis on the detailed modeling of the ecosystem itself (and its many components), as well as on the interaction of the economy and the environment. Also, ecological economics has a much broader tool-kit, in part because it is not so narrowly steeped in the neoclassical economics tradition.

The concept of resilience, as it is used in several fields, is often attributed to the ecologist Holling (1973). An extensive literature has evolved from his work in the ecological field itself and in ecological economics (e.g. Perrings 2001; Folke 2006; Folke et al. 2010). Most of the work is applied to the resilience of the ecosystem in general or various natural ecosystems in particular. However, an increasing amount of research is focused on an application of ecological principles to disasters (e.g. Carpenter et al. 2012), though, interestingly, this research has minimal overlap or even reference to the work of the natural disaster research community (e.g. Mileti 1999).

More recent research has extended ecological economics principles to the operation and survival of individual firms in terms of their richness of functions and response (Garmestani 2006). This work is very valuable in that it identifies factors that help firms survive. More detailed work on the effectiveness of resilience in relation to disasters has been undertaken by Rose (2009), Rose and Krausmann (2013) and Rose and Tierney (2013). Zolli (2012) has recently identified a major difference between resilience and sustainability that is especially important in relation to cities and climate change. He sees resilience focusing on disequilibrium situations and stability, in contrast to sustainability's focus on equilibrium paths. He points to the need for a reorientation of urban infrastructure, designed to be less brittle and more robust, and overall more flexible so as to be able to rebound. The author points out that many practices promoting sustainability do not necessarily promote resilience. A key example is new energy-efficient buildings, which include systems that promote longevity but not necessarily the ability to withstand or rebound from shocks.

Zolli (2012) also points to the importance of ecosystems in our future ability to deal with disasters to humankind. He points to the fact that the extensive flooding associated with Hurricane Katrina was due in part to deterioration of wetlands to the south and east of the city. These natural barriers were destroyed by human development, and this is just one of many examples of so-called progress neither being sustainable nor resilient.

Various points discussed in this section all help lead to the conclusion that a broad, holistic framework is needed to truly address both resilience and sustainability in urban areas. Although cities are not typically characterized in relation to natural ecosystems, the New Orleans/wetlands example demonstrates the connection, as would the small ponds in cities that would be breeding grounds of vectors carrying West Nile virus or other dread diseases migrating northward. Environmental economics is likely to be very useful for analyzing the operation of an individual firm or market. It is also very useful in designing policy instruments. However, the broader ecological economics framework is far superior otherwise. This is due not only to its broader set of methodologies and greater inclusiveness, but also to its greater ability to address key issues of resilience and sustainability.

Cities, and many of their major components, such as transportation, are complex systems, and no single discipline can do them justice. Complexity analysis in economics comes in many forms, but one is general equilibrium analysis, which examines the interactions in the economy as a whole through the working of markets. One empirical approach is computable general equilibrium analysis (CGE), which characterizes the economy as a set of integrated supply chains (Sue Wing 2011). Advances have been made to incorporate shocks into the system in the form of disequilibria (Rose et al. 2007). Resilience has been incorporated effectively into these models as well, primarily through parameter changes reflecting adaptive behavior (Rose and Liao 2005). Moreover, general equilibrium approaches have even been extended to pure ecosystems, including the calculation of equilibrium nutritional values (Finnoff and Tschirhart 2007).

Any approach to economics would be well placed to integrate with other fields, especially those that are holistic, such as planning. Godschalk (2003) and others have analyzed resilience in this vein, but there is still much more work to be done. Recent research on community resilience has also extended the boundaries to psychology and sociology (Norris et al. 2008; Cutter et al. 2010). A truly comprehensive, interdisciplinary approach is still far in the future, however.

IX. CONCLUSION

I conclude by first offering a broader definition of economic resilience that is intended to promote sustainability:

> The process by which businesses and households within a community develop and efficiently implement their capacity to absorb an initial shock through mitigation and respond and adapt afterward so as to maintain function and hasten recovery, as well as to be in a better position to reduce losses from future disasters.

Cities can be made less vulnerable to disasters through decentralization of key infrastructure services, reduction of transportation bottlenecks and more rapid emergency response systems. They can more readily bounce back from a disaster if they incorporate flexibility into their overall and infrastructure design, have back-up systems and alternative business locations in place, broaden their supply chains and maintain their internal and adjacent natural ecosystems. A key strategy is to translate ingenuity in coping with disasters in the short run into long-run decisions and practices that continuously promote sustainability. Resilience tactics to address resource shortages, such as conservation, input substitution and technology modification, can be further refined for long-run application. Disasters can also provide opportunities for transitions to more sustainable paths in the reconstruction process through revised land-use planning, downsizing and industrial targeting, in addition to enhanced structural mitigation.

Resilience offers many important lessons for sustainability. As noted by Zolli (2012), it places greater emphasis on flexibility and responding effectively to disequilibria, as opposed to smooth equilibrium time-paths. At the same time, resilience and its sustainability counterpart – adaptation – do not mean that we are giving up on sustainability or denigrating mitigation of short-run and long-run challenges, such as climate change. It simply means we are taking a more pragmatic approach to inevitable crises.

Following are some guideposts for implementing resilience in the short term and transforming it into capacity that will promote sustainability in the long term:

- Identify effective resilience tactics at the micro, meso and macro levels based on actual experience. For example, ingenuity in conserving or substituting for critical resources under extreme stress should be examined for their more permanent potential under normal conditions.
- Develop resilience indicators based on evidence of successful practices to monitor progress on resilience capacity. Even though disasters may be sporadic, the need to develop ways to mute their negative impacts should be a continuous process.
- Disseminate findings on best-practice resilience tactics and community response. Likewise, the continuous dissemination of information about resilience helps make it ingrained in daily life.
- Evaluate the cost-effectiveness of resilience. This helps ensure that resilience will be implemented as efficiently as possible, thereby helping to remain on or return to a sustainable path.
- Analyze the strategic tradeoffs between mitigation and resilience in terms of cost-effectiveness. Resilience should not be assessed in isolation from other major strategies, and that assessment should be done in terms of their ability to cope with short-run crises and to contribute to long-run sustainability.
- Identify ways to make resilience in the face of crises enduring, so as not to repeat previous mistakes. A good institutional memory contributes to both resilience and sustainability.
- Identify ways to transform short-run resilience responses into sustainability strategies. The view of resilience should go beyond consideration of individual tactics and should be evaluated in terms of broader community strategies that capture synergies.
- Steer the economy and related systems to greater flexibility in terms of resource provision and utilization. A key attribute of residence is flexibility, and ways need to be found to take advantage of this attribute, by broadening the array of sustainable future paths.

Although the world has witnessed a large number of major disasters in recent years, only those related to nuclear contamination seem to have threatened the survival of the host region (e.g. Chernobyl and Fukushima). Improvements in conditions underlying sustainability have helped in this regard, as has inherent and adaptive resilience associated with disaster recovery. Sharp breaks from the past do not appear to be the norm, but opportunities for major transitions that promote sustainability do increase in the aftermath of disasters. Climate change poses unprecedented challenges in this respect, however, because of its likely continuous and accelerating pace.

REFERENCES

Blanco, H., M. Alberti, R. Olshansky, S. Chang, S.M. Wheeler, J. Randolph, J.B. London, J.B. Hollander, K.M. Pallagst, T. Schwarz, F.J. Popper, S. Parnell, E. Pieterse and V. Watson (2009), 'Shaken, shrinking, hot, impoverished and informal: emerging research agendas in planning', *Progress in Planning*, **72** (4), 195–250.

Boettke, P., E. Chamlee-Wright, P. Gordon, S. Ikeda, P. Leson and R. Sobel (2007), 'Political, economic and social aspects of Katrina', *Southern Economic Journal*, **74** (2), 363–76.

Brennan, Timothy J. (1999), 'Discounting the future: economics and ethics', in Wallace E. Oates (ed.), *The RFF Reader in Environmental and Resource Policy*, Washington, DC: Resources for the Future.

Carpenter, S.R., K.J. Arrow, S. Barrett, R. Biggs, W.A. Brock, A. Crépin, G. Engström, C. Folke, T.P. Hughes, N. Kautsky, C. Li, G. McCarney, K. Meng, K. Mäler, S. Polasky, M. Scheffer, J. Shogren, T. Sterner, J.R. Vincent, B. Walker, A. Xepapadeas and A. de Zeeuw (2012), 'General resilience to cope with extreme events', *Sustainability*, **4** (12), 3248–59.

Chang, S. and M. Shinozuka (2004), 'Measuring and improving the disaster resilience of communities', *Earthquake Spectra*, **20** (3) 739–55.

Chernick, Howard (ed.) (2005), *Resilient City: The Economic Impact of 9/11*, New York: Russell Sage Foundation.

Comfort, Louise K. (1999), *Shared Risk: Complex Seismic Response*, New York: Pergamon.

Cutter, S.L., C.G. Burton and C.T. Emrich (2010), 'Disaster resilience indicators for benchmarking baseline conditions', *Journal of Homeland Security and Emergency Management*, **7** (1), Article 51.

Dovers, R. and J. Handmer (1992), 'Uncertainty, sustainability and change', *Global Environmental Change*, **2** (4), 262–76.

Finnoff, D. and J. Tschirhart (2007), 'Linking dynamic economic and ecological general equilibrium models', *Resource and Energy Economics*, **30** (2), 91–114.

Folke, C. (2006), 'Resilience: the emergence of a perspective for social–ecological systems analyses', *Global Environmental Change*, **16** (3), 253–67.

Folke, C., S.R. Carpenter, B. Walker, M. Scheffer, T. Chapin and J. Rockström (2010), 'Resilience thinking: integrating resilience, adaptability and transformability', *Ecology and Society*, **15** (4), 20.

Foster, Harold D. (1997), *The Ozymandias Principles: Thirty-one Strategies for Surviving Change*, Victoria, BC: UBC Press.

Freeman, A. Myrick (1993), *The Measurement of Environmental and Resource Values*, Washington, DC: Resources for the Future.

Garmestani, A.S., C.R. Allen, J.D. Mittelstaedt, C. Stow and W. Ward (2006), 'Firm size diversity, functional richness, and resilience', *Environment and Development Economics*, **11** (4), 533–51.

Godschalk, D. (2003), 'Urban hazard mitigation: creating resilient cities', *Natural Hazards Review*, **4** (3), 136–43.

Horwich, G. (1995), 'Economic lessons of the Kobe earthquake', *Economic Development and Cultural Change*, **48** (3), 521–42.

Holling, C. (1973), 'Resilience and stability of ecological systems', *Annual Review of Ecology and Systematics*, **4**, 1–23.

Kajitani, Y. and H. Tatano (2007), 'Estimation of lifeline resilience factors based on empirical surveys of Japanese industries', *Earthquake Spectra*, **25** (4), 755–76.

Klein, R.J.T., R.J. Nicholls and F. Thomalla (2003), 'Resilience to natural hazards: how useful is this concept?', *Environmental Hazards*, **5** (1–2), 35–45.

Kunreuther, Howard C., Mark V. Pauly and Stacey McMorrow (2013), *Insurance and Behavioral Economics: Improving Decisions in the Most Misunderstood Industry*, New York: Cambridge University Press.

Metz, B., O.R. Davidson, P.R. Bosch, R. Dave and L.A. Meyer (eds) (2007), *Climate Change 2007: Mitigation of Climate Change. Contribution of Working Group III to the Fourth Assessment Report of the Intergovernmental Panel on Climate Change*, Cambridge, UK and New York: Cambridge University Press.

Mileti, Dennis (1999), *Disasters by Design: A Reassessment of Natural Hazards in the United States*, Washington, DC: Joseph Henry Press.

Norris, F.H., S.P. Stevens, B. Pfefferbaum, K.F. Wyche and R.F. Pfefferbaum (2008), 'Community resilience as a metaphor, theory, set of capacities and strategy for disaster readiness', *American Journal of Community Psychology*, **41** (1–2), 127–50.

Pacific Council on International Policy (2010), *Preparing for the Effects of Climate Change – A Strategy for California: A Report of the California Adaptation Advisory Panel to the State of California*, Los Angeles, CA: Pacific Council on International Policy.

Perrings, Charles (2001), 'Resilience and sustainability', in Henk Folmer, H. Landis Gabel, Shelby Gerking and Adam Rose (eds), *Frontiers of Environmental Economics*, Cheltenham, UK and Northampton, MA, USA: Edward Elgar Publishing, pp. 319–41.

Robertson, C. (2009), 'In New Orleans, recovery is not enough', *New York Times*, available at http://www.nytimes.com/2009/08/31/us/31orleans.html (published online 30 August 2009).

Rose, A. (2004), 'Defining and measuring economic resilience to disasters', *Disaster Prevention and Management*, **13** (4), 307–14.

Rose, A. (2009), *Economic Resilience to Disasters (Report No. 8)*, Oak Ridge, TN: Community and Regional Resilience Institute.

Rose, A. and E. Krausmann (2013), 'Disaster resilience indicators: a critique and operational framework', *International Journal of Disaster Risk Analysis*, **5**, 73–83.

Rose, A. and S. Liao (2005), 'Modeling resilience to disasters: computable general equilibrium analysis of a water service disruption', *Journal of Regional Science*, **45** (1), 75–112.

Rose, A. and D. Lim (2002), 'Business interruption losses from natural hazards: conceptual and methodological issues in the case of the Northridge earthquake', *Environmental Hazards: Human and Social Dimensions*, **4** (1), 1–14.

Rose, A. and K. Tierney (2013), 'An integrated methodology for analyzing dynamic economic resilience', Proposal to the US National Science Foundation, February.

Rose, A., G. Oladosu and S. Liao (2007), 'Business interruption impacts of a terrorist attack on the electric power system of Los Angeles: customer resilience to a total blackout', *Risk Analysis*, **27** (3), 513–31.

Rose, A., D. Wei and F. Prager (2012), 'Distributional impacts of greenhouse gas emissions trading: alternative allocation and recycling strategies in California', *Contemporary Economic Policy*, **30** (4), 603–17.

Rose, A., G. Oladosu, B. Lee and G. Beeler-Asay (2009), 'The economic impacts of the 2001 terrorist attacks on the World Trade Center: a computable general equilibrium analysis', *Peace Economics, Peace Science, and Public Policy*, **15** (2), Article 4.

Rose, A., D. Wei, J. Wennberg and T. Peterson (2009), 'Climate change policy formation in Michigan: the case integrated regional policies', *International Regional Science Review*, **32** (4), 445–65.

Sheffi, Yossi (2005), *The Resilient Enterprise: Overcoming Vulnerability for Competitive Advantage*, Cambridge, MA: The MIT Press.

Sterner, T. and J. Coria (2012), *Policy Instruments for Environmental and Natural Resource Management*, New York: RFF Press.

Sue Wing, Ian (2011), 'Computable general equilibrium models for the analysis of economy–environment interactions', in Amitrajeet A. Batabyal and Peter Nijkamp (eds), *Research Tools in Natural Resource and Environmental Economics*, Toh Tuck Link, SG, Hackensack, NJ and London: World Scientific Publishing, pp. 205–306.

Tietenberg, Tom (2006), *Environmental and Natural Resource Economics*, 7th edn, Boston, MA: Pearson.

Timmerman, P. (1981), 'Vulnerability, resilience and the collapse of society: a review of models and possible climatic applications', *Journal of Climatology*, **1** (4), 396–438.

Vale, Lawrence J. and Thomas J. Campanella (2005), *The Resilient City: How Modern Cities Recover from Disaster*, New York: Oxford University Press.

Zolli, A. (2012), 'Learning to bounce back', *New York Times*, available at http://www.nytimes.com/2012/11/03/opinion/forget-sustainability-its-about-resilience.html?pagewanted=all&_r=0 (3 November 2012).

18. A systems approach towards sustainable procurement

Laurie Kaye Nijaki

Cities, like any large organization, require considerable and varied arrays of goods and services in order to meet the needs of constituents. At the most simplistic level, agencies spanning geographic scopes, from local agencies such as city and county governments to state and national-scale departments, all procure goods and services to serve the internal day-to-day function of the organization itself. Cities procure products such as janitorial products to clean facilities in which such public agencies operate. In other cases, public agencies procure services that impact the public economic and environmental sphere directly and are drawn from beyond their 'in-house' resources such as contracting private builders to construct public works projects. In doing so, they must weigh options between particular goods and services. As noted by the National Association of State Procurement Officials (2008), for example, 'the primary role of public procurement is to obtain quality goods and services to support an effective and efficient government'. The necessary functions of the city are supported through this process (Coe 1989; Murray 2007; New Economic Foundation 2005). In fact, procurement has been portrayed by scholars such as Thai (2001) as one of four major economic activities undertaken by government – including providing a legal framework, redistribution of income through taxation and spending, and the provision of public goods. This operation is, in theory, thus designed to produce public and commons goods to constituencies in the form of everything from enforcement of zoning decisions to the administration of parking permits.

Procurement decisions are not made in a vacuum. As market actors, city and regional governments can make considerable impacts on economic development and growth opportunities through the goods and services that they procure. Similarly, the goods and services that cities acquire undoubtedly have significant environmental impacts; such impacts can vary as cities pick and choose within a universe of potential goods and services. This chapter examines the potential role of government procurement in fostering sustainability goals at the city-based and regional level. Procurement is one potential policy tool towards attaining sustainable development goals. Seeking to achieve 'triple-bottom-line' results, the chapter examines how government procurement can be re-imagined in order to address sustainability considerations at the local and regional level. First, I discuss the municipal procurement process. Strategies going beyond 'lowest cost', as characterized by the relevant sustainability value, are explored. Second, I discuss how sustainability values can be integrated into the municipal procurement process. Through this approach, previously siloed procurement strategies based upon singular values can be merged together to achieve 'triple-bottom-line' solutions indicative of the full array of sustainability values. Through this approach multifaceted goals such as green jobs development can be bolstered, using sustainable procurement as a central tool within the broader toolbox explored throughout the chapter.

1. VALUES AND GOALS OF GOVERNMENT PROCUREMENT

Dating as far back as biblical time, public entities have procured goods and services. Much more recently, in the USA and Europe, procurement has long existed in its own right and has been used as a tool for social outcomes. In the 1880s, Oklahoma (a territory at the time) created a central purchasing board responsible for procurement of all goods for state agencies. Following suit, cities such as Chicago, Cleveland, New York and Los Angeles centralized purchasing throughout the nineteenth and twentieth centuries. The Uniform Commercial Code, created in 1951, standardized purchasing and was subsequently adopted by almost all states. Most recently, the American Bar Association created the first *Model Procurement Code*, which was updated in 2000 and is now known as *The 2000 Model Procurement Code for State and Local Governments* (Thai 2001).

Procurement is a complex process of weighing and evaluating options. Central to procurement as a municipal function is the question: how can and should cities evaluate potential goods and services? Traditionally, procurement has been undertaken at the lowest-cost basis (Murray 2009a; 2009b). In doing so, cities have aimed to acquire goods and services in the most economically efficient manner. At the start of this process, cities release a request for proposal for private contractors. They receive responses to their requests, often referred to as 'bids', from interested contractors. The city is often legally required to choose the lowest-cost bid; the city thus selects the contract that provides the good or service for the lowest price. Drawing on this definition of optimal, scholars have defined the act of procurement itself as the effort to 'obtain the most appropriate and highest quality good or service for the least cost' (McCue and

Gianakis 2001). Requests for proposals for goods and services are thus evaluated in order to acquire the desired good or service in the cheapest manner possible, thus saving the municipality money and bolstering its bottom line. Additionally, such procurement strategies have historically been driven by the need to provide regularity and transparency within the procurement process. City officials are thus required to evaluate different bids in a manner that is easy to describe, translate and defend. Through a lowest-cost approach, differences in goods can be evaluated and compared across a relatively simplistic and easily defensible methodology. Political feasibility is enhanced through the increased transparency engendered by the process. In the end, the process is kept a competitive one and contractor decisions are easily explainable by city staff facing outside challenges to their contractor decision.

Particularly in the current tight budget environment facing many municipalities, bolstering bottom lines is a laudable end. Nevertheless, saving money may not always be the singularly sought-after end for municipal decision-making. As reflected by this volume in aggregate, sustainability has increasingly been integrated into the local policy and planning context as a desired municipal goal (Jepson 2004; Wissenburg 2006; Zeemering 2009; Portney 2003; Berke and Conroy 2000). In its most simplistic terms, sustainability is often defined as incorporative of environmental, economic, and equity goals and values (Campbell 1996). How can procurement be altered in order to consider diverse values, and to bolster local quality-of-life benefits indicative of sustainability? Many cities actively seek to go beyond cost-effectiveness considerations in developing procurement policies; sustainability values can be utilized to frame such approaches. Seeking to characterize municipal strategies along sustainability values, this chapter briefly describes the way in which procurement policies have thus far integrated an increasingly diverse array of values going beyond the 'cost-efficient' or 'cost-effective' solution.

What sustainability values are frequently integrated into a city's decision-making criteria? Domestically, the integration of such values can conceptually fall within three broad and dichotomously realized values broadly related to sustainability, as summarized in Table 18.1. First, cities integrate economic development goals into procurement practices through the institution of buy-local campaigns. Adding distributional considerations into the economic development equation, equity-driven values are layered onto the procurement process through the integration of targeted procurement policies such as women and minority business requirements. Third, environmental considerations are integrated into procurement decisions by developing environmentally preferable procurement policies that seek to consider the environmental impacts of procurement decisions. Such

Table 18.1 Integration of sustainability values into procurement

Sustainability value:	Environment	Economic development	Equity
Procurement program type	Environmentally preferable procurement policies Recycled content programs	Buy-local programs	Minority and business requirements Programs for businesses with lower total costs of ownership Worker health and safety requirements
Example of implemented policies	City of Seattle: products meeting EPA comprehensive guidelines for post-consumer recycled content given 10% price preference. Lower toxic alternatives given 10% price preference (City of Seattle 2002; 2003)	City of Santa Monica: 1% preference for businesses located within the City Santa Monica (City of Santa Monica n.d.). City of San Jose: 5% bud preference for local business enterprises (City of San Jose 2004; 2011)	City of Portland: reorients procurement framework to focus on the 'greatest common good'. Provides training and workshops for minority women and emerging small businesses (Culver 2008)
Key implementation difficulties	Training staff to use new, less harmful products. Lacking scientific expertise to evaluate products. Complexity in determining green products Absorbing higher costs for the 'greener' alternatives	Ensuring competitiveness and transparency Supporting viable industries and ensuring economic compatibility in targeted industries	Ensuring competitiveness and transparency Supporting viable industries and ensuring economic compatibility in targeted industries Outreach to businesses and ensuring that the right businesses are able to access the process

Source: Adapted from Nijaki and Worrel (2012).

approaches, largely instituted in isolation from one another, are pursued by a range of cities from San Francisco to New York in their concerted attempts to revamp the range of values germane to the procurement process.

Procuring Economic Development Benefits

As cities reflect on their role in society, economic development considerations are increasingly layered onto the procurement process (Murray 2009a; 2009b) through the implementation of 'buy-local' campaigns. Such campaigns target local benefits from government procurement by giving preferences to locally sourced goods or services. Such approaches aim to bolster the economic opportunities within a defined geographic scope by fostering local business opportunities directly with the municipality. Through this approach, the municipality utilizes its own market-generating power to create growth opportunities for local businesses.

Spurring innovation is seen as a potential output of the process. Specifically, there is some evidence that procurement can be used as a tool for innovation in order to 'jumpstart' the wider availability of a desired commodity. Hemenway (1989) describes the origin of vehicular airbags as a standard commodity in autos sold to the general public. The federal government was the first entity to produce a demand large enough to spur the large-scale installation of this relatively new feature in vehicles purchased for public use in the 1980s, and, as such, sparked the widespread use of airbags. Hemenway (1989) notes that this is a public health victory, and says, 'Government purchasing power can be used to provide consumer information and to stimulate the production of beneficial commodities.' The authors support Hemenway's position two decades later, in their study of the innovation generated from this approach. In their study of over 1000 firms and 25 federations, over 50 percent of respondents pointed to demand as the main driver of innovation. By contrast, only 12 percent of firms said that entrepreneurship was engendered from new technologies within the company.

Many sub-national-scale governments are integrating buy-local approaches into their procurement practices. Qiao et al.'s survey in 2007 indicated that 26 states operated preferences for in-state bidders. More recently, the Institute for Local Self Reliance conducted a survey at the city-based level in 2011 (see Shahan 2011). It identified 140 cities with buy-local policies. Many of these policies create bid preferences for locally produced goods and services. For example, the City of New York operates a bid preference for local businesses aimed at local economic development goals (City of New York 2007). Multnomah County and the City of

Portland procure 45 percent of their county's produce from local sources (Portland Multnomah County 2005).

With a focus on innovation and business growth, the effort to implement buy-local campaigns has been supported by grassroots efforts within the sustainable business communities. The Business Alliance for Local Living Economies (BALLE) epitomizes advocacy in this realm. BALLE provides an advocacy and information exchange network of related locally sourced programs. Local chapters seek to develop local procurement policies in a strategy geared to provide local economic development opportunities. As noted by BALLE (n.d):

> One of the greatest things an individual can do to support his or her local community is to patronize its locally owned businesses. Compared to their national competitors, local independent businesses recycle more money back into the local economy and give greater support to a community's nonprofit and civic needs. They are better positioned to respond to the special needs of the community, and they are more tied to the community's future. Additionally, unlike a homogenized Anyplace, USA, a community with vibrant independent businesses retains its unique character as a great place to live and visit. In promoting a Local First campaign, a community supports a thriving local economy and its way of life.

As a national umbrella organization, BALLE offers local chapters a range of technical resources, including a 'leakage calculator' whereby they can measure economic linkage attributable to purchasing beyond municipal boundaries. Chapters often work collaboratively across small-scale sustainable businesses located in a particular area.

Procuring Equity and Social Justice Outcomes

Seeking to integrate equity considerations into the equation, economic opportunities can be further targeted at particular populations. Government agencies in the twentieth century in the USA and UK, for example, often focused on implementing fair wages and work hours for laborers, along with relieving unemployment through public works projects (McCrudden 2004). McCrudden goes so far as to say that the development of procurement grew up with and was used to achieve the goals of the welfare state. Policies such as Martin Van Buren's ten-hour workday requirement for government-contracted workers promoted fair labor practices. US twentieth-century policy promoted employment for the disabled through government contracts. The 1938 Wagner–O'Day Act encouraged employment of the blind under contracts with nonprofit organizations. Decades later, the Wagner–O'Day act expanded its purview to include 'other severely handicapped'. During the First World War, the federal government used contracting first to support disabled veterans, then later to support other disabled persons. The Great Depression and the Second World War introduced an unprecedented use of government procurement policies (mainly through labor contracting) to resolve widespread unemployment and poverty in the USA. For example, the 1931 Bacon–Davis Act required the government to pay local prevailing wages, effectively implementing a minimum wage based on the local jurisdiction (McCrudden 2004). The trend of government procurement for social ends continued into the late twentieth century, evolving into the use of affirmative action to promote racial equality in the workplace. The Public Works Act of 1977 required that a proportion of federal government contracts be given to black-owned businesses, and that 10 percent of local work grants be given to minority business enterprises. This trend towards anti-discrimination policy, enforced partly through procurement, also spread to other countries such as Canada, the UK and many nations previously colonized by European countries (McCrudden 2004).

Today, as the most popular expression of this, many cities integrate equity considerations into municipal procurement practices. Common categories of targeted 'business types' include small businesses, minority-owned businesses, and women-owned businesses. Small businesses are targeted for growth in order to jumpstart economic opportunities. In some cases, equity considerations are layered onto a buy-local approach. For example, the City of San Jose maintains a 5 percent bid preference for local business enterprises that is increased if the business entity is also a small business (City of San Jose 2004). Social justice considerations are more directly addressed through minority and women-owned business procurement programs. Popularly, minority and women-owned business preferences are sometimes required as a part of the municipal bidding process. Contractors often must seek subcontractors meeting this requirement in order to successfully bid for contracts. Cities utilize the point system within the request for proposal process to give preferences to minority and women business owners. In addition to bid preferences, bureaucratic assistance is likewise used as a strategy. The City of Portland, for example, provides training and workshops for minority and/or women-owned businesses (Culver 2008).

Procuring Environmental Benefits

Cities infuse environmental considerations into their procurement decisions through the integration of 'environmentally preferable procurement' or 'green purchasing' strategies. Most efforts towards integrating environmental considerations into procurement processes emerged following the

2002 World Summit on Sustainable Development (Preuss 2007; Murray 2001; Preuss 2009; Walker and Brammer 2009). The federal government defines environmentally preferable products and services as having 'a lesser or reduced effect on human health and the environment when compared with competing products or services that serve the same purpose. This comparison may consider raw materials acquisition, production, manufacturing, packaging, distribution, reuse, operation, maintenance or disposal of the product or service.' Cities integrate environmentally preferable procurement programs, polices, ordinances and green business certification programs as a mechanism to identify and then procure goods with smaller environmental impacts. Such strategies aim to integrate a variety of environmental considerations into procurement valuations, and provide opportunities for cities to purchase higher-priced goods because of their smaller environmental impacts. As noted by the EPA, 'Environmentally Preferable Purchasing (EPP) helps the federal government "buy green," and in doing so, uses the federal government's enormous buying power to stimulate market demand for green products and services'. Institutionally, environmental considerations can be integrated into day-to-day government operations. As advocated by the EPA, 'environmental considerations should become a normal purchasing practice, consistent with such traditional factors as product safety, price, performance, and availability' (US EPA 2000, p. 4).

Environmental attributes are multiple and complex. Increasingly cities and states are looking towards the integration of multiple metrics of environmental attributes. Towards that end, the federal EPA has been working with local entities to encourage the use of multiple metrics. They note:

> As federal, state, and local government definitions suggest, EPP involves examining the multiple environmental impacts of products or services throughout their life cycles, from resource extraction to ultimate disposal. While examining a single environmental attribute such as recycled content or energy efficiency is important when making purchasing decisions, EPP promotes the examination of multiple environmental attributes such as recycled content *and* energy efficiency *and* toxicity. An increasing number of state and local governments are adopting EPP definitions that embrace the multiple attribute concept. In practice, however, many of them continue to emphasize single environmental attributes, particularly recycled content. (Ibid.)

Providing the potential range of metrics, the federal government defines a variety of potential environmental attributes that can be the focus of a municipal procurement policy, including: energy efficiency; recycled content; recyclability; water efficiency; resource conservation; greenhouse gas emissions; waste prevention; renewable material percentages; adverse effects to workers, animals, plants, air, water and soil; toxic material content; packaging; and transportation. Moving away from traditional programs focused on recycled content, cities can seek to integrate environmentally preferable procurement across different combinations of such metrics.

2. SYSTEMS-BASED SUSTAINABLE PROCUREMENT

The preceding section sought to provide a more nuanced view of values that should be integrated into the procurement process, conceptualized along sustainability values. Moving beyond internal values such as cost-effectiveness, cities have integrated additional societal values into their procurement decision-making. How are diverse values in the procurement process being implemented by cities aiming to provide public goods through their purchasing strategies? As noted above, integration of such complex and textured goals within the procurement process has largely been incorporated in isolated tracks. Even when cities engage in a range of such policies, implementation tends to be siloed. San Jose provides such an example. San Jose maintains an environmentally preferable procurement policy. Through this policy, the city incentivizes services and products that reduce toxicity; conserve natural resources, material and energy; and maximize recyclable content. San Jose has a social-justice-oriented procurement policy. The city grants up to a 5 percent bid preference to minority-owned and women-owned businesses. San Jose has a buy-local policy. The city instituted a local preference policy that gives a 5 percent bid preference for local business enterprises and additional preference to local businesses that are also small businesses. However, such policies are largely disconnected from one another. Thus cities have tended to engage singularly in procurement for equity, procurement for economic development outcomes, or procurement for the environment. There is no coherence between such policies that might effectively create green jobs and incorporate the values of sustainability through a systematic approach leading to 'triple-bottom-line' ends.

The integration of such values individually is simply not enough to achieve truly sustainable outcomes. Sustainability necessitates the integration of environmental, economic and equity-driven values into the procurement process. Doing so may, in fact, call for a true systems thinking approach outlined in this book's introduction. Specifically, how can procurement reflect such integrated values within the sustainable city through systems thinking? As cities move towards sustainability goals, there is a need to consider how procurement can be altered within a burgeoning sustainable vision that symbiotically bolsters these disparate values. As municipalities' behavior is increasingly evaluated as a part of sustainability planning and climate action planning, a city's consumption behavior is perhaps the most obvious place to institute change and to look for leadership. This section will create a framework for sustainable procurement for the sustainable city. How can municipal procurement be utilized as a key component of a sustainability strategy? In concert with the 'three Es' of sustainability, such a sustainable and systems-driven approach will link equity, environmental and economic goals together. And in fact, within the move towards sustainability, procurement can be specifically utilized as a tool towards the creation of green jobs. Similar more systematic approaches are beginning to infiltrate the municipal discourse. As perhaps the best example of this, Portland and Multnomah County (2002) developed what they term a 'sustainable procurement strategy'. They imply a more systemic approach towards procurement through the text, noting at the outset:

> Prompted by a need to cut costs or by a desire to respond to community concerns or external political forces, public and private organizations are increasingly driven to evaluate the environmental, social, and economic impacts of the purchases they make. Local government, in particular, is expected to make purchasing decisions that support publicly stated values.
>
> Sustainable procurement is the process of integrating these environmental, social, and economic factors into purchasing decisions. This strategy provides a blueprint to implement sustainable procurement at the City of Portland and Multnomah County. It will move local government beyond the current state of ad hoc, often contradictory, inconsistently applied policies. It will move local government toward purchasing decisions that promote the long-term interests of the community.

Drawing on these sentiments, this chapter aims to provide an applied approach for integrating procurement into a comprehensive sustainable procurement strategy. And, through such an approach, the chapter seeks to reconceptualize sustainable procurement as a sustainable economic development or green jobs strategy.

In developing such an approach, this section will investigate the challenges that exist in devising and subsequently implementing procurement policies. Challenges are multiple. As discussed in detail below, a variety of governance challenges may persist in implementing sustainability procurement policies. By moving away from a lowest-cost basis decision-making metric, difficulties may persist in ensuring fairness and transparency in the process. Integrating such an approach into a city's current policy-making structure is likewise difficult. For example, procurement decisions are often made by general services departments and implemented without economic development and/or environmental focuses. Expertise from both departments organized around environmental preservation and departments organized around economic development is needed in order to craft strategies responsive to the full array of sustainability values. Second, challenges abound in evaluating the environmental impacts of products. Considering complex calculations such as life-cycle costs of products, ensuring that the products are rigorously evaluated for environmental impacts, presents a host of challenges.

As is often true in the context of sustainability strategies more broadly (Gunder 2006; Hemple 2009), implementing and operationalizing sustainable procurement is fraught with difficulties and ambiguities, as well as possibilities to bolster quality of life in communities. How can cities integrate economic development tools and lenses in considering what goods and services to procure, and then use procurement as a mechanism to begin to develop a market for green goods and services at the localized level? The implementation process for such an approach can broadly consist of implementation through a number of conceptual stages. First, each municipality must identify appropriate products purchased by the public sector in substantial volume that can reasonably be expected to be both produced locally and produced in an environmentally friendly manner. Second, cities can develop coherent and comprehensive strategies for policy implementation that incorporate an array of linked policies for green jobs growth. Fostering difficult connections, this section discusses how procurement can be linked with other policy mechanisms in a coherent manner in order to produce opportunities in the green economy. Third, cities must implement such approaches by tackling a range of governance challenges. They can seek to develop partnerships in the implementation of sustainable procurement strategies. Each of these topics will be discussed in some detail below; together they can compose a systematic green economy action based on systematic thinking around sustainable economic development.

Systems Thinking around Sustainable Procurement Product Identification

The first step in developing an implementation plan for sustainable procurement is to identify potential product categories that could be purchased by the public sector in substantial volume through a sustainable procurement strategy. Identified products should be reasonably expected to have the economic development potential to be produced locally. At the same time, they should enhance a city's environmental performance enough to be identified as a green good or service. Thus products must simultaneously fit the requirements of a buy-local program and an environmentally preferable program. How can particular opportunities be identified in terms of targeted product and service types, and their related industries and occupations? Where might the city have comparable/competitive advantage in the green economy? Making sure that there are linkages with economic realities underlies a comprehensive approach towards procurement. Broadly speaking, analysis can be undertaken on three related tracks: an economic development analysis; a policy analysis; and a stakeholder analysis.

First, conducting economic development analysis may be helpful in the development of a green jobs strategy centered on sustainable procurement for municipalities and corollary regions. The green economy is not a singular industry sector and incorporates a wide array of potential industries and occupations. Not all cities are equally suited for the same version of green jobs growth. A comprehensive sustainable procurement policy should target those areas that make economic development sense for the locale. To that end, the question of product selection for municipal procurement is ultimately a question of economic development, and should draw from traditional approaches to local economic development. Cluster analysis broadly around the green economy may provide an avenue for analysis. Location quotients, whereby the concentration of economic activity within particular sectors is based upon particular industries and occupations, may indicate areas of opportunity (Blakely and Leigh 2010). Comprehensive economic development analysis, moreover, is critical to ensure that the municipal government is not the only source of demand for selected green goods and services. Demand for green goods and services targeted through a sustainable economic development approach should also be engendered from the private sector. This will increase the size of the market and lend consistency to business opportunities regardless of changing politics within the municipality.

Second, locating areas of opportunity is linked to the policy direction at both the local and national level. Although green economic development is closely married to the mechanisms of economic development, industries related to green goods and services are often directly incentivized by particular policies. Conceptually, policies will fall in several key areas: climate action plans; sustainability plans; alternative fuels policies and transportation policies; water policies, including water efficiency and reuse policies; energy policies, including energy efficiency policies, solar plans and renewable portfolio standards. Policies should be examined for industry and occupational impacts; policies can be indicators of opportunities and should thus be considered as a sustainable procurement strategy aimed at market generation.

Third and finally, identifying areas of opportunity also necessitates consideration of relevant political players. As directly related to policies, the emergence of advocacy coalitions around the green economy may incentivize particular types of industries and occupations as they effectively push for particular policies. Sustainable business coalitions consisting of green business along with environmental organizations are active in many cities. Pushing for 'green-collar jobs' opportunities, alliances of environmental justice organizations and labor organizations are likewise increasingly involved in workforce development around the green economy. Looking at the range of such coalitions may, in fact, provide valuable insights into areas of opportunity. This may be particularly enhanced as nonprofit organizations directly provide training in particular areas, such as in green building retrofits and weatherization.

Systems Thinking around Sustainable Procurement Policy Development

The second conceptual step towards a sustainable procurement strategy can be broadly defined as policy development. Given the systems approach necessitated by sustainability, a comprehensive approach towards green jobs and sustainable development is needed. Sustainable procurement becomes one tool within a policy toolbox aimed toward such goals. Specifically, municipalities must determine a coherent array of policies necessary to bolster sustainable procurement opportunities. As noted above, one area where specific opportunities in the green economy can be located is the array of policies actively pursued or slated for the near future. However, the relationship to policies can be extended beyond simply understanding areas of potential opportunities. Procurement is one policy tool within a larger toolbox that can and should be strategically employed in order to bolster green economic opportunities at the local scale. Procurement should not be pursued alone, but in concert with such policies around a broader approach towards green economic growth.

What types of policy areas can be considered in bolstering procurement as a municipal strategy? First, cities can determine economic development strategies including incentives and industry incubation strategies that could be married to government purchasing to generate further demand for these goods. Second, cities can determine needed workforce strategies and work in conjunction with the workforce development community in order to achieve results.

Economic development strategies

A variety of economic development strategies can be pursued to bolster a comprehensive approach towards sustainable procurement. Such strategies can include financing strategies, business incubation and land-use-specific strategies. Financing mechanisms and other business incentives have been advocated as an economic development tool in order to provide a business-friendly environment. Local governments have traditionally offered incentives to businesses as a part of an economic development platform. As noted by Gabe and Kraybill (2002), 'the widespread use of incentives has generated interest in the effects of incentives on employment growth and the strategic interactions occurring in incentive negotiations where firms announce plans to create new jobs in exchange for incentives from the government'. Such financing efforts have been limited; many scholars have pointed to decidedly mixed results (Bartik 2003). Similarly, mixed results have also persisted around the use of empowerment and enterprise zones. Such failures have often come, as noted by Michael Porter (1997), when 'again and again businesses that locate in an area because of tax breaks or other artificial inducements, rather than genuine comparative advantages'.

Despite the limitations, opportunities may be spurred through business financing and incubation efforts. And by integrating sustainability ideals into the procurement process, the local government can bolster the business climate for targeted subsets of the green economy slated for procurement and identified through the economic development analysis described above. Previous research indicates that a variety of financing mechanisms is being actively employed at the local level, and is applicable to a comprehensive approach around the green economy attached to a sustainable procurement approach. For example, the City of Louisville operates four incentive programs that include the operation of a revolving loan fund. Similarly, the City of Seattle operates a financing mechanism and incentive scheme around green building. Most widespread, the local implementation of the Property Accessed Clean Energy (PACE) program provides a compelling example of needed financing mechanisms around the institution of green economy programs. Such approaches may likewise include targeting particular companies as a part of the efforts around the green economy. For example, targeted American Recovery and Reinvestment Act (ARRA) funding was utilized by the City of Omaha in order to bolster the development of an HVAC-related manufacturing facility. This created employment directly in an arguably green industry. Additionally, such an approach may allow a larger range of consumers to access technology and can therefore further bolster demand. Justice questions can emerge as to the fair distribution of the benefits garnered from green economic development. Equity considerations have been considered, for example, most widely in the context of building retrofits as a sustainable economic development strategy. For example, the Apollo Alliance chapters at the local levels provide financing tools designed to incentivize local markets around green building.

More time-intensive business incubation strategies can be utilized along with sustainable procurement. For example, green business certification strategies can be linked to a sustainable procurement approach. Certification of businesses along environmental lines has been implemented in counties in California through the Green Business Certification Program. Qualifying businesses receive marketing support and recognition, including a sticker to be displayed on their window. The program cites increased consumer demand for participating business as a likely result of the promotion provided through the county administered program. By linking sustainable procurement to green certified businesses, private and public markets can be linked and small-business development may be bolstered. Second, sustainable procurement can be linked to land-use considerations through the implementation of clean technology parks – geographical locales specifically cited for green goods and service providers. Incentives could be potentially provided for park residents, including bid preferences, through a sustainable procurement approach.

In the end, considering financing and other incentives for whatever green industry is ultimately targeted is an important step towards developing a targeted plan around green economy development linked to sustainable procurement. The key questions in implementing this policy element are: what economic development barriers may exist in developing or institutionalizing a local market around a particular green goods or service? Financing mechanisms and other incentives including land-use-specific strategies are thus an important policy component of a green economy plan linked with sustainable procurement that can further bolster targeted markets.

Workforce development strategies

Workforce development needs are important to the development of a comprehensive strategy of sustainable procurement. Human capital strategies are important, albeit somewhat overlooked, aspects of economic development approaches. Economic development theory suggests that human capital availability may provide incentives for employers moving to a particular locale (Mathur 1999). Having a readied workforce may provide an attractive incentive to bolster markets for the particular good and service that is being actively procured by the city through its sustainable procurement approach.

Towards that end, the application of workforce development theory and strategies may not be significantly different than traditional approaches and strategies when environmental values are introduced into the equation. When certain industries are targeted through the procurement policy, particular employment opportunities may result, and particular skill sets are needed. The politicized conversation around green employment has often focused on the desire for job growth. However, opportunities within the green economy may lie in retraining existing occupations for new environmentally sensitive skills. Such a process has been popularly referred to as 'greenifying' occupations (see Rivkin et al. 2009). Providing training for targeted industries and occupations in areas targeted by sustainable procurement may help to bolster the overall approach.

A workforce development perspective, moreover, can also be an area where equity considerations can be layered onto the policy implementation process. Specifically, integrating a sustainability perspective on workforce development may also buildon equity considerations in terms of the range of occupations that may be incentivized through a sustainability-driven approach to procurement. In considering equity, the key question to assess is the desired skill level that should be targeted in the training efforts. This determination lies at the intersection of the green-collar jobs movement (where job opportunities are targeted at the lower skills end of the spectrum), and the green technology movement (where employment opportunities are focused on high-skilled, high-technology strategies). In terms of implementation, training at particular levels (green-collar versus high-technology employment, for example) can provide different opportunities appropriate for different communities. At the relatively lower end of the skills spectrum, much impetus around green jobs training appears to be coming from community college districts. Moreover, municipalities must consider where environmental remediation, if any, from green employment should be targeted. Specifically, should clean-up activities be performed in places with a history of inequitable distribution of environmental hazards in order to redress past inequities? A sustainability-inspired procurement approach should integrate new stakeholders into the process through developing a coherent strategy incorporative of both workforce development and economic development considerations.

Systems Thinking around Sustainable Procurement Policy Implementation

Implementing purchasing of targeted products through a targeted and strategically advised approach to green procurement is the final conceptual and practical step towards the development of a sustainable procurement program. Indicative of the broader challenge of sustainable governance, implementing sustainable procurement is a considerable institutional challenge. Governance challenges persist in terms of implementing sustainability more generally, and in implementing sustainable procurement strategies in particular.

Institutionally, procurement is often specifically undertaken by dedicated procurement staff. These civil service employees perform the mechanics of goods and services procurement for the municipality. Procurement officials see their role within the city as distinctive and focused on the evaluation of products and services. For example, the National Association of State Procurement Officers (NASPO 2006) notes that 'public procurement professionals add value to every government function by: Providing efficient delivery of products and services; Obtaining best value through competition; Offering fair and equitable competitive contracting opportunities for supporters; Maintaining public confidence through ethical and transparent procurement practices'. They often work cooperatively across city government departments in the execution of procurement plans. Additionally, many city staff members participate in procurement of services specific to their department through the municipality's request for proposal process.

As procurement professionals and other municipal actors move forward in a governance environment that contains many actors and multiple layers of influence exerted by these actors (including citizen groups, private business coalitions or other government agencies), understanding the institutional realities dictating agency goals is helpful in crafting and communicating procurement practices that effectively support sustainable economic development. A basic institutional framework for achieving sustainable procurement ends hinges on two fundamental components of coordination that are discussed in further detail below: intra- and inter-governmental coordination. Together, systems thinking around government operations and sustainability approaches is thus required in order to effectively govern a sustainable procurement strategy.

Intra-governmental coordination

Can siloed departments foster systems thinking about sustainable procurement? Intra-governmental coordination is required for the development of a successful procurement policy aimed at sustainable local economic development. The successful pursuit of such policies will be characterized by the reversal of internal institutional silos that impede the effective implementation of such policies and programs. Government officials charged with implementation must learn to simultaneously view procurement as an economic development activity and an environmental policy approach. This municipal function may be conducted in a dramatically different manner from the traditional mechanisms through which procurement is often practiced within the municipality's pursuit of goods and services. Through sustainable procurement, government officials may find themselves working with departments and information that they do not customarily interact with. Specifically, procurement is often a part of the general services function of a city. Thus procurement decisions have not been routinely undertaken by staff with expertise in either environmental policy or economic development principles. This creates a dearth of technical skills and is not likely to lead to effective systems thinking around procurement as symbiotically an economic development and environmental tool.

How can sustainability thinking and requisite expertise be effectively brought to bear on procurement decisions? Given that one of the dangers in implementing green procurement policies is the creation of additional, inefficient silos, it is vital for departments to work cooperatively to devise and implement a sustainability-minded procurement policy. For example, municipalities introducing a new 'green' policy must consider whether or not to create new positions dedicated to implementing sustainability-minded procurement policies, or to retrain existing staff. Additionally, government agencies can holistically address their sustainability objectives by infusing broad managerial goals into their purchasing policies across all categories of good and services. For example, evidence shows that, in some cases, integrating procurement into an overarching governmental mission creates more successful initiatives for agencies (Coggburn 2004). Therefore, when procurement is a part of a larger sustainability agenda, a systems approach towards procurement is particularly important in order to integrate procurement across institutional silos.

Inter-governmental coordination

Can siloed municipalities foster systems thinking about sustainable procurement? Creating markets must be done in aggregate and thus requires coordination in order to create business opportunities. Municipal boundaries may not mirror economic ones – opportunities for growth in green industries and occupations will undoubtedly spill over. Economic conditions, environmental policies and other relevant factors in neighboring municipalities will undoubtedly impact each municipality's opportunity set. Given these factors, coordination across boundaries may be required in order to fully reap the benefits of implementing comprehensive sustainable procurement strategies. Parks and Oakerson (2000) note that, as regions expand and grow, and as globalization is increasingly impacting local decision-making processes, governance and institutional arrangements need to change in order to best serve constituencies. One of these changes is increased coordination among separate government agencies within a region. In order to successfully create and implement purchasing policies that produce environmental and economic benefits for the local community, there must be strong leadership across disparate governments, including municipalities, as well as an integrated public/civic coalition that can help push the agenda through the policy process. Thus, in the same way that governments are increasingly integrating regional solutions into climate change adaptation and mitigation, the old governance structure around both environmental and economic development approaches may not be ineffective in implementing sustainability goals.

Considerable progress in relation to sustainable procurement efforts may be garnered through the integration of collaborative procurement programs. At the end of the day, much of the potential of the policy instrument depends on the creation of reasonable markets. And such markets require considerable quantity. Thus collaborative procurement programs for sustainable procurement may lead to growing markets by allowing greater volumes of procurement for green goods and services by multiple-agency procurement across jurisdictional lines. Such collaborative procurement can extend beyond municipalities through public private partnerships with private corporations also desiring such goods and services. Targeted products, moreover, can be made further accessible by reducing the cost of such products through bulk procurement. Drawing on the remaining sustainability value, this approach can further bolster equity by allowing companies in lower-income areas to procure such products at lower cost.

3. CONCLUSION: COST, COMPETITION, AND CONSISTENCY IN INTEGRATING SUSTAINABLE PROCUREMENT VALUES

The previous section sought to reframe local government's procurement process specifically along sustainable values. This chapter, as a whole, centers on city-based efforts towards sustainability. Procurement is the very essence of municipal activities, and lies at the heart of municipal impacts. To that end, cities are increasingly considering sustainability values in their procurement decisions. And, as described above, a variety of considerations beyond price has been integrated into municipal procurement decisions. In fact, external values are increasingly pursued through procurement, and can be broadly characterized by their relevant sustainability value. Economic development is furthered through buy-local procurement policies. Environmental preservation is bolstered through the process of selecting environmentally preferable products. Finally, equity is fostered through women and minority business programs, as well as through procurement preferences for smaller businesses in need of a foothold in a local market. By moving beyond immediate cost considerations, such values can fundamentally change the metrics by which products and services are evaluated. Municipal procurement provides a mechanism for cities to become an exemplar of sustainability solutions.

Environmental preservation, equity and economic development may be laudable goals. However, the integration of sustainability values into the procurement process is not without its difficulties and opposition. Many procurement officials are opposed to the integration of such values as a violation of the competitive bidding process. Changing metrics to incorporate sustainability values will invariably have an impact on procurement decisions. In addition to impacting the value at hand (be it environmental preservation, equity or economic growth), revisiting procurement policies may change the good or service ultimately chosen by the municipality. The National Association for Procurement Officials, representing procurement officials nationally, has raised concerns about such potential changes to process and products. Exemplifying such concerns, the NASPO (2006) states that they have

> already described the commitment of the procurement professional to maintaining the openness of the competitive process. Socioeconomic programs that legislatures and city councils adopt to achieve some social goal through public procurement run counter to that commitment. Types of policies that fall within this category are environmentally and sustainability mandates, minority and gender-based set-asides and preferences, local vendor preferences, and prohibitions against doing business with vendors that have capital investments in countries considered to have violated human rights . . . Socioeconomic procurement mandates require a whole set of responsibilities that differ from the key tasks that are part of providing strategic services. For instance, procurement officers must devote time and dollars to maintaining a means of verifying that business or products qualify for a socioeconomic benefit such as a preference or a set-aside.

Thus such values are often seen as diametrically opposed to preserving a competitive process, and in providing the most efficient and effective good and service to the municipality.

Adding other considerations into the process and moving beyond cost calculations alone undoubtedly increases complexity of the evaluative process. However, it may not lead to a lack of a competitive process, as suggested by NASPO. The view of NASPO and of traditional procurement platforms is indicative of thinking that does not reflect the perspective of sustainability and instead focuses on a zero-sum game between economic development and other quality-of-life gains – including the pursuit of environmental preservation. In fact, integrating economic development considerations along with environmental ones may seek to further bolster competitiveness and ensure that the markets for governmental goods are in fact competitive ones along a more dynamic evaluative framework where goods have to compete on more than just cost. A good can be evaluated in accordance with its immediate costs, as well as its current and future environmental costs. Life-cycle costs, for example, can provide a more complex metric through which goods can be evaluated and compared. Demanding goods that are both good for bottom lines today, and that lower the environmental costs (both today and potentially into the future) of municipal operations, may further bolster competitiveness between contractors who seek to win city contracts.

Despite the difficulties and limitations, sustainable procurement may provide one initial tool for the future. The previous section aimed to provide a conceptual framework for the development of a sustainable procurement approach hinged on the creation of sustainable economic development for communities. However, given the differences that persist and are germane to each municipality' system, no one-size-fits-all approach is likely to be effective. For scholars and practitioners, working through such an approach requires engaging a number of key questions aimed at critical actors, and aimed at value considerations in policy development and subsequent implementation. Many of them can be framed as follows.

First, the municipality must consider the practicality of value considerations in integrating sustainable procurement as a strategy. Economic development considerations are key for municipalities, which must ask: how can sustainable procurement policies be effectively utilized as an economic development approach that fits within extant economic realities, capitalizes on areas of comparative advantage, and facilitates career ladders through job opportunities at different junctures on a spectrum of skill levels? Moreover, how can sustainable procurement policies be responsive to equity considerations by effectively targeting green employment opportunities specifically in green-collar jobs, or which aim to provide benefits to environmental justice communities? And how can governments effectively integrate sustainable procurement strategies in a manner that may effectively build upon minority and women business requirements in procurement as an equity-driven approach? Finally, what environmental impacts do products have both today and into the future through consideration of the environmental footprints of products, including life-cycle cost evaluations? Implementing sustainability into product procurement may ultimately require a balancing of equity, economic and environmentally driven values. At the end of the day, the municipality is ultimately tasked with finding the green goods and services that are most likely to be produced or acquired locally, in an effort to provide sustainable economic development.

Second, in addition to values, relevant actors must also be considered, as cities face a myriad of governance challenges to sustainability strategies. Many conceptual questions emerge related to municipal action. Specifically, how can sustainable procurement policies be framed within municipal goals and policy-making? What benefits may be associated with such an approach? And how can transparency and fairness be integrated into systems thinking around product evaluations that necessitates evaluation going beyond lowest costs? Moreover, as indicated above, governance extends beyond the municipality itself. Communities must consider what stakeholder groups are or should be involved in the integration of such policies. Particularly given the new emergence of green jobs alliances such as the Apollo Alliance, how can emergent green economy alliances utilize procurement policies as a basis for sustainable economic development plans at the municipal level? How can sustainability procurement policies be responsive to equity considerations by effectively targeting green employment opportunities specifically in green-collar jobs, or those that aim to provide benefits to environmental justice communities? And how can governments effectively integrate sustainable procurement strategies in a manner that may build upon minority and women business requirements in procurement as an equity-driven approach? Finally, how can cities build partnerships beyond their borders? Specifically, how can they build partnerships with other municipalities, regional institutions, and beyond in bolstering their purchasing power and their demand for targeted green goods and services? Similarly, how can public–private partnerships be structured to pool demand, and to offer green goods and services at lower costs that are perhaps more commensurate with the 'traditional' more environmentally costly alternative? In doing so, demand and thus corollary economic development opportunities can be further fostered within municipalities.

At the end of the day, in order to develop a viable sustainable procurement strategy, what is ultimately required is a systems approach towards procurement that seeks to specifically bolster sustainable economic development as a purposive policy and planning goal. As this chapter notes at the outset, sustainability fundamentally requires interdisciplinary, integrative solutions. As arguably a critical piece of the sustainability puzzle, procurement is not outside of a systems approach towards sustainability. Sustainable economic development, or green jobs growth, requires such systems thinking and will ultimately occur at the interstices of previously separately pursued values within the procurement process. Linking procurement for economic, equity-driven and environmental goals, sustainable procurement provides one tool through which results may be achieved. A comprehensive green jobs plan, going one step further, may in fact provide the coordinated action needed to reach the interdisciplinary solutions at the nexus of sustainability values. And, as such, such an approach may more comprehensively consider the impact and role of municipalities on both the local and global environment, and create sustainable economic development opportunities within municipalities.

REFERENCES

Bartik, Timothy J. (2003), 'Local economic development policies', Working Paper 03–91, Kalamazoo, MI: W.E. Upjohn Institute for Employment Research.

Berke, P.R. and M.M. Conroy (2000), 'Are we planning for sustainable development? An evaluation of 30 comprehensive plans', *Journal of the American Planning Association*, **66** (1), 21–33.

Blakely, Edward J. and Nancy G. Leigh (2010), *Planning Local Economic Development: Theory and Practice*, Thousand Oaks, CA: Sage Publications.

Business Alliance for a Local Living Economies (BALLE) (n.d.), 'Thinking Local First: Making the Case for a Local First Campaign', available at http://bealocalist.org/sites/default/files/Making%20the%20Case%20for%20Thinking%20Local%20First_0.pdf.

Campbell, S. (1996), 'Green cities, growing cities, just cities? Urban planning and the contradictions of sustainable development', *Journal of the American Planning Association*, **62** (3), 296–312.

City of New York (2007), 'Energy efficiency case studies', available at http://www.nyc.gov/html/nycwateless/html/at_agencies/govt_case_studies_energy.html.

City of Portland (2002), *Sustainable Procurement Strategy: A Joint City of Portland and Multnomah County Effort*, Portland: City of Portland and Multnomah County.

City of Portland (2004), 'Environmentally preferable law (5.33.080)', available at http://www.portlandonline.com/auditor/index.

City of San Jose (2001), *City of San Jose Council Policy (Council Action Number 9252001, Item 4.2)*, San Jose, CA: City of San Jose.

City of San Jose (2004), 'Local preference on procurement remediation, agenda 4/6/04', available at http://www.sjeconomy.com/businessassistance/pdfs/local.preference.pdf.

City of San Jose (2011), 'Local preference', available at http:///www.sjeconomuy.com/businessassistance/localpreference.asp.

City of Santa Monica (n.d.), 'Summary of sustainable procurement policies', available at http://www.smgov.net/departmeetns/ose/categories/buying_green/procurement_policies.aspx.

City of Seattle (2002), 'Chemical use policy', available at http://www.seattle.gov/environment-documents/chemicalusepolicy.doc.

City of Seattle (2003), 'Sustainable procurement policy', available at http://www.seattle.gov/environment/documents/sus-purchasing-policy11-06-03.

Coe, Charles K. (1989), *Public Financial Management*, Englewood Cliffs, NJ: Prentice-Hall.

Coggburn, J. (2004), 'Achieving managerial values through green procurement?', *Public Performance & Management Review*, **28** (2), 236–58.

Culver, A. (2008), 'Buying smart: experiences of municipal procurement pioneers', available at http://www.chej.org/ppc/archives/purchasing/file003.pdf.

Gabe, T.M. and D. Kraybill (2002), 'The effect of state economic development incentives on employment growth of establishments', *Journal of Regional Science*, **42** (4), 703–30.

Gunder, M. (2006), 'Sustainability: planning's saving grace or road to perdition?', *Journal of Planning, Education, and Research*, **26** (2), 208–21.

Hemenway, D. (1989), 'Government procurement leverage', *Journal of Public Health Policy*, **10** (1), 123–5.

Hemple, Lamont C. (2009), 'Conceptual and analytical challenges in building sustainable communities', in Daniel A. Mazmanian and Michael E. Kraft (eds), *Towards Sustainable Communities: Transitions and Transformations in Environmental Policy*, Boston, MA: MIT Press, pp. 33–62.

Jepson, E.J. (2004), 'The adoption of sustainable economic development policies and techniques in US cities: how wide, how deep, and what role for planners', *Journal of Planning Education and Research*, **23** (3), 229–41.

Mathur, V. (1999), 'Human capital-based strategy for regional economic development', *Economic Development Quarterly*, **13** (3), 203–16.

McCrudden, C. (2004), 'Using public procurement to achieve social outcomes', *Natural Resources Forum*, **28** (4), 257–67.
McCue, C.P. and G.A. Gianakis (2001), 'Public purchasing: who's minding the store?', *Journal of Public Procurement*, **1** (1), 71–95.
Murray, G.J. (2001), 'Improving purchasing's contribution: the purchasing strategy of buying council', *The International Journal of Public Sector Management*, **14** (6), 391–410.
Murray, G.J. (2007), 'Strategic procurement in UK local governments: the role of elected leaders', *Journal of Public Procurement*, **7** (2), 429–34.
Murray, G.J. (2009a), 'Improving the validity of public procurement research', *International Journal of Public Sector Management*, **22** (2), 91–103.
Murray, G.J. (2009b), 'Public procurement strategy for accelerating the economic recovery', *Supply Chain Management: An International Journal*, **14** (6), 429–34.
National Association of State Procurement Officials (NASPO) (2006), *Strength in Numbers: An Introduction to Cooperative Procurement*, available at http://www.naspo.org/documents/cooperativepurchasingbrief.pdf.
National Association for State Procurement Officials (NASPO) (2008), *State and Local Government Procurement: A National Guide*, Lexington, KY: NASPO.
New Economic Foundation (2005), 'Public spending for public benefit', available at www.neweconomics.org (accessed 15 December 2009).
Nijaki, L. and G. Worrel (2012), 'Procurement for sustainable local economic development', *International Journal for Public Sector Management*, **25** (2), 133–53.
Parks, R.B. and R.J. Oakerson (2000), 'Regionalism, localism, and metropolitan governance: suggestions from the research program on local public economies', *State and Local Government Review*, **32** (3), 169–79.
Portland Multnomah County (2005), 'Multnomah County corrections local purchasing', Food Policy 2005 Highlights, available at www.portlandonline.com/shared/cfm/image.cfm?id=133874 (accessed 4 July 2010).
Portney, Kent E. (2003), *Taking Sustainable Cities Seriously: Economic Development, the Environment, and Quality of Life in American Cities*, Cambridge, MA: MIT Press.
Preuss, Lutz (2007), 'Buying into our future: sustainability initiatives in local government procurement', *Business Strategy and the Environment*, **16** (5), 354–65.
Preuss, L. (2009), 'Addressing sustainable development through local procurement: the case of local government', *Supply Chain Management: An International Journal*, **14** (3), 213–23.
Qiao, Y., K.V. Thai and G. Cummings (2009), 'State and local procurement preferences: a survey', *Journal of Public Procurement*, **9** (3), 371–410.
Rivkin, David, Phil Lewis, Erich C. Dierdorff, Jennifer J. Norton, Donald W. Drewes and Christina M. Kroustalis (2009), *Greening the World of Work: Implications for ONET SOC and New and Emerging Occupations*, Washington, DC: The National Center for ONET Development.
Shahan, Z. (2011), 'Report: Buy Local Campaigns Help Independent Businesses', *Ecopolitology*, available at http://ecopolitology.org/201/02/03/report-buy-local-campais-help-independent-businesses/ (published online 3 February 2011).
Thai, K.V. (2001), 'Public procurement re-examined', *Journal of Public Procurement*, **1** (1), 9–50.
United States Environmental Protection Agency (1998), *The City of Santa Monica's Environmental Purchasing: A Case Study (EPA742-R-98–001)*, Washington, DC: EPA.
United States Environmental Protection Agency (2000), *State and Local Government Pioneers: How State and Local Governments Are Implementing Environmentally Preferable Purchasing Practices (EPA742-R-00–004)*, Washington, DC: EPA.
Walker, H. and S. Brammer (2009), 'Sustainable procurement in the United Kingdom public sector', *Supply Chain Management: An International Journal*, **14** (2), 128–37.
Wissenburg, M.L.J. (2006), 'Global and ecological justice: prioritizing conflicting demands', *Environmental Values*, **15** (4), 425–39.
Zeemering, Eric S. (2009), 'What does sustainability mean to city officials?', *Urban Affairs Review*, **45**(2), 247–73.

PART III

THE FUTURE

19. Urban design and sustainability: looking backward to move forward

Tridib Banerjee

In recent decades we have seen an explosive growth of books and monographs on the general themes of sustainability, but, more specifically, and of interest here, on urbanism, urban planning, urban design and landscape planning. Many of these publications have essentially repackaged many of the known principles, or included very specific and technical but partial responses to the challenges of sustainable design. But in the end not much of this new production is innovative or broadly applicable. In this chapter I do not aim to review the new materials. Rather, I return to the established literature in environmental and city design. This chapter scans the relevant literature in environmental design and culls the theories, principles, methods and measures pertaining to the goals of sustainability. This scanning is framed in a theoretical construct, and findings are presented according to a schema derived from it. My aim is to critically review urban design theories and movements to reveal how their theoretical roots relate to sustainability. Such a critical understanding will be fundamental to advance the theory and practice of urban design towards more sustainable cities in the future.

Accordingly, it is appropriate to begin by reviewing the legacy of important thinkers and thinking about sustainability in the literature of architecture, landscape architecture and urban design. I should note at the outset that, although the term 'sustainability' was not a part of the formal lexicon of these arguments, it is reasonable to infer that this legacy is based on what is commonly considered as sustainability today. We should note further that much of this thinking and writing occurred before the current crisis in global warming and climate change, and was focused on environmental damage and resource depletion.

As is common in the tradition of design, much of this legacy in defining, practicing and achieving sustainability goals is normative and speculative, and relatively few of its tenets have been applied in practice and are thus yet to be formally vetted through empirical studies or formal evaluation of the outcomes. Nevertheless, this review will be structured around two underlying dimensions of normative thinking in design theory and practice.

The first of these two dimensions has to do with what can be called the Platonic versus Aristotelian approaches. As we know, both Plato and Aristotle had normative ideas about optimal city size and the governance order of cities. While Plato had a very definitive view of what constitutes an ideal city, Aristotle based his reflections on the experience of real cities, and emphasized the process by which the ideal form and size may be achieved. This distinction was first suggested by Lisa Peattie (1987), from her experience of working as a field anthropologist, and a member of a MIT–Harvard team working on the planning and design of a new town, Ciudad Guyana, in Venezuela in the mid-1960s. The process, she argued, involved two parallel experiences and expectations. Thus '[T]he Platonic City of the designers appeared on schematic diagrams of urban form, renderings showing elegantly slim pedestrians strolling in the shade, prose which suggested that the Caroni Bridge may evoke the Ponte Vecchio' (pp. 57–8). In contrast, '[T]he Aristotelian City appeared as businesses and neighborhoods and as people with individual and collective purposes . . . It was a world of boosters, hustlers, prospectors, promoters, entrepreneurs, and developers' (p. 56).[1]

For the purposes of this chapter I extend the experiential parallels of Peattie's Ciudad Guyana to two conceptual if not philosophical parallels in approaches to design. Hence, by the Platonic approach I imply an authoritative, visionary, dogmatic, deterministic (based on fixed schemas) and perhaps non-negotiable approach to sustainable design, whereas the Aristotelian approach would represent the more possibilistic, experiential, provisional, dialogic, if not negotiated approach to achieving sustainability in design. One might also think of the Platonic approach as specification (or input) oriented, whereas the Aristotelian approach can be seen more as experiential, performance (or output) oriented. In the former the belief lies in the specific means to achieve a particular end – sustainability in this instance. The latter approach, in contrast, emphasizes the same outcome or end, but remains open to alternative possibilities as to the means.[2] In the former approach the challenges lie in establishing the causal link between the means specified and the end desired; in the latter approach the challenge lies in defining the performance measures of the desired end itself, that is, sustainability.[3]

The second dimension can be seen as one of an ecological versus anthropocentric approach to design. The former approach involves synoptic thinking involving the larger ecosystem, while the latter focuses on the human purposes and consequences of design actions and outcomes. In the former approach ecological imperatives dominate, thus relegating human aspirations, purposes, functionings and uses of land to a necessarily subservient status.

In combination, then, we can imagine a two-by-two space with four quadrants, representing four major conceptual approaches to sustainable form and design: Platonic–Ecological; Platonic–Anthropocentric; Aristotelian–Anthropocentric; and Aristotelian–Ecological. As I will argue, these quadrants tend to capture four major orthodoxies in the design literature represented by two authorities – Kevin Lynch and Ian McHarg – and two movements – new urbanism and ecological (or landscape) urbanism. This framing may not capture an exhaustive account of the design literature as it pertains to sustainability. One could argue that the ecological approach considers the design of the built environment and human settlements from a synoptic environmental perspective, with sustainability as the canon, while the anthropocentric approach imagines the built environment that best serves the human purposes, functionings[4] and livability, with sustainability as the limiting condition. On this approach sustainability can be achieved in many different domains and spaces of human functionings. In the combination of these two dimensions, then, we could derive a four-quadrant organizing schema, as shown in Figure 19.1.

I begin by reviewing the works of Ian McHarg and Kevin Lynch, the two authorities whose works have become somewhat paradigmatic in the field, followed by the two movements – new urbanism and ecological urbanism – which lately have gained considerable popularity in the professions.

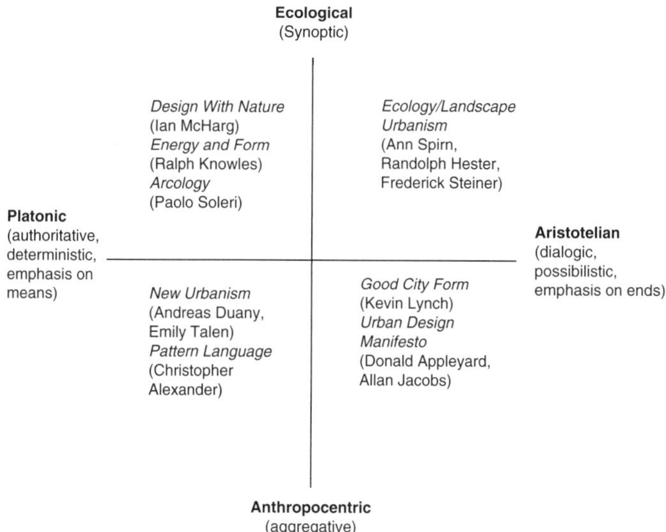

Figure 19.1 Normative models of sustainability through design

Design with Nature: Ecological and Platonic

When Ian McHarg, a landscape architect by training, first wrote *Design With Nature*, published by the Conservation Foundation in the late 1960s, it represented a major paradigm shift in the design and planning thinking. Although there has been a long, if spindly, tradition of writings about nature and landscape, and the imperatives of their inherent values in the organization and development of the built form and human settlement – notably the writings of Frederick Law Olmsted, Benton Mackaye, Patrick Geddes, Lewis Mumford and the like – very little of that legacy had influenced the aggregate urban outcome. Engineering, not design, with nature was the norm; market economy defined the imperatives.

The impact of McHarg's work was not limited to planning; his work joined the ranks of well-known environmental proponents like Barry Commoner, Rachel Carson, Luna Leopold and others. Collectively, their work marked the important beginning of the environmental movement in the USA.

McHarg believed strongly that much of the environmental degradation and loss of nature is a direct outcome of the Judeo-Christian values that had placed man in a competitive position *vis-à-vis* nature, ignoring the synoptic relationship between man and nature, which, in contrast, was intrinsic in the values of ancient religions. In *Design With Nature*, he asserted the primacy of ecological values over economic values, especially where uses of land are concerned. His prescriptions for future development of such ecological regions as the Potomac River Valley were strictly based on scientific analysis of the various interlinked environmental systems – climate, geology, physiography, hydrology, groundwater, soils, plant association, wildlife, mineral resources and the like. These analyses were mapped on multiple overlays showing specific ecosystem characteristics along with a matrix that evaluated the degree of compatibility between candidate land uses and environmental characteristics, which displayed, for a given pixel of land, the suitability for future uses in that location. The overall format and program for the built environment was essentially derived from this analysis. In this approach there is not much room for negotiation because the parameters of development are scientifically obtained. The Platonic and deterministic tenet of this approach was embedded in the synoptic and systemic analysis of the larger ecosystem within which future uses of urbanized land were to be located. In this approach, the planner's or designer's role is to apply this ecological analytic schema to achieve ecologically good urban form.

While McHarg's approach offered a methodology to determine the precise disposition of land use for a given site according to its component subsystems, his urban form prescriptions were limited to density and the siting of buildings. The guiding principle of this methodology was that economic value must be subservient to ecological values intrinsic to the site. He did not offer any urban design guidelines to dictate the height, bulk and spatial organization of such built forms. He did not, for example, suggest that a grid pattern might be more ecologically sustainable than a radial city form, or vice versa. We should note that his work was published long before the global warming and climate change issues worked their way to the forefront of public consciousness, if not conscience. Thus his prescription for scattered low-density clustering of homes to protect the ecosystem of a river valley, as opposed to more consolidated and compact urban form, in retrospect might have been responsible for the resulting sprawl effect and the much larger carbon footprint, just from increased VMT (vehicle miles travelled) alone, and even more so when the effects of increased infrastructure provision and energy consumption are included in the calculation.

We could also place in this quadrant the work of Ralph Knowles, professor of architecture at the University of Southern California, who devoted most of his scholarly work to energy and form, involving laboratory simulation of solar trajectories. He was able to define the precise 'solar envelope' necessary to maximize (or minimize, depending on the climate zones) solar exposure to an individual or a complex of buildings. He was particularly interested in developing zoning ordinances based on solar envelopes, and thus creating a more energy-efficient urban form from the ground up.

In many ways Knowles was ahead of his time, long before LEED certification and other green building technology came into vogue. The only caveat in placing Knowles in this quadrant is that his analysis may not have been as synoptic as that of McHarg. Nevertheless, his work is based on empirical and scientific work, deterministic in tone, and with promises for defining the criteria for the design of urban form.

We should consider also the work of Italian architect Paolo Soleri, who came to the USA to work with Frank Lloyd Wright. Not able to stand Wright's authoritarian style, he parted company but proposed several schemes for the ultimate compact city, a polar opposite of Wright's Broadacre City, but very much in the same visionary Platonic tradition, Unlike McHarg or Knowles, Soleri's vision was based on intuition, not scientific research. This visionary urban form aspired to cover the least ground area, in this way reducing the literal, and in current understanding the carbon, footprint of a city, as understood in the current terminology of sustainability. In some ways this was prescient of our efforts today to develop more compact cities as sustainable urban form.

Good City Form: Anthropocentric and Aristotelian

The writings and projects of Kevin Lynch had an important influence in shaping the pedagogy and practice of city design – a term he favored over the more commonly used term 'urban design'. A close associate of Gyorgy Kepes, a noted designer and visual theorist who was very much taken by the possibilities of cybernetic theory (see Boyer 2011) in designing the built environment, Lynch himself was more interested in the 'public image', that is, the aggregate of the individual representations of the city. This was the first time in design history that the theory and practice of urban design had been based on empirical research, very much in the tradition of social sciences, rather than on the intuitive and creative impulses of the architect designer.

Lynch's seminal work, *The Image of The City*, would have enormous impact on the field of planning and urban design, as well as many other disciplines in social sciences. His work inspired new interest in cognitive maps and mapping to study human behavior and social organization of cities. In the context of sustainability this work had very little to contribute. Yet, in his subsequent work, he wrote extensively about the natural environment, and how environmental sensibilities must be included in the design of the built environment. Much of this thinking at the site and project scale has been incorporated in his book *Site Planning* (1962), the most recent edition written with Gary Hack (1984). Lynch's major writings on environmental issues concerned regional and metropolitan scales, not unlike that of McHarg and the works of ecological or landscape urbanists reviewed elsewhere in this chapter (see Banerjee and Southworth 1990). Even at this scale, his writings included human purposes and the consequences of using nature's services; this is why we place him on the anthropocentric side of the schema. Indeed in his book, *Managing the Sense of the Region*, he develops guidelines for human purposes and uses in the large-scale regional and metropolitan landscape, in balance and harmony with the regional ecology and landscape that are becoming increasingly relevant today. Indeed the current writings on ecological landscape often invoke his works, especially the aforementioned book. In his practice career two projects are particularly noteworthy: a study of the natural landscape and ecology of Martha's Vineyard and polices for its future development ('Development and landscape: Martha's Vineyard', in Banerjee and Southworth 1990) and a study of the metropolitan landscape of the San Diego region ('Temporary Paradise? A look at the special landscape of the San Diego region' with Donald Appleyard, in Banerjee and Southworth 1990) that included policy recommendations for future development. In the twilight years of his career Lynch would become increasingly engaged in environmental issues, particularly the waste and destruction of the environment and ecosystems. In his frustration he composed scenarios of 'cacotopia', where the waste generated by modern civilization and the capitalist economy would overwhelm nature and the natural ecosystem as we experience it today. Entitled *Wasting Away*, and published posthumously (edited by Michael Southworth), this book is also a major testimony to Lynch's concern for protection and preservation of nature in the social arrangements and the built form of mass consumption societies. Curiously, the term 'sustainability' rarely appeared in the text of these essays. Indeed the index of the collection of his writings and projects edited by Banerjee and Southworth (1990) does not include that term.

Nor does the term appear in his other major publication, *A Theory of Good City Form* (1981) that bookends the corpus of his work with *The Image of the City*. Considered a major treatise on the performance of the built environment, this book develops the arguments for what Lynch considered a normative theory of good city form. He proposed five essential performance characteristics of good city form: vitality, sense, fit, access and control – and two meta-criteria that he defined as efficiency and justice. Of these five criteria, it is vitality that suggested measures appropriate for the sustainability goal. In elaborating the performance characteristic of vitality, he further suggested the following five specific dimensions:

a. *sustenance*: the adequacy of the throughput of water, air, food, energy, and waste;
b. *safety*: the absence of environmental poisons, diseases, or hazards;
c. *consonance*: the degree of fit between the environment and the human requirements of internal temperature, body rhythm, sensory input, and body function;
d. for other living things, how well the environment provides for the health and genetic diversity of species which are economically useful to man; and
e. the present and future stability of total ecological community. (Lynch 1981, p. 129)

While clearly the first three criteria – sustenance, safety and consonance – are fundamentally anthropocentric, both sustenance and safety refer to inherent limitations and constraints of a local ecosystem, and suggest the imperatives of subservience to such limits.

The last two criteria are clearly post-anthropocentric, and here Lynch clearly asserts the necessity of paying attention to the larger ecosystem of which we are a part. He argues that the health of human communities is inextricably related to the health of the larger 'ecological community', and that we should necessarily be concerned about biodiversity and plant ecology. According to Lynch (1981, p. 128):

> We can move from questions of human to the health of other species, or the entire biological community . . . We should also be concerned about maintaining

> genetic diversity among plants and animals of value to us. A human interest in the health of the entire ecological community can be justified on the grounds that we depend on the entire web of life, and may suffer when that web is torn. Thus the relative stability of the local ecological system should be a measure of some importance to us.

While one could read this as a self-serving plea for paying attention to our immediate habitat, it does have a hint of moral reasoning, not unlike John Rawls's notion of the 'veil of ignorance' (Rawls 1971) as the basis for establishing his 'difference principle' of distributive justice. Furthermore, this reasoning comes closest to the notion of sustainability developed from an anthropocentric position.

Indeed, it is interesting to speculate how Lynch would have addressed the question of sustainability if he were alive today. One wonders if he might have added sustainability as the third meta-criterion in defining the performance characteristics of good city form. In defining the meta-criteria, he spoke of them as a feasibility check, since the five performance characteristics are 'meaningless' on their own unless the questions of cost and equity are fully addressed: how much does it cost and who is getting what and how much (Lynch 1981, p. 119)? Today it might be asked in addition: is it sustainable? What is its ecological footprint? How does it mitigate global warming? and the like. Thus this meta-criterion serves the remaining apex of the 'three Es' triangle – efficiency, equity and ecology – that defines the essential scope of sustainability and the attendant tensions in planning as argued by Scott Campbell (1996). Or, would he simply have argued that the notion of efficiency includes sustainability, because efficient design would minimize waste and carbon footprint, would avoid overuse of natural environment and resources, allow recycling of non-renewable materials and so on?

Normative views of design strictly from the anthropocentric perspective were also typical of the writings of Donald Appleyard and Allan Jacobs, both of whom were influenced by Lynch's work (see Jacobs and Appleyard 1987). Quality of environment and landscape has been a leitmotif in their work also.

New Urbanism: Anthropocentric and Platonic

New urbanism has become an important movement today in the world of architecture, planning and urban design since its official inauguration in 1991, when a group of like-minded architects met in California to write a manifesto known as the Ahwanee Principles. Later these principles would be formalized as the 'Charter of the New Urbanism', very reminiscent of the Athens Charter of the Congrès Internationaux d'Architecture Moderne (or CIAM) that grew out such congregations of like-minded architects, planners and urban theorists, mainly from Europe (see Birch 2011).

The Congress for the New Urbanism (or CNU) Charter comprises a preamble of several declarations, followed by 27 principles grouped in three categories structured by the scales of environment: 'the region: metropolis, city, and town'; 'the neighborhood, the district, and the corridor'; and 'the block, the street, and the building' (CNU 2012). Thus the principles cover the entire spectrum of human settlements. But the essential premise of this organization and the Charter is that it

> views disinvestment in central cities, the spread of placeless sprawl, increasing separation by race and income, *environmental deterioration, loss of agricultural land and wilderness*, and the erosion of society's built heritage as one interrelated community-building challenge. (CNU 2012; emphasis added)

The Congress thus asserts a broad agenda ranging from social and economic inequality, and the loss of the urban heritage, to the protection of the environment.[5]

While environmental concerns remain integral to the new urbanist movement, it should be self-evident that it is anthropocentric in orientation, with a strong interest in the form of the built environment and the disposition of the use of space that leads to the human experience of urbanism. While social justice and equity remain a concern, their pursuit remains unclear in the specific principles. Indeed, environmental concerns notwithstanding, the sustainability goals remain muted and obscure. While the overall aim remains somewhat rhetorical, for example 'We dedicate ourselves to reclaiming our homes, blocks, streets, parks, neighborhoods, districts, towns, cities, regions, and environment', there is little hint about any possible role of the general public – the users of the environment – in their commitment to 'reclaiming' the continuum of urban spaces.

While the aim of new urbanism is somewhat amorphous, other than a passionate rejection of the contemporary urban development, the 27 principles that define the charter are quite specific and doctrinaire. Thus the emphasis of this approach is prescriptive of the means rather than of the end, in contrast to the performance characteristics of good city form discussed by Lynch.

Of the 27 principles prescribed in the CNU Charter, about five at the regional scale, four at the neighborhood scale and two at the block scale are explicitly or implicitly related to sustainability goals involving environmental benefits as commonly understood. Protection of natural resources and the ecosystem, more generally, reducing VMT (vehicle miles traveled) or auto-dependency through denser, compact urban form, with diversity of land use are implicit in most of the new urbanism guidelines.

The protagonists of new urbanism went beyond merely establishing guidelines. They seized the opportunity to design several planned communities as demonstration projects. Noteworthy among the earliest examples are Seaside in Florida, and Kentlands in Maryland by Andreas Duany, the spiritual leader of the new urbanist movement, Play Vista in Southern California by Stefanos Polyzoides, and Laguna West in Northern California by Peter Calthrope. Today there are many hundreds of projects either planned or constructed throughout the country that are certified by CNU as new urbanist design (see Garde 2004; 2006).

Beyond these examples of new urbanist communities, the movement has taken two major related initiatives to broaden its influence. These are (a) form-based codes (FBC) or 'smart codes' and (b) transect planning. One of the major targets of new urbanism has always been the long-established American institution of zoning, and associated land platting and subdivision regulations. They have identified these legal institutions that have defined much of the American urban and rural landscape for centuries, as principally responsible for the dysfunctional, inefficient, auto-oriented and ultimately unsustainable urban form (see, e.g., Talen 2012). This criticism of zoning and related institutions is not limited to new urbanists; others have leveled similar criticisms against zoning and associated codes and standards responsible for much of urban sprawl (Ben-Joseph 2005; Levine 2006). The argument for FBC or 'smart codes' over conventional zoning is based on two seemingly contradictory arguments. On the one hand, zoning is seen as too rigid and incapable of adapting to new circumstances. At the same time zoning is also seen as an institution constantly compromised by variance, conditional uses or special development agreements, and thus becoming too unpredictable. This latter is essentially a critique of zoning's vulnerability to the Aristotelian process. FBCs or smart codes are seen as offering predictability in the production of the urban form, more so than traditional zoning, according to some larger schema of things, such as transect planning (Duany and Talen 2002; Talen 2012).

As Duany and Talen (2002) acknowledge, the concept of a transect is drawn from the earlier work of renowned biologist–planner Sir Patrick Geddes (1915). It refers to the continuum of nature and human settlements based on the ecological relationships between human activities and the suitability or constraints of the landscape. The idea of organizing human settlements by scale and intensity according to such a continuum was also expressed by Lynch (1976) and McHarg (1969), as noted previously. The new urbanist formulation of the transect consists of a continuum of six 'ecozones' from 'Rural Preserve' to 'Urban Core', with 'Rural Reserve', 'Sub-Urban', 'General Urban' and 'Urban Center' as intermediate stages with growing urban intensity. This transect then becomes the basis for FBC or smart codes that specify precisely the building disposition, building configuration, building function and various standards for parking, landscaping, signs and so on for each of these ecozones (Duany and Talen 2002, p. 254). In developing this premise of transect-based planning, the authors derive considerable legitimacy from ecological principles, although codes are quite specific, and the application of deterministic design schema very Platonic.

The new urbanism movement and ideas have their share of detractors. The scope of this chapter will not allow a detailed review of the critique. In a recent article Cliff Ellis (2010) summarizes these critiques – some empirical, some ideological – but seemingly, according to the author, not always based on full understanding of the movement's aims and purposes.

We must also consider the important work of Christopher Alexander, if only briefly, in discovering timeless 'patterns' of relationship of human activities and functionings and the built environment. These 'patterns' then become the ingredients of effective and efficient urban design. Although sustainability was never an overt theme, one could revisit these patterns with sustainability in mind and may find some relevance. Nevertheless the pattern language was conceived largely as a Platonic approach to city design (see Alexander et al. 1977).

Landscape (Ecological) Urbanism: Ecological and Aristotelian

If new urbanism is a product of the profession of architecture, the roots of ecological or landscape urbanism lie squarely in the profession and tradition of landscape architecture. The challenge of balancing the production and consumption of natural resources in the built environment and its larger ecological context has been confronted for some time in the environmental design profession. Anne Spirn (2011) refers to the writings of Leon Battista Alberti in the fifteenth century, and more recently to such pioneers as George Perkins Marsh, Frederick Law Olmsted and Lewis Mumford. The essential normative position in these writings was that human settlements should be considered an essential part of nature and the larger ecosystem. Clearly this position is quite foundational, and while aware of human needs and purposes, the primacy of the ecological consideration was central to this genre of thinking. Accordingly, this approach belongs to the upper half of the chart.

The arguments and methods developed in McHarg's *Design With Nature* have considerably influenced landscape or ecological planning projects in the second half of the last century. But while McHarg's work was uncompromisingly Platonic, adaptation of his deterministic analytic schema, and method in the contemporary public planning context reflects the reality of the political and institutional structures of environmental decision-making – the Aristotelian imperatives, that is. The contribution of Frederick Steiner (1991), a student of McHarg, is noteworthy in this regard. His process model of ecological planning, while using technical methods of land suitability analysis, is exemplary in including participation of the community at large. This Aristotelian process in environmental design has been further advanced by the writings and projects of Randolph Hester (2006) of UC Berkeley.

But the notion of ecological (or landscape) urbanism today implies a larger, and assertive claim, about sustainability. This movement is led by the likes of Charles Waldheim (2006) and Mohsen Mostafavi (2010) of Harvard Graduate School of Design and their University of Pennsylvania compatriots. 'Landscape urbanism', claimed Waldheim, 'describes disciplinary realignment currently underway in which landscape replaces architecture as the basic building block of urbanism' (quoted in Scheer 2011, p. 612). In a more expansive note, Mostafavi (2010) argues that a 'key characteristic of ecological urbanism is its recognition of the scale and scope of the impact of ecology, which extends beyond the urban territory' and, further, '[T]his regional, holistic approach, with its consequent national and global considerations, demonstrates the multi-scalar quality of ecological urbanism' (p. 130).

These proclamations, lofty as they are, lack palpable aims and examples. Thus, according to Sorlien and Talen (2012), 'most Landscape Urbanism designs exist only on the drawing board'. Others have questioned the ambiguous nature of the concept, or whether it has anything new to add beyond the McHargian paradigm, and that it is only a new territorial claim of the existing domain of practice in landscape architecture and urban design (Andersson 2012).

While it is true that ecological (or landscape) urbanism remains provisional, indeterminate and organic, much in the manner in which landscapes change and evolve, some general principles and propositions of ecological urbanism have been articulated as suggested by Anne Spirn (2011, pp. 603–7), such principles capture the promises of this evolving movement:

- Every city has a deep, enduring context
- Cities are habitats
- Cities are ecosystems
- Urban ecosystems are connected
- Urban ecosystems are dynamic
- Urban design is a powerful tool of adaptation.

It should be apparent then that this north-east quadrant draws from both the north-west and south-east quadrants, but remains somewhat in opposition to the south-west quadrant.[6]

TOWARD AN INTEGRATIVE FRAMEWORK

I began by proposing a conceptual framework to organize the literature on sustainability from the perspectives of the design disciplines and professions. Now it is time to propose an integrative framework for combining multiple ideas on principles, standards, methods, processes, models and performance characteristics. Toward this end I have benefited from a recent synthesis of literature on sustainability and urban form offered by Yosef Rafeq Jabareen (2006) of Technion University in Haifa. He has been able to extract seven essential design concepts pertaining to sustainable urban form. These are: compactness; sustainable transport; density; mixed land use; diversity; passive solar design; greening. He observes further that the literature suggests four models of urban form derived from various combinations of these seven popular design concepts. These are: Neotraditional Development; Urban Containment; Compact City; and the Eco-City. Jabareen also attempts to show how these form types score against these criteria.

In Table19.1 I summarize the essential imperatives, initiatives, orthodoxies and normative directions for sustainability as might be achieved through city design. The field is evolving and the very concept of sustainability is a work in progress. The design responses to the sustainability challenge are very much influenced not only by professional predilections, but also by specific orthodoxies and movements. The design responses can be either ends or means oriented, or may involve aspects of performance measures, methods, processes, design concepts and principles, urban form models and so on. Table 19.1 is an attempt to capture these responses. Of necessity, details have been omitted, but the reader can track them down through the references provided in the text of this chapter.

I should conclude with a few caveats. First, Table 19.1 is not exhaustive in covering the bumper crop of books and monographs written on this subject, as noted earlier. Second, not all experts may necessarily agree with my classification. Third, I see this organizational frame as a work in progress, as is the concept of sustainability, the meaning of which is still questioned and debated, even among the academics.[7] I suggest that the way towards sustainable urban form should be informed by a critical understanding of our theoretical roots.

In a seminal book published in 1971, Harvard philosopher John Rawls wrote about a theory of justice, based primarily on what he called a conception of ‘justice as fairness’. Thirty years later he published another book, *Justice as Fairness*, a restatement of his original argument. He believed that his original argument did not make it clear ‘whether justice

Table 19.1 Toward an integrative framework

End	Four quadrants from Figure 19.1			
	Ecological-Platonic	Anthropocentric-Platonic	Ecological-Aristotelian	Anthropocentric-Aristotelian
Performance measures				Vitality, efficiency and justice
Form models	Eco-city	Neo-traditional design	Urban containment	Compact city
Processes			Ecological landscape planning	User control and participation
Methods	Land suitability analysis	Transect planning		
Design concepts, principles	Passive solar design	Form-based codes, density, sustainable transport, mixed land use	Greening, diversity, sustainable transport, mixed land use	Compactness, diversity
Means	Platonic	◄──────	──────►	Aristotelian

Sources: (a) Jabreen 2006; Author.

as fairness is a comprehensive moral doctrine or a political conception of justice' (Rawls 2001, p. xvii). In the restatement he asserts that 'justice as fairness is now presented as a political conception of justice'. The notion of sustainability involves similar conflict along the Platonic–Aristotelian dimension. The design profession would like to see cities designed as Platonic cities or, alternatively, shaped by ecological determinism. But in liberal democracies, cities are Aristotelian in character, works in progress, and the design dimension of sustainability will be ultimately determined by a 'political conception' of sustainability determined through an experiential Aristotelian process. This conclusion, I am sure, will be disappointing to some, but inescapable, I am afraid.

ACKNOWLEDGMENT

I would like to acknowledge constructive edits from Hilda Blanco. End notes 2 and 3 are verbatim inclusions of her thoughtful notes.

NOTES

1. I have used this dichotomy quite extensively to organize the literature pertaining to urban design in my editorial introduction to a forthcoming four-volume collection of major works in urban design. Entitled *Urban Design: Critical Concepts in Urban Studies*, which was published by Routledge in 2014.
2. A good example is the difference between traditional zoning – the Euclidean approach, with fixed and separate land uses – and performance zoning, where there are no fixed zones, but as long as one meets the performance standards or the goals, one can use any combination of means.
3. I would emphasize the basic distinction between a Platonic versus Aristotelian perspective as that between the Platonic emphasis on ideal fixed schema or forms, and the more experiential, socially focused Aristotelian approach.
4. I use the term 'functioning' in the sense Amartya Sen (1999, p. 75) defines it in his seminal book on development and freedom. According to Sen:

   > The concept of 'functionings,' which has distinctly Aristotelian roots, reflects the various things a person may value doing or being. The valued functionings may vary from elementary ones, such as being adequately nourished and being free from avoidable disease, to very complex activities or personal states, such as being able to take part in the life of the community and having self-respect.

5. The CNU Charter has been translated in Arabic, Chinese, Creole, German, Spanish, French, Polish and Swedish. According to the CNU website, translations in Hindi and other languages will be available soon.
6. Indeed the ideological tension between these two quadrants is captured in a recent publication of essays edited by two leading protagonists of new urbanism. See Duany and Talen (2013).
7. Note the PLANET posting by Martin Krieger, 'Sustainable, congestion for articles', 22 March 2013.

REFERENCES

Alexander, Christopher, Sara Ishikawa, Murray Silverstein, with Max Jacobson, Ingrid Fiksdahl-King and Shlomo Angel (1977), *A Pattern Language: Towns, Buildings, Construction*, New York: Oxford University Press.

Andersson, Thorbjörn (2012), 'Landscape urbanism vs. landscape design', in Tigran Haas (ed.), *Sustainable Urbanism and Beyond: Rethinking Cities of the Future*, New York: Rizzoli, pp. 159–61.

Banerjee, Tridib and Michael Southworth (eds) (1990), *City Sense and City Design: Writings and Projects of Kevin Lynch*, Boston, MA: The MIT Press.

Ben-Joseph, Eran (2005), *The Code of the City: Standards and the Hidden Language of Place-Making*, Boston, MA: The MIT Press.

Birch, Eugenie (2011), 'From CIAM to CNU: the roots and thinkers of modern urban design', in Tridib Banerjee and Anastasia Loukaitou-Sideris (eds), *Companion to Urban Design*, London: Routledge, pp. 9–29.

Boyer, M. Christine (2011), 'Two orders of cybernetics in urban form and design', in Tridib Banerjee and Anastasia Loukaitou-Sideris (eds), *Companion to Urban Design*, London: Routledge, pp. 70–83.

Campbell, S. (1996), 'Green cities, growing cities, just cities? Urban planning and the contradictions of sustainable development', *Journal of the American Planning Association*, **62** (3), 296–312.

Congress for the New Urbanism (CNU) (2012), 'Charter of the new urbanism', available at http://www.cnu.org/sites/www.cnu.org/files/charter_english1.pdf (accessed 30 March 2013).

Duany, Andrés and Emily Talen (2002), 'Transect planning', *Journal of the American Planning Association*, **68** (3), 245–66.

Duany, Andrés and Emily Talen (eds) (2013), *Landscape Urbanism and Its Discontents: Dissimulating the Sustainable City*, Gabriola Island, BC: New Society Publishers.

Ellis, C. (2010), 'The new urbanism: critiques and rebuttals', *Journal of Urban Design*, **7** (3), 261–91.

Garde, Ajay M. (2004), 'New urbanism as sustainable growth? A supply side story and its implications for public policy', *Journal of Planning Education and Research*, **24** (2), 154–70.

Garde, Ajay M. (2006), 'Designing and developing new urbanist projects in the United States: insights and implications', *Journal of Urban Design*, **11** (1), 33–54.

Geddes, Patrick (1915), *Cities in Evolution*, London: Williams and Norgate.

Hester, Randolph (2006), *Design for Ecological Democracy*, Boston, MA: The MIT Press.

Jabareen, Yosef R. (2006), 'Sustainable urban forms: their typologies, models, and concepts', *Journal of Planning Education and Research*, **26** (1), 38–52.

Jacobs, Allan and Donald Appleyard (1987), 'Toward an urban design manifesto', *Journal of the American Planning Association*, **53** (1), 112–20.

Levine, Jonathan (2006), *Zoned Out: Regulations, Markets, and Choices in Transportation and Metropolitan Land-Use*, Washington, DC: Resources for the Future.

Lynch, Kevin (1962), *Site Planning*, Boston, MA: The MIT Press.

Lynch, Kevin (1976), *Managing the Sense of a Region*, Boston, MA: The MIT Press.

Lynch, Kevin (1981), *A Theory of Good City Form*, Boston, MA: The MIT Press.

Lynch, Kevin and Gary Hack (eds) (1984), *Site Planning*, 3rd edn, Boston, MA: The MIT Press.

Lynch, Kevin (with contributions by Michael Southworth, ed.) (1990), *Wasting Away*, San Francisco, CA: Sierra Club Books.

McHarg, Ian (1969), *Design With Nature*, Garden City, NY: Natural History Press.

Mostafavi, M. (2010), 'Why ecological urbanism? Why now?', *Harvard Design Magazine*, **32**, 124–35.

Peattie, Lisa (1987), *Planning: Rethinking Ciudad Guyana*, Ann Arbor, MI: University of Michigan Press.

Rawls, John (1971), *A Theory of Justice*, Boston, MA: Harvard University Press.

Rawls, John (2001), *Justice as Fairness: A Restatement*, Cambridge, MA: Harvard University Press.

Scheer, Brenda (2011), 'Metropolitan form and landscape', in Tridib Banerjee and Anastasia Loukaitou-Sideris (eds), *Companion to Urban Design*, London: Routledge, pp. 611–18.

Sen, Amartya (1999), *Development as Freedom*, New York: Random House.

Sorlien, Sandy and Emily Talen (2012), 'Out of place: context-based codes and the transect', in Tigran Haas (ed.), *Sustainable Urbanism and Beyond: Rethinking Cities of the Future*, New York: Rizzoli, pp. 99–104.

Spirn, Anne Whiston (2011), 'Ecological urbanism', in Tridib Banerjee and Anastasia Loukaitou-Sideris (eds), *Companion to Urban Design*, London: Routledge, pp. 600–610.

Steiner, Frederick (1991), *The Living Landscape: An Ecological Approach to Landscape Planning*, New York: McGraw-Hill.

Talen, Emily (2012), *City Rules: How Regulations Affect Urban Form*, Washington, DC: Island Press.

Waldheim, Charles (2006), 'A reference manifesto', in Charles Waldheim (ed.), *Landscape Urbanism Reader*, New York: Princeton Architectural Press, pp. 15–19.

20. The future of sustainable economic development in cities

Edward J. Blakely

In all respects, since the inception of the field of economic development, the notion and practice of sustainability has been a core principle. As a founder of the academic and professional field of local economic development, my first edition of *Planning Local Economic Development* (Blakely 1990) is premised on the notion that local communities (cities, towns, neighbourhoods) could and should form themselves into economically viable units based on their continuous and replenishable resources. In this way, I argued, the basic foundation of sustainable economic development is endogenous (local resources) development. Local resources are described as human, physical, social, economic, organization/institutional and governmental or regulatory. Regional economies are not isolated units; they operate in a larger and increasingly global framework. However, central to the concept of local economic development is making choices within the global framework on what and how to use resources of the locality – no matter how place is defined. My concept of sustainable economic development grows out of more than 50 years of practice along with academic teaching. My concept rests on three pillars. First, economic development must be indigenous; that is, it should be driven by use of the human, natural and community resources in the place and not by external economic drivers. That is not to say that a firm attracted to a place is a bad idea. But the firm needs to fit the environment, instead of forcing the environment, human and physical, to be altered to fit the firm. Changing tax regimes, labour laws and the like to attract firms do not have sustainable outcomes. Eventually, the firms leave because they cannot compete without the actual or implied subsidies. Second, sustainability means adding value to and not extracting value from a place. Sustainable economic development builds community resources as it educates and gives back to the place and the people in the locale, continuously creating and adjusting to the environment. Finally, sustainable economics grows and spreads wealth, both knowledge and money, throughout the community, enriching the entire environment.

THE DIRECTION OF SUSTAINABLE ECONOMIC DEVELOPMENT

Sustainable economic geographies are based on interconnected spaces, which can be as small as a few blocks in a city or a small town covering thousands of square kilometres. Inherent in the notion of local place is the identity appended to the location. In most instances, a name denotes the economic space – St Leonards or Paul's Crossing as places where people live, shop and some work. But a large city is a local economic geography, too. New York City and London are celebrated name places with large interconnected eco-geographies within them. We know the sub-parts of these large metropolitan centres as well as we know the whole. Brooklyn and Westminster are visible operating units of New York and London respectively. Hollywood is part of Los Angeles. Hollywood is a small global hub in a larger economic system. People in Hollywood identify with the territory as a living place as well as a global economic entity. Therefore it is important to parse the concept of sustainable local economic development into sub-locations and venues that connect to larger places. In essence, we need to make every part of the system sustainable to have a larger sustainable economy. This is an easy concept to discuss but very hard to implement. In resource-extractive areas such as gold- and coalmines or oil wells, the local environment and the local community are often sacrificed for the larger global economic system.

Few towns from which natural resources are extracted are wealthy places. Most of these once-vital places are abandoned when the resource humans and minerals are depleted

My view of economic development is that all places deserve to be part of a healthy, socially robust economic system to be sustainable. It is not sufficient for a single housing development to claim sustainability because it has solar panels on roofs. Nor is it all right to live off the prosperity derived from mining and other natural resources, and say – 'that's their problem'. We must all work together to develop sustainable communities across the globe. Our individual actions are important. When we make purchases based on resource extraction, we are able, in some instances (not enough), to select those that have added wealth back to the place where the resource came from over those that simply rip it out of the ground and leave people and communities to fend for themselves. In this chapter, I will focus on local economic sustainability from the perspective of place continuity and enhancements as well as individual and collective actions that stimulate increasing sustainable outcomes for people and places.

An Old Paradigm, Renewed

Sustainable economic development is not new. For most of the history of man, preservation of the local landscape was part of survival. Early man could not deplete stream, forests or land. He had no equipment to move beyond his domain. Wheels and animal energy changed this situation and induced larger settlements. However, until the Industrial Revolution, these places depended on the accessible resources near them. Machinery has broken the link between 'what we get' and 'what we have as the means to attain it'. The fundamental goal of sustainable economic development is to restore these links. We have to change the assumptions that

- economic production is the *de facto* goal of society and must be the measure of all economic activity;
- knowledge is a good that can be traded and kept by owners;
- the only (legitimate and sanctioned) means of obtaining economic rewards is through work on a job;
- scarcity rules all exchanges; and
- natural resources are assets to be used for economic gain.

These fundamental assumptions have to be challenged, and for a changed economic system to take place we must replace them with a new and increasingly accepted set of notions that form the basis for sustainable economic development. These are:

- increasing the options and opportunities for people and places to participate in the socioeconomic system is primary;
- extending and preserving natural and human resources is fundamental;
- equity and equality are the best measures of the health of an economic system; and
- quality is more important than quantity in producing goods and services.

With this new set of assumptions, we can proceed to build a sustainable local economy in several ways.

We have to build a new system that is people- over thing-oriented. This means that all human resources are valued. This seems obvious, but it does not reflect the practice. In many places in the developing world, women, as well as tribal or ethnic groups, are excluded by rules from participation in the society's production systems. In advanced nations, some of the same barriers exist for females in various degrees, with discriminating impacts for female participation in the labour markets. Minorities and indigenous people fare no better in market-based economic models. In effect, the income gap is a clear measure of the sustainability of economic outputs. The wider the gaps between haves and have-nots by race, ethnicity or locality, the less sustainable the economy will be in the present and the future.

Second, we must move to an economy that redistributes wealth versus one that intensifies it into a few sectors of the economy and a few groups and organizations in control. In this way, a diversified economy is a sustainable economy generating wealth more evenly as well as ensuring deep democratic rights for people in the society.

Third, we must localize as we globalize. Marginalization of people in places is one of the by-products of a competitive global economy. Agriculture is a prime example. Farmers are growing more commodities all over the world but less food. Global prices make farming by small food growers uneconomic while driving up prices of nutritious crops and making it hard for the lowest-income earners to eat proper diets (Hazell and Woods 2008, p. 495).

A new paradigm for sustainable economic development emerged from the work of Schumpeter (1975), who argued that local development is the only form of sustainable development. If localities fail to take charge of their own direction, they will be the victims of the process of creative destruction. Witness how Detroit and much of the US Midwest, Southern Spain, Italy and Greece, former bulwarks of civilizations and economic productivity, are currently in disarray based on the assumption that people can move and communities can die as a by-product of global rationalization.

A NEW APPROACH

Sustainable economic development does not argue with globalization but takes issue with the processes of current globalization practices that are unsustainable and unaccountable. I suggest that the global economy needs to be based on locally based competition within a framework where all can participate. Large transnational firms that hoard access and information, operating outside the bounds of free trade agreements, currently dominate global trade. As a result, small nations and communities are forced to trade at a distinct disadvantage. In fact, global firms can destroy local communities. We have all seen the devastation of formerly strong downtowns as big multinational firms enter the market, underpricing local firms, and thereby making the central part of the city uncompetitive and uneconomic. As these giants control the market, they tend to introduce price regimes that are uniform, distorting economic reality and forbidding smaller merchants from participation. In effect, there is no market any more. My contention is that the playing field needs to be levelled.

The Levers for a New Economy

First, large multinationals should not be given subsidies and tax breaks for moving or establishing their branches in any nation, state or community. Removing this distortion would allow a genuine global competition where the smaller, more agile firms with Internet and other connectivity can offer goods at competitive prices anywhere. As Elkins points out, the 'highly integrated global economy of the 1990s, dominated by . . . a few hundred multinational corporations, bears little resemblance . . . to the rules conceived post war . . . nor to the models of perfect competition, which justified the emphasis on free trade' (Elkins 1992, p. 86).

I believe that removing the distortions in the market, and not adding to them as many global transnationals favour, can restore good, if not perfect, competition.

Extraction taxes and levies

Changing the tax structure to reflect the costs of extraction and environmental plundering as opposed to taxing work incomes is the central mechanism for government operations. Increasingly, extraction firms ask for fewer taxes and restrictions to move limited resources to global consumption markets. This is wrong-headed for two reasons. First, easing extraction means that the time to depletion is shortened. When the mines and people around them are exhausted, these firms move on or transform themselves into new institutions based on the capital they accrued while extracting the limited resource. Second, low taxes on both extraction and consumption, as in the case of petrol, means that the transition to other forms of living or energy occurs too slowly or too uneconomically for new entrants into the market who might offer better or more sustainable supplies. It is profoundly important that this link be broken for any form of sustainable economy to emerge. Last, local suppliers or entrepreneurs cannot compete with the internal subsides of the transnationals. As leading global agriculture scientists, Hazell and Woods (2008, p. 495) put it so eloquently,

> As a result of agricultural intensification, more food is produced today than needed to feed the entire world population and at prices that have never been so low. Yet despite this success and the impact of globalization and increasing world trade in agriculture, there remain large, persistent and, in some cases, worsening spatial differences in the ability of society to both feed themselves and protect the long term productive capacity of their natural resources.

Agriculture and soil

Agricultural reform is at the heart of sustainable development. Global agricultural practices have reached a critical stage. Soil exhaustion and depletion are rampant across the world. Agri-farms use land like big mining companies. They extract the nutrients from the land and move on. Moreover, farming and food are not synonymous. Much land is devoted to growing soy or other crops that are part of the plastics and chemical industries, and not the food chain. Again, farm subsidies, along with related governmental policies affected more by politics than economics, distort agricultural practices. This is not just a matter of how farmers make a living. Communities are directly affected by agricultural practices. In a seminal study of two towns in California's Central Valley, it was shown that agri-industrial farming led to the collapse of the small towns, whereas nearby small vegetable-producing farming communities were vital and viable places to live (Goldschmidt 1947). Food production is a central feature of sustainable economic development. Not only is food-growing important to the local economy; it alters the regional economies. Chicago is a classic example of the link between food production and distribution and poverty. As the food bowl around Chicago collapsed, good jobs in harvesting and moving crops, as well as in selling them, also collapsed, creating 'food and job deserts' (Chicago Community Trust 2002).

Globalizing agriculture is placing enormous pressure on soils. Farmers on the urban fringe sell out. One can argue that this land may some day go back into production – but at what cost? Others argue that food can be produced in the city. This is true, but we need to redesign local economies to do this in the same way that we must reconfigure power for solar or decentralized power generation to replace the grid. Good soils are not replaceable, so an urgent goal for sustainable economic development is land stewardship and preservation (Montogmery 2007).

Sustainable land development will require transfer payments to land managers (farmers) who are paid to maintain fertile landscapes for the larger society to enjoy clean water, fish habitats and similar valuable non-tangible resources. New York City is already doing this in Upstate New York along the Hudson River to ensure the purity of its water supply. Several European nations such as Switzerland are seeing the need to provide farm operators with land-care incomes (Robertson et al. 2009).

Energy

It is easy to argue that energy use is an addiction. People drive short distances as a preference and not as a need. People keep televisions and air conditioners on when they are not at home, even though the price is high. No matter the compulsion, the results are catastrophic. There is no need to recatalogue the consequences of energy abuse in this chapter. However, since energy is a cornerstone of every form of economic activity, its use is central to a sustainable productive pattern. Three choices are offered for energy:

1. Reduce energy demand – this is the rational strategy for more energy-efficient buildings and appliances. However, just changing the amount does not alter the direction of energy consumption. Sustainable economic development would suggest taking more energy uses out of the stream – for example by reducing the number of vehicles with higher taxes for owning them, and a similar policy for ownership and operation of television sets. This may seem silly but until recently everyone in the UK had to have a radio licence. Why not licences for energy-guzzling appliances like air conditioners and rebates for off-peak use?
2. Alternative fuels sound good. However, altered fuels, like bio-fuels, require production systems. As we grow more corn or sugar as bio-fuel, this affects the environment and the food supply. Doing with less use or fewer uses is a better alternative. Solar and similar new technologies are handicapped in the marketplace by larger utilities that control central distribution systems.
3. Changing living patterns holds the most promise, since different settlement patterns yield distinctive energy consumptions. For example, cycling and walking reduce the need for autos and reinforce social and community building. Higher density introduces all forms of friendly and economic mixes that can improve community energy uses and lead to decentralized energy generation preferences.

Mixes of these three approaches have to be employed over time in different institutional environments and based on current regimes. Energy must be the pivot for a local or higher-level economic development policy. To accomplish good energy use, national policy is required either to support it or not to get in its way. A case in point is the movement of many communities to decentralized localized power over the objections of centralized, legacy energy production systems. From these examples, it is clear that government policies can encourage new forms of energy, some of which might be wind farms, or regional solar water systems. These systems can generate power on private or government local lands. Energy presents an unusual opportunity to use decentralized energy production as a local economic development income stream. In California and some other places, small energy providers can already feed flows into the grid and distribution system. In the future, more sustainable economic development calls for more communities to disconnect from the main system and produce energy locally through collective neighbourhood-level approaches (Green Leigh and Blakely 2013).

Travel and transport

Travel and transport are closely connected to energy use. Sustainability cannot be achieved without large-scale changes in how people move and are transported. Collective travel can be achieved only with changes in how time is used. For communal travel to make a difference, work hours and work locations must be altered. The current practice of Monday through Friday 7:00 to 7:00 peak travel is a convention and not a necessity. Community travel is a matter of local business and government decision making. One of the larger opportunities in sustainable local economics is shifting work closer to homes. Moving work makes good sense because there are vacant lands, buildings and under-utilized space in many small towns that can be retrofitted for work purposes. Some research indicates gains in productivity when work is decentralized. Surely, if tele-work centres can move halfway around the world, back-office work can be moved a few kilometres to nearby suburbs. To accomplish this, local governments in suburbs or community organizations must become active in promoting the reuse of local space. Cities such as Sydney, Australia, are employing this approach to revitalize old shopping districts with fresh low-cost workspaces for new entrepreneurs and as nearby back-office locations.

Community economic development corporations

Community economic development corporations and/or neighbourhood development corporations can become a new wave of local governments providing platforms for new and existing businesses or social capital ventures such as housing, schools and community food stores. As part of this approach, old community markets are being transformed into large-scale business incubators in a new format where small businesses, new businesses and immigrants can make a start with new product services or different ways of marketing in open-air or enclosed markets. This is how central markets started, and now they are re-emerging in the suburbs where shopping centres once dominated the retail marketplace (Blakely 1990).

Environment and settlement patterns

Environment and settlement patterns are critical and central to every facet of sustainable development. Other chapters in this volume cover this topic. From an economic development perspective, sustainability is the ability of land uses to be fungible. That is, it should be possible to convert one building use into another without great costs. Today, too many buildings are built for a single purpose. Schools should be convertible into offices or housing, and the reverse should be true as well. In particular, business districts are hard to make into housing areas. In the CBD (central business district), such a direct functionality may make sense, but there are too many examples of single-purpose shopping malls scarring the landscape post use. Smart jurisdictions are requiring that community plans include good mixes of buildings and that many of these buildings on frontage streets be designed as multi-purpose buildings. In this way, the community can mature and change with minimum new investment. This adaptability in an era of climate change will become increasingly important.

Density and affordability

Although issues of density and affordability are covered elsewhere in this volume, they should be mentioned here. Social mix reduces economic isolation. Simply put, as low-income people mix with others, there is information transfer for work and social supports that helps to increase participation in labour markets and reduce welfare burdens. Pursuing affordability and density contributes to reducing economic physical distances, which in turn increases information for lower-income groups regarding jobs, improvement in school achievement and other related socioeconomic outcomes. This, in turn, reduces gaps that hold back economic regions and communities. There is plenty of evidence that more economically affordable places are more productive places, too (Goldsmith 2010).

New Roles and Rules

Economies do not operate in a government-free environment. Some recent neoliberal thinking suggests that government and its regulatory apparatus are at odds with markets, and that, as a result, government must be curtailed. Governments establish the rules for economic activity. If there were no government intervention, markets would be skewed to large conglomerates and competition stifled. One can argue, in light of the global financial crisis of the late part of the first decade of the 2000s, that this is our condition. Today, markets cannot produce the desirable outcomes because regulatory regimes are light or lacking. No matter where one stands on this issue, it is clear that some forms of government intervention are required, because, otherwise, markets are distorted away from communities and sustainability goals in favour of short-term gains. Sustainable development requires government at every level to set the boundaries of sustainable behaviour, for example by establishing how much of a resource can be depleted and the regime for replacing it, if this is possible. Government has to set sustainability targets as well. Requiring the auto industry to extend petrol kilometres (or gas mileage) changes the rules of the game. Similarly, safety and other regulations ensure that all firms are moving society in a common direction. Housing standards requiring insulation and water recycling to meet local sustainability standards are interventions into a failed market. As some firms exceed the targets, the economy benefits from innovations that these firms stimulate. Moreover, sustainability targets are incentives for new start-up firms to spawn creativity in the market system.

Economic value must also be part of the sustainability equation. One business practice might be cheaper, such as sealed windows when energy is cheap, but not sustainable when energy prices change. As a result, government has to provide the guideposts for longer-term public interests with respect to economic outputs.

Business

Offering goods and services is at the core of sustainability. Every firm, from sole proprietor to major corporation, is part of an economic system from suppliers to final demand delivery. Firms that think this through add value to the entire economic system. Amory Lovins (2012) suggests that the transition from today's resource-depleted and human-degrading systems can be made into a new economic order in the USA, generating millions of brand-new jobs and saving net $500 trillion in the coming decades (see Figures 20.1 and 20.2). Thus we argue that the movement to clean industries will be a more efficient system than the current one.

Fundamentally, the new role of business is not to resist regulations aimed at sustainability targets but to generate modern firms and open new sectors of the economy while shifting from goods-producing to information-based activities. How do we innovate in a new information-based economy when new resources are now ubiquitous? For example, the fresh-fruit office drink machine generates opportunities for machine manufacturing as well as options for software to blend drinks in new ways by machine, and opportunities for sustainable suppliers and reuse recycling processes. Thus an information economy is flatter in a hierarchy with few constraints on employees. This 'brave new world' is here. Workers are nested in firm environments with fibre-optic backbones. New, more nimble firms are hubs with a variety of access points. Stationary work sites will disappear for millions, and this in turn will allow people to be more creative about how and where they work. In these economies, barriers to entry such as physical handicaps, skin colour or background can be reduced. Employment justice is central to sustainable outcomes since the firm is a collective of skills rather than a container of people made to fit routine processes. This new open system is the starting point for future business sustainability.

Source: Lovins (2012).

Figure 20.1 Old economy

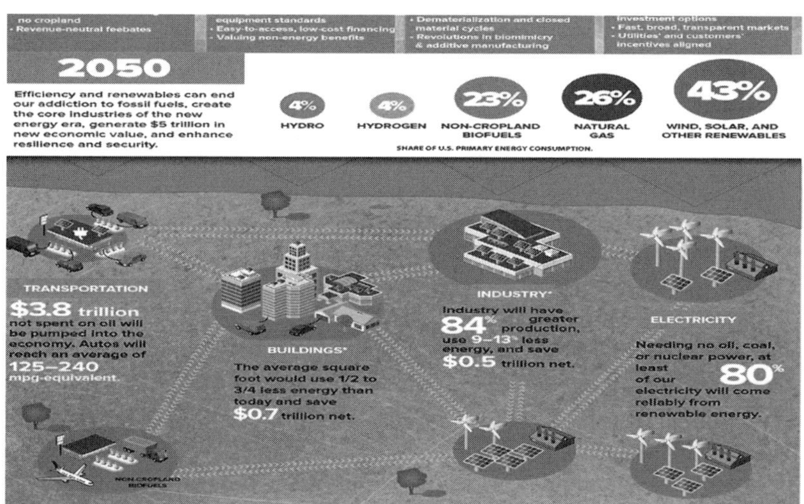

Source: Lovins (2012).

Figure 20.2 New economy

Technology

Technological processes that support the environment and prompt reductions in waste and consumption is an important principle. Much modern technology is energy intensive. Reducing energy consumption is a technological goal that can generate new firm start-ups in renewable energy, including solar, wind and tides, and other means, as well as through various forms of monitoring or 'process flow' regulatory systems that turn equipment on and off, and regulate building thermal performance. A myriad of new tech start-ups are coming into being, dealing with regional and national problems. Our current approach to capital raising for these ambitious new entrants is complex. Creating a new economy requires creating new capital formation organizations. For example, an idea being seriously considered is to develop low-capital-investment opportunities for people to invest in start-up firms where risks are elevated but with correspondingly high rewards. To date, only sophisticated investors can place money in complex vehicles for this purpose. This seems silly when there are no regulations on placing bets on the government-run lottery or in gaming casinos.

Glocalization

Glocalization requires every place to compete on a worldwide platform, as local nodes linking to global trade systems and not dependent on other larger places to be their gateways of trade. Local communities must become more self-reliant. De-linking from the global economy is not plausible. However, we can and should find ways for communities to adjust to the world from where they are. Communities can do this. There are many examples of communities that are thriving in a global world by maintaining and extending core assets such as tourism sites or celebrations and special crafts. These communities have connected into global systems without sacrificing local culture and values. Examples abound, such as Ashland, Oregon with its Shakespeare Festival and the villages along the 'walk of the Virgin' in Spain. Other communities, such as Orem, Utah, a computer software centre, and upstate New York, a new heart of web-based publishing and production systems, have entered global production by providing small-town village lifestyles for creative people. It is not size but community strategy and leadership that count. In each of these cases, strong sustainability values manifested in very different ways form the core of the communities. These local communities thrive in the global market through modern technology and not through its rejection. Sustainable economies and sustainable communities come in all sizes and shapes.

Taxation

Taxation is the key to how societies function. Taxes are the mechanism that distributes or reallocates money. Tax systems that reward farmers for converting their land from farms to houses by not imposing a 'value capture' tax ensure that the process of conversion will continue. However, basic tax regimes modelled on the principle of 'site value' would place taxes on the land rents of land and not so much on earners of employment income. In essence, land would be taxed for what it could produce, not for what it is being used. Therefore a property owner who let his building rot would pay taxes as if the building could draw a good rent if improved. Under this process, the Henry George approach, as many know it, land would always be performing at its maximum level. Under such land-value tax systems, inner-city derelict properties would be cleaned up and put on the market quickly. On the other hand, there would be less interest in building more in the suburbs, too far from infrastructure and government assets (George 1897). Sustainability requires a sustaining tax system. A site-value taxation approach would induce more sustainable economic behaviour.

Female and indigenous values

Female and indigenous values involve the instinct to preserve and protect. Several scholars have suggested that the natural feminine and native people's instincts of caring need to replace the pillaging character of current economic systems. There is little doubt that economics as currently understood and practised has fleeting regard for what comes next. Brand-new sets of values are essential to develop a sustainable economic perspective for cities of the future. Fundamentally, economics is a philosophy, and new guiding paradigms produce different outcomes, as we have witnessed in the shift from Keynesian to neoclassical economics.

PRODUCING A SUSTAINABLE COMMUNITY-BASED ECONOMY

Talking about economic transformation is easy. Making the transition to a local economy based on the principles discussed in this chapter is hard. I attempt to provide a framework for this process here (see Figure 20.3).

1. *Resource base*. Every community has to examine what their resource base really is. In too many instances, the resources are thought of in terms of local businesses, visitors or natural resources. However, in a global economy the prime resource is 'human capacity'. Communities need to develop an in-depth analysis of 'who is in the economic catch-

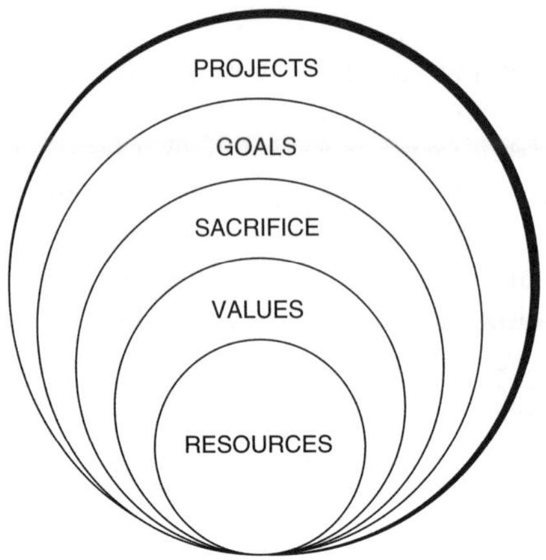

Source: Author.

Figure 20.3 Sustainable economic development process

ment', which is very different from what businesses or enterprises make up the community. For instance, many communities are ageing, so there are increasing numbers of retired people. Most of us think of these people as 'spent capital'. We look at what they did and not what they can do. Smart communities are surveying and human-resource-auditing people's skills. A woman who was a homemaker may also be a good project manager or accountant. A man who spent much of his life in manufacturing might be a talented actor or musician. Skills and opportunity audits are essential to assess the range of economic opportunities for a community. An excellent example is a community over 1000 kilometres from a major university in Western Australia. The community wanted to have a campus of the university in their town, both to keep young people and to enhance community life for seniors. A community audit revealed that the town had attracted a number of retired university faculties and former teachers. As a result, this community was blessed with the combination of the Internet and local people to offer degree programmes and continuing education. The social capital of communities is a major resource that can be tapped to generate, preserve or extend economic wealth.

2. *Determining the economic values of the community*. Many people say, 'everyone in our community shares the same values'. This may be true, until it is tested. When values are tested in action, such as in cases that call for increasing community density or adding bike lanes, values rise to the surface. It is important for a community to go through the long,

hard process of community consultation to determine where the community places its highest priorities for now and into the future.

3. *Sacrifice*. Sustainability requires sacrifice. In order to get something we frequently have to give up something. Communities need to look at their community eco-footprint to see what they have to do to become more sustainable economically and socially. Such an assessment will put money and action at the core of what can and what cannot be done, by whom and when.
4. *Goal setting for a new economy*. Setting goals in a renewed community is painful but necessary. Economic goals are the real goals for any community and redesigning tax and related economic income systems or forming new community development corporations will put pressure on community leaders. Putting money and accountability together are hard things to do. But economic goals have a life longer than council, state or national elections. This calls for goal formulation and goal-assessing instruments that will last until the goals are reached.
5. *Projects*. In order to reach goals based on sustainable principles, projects have to be developed with long time horizons and clear mandates. Good, clearly articulated, measurable goals lead to stronger outcomes. New directions do not come quickly. Patience is required, and long-term economic instruments, such as value-capture tax revenues and other systems, will need to be put in place to move towards long-term sustainable communities.

Sustainable local economies are linked internally within the locality and elaborated outwards to the region in which they are nested towards the larger world. Looking towards the future, I argue that unwieldy economic systems will not be able to deal with change and may harm people and places. Thus they are not sustainable. This not an argument against globalization, but a firm proposition that global economic strength arises from endogenous resource development that uses each component of the resource base carefully. A sustainable economy is not an end state but a constant process of adjustment to all factors in an economic system in order to generate wealth on a continuing basis for people and places.

REFERENCES

Blakely, E.J. (1990), *Panning Local Economic Development*, Thousand Oaks, CA: Sage.
Chicago Community Trust (2002), *Hunger Report*, Chicago, IL: Chicago Community Trust.
Elkins, P. (1992), *Wealth Beyond Measure*, London: Gala.

George, H. (1897), *Progress and Poverty*, New York: Henry George.
Goldschmidt, W.R. (1947), *As You Sow: Three Studies in the Social Consequences of Agribusiness*, Montclair, NJ: Allanheld, Osmun and Co. Publishers, Inc.
Goldsmith, W.A. (2010), *Separate Socities: Poverty and Inequality in US Cities*, Philadelphia, PA: Temple University Press.
Green Leigh, N. and E.J. Blakely (2013), *Planning Local Economic Development*, 5th edn, Thousand Oaks, CA: Sage.
Hazell, P. and S. Woods (2008), 'Drivers of change in global agriculture', *Philosophical Transaction of the Royal Society of Biological Science*, **363** (1491), 495–515.
Lovins, Amory (2012), *Reinventing Fire: Bold Business Solutions for the New Energy Era*, White River Junction, VTA: Chelsea Green Publishing Company.
Montogmery, T. (2007), *Soil Erosion and Agricultural Sustainability: Proceedings of the National Academy of Sciences in the United States*, Washington, DC: National Academy of Sciences of the United States.
Robertson, David, Christy Gabbard, Bruce Hull, Jerry Moles, Jim Stokoe, Scott Burge, Jeff Waldon and David Lowe (2009), 'Landcare in America: changing landscapes, lifestyles and livelihoods', available athttp://www.landcarecentral.org/References/Chapter%209_America.pdf.
Schumpeter, J. (1975), *Capitalism, Socialism and Democracy*, New York: Harper.

21. Sustainable cities and governance: what are the connections?

Daniel J. Fiorino

Is a city that cannot govern itself sustainable? The answer in nearly all cases is that it is not. A city that fails to meet the core expectations of governance – maintaining order, making and carrying out collective decisions, providing basic services – will not be able to sustain the ecological, social and economic aspects of the concept of sustainability. In this sense, effective governance describes a set of capacities that make sustainability possible in its broad dimensions. Yet the role of governance in defining and making a transition to a more sustainable society receives limited attention in the literature. It is, to a degree, captured in the social dimension of sustainability, but has generally been defined vaguely and wrapped normatively in issues of participation, equity and transparency. In *Our Common Future*, seen as a foundational document on the concept, the World Commission on Environment and Development (1987, p. 63) described sustainability as 'promoting citizens' initiatives, empowering people's organizations, and strengthening local democracy'. The empirical relationships of these goals with ecological and economic sustainability and the need for effective governance receive only limited attention.

The theme of this chapter is that the concept of sustainability as it has evolved over the last few decades has neglected the crucial role of governance. To be sure, several elements associated with effective governance are captured to some degree in the social dimension of sustainability. Values of participation, empowerment, civil rights and liberty, transparency and equity have been central to the definition and analysis of sustainability. However, discussions of the role of governance in sustainability have been limited in two respects. First, they have been embedded in the social dimension of the concept and not articulated as separate imperatives and capacities. Second, they have been considered largely from a normative standpoint (as values and characteristics that should be associated with a sustainable society) rather than from a more instrumental and empirical perspective. There is a difference between specifying equity as desirable in a sustainable city and assessing its role in making ecological sustainability possible. Appreciating the instrumental as well as normative contributions of governance to sustainability requires a better understanding of how it is linked with ecological, economic and social goals.

Two questions are important in thinking about sustainable governance in cities. First, what is sustainable governance in itself and what characteristics are associated with it? Second, what are the relationships between effective governance and the ecological, economic and social dimensions of sustainability? The first is an example of 'within-system' analysis and is one of the core topics of the discipline of political science. The second may be termed a form of 'inter-system' sustainability analysis that explores relationships among the dimensions of the concept.

This chapter focuses on the second question. It begins by setting out a systems-based framework for sustainability that identifies governance as a fourth system on a par with the ecological, economic and social ones. Next is an overview of what research on environmental performance suggests about the relationships between governance and ecological systems. The third part discusses governance and sustainability in American cities as a means of exploring particular issues in greater depth. The chapter concludes with discussion of issues for research or practice and reflections on the role of governance in the future of sustainable cities.

This chapter uses the term 'sustainability transition' to describe the process and goal of moving away from unsustainable policies, behaviors and relationships within cities to those that are more sustainable. This reflects a view of sustainability as less an end state or a set of specific policy, behavioral and institutional outcomes than 'a socially instituted process of adaptive change' that occurs over time at many levels of governance (Kemp et al. 2005, p. 13).

A SUSTAINABILITY FRAMEWORK: DIFFERENTIATING GOVERNANCE AS A FOURTH SYSTEM

Before moving to the specific issues associated with governance and sustainability in an urban setting, it is important to set out the framework for this chapter. It draws on a 1997 essay by John Robinson and Jon Tinker that presents the standard elements of sustainability – ecology, economy and society – as three 'interacting, interconnected, and overlapping prime systems' (p. 74). Each system defines a societal imperative (p. 77). The *ecological* imperative is 'to remain within planetary biophysical capacity'. The *economic* imperative is 'to ensure and maintain adequate standards of living for all people'. The *social* is 'to provide social structures, including systems of governance, that effectively propagate and sustain the values people wish to live by'. Each system is essential for collective survival; each affects the others in critical ways. As a matter of collective survival, no system should be allowed to threaten the existence of others. The goal of governance is to sustain each system while maintaining an appropriate balance among them. The political process ultimately determines where that balance lies (Fiorino 2010).

Three aspects of these 'interacting, interconnected, and overlapping' systems should be noted. First, the economic and ecological systems display complex and contradictory relationships, often to the point of being irreconcilable. After all, the economic system is dynamic and in a process of continual expansion, often exponentially (Victor 2008). The ecological system, in contrast, exhibits fixed limits that economic and population growth may not exceed, as many local and regional ecosystems attest and expectations about long-term global climate change illustrate. Second, there are normative and empirical aspects to the relationships among these systems, as suggested above. Advocates of enhanced participation justify it both as a right of citizens and for its asserted positive effects on outcomes and legitimacy (Berry et al. 1993; Rydin and Pennington 2000). Similarly, the case for preserving the rainforest may be argued on the ethics of protecting species from extinction or the economic value such resources provide. Third, the value accorded each system varies temporally and spatially. Once the global financial crisis occurred and recession took hold in 2008, for example, economic concerns displaced much of the attention previously given to ecological issues, as public opinion on climate change shows.

This chapter proposes a modification in the three-system sustainability framework by differentiating governance as a fourth interacting and overlapping prime system. By embedding governance in the social system, as it has in the past, the sustainability field has failed to appreciate the role of effective, legitimate governance in enabling societies to sustain the other systems and maintain an appropriate balance among them. The governance imperative and thus the scope of the governance system is defined here as the need 'to make and carry out decisions that are accepted as legitimate and ensure the survival of the other three systems'. It may be distinguished from the social system, which encompasses such goals as fairness and dignity, access to education and health care, social cohesion and harmony, and durable social institutions, among others. Such goals as political stability, freedom and rights, effective and accountable institutions, and legitimacy are seen within this framework as aspects of the governance system. In Tinker's and Robinson's terms, this formulation removes governance from the scope of the social system and establishes it as a fourth, enabling, system.

For this chapter, a useful definition of governance is the Worldwide Governance Indicators (WGI) project of the World Bank, which defines it as 'the process by which governments are selected, monitored, and replaced; the capacity of the government to effectively formulate and implement sound policies; and the respect of citizens and the state for the institutions that govern economic and social interactions among them'. Within this definition, six indicators are used: voice and accountability; stability and the absence of violence; government effectiveness; regulatory quality; rule of law; and control of corruption (World Bank 2013). The measures for each are drawn from a range of sources. The WGI provides a useful definition of governance for this chapter; it has been used in research on the effects of regime type and political institutions on environmental performance nationally. Because few studies examine the effects of governance at a city level, the national studies may be used to define a research agenda on city governance.

Performance on at least some of these governance indicators is an obvious requirement for enabling a sustainability transition. Highly unstable societies racked by violence are unlikely to be able to make progress in sustaining any of the other three systems or in maintaining the needed balance among them. As discussed below, the voice and accountability associated with democracies have been linked positively to high levels of environmental performance. There has been some research on the relevance of effective governance, elements of a rule of law, and the effectiveness of government institutions, although not a substantial amount. Much of the national research has focused on the effects of different institutional arrangements within democracies.

An advantage of the sustainability concept is that it applies at multiple governance levels. Indeed, the concept has been defined and analyzed in global, national, regional, corporate and local/urban settings. The focus here is on the role of governance in sustainable cities. However, research at several levels provides a starting point for considering the relationships among governance characteristics and the ecological, economic and social dimensions of sustainability.

RESEARCH ON GOVERNANCE AND ENVIRONMENTAL PERFORMANCE

The bulk of the research relating governance to environmental performance has been done at a national level (Fiorino 2011). It usually is designed with governance as an explanatory variable and a set of indicators of environmental performance as the dependent variable. One body of research focuses on regime type (as relatively democratic or authoritarian). It concludes generally that more democratic regimes exhibit higher levels of environmental performance than their authoritarian counterparts (e.g. Barrett and Graddy 2000; Farzin and Bond 2006; Li and Reuveny 2006). These findings are attributed to the availability of information, opportunities for protest and mobilization, independence of scientific research, and accountability of leadership in a democracy (for discussions, see Frederiksson and Wollscheid 2007; Neumayer 2002). Higher levels of democracy also are associated with growth in per capita income, which in turn is positively related to environmental performance on many health-based indicators. But the effects of the levels of democracy have been found to be significant independently of the income effects.

Another body of research studies the effects of institutional factors, such as presidential–parliamentary, federalist–unitary, proportional representation, and pluralist–corporatist systems on environmental outputs and outcomes. It is difficult to draw clear and consistent conclusions from this research, because of differences in the dependent variables, the complexity of the interrelationships among institutional factors, and the stage in the policy process in which the environmental effects are observed. Two factors that do appear to have explanatory value in these studies were electoral rules and the degree of corporatism within a governance system.

Many researchers have found that electoral systems based on proportional representation and multi-member districts exhibit higher levels of environmental performance than single-district, winner-takes-all ones. It appears that proportional representation lowers barriers for new parties to gain seats; legislators from multi-party districts may represent more diverse interests and advocate broader policies than those from single member districts (Frederiksson and Millimet 2004; Harrison and Sundstrom 2010, pp. 16–19). The success of European green parties flows in part from this feature.

More relevant for this chapter is performance of corporatist and neo-corporatist systems relative to their pluralist counterparts. Many studies have found that neo-corporatist systems like Sweden or Germany perform better on several environmental indicators than pluralist ones like the USA or Canada. Scruggs (2003, p. 123) found that countries with strong, centralized interest groups and consensual policy making exhibit stronger environmental performance than more decentralized and adversarial ones. Several other studies have reached similar conclusions (e.g. Crepaz 1995; Jahn 1998; Liefferink et al. 2009; Ward 2008). Scruggs attributes better performance in neo-corporatist countries to the better use of information; higher trust and business engagement that leads to better implementation; and the ability in such systems to link environmental and economic goals in ways that reduce conflict and promote synergy. Liefferink et al. (2009, p. 92) conclude that 'collective action problems inherent in environmental policy can be solved more easily in neo-corporatist "closed shops" based on trust and long-term reciprocity'.

Although these findings do not necessarily transfer to cities, they suggest directions for inquiry. Both the system of representation and the ability to integrate policy across systems could influence a city's capacity to implement a sustainability transition. Other research findings on national governance and its effects on environmental performance could be useful at a city level. Examples are the indicators of governmental effectiveness, regulatory quality and corruption. One empirical study linked higher levels of environmental performance to a country's stage of 'institutional development, with significant roles for private property protection, effectiveness of the legal/judicial system and efficiency of public administration' (Dasgupta et al. 2001, p. 173). A promising area for research on city governance, as suggested below, is to explore the effects of institutional and other factors in promoting a transition to sustainability in varied urban settings.

GOVERNANCE AND AMERICAN CITIES

A growing literature has examined the emergence of a sustainability agenda in American cities and their efforts to undertake a sustainability transition (Hempel 2009; Conway 2006). The topic of governance capacities and styles has drawn a great deal of interest in this literature. This interest has focused more on the process of engaging citizens and the role of citizen participation than on the institutional factors discussed above. Because citizen participation and engagement are such a central element of the governance system, however, it is worth considering the arguments and evidence from this literature on the role of citizens and democratic process in a city's transition to sustainability.

One of the central debates in the literature on American cities with respect to governance has focused on how 'communitarian' a transition to sustainability must and should be (Portney 2003, pp. 126–33; also see Portney 2005; 2009). This refers generally to the degree to which citizens should be engaged actively in the process of change. One school of thought views civic engagement as a defining aspect of sustainability; the other asserts that change may and even is most likely to occur as a narrower, technical process focused on policy and behavioral change.

These two governance models for a sustainability transition in cities differ in goals, scope, structure and normative arguments. From a communitarian perspective, a sustainability transition is a transformational process. It is as much (or more) about changes in individual and community values as it is about policy and behavior. For this transformation to occur, citizens should be actively engaged in defining a vision for the community. They should take part in deliberation and debate about their shared interests as a community and strategies for promoting those interests. They participate through multiple structures (public meetings, citizen juries, planning and advisory bodies) and processes. The scope of these deliberations is broad; it explicitly incorporates not only ecology and health but broader issues of economic fairness, jobs, housing, transportation, education and social justice. This communitarian view embraces the social system as fully as ecological and economic systems in defining sustainability.

At the more technical end of the continuum is a narrower view of the scope of and processes for change. In this view, the transition to sustainability occurs as a more traditional process of change, in which policy makers and community leaders decide on a set of measures (e.g. energy management, transportation options, zoning or redevelopment policies) for moving in a new direction. Some degree of citizen participation is needed, if only to gain community and political consent for the policy changes. The goal is to change policies, incentives, behaviors and outcomes, but not necessarily to create a strong sense of community or transform values. Structures and processes for participation may be limited to such conventional means as public hearings or meetings. The process of change is narrower; it focuses on reducing environmental and health risks, improving air and water quality, or increasing transportation options. Emphasis is placed on linkages between the economic and ecological systems rather than the social system.

The literature on sustainability in American cities provides examples of advocacy for both models of governance (Portney 2003; 2005). Illustrative of the debate is an analysis by Agyeman and Angus (2003). They differentiate the two in terms of the information-deficit (ID) and deliberative and inclusionary processes and procedures (DIPs) models and express a clear preference for the latter. In the ID model, the aim is to provide information that will support a process of community change. Although citizens may participate in various ways, they are mostly on the receiving end of the change process. The change process itself is viewed in narrow terms, as focusing on the ecological health of communities. The model fails 'to create the kind of transformative policies that are required to move societies toward broadly based sustainability' (p. 346). This model, the authors argue, perpetuates the status quo and does not support a durable sustainability transition, which they argue should be the objective.

In contrast, the DIPs model seeks to actively engage the community in a change process. It assumes that 'a civic renewal and regeneration of social capital is an essential prerequisite for any sustainable community' (p. 347). Only when citizens are engaged in creating a vision for the future and examining their values in light of that vision can a durable transition to sustainability occur. The DIPs model elevates the social and governance aspects of sustainability to the level of the ecological and economic aspects. From both normative and instrumental perspectives, it asserts a relationship between governance capacities or practices and a sustainability transition.

Two case studies in a recent collection illustrate the different paths a city may take to becoming more sustainable. Portland, Oregon is widely recognized as being one of the more active cities in the USA in its sustainability programs. Its current status may be seen as the outcome of a long process of demographic, cultural and institutional change. After being a relatively static city in terms of population and economic growth in the 1950s, the city began a process of economic development and associated population growth in the 1960s. In addition to seeking jobs, 'many of those who moved to Portland were attracted by the reputation the city was earning for livability and a high level of environmental awareness' (Slavin and Snyder 2011, p. 22). The city adopted many sustainability programs in the 1970s. In the 1980s, advocates 'fought for the inclusion of an explicit carrying capacity goal' in the city's planning processes (ibid., p. 25).

Structural factors also supported these changes. Portland is one of the few cities in the country where city council members not only exercise legislative responsibilities but serve as heads of agencies. In 2000, the council member heading the Bureau of Environmental Services created an Office of Sustainable Development. In 2009, the five-year economic development plan set the goal of building 'the most sustainable economy in the world' (ibid., p. 37). These initiatives 'emerged from a long tradition of environmental and planning activism and strong leadership' (ibid., p. 40).

A different case is Milwaukee, Wisconsin's program of sustainable 'redevelopment' for the Menomonee Valley, which was an old, blighted, industrial area. This was more of a project-scale (although a large one) effort than a broader process of city-wide change. The Menomonee Valley project was sparked by recognition of 'a high likelihood of problems resulting from more than a century of heavy manufacturing and land filling throughout the area' (DeSousa 2011, p. 49). Although economics motivated the redevelopment, the city injected equity goals by adopting a minimum wage and requiring a 'sustainable wage plan summary' from employers. It included stakeholder involvement; sustainability indicators; and a vision that 'incorporates family-supporting wages, sound design, ecological restoration, and connections to the community' (ibid., p. 64).

In contrast to the Portland experience, however, the scope and depth of the Milwaukee project was narrower, more consistent with a technical model of engagement than the more transformational one. Yet it constituted a formidable process of change that affected all the sustainability systems in the area. These two cases illustrate the different patterns a sustainability transition may take and the varying degrees of community engagement that may occur over time.

Indeed, research by Eric Zeemering (2009) confirms that the term 'sustainability' is used in many ways and may be associated with many initiatives in American cities. He identifies three patterns in how local officials view sustainability programs. In *aspiring* cities, they stress the integration of urban design (e.g. compact design, mass transit) and sustainability initiatives, with less attention to equity and other social goals. *Traditional development* cities, typically those that have undergone industrial and economic decline, stress business retention and redevelopment, not participation. As the label suggests, *participatory* cities emphasize citizen engagement in development decisions, with a strong neighborhood orientation. 'The results clearly show', he concludes, 'that the term sustainability is associated with distinct initiatives in each city' (ibid., p. 266).

As this analysis suggests, the approach taken to sustainability in cities, and the relevance of different models of governance, depends on local values, political culture and other factors. The Milwaukee project did engage all four of the sustainability systems, but it was focused on a particular area within the city and the redevelopment of an old industrial landscape. Whether this stimulates a longer-term process of a city-wide sustainability transition remains to be seen. The Portland experience reflects a longer-term process of demographic, cultural and policy change. It is no surprise that Portland usually appears at or near the top in various sustainability rankings. A theme of this chapter is the value of understanding not only the underlying process of change and scope of sustainability initiatives in different cities, but also the role of cultural, institutional, economic and social factors, along the lines of the national-level research discussed above.

Much of the research on the relationship of governance characteristics to sustainability has focused, explicitly or not, on the concept of social capital. In a frequently cited article, Robert Putnam (1995) defines social capital as the 'features of social organization such as networks, norms, and social trust that facilitate coordination and cooperation for mutual benefit'.

The first elaboration of the concept may be found in James Coleman's 1988 essay, 'Social capital in the creation of human capital'. He develops it in terms of two streams of explanations for social action. The first, mainly sociological one, describes actors as 'socialized and actions as governed by social norms, rules, and obligations' (p. S95). The second, coming from economics, is that actors behave independently and are 'wholly self-interested'. Neither, on its own, offers a sufficient explanation for social action. The first emphasizes context at the expense of defining an 'engine' to explain the basis for individual behavior. The second neglects the context defined by the social setting and relationships. Social capital is a way of linking the two.

Social capital may be compared to other forms of capital, such as financial, physical and human. Like the others, social capital serves a role in facilitating productive activity in society. Social capital differs from the others, however; it 'inheres in the relations' between and among actors (Coleman 1988, p. S98). It facilitates productive activity 'in generating trust, in establishing expectations, and in creating and enforcing norms' (ibid., p. S97). Higher social capital creates obligations and expectations, thereby increasing perceptions of the 'trust-worthiness' of other actors; improves capacities for information flows; and defines norms accompanied by sanctions that promote action on behalf of collective rather than purely individual interests. Societies tend to underinvest in social capital, Coleman argues, because 'actors who generate social capital ordinarily capture only a small part of its benefits' (ibid., p. 119). In this sense, social capital exists as a form of a public good that is created largely as a result of other activities in society. As is the case for other kinds of public goods, such as clean air or water or wilderness, government must take a leading role in generating and maintaining social capital, given its functions as a positive externality in society. This is a central feature of the governance system.

A fair degree of evidence suggests that social capital is necessary to support governance for sustainability. A consistent theme of the research has been that consensus-based political cultures with high trust and institutions for promoting dialogue are well suited to meeting the challenges of sustainability (Lafferty and Meadowcroft 2000; Janicke 1997; Weidner 2002; Liefferink et al. 2009; for a caveat, see Poloni-Staudinger 2008). If so, as Portney observes, 'pursuing sustainable communities can be just as much about building communities of people as it is about achieving sustainable development results or protecting the environment' (Portney 2003, p. 128).

This discussion has emphasized the effects of governance patterns and capacities on the ecological, economic and social systems. The other side of the coin, of course, is how the other three systems affect governance. The effects of economic failure on governance are documented historically. A growing theme in the sustainability literature, captured in the term 'environmental security', is that competition for scarce resources (such as water), deterioration of the ecological base on which life depends (such as topsoil or tropical forests), and long-term changes in patterns of precipitation (such as drought or flooding due to climate change) may lead to political instability, violence, and other effects on governance capacities and legitimacy at many levels (Matthews 2013). Although this aspect of the relationships among the governance and ecological systems is not explored here, it should be part of the research on governance and sustainability.

ISSUES FOR RESEARCH AND PRACTICE

This chapter makes several arguments about the role of governance in sustainable cities. One is that governance should be defined as a fourth sustainability system, both generally and in the context of cities. It matters not only as a critical system in itself but in enabling progress in the ecological, economic and social systems. Second, there is value in drawing lessons from research at multiple levels of governance. That is, the national research may help in analyzing the role of governance in cities. Third, the aim of sustainability studies should be to understand the relationships among the four systems. In this discussion, the central issue is the effects of governance capacities, structures and processes as they relate to sustainability. The chapter now moves to discussion of research needs on the role of governance in a sustainability transition.

1. Do Institutions and Structures Make a Difference?

The many studies of the effects of political institutions at the national level have not been matched by research at the city level. Although there are no hard-and-fast answers to many questions at the national level, several conclusions have been suggested in this chapter. There is evidence that more consensus-oriented political systems with the institutional capacity to integrate across policy sectors may be more effective in adopting and implementing a sustainability agenda. Experience from case studies of cities such as Portland, Oregon suggests variables that warrant empirical study. In Portland, for example, elected members of the city council also serve as the directors of city agencies. Could this fusion of authority contribute to a better capacity for implementing a sustainability agenda?

Other factors to consider at a city level are electoral rules, the form of representation in city councils, governmental structure (e.g. city manager, executive–legislative relationships), the presence and effectiveness of neighborhood organizations, local political cultures and diversity, and the structure of and relationships among administrative agencies. Although many such factors have been studied with respect to the interactions between economic and social systems, studies of the relationships with the ecological system define a useful area for future research.

2. How do the Four Systems (Governance, Ecological, Economic and Social) Interrelate at the City Level?

The research on national environmental performance suggests general conclusions about the interrelationships among the four sustainability systems. Many of these appear on the surface to be contradictory. Economic growth exacerbates many environmental problems, yet sustainability seems to require a degree of economic affluence if it is to occur. Many of the core aspects of social sustainability, such as access to health care, improved social status of women and educational opportunities depend on economic development. Effective governance also is linked with economic affluence. Yet the ecological consequences of changes in energy use, transportation, diets, habitat stress and consumption press the limits of ecosystems. The analysis of the relationships among the four systems, in particular for identifying policies that maximize positive relationships and minimize conflict among the systems, is a fruitful area for research.

One set of opportunities could come in developing a field of sustainability policy analysis and in building capacity for exploring inter-system relationships at different governmental levels (Baehler and Fiorino 2012). This would establish frameworks and analytical tools for analyzing strategies that reduce conflicts and increase synergies among the four sustainability systems. At least two organizations have proposed elements of a framework (Organization for Economic Co-operation and Development 2010; National Academy of Sciences 2011). The OECD's *Guidance on Sustainability Impact Assessment* sets out an eight-step framework for identifying issues, defining the scope of analysis, evaluating cross-system effects and engaging stakeholders. The National Academy of Sciences' *Sustainability at EPA* proposes an 'operational framework' for integrating sustainability into agency functions, on the principle that action furthering one of the systems 'should, to the extent possible, further the other two' (NAS 2011, p. 41). However, the methods for making these complex inter-system linkages and conducting integrated analyses are unclear.

3. Is Transformational Change Essential for a Durable Transition to Sustainability?

This debate has proceeded along largely normative lines. The premise of the communitarian argument is that an informed process of deliberation and debate will lead citizens and communities to an appreciation of their collective interests. As Portney (2005, p. 584) notes: 'this is an idea that is generally still in search of empirical support'. In future debates about sustainable cities, this will and should remain a largely normative issue. The degree to which a sustainability transition is more 'communitarian' or 'technical' depends on the local political culture, the demographic and economic composition of the city, the attitudes of the business community, citizen involvement, the quality of leadership, and the shared vision for the future that is established for the city. A process of systematic lesson-sharing, backed by action-oriented social science research, can inform policy makers and sustainability advocates of the effects of citizen engagement strategies.

4. To what Extent do Higher Levels of Government Determine Sustainability at the City Level?

The literature has shown a growing appreciation of the consequences of multi-level governance in shaping environmental policies. This is particularly important in the USA, where local governments are largely authorized by the states. At times, higher levels of governance may block sustainability initiatives at the city level. An example is the refusal by the New York legislature to allow New York City to assess fees on traffic into core areas of Manhattan in 2008 (Confessore 2008). At other times, higher levels of government may stimulate sustainability initiatives locally. A priority for research on sustainable cities is the effects of multi-level institutions and policies on the ability of local governments to achieve a sustainability transition (Bulkeley and Betsil 2005). Local governments are part of a complex of 'nested' systems at multiple levels of governance.

5. What are the Effects of Political Culture on the Ability to Undertake a Sustainability Transition?

Because sustainability affects so many aspects of urban lifestyles and behavior, political culture will be more influential than it is for environmental issues alone. Although a sustainability transition does not necessarily involve more heavy-handed government or more bureaucratic structures, as critics often claim, it does involve a willingness to engage in collective action of many kinds and to accept a vision of a city as more than a growth engine. A sustainability transition at any level will require a higher degree of planning, consultation, public–private partnership, and guided growth and development than a purely economic model. A highly individualistic, market-dominated political culture may find a sustainability transition (to the extent that the issue even is on the local agenda) to be challenging, at best. Part of the explanation that countries in Northern Europe (e.g. Norway, Sweden, Finland) consistently rank highly on the Environmental Performance Index and other such rankings may be a political culture in which a state role in economic relationships is more accepted (Emerson et al. 2010).

SUSTAINABLE GOVERNANCE FOR SUSTAINABLE CITIES: THINKING ABOUT THE FUTURE

The role of effective and legitimate governance in the transition to sustainability warrants more attention in the field. By proposing governance as a fourth system on a level with the other three systems that have traditionally made up the sustainability concept, this chapter has set out a framework for studying governance at multiple levels, especially in cities. The central question for cities (and, for that matter, any level of governance) is whether a transition to sustainability requires different kinds of governance capacities than have been common in the past. Can a 'business as usual' governance scenario provide the institutional capacities needed to meet the demands of sustainability transitions? Or will new capacities – in institutions, relationships, participatory mechanisms and political cultures – be required in the coming decades?

As the other chapters in this volume emphasize, sustainability in cities will require profound changes and new capacities of many kinds. Whether in the realm of policy instruments, analytical tools, participation, cross-sector integration, urban systems analysis, infrastructure planning or many others, business as usual is not a sufficient strategy. The same may be said of governance. Governance for city sustainability will require adjustments in many different arenas.

Even brief reflection on the issues discussed in Stephen Dovers's (1997) analysis of policy demands in a sustainability transition underscores the need for new governance capacities. Dover argues that 'sustainability problems are different from those in other policy fields, both in kind and degree' (p. 308). Among these differences are the temporal and spatial scales of sustainability issues; the irreversibility of lost resources, such as species or wetlands; the connectivity among and complexity of problems; the urgency of problems; and the 'absolute limits to human activities' posed by stresses on local, regional and global ecosystems (pp. 310–12). Although some of these apply to nearly any policy issue, they occur more often for sustainability. 'Existing processes,' Dovers argues, 'which have evolved around problems that do not as commonly display these attributes, can be suspected to have limited ability in coping with problems that do' (p. 313).

If sustainability presents distinctive and novel challenges to city governance, as is argued here, then what capacities will be needed to achieve a durable transition? Of the many capacities that could be discussed, this section considers four: connecting and even integrating across the three other systems and among the components within each system; creating the social capital for the collective action needed for a sustainability transition; developing processes and mechanisms for engaging citizens in change; and building the capacity for flexible and adaptive governance.

By definition, sustainability requires that a city maintain a balance among the ecological, economic and social systems, with governance as a critical enabling system. As a consequence, a core governance capacity for a sustainable city will be that of integrating cross-system policies.

In his research on national environmental policy, Martin Janicke (1996, p. 79) defines policy integration as 'institutional dialogue among the relevant actors concerning future dimensions of ecological and economic development'. William Lafferty and Eivind Hovden (2003, p. 1) argue that central to the sustainability concept is the 'integration of environmental objectives into non-environmental policy sectors'. Indeed, the ability to make long-term policy choices within a multi-systems framework may be what defines the more successful cities in the coming decades.

The integration of ecological and economic decision making will be especially important. This was recognized as one of the seven core sustainability principles in *Our Common Future*. A policy framework for integrating ecological and economic factors also is reflected in the efforts of many cities as they work with such notions as a 'green economy' and 'green infrastructure'. Examples are sustainability plans based on clean energy industries and low-impact development. The first seeks to define development strategies based on the manufacturing of clean energy technologies like wind turbines and solar panels, and is drawing particular attention in areas that have lost industry in recent decades. The second is the use of design principles and tools that link stormwater management with natural processes as a way to lower urban infrastructure costs.

One survey suggests that most cities in the USA are approaching sustainability *ad hoc* rather than within the context of 'an overarching development framework' (Saha and Paterson 2008, p. 22). Focusing on the interdependence among environmental, economic and social equity concerns, the study found that sustainability initiatives addressed economic issues (93 percent of the initiatives) more than environmental (79 percent) and equity issues (63 percent). The lack of an inter-systems and integrated sustainability framework, the authors argue, is a constraint, because sustainability is likely only 'when there is coordination across city departments, and officials working in the areas of transportation, land-use planning, public works, community development, and environmental protection sit at the same table' (Saha and Paterson 2008, p. 36).

A second set of governance capacities may be captured in the concept of social capital. A major advance in the sustainability literature was the recognition of natural capital on a level with conventional ideas of physical, financial and human capital. Natural capital is described in a leading book on the subject as 'made of resources, living systems, and ecosystems services' (Hawken et al. 1999, p. 4; also discussed in Hempel 2009, pp. 43–5). Like the other forms, natural capital makes possible a broad range of activities that support human well-being. It differs from the others, however, in the existence of inherent limits in natural capital, especially in the 'life-supporting services that have no substitutes and currently have no market value' (ibid., p. 9). The history of economic development is one of consuming natural capital (e.g. ecosystems or clean air). In these terms, the path to a sustainable future lies in preserving this natural capital and valuing it more appropriately than in the past.

It may be time to add the concept of social capital to this formulation of sustainability. If capital is seen as 'goods or ideas with which something else may be created or established', social capital should be part of the equation (Ryden and Pennington 2000, p. 161). Even in the terms of the more technical, top–down model of change, sustainability requires a capacity for collective action. Although it is difficult at this stage to support the argument empirically, there is a reasonable basis for arguing that greater social capital may facilitate sustainability transitions at any governance level. Because of the more limited scale, opportunity for direct contact, and likelihood of shared values at neighborhood and community levels, there may be more potential for creating and enhancing social capital within cities than at larger governance scales.

Research by Robert Putnam suggests that social capital is higher in more homogeneous settings. More ethnically diverse societies exhibit characteristics that undermine social capital: more distrust of neighbors; withdrawal from collective life; less civic activity, such as voting or giving to charity; and lower expectations from society. In contrast, in less diverse societies, there is less social distance, leading to 'a feeling of common identity, closeness, and shared experiences' (Putnam 2007, p. 159). Ethnic diversity is increasing generally, so social capital may decline in the short term. In the medium to long term, it may be possible to create new forms of solidarity and offset such effects 'by constructing new, more encompassing identities' (p. 138).

A third governance capacity involves mechanisms and processes for citizen participation. Even if a city does not aim for widespread and transformational change along the lines of the DIPs model, some degree of citizen engagement is important as part of a sustainability transition. The extent of participation that is achievable and needed will vary by setting. For some cities, the political, cultural and institutional setting is likely to require as well as support widespread citizen engagement. For others, a similar level of public engagement and dialogue may be difficult. Still, the collective aspects of sustainability will require expanded and more effective participation.

Much of the recent literature on sustainability has considered mechanisms and processes by which citizens participate in decision making. Embedded in the social aspects of the concept, the value of participation has been asserted normatively, instrumentally and often uncritically. A fundamental premise of the sustainability literature is that a vibrant and informed community dialogue enables citizens to realize that a transition to sustainability is in their collective interest. Assuming for the moment the transformational value of such dialogue, will it always lead to an appreciation of sustainability rather than to agreement on a more traditional agenda focused on maximum growth, regardless of evidence on the existence of ecological limits or social inequity?

If a community's underlying values accept the need for growth as an overarching priority, and if the local political culture is skeptical of collective action and is committed to markets, then shared values discovered in participatory processes may be hostile to a sustainability transition. This is an outcome that should be acknowledged in thinking about sustainability and governance.

Although citizen engagement and participation have been stressed for their relevance to all governance levels, opportunities at the urban and local scale are perhaps the most promising. The ability to engage in face-to-face interaction, establish recurring relationships that persist over time, and build trust and a shared sense of community (i.e. social capital) may be higher at a city scale than nationally. Portland, for example, is well known for its high degree of citizen awareness and engagement. Research on participation offers a foundation for understanding the role of citizen engagement. The environmental justice movement in the USA provides additional experience from cities (see, e.g., the discussion in Agyeman et al. 2002).

A fourth governance capacity is more difficult to define and even more challenging to build than the first three. Sustainability transitions involve an 'explicit appreciation of complexity and uncertainty, likelihood of surprise and need for flexibility and adaptive capacity' (Kemp et al. 2005, p. 17). This 'flexibility and adaptive capacity' will be a critical aspect of governance in the coming decades. This is due partly to the recent emergence of the sustainability concept and a lack of experience of applying it in practice. No tested roadmaps to sustainability exist. More importantly, however, are the characteristics of sustainability issues as outlined by Dovers and others. An advantage of a systems-based approach to sustainability is that it provides a framework for analyzing this need for flexibility and adaptive capacity in governance. By definition, systems continually adjust to various internal and external pressures to maintain equilibrium, just as the economic, governance and social systems must regularly adapt to pressures or shocks of climate change, water scarcity and other environmental issues.

At the level of sustainable cities, this flexibility and adaptive capacity may be developed in several ways. In general, there will need to be a shift from hierarchical, linear models of policy making to ones based on networks, adaptive management and sectoral integration (Hjorth and Bagheri 2006). In developing these capacities, the task of creating social capital and developing mechanisms and cultures for citizen engagement and participation will be important. A review of practices in American cities that are recognized as 'taking sustainability seriously' (Portney 2003; also see Hempel 2009; Slavin 2011) reveals a range of public–private partnerships, interactions among levels of government, cross-sectoral policy, feedback loops based on collectively defined sustainability indicators, pilot projects and other forms of flexible, adaptive planning and management. The extensive and growing literature on urban sustainability provides a number of directions for improving governance capacities and policies in the coming decades.

CONCLUDING THOUGHTS

This chapter has presented a case for thinking about the relationships between effective governance and the ecological, economic and social dimensions of sustainability. This case is based on a systems framework, with the addition of governance as a fourth, enabling system on a level with the conventional three. It has suggested issues for research and practice that may be applied at the city level, based partly on studies conducted at other governance levels. It also has argued that the distinctive challenges of a sustainability transition require that cities develop new or enhanced governance capacities. Among these capacities are integrating policy, enhancing social capital, improving participation, and making and implementing choices more adaptively.

A common observation in the literature is that the greatest progress toward sustainability in the USA is occurring at the local, city level rather than nationally. This is an uneven transition, to be sure, and many barriers to further progress exist. Still, sustainability, at least in the public sector, appears to be an issue in which leadership is coming more from the bottom up than the top down. It may be that cities cannot avoid the consequences of declines in systems – ecological, economic and social – for as long or as easily as higher levels of government. Or perhaps the differences in geographic scale, political culture and institutions enable cities to move more rapidly. Whatever the explanation, it appears that having effective, innovative and adaptable governance is a necessary condition for cities seeking a transition to sustainability.

REFERENCES

Agyeman, J. and B. Angus (2003), 'The role of civic environmentalism in the pursuit of sustainable communities', *Journal of Environmental Planning and Management*, **46** (3), 345–63.

Agyeman, J., R.D. Bullard and B. Evans (2002), 'Exploring the nexus: bringing together sustainability, environmental justice and equity', *Space and Polity*, **6** (1), 77–90.

Baehler, K.J. and D.J. Fiorino (2012), 'Sustainability policy analysis: what is it? What can it do for us?', Conference paper, Las Vegas, NV: American Society for Public Administration (presented 6 March).

Barrett, S. and K. Graddy (2000), 'Freedom, growth, and the environment', *Environment and Development Economics*, **5** (4), 433–56.

Berry, Jeffrey M., Kent E. Portney and Ken Thomson (1993), *The Rebirth of Urban Democracy*, Washington, DC: Brookings Institution.

Bulkeley, H. and M. Betsill (2005), 'Rethinking sustainable cities: multilevel governance and the "urban" politics of climate change', *Environmental Politics*, **14** (1), 42–63.

Coleman, J.S. (1988), 'Social capital in the creation of human capital', *American Journal of Sociology*, **94**, S95–S120.

Confessore, Nicholas (2008), 'Congestion pricing plan dies in Albany', *The New York Times*, 7 April.

Conway, M.M. (2006), 'Moving the middle ahead: challenges and opportunities of sustainability in Indiana, Kentucky, and Ohio', *Journal of Planning Education and Research*, **26** (1), 18–27.

Crepaz, M.L. (1995), 'Exploring national variations of air pollution levels: political institutions and their impact on environmental policy-making', *Environmental Politics*, **4**, 391–414.

Dasgupta, S., A. Mody, S. Roy and D. Wheeler (2001), 'Environmental regulation and development: a cross-country empirical analysis', *Oxford Development Studies*, **29** (2), 173–87.

DeSousa, Christopher (2011), 'Greening the industrial district: transforming Milwaukee's Menomonee Valley from a blighted brownfield into a sustainable place to work and play', in Matthew I. Slavin (ed.), *Sustainability in America's Cities: Creating the Green Metropolis*, Washington, DC: Island Press, pp. 45–67.

Dovers, S.R. (1997), 'Sustainability: demands on policy', *Journal of Public Policy*, **16** (3), 303–18.

Emerson, Jay, Daniel C. Esty, Mark A. Levy, Christine H. Kim, Valentina Mara, Alex de Sherbinin and Tanya Srebotnjak (2010), *Environmental Performance Index*, New Haven, CT: Yale Center for Environmental Law and Policy.

Farzin, Y.H. and C.A. Bond (2006), 'Democracy and environmental quality', *Journal of Developmental Economics*, **81** (1), 213–35.

Fiorino, D.J. (2010), 'Sustainability as a conceptual focus for public administration', *Public Administration Review*, **70** (S1), S78–S88.

Fiorino, D.J. (2011), 'Explaining national environmental performance: approaches, evidence, and implications', *Policy Sciences*, **44** (4), 367–89.

Frederiksson, P.G. and D.L. Millimet (2004), 'Electoral rules and environmental policy', *Economics Letters*, **84** (2), 237–44.

Frederiksson, P.G. and J.R. Wollscheid (2007), 'Democratic institutions versus autocratic regimes: the case of environmental policy', *Public Choice*, **130** (3–4), 381–93.

Harrison, Kathryn and Lisa M. Sundstrom (2010), *Global Commons, Domestic Decisions: The Comparative Politics of Climate Change*, Boston, MA: MIT Press.

Hawken, Paul, Amory Lovins and L. Hunter Lovins (1999), *Natural Capitalism: Creating the Next Industrial Revolution*, Boston, MA: Little, Brown.

Hempel, Lamont (2009), 'Conceptual and analytical challenges in building sustainable communities', in Daniel A. Mazmanian and Michael E. Kraft (eds), *Toward Sustainable Communities: Transition and Transformations in Environmental Policy*, 2nd edn, Washington, DC: CQ Press, pp. 33–62.

Hjorth, P. and A. Bagheri (2006), 'Navigating towards sustainable development: a systems dynamic approach', *Futures*, **38** (1), 74–92.

Jahn, D. (1998), 'Environmental performance and policy regimes: explaining variations in 18 OECD countries', *Policy Sciences*, **31** (2), 107–31.

Janicke, Martin (1996), 'Democracy as a condition for environmental policy success: the importance of non-institutional factors', in William M. Lafferty and James Meadowcroft (eds), *Democracy and the Environment: Problems and Prospects*, Cheltenham, UK and Brookfield, VT, USA: Edward Elgar Publishing, pp. 71–85.

Janicke, Martin (1997), 'The political system's capacity for environmental policy', in Martin Janicke and Helmut Weidner (eds), *National Environmental Policies: A Comparative Study of Capacity-Building*, New York: Springer, pp. 1–24.

Kemp, R., S. Parto and R.B. Gibson (2005), 'Governance for sustainable development: moving from theory to practice', *International Journal for Sustainable Development*, **8** (1), 12–30.

Lafferty, W.M. and E. Hovden (2003), 'Environmental policy integration: towards an analytical framework', *Environmental Politics*, **12** (3), 1–22.

Lafferty, William M. and James Meadowcroft (eds) (2000), *Implementing Sustainable Development: Strategies and Initiatives in High-Consumption Societies*, Oxford: Oxford University Press.

Li, Q. and R. Reuveny (2006), 'Democracy and environmental degradation', *International Studies Quarterly*, **50** (4), 935–56.

Liefferink, D., B. Arts, J. Kamstra and J. Ooijevaar (2009), 'Leaders and laggards in environmental policy: a quantitative analysis of domestic policy outputs', *Journal of European Public Policy*, **16** (5), 677–700.

Matthews, Richard A. (2013), 'Environmental security', in Norman J. Vig and Michael E. Kraft (eds), *Environmental Policy: New Directions for the 21st Century*, 8th edn, Washington, DC: CQ Press, pp. 344–67.

National Academy of Sciences (NAS) (2011), *Sustainability at EPA*, Washington, DC: NAS.

Neumayer, E. (2002), 'Do democracies exhibit stronger environmental commitment? A cross-country analysis', *Journal of Peace Research*, **39** (2), 139–64.

Organization for Economic Co-operation and Development (OECD) (2010), *Guidance for Sustainability Impact Assessment*, Paris: OECD.

Poloni-Staudinger, L.M. (2008), 'Are consensus democracies more environmentally effective?', *Environmental Politics*, **17** (3), 410–30.

Portney, Kent (2003), *Taking Sustainability Seriously: Economic Development, the Environment, and Quality of Life in American Cities*, Boston, MA: MIT Press.

Portney, K. (2005), 'Civic engagement and sustainable cities in the United States', *Public Administration Review*, **65** (5), 579–91.

Portney, Kent (2009), 'Sustainability in American cities: a comprehensive look at what

cities are doing and why', in Daniel A. Mazmanian and Michael E. Kraft (eds), *Toward Sustainable Communities: Transition and Transformations in Environmental Policy*, 2nd edn, Boston, MA: MIT Press, pp. 227–54.
Putnam, R.D. (1995), 'Bowling alone: American's declining social capital', *Journal of Democracy*, **6** (1), 65–78.
Putnam, R.D. (2007), '*E pluribus unum*: diversity and community in the twenty-first century', *Scandinavian Political Studies*, **30** (2), 137–74.
Robinson, John and Jon Tinker (1997), 'Reconciling ecological, economic, and social imperatives: a new conceptual framework', in Ted Schrecker (ed.), *Surviving Globalism: The Social and Economic Challenges*, New York: St. Martin's Press, pp. 71–94.
Rydin, Y. and M. Pennington (2000), 'Public participation and local environmental planning: the collective action problem and the role of social capital', *Local Environment*, **5** (2), 153–69.
Saha, D. and R.G. Paterson (2008), 'Local government efforts to promote the "Three Es" of sustainable development: survey in medium to large cities in the United States', *Journal of Planning Education and Research*, **28** (1), 21–37.
Scruggs, Lyle (2003), *Sustaining Abundance: Environmental Performance in Industrial Democracies*, Cambridge, UK: Cambridge University Press.
Slavin, Matthew I. (2011), *Sustainability in America's Cities: Creating the Green Metropolis*, Washington, DC: Island Press.
Slavin, Matthew I. and Kent Snyder (2011), 'Strategic climate action planning in Portland', in Matthew I. Slavin (ed.), *Sustainability in America's Cities: Creating the Green Metropolis*, Washington, DC: Island Press, pp. 21–44.
Victor, Peter A. (2008), *Managing Without Growth: Slower by Design, Not Disaster*, Cheltenham, UK and Northampton, MA, USA: Edward Elgar Publishing.
Ward, H. (2008), 'Liberal democracy and sustainability', *Environmental Politics*, **17** (3), 386–409.
Weidner, H. (2002), 'Capacity building for ecological modernization: lessons from cross-national research', *American Behavioral Scientist*, **45** (9), 1340–68.
World Bank (2013), 'Worldwide governance indicators', available at info.worldbank.org/governance/wgi/index.asp (accessed 11 February 2013).
World Commission on Environment and Development (1987), *Our Common Future*, Oxford: Oxford University Press.
Zeemering, E.S. (2009), 'What does sustainability mean to city officials?', *Urban Affairs Review*, **45** (2), 247–73.

22. Technology and city sustainability

Bill Tomlinson

INTRODUCTION

Information technology (IT) has a long history as a force multiplier of human endeavors – amplifying the capabilities of both individuals and organizations. From abacuses to printing presses to modern computational systems, IT has transformed the way humans live. As humans across history began living together in larger numbers and formed cities, IT has facilitated and coordinated the complexities that go along with close human cohabitation. Looking forward, if cities are to become sustainable systems, IT systems are likely to factor prominently into the process.

How IT influences human activities, though, is complex. IT has been instrumental in enabling the massive exploitation (and many would say overexploitation) of the resources that have supported the growth of human civilizations. Now, as humanity develops a greater awareness of the interdependencies among the ecosystems in which humans live, IT designers and engineers are beginning to build IT systems that support sustainability as an explicit goal (e.g. Millett and Estrin 2012). The design of a system cannot fully predict the role it will play (e.g. Lessig 2000; Benkler 2007); human history is awash in examples of technologies intentionally or accidentally misused for both good and bad ends. Nevertheless, the design of a system does exert a significant influence on how that system will change the contexts in which it is deployed.

This chapter highlights four key themes in the relationship between IT and sustainable cities, focusing on likely future outcomes of this relationship. Specifically, IT will help cities and their resources be quantified, smart, local and shared. These four topics lead into one another. IT will help cities be quantified by tracking a wide variety of factors, such as resource flows, personal habits and institutional activities. The results of this quantification process will then influence semi-autonomous (i.e. 'smart') control over myriad aspects of city life. Smart control can reduce the transaction costs of many kinds of activities, from dynamic regulation of energy consumption and generation, to small-scale growing of vegetables, thereby enabling local activities on a large, distributed scale. IT-enabled reduction in transaction costs coupled with the high population density of cities will enable many new kinds of IT-enabled sharing – everything from online markets for borrowing and bartering goods and services to the sharing of sensor data among computational devices.

Each of these four themes carries with it significant concerns, such as privacy (e.g. who can see the results of the quantification of my life), security (e.g. who is allowed to share my possessions) and authority (e.g. which stakeholders determine the default behavior for semi-autonomous systems). However, these concerns have accompanied many new technologies in the past, and human civilizations have a long history of addressing them, so perhaps they will not prove insurmountable.

There will probably be many other ways in which IT contributes to the sustainability enterprise; these four themes provide a brief sampling of the variety of effects that novel IT systems may have. Broad-scale adoption of these activities, though, like so many other cultural shifts, remains a cultural problem rather than a technological one (Toyama 2010). IT may support and enable profound cultural shifts, but it is unlikely to single-handedly bring about city-scale sustainable systems. But taken together with the other topics discussed in this handbook, IT is likely to provide a powerful force multiplier for bringing about sustainable cities.

QUANTIFICATION

The first means by which IT can support sustainability is enabling the quantification of a wide variety of aspects of city life. Quantification itself is not new – human civilizations have monitored their own processes for thousands of years. However, new forms of IT enable more diverse and more rapid tracking (see, e.g., the *ACM Transactions on Sensor Networks* journal) and more thorough analysis and understanding of both individual streams of data and the interrelationships among many different data sources (see, e.g., the *ACM Transactions on Knowledge Discovery from Data* journal).

New IT systems are sometimes seen as paving the way to a clean, unified and well-organized future. Both science fiction and academic publications often consider idealized utopias – 'Better Living Through Technology'. However, as with many things human, new ways of being accrete on the old. Terry Gilliam's film *Brazil* highlights this phenomenon – his dystopian future city is beset with layer upon layer of pneumatic tubes, all in various states of wheezing disrepair. The means by which IT systems will track events in future cities will be built on today's infrastructures (or, at least, the carcasses of those infrastructures).

Mark Weiser's (1991) vision of ubiquitous technology – that '[s]pecialized elements of hardware and software, connected by wires, radio waves and infrared, will be so ubiquitous that no one will notice their presence' – remains only partially realized. While many city-dwellers do expect continuous connectivity, the devices and infrastructures that provide that connectivity are frequently the source of interruption, incomprehension and irritation for their users. Many of the challenges of new technologies lie in their lack of thorough integration with previous systems.

Despite the challenges of equipping future cities with the IT systems necessary to sense and transmit large amounts of data, the process is well under way. Air conditioning systems in buildings rely on thermometers throughout. Lighting control systems frequently have motion sensors in every room. And power strips may now sense the activities in a space to determine when best to turn themselves off (Kaysen 2011). IBM's Smarter Buildings initiative (IBM 2011) is exploring the integration of these and related topics. Taken together with myriad other sensing systems, the 'internet of things' (Gershenfeld et al. 2004) is playing a more central role in providing the data through which human cities may be quantified. As technology publishing CEO Tim O'Reilly offers, 'we really are instrumenting the world, and that will allow us to solve a whole new class of problems' (Cheok 2012).

Quantification does not just revolve around the inanimate aspects of future cities. More and more people are engaging in life logging, for a variety of purposes. To study his health, technology pioneer Larry Smarr has been tracking a wide range of vital statistics and other information for several years (Bowden 2012). The company 23andMe provides a thorough analysis of a person's DNA, and a wide array of information about the implications of their genes, for less than the price of many smart phones. Websites such as MyFitnessPal and CureTogether harness the benefits of collective activity for weight loss and the healing of many different ailments. Some of these efforts have explicit environmental focuses, but most of them have at least incidental or indirect implications for efforts to support city-scale environmental sustainability. Regardless of their motivation, the data these efforts collect could all feed into the collective understanding of the flows of activities and resources in cities. (The privacy implications of various forms of quantification will be addressed separately below.)

One major challenge that remains unsolved is thorough integration across many different quantification efforts. Efforts are under way to engage in life-cycle assessment (LCA) of various production processes and other activities; however, the necessity of scoping as a key part of that assessment process limits the breadth that any particular LCA effort may achieve. Just as Wikipedia has provided a central clearinghouse for factual information on a vast diversity of different topics, there is a need for a way to bring together disparate data sources so that they may be understood together. Humans do not have the cognitive capabilities to understand and process millions of real-time data streams each providing millions of bytes of digital data per second; nevertheless, there are profound interdependencies among widely different topics being tracked. Some way of exploring the interactions among various data sources (e.g. a sort of 'Wikiquantification' system, through which interested people could contribute a variety of data streams) is needed to support this integration process. In the absence of such a system, there are still many efforts afoot to enable 'smart' control of human environments based on various data streams. The next section provides more detail on this topic.

SMART CONTROL

The proliferation of data about events in cities will enable novel forms of semi-autonomous ('smart') control over numerous activities (e.g. ICDSW 2005). This smart control will have profound implications for environmental sustainability.

The goal of semi-autonomous control is to conform to human preferences with a response time, consistency and ease that are superior to those available when a human is managing the controls manually. 'Human preferences' are broadly defined here, encompassing both immediate gratification of short-term human desires (e.g. 'make my room warmer') and larger-scale civilizational directions (e.g. 'let's not drive ourselves to extinction through overuse of scarce resources').

While humans may be able to manage the controls to satisfy the former constraints (e.g. turn up the thermostat), the human species is notoriously bad at effectively integrating the latter. Research suggests that humans take the latter constraints into account more effectively when thinking about events in the future rather than in the present (Trope and Liberman 2000). Therefore, creating computational systems that help facilitate humanity's adherence to these long-term and large-scale priorities is likely to support efforts to create sustainable cities. Taking these long-view priorities into account does not necessarily mean compromising humans' short-term satisfaction; often the barriers preventing adoption of more sustainable approaches are indifference, lack of information or inconvenient startup costs.

Even in contexts where an individual human's decision would match that determined by an autonomous computational system adhering to a large-scale societal preference, humans do not have the response time, reliability or interest to perform adequately many types of control. A human may adjust a thermostat a few times a day but not thousands of thermostats hundreds of times per hour. However, IT may enable us to transcend these limitations. As Tim O'Reilly puts it, '[a]pplications are being driven by sensors rather than being typed on keyboards' (Cheok 2012).

Perhaps the most prominent form of smart control being explored at present is the smart electrical grid (Massoud Amin and Wollenberg 2005). The goal of the smart grid is to use computer control to improve the production and distribution of electrical power.

A canonical example of the benefit of the smart grid involves renewable energy and washing machines. Many renewable energy sources such as solar and wind power suffer from the so-called 'intermittency problem'. That is, whereas fossil fuels can be stored readily and burned on demand, providing a steady supply of electricity, solar and wind are not able to provide the same degree of reliability. Some days are cloudy, and on some days there is no wind. While efforts are afoot to store energy from wind or sun economically at large scale (e.g. Abbey and Joos 2007), this problem has not yet been solved adequately for these power sources to compete with fossil fuels in this regard. Therefore renewable energy sources often lead to an uneven, and unpredictable, supply (and therefore cost) of electricity.

Washing machines seek to satisfy a human desire to have clean clothes. However, the exact time at which the clothes are cleaned is usually not critical. Therefore a washing machine that was under computer control could monitor the changing cost of electricity and choose to begin its cycle at the most economical time (e.g. in the middle of the night) and be more effective than one that only started when a human pushed a button on the front. The smart grid would be able to provide smart appliances with information on energy availability and pricing, and those appliances would be able to alter their behavior based on the implicit or explicit preferences of their owners (and/or other human stakeholders).

A key factor in the design of smart grid technologies will be the human–computer interaction (HCI) factors that enable human users to engage with them easily. Many homes now have smart thermostats; nevertheless, many people do not use them to their full potential. Thoughtfully designing the user interfaces of these system (e.g. Froehlich et al. 2010), coupled with growing societal awareness of the benefits of engaging with these interfaces, will be important to the success of smart grid technologies.

Another major area of smart control is transportation. As described earlier, many human activities reflect the impact of the accretion of generations of previous ways of doing things. Human production pipelines are a clear example of this issue. The locations of various factories are the result of the intersection of numerous disparate factors ranging from economics to zoning laws to the preferences of the management. Therefore the components of many products travel long distances before arriving at the point of use. Streamlining these processes and reducing total miles traveled could be another area where smart control could be deployed effectively.

To offer a concrete example, Ernst von Weizsäcker (2005) has cited work by Stephanie Böge at the Wuppertal Institute describing how the components of strawberry yoghurt traveled thousands of kilometers within Europe before being eaten. Modern supply chains benefit from a significant fossil fuel 'subsidy' (i.e. the current abundance of fossil fuels supports low prices), in particular because the costs of transportation remain low. Thinking about ways to streamline these production processes and enable products to be produced and consumed within a local area rather than being shipped around the world could substantially reduce the impact of human consumption decisions.

The possibility of broad deployment of electric cars also enables a new kind of smart control. While parked, electric cars could serve as a large, distributed battery system (Kempton et al. 2001). By drawing on and recharging those batteries dynamically, a smart control system could manage the availability of energy at different locations, potentially buffering some of the problems created by the intermittency of renewable power.

LOCAL ACTIVITY

Advances in IT for smart control may also enable a range of local activities. In human civilizations, certain kinds of activities are possible only because large-scale production and infrastructures minimize the effect of startup costs and transaction costs that render those activities unfeasible at smaller scales. For example, electricity might not have played such an important part of the twentieth century had it not been for centralized generation plants. However, new IT systems can help to reduce the minimum viable scale for various endeavors, thereby enabling them to be undertaken more locally than previously. Cities themselves are an example of the synergies that come from local activity; enhancing these synergies in new ways could offer powerful opportunities for sustainable living.

IT systems may support local activities via both the design of sociotechnical systems and the real-time management of those systems. At the design stage, IT may help model new ways of life and create the tools that enable them. For example, computational modeling of the power needs of a household or community and the availability of renewable power sources could inform the design of custom-tailored small-scale energy systems (cf. Pierce and Paulos 2012). Later, after the deployment of a particular tool, IT might help automate the efficient operation of the system of which that tool is a part, and support integration across that system and others that relate to it (see the discussion of smart grids above). IT could also help manage the real-time collection and utilization of energy in that system.

A design sketch based on this premise was developed as an in-class exercise during one of my undergraduate classes a few years ago. The sketch was set on a university campus. A student wished to buy lunch, but when she arrived at the dining hall, she found that her meal card did not have quite enough money for the sandwich she wanted. So she walked out into the sunny afternoon, spread out some collapsible solar panels (perhaps a solar umbrella or solar picnic blanket?) that she had in her bag, and plugged the panels into a nearby socket. She sat in the sun and waited, and before long her phone alerted her that she now had enough money for the sandwich. (At current rates for electricity, a human-scale set of solar panels might earn only a few cents an hour; however, increasing energy prices could make this design sketch more viable.) The class discussion anticipated a time when people will appreciate the sun falling on their shoulders as a source not just of warmth and Vitamin D, but also energetic abundance and a more intimate connection with the energy around them.

Another example of how IT can support local activities comes from the domains of permaculture and 'square foot' gardening. In a city, small plots of land already exist, or could readily be brought into existence – from street-side landscaping to apartment or house window boxes. Rather than simply providing aesthetic value, as they typically do now, these plots could also be used to provide food and other resources for the local communities. However, various challenges (e.g. which species to plant; when to water, thin and harvest; and whose job it is do to so) could cause these spaces to be utilized less effectively than they could be. A research effort currently afoot called the 'Domestic Plant Guild Composer project' (Norton et al. 2012; Tomlinson et al. 2012) seeks to use computational power and human–computer interaction techniques to help address these issues. The project's goal is to enable community members to input the location of a plot of land (e.g. address, GPS coordinates etc.), and the desired outputs of that land (e.g. food, building materials); the system would then guide the user through the process of creating an appropriate 'plant guild', that is, a viable set of species that can survive in that location. The goal would be to create a local ecosystem that could survive without the need for external watering, fertilizer and other enhancements, instead surviving on the native sunlight and rainfall, with various plant species providing for any other needs the other plants in the plot may have (e.g. fixing nitrogen in the soil). While the Plant Guild Composer does not yet exist, it points toward the type of project that could enable local production of food and other resources within the borders of a city.

Another effort working at a similar juncture of topics is the 'Bitponics'

Kickstarter project (Bitponics 2012). This project seeks to use IT to automate small-scale hydroponics systems. The system is designed to be open-source, so various people and communities can adapt it to their own needs.

These gardening examples demonstrate ways that people may have closer relationships with the ecosystems in which they live, and with the resource flows that underpin their lives. (Note that local activities are not always the most sustainable choice, but in a context of rising transportation costs, the frequency with which they are the most sustainable option is likely to rise.)

In addition to being potentially more sustainable, local activities may also lead to greater human happiness. The complexity of the modern world is, in many ways, hard for the human brain to fathom (Walsh 2011); enabling people to live and work among locally made artifacts and with locally produced food could help people understand and connect more readily to they world in which they live.

WIDESPREAD SHARING

The same reduction in overhead and transaction costs that might enable IT to support local activities might also foster new forms of IT-enabled sharing. This sharing might then reduce the redundancy of material possessions and other potentially unnecessary forms of resource consumption that currently accompany high standards of living. While increasing efficiency does not automatically lead to greater sustainability (Tomlinson et al. 2011), IT-supported sharing may enhance human efforts to adopt sustainable lifestyles.

IT systems can help overcome some of the limitations that have previously hampered efforts to share. For example, the Craigslist website makes it easier for people to list goods and services for sale and engage in other forms of impromptu commerce, thereby enabling more numerous smaller-scale transactions than were viable under newspaper-based want-ads or other previous systems.

Other examples of current or future sharing systems abound. Web-supported car-sharing services such as Zipcar enable more fluid sharing of vehicles. CouchSurfing.org enables people to stay with other members of that online community when they travel, reducing the need for resource-intensive hotels. The rise of 'little free libraries' (Little Free Library, Ltd. 2012), in which people lend each other books from their own personal libraries, is also facilitated by IT infrastructures. And my research group recently created an online system, called CanIBorrowYourGoat.com after an old Monty Python sketch, to support sharing of goods and services within a local faculty housing community at the University of California, Irvine.

Another form of sharing enabled by IT is less closely linked to existing practices than is the sharing of various goods and services depicted above. This form of sharing involves the automatic sharing of data. People already share data on occasion (e.g. by asking a passerby 'What time is it?'); however, enabling the automated sharing of data more widely could provide the infrastructure for people to live with a broader awareness of the sustainability implications of their decisions.

To provide a concrete example of this kind of sharing, imagine that a person wanted to know the atmospheric conditions (temperature, sunlight, wind etc.) at a particular location (e.g. in a window box). The naïve approach to this problem would be to augment the location itself with appropriate sensors for all those features. However, some of those phenomena might not change dramatically over distance and/or time; therefore a sensor on a neighbor's window box might provide data that are amply accurate for the task at hand (e.g. raising plants). Enabling devices to share sensor readings dynamically (e.g. via Bluetooth) could dramatically reduce the number of sensors needed to provide sensor services to the city population. Several of my students conducted an analysis of the necessary levels of sensor penetration to provide services at various levels of precision (Tomlinson 2010, pp. 103–4).

Sharing of both goods and sensor data tends to work better in conditions of relatively high population density, a condition that is met well in cities. However, sharing also tends to rely upon trust between lender and borrower, a condition that is not necessarily met among city-dwellers. However, digital reputation management systems (e.g. Malaga 2001), through which the reliability of individuals is tracked across multiple transactions with various partners, may help to address the trust issue (e.g. as one reputation system does in CouchSurfing.org).

A move toward greater sharing would be well matched to a shift from owning objects to buying services that is occurring in certain economic sectors, as well. Mobile phone companies, for example, are deeply invested in maintaining subscribers to their service, rather than simply causing people to buy phones. And Zipcar's business model is built around people easily renting, rather than buying, cars. Ubiquitous IT-enabled sharing could help move people away from a focus on needing their own instance of numerous objects (cars, vacuum cleaners, ladders etc.), and instead relying on the ready access to the services provided by their neighbors' possessions.

CONCERNS

Taken together, quantified, smart, local and shared activities, objects and services might usher in bold new forms of sustainable living. However, they are not without their challenges. This section addresses a few of the most apparent concerns raised by these new directions for city living.

A clear issue arising from the quantification of people's lives is how to deal with privacy. With vast data collection and storage documenting many facets of people's lives, the questions of who has access to the collected data, and for what purposes they may use them, become ever more critical. Already there are significant privacy issues arising from new (and sometimes quite creepy) forms of IT, from a location-stalking system called 'Please rob me' (Borsboom et al. 2010), to 'Girls Around Me', a system that helps men find out intimate details of women in their area by accessing their publicly available social media and location content (Girls Around Me 2012).

At the same time, how people perceive privacy is changing quite rapidly. The wide use of Facebook and other social networking sites (and ensuing questions about whether it is appropriate to upload photos of a person being drunk, high or otherwise indiscreet) is altering the thresholds of acceptable disclosure of private information, in particular among young people. There are no clear answers to the privacy concerns that are arising, and that are likely to continue to arise as IT changes people's lives. Excitingly, these issues are a topic of active research around the world, and are leading to substantial new efforts to understand their implications, for example the founding of the Intel Science & Technology Center for Social Computing at UCI (http://socialcomputing.uci.edu/) and several other universities.

A second topic that arises from new IT interventions is the question of security. Similar in some ways to privacy, security addresses concerns over who has control of and access to real-world systems. These systems may be controlled by a variety of human stakeholders (e.g. ordinary citizens, corporate employees, police officers), with varying levels of authority being exerted by corporate or governmental policies. But the control of these systems may also be dictated by autonomous computational systems (McDaniel and McLaughlin 2009). For example, a few years ago Amazon secured a patent for enabling autonomous computational systems to assign tasks to human workers (e.g. Harinarayan et al. 2007), via their Mechanical Turk system. Smart systems by their nature require sacrificing human control to automated systems. For many people and cultures (including to a large extent the US industrialized culture, from which this author is writing) this relinquishing of control is unwelcome; nevertheless, it is a common part of everyday life (from direct deposit of paychecks to timed sprinkler systems). Human fears of autonomous computers of various sorts are common in science fiction, for example in films such as *The Terminator* and *The Matrix*. Despite the broader range of contexts in which IT brings them up, security concerns are pervasive across human history. Trust is a critical human problem, not unique to technological contexts. As it has been for millennia, the reconciling of viewpoints of different stakeholders around questions of security and authority will continue to be an important concern.

Novel health care concerns also accompany the rise of these new ways of living together. Sharing of goods could encourage the spread of disease and contribute to epidemics. The health care industry, and germ prevention efforts in general, tend to focus on 'single-serving' approaches to the spread of disease, from disposable syringes to plastic-wrapped plasticware at restaurants. These efforts are presumably effective at containing the spread of disease, but they lead to a great deal of waste and thus may not be perfectly aligned with efforts to live sustainably. As with the previous concerns discussed above, this chapter does not present clear solutions to the health-related conundrums brought about by new IT-enabled lifestyles. Rather, these concerns remain important topics to grapple with as cities move toward these new futures.

CULTURAL SHIFTS

The possibilities enabled by new forms of IT, and their accompanying concerns, are all contingent upon broad adoption and cultural acceptance of the lifestyles that they involve. Many of the IT systems described above are already coming into existence in some form, whether as research prototypes or deployments in other specialized contexts. As science fiction author William Gibson once said, 'The future is already here – it's just not very evenly distributed' (Wikiquote 2012). It is hard to predict the numerous ways in which human lifestyles will change as these systems become more common in everyday life.

One challenge with all technological transitions is how to get 'from here to there'. Systems that require wholly new infrastructures are less likely to succeed than those that build on existing frameworks. As such, there will be many hybrid cultural forms as new ways of living arise. Even when a new system is likely to be superior to a preceding one, it is often unclear when is the best time to make the shift.

Despite the myriad directions in which IT may lead, ultimately the enacting of sustainable lifestyles at a large scale is a human cultural problem. IT may multiply the effectiveness of human effort, enabling people to enact their desires faster, cheaper, better and at larger scales, but the core motivation must come from the people themselves. In his opinion piece in the *New York Times*, Tim Jackson (2012) offers one proposal for such a cultural shift, involving a move away from labor productivity toward a greater focus on care-giving and craft-intensive lifestyles.

A large portion of the question about how best to enable the cultural shifts necessary to bring about city-scale sustainability involves education. In order to make well-informed decisions based on the sustainability implications of the various options in nearly every facet of their lives, people would benefit from skills in systems thinking (Jacobson and Wilensky 2006) and other ways of integrating across diverse content domains. Nevertheless, the best educational efforts are unlikely to address the sustainability problem unless there are modes of existence available to people that offer a higher quality of life than less sustainable alternatives. Significantly, quality of life is not necessarily correlated strongly with standard of living, especially at higher levels of both (Speth 2008). Supporting high quality of life may be done in ways that are not inherently resource-intensive.

The approaches described in this chapter seek to enable a high quality of life while reducing the material needs of a city. Local use and sharing of resources, for example, appear to be well aligned with human evolutionary history. It has been hypothesized that humans evolved to live in groups of approximately 150 individuals (Dunbar 1993), and that the stresses of modern life (which is often lived with many more than 150 people) may significantly compromise quality of life through cognitive overload (Walsh 2011). However, social support from friends and family appears to improve health outcomes in a variety of health care contexts (Uchino 2006). By helping people simplify their lives, reducing the social complexity with which they must grapple each day and yet increasing social ties with close family and friends, local engagement and sharing may help people become happier as they become more sustainable.

CONCLUSION

Cities often provide a test bed for new technologies, with city-dwellers being ahead of the curve in embracing new ways of living. As such, cities have the potential to be early adopters of IT support systems for sustainable lifestyles. This chapter has explored several main pathways by which IT may contribute to city-scale sustainability.

The four key themes presented here include broad-scale quantification, smart control, local provision of human wants and needs, and IT-enabled sharing. While not without substantial challenges, these four areas show promise in enabling more sustainable future cities.

While IT is likely to play an important role in enabling sustainability, IT is only effective in the context of human culture that puts it to use for particular ends. Therefore it is critical that stakeholders interested in enabling sustainability focus primarily on transforming the culture, and look to IT to support that transformation, rather than counting on new forms of IT to drive the transition. IT has enabled both the best and the worst of humanity; it is up to people, not machines, to become sustainable.

ACKNOWLEDGMENTS

The author would like to thank Don Patterson, the Social Code Group and the students in several offerings of UCI's Informatics 161 course, for discussions that contributed to the ideas in this chapter. This material is based upon work supported in part by the Donald Bren School of Information and Computer Sciences, the California Institute for Telecommunications and Information Technology, the National Science Foundation under Grant No. 0644415 and the Alfred P. Sloan Foundation.

REFERENCES

Abbey, C. and G. Joos (2007), 'Supercapacitor energy storage for wind energy applications', *Industry Applications, IEEE Transactions On*, **43** (3), 769–76.

Benkler, Yochai (2007), *The Wealth of Networks: How Social Production Transforms Markets and Freedom*, New Haven, CT and London: Yale University Press.

Bitponics (2012), 'Bitponics – your personal gardening assistant', Kickstarter, available at http://www.kickstarter.com/projects/1498890810/bitponics-your-shortcut-to-a-green-thumb.

Borsboom, B., B. van Amstel and F. Groeneveld (2010), 'Please rob me', available at http://pleaserobme.com/.

Bowden, M. (2012), 'The measured man', *The Atlantic*, available at http://www.theatlantic.com/magazine/archive/2012/07/the-measured-man/309018/#.UBlV1B31SK8.twitter (August 2012).

Cheok, A. (2012), 'What are the hot topics for young people?' available at http://www.adriancheok.info/post/27945925393/what-are-the-hot-topics-for-young-people-tim.

Dunbar, R.I.M. (1993), 'Coevolution of neocortical size, group size and language in humans', *Behavioral and Brain Sciences*, **16** (4), 681–93.

Froehlich, J., L. Findlater and J. Landay (2010), 'The design of eco-feedback technology', *Proceedings of the SIGCHI Conference on Human Factors in Computing Systems*, New York: ACM, doi:10.1145/1753326.1753629.

Gershenfeld, N., R. Krikorian and D. Cohen (2004), 'The internet of things', *Scientific American*, **291** (4), 76–81.

Girls Around Me (2012), 'Girls Around Me', available at http://girlsaround.me/.

Harinarayan, Venky, Anand Rajaraman and Anand Ranganathan (2007), 'United States patent: 7197459: hybrid machine/human computing arrangement', available at http://patft.uspto.gov/netacgi/nph-Parser?Sect1=PTO1&Sect2=HITOFF&d=PALL&p=1&u=%2Fnetahtml%2FPTO%2Fsrchnum.htm&r=1&f=G&l=50&s1=7,197,459.PN.&OS=PN/7,197,459&RS=PN/7,197,459.

IBM (2011), 'IBM – energy and environment: smarter buildings' available at http://www.ibm.com/ibm/green/smarter_buildings.html.

ICDSW (2005), *Proceedings of the Fifth International Workshop on Smart Appliances and Wearable Computing (Volume 05)*, Washington, DC: IEEE Computer Society.

Jackson, T. (2012), 'Let's be less productive', *The New York Times*, available at http://www.nytimes.com/2012/05/27/opinion/sunday/lets-be-less-productive.html (26 May 2012).

Jacobson, M.J. and U. Wilensky (2006), 'Complex systems in education: scientific and educational importance and implications for the learning sciences', *Journal of the Learning Sciences*, **15** (1), 11–34, doi:10.1207/s15327809jls1501_4.

Kaysen, B. (2011), 'Green Campus presents: iPAN power strip', available at http://www.youtube.com/watch?v=lpZmCb5keFM&feature=youtube_gdata_player.

Kempton, W., J. Tomic, S. Letendre, A. Brooks and T. Lipman (2001), 'Vehicle-to-grid power: battery, hybrid, and fuel cell vehicles as resources for distributed electric power in California. Report to California Air Resources Board and California Environmental Protection Agency', available at http://escholarship.org/uc/item/0qp6s4mb.pdf.

Lessig, Lawrence (2000), *Code and Other Laws of Cyberspace*, New York: Basic Books.

Little Free Library, Ltd. (2012), 'Little free library', available at http://www.littlefreelibrary.org/.

Malaga, R.A. (2001), 'Web-based reputation management systems: problems and suggested solutions', *Electronic Commerce Research*, **1** (4), 403–17.

Massoud Amin, S. and B.F. Wollenberg (2005), 'Toward a smart grid: power delivery for the 21st century', *Power and Energy Magazine, IEEE*, **3** (5), 34–41.

McDaniel, P. and S. McLaughlin (2009), 'Security and privacy challenges in the smart grid', *Security & Privacy, IEEE*, **7** (3), 75–7.

Millett, Lynette and Deborah Estrin (eds) (2012), *Computing Research for Sustainability*, Washington, DC: The National Academies Press.

Norton, J., A. Stringfellow and J. LaViola (2012), 'Domestic plant guilds: a novel application for sustainable HCI', *CHI 2012 Workshop on Simple, Sustainable Living*, Austin, TX: ACM.

Pierce, J. and E. Paulos (2012), 'The local energy indicator: designing for wind and solar energy systems in the home', *Proceedings of the Designing Interactive Systems Conference*, New York: Association for Computing Machinery, doi:10.1145/2317956.2318050.

Speth, James G. (2008), *The Bridge at the Edge of the World: Capitalism, the Environment, and Crossing from Crisis to Sustainability*, New Haven, CT: Yale University Press.

Tomlinson, Bill (2010), *Greening Through IT: Information Technology for Environmental Sustainability*, Cambridge, MA: The MIT Press.

Tomlinson, B., M.S. Silberman and J. White (2011). 'Can more efficient IT be worse for the environment?', *Computer*, **44** (1), 87–9.

Tomlinson, B., D. Patterson, Y. Pan, E. Blevis, B. Nardi, M. Silberman, J. Norton and J. LaViola (2012), 'What if sustainability doesn't work out? An informatics perspective on adaptation to global change', *Interactions*, **19** (6), 50–55, http://doi.acm.org/10.1145/2377783.2377794.

Toyama, K. (2010), 'Can technology end poverty?', *Boston Review*, available at http://bostonreview.net/BR35.6/toyama.php.

Trope, Y. and N. Liberman (2000), 'Temporal construal and time-dependent changes in preference', *Journal of Personality and Social Psychology*, **79** (6), 876–89.

Uchino, B.N. (2006), 'Social support and health: a review of physiological processes potentially underlying links to disease outcomes', *Journal of Behavioral Medicine*, **29** (4), 377–87.

Walsh, R. (2011), 'Lifestyle and mental health', *American Psychologist*, **66** (7), 579–92.

Weiser, M. (1991). 'The computer for the 21st century', *Scientific American*, **265** (3), 94–104.

Von Weizsäcker, E. (2005), 'Resource Productivity – Good for China, Good for the World', available at http://ernst.weizsaecker.de/en/resource-productivity-good-for-china-good-for-the-world/
Wikiquote (2012), 'William Gibson – wikiquote', available at https://en.wikiquote.org/wiki/William_Gibson.

23. Conclusion

Daniel A. Mazmanian and Hilda Blanco

We conceived of this volume as a way of bringing together between two covers a range of critical strategies for moving cities toward greater sustainability and a variety of methods for accomplishing this goal. Doing so has become imperative in light of the growing human global population, the migration of people to urban centers, and the extraordinary challenge this poses to the services provided by nature and the quality of the environment and health of all those affected.

In the introductory chapter we posited that, while the transition to greater sustainability is not and can never be restricted to cities, urban centers have become the leading edge and exemplars in charting more sustainable paths forward. We argued also that any meaningful path must weave together both intra- and intertemporal dimensions of this challenge into a more comprehensive and systems approach – one that brings together in as harmonious a way as possible the three central dimensions of sustainability; that is, the three Es of economic, environmental and equitable sustainability. Moreover, as depicted in Figure 1.2 in Chapter 1 (reproduced here), the relation is not of equals but of nested dependency, with economic activity providing the building blocks of and nested within human society, and with the economy and society ultimately dependent on the natural environment and the services it provides. This is an enormous and complex undertaking, as anyone who has begun down the path can attest, which is all the more reason for providing this book. Finally, in moving from the abstract to the more concrete, we defined a sustainable city 'as an active, evolving, organic community addressing problems of the present and foreseeable future while confronting ongoing challenges of economic development, equity and justice, and environmental protection'.

Our goal has been to bring together the very best thinking on strategies and methods of practice in moving toward greater sustainability in a series of chapters authored by respected experts in their field and proponents of sustainability, in a manner accessible to and for use by scholars, practitioners and students of the city.

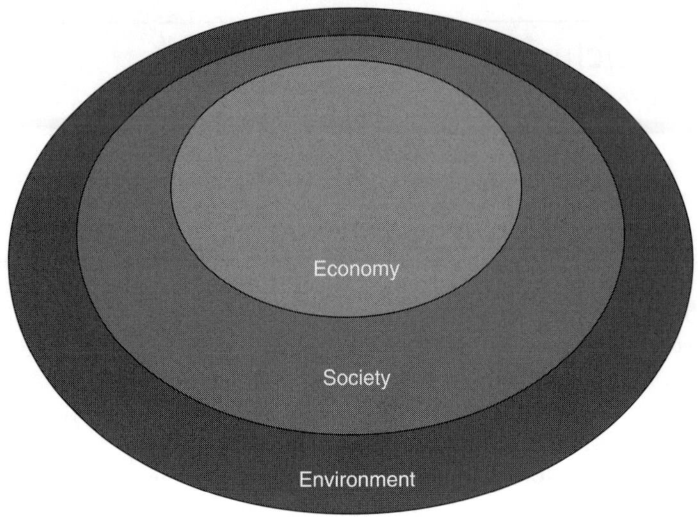

Figure 1.2 The nested relationship among the three dimensions of sustainability

STRATEGIES AS 'INTERVENTIONS' IN COMPLEX SYSTEMS

We begin with the premise that cities, like all complex systems, must be conceptually understood as a whole, but cannot be addressed as a whole. Rather, in order to chart a sustainable path, the system must be intervened on, or intercepted, at critical junctures that, in turn, redirect (steer) it in a new direction. These interventions are, as we noted at the outset, the strategies or points of entry into city activities in order to bring about change. To be successful, they require vision, leadership, capacity and a degree of good fortune. While there is no formulaic approach that can be universally applied, there are several promising emerging strategies and helpful examples. Under 'Strategies', the first part of the volume, eight such 'interventions' are presented, ranging from the necessity of envisioning the city as a sustainable system as the first step in the change process, to rethinking and redesigning existing approaches to well-established functions and activities of the city and, lastly, to gauging the result in terms of not one or two, but all three Es, with an emphasis on equity and justice.

Peter Newman leads off in Chapter 2 with an appreciation of the linkage between transport and urban form as a crucial conceptual building block upon which sustainability can be understood and acted on. Reducing vehicle miles traveled, which is the promise of more compact urban forms, can reduce urban air pollution and traffic congestion, and therefore has beneficial impacts on public health and the quality of urban life. Climate change has magnified the importance of the linkage between urban form and driving, since increasing automobile travel has direct impacts on fossil-fuel energy use and resulting carbon emissions. As a result, reducing vehicle miles traveled has become an important climate change mitigation strategy. In 'Rediscovering compact cities for sustainability', Newman outlines his vision of the compact city and why it is the critical starting point. Based on Italian physicist Cesar Marchetti's intriguing argument that there is a universal time budget of around one hour on average per person per day, and on the average speeds of major transport modes, Newman traces the evolution of urban form from the walking city (pre-urban rail) to the transit city (pre-automobile) to the automobile city. As he indicates, rail and auto modes allow a city to extend beyond walking cores, but, in the case of the automobile mode of transport that has enabled cities to extend as far as 50–80 km in all directions, as traffic congestion increases, cities may be reaching the limits of the Marchetti Constant. Newman suggests that, as commutes in automobile-oriented (sprawling) cities reach the Marchetti Constant, they begin to adapt by increasing density, providing greater access to rail transit, and facilitating walking and biking. He recognizes the value of a polycentric city model where small, walkable cities in the suburbs can be linked by 'fast, quality rail transit', and urges the use of old tools such as strategic plans, and new ones, such as value capture, to finance transit.

Strategies for making our cities more sustainable along several key dimensions follow in the subsequent chapters, beginning with the management of water, by Blanca Jiménez Cisneros (Chapter 3). Jiménez Cisneros takes a global perspective on the future challenges that urban water services face under climate change. Drawing on her international research on the urban water sector, she provides a comprehensive review of adaptation options in the sector. As she points out, adapting the water sector to climate change will be costly and require a 'portfolio' of adaptation options. She begins by providing an informative summary of the potential impacts of climate change on water supply, including higher evaporation losses, loss of snowpack, higher water temperature and its effect on water quality; corrosion of sewers, saline intrusion, decreases in precipitation, as well as the impacts of climate change on water demand, in particular an increase in consumption. She identifies the need to assess the vulnerability of the specific water services as well as of vulnerable populations. In addition, Jiménez Cisneros reviews the global cost estimates for providing sufficient municipal and industrial water supply around the world. Although the estimates are preliminary, the studies indicate a range in the order of $11–12 billion per year to 2030–50, with most of the costs required for developing countries. Jiménez Cisneros then provides a step-by-step approach for local water utilities to adapt to climate change. Beginning with a discussion of goal-setting, she then presents a comprehensive set of adaptation options or strategies and indicates the relative cost and difficulty of implementing each of these. Stressing the need for water agencies to develop plans that provide a portfolio of adaptation options taking into account various factors, Jiménez Cisneros emphasizes the need to consider demand management options and not just engineering solutions. The chapter also discusses climate change mitigation issues and options in the water sector. This is an important topic, since water and wastewater services account for 5–7 percent of total global GHG emissions. Overall, the chapter provides a state-of-the art planning guide for local water agencies as they begin to confront the impacts of climate change on these essential municipal services.

As Nevin Cohen points out, in Chapter 4, 'Urban food systems strategies', until the 1990s food was considered a rural, not an urban, policy issue, and food availability was seen as a 'private sector concern'. Cohen sets the stage for a discussion of urban food systems strategies by describing the drivers of food policy-making and the sustainability dimensions of the urban food system. In his fascinating account of this new urban policy field, he points to the problems that have led to this new field, such as global hunger and malnutrition, increasing rates of obesity in developed countries and emerging economies, and increasing threats to food safety. He discusses the shift from a focus on increasing food production to the provision of sustainable diets, and the emergence of notions of community food security and of food justice. In his discussion of strategies for sustainable urban food policy, Cohen identifies five major strategies: supporting regional producers; expanding urban agriculture; improving distribution and processing infrastructure; expanding access to and use of federal food benefits; and managing food residuals. In this way, he shows how the field is developing to apply leverage to points within and outside municipal boundaries to achieve a more sustainable urban food system. Cohen concludes the chapter with a discussion of how the strategies identified are implemented 'through a combination of conventional policy making and networked governance'. Insightfully, he notes the governance challenges that multisectoral local food policies face when they confront the traditional sectoral structure of local governments. The governance challenges of developing urban sustainable strategies and, in general, more sustainable cities is a major issue confronting all aspects of sustainability and it is an issue that Daniel J. Fiorino addresses from a more future-oriented perspective in Chapter 21.

In 'Sustainability strategies for consumer products in cities' (Chapter 5), Gregory A. Keoleian, Joshua P. Newell, Ming Xu and Erin Dreps define consumer products as any material good 'produced and distributed for sale . . . for [the] personal use, consumption or enjoyment'. Their goal is to provide a range of strategies for improving sustainability when viewed through the complete product life cycle, from raw material to ultimate disposal, through application of life-cycle assessment tools. Their breadth of strategies available to cities and overview of research and detailed information constitute a valuable reminder of the available options. They cover 13 strategies that span the life-cycle stages from production, distribution, use and post-use (end of life). The strategies range from local sourcing, digital delivery and online shopping, dematerialization in packaging, product sharing, to repair, reuse, recycling and more. The full range is nicely captured in their summary Table 5.4 where they also incorporate sustainability benefits, tradeoffs and major actors.

The strong message is that, through a range of policy approaches, extending from leading by example, providing necessary infrastructure, incentivizing and mandating, a city can help its citizens become more sustainable in their consumption, individually and collectively, to the betterment of all.

Chapter 6, 'Strategies for growing green business and industry in a city', by Karen Chapple, provides a valuable discussion of how and why sustainable cities should and, in two contrasting case studies – the City of Portland and the Riverside–San Bernardino region – do cultivate green jobs and industry. Moreover, doing so needs to be seen as an important aspect of a city's economic growth as sustainability becomes ever more important. Chapple devotes attention to clarifying what for most is unclear: what green industry is and how it should be measured. Detailed answers are provided, based on an extensive survey of the literature and the author's research. Stated succinctly, the green economy is defined as economic activity that 'reduces energy consumption and/or improves environmental quality'.

While the green economy is nascent and the concept still contested, cities can play a major role in fostering greening within their existing powers by adopting green standards and regulations for energy, green building incentives, environmentally preferable purchasing, and 'buy-local' initiatives. An important caution is that adoption of these policies alone may not help foster local businesses, which may require the addition of green local purchasing standards (an issue addressed in Chapter 18 by Laurie Kaye Nijaki). While cities can take the lead in fostering green industry and a green economy, Chapple is careful to note that they cannot do so alone and require supporting policies from higher levels of government. It also remains to be seen if the efforts under way in cities will precipitate the transformation of the overall economy within which they exist.

Urban infrastructure systems and ensuring their sustainability through infrastructure investment is the subject of Rae Zimmerman's 'Strategies and considerations for investing in sustainable city infrastructure' (Chapter 7). Without functioning urban infrastructure systems, such as transportation, water, waste disposal and so on, city living is not viable now or in the future. Yet, as Zimmerman points out, public opinion polls in the USA show 'that infrastructure categories tend to rank low as a priority', and infrastructures seem to be taken for granted. However, she argues, the increasing frequency of extreme events, with their huge demands for infrastructure investment, may yet change the public perception of infrastructure. The American Society of Civil Engineers (ASCE) tracks the condition of infrastructure systems – estimates of investment needs for infrastructure are based on conditions assessments – by issuing a national infrastructure report card every four years for the different systems. The report cards show an increasing need for infrastructure investment, more than doubling the need since 2005 to a current estimate of $3.6 trillion by 2020. This is a staggering estimate of the funds needed to address backlog needs for repair, replacement and renewal of existing infrastructure. The increase of climate-driven extreme events makes salient the importance of infrastructure. Recovery efforts in these disasters, with the federal government funding a large portion, also include funds for infrastructure repairs or renewal. But, as Zimmerman indicates, the real issue is whether the funds for recovery will make infrastructure systems more resilient against future extreme events.

On the demand side of infrastructure provision, she notes the recent trends in settlement patterns in the USA, where greater growth is occurring in smaller, more spread-out areas and points out the greater costs incurred in providing infrastructure services to outlying areas. While Newman's argument for compact cities is focused on the energy and emissions intensity of travel in lower-density, automobile-oriented cities, this argument focuses on the greater capital costs of providing infrastructure to more extensive urban areas. Low-density areas require more linear miles of water pipes, roadways and so on.

The investment needed to bring US infrastructure systems to a good sustainable condition by 2020, as Zimmerman points out, is enormous and will require investment by all levels of government, as well as private sector utilities. How the disruption or damage of infrastructure systems by extreme events will affect both public priorities and financing strategies to increase the sustainability of such systems is unknown. Our aging infrastructure systems in an era of climate change thus pose a fundamental challenge to the sustainability of urban life today and increasingly in the near future.

'Aligning fiscal and environmental sustainability', Chapter 8, by Richard F. Callahan and Mark Pisano, seems so self-evident that it barely needs mention; you cannot have the latter without the former. However, as the chapter illuminates, as city budgets and fiscal policies exist today, the focus is primarily if not exclusively on the present, whereas sustainable development requires looking over the horizon and aligning a city's fiscal decision making with the transition to a more sustainable economy. It requires investing in that future. This underscores the parallel between thinking about the sustainable economy and the way cities must move from thinking fiscally as a yearly or near-term endeavor to thinking about fiscal viability over time – that is, become more fiscally sustainable.

While the impetus for this shift has not come from concerns about sustainable development so much as from the funding constraints imposed from the federal and state governments within which cities are nested and the changing appetite of the public to fund government, especially if this results in higher taxes, the result is the same. Bringing together sustainable city and regional fiscal and environmental strategies is illustrated through case examples and the authors' own research into fiscal sustainability in eight different cities, and the role that leadership and institutional design play in successful strategies. Viewed through the lens of fiscal policy, the first step is to refocus the city's decision-making institutions and leadership from near- to long-term fiscal sustainability. Presumably, once headed down this path, the tenets of sustainable economic development (as in the previous chapter and others throughout the volume) will guide the choices made in ensuring a melding of the fiscal and environmental sustainability of a city.

In 'Gauging the health of a city: maximizing health and sustainability', Chapter 9, Alek Miller and Richard J. Jackson first provide an informative review of the renewed linkage between public health and urban planning issues, strategies and methods. The authors explore the shift in the health professions from the definition of health as the absence of disease to a more holistic conception of health as well-being, which encompasses the physical and social conditions that facilitate it. They then discuss recent research on the interaction of the built environment and public health, especially the influence of the built environment on physical activity and issues of food insecurity. They go on to explore several public health issues and strategies that have been developed to address them. At the neighborhood scale, for example, they discuss the complete streets strategy, that is, streets equipped for walking, biking as well as driving to encourage physical activity and transform auto-centric streets. At a regional scale, they discuss improving public transit to reduce driving. The chapter also discusses several tools or methods important for urban sustainability that address public health issues. For example, the WalkScore rating system provides a user-friendly guide to the walkability of neighborhoods. Miller and Jackson also provide an account of health impact assessments (HIAs), a relatively new evaluation tool, increasingly used in the assessment of the impacts of new policies or projects. HIAs place a special emphasis on equity and the elimination of health disparities, and constitute an important addition to urban sustainability methods. In the example they provide of the use of HIAs in the rezoning of Baltimore, the authors indicate the potential for such assessments to magnify positive health outcomes and reduce negative ones.

Miller and Jackson's chapter illustrates the interdisciplinary and overlapping nature of urban sustainability. For example, take the stream of research in public health and urban planning linking patterns of physical activity and their health outcomes to the automobile-oriented city, the latter of which is the focus of Peter Newman's chapter. While Newman emphasizes the energy, traffic congestion and carbon emissions of the automobile city, the built environment–physical activity field of research emphasizes the health outcomes of such cities. As relevant is the concern in public health with food insecurity issues in low-income communities – the focus of Nevin Cohen's chapter on the emerging urban food policy field of studies. These linkages illustrate the interdisciplinary nature of urban sustainability, and indicate both the promise of greater integration among the disciplines, as well as the standing institutional challenges to implementing more holistic sustainable solutions.

In Chapter 10, 'From information provision to participatory deliberation: engaging residents in the transition toward sustainable cities', Michaela Zint and Kimberly S. Wolske present the rationale and strategies for engaging citizens and stakeholders in a city's transition to a more sustainable future. While virtually all discussions of the needed transition emphasize the importance of education of and communications with the general public, it is evident that most rely on information-based approaches. As important as these are in informing, the very important message is that research has repeatedly shown that they fall well short of motivating behavioral changes. In essence, a far more engaged process is required and there is a growing number of models and examples to draw upon among cities and communities that have begun down the path toward sustainability. Zint and Wolske add to the emerging discussion both conceptually and through illustrative cases that have successfully led to changes in behavior.

Conceptually, they focus on knowledge of behavior change gleaned from psychology and the lessons learned from the growing utilization of deliberative participatory process in developing community goals and fostering new public policies. Cases of how this has been helpful in several different-sized cities are presented. The authors develop a set of recommendations for any city that intends to employ an active engagement strategy as part of its sustainability initiative:

- Support efforts to document and disseminate information about cities' sustainability engagement programs.
- Draw on research and resources from related disciplines to inform cities' sustainability engagement efforts.
- Encourage researchers to investigate questions surrounding sustainability engagement strategies in cities.
- Strengthen collaborations and partnerships with a range of stakeholders.

They conclude with the observation that an effective engagement strategy requires time and effort, especially so in view of the significant changes in thinking and behavior required in the transition to sustainability.

Recognizing the limitations of an information-based approach to engaging residents in policies towards more sustainable cities, in Chapter 11 Connie P. Ozawa's 'Developing effective participatory processes for a sustainable city' provides an approach grounded in urban planning theory and practice. She first recognizes the need for participatory processes to engage citizens in transitions to more sustainable urban living, given the uncertainty surrounding future-oriented policies and the need to develop agreement on an ongoing path to sustainability. She argues that public involvement in sustainability requires greater attention to strategies that build on information sharing, strengthen the adaptive capacity of relations among actors and deepen the sense of collective responsibility. Ozawa emphasizes how going beyond traditional strategies such as public notices, meetings and hearings, basically aimed at informing the public, participatory strategies used to further the sustainability of cities need to engage the public in gathering and not just sharing information and in deliberating and negotiating. Only through such active participatory strategies can community capacity and a sense of citizenship be increased. She argues that a community that understands the reasoning behind actions and objectives will be better prepared to build social capital and remain adaptable to changing conditions.

Ozawa then discusses three strong public participation strategies: community partnerships, participatory planning, and community benefits agreements. In her examples of these strategies, she explains how the strategies engage communities in building social capital and a sense of shared citizenship. Among these strategies, participatory planning appears to be the most appropriate to respond to the challenges of urban sustainability and climate change, since it is a strategy that, as developed in Ozawa's example of the participatory process involved in planning for East Portland, involves ongoing community engagement with public officials in a planning and implementation process. Given our limited experience with community involvement in urban sustainability efforts, however, we still lack evidence on the outcome of such participatory processes. To gain such evidence, we require experiments that reorganize local institutions, enabling all the neighborhoods in a city to engage in strong participatory processes on issues relating to future sustainable options involving uncertainties and trade-offs.

The strategies section of the book concludes by arguing the case that justice and equity are not only an important moral and ethical part, but also an essential pragmatic component, of the sustainable city. Manuel Pastor (Chapter 12), in 'A measure of justice: environmental equity and the sustainable city', brings to light several aspects of environmental justice that are central to strategies for the sustainable city. The first is that research shows that economic viability and sustainability are both diminished, the greater the inequality of place – city, state or nation. This, he argues persuasively, provides 'a political economy reason why more equity might produce a better environment: by paying attention to communities that may face the worst environmental conditions, we can strengthen the base of public support for sustainability'.

In addition, the definition of environmental justice has evolved into a more holistic concept that goes well beyond the initial focus on environmental and health harms to minority and underrepresented populations. His third key point is that, if justice is to be achieved, if sustainable development is to be realized, then the focus must extend beyond the conventional city lines to the metropolitan or regional scale. Finally, while Pastor favors the cumulative impact metric for gauging equity and justice developed in California as reflecting broader thinking about justice, there are several other environmental justice, climate change and health-related tools that cities can choose to gauge their progress, and through which they can compare themselves with others.

In brief, the cumulative approach Pastor highlights needs to incorporate 'the multitude of sources that impact people at a neighborhood level and account for social vulnerability'. This is spelled out in detail in the chapter and summarized in Figure 12.1, bringing together a proximity to hazards and sensitive uses score, a health risks and exposure score, and a social and health vulnerability score. Other tools are outlined in Figure 12.3. This is an important discussion in explaining the centrality of justice to sustainable development, strategies for incorporation of equity and justice into a city's approach, and how to gauge the degree of success in doing so.

METHODS FOR ACHIEVING SUSTAINABILITY

In their paths towards more sustainable futures, cities must first determine their current sustainability status. A major assessment method to determine the biophysical flows within a city, urban metabolism (UM) analysis, is the subject of Chapter 13 by Christopher Kennedy, Larry Baker and Helge Brattebø, 'Analyzing a city's metabolism'. A major advantage of UM when compared to other popular methods, such as greenhouse gas inventories or ecological footprints, is that UM is systems-oriented. It aims at providing a quantitative analysis of the inflows and outflows of energy, water and materials within an urban boundary. Another advantage of the approach is the system diagrams used to represent the results of the analysis. Such diagrams serve as memory aids that reinforce system interconnections. Since data inputs are essential for applying this method, in their useful, step-by-step guide for conducting UM analyses the authors discuss the types of data needed for each of the different inputs, their availability and several data options when optimal data sets are lacking.

By providing an analysis of the biophysical aspects of a city, and since the data inputs for this type of analysis can be used for other types of analysis, such as GHG inventories or ecological footprints, the use of UM analysis indicates a fundamental change in the way we conceive and plan for cities. Until recently, planning of cities has been driven by population and economic projections, as well as the existing land uses in an area, including open spaces and parkland. These drivers will doubtless remain important. But increasingly, as we face sustainability challenges, especially climate change, in our urban plans and programs, we will need to pay attention to patterns of urban energy production and consumption, materials, especially building and infrastructure materials, water use and the resulting solid waste, and air and water pollution, patterns that UM analysis documents and illustrates.

In Chapter 14, 'Developing sustainable cities indicators', Kent E. Portney takes to heart the old adage that you get what you measure. As the author of one of the more comprehensive metrics of sustainable cities in use today, in this chapter he focuses in on a select number of cities (six) and how they have adopted different targets and methods of measurement as an indispensable component of their sustainability initiatives. While the indicators approach may be arrived at through different routes, through the initiative of nonprofit community or civic organizations, or city governments, they all share the objective of providing for public view a kind of report card on progress toward a community's objective, in these cases, toward their aspirations to make their city more sustainable. What they all share, also, is including not one but all three of the three Es of sustainable development.

The cases show that there is no one right or best method of developing and utilizing indicators as a means of providing information and transparency, and demonstrating in measureable ways progress toward sustainability. The cases also underscore some of the challenges in selecting and utilizing indicators, not the least of which is agreeing which indicators are the most relevant for a given city and, then, having available systematic and reliable data for measuring them. Most important, however, is that no sustainable effort can be credible or effective absent some method of measuring, continuously over time, action taken by a city toward achieving the goals of its sustainability initiative.

One of the most salient issues facing cities today is climate change, and, as an important dimension of sustainability, cities need an operational mitigation plan, addressed by Michael R. Boswell, Adrienne L. Greve and Tammy L. Seale (Chapter 15). Many cities around the world, especially in the USA, are not waiting for national plans for reducing greenhouse gas (GHG) emissions, but have taken the initiative to develop local climate action plans (CAPs), which have, until recently, focused on reducing carbon emissions or mitigating climate change. As the authors point out, in the USA alone, over 200 cities have already adopted such plans, and as many are in the process of preparing them. The analytic core of CAPs is the inventory of GHG emissions and the forecast of emissions based on growth projections. Other planning processes include setting targets for future emissions, and identifying the actions to achieve such targets. The authors then unpack this planning process into several phases and steps that include community education and engagement as well as implementation. In this useful set of guidelines, the authors also provide a list of resources to further help communities develop such plans. CAPs represent a relatively new type of community plan, and because the motivation for such planning varies, their implementation and how the plans relate to existing community plans ranges from visionary, inspirational statements to the adoption of such plans as chapters or sections of sustainability or comprehensive/general plans. Also, because of their interdisciplinary nature, often involving transportation, energy, land use and waste management, their implementation relies on commitment of several different agencies in local government. This raises the issue of their legal/official status. The legal status of CAPs as relatively newcomers in local policy and the extent to which they require multisectoral commitment for implementation raise important government issues in efforts to improve the sustainability of cities.

In 'Climate change adaptation', Adrienne L. Greve and Michael R. Boswell (Chapter 16), turn to the process of cities adapting to the unavoidable impacts of climate change. As they point out, CAPs increasingly address climate change adaptation. While the global reduction of GHG emissions requires national and international action to be effective, climate change impacts vary regionally and locally. Thus the appropriate scales for planning for climate change adaptation are regional and local. The authors point out that, although climate change adaptation planning may be a more recent development, cities may already have plans in place, such as local hazard mitigation plans, or public health plans, that can incorporate climate change adaptation strategies. Thus adaptation plans need not be stand-alone plans but could be integrated throughout existing city government functions. The authors identify major climate change impacts that cities may face, and major aspects of the adaptation planning process, including the formation of a local government cross-sectoral team in charge of preparing the plan, the development of a vulnerability assessment, and strategy development. Included is an insightful discussion of how to assess adaptation strategies, and how to prioritize such strategies given the expected timing of the impacts. Importantly, the authors stress the long-term monitoring of systems and feed-back loops.

Climate adaptation plans, because of their long-range nature, raise another institutional issue. How can local government, whose leadership changes with political administrations, ensure long-range adaptation, or, in general, sustainability strategies?

Adam Rose provides a valuable approach to the economics of sustainability in Chapter 17, 'Economic resilience and the sustainability of cities in the face of climate change: an ecological economics framework'. He begins by linking the study by economists of resilience, as a well-defined field addressing short-term shocks, to sustainability, which focuses on long-term survival and at a non-decreasing quality of life. To the extent that the methods of strengthening a city's resilience to extreme natural events serve also the needs of adaptation to longer-term changes brought about, in specific, by climate change, the two begin to merge. Extending resilience methods is a point relevant to theory though not immediately to practice at the city level, and Rose does not believe that it goes far enough, favoring the approach of ecological economics, 'where the economy and the environment are at least on par', and where 'emphasis is on the detailed modeling of the ecosystem itself . . . as well as the two-way interaction between the economy and the environment'.

As practical advice he offers a set of guideposts for cities extending from the lessons learned in resilience in becoming more sustainable, including:

- Ingenuity in conserving or substituting for critical resources under extreme stress should be examined for their more permanent potential under normal conditions.
- Disseminate findings on best-practice resilience tactics and community response.
- Evaluate the cost-effectiveness of resilience. This helps ensure that resilience will be implemented as efficiently as possible, thereby helping to remain on or return to a sustainable path.

In the final chapter of Part II, on Methods (Chapter 18), Laurie Kaye Nijaki presents, in 'A systems approach towards sustainable procurement', the case for assessing the economic value of ecosystem services to a city; a very concrete transformative way of doing so is through the city's purchasing practices. Of importance is that cities can lead by example and through the purchasing of goods and services, they can not only model sustainable behavior but affect the marketplace, at least within their sphere of influence. This involves both a purchasing strategy, on the consumption side of the equation, and a green jobs and training component to bring production of greener goods and services to the city. Moreover, when both consumption and production are framed through the lens of the three Es (the triple bottom line), the city will also be able to ensure that equity and justice in procurement practices and job training and capacity building are woven into a single whole. How this can come together in practice is outlined with examples in Table 18.1, 'Integrating sustainability values into procurement'.

The chapter is rich in information about green products used by cities, purchasing practices, and a step-by-step guide on how to evolve from a traditional purchasing approach to a more strategic, integrated and, across departments, cooperative sustainability procurement process.

LOOKING TO THE FUTURE

As indicated in the introductory chapter, to complement the sections on strategies and methods applicable today in fostering sustainable cities, we invited scholars who are looking over the horizon to imagine what the more sustainable city will look and feel like. Four future-oriented thinkers offer their thoughts on the form of the city of the future, a sustainable economy, governing sustainably and contributory technologies.

In 'Urban design and sustainability: looking backward to move forward' (Chapter 19), Tridib Banerjee critically reviews urban theories and movements to show how their roots relate to sustainability. He conducts this review of normative models of sustainability through a theoretical lens that distinguishes theories and movements along two axes, one focused on the degree of authoritarian (Platonic approach) versus experiential (Aristotelian approach) and the other axis focused on the extent to which the approach gives primacy to ecological versus anthropocentric values. He then goes on to show how different approaches, for example, Ian McHarg's approach in *Design With Nature* belongs in the Platonic/ecological quadrant, and Kevin Lynch's approach in *Good City Form* belongs in the Aristotelian/anthropocentric quadrant. In his suggestive comments on developing an integrative framework for the urban design literature on sustainability, Banerjee indicates how current design concepts related to sustainability, such as Eco-City or Neotraditional Development, or urban containment models relate to the quadrant analysis.

He comments on the tendency of designers to impose Platonic forms on cities, and concludes that cities are more Aristotelian in character, 'works in progress', subject to messy political processes. It is clear that the very nature of scientific inquiry, which even designers must recognize, is experiential, and thus a less dogmatic approach to design is not only preferable but more objective. However, the long-term sustainability of ecological versus anthropocentric approaches is open to debate. Yes, if we do not take into account human values and political processes, we are blind to ourselves as part of nature, and will probably not get very far in implementing our plans. On the other hand, failing to incorporate ecological values into our valuation processes will intensify and multiply the sustainability challenges that we face today.

Edward J. Blakely, in Chapter 20, 'The future of sustainable economic development in cities', argues that the field of local economic development has always incorporated the idea and practice of sustainability. He contrasts this approach with prevailing economic views and identifies the levers for a new economy, including extraction taxes and levies, agricultural reform, and reducing energy demand through changes in living patterns. Blakely argues that sustainable economic development must be based on the human, natural and community resources indigenous to a place rather than on external drivers, and that it should add value and spread wealth throughout the community. Along with his vision of sustainable community-based economies, he provides a framework or process for achieving such economies. First, communities need to undertake an analysis of their resource base, especially its human resources. This should be followed by community processes to determine their economic values, as well as to identify the sacrifices they are willing to make to become more sustainable. Communities, on the path to sustainability, then need to set economic goals, and finally identify and engage in projects to achieve such goals. His vision directly challenges the dominant economic system and illustrates how sustainability approaches at the urban scale could influence larger-scale economic practices in the future.

In Chapter 21, Daniel J. Fiorino contends that governing a sustainable city will require substantial redesign in the institutions of governance and policy implementation. In 'Sustainable cities and governance: what are the connections?', Fiorino ask what direction these changes will take. He reflects on the emerging though limited literature on sustainable governance, tracing the communitarian versus a more technical framing of sustainable development – one transformational, the other more focused on specific goals, such as green procurement and jobs. He also develops a set of questions for all those concerned with governing relevant to the difference between present practices and a more systematic and integrated way of governing.

This leads to his most intriguing observation and challenge to us all. To date, the discussion of sustainability has centered on the need to better understand and integrate the ecological, economic and social dimensions of a more sustainable society. As difficult as this is proving to be, it is unrealistic to image the parts coming together without a form of governing commensurate with the complex systems problems in weaving the three together. His conclusion is that we need to add a fourth dimension to our framework for sustainability, which is a design for a governing system capable of performing the perennial tasks of any effective governmental system, such as providing political stability, freedom and rights, effective and accountable institutions, and legitimacy, with the needs, scope and complexity of the other three systems. The challenge is captured best in his own words:

> The central question for cities (and, for that matter, any level of governance) is whether a transition to sustainability requires different kinds of governance capacities than have been common in the past. Can a 'business-as-usual' governance scenario provide the institutional capacities needed to meet the demands of sustainability transitions? Or will new capacities – in institutions, relationships, participatory mechanisms and political cultures – be required in the coming decades?

His answer is that we are moving into uncharted territory in the effort to effectively balance the needs of people, as they are congregating increasingly in the mega-cities of today, with the ecological systems that provide 'nature's services' for them. There is no prescribed path for doing this, although it is clear that the new form of governance must be in keeping with the systems thinking pervasive throughout the previous chapters. It will be a learning and adaptation process, which he labels the 'sustainability transition', as we move away from the clearly unsustainable practices of the past to those policies, behaviors and relationships that are both more integrated across social and ecological spheres and more sustainable. While the path forward has yet to be charted, all the evidence points to the fact that it is being led by a multiplicity of attempts – real-world experiments – from the bottom up, from cities.

In Chapter 22, 'Technology and city sustainability', Bill Tomlinson opens our eyes to a very different world than most people can imagine, extrapolating as he does from the transformational changes being brought about through innovations in information technology. What he foresees will in all likelihood help address many of the challenges identified in the previous chapters. Without being Pollyanna-ish, and recognizing the importance of the human–technology interrelationship, Tomlinson contends that IT can facilitate the transition to sustainability in cities. Organized around four themes in IT, cities will be better equipped to collect and monitor data, develop better system-level models and management systems, become more efficient, and manage flows throughout the city in a variety of arenas more intelligently, hence improving the quality of life for all involved.

He spells out how this is coming about through the ways IT 'will help cities and their resources be quantified, smart, local and shared'. The ability to collect, maintain and analyze large arrays of data is central to managing complex systems, and developments in IT are making this easier by the day. From a governance perspective, for example, this can facilitate the integration of ecological, social and administrative systems called for by Fiorino and the UM modeling by Kennedy, Baker and Brattebø. Similarly, the proliferation of hand-held communication devices, with the instant connectivity and dissemination of information they provide, has the potential to dramatically reduce the need for personal transportation for smart growth, for enabling better – less environmentally harmful, more functional and more efficient – food and product choices. Importantly, however, Tomlinson reminds us that technology is only enabling, not determinative. How it is used is culturally and humanly defined. Applied to the needs of fostering a more sustainable world, it can help immeasurably. He also reminds us that 'IT has enabled both the best and the worst of humanity; it is up to people, not machines, to become sustainable'.

CONCLUDING THOUGHTS

As befitting the interdisciplinary and systems-oriented nature of urban sustainability, the strategies covered in the chapters of this volume have an extraordinary range. While some are clearly focused on conserving an environmental resource, such as water supply, they may focus on changing social ideals and behavior, such as changing homeowners' preferences for outdoor landscaping or the length of showers, or building codes; or on using strategies to capture more precipitation, such as rainwater harvesting or stormwater capture. The variety of strategies illustrates the multiple levers for achieving greater sustainability in urban systems. What is still to be determined with respect to many of these systems is the effectiveness and interaction of these strategies, especially within their institutional settings. For example, to continue with the water supply illustration, water conservation pricing schemes that increase water rates with greater use have long been considered, especially by economists, as an effective strategy for reducing urban water use. However, this strategy runs into the problem of its own success. That is, if the strategy is successful in conserving water, it reduces water agency revenues. It may also mean a disproportionate reduction of water for the less well-off. These effects can be anticipated and addressed through policy choices and organizational change, but, in practice, short of a more sustainable governing framework within which decisions are made, they seldom are (Blanco et al. 2012).

The strategies focused on social aspects of sustainability also display the systemic nature of the approach. For example, take food justice in the emerging field of urban food policy. Strategies range from information and educational campaigns aimed at changing individual/family food preferences, to introduction of healthier foods in school lunches, to the regulation of fast-food restaurant locations; and to providing local government incentives for large grocers to locate in low-income neighborhoods.

Likewise, economic, fiscal and institutional aspects of urban sustainability pose formidable challenges. The promise of greening our local economies and using local government procurement functions for this purpose is an exciting prospect that does not essentially challenge existing local government structures. But it is clear that fiscal reform at local and other levels of government is required, especially given the backlog in infrastructure investment, to attain greater local economic and built environment sustainability. The interdisciplinary nature of sustainability and the long-range nature of strategies to achieve it, when pitted against the compartmentalized organization, vested near-term interests of local governments and thus short-term nature of local decision making, highlight the obstacles to be overcome in achieving urban sustainability.

The volume provides a range of methods useful for achieving greater sustainability in our cities, from urban metabolism, climate change mitigation and adaptation plans, indicator approaches, cumulative impact methods to gauge environmental justice, and health impact assessments. Some of the methods, such as environmental justice screening methods and health impact assessments, expand traditional environmental assessment methods to encompass more social dimensions of sustainability and can be applied at the project and community plan scales. Other methods, such as urban metabolism or climate action plans, are new types of assessment that incorporate biophysical environmental aspects of sustainability going beyond the environmental aspects of local decisions incorporated in traditional plans and impact reviews. Yet other methods, such as sustainable indicator rating systems, enable local governments to track their progress over time along agreed sustainability metrics.

In the future-oriented chapters, the authors identify challenges and present desirable and, we can only hope, likely futures, focused on a more sustainable urban form, locally based economies, more coherent and future-oriented governance, and technological innovations in information management, transmission and utilization that complement if not actually facilitate the changes described by the others.

While not covering every imaginable aspect, the book accomplishes our objective of presenting many of the most important aspects of a city's path to sustainability. As editors and authors, we take from the range of strategies, methods, and array of thoughts and ideas proposed, five overriding guiding messages running throughout:

1. The process of transformation to a more sustainable world is under way, and cities are in the vanguard of the changes needed.
2. Accomplishing the three Es is possible, though doing so needs to be woven into to the overall sustainability plan of a city.
3. There is no one path forward; indeed, it appears that any one of the strategic interventions can be a starting point, depending on the particular circumstances of the city.
4. Institutions and past practices and behavior will need to change, and this is often the most difficult part of the transformation before us.
5. Leadership matters – civic, business and political.

REFERENCE

Blanco, H., Newell, J., Stott, L. and Alberti, M. (2012), *Water Supply Scarcity in Southern California: Assessing Water District Level Strategies*, Center for Sustainable Cities, University of Southern California. Available at http://sustainablecities.usc.edu/news/water-scarcity-in-southern-california.html.

Index

Academy of Nutrition and Dietetics 183
Alberti, Leon Battista 391
Amazon.com, Inc.
  Mechanical Turk system 443
American Bar Association
  Model Procurement Code 355
American Nurses Association 183
American Planning Association
  Planning and Community Health Research Center 183
American Public Health Association 183
American Public Transportation Association (APTA)
report of trends in funding for public transportation 137–8
American Society of Civil Engineers (ASCE) 136, 148
  estimation of spending trends 137–8
  infrastructure ratings 139
American Water Works Association 138
AmeriCorps
  staff of 197
Apollo Alliance 367
Australia 22–3, 25, 100, 196, 200–201, 410
  Melbourne 19
  Sydney 16, 19
Austria
  Vienna 24, 261

Bangladesh
  Dhaka 16
Behaviour, Energy, and Climate Conference 204
Belgium
  Brussels 276
Bilan Carbon 257
Böge, Stephanie 439
Boston Foundation, Inc. 295
  Wisdom of Our Choices: Boston's Indicators of Progress, Change, Sustainability, The 287
Brookings Institution 22, 144
Brown, Jerry
  lawsuit against San Bernardino County 130
Brundtland, Harlen 4
Brundtland Commission 3–4, 296
Commission on Environment and Development Report (Brundtland Report) (1987) 4
Bureau of Economic Analysis 136

Cal-EnviroScreen 242
Cal State San Bernardino 129
California Air Pollution Control Officers' Association (CAPCOA)
  Quantifying Greenhouse Gas Mitigation Measures: A Resource for Local Government to Assess Emission Reductions from Greenhouse Gas Mitigation Measures 315
Campbell, Scott 388
Canada 27, 58, 77, 417
  Ontario 161
  Toronto 80, 269, 277
  Vancouver 16, 69, 267
carbon credit savings 52
Carpenter, Novella
  'Ghost Town Farm' 79
Center for Disease Control and Prevention (CDC)
  Communities Putting Prevention to Work (CPPW) Initiative 79
  Healthy Community Design Initiative 182–3
Central Arizona-Phoenix Long-Term Ecological Research Project (CAP-LTER) 276
Chevron 164

China 6
  Hong Kong 16, 277
  Shenzhen 16
city indicators of sustainability 283–301
challenges 298–9
early projects 283–4
indicator categories 291–7
  air quality 293–4
  economic indicators 296–7
  energy 295
  environment 293
  social indicators 295–6
  solid waste management and recycling 294–5
  water quality 294
indicator projects 284–99
  Austin, TX 287–8, 291, 293, 297, 299
  Boston, MA 285, 287, 292, 295–9
  Jacksonville, FL 286–7, 299
  Minneapolis, MN 284–5, 287–99
  Santa Monica, CA 285, 288, 291–2, 294, 296–7, 299
  Sustainable Seattle 284, 286–7, 290, 292–8
intersecting indicators 297–8
purposes 284
CivicEvolution 201
Clean Energy Works
  aims of 128
Clean Water State Revolving Fund
  funding provided by 149
Climate Access
  Climate Communication and Behaviour Change 204
climate action planning (mitigation) 302–19
  definition of 302
  goals of 303
  implementation and monitoring 315–17
  number of cities within 302
  plan development 309–15
  preliminary activities 305–9
  resources 317–19
  steps in process 303–5
climate action plans (CAPs) 302–3, 315
  adoption of 305–7
  climate action team (CAT) 304–5, 307
  climate adaptation strategies 313–14
  community 305
  GHG inventory 307, 310–11
  public participation 308
  updating of 317
climate adaptation planning 320–335
  climate impacts 321–3
  definition of 320
  implementation 333
  strategy development 330–2
  decision matrix 330–1
  prioritizing strategies 332–3
  vulnerability assessment 325–30
  adaptive capacity 329–30
  exposure 325–7
  Cal-Adapt (PIER) tool 327
  NOAA sea-level rise viewer 327
  Sensitivity 327–30
climate change 32, 190, 338, 344–5, 351, 415
  change in precipitation 36–7
  extreme events 37–8, 322–3
  impact on ecosystem 322–3
  impact on municipal water services 33
  impact on public health 322
  impact on urban water services 32, 38–9
  increased ambient temperature 33–5, 321
  sea-level rise 35–6, 322
Clinton, Bill
  Executive Order #12898 228–9, 234
Club of Rome 162
cluster initiatives
  concept of 122
  technology transfer facilitated by 123
Coleman, James
  'Social capital in the creation of human capital' 421–2
compact cities 28–9
  automobile cities 16–17
  densities to facilitate walking and transit 17–22
density 15–16
energy use of transport 17–20
Marchetti Constant 24–5
  peak care use 22–4

causes of 24–8
role of transport 15–17
transit cities 16
urban form, history of 15–17
walking cities 16
compact fluorescent lamps (CFLs) 197
computable general equilibrium analysis (CGE)
concept of 348
Congrès Internationaux d'Architecture Moderne (CIAM)
Athens Charter 388
Consolidated Edison 141

East Bay Green Corridor Partnership 122
economic development 397, 410–11, 420
economic value of community 410–11
green economy and 358–9
in sustainable development 358
procurement policies and 358–9
strategies 366–7
sustainable 397–401, 409–11
taxation 401, 409
economic resilience 336–53
business interruption (BI) 340
climate change adaptation and 344–6
definition of 339–40
direct state economic resilience (DSER) 340–1
ecological economics and 347–9
environmental economics and 346–7
options for achieving 342–4
quantification of 340–2
sustainability and 338–9, 348–9
total static economic resilience (TSER) 341
urban vulnerability and resilience 336–8
Edison Electric Institute 137
Emerald City status
concept of 129
engagement strategies 192–205
case studies 192–202
Ann Arbor MI energy challenge 193–4
Australia's Clean Run Behavior Change Initiative 196
Baltimore's Energy Challenge (BEC) 196–7
Chicago's City-Community Partnerships 199–200
Denver's Clean Air at Schools: Engines Off! (CASEO) 195
EcoTeam programs 197–9
Geraldton 2029 and Beyond, Western Australia 200–2
Toronto's Turn It Off program 194–5
guides for engagement 188–9
strategies for engagement 189–92
information provisions and persuasion 189–91, 193–4, 202
psychology-based tools 191–9
Community Based Social Marketing (CBSM) 194, 196
participatory deliberation 189, 192, 199–202, 205
strengthening engagement strategies 202–5
environmental economics 346–7
concept of 346
view of resilience 346–7
environmental justice (EJ) 228–52
definitions of 232–3, 235–6
history and issues 228–30
measurement of 233–41
community involvement 239–41
cumulative approach 235–9
Environmental Justice Screening Method (EJSM) or CAL-EnviroScreen 237–9, 242
EPA EJSEAT program 242
local and regional scale 232–5
other environmental health/justice tools 243–4
relation to sustainability 230–2
Environmental Justice Advisory Committee (EJAC)
recommendations of 241
Environmental Protection Agency (EPA) 98, 138, 143–5, 240–2, 293, 316–17, 362
drinking water criteria 38
EGrid Model 96
Energy Star 313

Environmental Justice Strategic Enforcement Assessment Tool (EJSEAT) 242
Environmentally Preferable Purchasing (EPP) 361
funding provided by 316
Pollutant Standards Index 293
European Union (EU) 51
TRUST project 267

Fair Food Network 73
Field Museum, The 199–200
Finland 426
First World War (1914–18) 359–60
fiscal sustainability 154–65
connecting fiscal and environmental decision-making 157–8
connecting land use, housing, transportation and air quality
California's Cap and Trade program (case) 159
Southern California Association of Governments (case) 158–9
environmental sustainability 154–5
Alameda Corridor, Los Angeles County (case) 154
linking long-range planning and budgeting
City and County of San Bernardino (case) 160–2
political strategy for 162–4
shifting from short-term to long-term fiscal planning 156–7
urban budgeting 155–6
Florida, Richard 15
Food Action Plan 75–6
recommendations of 76–7
Food and Agriculture Organization (FAO)
definition of sustainable diets 60
Food Retail Expansion to Support Health (FRESH) 72
food supply chain/system 71, 79–80
mobile food vending 71
regional 66–7
relationship with urban environment 63–4
waste reduction strategies 74–5, 80
Food Trust, the
Pennsylvania Fresh Food Financing Initiative 72
Forester, John
Deliberative Practitioner, The 216
France
Agency for the Environment and Energy Management 257
Nantes 267, 269
fuel prices 19
rise of 28
Futerra
Engage: Campaign Guidebook for Cities 204

Garrison Institute 189, 204
Geddes, Patrick 384
Germany 161–2, 417
Freiburg 162
Hamburg 261
Leipzig 261
Giuliani, Rudy 68
Global Cities Database 15, 17–18
expansion of 23
Global Financial Crisis (2007–9) 28
impact on urban food systems strategies 59–60
globalization 58, 371, 400, 411
economic 6
of agriculture 402
Good Food Purchasing Pledge
good food criteria 65–6
governance of sustainable cities in future 413–33
as fourth system 414–15
city-level 423–4
corporatist 417
definition of governance 416
deliberative and inclusionary processes and procedures (DIPs) model 419–20, 429
governance and sustainability in American cities 418–23
impact of economic failure on 422–3
information-deficit (ID) model 419
legitimate 415, 426
neo-corporatist 417–18
networked 75
new governance capacities for local sustainability 426–31

relation of governance to environmental performance 416–18
research needs 423–6
role of governance in sustainability transition 413–14
Great Depression 360
Green Action Plan 129
green business and industry 116–32
  case studies of green businesses
  energy efficiency retrofits in Portland, Oregon 127–8
  Green Action Plan of Riversdale, California 127–30
  evidence of green business and industry 125–7
  green economy, definition of 117
  green economy and economic development 117–20
  growth vs. development goals 120–3
  strategies for greening local economies 123–5
Green Business Certification Program 368
Green Developer Agreement (GDA) 70
green economy 116–17, 125, 365
  concept of 117
  consumption 119–20
  development of 118–19, 121, 124–7, 130–1, 365
  production 119
  regulation and standards in 123–4
  use of business incentives in 121–2, 125–6
Green Valley Initiative (GVI)
aims of 129–30
Greenest City 2020 Action Plan 69
greenhouse gas (GHG) emissions 3, 52, 86, 107, 255, 261, 269–70, 294, 302, 306–7, 316–17, 345, 361
  carbon dioxide (CO2) 159, 194–5, 265, 268, 270
  contribution of infrastructure to 145
  inventory 307, 310–11
  life-cycle 67, 257
  national 51
  reduction of 50–1, 53, 96–7, 145, 159, 172–3, 270, 303, 309–10, 312–14, 320, 323
  sources of 50
Hayes Valley Farm 70
Haynes Foundation 154
healthy cities 166–87
  density and health 167, 172
  extreme weather events and health 170, 172
  health, definitions of 166–8
  Healthy Cities Initiative (WHO) 183
  nutrition and access to healthy food 170–1
  organizations promoting healthy communities 182–4
  physical activity and built environment 169
  social capital and public places 171
  sustainability and human health 166
  tools for measuring health in cities 178–82
  Health Impact Assessment (HIA) 180–2
  City of Baltimore's HIA (case) 181–2
  LEED certification 178–80
  WalkScore 179–80
urban heat island effect 176–7
  urban planning and public health 167, 169–78
  building scale
  city scale
  neighbourhood scale
  region scale
Healthy Food Financing Initiative 72
human capital 421, 428
  worker 122
human social organizations 4

ICLEI – Local Governments for Sustainability 60, 188, 204, 305, 314, 317
  5 Milestone Process 303–4
India
  Mumbai 16
Indonesia
  Jakarta 16
Industrial Control Systems Cyber Emergency Response Team 143
Industrial Revolution 399
infrastructure facilities, definition of 136

Inland Empire 130
  development of 128–9
Inland Empire Economic Partnership 129
Institute of Medicine 167
Intergovernmental Panel on Climate Change (IPCC) 147
International Business Machines Corporation (IBM)
  Smarter Buildings 436
Israel
  Haifa 393
International City Management Association 285
Italy
  Turin 267

Jabareen, Yosef Rafeq 393
Japan 6
  Kobe Earthquake (1995) 343
  Tokyo 16
Jonathan Rose Companies 70
Jordan
  Amman 277

landfill disposal
  EPA regulation of 98
life-cycle assessment (LCA) 91, 102, 111, 266, 270, 436–7
  concept of 90
  environmental 268
  life-cycle inventory (LCI) 90–1
  social 91
  spatially explicit 91
local human development 119
location theory
  concept of 125
Loveridge, Ron
  Mayor of Riverside 129

Mackaye, Benton 384
Marchetti, Cesare 15
Marsh, George Perkins 391
Menomonee Valley project 420–1
metropolitan planning organizations (MPOs) 245
Mexico
  Michoacán 200
Mostafavi, Mohsen 392
Mumford, Lewis 384, 391

National Academy of Public Administration 162
National Academy of Sciences
  Sustainability at EPA 424
National Aeronautics and Space Administration (NASA) 162
National Air Toxics Assessment 232
National Association for the Advancement of Colored Peoples (NAACP) 228
National Association of State Procurement Officials (NASPO) 354, 370, 373
National Audubon's Society
  Tools of Engagement 204
National Bridge Inventory 139
National Center for Environmental Health
  Division of Emergency and Environmental Services 182
National Science Foundation
  Climate and Urban Partnership 205
National Transportation Safety Board 139
New Zealand 17
non-governmental organizations (NGOs) 59, 65, 69–70
North American Association for Environmental Education
  Guidelines of Excellence (series) 204
Norway 426
  Oslo 266–7, 269

Obama, Barack
  administration of 134, 141
Olmsted, Frederick Law 384, 391
O'Neil, Tip
  US Speaker of the House 155
Organization for Economic Co-operation and Development (OECD)
  Guidance on Sustainability Impact Assessment 424

participatory processes 210–27
  Community Benefits Agreements (CBAs) 221, 224–6
  Los Angeles' Staples Center district (case study) 222

community partnerships 218, 223
Oregon Solutions (case study) 218–19
Diversity, Interdependency, Authentic Dialogue (DIAD) 214–15
elements of 214–18
methods 212–13
participatory planning 219, 223–4
East Portland Action Plan (case study) 219–21
Public Outreach and Engagement Liaisons (POELs) 216
social capital 217
Pedestrian Environmental Quality Index (PEQI) 180
Penn Future 122
Pew Research Center for the People and the Press 133
survey (2014) 134
Poland
Kraców 16
Portland Business Alliance 128
Portland State University
National Policy Consensus Center 218
Portugal
Lisbon 261
procurement policies 354–77
buy local approaches 358–9
Business Alliance for Local Living Economies (BALLE) 359
concept of 354
economic development and 358–9
environmental benefits 360–2
equity and social justice and 359–60
intergovernmental coordination 370–2
policy development 366–9
policy implementation 369–70
product identification 364–6
sustainability values and 356–7
systems-based sustainable 362–4
values and goals of 355–6
Property Accessed Clean Energy (PACE) 367
Putnam, Robert 428
definition of social capital 421

Rawls, John 388, 393
Justice as Fairness 393–4
Recipe for Healthy Places, A (2012)
provisions of 78–9
Recyclebank
rewards program of 99
Recycling Market Development Zones
concept of 121
Reinvestment Fund 62
Republic of Ireland
Limerick 261
return on investment (ROI) 159
Richmond Build 123

Safe Routes to School
aims of 183–4
Second World War (1939–45) 360
Sightline Institute 148
Singapore 16
SNAP 65, 72–3
increased enrolment in 59, 76
Solar Energy Industry Association 127
SolarTech 127
Soleri, Paolo 385
Spain 51–2
Barcelona 16–17
substantive flow analysis (SFA) 272
sustainable economic development in future 397–412
change in economic assumptions 399–400
framework for transition 409–11
levers for a new economy 401–9
agriculture and soil 402
business 406–7
community economic development corporations 404
density and affordability 405
energy 402–4
environment and settlement patterns 404–5
extraction taxes and levies
female and indigenous values 409
glocalization 408
new roles and rules 405–6
taxation 409
technology 408
travel and transport 404
role of local places 398
sustainable foundation of local economic development 397

sustainability 3–4, 6, 9–10, 28, 77, 107, 184, 189–91, 199, 203–4, 210, 225, 232, 236, 240–1, 245–6, 356, 362–4, 381, 393–4, 406, 413, 424–5, 427–9
initiatives 1–2
long-term 178
promotion of via public health 172–3, 180
public involvement 211
relationship with resilience 338–9, 348–9
role of governance in 413–15, 422, 428–30
role of infrastructure in 145
  transit access 22
  transitions 414, 416, 418–21, 423, 425–6
urban 8, 58, 86, 385, 456, 458, 466–7
Sustainability Community Program
proposed development of 158–9
sustainability, definitions of 3–6, 230
Sweden 417, 426
Stockholm 24
Switzerland
Zurich 24

Thailand
Bangkok 259
technology in cities in future 434–48
adoption and cultural acceptance 444–5
health care concerns 444
  human-computer interaction (HCI) 438
information technology (IT) as force multiplier 434
  local activity 439–41
quantification of 435–7
privacy concerns 443
security concerns 443–4
  smart control 437–9
  widespread sharing 441–2
transit
growth of public 25–6
triple bottom line (TBL)
concept of 4
Twin Cities Household Ecosystem Project (TCHEP) 276

UC Riverside
  College of Engineering-Center for Environmental Research Technology (CE-CERT) 129
United Church of Christ (UCC) 228
  Commission for Racial Justice 228
United Kingdom (UK) 15, 359, 403
  London 16, 24, 261, 398
United Nations (UN) 3, 144, 189
  Environment Program (UNEP) 147
  Millennium Development Goals (MDGs) 32
  World Commission on Environment and Development 166
United States of America (USA) 17, 25, 27, 51, 58, 62, 64, 77, 86–7, 96, 102, 106, 148, 154–5, 167, 169–70, 174, 213, 217, 230–2, 246, 263, 271–2, 276, 283, 285, 302, 306, 341–2, 359, 384, 417, 427, 430–1
  9/11 Attacks 338, 341–2, 344
Affordable Health Care for America Act 73–4, 79
  Air Force (USAF) 162
  American Public Transportation Association (APTA) 137–8
  American Recovery and Reinvestment Act (ARRA) 137, 367
  Ann Arbor 97
  Atlanta 17, 24, 125
  Austin 122, 234, 283
Bacon-Davis Act (1931) 360
  Bureau of Census 273, 285–6, 299
  Chicago 69, 71, 80, 147, 337, 402
  Clean Air Act 136, 178
  Clean Water Act 70
  Congress 133, 141
  Congressional Budget Office (CBO) 136–7, 149
  Council on Economic Advisors 135
  Department of Agriculture (USDA) 62, 72–3, 93, 170, 183
  Department of Energy 128, 140, 146–7, 273
  Department of Health and Human Services 170, 181
  Department of Homeland Security (DHS) 142–3

Department of Housing and Urban Development (HUD) 141, 242
Department of Transportation (DOT) 141–3, 148
Department of Treasury 135, 170
Detroit 68, 73, 336
Disaster Relief Appropriations Act (2013) 141
Federal Emergency Management Agency (FEMA) 140, 142
Federal Highway Administration (FHWA) 148, 184
Food, Conservation, and Energy Act (2008) 64
GDP per capita 137
General Accounting Office 228
Government Accountability Office (GAO) 139, 143
Healthy Hunger-Free Kids Act (2010) 73
Houston 24
Hurricane Gustav (2008) 140
Hurricane Ike (2008) 140
Hurricane Katrina (2005) 140–1, 144–5, 336, 343, 345, 348
Hurricane Rita (2005) 140
Hurricane Sandy (2012) 140–1
Jacksonville 283–4
Los Angeles 24, 60, 65, 71, 79–80, 100, 128–9, 163, 176, 398
Medicaid 298
Medicare 298
military of 62
Minneapolis 69, 74, 80, 272
MSW of 94, 97–8, 101
National Environmental Policy Act (NEPA) 135–6
National School Lunch Program 72
New Orleans 144, 336, 338, 341, 345, 348
New York 16, 58–9, 64–71, 73, 7, 80, 93, 125, 141, 144, 147, 167, 198, 236, 341–2, 358–9, 398, 408, 425
obesity rates in 93
Omaha 367
Portland 99–100, 117, 360, 420–1, 423, 429
public school system of 66
Public Works Act (1977) 360
real estate sector of 28
renewable energy sector of 146–7
Sacramento 122
San Bernardino 117, 127–30, 154–5, 163
San Diego 128, 237, 385
San Francisco 24, 68, 70, 74, 121–3, 125, 338, 358
San Jose 360, 362
Santa Monica 283–4
Seattle 75–7, 79–80, 216, 234, 283
Silicon Valley 127, 129, 234
Special Supplemental Nutrition Program for Women, Infants, and Children (WIC) 72
Superfund Amendments and Reauthorization Act (SARA) 221–2
Supplemental Nutrition Assistance Program 72
Wagner-O'Day Act (1938) 359–60
Warren County Protests (1982) 228–9
Washington DC 125
United Way
Caring Index 296
University of California, Irvine (UCI) 442
Intel Science & Technology Center for Social Computing 443
University of Southern California
faculty of 385
urban
definition of 6
urban agriculture 57, 69–70
expansion of 67
growing space 68
potential use of contaminated soil in 68
Urban Agriculture Policy Plan 69
urban complexity 8
urban consumption patterns 86–115
life cycle of products consumed in cities
municipal solid waste (MSW) illustration 86–9
sustainability for urban consumption 91–111
consumer product design 92
dematerializing packaging 101–4
distribution efficiency 105–6

distribution strategies 102, 104–5
energy efficiency/Grid Mix 96–7
local sourcing 105–7
optimal product replacement 95
plastic bag policies 100–1
product sharing 93–4
recycling 97–100
reducing food consumption 92–3
repair 94–5
urban design 381–96
Ahwanee Principles 388
Alexander, Christopher 383, 391
Appleyard, Donald 383, 386, 388
Aristotelian vs. Platonic approaches 382
Congress for the New Urbanism (CNU) 389–91
Duany, Andres 383, 390
ecological vs. anthropocentric approaches 383
Hester, Randolph 383, 392
integrative framework 393–4
Jacobs, Allan 383, 388
Knowles, Ralph 383, 385
Landscape (Ecological) Urbanism 383, 391–2
Lynch, Kevin 383, 386
matrix of normative theories 383
McHarg, Ian 383–5
New Urbanism 383, 388–91
Peattie, Lisa 382
Soleri, Paolo 383, 385
Spirn, Ann 383, 391–2
Steiner, Frederick 392
Talen, Emily 383, 390, 392
theories and movements 381
Wright, Frank Lloyd 385
urban food systems and plans 57–85
comprehensive plans for food production 69–70, 78–9
drivers of food plans and policy making 58–60
environmental impacts of food production and distribution 63–4
farmers' markets 64–5
federal food benefits 59, 72–4
food deserts 62
food insecurity 61–3
food residuals 74–5
food system sustainability 60–1, 63–4
governance of food systems 75–8
history of 57
local trap criticism 66–7
obesity and health effects 61–2, 92
school procurement of local food 65–6
strategies for sustainable urban food policy 64–70
urban food distribution and processing
zoning changes for local food production 67–8
urban flooding
efforts to prevent 8
urban infrastructure investment 133–53
age of infrastructure 139–40
alternatives to traditional infrastructure 146–8
ASCE rating of investment funds 139
demand characteristics of infrastructure 143–4
equity and infrastructure 144–5
GHG emissions of infrastructures 145
impacts of extreme events on infrastructure 140–2
multiplier effects from 135–6
need estimates 137–8
public priority of 133–4
resource use of infrastructure 146
sources of investment funds 138–9
streets as finance engines 147–8
use of IT in infrastructure operation and maintenance practices 142–3
urban intensity 390–1
relationship with household income 19
urban metabolism (UM) 8–10, 107, 255–82
combined heat and power (CHP) 260
data requirements 258–75
energy 259–61
material flow analysis (MFA) definition 272
material stocks and flows 261–3
MFA of nutrients and salts 271–5
nitrogen, phosphorus, salts 271–2
water 263–7

water-energy-CO2 nexus 266–70
description of method 255–7
diagrams 276–9
urban planning 381–3
emergence of 167
form-based codes (FBC) 390–1
transect planning 390
urban sprawl 390
reversal of 26–7
Urban Sustainability Directors Network 188, 204
urban water services and climate change 33–56, 266–7
adaptation goals and options for urban water sector 41–3
Brisbane, Australia (case) 43
concept of 32
cost of adaptation 39–41, 51
efforts to reduce GHG emissions in 50–1
impact of climate change on 32, 38–9
mitigation options for water services 43–52
Melbourne, Australia (case) 52
Rhurverband Water System, Germany (case) 51
Philadelphia, Pennsylvania (case) 37
Schoharie Creek basin, New York (case) 35
Wuxi City, Jiangu Province, China (case) 35
urbanization 1
suburbanization 144
US Computer Emergency Readiness Team (US-CERT) 143
US Conference of Mayors 61
Climate Protection Agreement 302, 305
US Geographical Survey 263
US Green Building Council (USGBC)
Leadership in Energy and Environmental Design (LEED) 86, 121, 129–30, 178–80

Van Buren, Martin 359
vehicle miles travelled (VMT) 385
reduction of 177–8, 389
Venezuela
Ciudad Guyana 382
Via Campesina 61
Via Verde 70
Vietnam
Ho Chi Minh City 16

Waldheim, Charles 392
Weiser, Mark 435–6
Wholesome Wave 65
Wikipedia 437
workforce development theory 368–9
programs 123, 369
World Bank 135, 255
World Governance Indicators (WGI) 416
World Commission on Environment and Development
Our Common Future 413, 427
World Environmental Education Congress 2013 189
World Health Organization (WHO) 144
definition of 'health' 166–7
Healthy Cities Initiative 183
water quality standards 271
World Trade Organization (WTO) 59
Wuppertal Institute 439

Zeemering, Eric 421